The Modern Legal Philosophy Series

III

Comparative Legal Philosophy

The Modern Legal Philosophy Series

Edited by a Committee of the
ASSOCIATION OF AMERICAN LAW SCHOOLS

COMPARATIVE

LEGAL PHILOSOPHY

Applied to Legal Institutions

BY

LUIGI MIRAGLIA

Professor of the Philosophy of Law in the University of Naples

TRANSLATED FROM THE ITALIAN BY

JOHN LISLE

of the Philadelphia Bar

WITH AN INTRODUCTION BY
ALBERT KOCOUREK
Lecturer on Jurisprudence in Northwestern University

AUGUSTUS M. KELLEY · PUBLISHERS
New York, New York

ROTHMAN REPRINTS, Inc.
South Hackensack, New Jersey

1968

First Published 1912
(Boston: The Boston Book Company)
Reprinted 1968
By Arrangement with the Macmillan Company

Library of Congress Catalogue Card Number
68-54751

AUGUSTUS M. KELLEY · PUBLISHERS
24 EAST 22ND STREET
NEW YORK, NEW YORK 10010

———

ROTHMAN REPRINTS, INC.
57 LEUNING STREET
SOUTH HACKENSACK, NEW JERSEY 07606

PRINTED IN THE UNITED STATES OF AMERICA
by SENTRY PRESS, NEW YORK, N. Y. 10019

GENERAL INTRODUCTION TO THE SERIES

By the Editorial Committee

"Until either philosophers become kings," said Socrates, "or kings philosophers, States will never succeed in remedying their shortcomings." And if he was loath to give forth this view, because, as he admitted, it might "sink him beneath the waters of laughter and ridicule," so to-day among us it would doubtless resound in folly if we sought to apply it again in our own field of State life, and to assert that philosophers must become lawyers or lawyers philosophers, if our law is ever to be advanced into its perfect working.

And yet there is hope, as there is need, among us to-day, of some such transformation. Of course, history shows that there always have been cycles of legal progress, and that they have often been heralded and guided by philosophies. But particularly there is hope that our own people may be the generation now about to exemplify this.

There are several reasons for thinking our people apt thereto. But, without delaying over the grounds for such speculations, let us recall that as shrewd and good-natured an observer as DeTocqueville saw this in us. He admits that "in most of the operations of the mind, each American appeals to the individual exercise of his own understanding alone; therefore in no country in the civilized world is less attention paid to philosophy than in the United States." But, he adds, "the Americans are much more addicted to the use of general ideas than the English, and entertain a much greater relish for them." And since philosophy is, after all, only the science of general ideas — analyzing, restating, and reconstructing concrete experience — we may well trust that (if ever we do go at it with a will) we shall discover in ourselves a taste and high capacity for it, and shall direct our powers as fruitfully upon law as we have done upon other fields.

Hitherto, to be sure, our own outlook on juristic learning has been insular. The value of the study of comparative law has only in recent years come to be recognized by us. Our juristic methods are still primitive, in that we seek to know only by our own experience, and pay no heed to the experience of others. Our historic bond with English law alone, and our consequent lack of recognition of the universal character of law as a generic institution, have prevented any wide contact with foreign literatures. While heedless of external help in the practical matter of legislation, we have been oblivious to the abstract nature of law. Philosophy of law has been to us almost a meaningless and alien phrase. "All philosophers are reducible in the end to two classes only: utilitarians and futilitarians," is the cynical epigram of a great wit of modern fiction.[1] And no doubt the philistines of our profession would echo this sarcasm.

And yet no country and no age have ever been free (whether conscious of the fact or not) from some drift of philosophic thought. "In each epoch of time," says M. Leroy, in a brilliant book of recent years, "there is current a certain type of philosophic doctrine — a philosophy deep-seated in each one of us, and observable clearly and consciously in the utterances of the day — alike in novels, newspapers, and speeches, and equally

[1] M. Dumaresq, in Mr. Paterson's "The Old Dance Master."

in town and country, workshop and counting-house."
Without some fundamental basis of action, or theory
of ends, all legislation and judicial interpretation are
reduced to an anarchy of uncertainty.   It is like mathematics without fundamental definitions and axioms.
Amidst such conditions, no legal demonstration can be
fixed, even for a moment.   Social institutions, instead
of being governed by the guidance of an intelligent free
will, are thrown back to the blind determinism of the
forces manifested in the natural sciences.   Even the
phenomenon of experimental legislation, which is peculiar to Anglo-American countries, cannot successfully
ignore the necessity of having social ends.

The time is ripe for action in this field.   To quote the
statement of reasons given in the memorial presented at
the annual meeting of the Association of American Law
Schools in August, 1910: —

The need of the series now proposed is so obvious as hardly to
need advocacy.   We are on the threshold of a long period of constructive readjustment and restatement of our law in almost every department.   We come to the task, as a profession, almost wholly untrained
in the technic of legal analysis and legal science in general.   Neither
we, nor any community, could expect anything but crude results
without thorough preparation.   Many teachers, and scores of
students and practitioners, must first have become thoroughly
familiar with the world's methods of juristic thought.   As a first
preparation for the coming years of that kind of activity, it is the
part of wisdom first to familiarize ourselves with what has been
done by the great modern thinkers abroad — to catch up with the
general state of learning on the subject.   After a season of this, we
shall breed a family of well-equipped and original thinkers of our
own.   Our own law must, of course, be worked out ultimately by
our own thinkers; but they must first be equipped with the state
of learning in the world to date.

How far from "unpractical" this field of thought and research
really is has been illustrated very recently in the Federal Supreme
Court, where the opposing opinions in a great case (*Kuhn* v. *Fair-*

mont Coal Co.) turned upon the respective conceptions of "law" in the abstract, and where Professor Gray's recent work on "The Nature and Sources of the Law" was quoted, and supplied direct material for judicial decision.

Acting upon this memorial, the following resolution was passed at that meeting: —

That a committee of five be appointed by the president, to arrange for the translation and publication of a series of continental master-works on jurisprudence and philosophy of law.

The committee spent a year in collecting the material. Advice was sought from a score of masters in the leading universities of France, Germany, Italy, Spain, and elsewhere. The present series is the result of these labors.

In the selection of this series, the committee's purpose has been, not so much to cover the whole field of modern philosophy of law, as to exhibit faithfully and fairly all the modern viewpoints of any present importance. The older foundation-works of two generations ago are, with some exceptions, already accessible in English translation. But they have been long supplanted by the products of newer schools of thought which are offered in this series in their latest and most representative form. It is believed that the complete series will represent in compact form a collection of materials whose equal cannot be found at this time in any single foreign literature.

The committee has not sought to offer the final solution of any philosophical or juristic problems; nor to follow any preference for any particular theory or school of thought. Its chief purpose has been to present to English readers the most representative views of the most modern writers in jurisprudence and philosophy of law. The series shows a wide geographical representation; but the selection has not been centered on the notion of giving equal recognition to all countries. Primarily, the desire has been to represent the various schools of thought; and, consistently with this, then to represent the different chief countries. This aim, however, has involved little difficulty; for Continental thought has lines of cleavage which make it easy to represent the leading schools and the leading nations at the same time. Germany, for example, is represented in modern thought by a preponderant metaphysical influence. Italy is primarily positivist, with subordinate German and English influences. France in its modern standpoint is largely sociological, while making an effort to assimilate English ideas and customs in its theories of legislation and the administration of justice. Spain, Austria, Switzerland, Hungary, are represented in the Introductions and the shorter essays; but no country other than Germany, Italy, and France is typical of any important theory requiring additions to the scope of the series.

To offer here an historical introduction, surveying the various schools of thought and the progress from past to present, was regarded by the committee as unnecessary. The volumes of Dr. Berolzheimer and Professor Miraglia amply serve this purpose; and the introductory chapter of the latter volume provides a short summary of the history of general philosophy, rapidly placing the reader in touch with the various schools and their standpoints. The series has been so arranged (in the numbered list fronting the title page) as to indicate that order of perusal which will be most suitable for those who desire to master the field progressively and fruitfully.

The committee takes great pleasure in acknowledging the important part rendered in the consummation of this project, by the publisher, the authors, and the translators. Without them this series manifestly would have been impossible.

To the publisher we are grateful for the hearty sponsorship of a kind of literature which is so important to the advancement of American legal science. And here the Committee desires also to express its indebtedness to Elbert H. Gary, Esq., of New York City, for his ample provision of materials for legal science in the Gary Library of Continental Law (in Northwestern University). In the researches of preparation for this Series, those materials were found indispensable.

The authors (or their representatives) have cordially granted the right of English translation, and have shown a friendly interest in promoting our aims. The committee would be assuming too much to thank these learned writers on its own behalf, since the debt is one that we all owe.

The severe labor of this undertaking fell upon the translators. It required not only a none too common linguistic skill, but also a wide range of varied learning in fields little travelled. Whatever success may attend and whatever good may follow will in a peculiar way be attributable to the scholarly labors of the several translators.

The committee finds special satisfaction in having been able to assemble in a common purpose such an array of talent and learning; and it will feel that its own small contribution to this unified effort has been amply recompensed if this series will measurably help to improve and to refine our institutions for the administration of justice.

EDITORIAL COMMITTEE OF THE ASSOCIATION OF AMERICAN LAW SCHOOLS

INTRODUCTION TO THE TRANSLATED VOLUME

By Albert Kocourek[1]

Now that we are having placed before us, in an
approachable form, the best modern materials of the
European continent on philosophy of law, it will be
possible for us to ascertain, at first hand, what of value
there may be in this kind of learning.

Philosophy of law, if not wholly an alien phrase, is,
at least for us, an obscure collocation of words.   In a
vague apprehension of its content and limits, we associate with it all that is sublimely elevated and
fundamentally basic in our legal life — and pass on.   It
resembles the anthropomorphic God of the Hebrew
Scriptures.   Residing at a distance, it influences our
everyday concerns with a power too remote, and too
mysterious, to enter into our practical cause-and-effect
ideas.   It is to the practical mind at once too lofty,
and too metaphysical, to coördinate with the median
plane of experience.

There are even those among us who, seeing only the
undeniable elements of brute force and material egoism
within life, and the resultant expression of an organized
social power which restrains the clashing and warring
instincts of a herd of human wolves, deny that there is
any philosophy of law, and seek the ultimate notion
of the law in the will of the sovereign.   This denial
(without pausing to find what becomes of that search
after the finalities of truth which has been pursued

---

[1] Lecturer on Jurisprudence in Northwestern University, Chicago.

from the beginning of history) carelessly brushes aside the entire structure of philosophy of law as an unnecessary and unreal creation — an invention which has no sensible contact with the political world founded on command and obedience, and no existence therefore in relation to anything within the compass of our experience.

But we have not been either more or less fortunate than other countries in our traditions and our inherited ideas. Our racial sense of immediacy — the immediacy which has gripped up to the exploitation of the direct, the special, the local, and the concrete in life — has only had the effect of temporarily staying the progress of philosophic thought. Like other countries, we too have been caught between the nether millstone of a form of political materialism which disavows everything but the imperative element in law, and the upper stone of a form of juridical idealism which claims too much.

Until the middle of the 19th century, the notion of natural law, under its variety of disguises and protean shapes, remained ascendant as the final hypothesis of legal truth. This natural law was thought to consist of certain fixed and universal principles adaptable for all times to every system of law by direct incorporation, and applicable to the concretest expression of legal standards. This unmitigated form of natural law has been abandoned wherever philosophy of law has become a discipline of thought. Its elimination has not been effected, however, without a struggle. In the language of Windscheid it is an "ancient, never-ending dream of mankind."[1]

---

[1] On the continent, its essential idea has again been vigorously proclaimed, as a natural law "with a variable content," by the neo-Kantian school, chiefly through Stammler in Germany, Del Vecchio in Italy, and Charmont in France, all of whom will be represented in this series. This modified doctrine is not to be confused, however, with the unrelenting natural law of the eighteenth century.

It is curious to observe the dualistic phenomenon of practicing an imperative theory of law, and believing in a metaphysical law of nature. Nourished on the pseudo-philosophy of Blackstone, the notion of an unalterable standard of justice has entered the very stronghold of the law in the English-speaking countries, and finds its strongest support among our practical lawyers and judges, who might be expected to be the first to deny that there is any philosophy of law. Justice and its companion term, Reason, have long been established as the inviolable and transcendent metaphysical arcana of positive law. Judicial decisions and the traditions of legal speech are full of the jargon of reason and justice. The changes that have been rung on them in legal phrase have all but exhausted the poetic possibilities of our language; but the inquiry is not pushed to determine their nature or their scope. They are idols to be revered upon their pedestals, but not designed for other use. That this judgment may not appear as without basis, let the following typical characterization (taken at random) speak as the declaration of one of the ablest and most practical of judges; it asserts of justice that "Truth is its handmaid, Freedom is its child, Safety walks in its steps, Victory follows in its train; it is the brightest emanation from the Gospel, it is the attribute of God." A thing so deserving of praise should not be obscured. It should be (as Berolzheimer says of philosophy of law) not an appendix to the law, but rather a prospectus.

Our literature is not destitute of anticipations, at least, of legal philosophy. We had at one time the dogmatic conception that justice is the word of God. That solution having been found unworkable in an unbelieving world, resort was had to the imperative idea that justice is the command of the sovereign. We are still swayed by the rationalistic conception that there is an inherent standard of justice as ever-present and inflexible as the law of gravitation and capable of approximation by the positive law. On the other hand, we have also had the historical explanation of law chiefly through the writings of Sir Henry S. Maine. Finally, Professor T. H. Green has given us a neo-Hegelian insight into legal institutions, and Professor Pound has shown us the value of the sociological point of view. This enumeration touches, perhaps, all the well-recognized aspects of the nature and function of law. And yet we have no philosophy of law. Our legal philosophy is fragmentary, occasional, and unread. It would be strange if we should first learn to estimate the position of Bentham, Maine, and Spencer through the judgment of Italy, and yet this seems to be the reasonable probability.

England and America are slowly, very slowly, coming to realize that an analysis of fundamental legal ideas, and a study of the formal scope — the osseous tissue of the *corpus juris* — are indispensable in a refined and scientific administration of justice. The intolerable burden of mountains of cases is compelling this unwilling belief. We cannot, however, expect to rest with a mastery of the form of the law; we must investigate in a scientific way its substance, its relation to life, and all other reality, employing all the aids that learning can afford. We must clothe the skeleton of formal law with tissues, and provide it with organs that will make it fit for its environment and its mission in the scheme of life.

Law is not a thing detached and isolated. It is not disposed of by pronouncing a humanly conceived formula. It has an inherent relation to all other facts. It must therefore be studied in connection with and as a part of the combined reality of the world. It cannot be limited (as by Hobbes) to the politically sovereign organization; its mission is not understood by simple reference to the promotion of happiness or the suppression of pain; nor its nature known by pointing out its similarity to language in psychological development. The historical incidents of the creation of law, the assembled facts of legal evolution, and the accidental phases of what law has wrought in the history of the world under varying social influences, do not touch the reality within.

If we can go as far as this, we are prepared to believe that the mere nature of legislation and its interpretation do not sound the depths of legal institutions. These studies are the immediate tools of the legal workman, but they do not employ the ultimate forces of the law. We may have successful and skillful lawyers who know nothing and seek nothing beyond a traditional and astute application of legal rules, just as we may have useful, successful, and skillful bricklayers who are not burdened with any learning beyond the proper laying of bricks. The hewer of wood and the drawer of water, while performing their necessary functions in the progress of the world, do not, however, by their numerical preponderance or by the admitted necessity and useful dignity of their labor, render dispensable (or at least do not make valueless) a knowledge of the organic unity of the world, the facts of which are stated by the sciences and explained by philosophy.

The practical aspect of philosophy of law is manifested in the two principal legal activities in which the human will exerts itself as the sole or at least as a contributory force; that is to say, in the making of legal standards, and in the application of legal standards.

I. With respect to the creation of law, it is self-apparent that legislation cannot be based on mere caprice, conjecture, or fancy, and at the same time be regarded as an enlightened cultural activity. In the words of Ihering, the object is the creator of the law, or in the thought of Socrates, life is to be considered as a system of ends.

Several choices of viewpoint are conceivably present in the creation of legal standards. First, we may supinely yield to a blind determinism. We may regard the making of legal standards as the mechanical expression of inherent forces whose fixed causal chain involves even the processes of the mind, and which we are impotent to control, and could only ineffectively seek to understand. This standpoint is reminiscent of the conception of the Historical School which thinks of law as the unconscious unfoldment of the spirit of the people.

Secondly, we may regard legislation as the product of a conscious egoism — the varying phenomenon of a conflict among the asserted interests within the State. This view, by reason of its proximate relation to the motives most strikingly apparent in life, finds a ready acceptation, and perhaps sums up the average man's conception of the nature of legal development. No doubt, also, it contains an obvious element of objective truth. This standpoint may admit of a modification allowing the intervention of a predominant ethical element, realized in a formula such as that of Bentham, that every institution and every action must be judged according to its tendency to promote happiness or arrest pain; or some similar and equally futile mechanical or arithmetical attempt to find a solution of the complex problems of human existence.

Or thirdly, the conscious process of legislation may proceed experimentally, without an underlying formula, and without the aid of the social sciences, and with no crystallized idea of what social end is to be attained. This indeterminism of legislative method and legislative purpose can lead only to the most incongruous social results. Only after the effects are seen does it know what legislation may accomplish. It is the unplanned labor of children playing in the sand, who lay out now one pattern and then another without reason or purpose.

Fourthly, we find the causal explanation of legal institutions. This looks to whole domain of empiristic knowledge, and especially to biology, psychology, and economics. This, the sociological standpoint, goes beyond a mere political or historical interpretation of law. The causal conception provides not only a method, but also an explanation. Its tools are experiment, observation, and induction — rarely, if ever, deduction. It seeks to provide and employ, by conscious impulse, the scientific materials for a legislation that will accomplish definite and predetermined social results. It looks for its generalizations of social destiny to the objective and sensible world. As an explanation, it represents the law as an evolutionary growth, adapting itself from age to age to variations in social conditions and responding to the ideals of the time. Causality does not involve the blind, unconscious, or mechanical unfoldment of social institutions implied in a Darwinistic evolution. The element of hazard is present, but the voluntary element persistently overrides the spontaneous factor of growth. This view of legal institutions is one which may confidently be expected to find among us an approving reception when it is better understood. "The English do not care to shoot in the air," says Mr. Höffding. "They prefer to hit the mark even should the roar of their artillery be less imposing."

That a method so constructively helpful and so consonant with our close-to-the-ground mental inclinations should have been almost wholly neglected illustrates the persistence of ideas. We have become so much attached to the natural law conception of a monad theory of justice operating under an official guidance, that we have missed the notion of law as a social product. We have likewise resolved all its possibilities into an exclusively individualistic legal purpose, which is becoming more and more unworkable, and which is accordingly exerting heavy strains on our fundamental legal theories.

Lastly, there remains another aspect of legal development which bears the name of Finalism. It assumes an ultimate destiny in human institutions, projected from the beginning of time. From this point of view, legislation is an instrument for the attainment of definite, concrete, and isolated objects, which harmoniously conform, in detail, with the aggregate plan of life. Even the acceptance of the Hegelian formula that "all that is real is rational" does not exclude human effort and the actual manifestation of a real will as to the particular aspects of social life.

The objective world may be said to consist of special realities. These isolated facts must be dealt with in an isolated way by the temporal and local forces under our control in the form of commands and prohibitions — laws, standards of conduct — applicable to the various concrete conditions of life. Man's function in the world is not of less importance, even though we admit that the total reality transcends his understanding, and is beyond his control. His will is not less real because the world moves on by a constant progression. We may even admit (without violence to anything conceived to be practical) that the unified process expresses reason, and that man's activity is only relative, and that this activity being relative, frequently opposes, temporarily at least, the general current of cosmic evolution.

Our interest in the universal and our efforts to mark out with our finite intelligence, from the moving shadows on the wall of objective appearance, the full meaning of the reality passing behind us, lies in our relation to the absolute and the desirability that the particular under our control shall not be in conflict with the universal.

II. The application of law is the second point of practical contact between legal institutions and philosophy of law. It may, perhaps, here, be sufficient to point out that mere words cannot circumscribe the infinite variations of life. The permutations of conduct are not to be reduced to a set of words, or to any number of sets of words. The legal rule applied in a special and concrete case may arise from another rule (a principle) of higher generic order, but the latter, being necessarily abstract, cannot nourish a fruitful consequence without a spirit. Every legal system has its own soul. The spirit of legislation, and its relation to the totality of knowledge, cannot be adequately understood by the culminating generalizations derived from an induction of legal rules. The essential necessity of philosophy of law to attain this completion of thought suggests itself, without any manner of resort to that species of philosophy of law which has disparagingly been called speculative.

Even that vague idea of ultimate legal principle, which is always current, reaches out helplessly into the ocean of philosophic idea, and manages always to attach itself to one of those islands of foam which are called reason, justice, or truth. In the most highly developed legal systems the province of law (legislation) never completely covers the territory of fact. Something must always be left to discretion, and the present tendency seems to be even in the direction of extending the scope of discretion or fact, as against the domain of mere verbal formalism, which frequently works counter to the very objects which may be assumed to be sought. The discretion to be employed must be a discretion which is in harmonious accord with all the facts and tendencies of life. It must be a discretion with an end, otherwise it becomes either a chaos of vacillation and impermanency, or a dominion of arbitrary formalism.

A recent writer[1] comments on the uncertainties of philosophy of law. In truth, however, these conflicts are much less serious than they superficially appear. It is true that we have a school which seeks to find the truth from within, that is to say, subjectively. We have another that looks wholly to the objective world. Then again there are varieties of standpoint, which in one way and another combine the subjective and objective viewpoints. There are indeed these differences of method and conflicts of explanation. But there is essential agreement among all schools of philosophy as to those things within the purview of our mental powers, and as to things of interest to us here and now. The problem of the validity of knowledge may always be with us, and the ultimate reality may perhaps always be beyond us; but these foundations of controversy, and these allurements to lead on our aspirations, argue nothing against the effort to unify and coördinate the isolated particulars of our common sense. All modern philosophy accepts the sciences. It accepts the facts of life as they are understood by the average man. But it goes beyond the mere fact to the internal relation of all facts to each other. It is often "taken for granted that when you entered a philosophic class-room you had to open relations with a universe entirely distinct from

---

[1] G. Aillet, in "Revue de Métaphysique et de Morale," March, 1911.

the one you left behind you in the street";[1] and this
mistaken notion is difficult to eradicate.

Whether the philosophic method adopted is idealistic
or materialistic, and whether it holds to monism, dualism, or pluralism, is a matter of little consequence, if
the results reached from the different angles of approach
are in substantial agreement as to the purpose of life.
The higher truth of philosophy does not scorn the results
of the special sciences, and while adopting their con-
tributions, discovers in them, by methods of its own, a
relation and a unity which they alone are unable to
furnish. We do not discard religion simply because
there are multiform sects, creeds, and beliefs. Religion
and philosophy are twin activities; one seeks the highest
reality by faith and inspiration, and the other aspires
to the ultimate by demonstration and intuition.

As there are thus degrees and kinds of philosophy, so
we may expect to find different varieties of philosophy
of law, since philosophy of law is only an aspect of
general philosophy, and perhaps one of the most important of its aspects.

A little reflection shows us that we have positive law,
jurisprudence, legal sociology (*Rechtspolitik*), and philosophy of law in an ascending series. Positive law is
the concrete law existing and applied within the State;
jurisprudence is the scientific study of these concrete
details in a systematic arrangement from an abstract
standpoint; legal sociology goes beyond the positive
law and deals with its relation to all other social sciences;
while philosophy of law crowns the edifice of the legal
system, and exhibits its relation to the totality of existence. Philosophy of law, to claim the serious attention
of practical lawyers, must have a vital, inherent, and

[1]James: "Defense of Pragmatism."

direct contact with the practical administration of justice.   It must be more than a "ballet of bloodless categories."   Nor is it sufficient that it be an auxiliary
embellishment; for its claim could then be asserted no
further than similar claims for divers other forms of
knowledge which may be indirectly useful and promotive
of a more refined administration of justice.

But it is not necessary or desirable that any system of
law be dominated by a highly speculative and undemon-
strable metaphysic.   We should not expect a revelation
of absolute truth.   No friend of philosophy of law will
go to this length.   No developed system of law, however, can afford to decline the direct advantages afforded
by philosophy of law, both in testing by analysis the
character of our legal ideas, and in refining by its syntheses the functions of legal justice, and in elevating it
from the stupidity of a mere experimentalism.   We
need not go so far as to deny everything that transcends
a positivistic explanation of the universe.   We should
not expect of philosophy of law the unattainable.
In the language of Kohler, "To ask of the philosopher the
impossible is to compel him either to offer a fantastic
substitute for metaphysics or to renounce it altogether."

The philosophy of law demanded by the twentieth
century is not one that attempts to represent the law as
it ought to be, and is therefore always in advance of the
fact; nor yet a philosophy of law that is always too late
to be of any use in life.   It must relate to the present,
and must be connected, inherently and organically,
with the problems of our daily experience.   It must be
drawn from the clouds into the thick of life,—not with
the expectation that every man will be a philosopher,
but that every man may be.   The hierarchy of modern
specialism is not to be disturbed or assaulted, but directly
and consciously furthered.

Bentham and Austin have given us in our own tongue
the juristic foundation for work that must soon be seriously prosecuted by us if we are to have any relief from
the perpetual deluge of our oceans of cases. With the
presentation of this series, of which this excellent book
of Professor Miraglia is one of the introductory volumes,
Dr. Wigmore, who is the author of the idea and who has
been the leading spirit in its realization, is making it
possible for the English-speaking world to attain direct
knowledge of the foundations for real legal thought in
the large substantive problems common to every system
of law. The conception of such a series was a bold one,
and it is only to be feared that it may be many years
before we are prepared fully to appreciate its true value.
It may, however, reasonably be hoped that this notable
addition to our equipment of knowledge will plant the
seed that will (if not in this, at least in some other generation) grow into a cultural harvest, and thus most
fitly and acceptably honor the scholarly mind that conceived its purpose. It is not unlikely that this series
of books will produce a result perhaps entirely un-
reckoned, in stimulating an interest in general philosophy.
If this comes to pass, a cobwebbed academic highway
will owe something more than politeness to the mere
jurist.

Germany is looked upon as the seat of the decisive
conflicts in philosophy of law; but the thinkers of Germany have perhaps been too near the clamor of
battle to give us an account of the struggle for a Philosophy of Law free from the color of strong partisan
bias. The presentation of this treatise at this point
in the series, while determined by the value of the work
itself, is secondarily a tribute to the country from
which it emanates. When philosophy of law was dead
in all the rest of the world, Italy, the land of Vico,

Spaventa, Romagnosi, and Vanni, the country which gave us in the *Corpus Juris* the greatest historical monument of private law — Italy alone nourished its vital spark and spread its living products over the map of Europe.

Since Philosophy of Law must rest upon foundations sufficient to support universal knowledge and universal reality, Professor Miraglia commences with a discussion of the basic propositions of the leading general philosophies, treating the subject from a critical and comparative standpoint. With this necessary orientation accomplished, he passes to the notion of law, and treats in detail the various institutions which appear in society as phenomena of the law, employing the same critical and comparative method which distinguishes the general part of his book.

If it has been necessary at the beginning to soar in the ether of pure reason, no just complaint can be raised, since the author has been able to effect a substantial landing-place in the midst of the most tangible and familiar practical concerns. Little formative influence will follow even a philosophical explanation of such settled institutions as property, obligations, and the family. They are coeval with the history of civilization, and have attained their highest theoretical form. It is, however, true that on the practical side much remains to be done in adjusting these institutions to the harmony of the world-movement, and it is here that philosophy will exert its most important service in laying open the internal relation of these legal conceptions to the facts of life, for their further refinement. But a problem greater than the mere explanation or simple refinement of legal institutions remains. Shall these institutions continue to exist, and if not, what is to take their place?

This work is primarily a book of instruction, but it is not a closed vehicle for a theory. It is true that the author has a point of view, but it is not rudely obtruded on the readers' attention to the exclusion of all other points of view. Kohler's great book is plainly labelled a book of instruction, but it is limited to his own new system of philosophy.

Professor Miraglia covers the whole field not only of the subject-matter of Philosophy of Law but also of the philosophies bearing on this subject-matter. As might be expected, the emphasis is largely placed on the Italian thinkers, but the available German, English, and French materials are treated with broad and sympathetic intelligence and conspicuous fairness. The wide horizon inspected, and the richness of view attained, testify eloquently to the author's industry and scholarship.

Italy has been easily the most prolific country of the world in Philosophy of Law, and the latter years have witnessed no diminution in this literature. It may be regarded as unfortunate that the time of the last edition of this treatise was such that the prevailing currents of thought in Italy could not have been taken into account. This deficiency will, however, be remedied by other works in this series.

To conclude, has Miraglia any position of his own in philosophy of law, and if so what is it? It can hardly be said that there can be extracted from this work any independent standpoint. It is a strong argument in favor of this treatise that such is the fact. A work of this extent could not, however, be written without manifesting philosophical preferences. Classified in a word, Miraglia is Vico modernized. History and metaphysics are reconciled, and the inductive and deductive methods are combined. Law, says Miraglia, consists of the true and the certain. One is the metaphysical element; the other is the historical factor. It is at once idea and reality. Just how he unites them is perhaps not entirely clear. Does he rely on the Kantian bridge between thought and thing, or the Hegelian principle of identity, or is the relation between idea and reality simply treated in a pragmatic sense?

Mirgalia's metaphysics is clearly not that of Hegel or of the neo-Hegelian school, nor yet of Hume or Kant. The Hegelian metaphysics is speculatively constructive. The Critical philosophy, on the other hand, tells us that we can know nothing about it except that it is unknown. Miraglia inclines toward a scientific metaphysics, but the point of stress is on the certain — the historical element. Kohler's metaphysics, for example, is also a scientific metaphysics. He justifies it in the same way that science affords information concerning celestial bodies that are beyond the power of telescopes; but Kohler's metaphysics is transcendental and ideal.

Miraglia's ideal element admits of the Hegelian view of the State as an ethical unity, but he does not assimilate his dialectic process. A metaphysics such as this, which does not leap too far into the dark, and yet holds something up to our aspirations toward knowledge, will frighten no one away from philosophy of law. The Italians have been greatly influenced by English thinkers, and their philosophy has accordingly followed a very conservative course.

This treatise adequately covers the ground that the author has laid out, and in connection with Berolzheimer's volume practically exhausts the historical part of this subject. Philosophy of law can be popularized no more than the integral calculus. But this work affords an excellent means of approach to a difficult matter; if the inherent problems are not made easy, their aspect is at least robbed of a too forbidding severity. It is fortunate, also, to find in its translator a happy realization of the combination of scholarship, linguistic skill, and technical knowledge, necessary to present this book to English readers.

BIOGRAPHICAL NOTE ON THE AUTHOR

LUIGI MIRAGLIA was born at Reggio in Calabria in 1846. He took his degree at Naples in 1866, and, after several years of teaching in subordinate posts, was appointed to the chair of philosophy of law in the University of Naples. He was at the same time professor of political economy in the Agricultural Scientific School at Portici. Among the other posts later filled by him at various times were those of Secretary of the Academy of Political and Moral Science, and of President of the Society for the Advancement of Naples. A final distinction — often conferred in Italy for juristic and literary eminence — was the royal appointment as Senator of the Kingdom. He died in September, 1903.

Among his numerous books and essays are the following: "The Fundamental Principles of the Various Systems of Legal Philosophy, and Hegel's Ethico-Juridical Doctrines" (1873); "The Modern Philosophy of Law in its Relation to Industrial Law" (1874); "The Primitive Family and Natural Law" (1877); "History and Theory of the Right of Prize-Capture in War" (1871); "Studies in the Science of Education" (1871).

The first work above-named received a second edition in 1893; and the third, enlarged edition, in 1903, bearing the simple title, "Philosophy of Law," is the work here translated.

To the Memory of
My Father

PREFACE

This book is a complete course in the Philosophy of Law, intended for the use of undergraduate students of law. It can be easily seen that a course in the Philosophy of Law in a law school cannot have the same character and the same scope as a similar course in a school of philosophy or art. But the Philosophy of Law must necessarily be a part of philosophy, and therefore must not be confused with an introduction to the study of positive law. Taught in a law school, it should sketch with a free hand the organism of legal institutions according to the principles of reason, and should have regard to the multiplications and intimate relations of philosophy with the legal, social, and political sciences. The second part of this book has no other object than to extend philosophical thought over various subjects that for a long time have been considered apart from any such relation.

LUIGI MIRAGLIA.

TABLE OF CONTENTS

INTRODUCTION

BOOK I

GENERAL PART

CHAPTER I

Philosophy and the sciences. The character of modern philosophy as foreshadowed by Vico. Philosophy of the law as part of philosophy. The human idea of law according to the doctrine of Vico, and the definitions of Kant, Hegel, Trendelenburg, Romagnosi, and Rosmini. The social and legal theories. Law and positive philosophy.

CONTENTS

BOOK II

PRIVATE LAW

———

CONTENTS

CONTENTS

Comparative Legal Philosophy

Comparative Legal Philosophy

INTRODUCTION

A SURVEY OF PHILOSOPHICAL SYSTEMS

I

GREEK SPECULATION AND ROMAN DOGMA

The fundamental principle of things and of knowledge is to be found, according to Greek speculation, always outside the mind in the object. The object for the Ionics is water, the primitive material without determinate quality (that is, infinite), and the air; for the Pythagoreans, it is number, the essence of things; for the Eleatics, it is pure, abstract, and immovable being, that has no beginning, nor end, that is not divisible, that does not go from place to place, but is always one and perfect. The origin of beings, according to Heraclitus, is birth or the perennial flow; according to Empedocles, it lies in the complexity of the four elements, water, air, fire, and earth, originally different in quality, from whose union and separation things are born and perish; and for Democritus, it consists in the indefinite plurality of atoms without qualitative difference and various only in form.

Anaxagoras builds up the Whole with primitive elements of diverse nature, called by him "seeds" and later "homoiomerei," and with the Noos or intelligence that gives them their order. The SOPHISTS show that truth cannot be found by natural knowledge, because phenomenon is variable and contradictory. The reality of things is different from our knowledge, and therefore thought is only a belief, and happiness lies in pleasure and utility. SOCRATES discovers the ideal object, and teaches that true knowledge is founded on the concept of things, separated by induction and determinated by definition. PLATO raises the Socratic concepts (now become ideas) and gives them their order by dialectics. Belief, in his mind, is connected with sensible phenomena, while the concept corresponds to the real and immutable essence or idea, as a metaphysical principle. ARISTOTLE makes the Platonic idea the form of reality, because there can be no essence without phenomena.

After Plato and Aristotle came the philosophers of the ideal objectivity, with the belief that the principle of things is not yet found, and that, consequently, it is convenient to let practical interest prevail and to lull the spirit to sleep with internal satisfactions. STOICISM, EPICUREANISM, and SCEPTICISM express the same tendency of the subject to renounce the possibility of self-satisfaction. The Stoics and the Epicureans consider knowledge as a means of practical life, whose object is the happiness attainable only by reason freed from passion, that is, by virtue, according to the first, or by sense and pleasure aided by calculation, according to the second. The Sceptics believe that the satisfaction of the spirit is not best attained by knowledge because things are unknowable and indifferent for us, for we can attribute to them different and contradictory predicates. If things are indifferent for us, the spirit should not be disturbed, whatever happens. Scepticism is the demonstration that truth cannot be learned by reason; differing from the teaching of the Sophists, which is the demonstration that truth cannot be attained by natural knowledge or sense. Therefore, Socrates opposes the Sophists and says that if truth cannot be learned by sense or belief, it is found in knowledge, or the concepts.

Since we cannot learn truth by reason, conclude the NEO-PLATONISTS, it must be higher than reason and must be regarded as a principle transcendent, supra-intelligible, ineffable, an object of faith, ascetics, and ecstatics. The supra-intelligible in Neo-Platonism is nothing more than the old Greek intellect, which by its nature always seeks the principle of things without itself, since it is without its own content; that is, truth which is felt in an objective manner.

The Ethos, given such a character in Greek philosophy, cannot fail to be objective and to be established, therefore, in the form of a natural organism. In such, the part is always medial and never ultimate; hence the defect of any true personal and private right in Greek society. Pythagoras sees in justice a number; Socrates discerns the measure of all things in the common nature of men, all eager for happiness, who attain it in its truth, through the realization of the concepts, that represent the ideal object. Plato places the Ethos in the idea of happiness, which controls in the spiritual world, having actual substance, as supreme as the sun, which does not depend upon the beholder but sheds its light over all. Such an idea (which has no part in reality, although reality can mould itself thereon) cannot be better incarnated than in a beautiful and artificial state, all complete, as Minerva, springing fully armed from the head of Jupiter. The Platonic state is ideal, exemplary; it represents man in the abstract, and unites in itself the variety of individual potentialities by that same force by which the internal principle of life interpenetrates the organs.

According to Aristotle, the Ethos must be found in reality and the purpose of nature; whence the maxim that no institution is good unless it conforms to nature, and also the value of the methods of comparison and analogy with which he builds up his politics. He holds that the State, not any of its components, is the child of the need which human beings, being neither animals nor gods, feel for unity and development; the State makes for the consummation and happiness that is the result of the unification, desired by nature, of all human activities and, therefore, it has the duty of making good and just citizens. Aristotle criticizes Plato for having recognized a separate ideal essence, while giving to the State an attribute which he denies to its components; Plato criticizes the master because he has conceived the State as a mere empty unity, while harmony is not derived from a single tone but from many; and yet he excludes slaves, farmers, and artisans from effective participation in that ethical eudemony made, by him, the basis of the State.

In general, the Greek State is not of the highest type because it is a natural organic body and not an ethical or human organization. It can be said to be gifted with classic beauty but it lacks the nobler and higher qualities contained with such potentiality in the Christian faith. Stoicism places wisdom above the State, withdrawing from the world and condemning itself to complete impassivity; for, in this belief, individual life is lost in that of humanity, and the life of humanity is confused with universal life. For the Epicureans, suffering is evil and the wise man works for lasting peace. Scepticism, on account of the confusion of phenomena, forms no judgment and lives in apathy. The wise man among the Neo-Platonists hopes to be included by the inconceivable principle of the whole through asceticism and ecstaticism by which PLOTINUS was made happy in three or four visions.

The ROMAN world is the world of the will, and, therefore, of law and politics. The will, in such a world, on the one hand, is continuously seen in the controlling and inflexible order of the State, and, on the other, begins to develop in the form of individual rights. With the development of the principle of will with its subjective nature, private rights cannot fail to arise, and the State cannot long preserve the rough semblance of a natural organic object. In Rome, private law was at first strict, ironclad, and cramped. Then it extended, becoming facile, general, supple, and equitable; for equity guards the right, which the law, in its generality, cannot protect. And finally it became human law, and, consequently, proclaimed the principle that slavery, an institution of mankind and contrary to nature, does not control the spirit, and that men, in natural law, are free and equal.

CICERO, the greatest philosopher of the Roman world, having no scientific knowledge of the manifestation of subjective rights as the act of the abstract power of the will, is inferior to Roman realism. He is not the author of a philosophy of his own, but he follows, as an eclectic, the Greek writers; he professes his doubt; he does not believe that mind can be absolutely sure, but thinks that it is satisfied with simple verisimilitude. In Ethics, he eliminates doubt, on account of its dangerous consequences, and appeals to the immediate consciousness, in which are found the germs of virtue, and to the consensus of mankind to define the honest and establish some speculative foundation for it. He prefers the ethical principle of the Stoics, which as a practical man he modifies; he derives law not from the statutes of the Twelve Tables or the Edicts, but from human nature; he reproduces the Aristotelean theory of the State, but assigns it a mixed form, proper to the political organization of Rome.

II

THE PHILOSOPHY OF THE MIDDLE AGES

The empty subject, represented by the Neo-Platonists as an object, received in the Middle Ages all its concreteness and, in the terms of Christianity, was defined as the Word or absolute mind. Philosophy, henceforth, became a subjective principle. Man, the image of God, and the incarnation of the Word, came to his own; and the ancient State, losing its high significance, was constricted within closer bounds. The more intimate part of the individual was no longer subjected to the political power, but rather to new beliefs that originally kept within the celestial realm in which they were born and acted in opposition to the pagan régime. The Apostle created a contradiction between the desires of the flesh and the impulses of the spirit. LACTANTIUS believed that true justice lay in the worship of the one God, unknown to the Gentiles. AUGUSTINE speaks of a celestial city, the seat of truth and justice, in contradistinction to the terrestrial city, the den of thieves and the product of original sin. The terrestrial city can acquire an ethical value by giving itself over to the defense of the Church, which had not at this time acquired its character of ruler or its mundane interests.

The struggle between Christianity and the world was much diminished when, through the work of religious phantasy, the celestial city was populated by an host subject to divine command, possessing an history, and the earth became holy through contact with the Church; which, in its turn, became a temporal instead of a spiritual communion. The conciliation was effected through a new conception of participation, of which THOMAS

AQUINAS was the founder. Aristotle had said that the universals are second substances, and he had further asserted that they were qualities. REALISM developed the side of the Aristotelean system in which the universals appear as separate forms. NOMINALISM was in its turn based on that side in which primal reality seems placed in the individual. Nominalism, not being easily correlated with any dogmas, was soon condemned; Realism, being analogous to the heterodox transcendentalism of the Arabian commentators, met a similar fate. Aquinas, in the footsteps of ALBERTUS MAGNUS, tried a compromise, claiming that the universals are models of creation before material existence, and that in material existence they are the substance of our conceptions.

There is, for Aquinas, one eternal law in God; a natural law, which is a participation in the eternal, the light of knowledge and the norm of ethical and juristic acts; and a human or positive law, a shadow of the natural, just as that in its turn is a shadow of the eternal. But he did not succeed in his project of conciliation; for the supernatural remained in its transcendence in the divine intellect, and the sphere of the king (who must obey Aristotle) remained in opposition to the sphere of the priest (who must obey the Bible). Hence the existence of contradictory sentences in St. Thomas, who now derives the State from the social nature of man, and assigns happiness for its object, and general consent for its base, and yet at the same time considers it the realization of the divine kingdom in its temporal aspect. The amalgam dissolved, the Aristotelean elements finally concentrated in the political doctrines of MARSILIUS of Padua, and the traditional in the dynastico-hierarchical doctrines of PETER of Andlo. While EGIDIO COLONNA, on the one hand, exaggerated the religious principle, presenting the type of hermit-prince lacking confidence in his own power and love of glory, and advised the pursuit of happiness in God, on the other hand he reproduced the ideas of the Stagirite and gained from his contemporaries the title of "doctor fundatissimus."

DANTE conceived law as the personal and real relation between man and man, and therefore distinguished it from morals, by which an action is good or bad of itself without relation to the rights of another. He knew how to distinguish with fine acumen the difference between legal freedom and untrammelled caprice; because the former, according to him, is the power that makes every individual competent to work in accordance with the judgment that he himself has made about the rectitude of his acts without being disturbed by others; the latter is only governed by desire. The object of civil society, in his mind, is the increase of civilization, which lies in the greatest possible development of the mind. Law strengthens it; otherwise, it does not deserve its great name. The State looks to the attainment of the transitory aims of human nature, while the Church, concerned with non-transitory objects, cannot exercise civil dominion. Dante solved the political problem by a system of free and independent municipal States, each the head of its own territory, with power to resist possible discordant ambitions vested in a king or supreme magistrate of the republic of the States, who would govern according to fundamental laws and be the agent of all the States. The principle of unity is present in the mind of Dante on every side; because of the predominating divine analogy, because of the classic remembrance of the Empire, because of the constitution of the Church, equally catholic, and because of his purpose of avoiding struggles between nations.

BARTOLUS, who deserves credit for having extended the sphere of jurisprudence by collecting analogies from the cases decided by the Roman jurisconsults and for having freed judges from many difficulties and accused persons from corruption on the part of the judges, does not consider (because he is a writer on practical law) the history of the philosophy of law. For the same reason all the commentators disregard it, however keen they may be in the discovery of equitable principles, and in the application of the dialectics of Arabian philosophy to the treatment of various subjects. So Bartolus disregards it in the sphere of civil law (as Gravina has said). The Thomists and the Scotists, irreconcilable in all else, agree in admitting an idealistic and realistic duality. Occam destroys such intermediaries in the order of cognition and recognizes direct communion of subject and object; on the practical score, he, the enemy of intermediaries, shows in a concise way the necessity of the separation of State and Church. Occam separates also theology from philosophy, and discusses the contradictions of dogma and reason. For him, reason is insufficient, and the only means of salvation is faith. Theology, separated from philosophy, is thought safe because its enemy is no longer by its side, and Philosophy becomes freer.

This is the moment of the dissolution of Scholasticism, which had represented a progressive step from Patristicism. Patristic philosophy is the elaboration of dogma by philosophic reflection. Scholasticism is the systematization of definite dogmas and the demonstration of their coherence. Both Scholastics and Patristics rely on dogma, to which the Scholastics apply rationalistic methods, distinguishing, therefore, belief from faith. Faith and reason, at first, are in accord, though the latter depends upon the former. Later, the two terms are found in disaccord, and separate, resulting in the downfall of Scholastics. Here it is useful to remember that even from its beginning Scholasticism had two diverse directions; Duns Scotus says that authority comes from reason, and Anselm of Aosta teaches that there is no need of understanding in order to believe, but that belief is necessary in order to understand.

In the days of Scholasticism, other systems appeared, which, though not generally received, are important because they contained the germs of future speculation. These systems depend also on the hypothesis of transcendentalism, although they are not logically harmonious therewith. Roger Bacon recommends the study of language, to understand the sources, and he relies greatly on mathematical and natural sciences, and states that without experience nothing can be known, and that experience alone should control speculative studies. But he connects internal experience with mysticism and places theology above philosophy; teaching that knowledge is vain if it has not the divine for an object. Raymond Lully considers demonstration more important than faith; in the "Ars Magna," a logical and mathematical method of unifying the concepts and of resolving scientific problems, he tries to constitute an a priori science and faith. Nicholas of Cusa admits that the mind can raise itself to infinitude as a principle in which contradictions coincide. Such coincidence cannot be understood by science, and therefore there is a state of learned ignorance. For him, God is the absolute greatness in which all being is bound; the universe is the concrete greatness that contains explicitly what God contains implicitly.

III

THE RENAISSANCE

Scholastic philosophy deprives the mind of truth (which is contained in the definition of faith), and does not include nature in its categories. The ensuing philosophy, a complete criticism of Scholasticism, is sceptic because truth placed above the intellect cannot be attained; and it inclines to Naturalism, because, according to the thinkers of the Renaissance, in nature alone can be seen the traces and later the very substance of truth, abstracted by mind and encompassed by dogma.

The conviction of the divine worth of the world and of man arose after humanity grew hungry in its inability to find God either in the Church (become too terrestrial with its wealth and its government) or in the Holy Sepulchre (the aim of the Crusades). This was the cause of the renewal of classic culture, which implied an attentive study of phenomena, a respect for work, a general need of reform, and the end of political feudalism (so closely connected with religion and speculation). By this conviction, largely, were caused many of the important characteristics of the new age, such as the increase of commerce (following the Crusades), the voyages for the discovery of new lands and a new continent, the independence of lay authority, and the formation of absolute monarchies. These destroyed the feudal power and laid the foundation stone of nationality, of Protestantism, and of the Catholic Restoration, with the decrease in papal authority. The invention of printing expressed the first unity of popular thought. So the man of the Middle Ages was transformed into that new man who follows a thousand industries, who is tenacious of his profession, who concerns himself with the facts of this world in popular assemblies, who no longer runs to liberate sepulchres, nor attends tourneys, but laughs in his sleeve at the stories of the investiture of popes and kings.

In Italy, the new man was incarnate in MACHIAVELLI. Completely dominated by the spirit of his time, he did not seek the aid of metaphysical and theological elements for social reconstruction; these he held up to scorn with fine irony, when he discoursed about the ecclesiastical principalities. He went deep into the effectual truth of things, and was not satisfied with its image. His purpose was to make Italy a State. He saw that, in his day, this could not be attained by moral methods; and, having before his mind the ineffectual attempt of SAVONAROLA, he fought a practical battle without hesitation over the morality of his means. He conceived of the State as a distinct institution — essentially civil, and having in itself a reason for existence, and strong in its own force. Machiavelli did not go out of the circle of political types designed by POLYBIUS; and, like Polybius, he preferred the mixed type (of which Paruta later accurately measured the difficulty).

PROTESTANTISM was an act of the new man. After starting with honest principles, it was not perverted by LUTHER (as Guicciardini maintained); nor was it the result of mere opportunity (as the Jesuits and Voltaire have said). Protestantism destroyed the hierarchy. It wanted the divine Word to be interpreted by free and independent reason, by the individual soul; it proclaimed in concise manner the individuality of conscience. In Italy, the Lutheran movement was not successful, because Italy possessed a literature and philosophy greatly superior to the Protestant idea, as

FLORENTINUS pointed out.   In Italy, the land of so many religious sects and of so many tentative reforms, the recovery of Greek culture had already inspired the study of Aristotle in the original, while in Germany they stiil studied a translation of the Old Testament.   The Italians were emancipated by the exclusively rational character of their studies.   Among Luther's compatriots Protestantism was a national slogan; it signified the destruction of Frederick's following, and by its religious character it became popular.   But Protestantism in its first moments so exaggerated the intimacy of man and God as to make faith, and not good works, the only dispenser of salvation; the only means was grace, excluding all human coöperation and free will. Ethics cannot fail to be prejudiced by such an exaggeration.

In the glorious days of the Renaissance, there flourished the renowned followers of Plato and Aristotle — originators and reformers of philology, all of whom had more or less sceptical tendencies and depended upon nature and experience.   They honored, for example, among the Aristoteleans, POMPONAZZI, among the new philologists, VIVES, among the reformers, MELANCHTHON; — which is a proof of what we have stated. Pomponazzi believed that our knowledge is only a shadow and trace of mind, that man is but a figure of the immaterial and knows but little of his nature; that sense is more powerful than reason.   On the other hand, he shows that man can in action attain that perfection which he cannot attain with the mind, and that theoretical and practical intellect is impossible without the body.   Vives held that human science is limited, that it only attains verisimilitude, and that the practical element should be preferred to the speculative.   This famous philologist (not logical in his sceptical principles) made the distinction (which Vico made later) that in human affairs, and therefore in law, there are two elements, absolute truth and mere probability, and observed that the true should be the aim of the probable, established by the free will of men for common utility. Such a distinction is found in the books of Plato. In treating of truth and belief, Vives placed natural law in superiority to divine law, and regarded the former as the sanction of the latter. He separated the office of philosopher from that of jurist, and consequently recognized a law of humanity distinct from that which is evolved from the various circumstances of time, place, and need. Melanchthon, who wrote books of moral philosophy, as Olendorp and Winkler wrote books of natural law (full of positive religious data and without scientific base), thought that man could not know absolute truth; that he should remain within the confines of experience; and that he should follow not only virtue but also life and the good things of life — that is, matrimony, society, and the well-ordered pleasures which the gods concede to men.

In the first period of the Renaissance, Greek thought was reconstructed by direct interpretation from its sources, diluted by Christian elements added in the Middle Ages. Marcello Ficino and the Florentine Academy represent the return to Plato. Pompanazzi represents the return to Aristotle. The Latin commentary on the works of the Stagirite was laid aside, and the Arabian of Averroes and the Greek of Alexander of Aphrodisias were used. The first tends to the transcendence of the intellect, to its existence separate and independent of the body; the second to the immanence of thought as an intrinsic form.

After this period of the reconstruction of the Greek philosophy, comes that in which there is a tendency to open a new life to the speculative spirit. TELESIUS, the first of the new men, as Bacon called him, did not follow theological or Aristotelean principles but considered the nature of things according to principles of his own. For him, all knowledge was a derivative of sense, which was connected with motion. Everything in nature was reducible to matter and force. Force was shown in the heat of the sun and the cold of the earth; heat was confused with motion.

BRUNO and CAMPANELLA are the greatest philosophers in this second period, and are authors of a new philosophy very different from the Aristotelean. Bruno brought to life the principle of the infinity of nature. According to him, all is God-Nature; God outside the world is left to the theological believers; the universe is the infinite creature of an infinite creator, who is infinite in his complications and in his sum, while it is explicitly but not totally infinite. Individual things are mere figures or accidentals. The ethical doctrine of Bruno is lighted by the divine intellectual sun of truth, the substance of moral action and of morality, which it penetrates as a temporal power or prudence. Law should be informed by reason and should result in utility. Government is strength; the act of the law is judgment or legal punishment, which should not condemn words or acts that do not affect the tranquility of the State.

Campanella, as a metaphysician, thinks that nature, if not itself God, is certainly his living image. As a psychologist, his motive is sense, and he recognizes its final connection with motion. He distinguishes the "sensus abditus" from the "sensus additus," in that one is native and occult, and the other derivative. He says that intellect is languid and rarified sense. The "sensus additus," that is, concrete, determinate sense, is founded on the original, "sensum abditum." He writes, "Nos esse et posse, scire et velle, certissimum principium primum." Campanella, however, recognizes the divine more in religion than in nature. He believes in progress, but in a theocratic manner, admitting community of possessions and of women, the governmental control of marriage, and the control of society as an institution (whence the frugality and poverty of the Solari), and he would govern the world as a kind of universal pontifical monarchy.

God is revealed not only in religion but in nature as well, according to the Neo-Platonists; at whose head is Ficino. Nature therefore is not only the means for the action of God but comprehends divine virtues and properties, which are open to the knowledge and utility of man. Theosophy is the knowledge of God, in that it is founded on a knowledge of nature. Nature is the grand mystery, the key to which is the Cabala. This has been defined as the Jewish gnosis. The gnosis (whatever be its religious content) considers fact as a veil under which the idea is hidden, and the value of such content is its explanation of the world, that is for speculative intent. The Cabala attests the presence of the divine force of nature; Magic is the study by which man tends to conquer it. Alchemy studies the elementary occult forces, and Astrology tries to determine the influence of the stars on human acts.

BODIN works to acquire an exact knowledge of the real elements of Politics and of the utility of social order without searching out the necessary fundamentals. In his process of examination, he follows Aristotle. Grotius points this out, saying that Bodin converts morals and law, at his own free will, into politics. He deserves, however, the honor of having noted the influence of climate on social institutions before MONTESQUIEU. This does not show (as Filangieri claimed) that

Montesquieu had no originality.   Many have held that the wise legislator should note the influence of climate, and among them are Plato and Aristotle, as well as Bodin; but none like Montesquieu made it the basis of his system.

In this epoch, in which the criticism of Scholastic hypotheses was strengthened and high consideration was given to nature, the State was no longer looked upon as an entity without ethical qualities, as an institution of fratricide and the result of sin; nor yet as a means at the disposition of the Church for the destruction of heresy.   Its object was not terrestrial virtue, dependent upon celestial virtue, neither was it a body, in respect to the Church, which was likened to mind; but was considered as an aggregate of forms, whose combination and disintegration was studied by Machiavelli as a natural human institution, which contained in itself that divine principle existing in the world.   The State existed of itself, and had no need of being connected with the Church to become legitimate.   It was a complex of forces, the centre of which was the king and later civil society.   It took the form of an absolute monarchy and was a factor in the development of nationality; except in Italy, where those obligations towards the Church, which Machiavelli records, were too strong for it.

IV

BACON, DESCARTES, AND GROTIUS

Modern philosophy, the daughter of the Renaissance, was born of doubt. Its chief founders, BACON and DESCARTES, sought for a secure basis of knowledge, free from the doubt of the ancient hypotheses.

BACON placed, over against the Aristotelean Organ, the "Novum Organum," in which induction, as the primal factor, acquires a new experimental character. Man, in his opinion, could not conquer nature without a knowledge of her laws, without interpreting her. And the interpretation of nature demanded experience. Experience should be free from all that the mind introduced therein of itself; that is, from prejudices or dogmas. It should use the form of induction, based on facts in which the law of the phenomena was exemplified; such a fact is called by Bacon a prerogative instance.

DESCARTES to reconstruct science turned to thought. He followed a movement opposed to that of Bacon. For Descartes, the senses are not true witnesses; the only indubitable knowledge of existence itself is from the "cogito ergo sum." This knowledge, which is primal, is clear, because the ego is present to itself; and is distinct, because thought is the characteristic by which the ego differs from all other entities. From this primal knowledge, from the knowledge of self-existence, are born through deductive processes all cognitions. Science always exists where a clear and distinct knowledge of things can be had; the mind doubts, because it is imperfect. If it believes itself imperfect, it must have the idea of the perfect or infinite. If it has the idea of the infinite, it means that an infinite cause has impressed it.

Inherent are the ideas of the ego and of God; acquired are the ideas that man forms, whose cause lies outside of him. The representations that refer to external objects are not entirely derivative from bodies, because there is in them some of our methods, for example, color, smell, sound, and taste. Extension alone is not one of our methods, but rather the very essence of external nature. Thought is spirit, extension is body; the spirit is active and the body inert.

Bacon wishes to transform by experience the natural and moral studies; yet with the latter he occupies himself little. He inclines to the thought that the moral and political sciences are founded on belief, and not directly on fact; and that the duty of public law is not only to protect private law, but to take care of the education and welfare of the citizens. Bacon's political doctrine, which follows a line between moral principle and legislation, and is contrary to an ideal type of absolute perfection of society, looks to mutual intercourse, trade, and the commonwealth. In his theory of mutual intercourse, there is a noticeable confusion of the right of society in its relation to law with the right of society in its relation to education; in that of trade, there is much erudition and many maxims of prudence. In his third book, he does not speak of the preservation of the kingdom and of the method of making it happy, but of the manner of extending its boundaries. It must not be forgotten that the book was dedicated to the King of England. The Chancellor's treatise on the sources of law is a study not so much philosophical as practical, containing wise precepts for legislation and entirely dominated by a political principle. With this understood, it is manifest that Francis Bacon should not be ranked (as Lampredi ranked him) among the writers on natural law.

Descartes considered God as the principle of thought, the extension of knowledge and motion. In man, the unity of spirit and body is brought about in the passions that owe their origin to both. Ethics aim to free man from the sway of the passions. Freedom cannot be gained without a true knowledge and comprehension of them. Bruno had here foreshadowed this epoch by his idea of Ethics founded on reason, and of a freedom of the soul (as mind) from its union of God.

With the Cartesian philosophy, this new and great movement which puts thought at the head, free from external and traditional elements, as the source of the honest and the just, and as the measuring rod of the legitimacy of social institutions, is brought to the fore and given a conspicuous position. This thought is abstract. It is first looked upon as a faculty of the individual man, and interpenetrates with the will of others. The principle of subjectivity is the foundation of modern philosophy, whose motive is either thought or experience. Experience is resolved into external sensations, into pleasures and pains, into the utilities of man, conceived as an individual; for the sensations are essentially individual. In experience, the subject prevails, as sense or tendency to pleasure, aided by hedonistic calculations. The principle of subjectivity was manifest also in the Reformation, which emancipated the religious consciousness and recognized the rights of the individual soul. And it is seen in all the series of attempts made by the individual to obtain at least his liberty, in these latter days. The individual, absorbed by the community, reasserts himself, opposes it, and believes that he is its origin and end; imagining even that he has lived without it (that is, in a hypothetical state of nature). At this point the ethico-juristic system begins, which is called the "theory of natural law"; for it is founded on the reason and experience of man more as an individual than as a society.

Hugo GROTIUS is the author of this system. Though partly foreshadowed by Bruno, he deserves credit for his lucid conception of a primitive and natural jurisprudence founded on reason itself, immutable, the source of every other jurisprudence. It was a time when the jurists venerated Roman Law as written reason—when the politicians publicly appealed to the right of might — when the Catholic theologians hoped to destroy royal power in favor of divine papal authority, by deriving the former from the people — when the Scholastics continued to weave subtleties — and when the Protestant theologians endangered human freedom.

Grotius developed the principles of the new science by treating the important subject of peace and war. Here the sad effects of an ignorance of the law of nature are more deplorable than elsewhere. He begged those who could remedy this miserable state of affairs to read his book and learn his new ideas. The first writers on the rights of war who had been illumined, as it were, by the light of the law of reason, were the Milanese Giovanni DI LIGNANO, Giovanni LUPO of Segovia (theologians whom Grotius mentions), Martino GARATI of Lodi, and Pietro BELLINI (counselor of the Duke Emanuele Filiberto of Savoy, of Francis Ariasdemesa, and of the Neapolitan Paris del Pozzo), all four of whom were jurisconsults, and, above all others, Alberico GENTILE (of whom Grotius makes honorable mention). Gentile was the first to formulate a system of rules of warfare, and to separate the notion of war and religion, placing the former within the rigorous limits of law. However, the law thought of by him is Roman and not rational. Furthermore, he keeps his eyes on the single fact of **war** and pays little attention to peace, the normal condition of humanity, so that he cannot put a just valuation on the former.

Grotius defines natural law as the sum of the principles of right reason by which we discern the wrongness or rectitude of an action, through the discordance or agreement of the action itself with rational and social nature. The mother of natural law is human nature itself, which prompts us to seek intercourse with our fellow-beings. Natural law is immutable; it would exist even on the hypothesis of the non-existence of God (to conceive of which is a horrible crime). Law in its broad sense embraces morals; and law in the strict sense includes imperfect and perfect right, capacities, and merits. It is distinguished, however, from the art of allotting just rewards to things pleasant and unpleasant, useful and harmful, present or future — that is, from politics. This distinction, indeed, between law and politics had been made clearly (although incompletely) some years before Grotius, by the Cosentine, Giovanni DA PALAZZO in his book on Government and the true rationale of the State.

Natural law, however, is conceived by Grotius solely as the right of individual man. Individual property, as following the primitive community of goods, is based by him on an express or tacit agreement. Intestate inheritance is based on the natural estimate of the will of the deceased. From the field of private law it enters that of the State through contract. It is the duty of natural law to protect agreements; those who constitute the State promise by express or tacit agreement to obey the majority, to whom the power is given. Obligation by consent is the basis of all civil law, according to the teachings of Grotius. The State, a perfect body of free persons, united for the purpose of enjoying their own rights through a common utility, is the people, affecting a stability of powers and obligations in a republic or an empire. The common subject of sovereignty is the State; political forms are derived from common consent. From the consent of the criminal, given implicitly by the criminal act, arises the right of punishment. There are laws and powers making for the exclusive advantage of certain classes. There is an international law common to all nations. The free development of the rights of society demands free trade; therefore the prohibition of the entrance of any product into a country is a just cause of war on the part of the importing nation. A people cannot prohibit the free transit of foreign merchandise since it should not place obstacles in the trade between nations. But the consent of nations justifies the restrictions of custom-houses or the prohibition of importation. The sea is free, for physical and moral reasons. This double reason ceases in the case of a body of water lying entirely within one nation's boundaries.

V

HOBBES, SPINOZA, AND LEIBNITZ

HOBBES, LOCKE, BERKELEY, and HUME agree with the philosophy of Bacon.

HOBBES admits only matter and motion; reduces thought to sense; and derives sense from motion. He accounts for the whole life of the spirit by the external laws of association; thus he is looked upon by LEWES and the modern psychologists of association as their earliest predecessor. Like Grotius, he begins with the nature of man; but he differs from Grotius in saying that it is founded on egoistical tendencies and not on the social desire for the general good. Society is sought through self-love, not through love of others. The origin of the great and enduring societies is not reciprocal benevolence but reciprocal fear. In the state of nature, there was a constant struggle, every man against his neighbor, through cupidity and the inter-collision of rights; for each man had a right to everything. Now the law of nature is the instinct of self-preservation; thus was felt the need of growing out of this state of insecurity and of finding peace. Unlimited fear forced men to transfer by agreement all their rights and powers to a civil committee; this is the origin of the civil contract. Thus an absolute empire was formed, destined to define the honest and the just, and to decree what must be believed. Honesty, justice, and religious beliefs are the product of social laws. Hobbes, like Grotius, believes in the principle of human nature in its individual form, and makes everything depend on contract — the begetter of natural law.

LOCKE combats the innatism of Descartes. He tries

to prove that the intellect is a blank tablet ("tabula rasa") on which the senses print characters. Our ideas are born of sensation and reflection; reflection elaborates the data of sensation, uniting, separating, abstracting, and generalizing. The idea of substance is a collective idea and does not express entity because we perceive only the methods — the ego is found by reflection only in its world of thought and not in substance. The entity of the ego lies in the continuity of representations and not in its real unity. If there are substances (and perhaps there may be), they must remain unknown and unrecognizable to us. Locke makes the validity of conduct consist in the conformity or non-conformity of an action to the law, which operates through the power of the law-giver, to punish or reward us. He departs from the hypothesis of the state of nature, in which there arises (his philosophy differing here from that of the other philosophers) a comprehensive system of rights to life, liberty, and property, and of punishment (to a limited extent, a power of the individual). In his opinion, the State grows out of contract and makes for the protection of the individual. He admits the principle of the sovereignty of the people, as a consequence of which he thinks that the people should make the laws and the princes obey them. Finally, he believes in the separation of Church and State.

Locke's division of power into legislative and executive, the former belonging to the people and the latter to the kings, leads to the constitutional doctrine which was soon to be formulated by Montesquieu. This philosopher, who outlined the perfect mechanism of the elements of representative government, as exemplified in the English Constitution, was the first to propound the theory of the division of powers into legislative, executive, and judiciary, with its corollary that one power would restrain the other, acting reciprocally as check and countercheck.   He is also the creator of historical climatology; but he exaggerated its significance; for (as Comte said) Montesquieu failed to perceive that in some instances history shows variations, while climate remains uniform; and he thus lacked a true conception of progress.   Montesquieu did not concern himself with the philosophy of law; yet his book is one wherein (as he says) every nation can find the reasons, on which its maxims of jurisprudence are based.   Of the work of Grotius, so popular in his day, Montesquieu makes no mention; and in the three places in the "L'Esprit des Lois," in which he speaks of natural law, he is really treating of morals.

Locke bases knowledge on perception; he teaches that we learn only the methods; he lays stress upon the objects whose substance we cannot perceive.   BERKELEY is more coherent.   For, starting with the premises of Locke, he shows that basically only ideas are real and not things, because the reality of the former is created by our very perception.   The true being of things is its perception, and in the perception lies their reality.

HUME completes the work of Locke and Berkeley, making a criticism of the concept of causality.   In his opinion causality is not an object of sensation, perception, nor deduction.   It is not an object of perception, because it lacks a corresponding impression, experience giving us the simple conjunction of two facts and not their connection.   Neither can it be discovered by the analysis of a concept, because this includes logical notes and not existence.   In other words, one cannot discover the real existence of the effect from the mere causal conception; that is a logical proof but nothing more.   On the other hand, it is not a subject for deduction, because there is no medial term between cause and effect.   Causality, therefore, has no scientific value, and we must doubt everything except mathematics, because everything presupposes a cause, with that one science excepted.   Causality rests in habit, in dogma, and in expectation.   With the repetition of one fact in sequence to another, we believe, or have faith that the first is the cause, the latter the effect.   Even if this dogma or expectation has no theoretical value, it is a more than sufficient norm for life and conduct.

MALEBRANCHE, SPINOZA, and LEIBNITZ are followers of the Cartesian philosophy.   In the mind of Descartes, the idea of God was innate in the human soul.   Malebranche, the Cartesian Averroes, again puts the origin of thought in a region outside of man and affirms that knowledge is an intuitive influent, a vision of the idea of God.   Extension, opposed to thought, is thinkable because it is seen in God.   God is the sole cause that works in reality; his creatures are occasions of divine action.   Thinking that truth lies in God, we can love and work with Him.   Man should take for a norm of his conduct the relations of perfection that exist in things; relations constituting the content of that love with which God loves Himself.

SPINOZA tries to reconcile the opposition between substances of extension and of thought (which Descartes admits, and which Malebranche believes eliminated by the intuition of extension in God) by the presupposition of a single substance of which thought and extensions are attributes.   He unites extension and thought in a single unity, which is indifferent of itself, in substance or nature, and includes all reality (as the Cartesian philosopher says that the idea of substance involves its existence).   Substance is active, self-causal, and develops in the two infinite attributes of extension and thought.   Each of the attributes expresses substance of its own mode, through an infinity of methods. Each is unconnected with the other. The modes of the two attributes have no reciprocal causality, but correspond and are parallel. Substance, with the two attributes, is "natura naturans," and the universe is "natura naturata" and is also infinite, while the particulars are simple modes. Substance is not determined by anything but itself. It is free; man is not free because he is a mode limited and determined by other modes. Man is a natural force with the illusion of freedom. The modes, particular objects, are ideas and bodies. We, *qua* spiritual, are the cause of ideas, and *qua* corporeal, are the cause of passions. In respect to ideas, we are active, if they are adequate and fully comprehend their object; in respect to passions, we are passive because they are derivatives of our and other bodies; and of neither one nor the other have we full consciousness. Passivity consists always of inadequacy, obscurity, and confusion of ideas. Man, *qua* mind, is free from sentiments, affections, and passions, because he knows God and the necessary connections of things, reaching adequate cognition by love of God.

Every entity strives for the preservation of its existence; man also has this tendency, in which the ethical principle is found. Law is the power of the nature of man, that is, the force by which he perseveres in his existence. The law of nature is the very power of nature. Man's right is equal to his power as a cause or force. The greater union gives greater force, and therefore greater right; whence the great power of the State, the result of the alienation of the powers of many. The object of the State is to stop the terrible struggle between men due to their conflicting passions and interests. It is founded on agreement; but this does not result, as Hobbes says, in the transference of all the rights of the individual to the State; for whatever is not subject to force does not become subject to the State (acts, therefore, can be controlled, but neither opinions nor creeds).

LEIBNITZ tries to reconcile the Cartesian dualism between the substances of thought and extension (which Spinoza attempted to eliminate through the principle of one substance with two infinite attributes). He shows that all substances are forces, and therefore active and not inert. He believes that all substances are representative, in that they are the result of monads, which are not physical atoms, but metaphysical points, unextended elements, unmodelled, indivisible, indestructible, impenetrable, and capable of perception and representation. Each monad is a simple force with a special original determination, not derived from without, having within itself the representative scheme of the universe. Bruno, the author of the monad theory, known to Leibnitz, says that each monad is a contracted universe. A monad as an active substance represents itself, and as an individual and limited substance it represents the others. In the doctrine of Leibnitz, there is not one substance but as many substances as there are forces.

From substance, which is the whole, he contradistinguishes the simple monad, with its representative virtue, developing through three progressive grades. For representation begins with simple and obscure being, it becomes clear when joined with sensation, and distinct when accompanied by knowledge. The power of the monad to pass from one conception to another is connected with this graduation. This power is a special activity in living beings, instinct in animals, will in man. In the monad, there is a continuity of states. In the spirit monad, the state of conscious knowledge

is a derivative of the state of unconsciousness and therefore the will is determined by the unconscious states
and cannot be caprice. The life of the spirit is that gradual passage by infinitesimal steps from unconsciousness to clear and distinct knowledge. Each monad
has a special disposition peculiar to it from the beginning;
it contracts the universe in its own manner, and in conformity with its disposition, it develops through a continuous succession of states. No monad is born of
another or exerts any influence over another, but between
them there is a fixed harmony from God.

Mind presupposes (teaches Leibnitz) sensible representation, but is not its cause. It is not a blank tablet,
but rather a containing energy — virtually the principles
of identity and of sufficient reason, distinguished as
causality and finality. The identity looks to the monad
in itself. The sufficient reason has to do with the
harmony between all the monads. The principle of the
sufficient reason is the base of the concrete sciences,
and therefore of morals and law. The spirit is mind and
will; will is a conscious tendency and makes for happiness.
Through clear and distinct cognition, the spirit feels
that it is an element in a great whole and that it has the
duty of acting so as to further the common good.   Only
through clear and distinct knowledge comes the tendency
to the generally useful. Law is founded on the essence
and not on the will of God, and is manifest in the form
of rigid law, of equity, and probity. The first consists
in commutative justice and is founded on the precept
of "Do no wrong." The second is based on distributive
justice and on giving each his due. The third is connoted
by the maxim of "Live honestly." The object of law
is perfection. Every kind of community proposes the
happiness of man as its object. The State looks especially to the good of external security. The practical

idealism of the Leibnitzian system consists in a community of spirits in immediate dependence on God, placed in the sphere of morals, with concentric circles comprehensive of rights.   It resembles the Stoic Republic.   Christian principles interpenetrate with Greek philosophy in an attractive manner; but we must remember that Leibnitz began with pure rationalism and then turned to eudemonism, and ended in the confusion of morality and religion.

VI

PUFFENDORF, THOMASIUS, AND WOLFF
ROUSSEAU

PUFFENDORF, who coupled in a somewhat arbitrary manner to the Cartesian philosophy his theory of natural law and of the law of nations, makes clear the psychological basis of law and the theory of imputation (erstwhile the doctrine of Grotius). But his development of his doctrine is neither profound nor exact; because he pleads especially for the interpretation of the social instinct (admitted by Grotius), not as benevolence but as common need, and because of his confusion of morals and law (not found in the works of Grotius) and his tri-division of morality into duties towards God, our neighbors, and ourselves. Puffendorf's conception of law is inferior to that of Grotius, because law and all that is honest depend, according to him, on the will of God and on divine imposition. Leibnitz does not think highly of this philosopher and very seldom mentions him in his work on natural law. The followers of Puffendorf are BARBEYRAC, BURLAMAQUI, and DE FELICE. Barbeyrac, a most erudite man (of whom it was said, in looking at his notes on Puffendorf and Grotius, that it was difficult to decide whether greater genius was required for the creation of the systems than for their annotation) is not clear in his understanding of rational law, though he gives it a new development and illustrates scientifically the difference between morals and law. In Burlamaqui, we find traces of Barbeyrac, and a blind obsequiousness to Puffendorf's ideas. De Felice is distinguished for his writings on public European law and for his bibliographic notes of the writers on the philosophy of law;

but he adds nothing to the system of his author and principal followers. He was ignorant of the attempts of the German philosophers to distinguish morals and law, begun before the death of Burlamaqui.

The works of Grotius and Puffendorf met opposition on all sides. The Romanists, even more irate than the theologians, accused the philosophers of aiming to create for equity an intellectual dominion over the world's greatest achievement — that is, Roman law; although the nature of this cerebrine equity was a thing about which they themselves could not agree. The theologians, especially the Protestants, confuse rational research in law with atheism. Both make much of the discords of the schools of natural law. SELDEN, not wishing to base natural law on reason, states that law is a derivative of the nature of God; that it is partly obligatory and partly permissive; and thàt the divine laws, which all must obey, are revealed in the Scriptures. Puffendorf, LeClerc, and Barbeyrac are almost unanimous in their criticism of Selden, because he deduces the principles of law from the Decalogue and especially from Judaic tradition. Cocceius agrees with Selden for polemic reasons, but has a superior principle, from which he derives juridical precepts directly — that is, the divine will, known from its acts or inferable from the perfection of the divine essence, without reliance on revelation.

Thomasius founds law on reason, independent of all revelation. He admits a state of nature, which was neither a state of war nor one of peace, but was a chaos. Human actions should depend upon a norm; and law is the norm for external actions and the guaranty of social peace. Thomasius avails himself of the three grades of law made by Leibnitz to show the separation of law from morals in his belief that moral duties are incoer-

cible or imperfect, and secure internal peace, while the
legal duties are coercible or perfect, and secure external
peace. A consequence of this is that the State should
abandon the moral and religious sphere to free conscience.
Thomasius, after indicating the various meanings of
the phrase "the law of nations," observes that there
cannot be a true law among nations, because there is
no higher authority that can enforce its obligations.
It is clear that in this he differs from Grotius and takes
a backward step.

WOLFF explains philosophy systematically for the use of
the schools, and follows the doctrines of Leibnitz. He
does not accept all of them, however, without some
modifications; for example, he does not believe that
all the monads have representative virtue (which according to him is an attribute only of the spirit monad). His
ethical principle, the result of an organic concept of the
world and of the teachings of Leibnitz, is perfection.
Wolff speaks of perfect and imperfect duties, but he does
not define their difference. He does not supply, like
Thomasius, a criterion for their separation and distinction.
Morals and law, therefore, are again confused, and
science from that point of view takes a retrogressive step.
Wolff thinks that he derives natural law from the human
essence by a rigorous deduction. The law of nature
imposes the duty of doing all that tends towards the
perfect and good. Natural law, founded on the nature of
man, is the law of what he should or should not do.
Natural law has its ultimate foundation in God, because
God is the author of the order of things or of the order of
nature. The Wolffian principle should not be interpreted in a too individualistic sense. For it holds
that good actions tend either to the preservation of essential, or to the acquisition of accidental perfection, or to
the consummation and perfection of mankind, more

especially of the family, nation, or State. Wolff and his disciple, VATTEL (following the way trodden by Grotius in the field of international law) assign absolute authority to positive law, but recognize the natural law of individuals and nations as its source. Among the Italians, LAMPREDI believes that it owes its origin to this source (thus following Wolffian doctrines). He goes so far as to say that if a law between armies could be defended, his pen would take up the task, and cites naval warfare in treating of the great principles of humanity. Lampredi (like Wolff) supplies no criterion of the difference between morals and law. He considers natural law as the comprehensive formula of natural laws, tending towards happiness and perfection, but he does not show of what it consists. He introduces and discusses, in the science of law, hypotheses and theories of ethics, as, for example, the hypothesis of a God who is judge of actions, and the analysis of moral imputability. Law, in Lampredi's mind (since he is a follower of Wolff), is the faculty of availing oneself of what is necessary for the fulfillment of obligations which may be universal, primitive, and innate, or particular, derivative, and hypothetical. Ownership presupposes, according to both authors, a positive community of things, and owes its origin to the appetites of animal life. Lampredi develops the doctrine of contract in exactly the same manner as Wolff, in the discussion of society as a consensual contract, thus opening the way to the discussion of society in general, which is founded on the consent of him who creates laws and government. And here Lampredi's chief error is apparent, that is, his failure to distinguish the principles of public from private justice; an error in that time common to the greater number of writers on natural law.

Hume represents the complement of Baconian philosophy, as Leibnitz represents that of the Cartesian. French Sensualism and Materialism, the general consensus of the Scotch philosophers, and German Syncretism of the past century, add nothing new in the sphere of speculation. French Sensualism originated in the doctrine of GASSENDI, a contemporary of Bacon and Descartes. Gassendi says that the only source of our ideas is sense; that the certainty of our being is not born of thought only, but also of sensible facts; but he can form no notion of substance. Later, after Locke, CONDILLAC reduces to mere sensation the origin of consciousness, sensation, and reflection, and shows that the life of the spirit is nothing but transformed sensation. BONNET and HARTLEY laid stress upon the sensations, in that they are reproduced, associated, and preserved under the laws of motion. LAMETRIE and HOLBACH express the principles of materialism in a clear and popular manner. The "I think, therefore I am" of Descartes became the "I feel, therefore I am" of Saint Pierre. Ideology, through the work of TRACY, became confused with zoölogy. The moral sciences are considered by CABANAS (who speaks of intracranial reflection and thought as secretions of the brain) as parts of natural history. Freedom is a supra-intelligible power, and the will wills as fire burns.

Locke maintains that man is urged to work not through cognition but through internal discomfort. This consists of a feeling, and therefore we must alter the foundation of ethics. Ethics are no longer based on reason but on feeling, in the teaching of the English moralists. Emotions and not ideas are the motives of work; and the criterion by which we measure actions is a special sense — the moral sense. This sense is not original (say some of the writers of the English school), but is derived from certain external elements. It is formed step by step, and is refined, appearing in all its grades as a product of psychological association. Through association and habit egoistical acts become moral; because one begins by wishing another's good for one's own ease and pleasure, but ends by wishing it for itself without other motive. To such conceptions (more or less) can the theories of SHAFTSBURY, BUTLER, HUTCHESON, Hume, and ADAM SMITH be reduced. Smith says (in accord with Hume) that the judge of morality is the impartial spectator, and that the basis of judgment is sympathy. Sympathy with him who receives a good or bad action results not only from participation in another's pleasures and pains (according to the writings of Hume), but also from partaking of the stimulus of rendering good for good and evil for evil. In this lies the principle of social justice.

Hume says that in morals the subjective element is feeling, the objective element utility. HELVETIUS founds conduct on egoism, on individual pleasure and utility. BENTHAM (who is by nature not a philosopher but a legislator) looks to the general utility alone, and makes it the basis of ethics, without that psychological analysis of principles which Hobbes and the other English moral philosophers make. Believing ingenuously in the originality of his doctrines (which belief showed him unacquainted with philosophical thought), the pursuit of pleasure and the avoidance of pain constitute in his mind the motives of action. In this, he is in accord with Hobbes and Locke, though he believes that such a principle cannot be demonstrated. Bentham opposes the systems which place the criterion of conduct outside the calculation of consequences, and builds up a moral arithmetic and social dynamics.

The SCOTCH philosophers base certitude on internal and inexplicable suggestion and make common sense (the extension or amplification of the moral sense) the measure of truth. The GERMAN philosophers of the Renaissance (the epoch of so-called sane or popular philosophy, a little anterior to Kant) waver between the empirical movement of Locke and the idealism of Leibnitz, inclining towards scepticism.

ROUSSEAU admits all the presuppositions of the system of natural law — that is, the basic freedom of individual man, the state of nature, the formation and destruction of the State by contract, the rights of individual defense and utility — and therefore the maxim of popular sovereignty. (To these Sidney and Locke had already added the right of rebellion; this had its origin in the belief in the rights of the Christian community in ecclesiastical affairs, and was brought to perfection in the papal interest by the Jesuits, who, in their desire to overthrow civil power, taught that it was born of the will of the people while pontifical authority came from God.) Rousseau gives to the system of natural law a new attribute, lacking in Grotius and in later writers, that is, the inalienability of freedom. He repudiates the usual view of individual freedom and does not hesitate to place Grotius together with Hobbes among the champions of human slavery. Accepting the principle of inalienable freedom, Rousseau, to solve the problem raised by it, discovers a kind of political union, in which freedom is not alienable. Every man, in obeying the State, obeys himself, with a full and reciprocal renunciation of all individual rights in favor of the community; — hence his doctrine of the "general will," the inalienable, indivisible, and non-representable sovereignty, and hence his criticism of the mechanical, constitutional régime. Rousseau recognizes representative government in the exercise of executive power only; this, under a system of restraints, can be entrusted to a king or commission. The object of the activity of the

State is public good (understood in an abstract manner
and not in the sense of the good of all) under various conditions of life, but in a uniform mode.   Later philosophy has of course shown us that Rousseau's state of
nature is an hypothesis contrary to reason and experience; that contract, its prerequisite, is not possible
without the State's guaranty; that law is and must be
existent, while contract need not exist; that to obtain
this supposed uniformity of interest and hypothetical
equality, it would be necessary to remove not only the
difference of legal conditions, but the indefinite variety
of all the elements of life as well; and that to admit a
distinction between the general will, and the will of all,
would set the latter free from every rational bond.

The French Revolution realized the system of natural
law, as taught by Rousseau.   It was not a sudden movement, but the result of a long preparation into which
many factors entered.   The new man evolved by the Middle Ages, the Renaissance, the Baconian and Cartesian
philosophies in all their phases, the religious wars,
the English Revolution, the English philosophical doctrines, the progress of the American government, the
abuses of the past, and the Encyclopedia, all contributed
their quota.   Similar elements in the less civilized nations
found in France a favorable place to concentrate and
strike the great blow.   With the "general will" separated
by Rousseau from all ethical essence and law, the
Revolution sought liberty (not within but beyond
all limits), and destroyed all secular obstacles opposed
to the development of men.   Liberty, now become
untrammeled caprice, soon felt the need of re-establish-
ing limitations; and various reconstructions appeared in
all branches of human activity.   But all were the temporary illusions of fancy.

VII

VICO

Vico is the author of the only new movement (with the exception of Kant's) since the days of Hume and Leibnitz. Principles (he says) govern the origin, development, and termination of facts. Providence, which is, in the last analysis, mind or thought, develops first in the natural and then in the human order — that is, first as natural, then as human providence. Providence is not a transcendent or extramundane principle, but is immanent and intrinsic in cosmic reality and history. Such a principle develops first in nature and then in the spirit; first in the natural world, then in the world of human reason; whence the double motion of entities from thought, their beginning, towards thought, their end, — a progress and regress, a double cycle. Science cannot enter the immediateness of thought, as Descartes believed, because the nature of things is nothing but a stage in history. The immediateness of thought does not reveal the cause of that relation of the certain and the true which science desires. From the certain, step by step, comes the true; the mind learns the true from the certain. The certain is part of the true. It is one of its extrinsifications, and therefore the true is contained in the certain. The true is the idea, the certain is the actual or reality.

The conception of immanent Providence, towards which his "Diritto Universale" pointed, is clearly shown in the "Scienza Nuova," but not in "Dell' Antichissima Sapienza degli Italiani," in which Providence is supramundane and analagous to the Platonic idea of the good. This book (the first manifestation of his genius, which aimed at the reconstruction of history from the rich field of Linguistics) contains two suppositions, which Vico himself later abandoned: The wisdom of our ancient ancestors, later called by him "the pride of nations and the learned"; and the invention by man of mathematics alone — a restricted application of the important principle of the conversion of the true with the actual. In the "Diritto Universale" and "Scienza Nuova" he holds that man is the author not only of mathematics but of all the sciences, which develop with the history of human ideas, that is, of the civil world (with its principles lying in the modifications of the human mind itself), and of religion (which changes with the development of the mind; for the ancients, with robust senses and vast imagination, pictured God according to their idea).

Man is knowledge, will, and power. His power is bounded only by his will, and his will by his knowledge, but mind is the principle. In mind, man is first sense, then imagination, and lastly reason, and therefore his history must run through three ages, the divine, the heroic, and the human. To knowledge, will, and power, correspond ownership, freedom, and perfection — the three elements of the law-idea, derived from the force of reason, which acts against cupidity as an ethical virtue and looks to equalizing the useful among men by means of law. Law has the useful as its occasion but not its cause. Ownership, freedom, and perfection make authority, which is monastic, economic, and civil. From ownership, freedom, and perfection are derived the three forms of government — monarchy, democracy, and oligarchy.

The science of law is based on reason or philosophy and on authority or philology. It considers the true and the certain, that is, reason and authority; authority is part of reason and not of caprice; the certain is part of the true.

Hence the distinction between the rationale of law, which looks to the true, and its reason, which looks to the certain; hence also the union between rational and positive law. Positive law, when the distinction between the true and the certain is understood, is seen to be not entirely identical with nor entirely opposed to the rational. It realizes ideal law according to the laws of the development of knowledge, or temporal evolution. It is, therefore, in its arboreal state, violence, which afterwards is subjected to restraint, and finally attains perfection through absolute truth and generous reason. The best law is not strict, ironclad, and cramped, but like that of the oligarchs in the early governments and under the Quirites in Rome. At Rome it was just and exemplary before the Twelve Tables, rigid under the Republic, benign under the Emperors, becoming divine again, as in the first ages, when it sprang from customs deep-dyed with religion and piety.

Government at first lay in the power of family monarchies and then passed into the hands of the heroic oligarchies and later to the people in popular republics, but finally returned to the individual in the civil monarchies. Mixed forms are born of the need of fostering the people's faith in the government. Law at first was seen in custom; then in legislation. Grotius, Selden, and Puffendorf are wrong in beginning at the first ages of uncivilized nations, and with men enlightened by a natural reason fully developed — that is, from the period in which the philosophers began to develop a true idea of philosophy. With the beginning of nations began the subject-matter of the natural law of people. Grotius was wrong, too, in saying that we should attribute the origin of feuds to the barbarians, because feuds date back to the earliest people; they were ancient before Homer and the days of the Heroes.

Vico's doctrine about the relation of reason and authority, of the true and the certain, and his criticism of the representatives of the abstract school of jurisprudence (that is, of the principles of natural law, from a number of which it would be necessary to exclude Selden, who abandons rational criticism and allies himself with theological data) show the broadest conception of law. In fact, if the certain is part of the true and authority is part of reason, law, on the one hand, cannot fall into that historical relativism which lies more in the "fieri" than in the "esse," denying the ideal and constant elements of right; on the other hand, it will be no longer possible to conceive of law as an abstract ideal without a history, as a truth without a relative certainty. We must remember that science, according to Vico, should develop with the history of human ideas, and therefore the idea of law without history would not be human.

Vico's criticism of the opinion of Grotius on feuds comes from his conception of the progress and regress of times and institutions — the denial of a history which moves not only constantly but variously and progressively. The concept of progress and regress prevents Vico from fully realizing the deep significance of Christianity; he is like Polybius, Machiavelli, and the Egyptian philosophers. MARIUS PAGANUS (who deserves credit for showing the influence of foreign causes in Vico's doctrine) falls into the same error.

Machiavelli is not a mere follower of Epicurus. He believes (contrary to Livy and Plutarch) that the greatness of Rome was the result of worth, notwithstanding that the reward of merit is given by fortune. He does not fully accept the mechanical hypothesis. We must note that the unscrupulous (some call it "diabolical") nature of the advice given in Machiavelli's "Principe," and the sincere admiration of the hermit of Saint Casciano for

Cæsar Borgia, are not, if one accepts the ideas of Vico, necessarily inconsistent with this reliance on the workings of an all-rewarding Providence. The same Providence (in Machiavelli's scheme of life) out of bestial lust developed the chastity of marriage, — out of the abuse of seignorial liberty brought popular freedom, — out of the dissoluteness of peoples the control of the stronger nations. Through the instrumentality of Polyphemus it spread obedience in mankind; by means of the proud Achilles and the just Aristides alike, it paved the way for popular liberty; it established monarchy through Tiberius (a sorrowful man, much given to meditation). And so may not Cæsar Borgia himself have been a sorrowful man, much given to meditation, and endowed with the qualities necessary in that age of corruption to make Italy a State? In many places in the "Scienza Nuova," Vico advances a criterion of political morality very different from that which governs in other spheres of life.

VIII

KANT

KANT believes that knowledge is a complex fact,
the result of rational and sensible elements; and that
it must be considered in its integrity, and not in one of
its parts, as Locke and Leibnitz considered it. Locke
tried to solve the problem of knowledge by the consideration of the single factor of sense; Leibnitz on the other
hand based all his theory on the other factor, mind.
Kant's object is to unify these two movements. In his
belief, time and space are not concepts, but intuitions of
sensibility. Space is the form of external and time of
internal sensibility. There are, however, these two
intuitions or forms of the primal reception of various
sensibilities, of which there is no corresponding object
without ourselves. Experimental knowledge is possible
under certain *a priori* conditions through the categories
of pure and original concepts, constituting the functions
of the mind itself applied to empirical intuitions. It is
an *a priori* synthesis, in that the categories are ideal centres about which phenomena group, because objects
are understood as they appear, and not of themselves.
The phenomena and the concepts intercommunicate
between themselves. There is an original synthetic unity
of intuition and category. This unity makes knowledge
possible and is its chief foundation. The objects not
given by experience, for example, the soul, the world
and God, are not knowable. The possibility of knowledge
of an object lies in its power of being experienced;
and to the three above ideas there are no corresponding
intuitions. The three ideas are not knowledge, but are
rules to bind the absolute, which is not given by experi-

ence. For the absolute must exist. It is a demand of
reason, but the science of the supra-sensible is entirely
eliminated from the "Kritik der Reinen Vernunft."

In knowledge, there are the two elements noted above,
the data of sense, and the category; in morality, likewise,
are found emotion, or sensible stimulus, and moral law.
Morality is the autonomy of will, as pure reason — free
from all prejudice, emotion, or passion. The heterono-
mous will, which is determined by secondary selfish
objects and generally by sensible stimuli, is not moral.
A desire of happiness, or a resolution under even a noble
passion, such as Christian charity, clouds the purity of
the will. The good should be desired *per se*, independent
of every extrinsic consideration. The categorical imperative is that the motive of action should be one with the
law, and should be the principle of universal legislation.
Morality is pure will. To it all our acts should conform.
The will, determined of itself, is an end for itself, and
therefore the categorical imperative demands that the
will be always treated as final and never as medial.
The categorical imperative is absolute, comprehending
pure and unlimited will; whence it follows that the
absolute of the "Kritik der Praktischen Vernunft" must
exist. Reason demands its existence. Freedom, the immortality of the soul, and the existence of God, are
three postulates of "Practical Reason," three presuppositions of ethics, and not knowledge. Free will is not an
object of cognition. It should presuppose the latter, in
order to be moral. Since there is a relation between virtue
and the time necessary to obtain it, the immortality
of the soul must be admitted. The harmony between
virtue and happiness implies the existence of God.

Kant lays bare the original synthetic unity of intuition and the category — of the real and the ideal,
of nature and mind; but he does not succeed in explaining

it.   He does not reconcile the two terms, and in the "Kritik der Reinen Vernunft," with the presupposition of the unknowable, he enters the confines of abstract, empty, and formal thought.   And in the "Kritik der Praktischen Vernunft," he does not overcome formalism, because morality is a pure form of reason, alien, and therefore contradictory to any kind of emotion or interest.   The categorical imperative, as formulated, does not in the least prescribe what must be done to be honest; it lacks concrete content.

As the "Kritik der Reinen Vernunft" fixes the conditions, laws, and limits of knowledge, so the "Kritik der Praktishen Vernunft" deals with fundamental notions of a practical order.   Such notions are moral and juristic, and constitute in their complexity the metaphysics of custom — a science built up by the mind of Kant alone. Morals differ from law, Kant thinks; because the former have to do with internal acts and intention, and can command in its own manner what law commands; while the latter, excluded from the realm of intention, embraces external acts and cannot enforce moral precepts. Here the separation and opposition of morals and law in the Kantian system are made clear, for since he has not completely grasped the ethical idea, it cannot appear to him as their common source.

Law, in Kantian philosophy, partakes of the general defects of his system, in being formal.   It is the sum of conditions under which everybody's unbridled freedom can coexist with the liberty of all, thanks to a universal law; but of exactly what this sum and this universal law consist, Kant does not tell us.   The essence of law, as he analyzes it, is limitation and coexistence.   It would be useless without a power of enforcement. Law is private and public.   Private law regards property and includes corporeal objects, obligations, and the status of individuals (whence the division of law into real, personal, and mixed). Public law is the guaranty of private law. Reason forces us to pass from the natural state (which, in Kant's mind, is an idea and not a fact) to the social. Public law is constitutional. It is the law of nations, and is cosmopolitan. The State arises from contract; but its content is not capricious, because, in the State, man has true liberty, equality, and independence. The State has no other mission than to look to the coexistence of the liberty of individuals. Thus it follows that the Kantian State, whatever be its law or policy, must, since it is based on reason, develop from a system of natural law. The State, like an individual, necessarily must advance from the natural to the social.

IX

GENOVESI, FICHTE, SPEDALIERI, AND ROMAGNOSI

After Vico came GENOVESI, not a follower of Wolff and Locke, though an admirer of the latter (and likened by him to a tall and noble but sterile cypress). He is eclectic, in fact, though showing but little scepticism. His teaching of eclectic freedom in philosophy emancipates it from slavery to the masters, both in Italy and elsewhere; for we must not forget that the principles of the Neapolitan philosopher were applauded and received in Germany. In ethics, Genovesi follows Locke closely. Man, according to the author of the "Diceosina," tends towards happiness, which is obtained by the harmony between individual cupidity and social rights. The law that effects this harmony is moral law. It is one, certain, unchangeable, and obligatory, enforcing the observation of rights, and their reëstablishment if violated. A right is an essential property given to rational beings and guaranteed by the universal law. It is a means to happiness. There is an equality in respect to inherent rights — an inequality in the different orders and species of things. Every right, acquired by means of an activity, is reduced to individual control which has its origin in a need. There is a right to occupancy, if work is done on the thing occupied. Whoever violates a right deprives someone of his property. The true natural state is not that of Vico and La Metrie but the patriarchal. Social coexistence, the effect of the existence of man, is the basis of sovereignty, which presupposes express tacit consent. The laws should be enacted by a body of learned men. The mixed form of the Spartan and English Constitutions is a divine invention. The State has the right of eminent ownership; the duty or right of education, and the temporal rights of the Church are really prerogatives of the State. Law demands full respect of neutrality, of allegiance, and of embassies, and is opposed to conquests made under the pretext of civilizing the conquered people.

Genovesi is a follower of Locke's utilitarian doctrines. He believes that the end of man is happiness, and therefore the motives of action can only be the desire of reward and the fear of punishment. The author of the "Diceosina" considers rights as property; but he does not show to what extent rights can be alienated. He does not believe in a state of nature, and yet he speaks of certain rights ceded to the State for common security. He develops an antagonism between natural and civil law, such as had not been asserted since Vico's time. His works contain disquisitions on punishment; on sovereignty as the effect of social coexistence; on certain of the statutes; on the regulation of private gentlemen or the middle class (called by him "pagliettismo"); on the body of learned law-givers; on the necessity of making ownership free, easy of transfer, individual, divisible, and accessible to all; and on the unity and sovereignty of the State. His views on the necessity of altering the rules of property can be found in the "Lezioni di Commercio," which outlined, even before Adam Smith's work, the science of the wealth of nations and of population — a science taught for the first time by Genovesi in the chair endowed by Intieri in Naples. He did not treat his subject, however, from the point of view of labor; this was first considered by Smith, who agrees with Genovesi that wealth comes from work as manifested in the arts, crafts, and trades. The idea of unity lies in sovereignty of the State, which, he says, in Naples expressed a new triumph of the laity through the efforts of a priest. Genovesi himself combatted as a philosopher the doctrines of Argento, Riccardi, Capasso, and Giannone, all of whom, controlled by civil history and canonical influences, believed in the claims of papal Rome.

After Kant came FICHTE. In his system, the original synthetic unity of intuition and category, of sense and mind, becomes auto-consciousness; is self-producing; and, as such, develops in thesis, antithesis, and synthesis. For Fichte, knowledge means that the subject, or the ego, is also in itself the non-ego or the object. In other words knowledge demands that the object, the non-ego, should have the same ideal form as the ego; whence the principle of the ego as ego and non-ego. But the ego of Fichte does not act as a real ego; neither does the non-ego act as nature; it is the form and non-reality of knowledge, and therefore is not truly absolute. From this, come the Fichtian subjectivism and relativism, shown both in his ethics and his natural law. In fact, moral action, which, according to Kant, presupposes conformity to necessary and universal law, is derived by Fichte from the action of the ego through conviction, and reaches fulfillment in enthusiasm or reciprocal excitation. Fichte does not tell what this conviction consists of, or rather he does not indicate its content, thus become a condition of morality. For Kant, juristic freedom is from its creation limited by universal freedom; for Fichte, it originates from the individual and real existence of the ego; is based on the right of a rational being to act as the sole cause in the sensible world; and is of itself unlimited, like the coercive faculties which inhere in it. But since one ego must admit another ego's existence, it must, by that admission, attribute to the other an unlimited power like its own. Thus the powers of both mutually lessen and limit one another. At this point, freedom is transformed into license, or into a power deprived of any law. Fichte perfects (with Rousseau) a system of natural law, paying no attention to those germs of speculative juristic philosophy left by Kant, who saw the great difference between license and freedom, and tried to realize the latter, while maintaining equality and independence within the State.

Fichte cannot deduce a permissive law from the absolute moral law of universal jurisdiction. In a rational being, there is love of duty for duty's sake (a tendency, absolute and obligatory) and love of one's self and of one's fellows (a power, and not of the same character, because it can be reduced to unlimited freedom, which excludes every law). The attainment of freedom depends on freedom itself, and therefore the law and the State are secondary. The State can be destroyed and remade at will. But in a second phase of his speculation he modifies his first doctrine, because he leaves subjective idealism and takes up the theory of the absolute ego, and consequently corrects his early legal notions.

SPEDALIERI, like Genovesi, starts out with the tendency of man to happiness, to which rights and obligations are medial. For him, natural law is a power conforming to reason — arising not from the act of man, like positive law, but from the essential qualities of man's nature. The principles of natural law are necessary and immutable truths; not so those of positive law. The natural rights, which belong to man, as man, look to his preservation, self-protection, and property; and there is a right to be free to act in pursuit of these three rights, as well as a free right to thought, to self-defense, and the aid of one's fellow-beings (an imperfect right in all cases, except of absolute necessity). As soon as the mind, says Spedalieri, sees that such a thing should be done in such a way, man enters into a true obligation, into

a necessity conforming to reason, although he contracts with no one.

The kinds of obligations are as numerous as the kinds of
rights. The notions of good and evil, of the just and the
unjust, contained in natural law, do not come from human
invention or the free will of God, but are the sequence of
things, expressing necessary eternal truths that God
cannot fail to approve. It is evident that Spedalieri,
with these three concepts of law, obligation, and natural
law, with the entirely rationalistic system which he emphasizes in his first book, goes back to the great principle
of the modern philosophy of law — that is, to reason
as the source of the Ethos, to the reason that is the very
system of the universe, and therefore to an objective will
and not a capricious and subjective one (like that on
which the whole system of natural law, so called, which
had its last expression in Fichte, was founded).

We can observe the same thing, when Spedalieri goes
on to contrast the state of nature with civil society,
and to conjecture about the origin of the latter. At
once, certain advantages and disadvantages are seen,
common to both states, derived from the nature of man
and its necessary effects. Thus, for example, in the
state of nature, since man tends towards happiness and
is gifted with powers capable of various development,
there should be (as in civil society) an equality of rights
and natural obligations, and an inequality in the material
of these rights. Looking more closely, it is seen that
man is infinitely better in civil society than he would be
in the state of nature, at least so far as physical conditions
are concerned.   Lastly, in regard to the spirit, the advantage is wholly on the side of civil society. If it, the state
of nature, therefore, could exist (concludes Spedalieri),
it would be infinitely worse than the present social
conditions. But it is more than likely that this state

never existed, because men in it, being savages, would
have been able only with the greatest difficulty to form
a conception of a system of society in order to realize it;
unless we suppose that God himself, by a single act of
omnipotence, created everything — mankind, civil society, language, and abstract ideas (at least those ideas
most necessary to physical existence and moral conduct).
Now there can be no doubt that these reasonings of the
Sicilian philosopher destroy, on the one hand, one of
the bases of the system of natural law, that is, the hypothesis of a state of nature; and on the other, show that the
inherent rights (thought to belong to a state of nature)
exist only in a state of society. for the part cannot exist
without the whole or the person without the ethical
organism.

And yet Spedalieri cannot rise entirely superior to the
influence of the principles of his time. After raising the
idea of an objective nature to the plane of ethico-
juristic criticism, and denying the state of nature, he
still maintains that contract is the base or intrinsic
rationale of civil society. In the first place, he says,
we must distinguish the actual from the ideal. It is
one thing to search out what has happened in fact,
and another to discover what should be done by right;
and it can be shown, as an historical truth, that man
can be born or remain outside of society, and at the same
time that an implied contract is the basis of rights
in civil society. In whatever state man is found (providing that it is one in which he can exist) he must
be there by his own will and consent, otherwise there
would be violence done to his imperishable right of freedom. But here Spedalieri's earlier principle, that of the
necessary and eternal sequence of things, which God
cannot fail to desire, is ignored, and an empty subjective principle of consent is substituted — a principle

not important in the various situations of life, and not all-controlling; for the subjective will should conform to the substantial and objective will, which is the norm and order of things.

ROMAGNOSI, as a philosopher, is not one who merely reproduces the thought of Locke, Condillac, and Bonnet. He is a close follower of the doctrine of Campanella, who considered the cognition of external things, called by him "addita," as founded entirely on the certainty of "abdita" cognition — that is, on the consciousness of being, power, will, and knowledge. It is evident that the conception of an original "abdita" knowledge, or primitive spontaneity of mind, is directly opposed to the system of the modern sensualists, who affirm that ideas come from without and that the spirit attains knowledge of external objects before it attains knowledge of itself. But according to Romagnosi, the perceptions are not copies of external originals, but are derived from the indeterminate energy of the ego or its unity, as shown by the consciousness of the functions of knowledge, will, and purpose, variously affected by the influences of external stimuli; and they should be regarded as signs to which existing things and methods correspond. The mind (says Romagnosi) knows with truth and acts with effect. He distinguishes the ages of mental development into epochs of personified, imitative, and philosophical doctrines (the last, in which true cognition of things is deduced from their assignable cause, was begun by the work of Galileo). Opposing the fanatic realists, he concedes there has been great abuse of this truth by gratuitous abstractions and speculations sanctioned by the Church; but insists that we should not fall into the other extreme; there is a middle course between Scylla and Charybdis; here Romagnosi makes good use of Bacon's maxim.

As to morals, law, and politics, Romagnosi distinguishes five schools — the mythical, transcendental, theological, fictional, and philosophical. He criticizes the first for basing law on an hypothesis of savage solitude; the second, for not giving equity a controlling interest; the third, for putting the divine will in place of the human; the fourth, for creating fictitious men and qualities. The fifth, he bases on indubitable fact, undeniable laws, and distinct norms. It assumes the natural tendencies of man as fundamental, and tempers legal acts with a necessary equity. Social power should be considered as the resultant effect of this intermingling; and from it canons and laws should be deduced, with due regard to the action of time and chance (which Romagnosi respects), keeping in view the perfecting of civilization, and regarding it as an art; whence the concept of the arbitrary transmission of the fact of civilization. This philosophical school is not really Baconian (because it makes facts, not dogmas, the basis of the moral and political sciences), nor is it Benthamic. Bentham, says the Italian, is the most famous among those modern philosophers who preach the atheism of law and morals; they do not distinguish between the regularly and irregularly useful; they present ethical notions without their fundamental causes; they hold both natural law and that of the nations to be fictitious, but only because they cannot rise to the conception of a useful existent before positive law — that is, to Vico's principle of the equitable good.

Natural law, he maintains, is a science. It is the systematic cognition of the rules governing human acts, deduced from the real and necessary natural relations, in order to obtain the good and avoid the evil. It lies in the pursuit, by means of society, of the best preservation of man, accompanied by the quickest and fullest

means for the perfection of the ego. This definition does
not take account of the difference between morals and
law, though human acts can be either entirely ethical or entirely juridical. It reproduces the idea of law according to
Clarke and Montesquieu; it is in accord with the positive
direction of Romagnosi's philosophy, who always seeks
the idea in the act. It presents the conception of nature
as a spontaneous and necessary sequence of events —
as an order of reason, as a moral necessity, not coercive.
It unites the utilitarian formula of happiness with that
of the equitable good of Vico. If natural law, writes
Romagnosi, is to attain to the Viconian doctrine of the
true and certain, it must be one of necessary and immutable reason, and of mutable position when there are
changes of nature or chance. And from this point
of view it is as extended, pliant, and multiform as circumstances demand — whence the socialization of necessary
law and the conception of an economic law. Herein
is seen a sanction of the liberal theories of Adam Smith,
and of the maxim of Genovesi that he who governs too
much governs badly.

The ruling maxims of practical jurisprudence, as
developed by Romagnosi, can be· reduced to four.
First, there is the formula of the equality of exchangeable utilities (except of the inviolable exercise of common
liberty), to which the laws of contract and quasi-contract (including trusts and the rules of intestacy)
are referable. Second, there is the idea of a legislative
survey comprehending the complicated relations of
social circumstances and of their control. Great reliance should be placed on statistics, which Romagnosi (here opposed to Say) thinks should aid
a politically strong State, with active control over all
objects within its sphere. Third, comes the concept
of the connection between law and economics, where

social justice makes common cause with truth and common utility, and is limited by the social power. Lastly, comes the idea of comparative legislation, which leads our author to say that there is no nation more advanced than the Roman in the art of comparing utilities — an art that is found to-day, he says, in the existing civil code of the Kingdom of Italy.

X

THE WRITERS OF THE REACTIONARY PERIOD — THE HISTORICAL AND PHILOSOPHICAL SCHOOLS—SCHELLING AND SCHLEIERMACHER

The powerful and extensive movement, begun in the name of the rights of the individual, resulted (as we have already said) in the theoretical and practical glorification of license. This can be seen in the systems of Rousseau and Fichte, and the immense revolutionary current of the past century. The individual, aiming to reaffirm his personality, produced an empty ego and then tried to reconstruct the human world by will alone, without giving it an ethical content. But this effort (because contrary to nature) was not crowned with success; and soon there was a reaction in the form of a new movement, based on the principle of an objective will. This principle was destined to lend substance to the empty, rational, and universal forms of Kant, reëstablishing the idea of a higher ideal necessity, and emphasizing the part of man that is more intimately related to the community. At this stage of events, the ancient State was an object of admiration. Yet we must note that the idea of the community never regained its former value in its redevelopment in history after the period of individualism. For, since the age of individualism, the need of a harmonic agreement between the two elements was clear — a harmony which the concept of an ethical organism alone is capable of producing.

In Italy, the principle of an objective will was not entirely lost sight of by the writers of the past century or their followers of to-day. In fact, Genovesi was moved to pity by their exaggerated doctrines. He held that we must preserve our rights, and must reëstablish them if violated. Lampredi looked upon a right as a faculty of doing what is necessary towards the fulfilment of an obligation; it was derived (in his mind) from the dictates of reason and a sensible impulse towards happiness. He believed that obligation is based on the nature of things itself and therefore on the will of God, the supreme creator and preserver of the laws of the world. Spedalieri did not believe in the state of nature, and advanced a belief in a general objective scheme. Romagnosi based his system on the necessity of nature, and freely criticized Rousseau.

The Italian authorities who inclined towards the maxims of the Encyclopedists (by whom they were extravagantly praised) are GALIANA, BECCARIA, and FILANGIERI. Galiana, economist, publicist, and writer, is not occupied with the search for the real principles of law. Beccaria (to whom Europe owes the reformation of a barbarous system of penal law, inherited from the Roman Empire, illustrated in Carpzovius, Clarus, and Farinacius) departs from the hypothesis of the social contract in order to establish a right of punishment. He denies the legality of capital punishment. Here he differed from Rousseau, who taking the same point of departure concludes in favor of it; for (says the latter) such a right is given to society by the individual, who risks his life in order to save it. The great reformer's principles of penal law and the laws of the division of labor are methodically set forth by RENAZZI, who borrows his practical criterion, his equity and his criticisms from the Roman jurisconsults and Malthus. Renazzi believes in the state of nature and in the social contract; but he does not decide the question of capital punishment, being content to combat barbarous punishments. Filangieri is a close follower of the abstract French philosophy, believing in the omnipotence of legislative license, which ought to abolish immediately the laws handed down from the brigands of the Middle Ages, and to create wise men and philosophers by the touch of the wand of honor. Always guided by abstract ideas, he recognized the possibility of laws which would be good for all times and places — thus departing from Montesquieu, who thought that law should answer the needs of each country and age. We might say that Filangieri shows what should be done and Montesquieu what has been done. But the connection between the science of legislation and the French theories is peculiarly manifest, when Filangieri accepts the distinction between the state of nature and society, and discourses upon the surrender of individual rights to society; among these he includes the right of killing an assailant, the foundation of the legality of capital punishment.

Outside of Italy, the new movement is represented by three groups — the so-called writers of the REACTIONARY PERIOD; the followers of the HISTORICAL SCHOOL; and SCHELLING and SCHLEIERMACHER.

The REACTIONARIES hope for the return of that ethical objectivity, existing prior to the great revolutionary movement, and conceive of a restoration of affairs, according to various national traditions. So DE MAISTRE, who extended theocracy to princes and nobles, and founded the theory of the papal system, reproduces the conception of the old French monarchy. BURKE, an admirer of the cavaliers, of the sentiments of honor and religion, but without any theocratic notions, combats the Revolution, with the aid of English civilization and conservative ideas. And HALLER, who attributes a character of private right to royal power, draws his inspiration from the principles of the ancient German territorial constitutions.

The partisans of the HISTORICAL SCHOOL (who want it regarded as a positive and not a philosophical school of jurisprudence) start out, as STAHL says, with the connection between law and the national conscience. Considering law as independent of individual will, they distinguish it from the statutes, and look on it as a varying, progressive, slow, and lengthy formation by society — thus making the State not a mechanism but an organism.   They distrust abstract metaphysics, and recognize in the State the continual succession of a change of forms, in which the highest intellectual unity of a people is shown.   They manifest the greatest respect for what exists, and great aversion to sudden innovations and destructions.   SAVIGNY, the head of this school, believes in the old law, and is inclined by birth and disposition to conservative ideas.   THIBAUT, the head of the philosophical school, attacks the old law, preferring the rational element, and is urged by his convictions to enter the field in support of progress.   We must remember, nevertheless, that Savigny did not deny himself the aid of philosophy, nor deny progress.   He recognized the principle of the continuity of the development of legal forms in connection with all other social facts; although he defended tradition, it was in a liberal spirit. On the other hand, Thibaut declared that he did not know a single jurisconsult who in the hope of a better future did not despise the past and the present.   He was a great admirer of NIEBURH and proclaimed with ardor the necessity of reforms not opposed to historical conditions.   The historical theory, like a philosophical principle, has its unity in Vico's immortal doctrine of the true and the certain, where they are joined and produce a harmony.

SCHELLING[1] posits the speculative principle of reason,

---

[1] See *infra*, p. 79.

as the identity of nature and spirit; and explains the reality of knowledge — left unexplained by Fichte. He attains such identity through intellectual intuitiveness. Conforming to the fundamental doctrine of his philosophy, Schelling bases Ethics on an absolute will, superior to the particular wills that develop in the various moral organisms. The State (in his mind) is the harmony of necessity and freedom in the realm of reality; while the Church is the expression of the same harmony in the spiritual realm of faith. The State is the resultant of the one and the many; and upon the various methods of equilibrium depends the history of nations. In antiquity, the one prevailed; in modern times the one, as a monarch, is placed over against the many, represented by the people, conscious of their power. The one, in the actual State, is abstract, not true and concrete, whence arises the need of the union of the State and Church, which expresses the unit in the ideal.

The starting point of SCHLEIERMACHER is analogous to that of Schelling. It is reason, the universal objective power, which in its development forms nature and the moral world. The moral world (according to Schleiermacher) is explained through Ethics, which include the rational laws of custom, right, the State and Church, as well as the history or realization of such laws. The essence of Ethics is derived from the interpenetration of reason and nature — an interpenetration that is never complete. The organic functions, by which reason subjects nature and makes it its symbol, constitute the methods of interpenetration. Law is based on Ethics, and consists in the moral coexistence of individuals, connected in their various relations, which constitute a necessary ethical process, because reason demands the moral communion of men. This is realized in the State by the submission of nature to the control of a national group of individuals.   If we once admit this definition of the State, it is clear that speculative thought or scientific communion, the free social idea, and religious sentiment, (although in the form a communion), should not be placed under the control of the State.   If the constitution of the State depends on various national elements, it follows that no political Metaphysics, but only a simple Physiology, will be possible.

XI

HEGEL

Schelling started out at once with the highest principle, — with an intuition (like a cannon ball, as
Hegel says). HEGEL does not believe in the presupposition of an intuition. He reaches absolute knowledge
by a series of acts so connected that one follows from
another. He develops his theory from the most elementary knowledge, or sensible consciousness (in which
the object, seen confusedly, is hardly distinguished from
the subject), to representation (which considers the object as something with determinate properties). From
this form of knowledge he comes to reason, which understands things as forces or causes, or individual objects;
from reason he goes on to auto-consciousness, in which
one ego considers its relation to another; and from
auto-consciousness he is led to the sphere where the spirit
is identity, always, however, distinct in itself from object
or subject. The determinations of this identity are, therefore, objective and subjective; such determinations are
the categories (the material of logic, a science of primal
reality or metaphysics). Logic is divided into Being
which develops in the categories of quality, quantity,
and measure; Essence, which includes all the categories
of relation; and Notion, which has its movements in immediate perception, its division in judgment, and its rein-
tegration in syllogism. Being is the thesis, Essence the
antithesis, and Notion is the unity of Being and Essence.
The entire process of the categories depends on the "idea."
"Idea," complete in itself, when fully understood, is sensible reason; nature is derived from the spirit, the immediateness of the idea; whence it appears always as posited,

created, and has a rationale of means in regard to it. The primitive categories of nature are space and time, indicative of pure exteriority. Matter is concrete space. It was first inorganic and then assumed organic and living form. Life has its degrees; vegetable life assimilates and exhales matter; in animal life there are also assimilations and exhalations, but the animal assimilates through the senses and exhales through the appetites.

The spirit, first as an indeterminate sense of self, and then as a concrete or individual sense, is mind made one with body. It participates in the life of nature, from which it receives various influences; hence differences of race, temperament, and the peculiarities of waking and sleeping, and of sex. When the mind becomes a concrete sense of self, interpenetrated with self, it is the ideal identity, knowledge, consciousness, the distinction of the ego from the non-ego. Consciousness, through its diverse forms, as we have said before, develops into mind and attains objectivity and certainty. Mind, this identity of the object and subject in subjective form, is theoretical. The theoretical mind begins by being an intuition, and becomes representation and reason. Since the mind produces the subject, the universal, or the concept, from theoretical, it becomes practical, that is, identity of object and subject in objective form. The practical mind is at first practical sentiment or unstable appetite, then inclination, desire, passion, and license, and finally reasonable or moral freedom, realized in custom. With the attainment of rational freedom, practical mind becomes ethical spirit, the unity of the theoretical mind. Such spirit is the activity which produces, not objects of sense, representation, and reason, but those that are ethical or juridical. Soul, consciousness, and mind are found in every individual. They do not constitute worlds; the spirit, as Ethos, is a community of subjects

and therefore a world. But, in fact, the struggle of
the passions does not disappear, whence the necessity of
a higher sphere where the spirit can be all-important
and can attain the Absolute through art, religion, and
philosophy. The Absolute in art lies in sensible intuitions, in religion, in sentiment, and faith; and in philosophy it is shown by the evidence of reason. It is in
philosophy that the spirit acquires full and complete
auto-consciousness and development through the mind.

The philosophy of law, according to Hegel, has for
its object the idea of the law and its realization. Law
is external freedom. It is the existence of freedom, which
is first determined in particular objects by ownership,
and then in agreement over one object by contract. In
ownership, there is the will that realizes itself in the things
possessed. As these are, by their nature, accidental, it,
too, is accidental. The accidental will or caprice denotes
a possibility of the alienation and also of the violation
of rights, though the latter entails a punishment. Punishment is the vindication of a violated right, by which
true and good reason is substituted for false and de-
praved reason. Thus freedom advances from the state
of external to one of internal existence. Internal freedom
is morality, which lies in the practical virtue of the
spirit to direct the sensible desires according to reason.

The spirit, after being shown in act as juristical objectivity and moral subjectivity, makes for the unity of
law and morals, of external and internal freedom. The
simple observation of the law has no virtue in it, nor
an abstract belief in the good *per se*, the law can be
obeyed without a belief in the good, and a belief
in the good is not a sure sign of respect for the law.
The belief should be shown in a manner not entirely
subjective, accidental, and temporary, but stably and
substantially — that is, in ethical habit, ordinary ac-

tion, and custom.   Custom presupposes the community
of subjects or minds.   This community is, first the family,
then civil society, and lastly the State.   The family is a
community existing in sentiment and love.   This unity
has a tendency to become more rational in form, the
family developing, when the children acquire full consciousness of their being and assert themselves with
their individual interests.   The systemization of these
particular interests is civil society.

Sentiment and interest cannot exhaust the concept of
man, therefore a new form of community is created,
in which the spirit can develop as reason or universal will.
The new form is the State, an ethical organism, containing universality in its legislative power, particularity in its governing power, and individuality in the
power of the king.   The predominance of one of these
factors over the others generates the various political
types, for democracy corresponds to universality,
aristocracy to particularity, and monarchy to individuality.   In representative monarchies, all the factors in the
concept of the State are fully realized.

International public law is a derivative of the relations between States, based on the common nature and
autonomy of nations.   War, a relationship between States,
is the only means for the settlement of their disputes;
it is like the salutary movement of the air.   Constant
peace presupposes an agreement, which, based on relative
motives, can only be accidental.   National existence
lies entirely in the power of the absolute spirit, which
exercises full jurisdiction, putting out of existence the
nations that have fulfilled their mission, and creating
others to express new concepts.   Whence it is that the
history of the world is the manifestation of universal
justice.   Absolutely spiritual are the beginning and end
of nations, which represent the grades of their develop-

ment. The historical entity of nations, their special mission in the world, are derived from the absolute spirit, which Hegel made all-important, believing in the ethical and mundane spirit as a complexity of law, morals, and politics.

XII

ROSMINI, HERBART, TRENDELENBURG, AND KRAUSE—THE VARIOUS PHASES OF SCHELLING'S PHILOSOPHY—STAHL AND SCHOPENHAUER

Italian philosophy did not remain uninfluenced by the movement of German thought, and especially by the Kantian movement.   SPAVENTA showed the influence of the former with great acumen, in his examination of the doctrines of GALLUPI, ROSMINI, and GIOBERTI. Gallupi follows experience, which for him is the elaboration of the data of the senses in the relations dependent upon the synthetic activity of the spirit, such as identity and difference. He starts out with the Kantian form of knowledge, that is, distinction, as the base of empirical knowledge, teaching that perception outside of myself is inseparable from consciousness of myself. And he follows Kant in his recognition of synthetic judgments *a priori* practical, and of ideas born of the spirit synthetically an unit. Rosmini bases knowledge on the transcendental idea of entity. Like Kant, he sees in the fact of knowledge, intuition or sensible data, and the category or innate idea of the entity; and in intellectual perception, the reduction of the latter to the former. But the idea of the entity through its very indefiniteness cannot lend itself to the connection of the pure concepts, of the categories; neither can the latter come from the senses, and therefore (thinks Gioberti) Rosminian transcendentalism results in nullism; and we are in need of a concrete principle of knowledge, suitable to the creation of the categories. Such a principle is the ideal formula of Gioberti; being creates the existent.   To explain knowledge, Gioberti does not have recourse to an empty and inert idea, like that of a possible entity, but to an idea which comprehends and originates everything, to the creative idea, a new form of the original synthetic activity of sense and intellect, of the ideal and the real, of nature and spirit.

Of the three Italian philosophers, Rosmini alone has a complete and fully developed philosophy. He starts out with the ethical principle, recognizes being in its place and respects it for what it is worth. From the practical recognition of being is derived happiness, consisting in the satisfaction of our capacities, by their attainment of their proper ends. Moral law prescribes the practical recognition of being, in its sphere or as it is; which means that in an intelligent being, all the activities proper to it should be recognized and respected. Respecting all the activities of an entity implies the duty of not hindering it in the exercise of its rights. The activities of a being, considered in relation to the law, whose respect they command, become as numerous as the rights to which they belong. And since the activity of a being is connected with its well-being, so right, subjectively considered, is the faculty of doing what one pleases, protected by the moral law which enjoins its respect. The science of law is connected with eudemonology, which shows the material or good of enjoyment, and with ethics, which show the form, that is, the nobility; they guarantee the well-being of man. Ethics are concerned with duties; the law's object is the power of action. The former are of an essentially moral, and the latter of an eudemonic nature but influenced by its relation with moral law, in which law is subordinate to ethics. From the definition of law, it can be easily seen, as morals must end in an intelligent principle, that there cannot be any rights except in intelligent beings, whose activities moral law protects. Moral law, too,

prescribes absolute respect of personality, which alone
is ultimate, and prescribes through it the respect due to
all the immediate or mediate activities that are man's.
The general characteristic, which marks activity as the
subject of a right, not only in relation to the inherent
rights but also in relation to rights in general, is property.
Property, in its broadest signification, means the conjunction of one individual thing to another, a stable and
complete conjunction, so exclusive, in fact, that one
object is called the other's, and can be bound in the same
degree to nothing else.   Rights are innate and acquired.
The second presupposes the first, as the act requires
its potentiality.   Only those rights are alienable which
are not essentially bound to the person.   Rights are
maintained by legal or by personal force.

The ideal being and the first law (says Rosmini) are identical for all men and intelligences.   All the intellectual
activities, therefore, and all the purely personal rights
of the beings, which form the human race, are joined,
thus binding men together in a state of natural society.
The concept of a society is that of many persons, who
have united for a common purpose, or the good that they
hope to obtain together, using to win and obtain it the
activities that each has a right to assign.   All men are
united in the ideal being; all men aspire to it, wish to possess and enjoy it.   The tendencies to being and well-
being generally start from the personal activities,
which cause the being in the first instance, and form
the nature of man.   If men propose for themselves other
more particular advantages, concepts of other societies
will arise within the first.   From the purely personal
rights comes the society of mankind; from individual
acquired rights spring the roots of all the other particular associations, with their determinate ends.   In such a
way, individual rights generate social rights.   But being is

ideal, real, and moral.   And three kinds of advantages
(objects of the society of mankind) correspond to these
three of its forms.   The tendency to happiness leads to
being as the real, the tendency to truth leads to being
as the ideal, the tendency to virtue and justice leads
to morality.   As each form of being demands the other
two, so, in each of these tendencies, the other two are contained.   The initial society of mankind can, therefore,
give place to three diverse societies, domestic, civil,
and theocratic or divine.   Domestic society places man in
relation to the reality of existence through sentiment and
procreation, and has the rationale of a principle.   Civil
society (a discovery of the human intellect) is the safe-
guard and protection of the exercise of rights and has the
rationale of a means.   Theocratic or religious society
consecrates rights by a new virtue, which bases all
entities and objects upon the principle from which they
spring, and it has the rationale of an end.

To the absolute idealism of Hegel is opposed in Germany the metaphysical and individualistic realism of
HERBART, founded on the Kantian principle of things
in themselves.   Kant began with the sensations; Herbart
begins with the formal concepts of experience, containing
contradictions which must be eliminated by metaphysics.   We know the phenomena of an object as
it appears; the phenomenon is not explicable without
the being in which it appears; the being is not an element of a concept, but is without it.   It is absolute
position, and is, as such, single, indistinct, simple, irrela-
tive, and immutable.   The contradictions, contained in
the concepts of things, properties, changes, and causes,
are derived from a presupposition of inherence (something
with diverse quality) and from the demand of change (a
partial alteration of the thing), while being is single, of
but one property, simple and not capable of change.

Inherence and change are referable to phenomena, not to being. Being consists in many "reals" or monads, simple and immutable, existing in themselves and of themselves. All these, united, give a result which each alone cannot give. Phenomena arise from the relations between the close, impenetrable monads, placed one against the other. If a monad touches another, the contact is always external, the disturbance extrinsic, but the monad, that is touched, preserves its qualities, and responds by an act of preservation, wherein lies the effective appearance of things, in other words, representation. The ego, as a principle of representations, is single and many. It contains the contradictions revealed in the conception of things and properties. The contradictions end when the ego is regarded as a point-movable, in which many series of representation intersect.

Now it is manifest that this kind of realism cannot overthrow idealism, because the "reals" are metaphysical presuppositions, which express thought in its simplicity and distinction. The difference (from this point of view) between Herbart and Hegel is that Hegel considers thought explained in his system of determinations as the concrete connection and truth of experience, while Herbart bases it on intuitive thought in its indistinction or the true substance of the "reals." Herbartian realism, in ethics, is mere formalism, because it is based upon purely abstract conceptions of harmony and æsthetic accord. Æsthetics, differing from metaphysics, depart from empirical data, and develop through a series of judgments, expressing contentment or displeasure. Ethics are a part of æsthetics, whose judgment contains approval or disapproval of actions, in comparison with some model concepts, which give no positive commands. If the action accords with such an original model, it is worthy of approval; if it does not, it is disapproved of. Such concepts do not show what should be done; they are not imperative; and ethics, therefore, are without a content of action, and are essentially formal. There are five model concepts, which deal with freedom, perfection, benevolence, law, and equity. Law is the harmony of the majority of wills to avoid struggle. From these five ethical concepts, not reducible to a single concept, there arise five social concepts. The concept of animated society rose from the concept of freedom, the concept of the system of education corresponds to that of perfection; beneficence comes from benevolence; the concept of the juristic society corresponds to law, and a system of retribution presupposes equity.

TRENDELENBURG, who thinks that in the Hegelian dialectics intuition is artfully hidden, and that, without intuition, there is no real progress, exalts above all the principle of simple original motion, common to thought and being. He, however, is unwilling to admit that motion, thus conceived, in an idealistic system such as his, must in its essence be the same as Hegelian growth. In Hegelianism, growth is derived from the nature of thought itself, which is an action of union and distinction, relation, motion. Motion, in which there is a communion of thought and of being, is not corporeal, according to idealism; and can only be the result of thought. For thought alone is capable of containing in itself being, of going out from itself and returning to itself. Motion, thus regarded, is reducible in the last analysis to the original synthetic activity of Kant. Trendelenburg, therefore, is not an effective opponent of Hegel but rather of Herbart, the enemy of motion. He thinks that the contradictions with which Herbart starts out are not true; that if they were true, they could not be resolved; and that even if they were resolved, the highest, that of the end, would not be explained.   He denies the atomic conception of the world and Spinoza's conception of indifference.   He prefers the organic teleological definition of Plato and Aristotle, and bases law on ethics.

Natural law, like ethics, has its presupposition in metaphysics, which give the organic conception of the world, and in psychology, that shows the essence of man. Metaphysics create the idea, the principle of organic conception and of all necessity.   Law, in that it rises to the elevation of the idea, participates in the necessity which is logical, physical, and ethical.   The necessity in law at first is ethical, because it contains a norm of reason.   Then it is physical or compulsory, because force is a means for the realization of the norm among recalcitrant wills;   and finally it is logical, because law must appeal to the intellect and has need of method in its formation and application.   Law, therefore, has three sides— ethical, physical, and logical.   From the first point of view, law, as ethics, should be founded on the essence of man lying in the depth of his ideas, and on the fullness of his historical development, because a single rational element leads nowhere, and a single historical factor is useless. The idea of man is the idea of a community: "unus homo, nullus homo."   The human community is essentially a whole, an ethical organism, in which control and organization are shown.   The control affects the individuals, who aid one another to obtain their particular ends.   The organization concerns the ends of the community, effectuated by man in general.   The control and organization should harmonize;   neither should prevail at the cost of the other.   If the first is absolute, it results in atomism and anarchy.   If the second has exclusive control, individual personality is denied.   Now law, the norm of control and organization, is the complexity

of those universal determinations of action, which
render the preservation of the ethical whole and its parts
possible. It works for the realization by force of the
ethical whole. Ethics are the objective realization
of the human essence; morals and law represent
more the subjective realization, one considering the intention and the conscience, the other considering
action, external relations, and coexistence.

The philosophy of KRAUSE shows an attempt to unite
the subjectiveness of Fichte and the objective principle
of Schelling. According to this philosophy, God is a
personal and living principle; the world is the revelation of a living God, who is the original essence through
autonomasia. AHRENS, who applies the ideas of Krause
to the sciences of law and of the State, holds that the
theory of this philosophy harmonizes the two general
methods, the analytic and the synthetic (resting on an analysis of all its relations of human nature in which law
appears as the principle of order); he reduces man
and humanity to God. The conception of law is therefore analytic in one aspect and synthetic in another.
Justice is a divine and human idea, and consists in the
untrammeled regularity of the life of all moral beings,
that is, in the organic complexes of conditions created
by God and humanity, so that reasonable beings may attain their rational ends. Law, on the one hand, is distinct
from morals and religion and, on the other, is intimately
connected with them, in that it represents their conditional side, giving conditions suitable to existence and
development to all the fundamental elements of life.
There is no side of life with which law has no relation.
Law not only limits and protects, but tends to
fulfill and aid the individual activities. In every
subject, it recognizes two elements, the personal and the
social; and tries to reconcile them in the various insti-

tutions.   The State represents the law; it does not
absorb the individual or society.   The rules should
be different for the spheres of science, art, industry,
commerce, morals, and religion.   The State's duty is to
maintain the social development in the life of justice
and to assure the means of perfection to every branch
of human knowledge.   The State may be called the medi-
ator between the individual and society, but it is nothing
more than one of the principal organs of the vast organism of society.   Society is an organic whole, resulting from diverse institutions, each of which is referable
to an important side of human life.   All institutions
are higher forms of existing society in epochs of
maturity and social harmony.

Between Kant and Hegel there are philosophical doctrines based on an irrational principle of the world.
JACOBI regards the absolute as not irrational in itself
but as unknowable for us.   The absolute for him was only
an object of sentiment and faith; Schelling passes from
rationalism to irrationalism,[1] when he abandons the presupposition of the identity of the real and ideal as reason
and yet (remaining a monist) teaches that everything
is derived from an unconscious will, which is force.
In mechanics, life, sensation, and instinct, the unconscious will (universal force) is blind and fatal.   In history
there is an internal individualization of the principle
of force accompanied by consciousness.   History begins
with the separation of the will as an individual conscious
force from the will as a cosmic force; and in this separation lies the origin of evil.   History proceeds with the
conscious and untrammeled prevalence of the general
will over the individual, that is, through the intelligence
and the spontaneous dedication of the individual wills
to the ends and purposes of the general will.

[1] See *supra*, p. 63.

Also, in the last phase of his philosophy, Schelling abandons realism. Existence, *qua* existence, is a fact for the mind, which alone can have a conception of it. Our knowledge is exclusively based on experience which, understood in its common meaning, cannot include the absolute. But there is an experience of another kind, human experience, or the religious consciousness of man in his historical development, which is capable of revealing spontaneously the absolute principle.

On the last phase of Schelling's speculation, STAHL, (who has a great reputation among the critics of the historical school) bases his arguments. Stahl admits that the world is the effect of the free creation of a personal God (the object of a higher experience), and that in history sovereign intelligence and divine control are shown. The great progress, he says, of our century in the philosophy of law and politics is due to the principle of objectivity, understood even by Hegel in a logical sense. It is necessary to understand objectivity in a real sense, and therefore to raise as a rule of law the effective and concrete order of life, that is, the structure and economy of the human family, made by a power superior to man with ethical or final laws, immanent in all relations. Stahl is the author of a doctrine of a historico-theological character.

SCHOPENHAUER considers the world as representation and will. The representation is phenomenon, illusion; the will is real, noumenon, placed outside the representative sphere. Man does not represent only the body, but feels immediate dependence on the will, as the latter's true and direct expression. Pleasure and pain indicate the agreement or disagreement of corporeal motion with acts of will. The will is the principle of the world inasmuch as it is separate from consciousness, and

in its infinity is a cosmic force. Will is gravitation, magnetism, the force of sorrow, instinct, the intentional
acts of man, which are the effect of the necessary determination of motive. Will is a blind force, a tendency to
objectivity and life. Phenomenon exists through the
objectivation of the will, and the will becomes objective
through its exercise. Hence, cognition is explained by the
will, the essence of the world. Human will cannot go beyond representation for its motive and purpose, and it
cannot equal the single and blind will as a cosmic force.
It suffers from this hindrance; and hence pain and
grief. We can free ourselves from phenomenon in an
essentially ethical manner. Will produces the individuals
in whom there are two stimuli, egoism and altruism,
the one referable to us as intellect, the other as will.
Egoism will not take us outside our individuality; altruism places us in a general relation. Man should struggle against egoism and participate in another's pains,
and so obtain moral perfection. But since our will cannot be separated entirely from representation, the only
virtue lies in self-resignation to fate. HARTMANN follows
Schopenhauer and places the primal principle of things
in the unknowable. Hartmann's unknowable is the absolute, the unconscious, the unity of the will and idea,
that is, of force without thought and of thought without
force.

XIII

MATERIALISM, POSITIVISM, AND CRITICISM

Irrationalism confuses the absolute with the data of experience or force; but force cannot be conceived of by itself, without thinking of the real as a substance; whence it follows that the irrational essence of the world is matter. Such is the logical bond between the accentuated forms of rationalism and materialism. The principles of contemporary materialism are the unity, transmissibility, and constancy of matter and force, and the circulation of the latter. From these principles it infers that mental force is a property of matter, that thought circulates as all other forces, and that psychic force is reducible to motion.

Everything is derived from matter and motion. With the different groupings of the atom, and the transformation by motion, everything is explained. Nothing is known of spiritual entities apart from matter; and therefore one cannot speak of their reciprocal action. The series of physical actions develops parallel to that of the psychological actions, and so the same phenomenon has two aspects and is bilateral, because from an objective point of view it is related to the former series, while subjectively it is referable to the second.

The positivism of COMTE declared impossible absolute knowledge or the knowledge of the primal cause, of essence and finality; it limited cognition to law, that is, to the constant relation of phenomena. Positive philosophy adopts the methods of the logical and classical sciences, of which it is a generalization, and therefore unifies the most general laws of knowledge and gives methods of discovery and proof, and establishes the control of the sciences themselves.   The mind, according to Comte, who in this has followed TURGOT, passes through three states, the theological, metaphysical, and positive.   In theology, the principles of things are divine entities; in metaphysics, abstract conceptions rule as real causes; in positivism the ever-changing phenomena, found by the aid of experience, govern all relations.   The phenomena are more or less complex; the more simple are the more general, and the more complex are the more particular.   Their general application is in inverse ratio to their complexity.   The sciences, therefore, can be classified as follows: First, Mathematics; second, Astronomy; third, Physics; fourth, Chemistry; fifth, Biology; and sixth, Sociology.   This classification is made on the ground that the last science presupposes all the others and that the first presupposes no other. Astronomy presupposes Mathematics, Chemistry, Physics; Biology leads to the development of Chemistry, and the other sciences in the prior grade of the classification.   Sociology is the last science.

All sciences pass through the three states, except mathematics, which has no precedent theological state. Progress lies in the gradual succession of states; Sociology is still concerned with metaphysical entities, and must be developed into a state of positivism.   In the theological state of social science, the regulation of conduct is given to God; in the metaphysical state, duties, rights, and authorities govern human nature, understood abstractly and hypothetically.   The principal theories of liberalism (for example, equality and popular sovereignty) belong to this phase, which now should belong to the past.   The revolutionary doctrine of equality is abstract and metaphysical (containing only the negation of fictitious and artificial inequalities). The principle of popular sovereignty is not positive, because the people are not capable of controlling the State; it can be received only as a conception from which the people's right to escape oppression may be derived. Sociology will effectively enter the third phase, when it is based on experience and considers man not as an abstract but as a historical entity. Historical experience determines and deduction proves the laws of society, reconstructing them, according to the laws of human nature, which are as fixed as those of biology. The law, discovered by historical experience, is true and necessary, if it harmonizes with the principles of human nature. Sociology proceeds from the whole to the parts (differing from the other sciences), because it is based on a collective fact. A social phenomenon has no meaning unless it is put in relation to all the others to which it is connected, and unless it is studied from all its aspects. Sociology is divided into two parts: Statistics, considering the laws of equilibrium and the conditions of the existence of the social elements; and Dynamics, referring to motion and progress. Progress is the prevalence of the highest human activity. Its great factor is the development of the intellect.

Positivism does not remain in its first phase, but becomes constructive and critical. The immense progress of the natural sciences, their rapid and important discoveries, and the new physical, chemical, and biological theories furnish a more ample content to positive philosophy. Founded on the sciences, it cannot fail to be developed and modified with their advance. The doctrine of evolution, which has gradually developed in realm of the natural sciences, with essentially an objective, experimental, and mechanical character, has made positivism evolutionistic. From now on, positive philosophy will be the general theory of evolution and transformation. As the particular sciences advance, increasing the quantity of principles applicable to a growing number of natural phenomena, it is not possible to hold that the essences and the primal causes will remain eternally hidden. Scientific experience refutes such a statement, therefore the mind must not be forbidden to search for the primal elements of things created in the breast of positivism. On the other hand, mechanical evolution cannot be applied in its purity and simplicity to the phenomenon of higher orders; and this necessitates giving evolution different means according to its grade of existence. Of this new phase of positivism, and, in particular, of the philosophy of Spencer, we shall treat at length in the following chapters.

The ancient metaphysics were destroyed by Kant, who corrects the ancient empiricism with the principle of the spontaneity and originality of thought. After Kant, absolute idealism attempted the reconstruction of realism by dialectics. And positivism made the same attempt, using science and experimental proof. Both movements were unsatisfactory to many philosophers, who believed that the first gave thought an objectivity independent of experience and separated it from reality, and that the second resulted, in the last analysis, in materialism, reducing everything to matter, motion, and mechanical laws.

The modern philosophers on whom we would lay emphasis are the followers of the NEO-CRITICISM, who consider the analysis of knowledge made by Kant as a fundamental physical doctrine, when purified of the dogmatic residual of "the thing in itself." The Neo-Critics agree in stating that metaphysics are an illegitimate production of the mind, and that módern experimental philosophy has not a strictly scientific character, in that it contains some presuppositions of theory not verified nor verifiable. Some of them think that experimental speculation (though it has not always a truly scientific character) is the best manner of contemplating reality, because evolutionary monism is the concept that best corresponds to the present state of cognition furnished by the various sciences, but we must not believe that the first principle has been determined or the supreme law of evolution shown. External observation (say these Neo-Critics) gives us only matter and motion; internal observation gives us thought already formed and does not show us how thought joins to the mechanical fact. In conclusion, evolutionary monism, according to these philosophers, is more a contemplation than a demonstration of the real. It is a useful hypothesis, and has more value than dualism, the worst of the metaphysical systems.

It is easy to deduce ethical ideas from the principles upon which the diverse movements of contemporary thought are based. It is plain that hedonism must be the basis of ethics in the greater number of these doctrines, which are founded on the stimulating effect of pleasure and pain, on organic needs and utility, and proceed in harmony with the laws of association, custom, heredity, and public opinion. To such ethical, juristical, and political ideas, and to the theoretical principles from which they spring, there will be ample consideration given in the general part of this work.

BOOK I

CHAPTER I

THE IDEA OF THE PHILOSOPHY OF THE LAW

PHILOSOPHY AND THE SCIENCES.—THE CHARACTER OF MODERN PHILOSOPHY AS FORESHADOWED BY VICO.— PHILOSOPHY OF THE LAW AS PART OF PHILOSOPHY.—THE HUMAN IDEA OF LAW ACCORDING TO THE DOCTRINE OF VICO, AND THE DEFINITIONS OF KANT, HEGEL, TRENDELENBURG, ROMAGNOSI, AND ROSMINI. —THE SOCIAL AND LEGAL THEORIES.— LAW AND POSITIVE PHILOSOPHY.

§ 1. *Philosophy and the Sciences.* The mind is suited by its very nature to develop from common and superficial knowledge of things to scientific reflection indicative of causes and reasons, and from that to Philosophy, which looks to the ultimate principles and supreme reason of entities as parts of the universe. Philosophy is the most general and elevated system of the fundamental principles and concepts of the mind, because it tends to correlate fully and intimately the mother-ideas, from which the different sciences spring. From this, it follows that there is and can be no natural disagreement between the Sciences and Philosophy.

§ 2. *Sciences Make for Unification.* The demand for a system or deep organic correlation of ideas (in which none can stand without the others, and all, interpenetrating, are derived from a common principle) is shown by the history of the positive and speculative sciences, which tend constantly to the acquisition

of such a form of coördination.   Physics, for example,
reviving the Cartesian concept, makes clear the genetic
development of forces with only two presuppositions,
matter and motion, because it is enabled through the new
and important discoveries to reduce the phenomena of
electricity, magnetism, heat, and light, to the unity of
molecular mechanics.

§ 3.   *Philosophy a Part of every Science.*   If the mind
feels the need of the systemization and genetic development in the particular branches of knowledge, it cannot
fail to feel it in the broader sphere of complete knowledge. And thus it is that with the growth of the quantity of notions the necessity of their coördination arises.
Philosophy, which is the ultimate ideal of coördination
(although not recognized in that form but rather as
the absolute centre of all codes of knowledge), gains
new life in the realms of the particular sciences, which
are thus prompted to exceed their proper bounds.   The
physics and chemistries that deny philosophy become
metaphysical and metachemical, and at the same time
are based on a philosophical theory of an original
atomic constitution.   Such a theory can be called
philosophical because there is no microscope in the
world that can show the intimate and actual structure of matter.   No one of the followers of studies
of nature, who are enemies of philosophy, keeps
within the bounds of his proper sphere.   The phy-
sicist would explain chemical phenomena by mechanics;
the chemist invades the realm of the physiologist;
and the physiologist usurps the office of the psychologist.   Each constructs a kind of philosophy in the restricted field of his chosen study and nevertheless all
of them deny philosophy.   At one time the Romanist
was as irate against science as the theologian, because
he thought that the dictates of Roman legislation were

oracles of written reason, and he unceasingly accused the philosophers of a desire to place their cerebrine equity at the head of human knowledge. The anger has notably decreased among the new school of Romanists, but the tendency still exists and is often shown. So it is that, with the purpose of exchanging rational for positive law, philosophy is denied on one hand, and recognized in a manner of its own on the other, by the acceptor of the "jus positum in Romanâ civitate" as "ratio."

§ 4. *Philosophy Depends upon the Sciences.* Since philosophy is the science that systemizes the mother-ideas of the particular sciences, it is evident that it cannot be separated from the latter. The naturalists seem to desire to make plain the schism by holding up the speculative processes to ridicule; but this is more apparent than real, because, in the last analysis, they only wish to free the natural sciences from the concepts of the old philosophy of the Middle Ages, which placed divine mysteries in the midst of sensible phenomena and confused them with human purposes, sympathies, antipathies, and senses. We all know that Galileo banished mystery and human prejudices from the realm of nature, to which he restored its proper language by recognizing a profound and real connection in its various transformations. And apart from the question of Galileo's conclusions, it is no longer a subject of doubt that from the coördination and subordination of the most general concept of various branches of knowledge regarding nature, there is derived a natural philosophy not disjoint from the positive sciences nor existent without their progress. Likewise, we must admit the possibility of a supreme science of history, in which will be joined all historical studies and auxiliary pursuits, and of a philosophy of linguistics, which will develop with an extended and profound knowledge of the development of words and with the long and tedious work of comparing the forms of various languages.

§ 5.   *Metaphysics and Necessity.*   "No more metaphysics," is the cry of many.   Distribute the objects they comprehend among the different particular sciences.   From the criticism of philosophy, they add, arises its denial.   But some recent positivists point out that the very denial of philosophy connotes philosophy; because it is necessary to show the impossibility of transcendental knowledge, this proof is essentially speculative and philosophical, and cannot be made except by searching the conditions and possibility of real knowledge, constructing thus a theory of cognition and a science, that is, logic.   Neither the origin nor value of knowledge can be determined without attention to the relation between knowledge and its objects; whence the cosmological doctrine.   From another point of view, the mind is urged to discover the meaning of existence and of the reality of things in regard to the ends of life; and this is the origin of ethics.   Philosophy is the unity of the sciences, those positivists continue; it is the systemization and critical analysis of the mother-ideas, to which they are reducible.   The sciences presuppose such ideas.   Philosophy is needed in their discussion, and therefore the state of dissension between this system and the philosophical schools should be no cause of wonder.   If the sciences, because of their constitution, do not contain serious grounds of disagreement that make the progress of philosophy hard, it is because they do not seek fundamental ideas.   Every science, in its development, discovers relations always more general, and approaches the rules of law that are common to the phenomena of different sciences.   These laws can be called cosmic, since they connect mechanical, chemical, and biological truths. As the sciences approach such principles, the need of metaphysics is felt, which cannot fail to be experimental and scientific in our days, and which should be admitted, according to Lewes, Wundt, and Anguilli, for the reasons above indicated. Be that as it may, it is clear that Metaphysics arise from the grave to aid the work of these very positivists. Positivism, says Anguilli, in "La Filosofia e la Scuola," cannot remain dogmatic, cannot renounce the search of the principles of knowledge and existence, when all the sciences are aimed at raising the veil that covers their origin. Positivism should be critical. It should leave the questions about the possibility of the knowledge of essences and causes open. It cannot be said *a priori* that the essences and causes are not knowable and that it is not possible to discover first principles. This was the mistake of Comte, who has reduced philosophy to a mere codification of natural law and a classification of the sciences, ignoring its higher duty to systematize the mother-ideas.

§ 6. *The Philosophy of Law.* The PHILOSOPHY OF LAW, a part of philosophy, is the science of the highest principles of law. It should not, therefore, be separated from the complexes of positive and historical studies of jurisprudence and of social and political sciences. It is not in the least possible to determine the remote rationale of the law considered by itself and in its relation to the individual, society, and the State, apart from its mediate and proximate principles. The mind ascends from what is particular and close to sense to what is universal and distant. It develops from what is only primal for us to what is primal for nature, according to Aristotle. Of course, whatever is particular and positive is not the direct and proper object of philosophy, but constitutes the necessary

foundation of it.   Physics, chemistry and biology are
not of themselves the philosophy of nature, but it
cannot be developed without great reliance on such studies. Philosophy is always the last to make its appearance;
life must be mature and the particular scientific modes
of knowledge must be numerous and developed before
we can have a philosophy. The black bat of Minerva,
as Hegel says on this subject, wings his flight only in
the night.

§ 7. *Character of Modern Philosophy as Foreshadowed
by Vico.* Modern philosophy has an original tendency
to keep itself free from blind empiricism and from the
metaphysics of abstract and empty thought. It is
fundamentally one with the metaphysics of the
human mind discovered by Vico, which advance
with the history of human ideas. What is this human
idea? Several places in the "Scienza Nuova" explain
it clearly. The nature of things, writes Vico, is nothing
but their origin in certain times and certain forms; and
as the times and forms are, so and not otherwise are things
born.   Now this means, on the one hand, that the
true nature of things is shown in motion and evolution
and does not lie in quiescent essences, placed beyond the
sphere of phenomena; and, on the other hand, it indicates the principle of necessity relative to certain times
and certain forms, very different from the abstract,
purely absolute logical necessity. And from this comes
the other dictum, that theory should begin at the time
when the matter of which it treats begins. The true object of science is to determine the nature of beings, and
this lies in their genesis of birth.

§ 8. *Vico's Philosophy is Historical and not Abstract.*
To discover the nature of human things, continues the
Neapolitan philosopher, we must institute a severe
analysis of thought concerning the necessities and

utilities of social life, which are the two perennial sources
of the natural law of mankind. And through such a principle, this science is the history of human ideas on which
it seems the metaphysics of the human mind should be
based. At this point, we should remember the first un-
doubted principle of Vico, which is that the world of
nations should find its form within the modifications of the
human mind. He founded on this a science that deals
with idea as it is shown by actions — a science that originates and moves with life. He was the discoverer of the
philosophy of history. The new science withdraws
from the empty and transcendental speculation of the
Middle Ages and advances to ideas intrinsic in the deed,
that is, to historical or human ideas. In this lies the
great discovery and the great merit of Vico.

§ 9. *Vico's Philosophy is Practical.* The conception of the intimate conjunction of philosophy with
history is illustrated by Vico in three other "golden
passages" (as he was wont to say in speaking of the
words of wisdom of the classical writers). Philosophy
contemplates reason, whence arises the science of the true;
philology observes the authority of the human free will,
whence comes the knowledge of the certain. Human
free will, of a nature most uncertain, becomes certain
and determinate through the common sense of men in regard to human necessities and utilities. This common
sense is a judgment without any reflection, commonly
felt by a whole class, people, or nation, or by all of
mankind. The certain is referable to the language and
acts of people; thus, at home it is shown as customs
and laws, and abroad as peace, war, alliances, voyages,
and trade. Those philosophers who do not make certain their rationale under the authority of philology fail
in their sphere. The philologists fail who do not prove
their authority by philosophical reasoning. If this had

been done, they would have been more useful to all countries and would have been foremost in developing this science.

§ 10. *Vico showed the Different Bases of Rational and Positive Law.* Vico teaches, in conformity with these principles in his book, "De Universi Juris Principio et Fine Uno," that the science of law should be based on reason or philosophy and authority or philology, because the law concerns the true and the certain, that is, reason and authority. The certain is part of the true, and authority is part of reason and is not license; hence the distinction between the reason of the law, which makes for truth, and the mind of the law, which regards the certain. And from this comes the speculative thought of a conciliation between positive and rational law. But this last thought has its origin in a concept of the philosophers and Roman jurisconsults. According to Cicero, the "jus naturæ" depends upon the "naturalis ratio," as civil or positive law gets its being from "civilis ratio." Gaius defines the "jus gentium" as "Quod naturalis ratio inter omnes homines constituit." For Cicero and Gaius, therefore, the "naturalis ratio" is "constitutivum" and the common observation of it by the people is the "consecutivum."

§ 11. *The Difference and Similarity of Rational and Positive Law.* Admitting the difference and at the same time the connection between the true and the certain, positive law is not entirely identical with nor entirely opposed to rational law. "Jus civile," says Ulpian, "est quod neque in totum a naturali vel gentium recedit nec per omnia ei servit; itaque cum aliquid addimus vel detrahimus juri communi jus proprium id est civile efficimus." It realizes the ideal law, following the law of the evolution of ages, which is the same law as that of the development of knowledge. Man's power is only bounded by his will, and his will by his knowledge. As to knowledge, he is first sense, then imagination, and finally reason; and therefore the State must pass through three ages, the mute, the heroic, and the human. Law in its arboreal state is legitimate violence, later it becomes more gentle, and attains perfection through naked truth and generous reason. Grotius, Selden, and Puffendorf are wrong, because they do not begin their theory from the time when nations began, but start with their researches further on, that is, from the first days of the ennobled nations and of men enlightened by fully developed natural reason. From such nations came the philosophers who developed by meditation a perfect idea of justice. The system of natural law cannot fail to be governed by the principle that the order of ideas must proceed in accordance with the objective order. The natural law of nations has come out of the customs of the nations mutually in accord in common sense, without reflection and without using one another as an example.

§ 12. *The Philosophy of Law cannot be Based on "a priori" Principles.* If law is a human idea, if it has truth and certainty, it is not possible to base the philosophy of law on its *a priori* principles alone, considering the fact merely as an example, as Kant states in his "Metaphysische Anfangsgrunde der Rechtslehre;" because the certain is always part of the true and enters into a philosophy not as particular and separate entity, but as a generalized whole. Philosophy should not be occupied with this or that reality in kind, but should rather comprehend and explain reality of itself. Philosophical reality is ideal, rational, conscious, as true ideality is of itself real. Kant is wrong in excluding the certain in general from the philosophical system of law, although he is right when he recognizes in cases of experience, that is, in particular and secondary forms, so many objects of positive or historical law which cannot furnish philosophy with more than material of example or illustration. These cases no longer belong to positive law, and cease to be cases when raised by speculation to phases or moments of the human idea of law.

§ 13. *Vico's Theory Upheld by Modern Philosophers.* Vico's conception of law and his philosophy are substantially reënforced in the definitions of the greatest modern writers. Hegel, for example, says ("Grundlinien der Philosophie des Rechts,") that such a science has for its object law and its effectuation. We must not forget that in his mind the ideal is real and the real is ideal, and that thus the idea by its essence becomes fact and the fact is part of the idea of truth, taking the form of the certain, as Vico teaches. In Hegel's mind, not everything that happens is ideal, although what happens and is, as he expresses it, is necessary and permanent in moral cosmics, and is therefore the actualization of reason. Yet he warns us not to put the relative in the place of the absolute and to confuse historical explanation with judgment on the intrinsic legitimacy of fact. Trendelenburg, in his "Naturrecht auf den Grunde der Ethik," writes that the philosophy of law should be concerned with the highest principles of law, which can only be discovered in history (wherein lies, as Aristotle says, the test of the worth of all theories). He adds that the rational and historical conceptions, sometimes seemingly in opposition, are fundamentally one; that man is essentially an historical being, and that it is not foreign to profound philosophical comprehension to determine what is the ideal in each stage or moment of the life of a people. Among the Italians, Romagnosi, who follows Vico's doctrine about the true and the certain, admits, in his "Assunto Primo della Scienza del Diritto Naturale," that natural law is controlled by coercive reason, which affects objects

according to their position, and that under this second
aspect it is as pliant and variable as the circumstances
and changes of opportunity.   Finally, Rosmini in his
"Filosofia del Diritto" very willingly agrees with the German philosophers, who are the followers of Kant, that the
historical element of fact does not enter into a science
which is wholly speculative reason.   Nevertheless, he
speaks of an universal philosophy of law that has three
parts: Rational law, the theory of positive law, and
their critic.   The theory of positive law and the critic
form the philosophy of positive law.   Rosmini declares
that he desires to treat of rational law, denominated by
him philosophy of law, because this title indicates the
above fusion of the three parts.   In other words, he
finds the intimate connection between the true and certain in the separation of the supreme science of law,
although he does not conceive of law as the human idea,
as an idea-fact.

§ 14.   *Vico's   Theory   is   that   of   the   Positivists.*
Positivist philosophy can be reduced to Vico's theory,
which conceives of law as a phenomenal reality, as a natural formation, seeking for its causes in the social
element, in the physio-psychical activities of common
life, in the forces that precede development, and in
the evolutionary motion of things.   They agree in
explaining that this natural formation is intimately
connected with a series of social idealities, anthropology, psychology of peoples, ethnology, the history of
civilization and of juridical institutions, and comparative jurisprudence.   Research, as can be seen, gives
preference to the doctrine of evolution, and is psycho-
genetical and historical, because law is particularly a fact
depending upon thought and will, and develops in human
life.   In other words, it is an ethical and historical fact
whose primal elements, genesis, and transformations

philosophy can discover.   Now, Vico says it cannot be
denied that law is a phenomenal reality, since it contains the certain; and can be called a natural formation, inasmuch as its nature is its origin, and as it is
derived from the analysis of thoughts about the necessities and utilities of social life, and from the modifications of the human mind.   These social idealities
which the law comprehends and of which it is born,
upon which positive philosophy often lays emphasis, are
really nothing more in Vico's words than the necessities
and utilities of social life.

§ 15.   *Vico's Theory Considers the Influence of Economics.*   The two perennial sources of the natural law of
nations are also connected with another doctrine now in
vogue, that is, with the doctrine that considers law in its
social aspect in relation to the purposes, needs, and interests of life.   The doctrine is not new, because the more
idealistic philosophers have always believed in the influence of the conditions of life on law.   Among the Italians,
Romagnosi is distinguished for his study of the relations of
law with life, and particularly with the latter's economic
factors.   In Germany, Krause and Ahrens, in their definition of law, lay stress upon its relation with the
conditions of life.   Vico's necessities and utilities of social
life correspond to the action of the economic factors,
though not considered predominant as Marx, De Greef,
and Loria claim they should be; they interpenetrate with
the two generating forces of law in the concrete sense,
which are, according to Stein, economic conditions and
the activity of the State.   Such activity follows the
thoughts already indicated.   The two perennial founts
are not foreign either to the theory of Ihering, who teaches
that there is a creative power in the law, and that it lies
in guaranteed interests.   Ihering sees in the law a system
of protected powers and interests, that is, a system of

necessities and utilities of life. The two sources mean simply the adaptation of human nature in its external and social relations to this necessity and utility, an adaptation which is the chief feature of positive and evolutionistic philosophy.

§ 16. *Law must Consider the Social Relations.* The social theory of law is not separable from the juristic, if we must consider law as the human idea. Pachmann has recently attempted such a separation, but the attempt was not successful. He says that law is the measure of the external freedom of man in common life. Law is thus reduced to a system of norms which regards the extrinsification of wills and actions, and limits their measure; the mission of the juristic science, properly so called, is to show the relations, become norms or principles, and to work them into a system, without considering them as facts. Such relations, as facts, enter the domain of other sciences and can there form objects of the social theory of law, in which the measure of freedom is studied in respect to purposes and interests. The true juristic theory is dogmatics, which take the measure as fixed in amount and determine the limits of external freedom independent of objects as ends or interests. It does not take much proof to show that the juristic theory so conceived is an empty, abstract formula and can be defined as mathematical, a computation of concepts, a crystallization of the relations of life into a mere sum, or a logical whole resulting from minutely modulated rules and maxims. In such a theory, law lacks concrete content and is separated from life and the conditions of existence, becoming a bare mathematical form. History and reality have no longer anything in common with law, thus transformed into a rigid formula. The very definitions that we find in dogmatics are not all possible, because not a few of them have ele-

ments derived from the nature of things. The system and
its technicalities grow into simply mental schemes
divorced from life. Law ceases then to be a reality
and a human idea.

§ 17. *Vico believes that Phenomena are Based on Reason.*
The base of phenomenal reality is, in Vico's mind,
reason, which is also the base of law, since history in
his mind represents the true. Reason immanent in
reality, the true intrinsically one with the certain, are
resolved in the last analysis into a concept of conditions
necessary to existence, and the order and constitution
of things, and also into the unavoidable effects of acts
about which those positivists disagree who do not admit
absolute transformism. In this concept they place the
objective and necessary substratum of law, reproducing
the principles of Romagnosi. Law should be based upon
the real relation of things, and the connection of their
cause and effect, so that it should be observed in conduct
in order to obtain the good and avoid the bad. Here
the order of things is not transcendental, neither is
it beyond knowledge, but can be seen by the mind. The
ancient natural law is wrong, they add, because it starts
out with an *a priori* idea resting outside of experience
and life and not because it seeks a necessary and universal principle.

§ 18. *Vanni's Philosophy of Law.* The philosophy
of law in critical positivism, writes Vanni, in "Il Pro-
blema della Filosofia del Diritto," is the science of the
first principles of the genetico-evolutionary theory. It
is the analysis of the possibility and value of juristic
knowledge. It is the doctrine of the norms of action
coördinated in a purposeful system. In its first aspect,
it is the synthesis of the mother-ideas of all branches
of positive and particular knowledge, and there can be
no doubt on this point when we have once recognized

the existence of such a study. Also, it cannot be denied that it has also a critical duty and practical function, because it is called upon to analyze the idea of law and to determine its value by an examination of the logical processes which are applied to it. Is not this philosophy perhaps essentially a theory of knowledge? And can philosophy cease to be a criticism of knowledge when it treats of law? If philosophy of law is a part of ethics and if ethics explain the first principles of conduct, it is clear that it should give norms for conduct. When it is a question of a fact of conduct, the study of the phenomena is not enough, but we must know the reasons that induce us to favor or disfavor its continuation in conformity to an ideal. It is said, and correctly so, that ethics are a practical science, that they not only seek the laws of moral acts but determine the methods best adapted to changing them in order to reach a state of perfection that does not yet exist.

§ 19. *The Positivists are Wrong.in Denying Special Philosophies.* There are positivists who do not wish to recognize special philosophies and therefore deny the philosophy of law, with the others. They say that there is only one philosophy which unifies all knowledge (as Spencer taught). The highest truths about one branch of knowledge regard determinated orders of fact, and form one or more sciences but never a philosophy. These positivists do not reflect that if special philosophies are part of the great philosophy, or the system of the supreme principles of entire knowledge, they should not, therefore, be deprived of a distinct existence. The special philosophies presuppose the coördination of the first principles of all knowledge, but they develop it fully with respect to the few objects to which they apply, determining their particular method of existence and emphasizing the differences or proper forms in relation to such objects. The special philosophies are not detached and independent of philosophy, they cannot be separated from philosophy, but lead to theories which show the various contact of first principles with the diverse entities whose elements they search for. Certainly, philosophy in general without the special philosophies would not be able to give sufficient development to the treatment of supreme principles, since they apply in different manners to different objects. We will see in the following pages whether it is possible to apply purely and simply the more general laws of the cosmos, for example, the physical and mechanical laws, to all the products of evolution. Whoever attempts to do it runs the risk of not explaining the nature and value of the higher products of historical and ethical facts. It cannot be doubted that they who will not accept the special philosophies because of a single philosophy, obscure the real difference of entities and tend to show unity or identity where none exists. Scientific and philosophical discovery should be complete and should not disregard a difference because of a preconceived unity, nor sacrifice unity to a preconception of difference. It is not its duty to alter the effectual truth of things.

§ 20. *Distinction between the Philosophy of Law and the Science of Legislation.* We must guard ourselves, in considering the philosophy of the law, against an error contained in the books of Sumner Maine on the history of primitive institutions and of law. Maine believes that the attempt to build up a system of jurisprudence on observation, comparison, and analysis of ideas is due to Bentham, and even more to Austin, who are very unjustly not known out of England. Austin and Maine think that the object of jurisprudence is positive law and that jurisprudence can either be particular and

national or general and comparative. This is the result
of abstraction, because the identical principles of the
various legislative systems are the same. General jurisprudence is called by these two writers the philosophy
of positive law. The philosophy of positive law differs
from the science of legislation, because the former
studies the laws as they are, and the second, a branch of
ethics or deontology, shows how the laws should be made
so that they will conform to a type, that is, the divine
law identified with the principle of general utility.
Putting aside this last element of the theory, which
Maine denies, because such identity is not proved or
provable, it is undoubtedly true that general and comparative jurisprudence is very remote from the philosophy of law in the true sense of the word. Philosophy
of law is the search of first and supreme principles, while
general jurisprudence recognizes similarities of fact,
or homonyms, and does not consider the reasons. The
analysis of ideas in which this jurisprudence is so valuable
never reaches a philosophical height. Rosmini's philosophy of law is something very different, it is a higher
study. It is not purely rational law, but is rational law
applied to the science of legislation and to the critic of
law.

CHAPTER II

THE IDEA OF LAW AND LOGICAL METHODS

INDUCTION AND DEDUCTION. — INDUCTION, OBSERVATION, AND
EXPERIMENT. — THE IDEA OF NATURAL LAW AND THAT OF THE
CIVIL GOOD (OF AMARI) AS SHOWN BY INDUCTION. — THE IM-
PORTANCE OF THE COMPARATIVE HISTORICAL METHOD USED BY
VICO, AMARI, POST, AND MAINE. — PARALLELISM IN THE DEVELOP-
MENT OF LANGUAGE AND LAW. — STATISTICAL INDUCTION. —
THE DUTY OF DEDUCTION. — THE ABSTRACT AND CONCRETE
UNIVERSALS AS PRINCIPALS.

§ 21. *Law must be both Abstract and Relative.* If law
has in it elements of the true and certain, it cannot
be explained in its integrity by abstract rationalism developed in a series of schemes fixed by reason, nor by
absolute relativism which sacrifices the ideality and
necessity of the law to the continuous and contradictory
happening of events.

§ 22. *Law must be Developed Inductively and Deductively.* Vico himself determined the logical process by
which the idea of law should be developed, in these words:
The order of human ideas is to observe like things, first
to know and then to prove them; that is, first with the example, content with one thing, and later by induction,
which has need of more. Socrates, the father of all philosophical schools, introduced dialectics with induction
and later Aristotle completed them with the syllogisms
which have no application without a universal. Hence
it follows that the human idea is first inductive and then
deductive. In fact, the mind proceeds from the partic-

ular to the discovery of the laws and causes of phenomena. It does not, however, develop the rational necessity of the discovered law, nor the method of causal action within the empirical confines of induction. It is a deductive process that leads to the proof of the rational necessity of law, deriving it from a general principle, and making clear the manner in which one condition joins another to produce a phenomenon. When these ideas are accepted, we can infer that the more the certain is studied in juristic, social, and political questions, the broader will the true become. The certain in such a subject assumes the form of an historical fact or event, which becomes a numerical series or statistical element, thus furnishing material for historical and mathematical induction.

§ 23. *The Four Methods of Induction.* Historical induction is based more upon the observation of social phenomena, including juristical and political events, than on experiment, because the social phenomena are even more complicated than the natural (especially the physical and chemical) and therefore lend themselves less to artificial reproduction and voluntary variation. Experiment can be made in four ways, that is, by the method of agreement, by the inverse method of difference, by the third, of concomitant variations, and the last, of the residues. The first is reducible to the elimination of various conditions and to keeping one as the antecedent of a phenomenon. The second, on the contrary, consists in the abstraction of identical conditions and in keeping to the one that varies as cause. The method of concomitant variation is based upon the principle that a phenomenon that varies in accordance with another is its cause or effect or is at least connected with it by a chain of general causality. The fourth is governed by the following law:

"Subduct from any phenomenon such part as is known by previous inductions to be the effect of certain antecedents and the residue of the phenomenon is the effect of the remaining antecedents."[1]

§ 24. *The Experimental Methods Possible in Physiology.* There was a time when it was believed that the use of experiment would not be possible in biological research. In the century just past, Cuvier stated that physiology was the science of mere observation, but in our own day vivisection has taken remarkable strides. All the famous physiologists adopt experimental methods, although they freely state that experiment in physiology has not the extension and logical force which it has in physics and chemistry. They show the laws of the union of the internal principle with the body, that is, the union of psychical and organic action through the method of agreement. In a great number of cases, this agreement can be established, though in others the profundity of the reflective operation and the subtleness of the physical act escape observation. But even if these cases do not confirm the results of agreement, they fail to prove the contrary. Through this same method, associated with the other of concomitant variations, the modern physiologists show the law of relativity; that is, the connection between the cause of an impression and a state of consciousness, and through the agreement of all the experimental methods are illustrated the laws of memory and the conception of similarity.

§ 25. *The Experimental Methods Possible in Political Sciences.* Bain, in his "Logic," determines the principle of the logic in the political sciences and recognizes, in opposition to Stuart Mill, that in politics the above methods offer useful help when they are applied with all the limitations and cautions suggested by the particular

[1]Mill's Fourth Canon.

nature of social science (which is by far the most complicated). Mill excludes experiment from political
economy because the phenomena of wealth are extremely
complicated. Experiment in social science (Bain points
out) does not mean the application of processes adapted
to the discovery of natural laws. So, for example, the
method of difference is not conducive to certain results
about the facts of civil life, since one cannot be sure that
the condition found is the sole effect or that there are not
unknown causes. But such uncertainty is lessened if a
force suddenly introduced is followed instantly by a
change. Take, for example, a suspension of diplomatic
relations between two nations coinciding with a marked
change in commercial values. On such a hypothesis
there are reasonable grounds for believing that the
severance has produced the disturbance.

§ 26. *Vico's Human Idea of Law proved by Historical
Induction.* From historical induction, founded more
on observation than on experiment, is derived the
human idea of the law. In fact, the mind forms
of itself the concept of a natural law common to all,
after gathering and comparing many homonyms or
similarities between the diverse positive laws of different nations. In a universal consensus, in uniformity, or in the constancy of jurisprudence, there
is not a "ratio juris" but the "principium cognoscendi."
Uniform ideas, writes Vico, appearing among entire
peoples, unknown to each other, must have a common
motive of truth. This shows the great principle that
establishes the general consensus of opinion of mankind
as the criterion taught the nations by divine Providence
to define the certain in relation to the natural law of nations. And even before Vico, Grotius stated that there
was *a posteriori* proof of natural law, if not absolutely
conclusive, at least highly evidential, by which we must

consider as law what is held as such by all nations or by the more civilized nations, because a universal effect supposes a universal cause. A universal belief cannot arise except from what is called the general consensus of opinion. Cicero had already written, "Omnium consensus naturæ vox est." "Omni autem in re consentio omnium gentium lex naturæ putanda est." And Aristotle had not failed to notice that there was something which all alike believe and which was by nature common and was called law or justice, although there was no agreement or communication. Socrates was the first philosopher to speak of the unwritten laws of the gods — of universal observance. He gives as examples religion and ancestor worship. Uniformity is the cognitive criterion of natural law as shown by the very arguments of those who do not believe in it. Carneades, Sextus Empiricus, and their followers denied that there was a natural law putting antinomies in place of similarities, which shows that they implicitly admitted the above criterion; they did not believe that there was a law of nature because the discrepancy and contrast between the laws of nations were so great that they could not believe in a true and extended harmony. If this were not so, and the concordance reducible to a fractional part (they said), there would be a natural law and they would recognize it.

§ 27. *Induction is Used in the Critic of Law.* In the other parts of philosophy of law and especially in those composing (according to Rosmini) the philosophy of positive law, that is in nomothesis and in the critic of law, historical induction furnishes the first concepts. Nomothesis and the critic of the law are not possible without the principle of the just, which is always the human idea, and without the concept of the civil good, of which Amari treats in "Critica di una Scienza della

Legislazione Comparata," or of the just in given form
in relation to the time and place and condition of a
determinate life. The mind raises itself in such a principle inductively through the collective similarities of
law and their equation. It is not difficult to see that the
concept of civil good is formed in this way through
the long experience of social institutions and domestic
and foreign laws. Plato, the great idealist, compared
the laws of different nations; he taught that the City
would never be happy and civilized while ignorant of the
good and evil of the regulations of other countries.
Aristotle collected notes on many constitutions and
placed great reliance on legislative comparison distinguishing the absolute good from the possible and conditional. Thus he founded the school that gives great
importance to the comparison of the laws, which was
taught by Theophrastus, Dicearchus, and Demetrius
Phalareus.

§ 28. *Followers of Vico and the Historico-Comparative
Method.* After Vico and Amari, the historico-comparative
method was applied by Volcraff, who, however, did not
have sufficient material at his disposal, and by Bastiat,
who had made ethnological researches without philosophical intent, and by Post, who in his "Einleitung in die
Studien der Ethnologische Jurisprudenz" tends to an
experimental philosophy of law founded on ethnological
data and on the principle of the dependence of the juridical fact on other precedent facts in the cosmic series.
Maine is the author of very important studies of an
historico-comparative character. He is a thinker, however, and not a philosopher, although he rises to generalizations that are close to philosophical. He reconstructs
the fragments of the social and juristical life of the Aryan
peoples of a primitive age and gives us a paleontology,
an archeology, and a moral embryology, and tends to

show the development and indicate the evolution of the idea of law in the consciousness of that race, developing sometimes into the philosophy of the history of law. Vanni in "Gli Studi di Somner Maine e le Doctrine della Filosofia del Diritto" determines clearly the nature of the complete researches of this writer and notes the difference between his work and that of the others. Maine applies the comparative method to the progressive or undeveloped nations of different races. He is circumspect and diffident about great syntheses and ethnological theories and does not put great weight upon the analogies between modern savages and primitive people. Most sociologists, on the contrary, love great syntheses, prefer ethnological intuitions, and use without scruple the above analogies. Since Maine was an historian and not a philosopher, it is useless to search his works for a complete and satisfactory doctrine of the genesis of law. His observations begin with a state of evolution relatively advanced and refer to law when it is already formed, and therefore do not contain a true social and juridical embryology.

§. 29. *Parallelism in the Development of Language and Law.* The inductive formation of the above two branches of the philosophy of law, understood in a broad sense, is revealed in the parallel between languages and law, first noticed by Plato and later by Vico, Savigny, Puchta, Amari, Ihering, and now outlined among the Italians according to the results of positivism by Gaudenzi in his book "Lingua e Diritto." The parallelism is real, because language reflects the thought and law manifests the acts of man; the intrinsic connection between thought and action is known. In concrete, the productive genius of a people has the same powers in language and in law. A proof of it is the character of Latin language in civilization and the historic meaning of Roman law. Action presupposes will and thought and is posterior to them; therefore the development of language must be antecedent to that of law. When Rome was founded the Latin language was formed, but the Twelve Tables appeared three centuries later. The literary language was perfect at the fall of the Republic, but the development of law was only complete towards the end of the Empire. There are local provincial dialects and national languages as there are customs of county and statutes and national law. Experience teaches us that language and national law are always derived from the generalization of a local dialect, and of the customs or laws of a particular province. At the beginning, language had only enough words to express sensible objects and law was active only in the confines of material facts; later there appeared the metaphor in language and the law developed through symbols. The metaphor and symbol raised the mind from the simple perception of the object of sense to the conception of intellectual facts and abstract ideas. Language went through three stages. The first is called monosyllabic, and is formed of independent roots which do the duty of both nouns and verbs; the second is called agglutinative, because the roots are placed together, though without internal variation, to express the various relations of thought; and the third, in which the associated roots are welded together in a homogeneous whole, is called inflective. In law, there are three such distinct periods, because the elements of juristic action are first shown in a distinct and independent existence, then they unite mechanically, and finally interpenetrate in a single logical whole. The customs of barbarians, composed of a most complicated system of petty rights, joined together only by tradition in the main, correspond to the agglutinative stage. In the first steps of civilization, states are found connected by language or by law for commerce or for some other reason. Grammar or the nomothesis of language and criticism appear with the development of language and art. First came Homer and Pindar, and then Praxiphanes and Aristarchus; first Ennius and Plautus were admired and then came Orbilius and Opilius. The same happened in respect to law, which preceded the science of law and philosophy. Plato and Aristotle were only possible after Lycurgus, Solon, and the other legislators. Later philological studies consisted in the researches of etymology, to which the first labors of the Greeks are referable. After laws had been established, jurisprudence investigated their genesis, and the most celebrated jurisconsults, such as Labeo, Gaius, and Ulpian wrote on this subject. From etymology joined to grammatical studies there was an infinite distance to a science of comparative linguistics, as there was a veritable abyss between the parallelism of laws joined to nomothesis and a science of comparative legislation.

§ 30. *Statistical and Mathematical Induction.* In the juristic, social, and political sciences, mathematic or statistic induction is joined to the historical. The order of numbers, observes Vico, although of simple and abstract things, is a help to the large and compositive order of human and civil affairs. (Statistical induction, starting out with a group of homogeneous or comparable facts gathered in the greatest number, reduces them to an average which represents the mean between the various extremes, a determinate quantity which is the most approximate sum of the many diverse numbers of like and various terms.) The mean itself is a numerical formula of the constant law that governs the quantity of a social fact in a period, and therefore shows a general condition. Mathematical induction (that succeeds to such a mean) is a proper instrument of a statistical science, that is, the systematic position of the social life of man and of the laws which arise from it, based on observation in mass. Mathematical induction *per se* is the mainstay of logic and is applied without distinction to social and natural facts. But it remains a method for natural facts, and constitutes an autonomous study of social facts and is called statistics. The reason of this is shown by Rumelin in his treatise on statistics, when he says that in nature unity is typical, and in the human world it is individual. In the observation of a natural fact, all the facts of the same kind are observed; but when a person is the subject of observation, society is not included in it. Since society is a composite of very dissimilar individuals, the principal means to find the roots of the laws of that organism must lie in the observation of the mass. Experiment in this field of research takes a secondary place and observation of the mass prevails; in the natural sciences the contrary is true. Wagner in "Statistische Anthropologische Untersuchung der Gesetzmässigkeit in dem Scheinbar Willkürlichen Menschlichen Handlungen" thinks that Rumelin generalizes too much, because it is true only in physics and chemistry that every case is typical and true, and not in biology. Physiological processes bring in constant and accidental causes which combine in a various and indefinite manner, and therefore the phenomena of this kind present irregular and peculiar characteristics. Certainly in the higher grades of the evolution of nature there are found phenomena more complicated, changeable, and irregular than in the lower. But the combination and the variety of the superior forces of nature should not be exchanged for human individuality that results from auto-consciousness and auto-determination, which are shown in the duosyllabic ego. In this sense, Rumelin is right in recognizing that as we ascend in the series of organisms, a greater number of factors are seen in organic life, the combinations become more complex, and the field of variations extended, and that in the physical and human world there is a gradation and not an absolute separation between what is typical and what is individual. No grain of sand, no blade of grass resembles exactly another grain or blade, but here the dissimilarities are small in comparison to the similarities and are due to external circumstances. In the human world, the savage is less individual than the civilized man, the negro less than the white, the man of the Middle Ages less than the man of to-day, the woman less than the man, the ignorant less than the wise, the brute less than him of gentler feelings.

§ 31.   *Need of Statistics.*   Statistical induction shows through numbers the constancy and regularity of social phenomena, and increases the measure of the certain, completing the work of historical induction, which shows their quality. Numbers, weight, and measure are not elements foreign to law, because it is generally thought of as a rule of proportion, and by the Pythagoreans was confused with numbers themselves. The intellect attains more easily the idea of measure or proportion of reason, in which the law rests, after noting the certain by observation and after measuring it by mathematical induction. Numbers logically considered are intermediate elements between the sensible fact and pure imagination, and therefore Plato and Galileo placed mathematics between physic and metaphysics. This helps us, because the progress of the physical sciences, lying principally in substituting the expression of quantitative for qualitative functions, leads also to an increase of the rational and apodeictical parts of the same study. The relation between statistical induction, nomothesis, and the critic of law is manifest, because the concept of the civil good presupposes the concept of varying social conditions, which are shown in statistics, that is, the "nosce teipsum" applied to the civil union and the State, and represents the balance of the forces. There is no important act of republican administration that can be separated from the knowledge that the State should have of itself or be entitled to as the measure or the degree of its own power. And here is the first reason why in our day statistics perform a public service. But there is a second, and it lies in the demand of unlimited publicity, since the government is free. And even those who profess individualistic theories and look upon the State as only a means of legal protection, allow it such a function, because statistics are not a business and cannot be gathered by private citizens without the State's intervention.

§ 32. *The Duty of Induction.* If experience without a concept is no guide and the concept without sensible data is useless, science is not possible without both induction and deduction. Induction without deduction is an empirical process only and does not show the necessity of the causal law or its method of action. Deduction not preceded by induction is building castles in the air of reason — making theories without a basis of fact. When a law is discovered through induction, the mind feels a need of explaining its existence and derivation. In such a case, the deductive process is adopted, through which one can come upon principles already known. One can conceive elements essentially, or conditions organically, united and discover the method of their combination which produces the effect or constant fact, that is, the derivative law. It is not true that the universal, from which the deduction starts, is furnished with the character of necessity and is reducible to an abbreviated formula of many particulars, as Stuart Mill states in his "Logic." The universal of this philosopher is a form distinct from the particular, but it is not a true and full universal, because it lies in the sum of qualities accidentally common to several things. It is discovered by the abstraction and comparison of singular data; it is of value only for them and not for others, and is only shown by them. The philosophers call such a universal, which has not the character of necessity and will not go beyond the confines of representation (differing from a concept), an imagination or common notion. Representation is accidental, particular, various, and objective; a concept is necessary, universal, constant, subjective, in that it expresses the essence of things, and is the product of a function higher than representation, that is, of thought. From thought alone can necessity and universality be derived which experience does not give us; from thought alone can arise the generalization by which the true universal is formed which is the essential unity of all possible objects in all times and places. A concept is the true and full universal, a principle of deduction, and comprehends all the necessary notes or conditions of the existence of things, and is one with their effective cause. It is the middle term which completes the syllogism (teaches Aristotle), exercising the same office as the cause in nature, and therefore shows the particular cases according to their power. The true universal is shown only by the reciprocal interpenetration of those necessary elements and conditions, from which comes organic unity. The method of concomitant variation shows us that the tide is a lunar phenomenon because the changes of the sea respond in equal measure to those of the moon, but does not show the reason of such inductive law, which ceases to be empirical when it becomes a means for the deduction of the resulting necessity of the principle of the attraction of the earth and the moon. History teaches us that the results of activity of the slave are

poor in relation to the better labor of the freeman.
When this generality is formed, it is connected with the
notion of the principal motives of work, which are fear
and hope. It is evident that the mind, though it hardly
completes the thought, sees the necessity in the above
phenomenon. One can by means of induction form a
conception of the influence of despotism, but only 'deduction can explain its causes, starting out with the valuation
of the love of power and other motives. Allowing the
concept of a person or entity which has a sense of itself,
consciousness, and freedom in a proper organism, we
must infer that it has a natural right to physical and moral
life. Proceeding on the same principle, we find as another
logical consequence respect for property, because it is
the projection of the person or the freedom of man applied to things.

§ 33. *Law is Physiological and Historical.* From
what has been said, it is clear that science in general,
and the juristic, political, and social sciences in particular, are not limited to the illustration of what exists,
but should extend to depicting what should exist.
Phenomenon is only what is actual; law expresses what
should be, if it is obtained through deduction from
a complete universal. Whatever is has its rational
and scientific base on what should be; the real is founded
on the ideal and the certain on the true. Change, therefore, has its origin in an immutable type and history
springs from an eternal idea. Vico emphasized this conception when he spoke of an ideal eternal history, and
of an eternal law that runs through all time, and of a
constant perpetual succession of civil affairs. There is
in the course of social and national life a final, necessary,
ideal principle which is always the same in the definite
variety of forms and change of events. This principle
is the idea of man or of common human nature, which

acquires knowledge of its own unity through a gradual development and continual movement, and uses it to conquer multiplicite and discrepant special characteristics. If these fail, human nature would no longer be able to develop and progress, since it would have no restraints to overcome. There is no development, progress, or evolution, where no defect is met or where there is no imperfection to conquer. From this, it is clear that we must lay aside the historico-physiological method and the purely rational and abstract deductive method. The first is repugnant to the conception of a science, which seeks and determines the necessary and universal; the second is formal and does not include the real. The historico-physiological method finds only the fact, the certain, the authority in law, and is adapted to illustrate the "mens" and not the "ratio legis." The abstract deductive method considers only a part of the true in law, and does not go beyond the bounds of pure reason, which is always foreign to the very life of the law and the rich and real variety of the certain. It is based on the simplest elements of human nature, which it considers in the abstract, disregarding all difference of clime, race, nationality, heredity, and time, considering them causes of social phenomena as determined and sure as the factors and laws of mathematics. Proceeding under this method, human nature would appear as a complex of properties always equal and quiescent and would be placed outside of history and life — which is absurd. Law would no longer be a human idea if determined under either of these methods. Law should be the object of that science which is, Vico says, history and philosophy at the same time. As philosophy, it sees a well-developed series of reasons, and as history it is the perpetual sequence of human acts in conformity with these reasons, since a cause produces its own result.

CHAPTER III

THE INDUCTIVE IDEA OF LAW

THE STUDY OF THE ETHICO-JURISTIC CONSCIOUSNESS OF
VARIOUS PEOPLES. — THE CONTRIBUTION OF THE ARYAN AND
SEMITIC RACES TO THE HISTORY OF CIVILIZATION. — THE IDEA
OF LAW AS THE MEASURE OF THE ARYAN RACE. — MEASURE BASED
ON THE PHYSICAL ORDER, ON POSITIVE LAW, AND REASON.

§ 34. *The Aryan and Semitic Races are the most Important.*
The inductive process of the philosophy of law should
begin with the study of the various ethico-juristic consciousness of peoples. Two races are the principal makers
of the web of history, the Semitic and the Aryan. China
can be called a world apart. Egypt, while neither Semitic nor Aryan, plays a considerable part in the life of the
human race, Babylon is not purely Semitic, the Tartar
races act as natural forces of a destructive nature, but
the value of the contribution of these nations to the progress of civilization is not comparable with that of the
above two races. There is nothing of such grandeur,
writes Renan, to be found in their history that it can be
compared to the invention of writing, to the mission of
Moses, to the conquests of Cyrus and Alexander, and to
Greek philosophy.

§ 35. *Difference between the Semitic and Aryan Races.*
Renan gives a true picture of culminating differences of
the two races in his work "De la Part des Peuples Semit-
iques dans l'Histoire de la Civilisation." First of all,
the Indo-European peoples have not the eloquence of
the Hebrew prophets, the Koran, or Psalms, but they
possess epics and tragedies that the Semites lack. Their
genius is not essentially philosophical, because it only

reproduces Greek thought with Arab commentaries. Science is declared useless in the Book of Job and Ecclesiastes. In invention and art, the Phœnicians were the first to teach writing, the elements of industry and manufacture, and to give themselves over to trade, afterwards developed in the Middle Ages by the Arabs and Hebrews. Comparative mythology shows that the Aryan peoples at first professed a worship of natural forces, later transformed by speculative thought into a kind of pantheism. On the other hand, the Semitic religions have an absolute dogmatic and monotheistic character. The Semites have the great religious mission in history: Judaism, Christianity, and Islamism are their creations. The Aryan race (with the exception of India and Persia) received Semitic beliefs, although its ethico-religious sentiment was more delicate and profound than that of the Semites. Semitic morality is high and pure, if it may be judged from the Mosaic laws, the sentences of prophets, and the Old Testament. It is based on the severe, narrow, and egostic mind of the people in which it is born. The Semites lack the great nobility, the ethical sense, and tenderness of affection that confer on Aryan morals their distinct, admirable quality.

§ 36. *The Aryan is a Juridical Race.* The Aryan race has always had a true conception of law and political life. The greatest juridical monuments of antiquity, the Indian books, the Roman law, and the Germanic laws belong to this race, which tends to reconcile the authority of the State with the freedom of the individual. Among Aryan peoples, there has never arisen that all-controlling despotism which blots out man, as in Egypt, Babylon, China, among the Mussulmans and the Tartar tribes — or if it has appeared it has not been of long duration. The Semitic Orient is in constant upheaval between the anarchy of the Arab nomads, a

continuous and bloody despotism, and theocracy. Solo-
mon, the wisest of rulers, was as cruel as a sultan; the
prophets struggled against the kings in the name and
interest of theocracy. Individualism had great weight
among the Semites, who did not succeed in making a dur-
able State. In fact, the history of the people of Israel is
a series of constant revolutions which hindered political and civil stability. The Semites were inclined to live
in small communities and out of their own country,
preserving, nevertheless, their original character and
a keen consciousness of their own nationality. The
Phœnicians (except in a few colonies), the Hebrews and
Arabs lived and still live in this way. It has been well
said that the Semite has an adopted, accidental, and secondary country, which confers on him rights and benefits,
and a country by nature, constant and fundamental, which
offers him aid and a refuge among all nations. The Semit-
ico-Hebraic faith, Kerbaker adds, harmonizes with
their political ideas in opposition to those of the Aryans,
who have religions that make man feel all his dependence
on external circumstances, and therefore urge him to
conform his conduct to a conception of natural necessity.
In nature there are inequalities against which it is vain
to struggle. The Hebrews, on the other hand, have three
conceptions, one of a personal and omnipotent God
who gives the laws according to His will, another of
a social law realizing the kingdom of God on earth, and
the third of human cosmopolitanism (notwithstanding
that the Hebraic hegemony was dominant). These three
conceptions contain the belief in the abstract freedom of
man, dependent only upon a divine, inexorable will and
not on the intrinsic necessity of entities, and a belief in the
abstract equality and concord of nations. In general, the
political life of the Semites did not develop beyond
patriarchal form; it is simple and not complicated, differ-

ing largely, therefore, from the Aryan political life, which
from the very beginning proceeded with its famous
government composed of a king, a senate, and a general
assembly through discussion. It cannot be doubted,
says Bagehot in "Physics and Politics," that the passage
from slavery and immobility to a free state is due to the
régime that is based upon the discussion of principles and
the questions of common interest, because discussion
makes the mind acute, increases originality of debate,
and presupposes tolerance.   But Bagehot, however,
admonishes us not to believe absolutely in the political
primacy of our race, since there are in the Orient the
Bengalese of Aryan race who are the most servile
people in the world, and among the Semites the citizens
of Tyre and Carthage, who were capable of enjoying
freedom.

§ 37. *The Aryan Language shows the Juristic Tendency.* From an examination of the various ethico-juristic manifestations of the consciousness of nations, we
find that law has always been conceived as a principle of
direction towards a moral object, and a rule, measure,
harmony, or proportion. In the Aryan mind, this notion
is very well marked and forms the main base of civil
life. Philology, since Vico's time, has had the same relation in respect to philosophy that paleontology has
towards biology, and language containing a spontaneous
knowledge shows the truth of this.   It teaches first
that the full development of philosophy, of poetry, and
of the State among the Aryan peoples is intimately connected with the fact of the independence of the verb
from the inflective endings for the nouns in the languages
spoken by those peoples. We may note that the verb is
the most abstract part of speech and therefore indicates
the power of universalization, a power necessary to philosophy, poetry, and the State.   The Greek word δίκαιον,

the Italian "diritto," the French "droit," the German "recht," the English "right," the Slavic "pravo," all express the principle of direction, or measure. According to the modern philologists the Latin "jus" comes from the Sanscrit root "ju," which means to bind; whence "jus" is what binds or harmonizes. Thus are explained the other words in which the same root is seen as "jungere," "jugum," "conjugium," etc. The word δίκαιον has for its root "dik," common to both Greek and Latin, and means to indicate, to point out, to direct. In Latin, the same root is found in the words "dicere," "digitus," "indicare," and in combination with "jus" forms "judicare," to show the right.

§ 38.   *Vedic Law is Harmony.*   From the Vedic hymns, it is seen that the Indian Aryan distinguished three worlds and three families of God, that which remained in the celestial grade, the second of the immovable earth and its depths, and the third that lay in the world of air, in which plants and animals live, and men work. In the Brahmans, in the Sutra, wherever philosophical meditations are enjoyed, the Vedic trinity of worlds does not disappear but changes, as Merlo in "Armonie nelle Antiche Dottrine Antropologiche e Morali dell' India e della Grecia" explains, into three abstractions, into the "tamas," or torpid obscurity, the "ragias," or headlong motion, and into the "settva," complete and quiet happiness. These are the three primal qualities to which the earth, the air, and the heavens correspond. In man, there is a triplicity of sense, will, and intellect, and a celestial part obscured by the vapors from the earthy part. The triplicity is observed also in the civil State, in its division into three castes, because, in ancient India the fourth class of Shûbra represents what is elsewhere the slave class, and is the link between man and brute. The Sudri have but one virtue, to serve with absolute devotion the three other castes. In the Brahmans meditation prevailed, in the Kshatriya, bravery, and in the Vaishya, temperance. It is enjoined upon everyone to keep his proper place in the caste without a desire to change it. In consequence the Aryan Indian cannot fail to consider justice as a harmony of all these elements and castes. The similarity between the Indian and Greek conception of justice is remarkable. According to the latter, justice is always harmony. Plato defined it as the accord of the three powers of reason, courage, and sense, of the three virtues, wisdom, bravery, and moderation, and of three classes of philosophers, warriors, and artisans.

§ 39. *The Mute Age. Ancestor Worship.* The Aryan conception of law as measure or accord passes through various phases, because man is sense, imagination, and reason, and because his history must pass through the mute, heroic, and human stages. Vico outlined at great length the characteristics of such ages, and his words are confirmed by the analyses of modern science. In the mute age, human nature was proud, haughty, entirely dominated by sense and the superior world, whose forces it called divine. It was overcome by fear and fright before those gods that it itself imagined. Law in such an age was essentially divine, hidden in oracles or commands of the gods, who dominated all, man and things. The oracle was the principle, or the measure of conduct, and jurisprudence a divine wisdom, a science of divine words or of the comprehension of the mysteries of divination, a science of auspices. There was a divine mental language for mute religious acts and divine ceremonies, in which lay the just. The first customs are redolent with religion and piety. The governments were of a theocratic character, because men believed that the gods commanded everything. Justice lay in repaying the gods for sudden crimes. It is "implorare deorum fidem," which means "deos obtestari." After such beseechings, that is, after the accusations and defenses (which form the first orations in the world), one comes to the act of execrating the culprit, of consecrating him to the Furies, and finally of killing him.

§ 40. *Modern Researches in Ancient Law.* The most profound studies of the moderns on the laws of India do not reach conclusions really different from the ideas of Vico. It is even proved by Max Müller, and by Sumner Maine in his "Dissertations on Early Law and Custom," that, according to the juristico-hierarchical schools of India (a kind of spiritual family), science is found in the sacred and inspired literature from Vishnu and Vasishtha to Apastamba and Gautama, and from these to Manu, and from Manu to Nerada, and contained therein is what man should know and what he should do. Law enters as a second term in the division. The juristic books are principally treatises on religious observances and sacerdotal duties, in which the principles of conduct imposed upon the Indian of the three higher classes are found—to live as a student of the sacred works taught by Brahmans in his youth, as head of a family in his mature years, and as an ascetic and hermit in his old age. In these precepts stands the law entirely based on religious beliefs and especially on those regarding the destiny of man after death; that is, the heavenly rewards and infernal punishments, the transmigration of souls and ancestor-worship. The principle developed in these books is that the destiny of man after death is the consequence of his acts. It depends on the man whether he becomes in the future life a plant, a reptile, a Brahman, or a demigod. The reward belongs to the other life; in this life lies the penance. But if the penance is not fulfilled, the king, aided by his priestly councilors, will threaten bodily punishment. The ritual of ancestor-worship, so closely connected with the right of inheritance, is found in all these juristic books. In our day this cult is explained in a psychological manner through the phenomenon of sleep and the primitive imagination. For a long time, writes Lubbock, in "The Origin of Civilization and the Primitive Condition of Man," man did not understand death, and confused it with sleep. The savage knew that during sleep the spirit lived although the body seemed dead, and it was natural that he should try to arouse the dead and placed food near the corpses. The prayers addressed to those who are no more, represent a logical deduction from such a conception, since the dead living in another world can exercise a considerable power over human affairs. Spencer in his "Principles of Sociology," in conformity with the above theory, classified the different societies according to their belief in spirits. The principle of the psychological theory did not escape the mind of Vico. He taught that posterity, who bury the dead of their ancestors according to the order of their mortality, were persuaded that the soul was not the body but an image of it, its simulacrum and shadow. This belief begins and is developed when posterity deify the ancestors of the race. It is not necessary to insist upon the agreement of recent studies with Vico's thought about ceremony. Spencer has gone so far on this subject as to hold that the customs expressing obedience to an invisible or visible sovereign precede the religious and civil obligations prescribed by it.   Before the law appears, there are religious duties. There must be, he says, subordination to a power which establishes this and imposes that and therefore the rule of the ceremonial is primitive and precedes religious and civil government.

§ 41. *The Heroic Age.* In the heroic age, man no longer feels himself a slave of his senses and the external world, but begins to have knowledge of himself and his position, although imagination prevails. Man really, writes Vico, is only body, breath, and mind. The breath or imagination is placed in the midst of the body and the mind. The spirit or imagination is nurtured by phantastic generations, by poetical universals, by formulas of words, as the mind has within itself intelligible universals. Heroic nature is believed by these heroes to be of divine origin and themselves to be children of Jupiter. Being born under his auspices, they boast of their natural nobility over those who, for safety from the ruin produced by infamous bestial communion, sought their asylum; whom, destitute and godless, they held as beasts. All the civil advantages, therefore, are contained within the reigning order of heroes, and to the plebeians, thought to be of bestial origin, is given only the use of life and natural fruition. The heroes had choleric and caviling customs, that is, a strong sense of personality, which they made good by force. Their law is that of Achilles; the measure, in that age, is reason estimated by fortune; it is force not bestial but purified by religion and animated by imagination. The rulers are the nobles, that is, the strongest, who work always to keep control and to hold their boundaries to prevent the communion of the outlaws. Wisdom is contained in solemn formulas and jurisprudence is bounded with certain words of its own, like the wisdom of Ulysses. In the heroes lay all the authority that formerly was part of faith and now is part or form of the solemn formulas of the laws and action in respect to judgments.

§ 42. *The Human Age.* The human age succeeded the heroic, when our nature became modest, benign, and reasonable, and custom became developed reason.

Jurisprudence was founded on natural equity, of which the free, generous, and magnanimous masses were capable, and it looked to the truth of facts and fulfilled benignly the reasons of the laws as demanded by justice. The truth of facts, good faith (the product of humanity), customs suitable to free republics and generous monarchies prevailed in the judgments. All are equal before the law in human governments because of the equality of intelligent nature. Authority is no longer the same as mysterious and secret counsel, chance, or hereditary nobility, but is one with reason: "Auctoritas ex ratione."

§ 43. *The Family was the first Unit of the Law.* Admitting the laws of the three ages, it can be seen that in the first the moral and juristic order was confused with the physical. Measure and harmony are found in nature and therefore ignorance and fatality cannot fail to enter into formation of the ethical concept. The act of man through this confusion is valued without consideration of the intention, and the fault becomes original and hereditary. Ate, the Homeric Nemesis, pursues whosoever wilfully or unconsciously disturbs the harmony of nature. The disturbance in every case demands expiation and the penalty falls upon the author and his descendants, because the basis of primitive law was the family community and not the individual. The confusion disappeared in Greece, the land of art, through the lyrics and tragedies, as Florentinus points out in "Ideale del Mondo Greco." Theognis demands that Jove punish the descendants, and Bias ironically likens the gods to doctors who give medicine to the children of the sick. Æschylus shows in "Prometheus," the stealer of fire who was bound to a rock for the eagles, the first act of personal punishment, but Prometheus is a demigod and not a true man. In the "Orestiad" there is the idea that a guilty man can redeem himself. Orestes is acquitted by a tie vote in the celestial Areopagus on the defense of the two young divinities, Apollo and Minerva, who, pleading in favor of a new law, are accused of offending the ancient laws which confuse the two orders of heredity and fault. The new law is based on intention and on ethics. Orestes, however, does not take part in the judgment and knows nothing of the contest on Olympus about his fate. Sophocles alone, in Œdipus, represents a man guilty without knowing it of parricide and incest, who is not punished because of the lack of guilty intent.

§ 44. *The Seven Sages and the Early Sophists.* In the human age, the measure, of which the Aryans made law consist, was no longer identified with the physical order, but rather with civil and positive law. The axioms of the Seven Sages, the first philosophical reflections, regard practical life and rules of social conduct, because in the Greek period the source of ethical notions and speculative activity itself was found in civil reality. The Seven Sages were not philosophers, but men of great experience living at the time of the struggle of the "demos" against the oligarchs. All their axioms make for clearing and reinforcing the Hellenic concept, that the State should realize harmony. Solon, for example, teaches that injustice disturbs this harmony. Bias teaches that obedience to the law is the principle of agreement. Anacharsis says that the harmony of the whole exists where the members are equal, and where virtue occupies the higher position and vice the lower. Archelaos tries to show that animals and men arose from the dust, and that the laws have their origin within the State after the separation of men from beasts. He adds, agreeing with the Ionic school, that the just is the measure of harmony in the State and is not decreed by nature, but by the laws of the city. The Sophists, says Chiappelli, in his book "Sulle Teorie Sociali dei Sofisti Greci," found themselves confronted with the idea of nature as portrayed by precedent thought, and were forced from the first to consider it as the basis of moral life. Hippias did not ·recognize the identification of the just with the legal, but believed that the laws were the variable and contradictory effect of agreements between men, and that the just, which could be found in the contrast of the principal branches of the legislation of different peoples, lay in the unwritten law of nature and in divine action. As the first movement of Sophism shows the applications of physical concepts to ethics, so the second shows the separation of moral thought from nature. Pythagoras observed that nature has neither constancy nor universality, but continuously changes, and man only knows it to the extent that sensation, which is variable, gives witness to it. What is honest and just is such because it is so held by the city, that is, by positive law. As things honest and just are true of every city, so they are made such by cities. The principle of Hippias that nature and not law is the principle of life served Callicles in his statement that the just is the will of the stronger, because the condition of nature is not equality but prevalence of strength. And so in nature, says Callicles, whoever has the strength is right. If the just lies in the law and State, as Pythagoras teaches, and the laws and the State are the product of force and caprice, Thrasimachus is not illogical in concluding that justice should be placed in prevalence of the strong over the weak, and that law is reducible to the interest of the strong. Thus, by two opposite ways, Sophism comes to the recognition of the individual subject, more sensate than intelligent, as the measure of everything.

§ 45. *Socratic Philosophy and Aristotle.* At last, the measure was not sought in the positive law but in a rational principle. Pythagoras had already taught that justice is harmony, quadrate and apart, always the same, counter-exchangeable; and that harmony is the state of the cosmos. The consequence of this, not shown by him, is that the just cannot originally lie in the laws of the State. Socratic truth and measure are not sought in nature and out of the sphere of knowledge, but in knowledge and the concepts. The principle of Socratic ethics is the identification of virtue with knowledge and of evil with ignorance. Whoever knows the good cannot fail to pursue it; whoever does the evil is ignorant of the good. In this knowledge is found happiness, just as virtue is allied with knowledge. On this side, Socrates agrees with Ionic philosophy and Pythagoras. On the other hand, he approaches the doctrines of Hippias in admitting unwritten laws given by the gods as the basis of the written laws. This distinction of laws made by Socrates should, however, always be placed in relation to his principle of knowledge. Plato thinks justice is a higher idea than law, consisting as it does in wisdom, and in the harmony of the three powers, virtues, and classes. Aristotle, following Plato, rises to the notion of justice independent of the orders of the State. In the mind of the Stagirite the just is the mean between the two extremes of the illegal or unequal and the strict law. "Summum jus, summa injuria." Commutative justice follows an arithmetical proportion, and is the mean between giving and having, between advantage and loss. Distributive justice looks to merit as its object and follows geometrical proportion. The Stoics admit a law that is the divine and vital manifestation of the reason of nature. " Jus vero, Stoici dicunt, esse natura," say Stobæus and Cicero.

"Lex communis quæ est recta ratio in omnes diffusa,"
is a sentence from Zeno. Chrysippus, in the beautiful
fragment translated by Martial, teaches, " Lex est
omnium divinarum et humanarum rerum regina.
Oportet autem eam esse præsidem et bonorum et
malorum, et principem et ducem esse."

§ 46. *Roman Philosophy*. Among the Romans the
same phases of the idea of law were reproduced, but
with differences growing out of the different national
characters. In Greece, the human mind developed,
and for the first time asserted its independence of
nature through art and philosophy. By art, man
reproduces and recreates nature, expressing his ideas
in the most adequate and sensible forms. The freedom of the mind, as thought tending toward distinction, is shown even better in the rapid, although
always gradating conversion from the mute to the
articulate that was observable in Greece. Distinction
is the basis of personality while imagination, the power
of art, is always wavering and confused. It is uncertain
and forced. This conversion took place through philosophy, and has its exemplified formula in the " Know
thyself " of Socrates. But the Logos in Greece came to
be recognized as different from imaginative thought,
but not separate from it, and did not develop outside the
realm of art, the special prerogative of the Hellenic
people. If Greece is the world of philosophy and art,
Rome represents the world of the will and therefore of
law, politics, and war. The concept of measure was
clothed in Greece in all the charming forms of beauty,
in the common thought and meditations of the philosophers; in Rome it became the basis of the juristic
intellectual, and political sciences and military wisdom.
In the Roman world, will on one hand was born in the high
organisms of the State, and on the other began to develop

as individual law.   With the principle of will and its subjective nature, private law could not fail to arise and
develop, as we have said above.[1]   According to Vico, law
is at first strict, iron-bound, and rigid, then it is amplified
and grows supple and elastic, moderated by equity.   It
is not gotten from the Twelve Tables or the Edicts, but
rather from human nature itself, as Cicero, the follower
of the Academico-Stoical philosophy, said, " Lex est
ratio summa insita in natura"; that " Recta ratio est
naturæ congruens, et natura fons est legum et juris, stirps
juris, tota causa universi juris.   Natura quidem jus est
quod non opinio genuit sed quædam innata vis inseruit."
In the minds of the ancient jurisconsults, the followers
of the Stoic law, it is the effect of the " naturalis ratio
quasi lex quædam tacita," and consists in the "equum
bonum " in the "id quod semper bonum et æquum est,"
in the " ars boni et æqui," and in a proportion of the
utilities.   There is, according to the Stoics, a "ratio"
that has in itself a basis of the common natural knowledge.   This natural knowledge contains, in the minds of
the jurisconsults, the knowledge of the "equum bonum."
At the end of the Republic the doctrines of Epicurus
flourished, who thought " Justum natura est utilitatis
pactum," and those of Lucretius who said, "Magistratus
partim docuere creari juraque constituere ut vellent
legibus uti . . . Genus humanum defessum . . . sponte sua
cecidit sub leges arctaque jura."   Almost at the same
time appeared the authors of the empirical theory with
Esidemus and the Sceptics, all enemies of the natural
law. Sextus Empiricus reiterates that law is the mutable
and variable product of human license. The sensualistic
doctrines were enthusiastically received by the Latin poets
and writers, if not by the jurisconsults whose various
schools resist more or less the influence of the Stoics and

[1] *Cf.* Intro. p. 5.

agree in proclaiming the existence of a natural law founded on the "naturalis ratio": "Omnibus ratio jus igitur datum est omnibus," said Cicero.

§ 47. *Later Philosophy.* In the modern and truly human epoch, the principle of the proportion or measure is developed wholly in the light and evidence of reason. Ever since the Middle Ages the beginning of this development was apparent in the works of Thomas Aquinas and Dante. Aquinas distinguished three kinds of law, — " lex æterna," that is in God, "lex humana" or positive law, and "lex naturalis," which lies between one and the other, in that it is a part of the first and the model or type of the second. For him justice is proportion; "justicia a justare." Dante defines law explicitly as, "Personalis et realis proportio hominis ad hominem quæ servata servat corrupta corrumpit societatem." At the time of the Renaissance, Bruno conceived of an ethical doctrine resplendent with the divine light of truth, which is the very substance of moral action attainable by a temporal discourse that is prudence. Law, says Bruno, should conform to reason and result in the useful. Reason is the measure, the directive principle of law. But the above development was fully realized by the father of natural law. Grotius conceived, with absolute clearness, of a natural jurisprudence, founded on reason and the source of all other jurisprudence. According to him natural law is the sum of the principles of right reason and could exist on the hypothesis of the non-existence of God. And thus the measure of goods or proportion of utilities, the constant object of the deductive definition of law, becomes human enough to separate from the original ties which bound it to God and tries to stand by itself.

CHAPTER IV

THE THEORETICAL PRESUPPOSITIONS OF THE DEDUCTIVE IDEA OF LAW

THE PRINCIPLE OF PERSONALITY. — THE ORGANIC AND SPIRIT-
UAL ELEMENTS OF THE PERSON AND THEIR CORRESPONDENCE. —
THE UNFOLDING OF MATERIALISM. — THE THEORY OF EVOLU-
TION. — THE CRITICISM OF MECHANICAL EVOLUTION.

§ 48. *Man as an Organic Spiritual Subject.*   The
concept of law as the measure or proportion of benefits
from inductive becomes deductive when based on the
principle of personality.   Man is a person, that is, an
organic and spiritual subject capable of wisely attaining
his own ends by the election of means, and of subjecting
the world to his will.   A person, as man, presupposes the
organism and spirit.   We must now go back to the first
elements and even to the original activity from which
the person is derived.   This subject cannot be briefly
treated, and we must go into what properly belong to
philosophy in general.

§ 49. *Bacon's Materialism.*   The correspondence often
shown between the organism and the spirit is used
as an argument in favor of the materiality of the
latter by those who agree with Bacon that the cause
is what comes first; and the sequent fact by alteration, change, and suppression implies development.
Since the spirit is a fact, it follows when the body is
given, and develops and changes with it and fails when
there is no body.   We can conclude (under the Baconian
method) that the spirit has the same nature as the organism, not being another kind of substance beyond the

material, and that it can through the perception of the
senses know the methods of the generation, combination,
and action of beings.

§ 50. *Bacon's Materialism is the Result of Illegitimate
Deduction.* The mistake of those who reason thus does
not lie in their continuous appeal to experience, but in
exceeding its data in their conclusions, because strict
reason cannot infer from the before mentioned correspondence that the organs are not subject to psychical
phenomena, but are only conditions essential for the
appearance and explication of the life of the spirit.
In such a case, they would not go beyond on the
sphere of experience, and spiritualism would be safe.
It, however, suffers at the hands of the modern believers in the persistence and transformation of
force; because from motion to heat there is only a
movement of molecules, and there is not that heterogeneity of change that lies between vibration and sensation. Now, until the series of medial termini is shown
through which one can see the change from molecular
motion to sense, it will always be right to consider
motion as a condition and not the cause of sensibility, to
keep the two things distinct. Vibration, it is said, is in
respect to sensation what the grain is in respect to powder.
The grain is the condition of the explosion, but its cause
lies in the chemical virtue of the powder. In sensation,
conceived as a complex phenomenon, we must distinguish
three processes, the physical, psycho-physical, and psychical. The physical process regards the action of external
force, that is, of the stimuli; the psycho-physical has reference to the structure and functions of the organ; the psychical is connected with the simple and indefinable internal
state of the spirit, that is properly called sensation. Modern physicists and physiologists of great reputation agree
that the second process is not the reproduction of the first,

as the third is not the copy of the second.   Sensation is
not the copy of external objects, but is only their symbol
and sign.   Helmholtz says that the knowledge furnished
us by sensation about the qualities of external objects is
no truer than that which words give to a blind man
about color.   This means that the stimulus is more
occasion than cause.   The materialists admit that
psychic phenomenon is not a fact, distinct in substance
from physiological fact, but claim it constitutes its subjective aspect, holding, therefore, that the two facts are
not identical, nor their relation formulated by an equation, because if that were possible the distinction between
the internal and the external, between the subjective and
the objective, would disappear.   Subjective manifestation here is a new fact.   It is a conscious, new and more
perfect reality.

§ 51.   *Psychological and Physical Materialism.*   Materialists, since Kant's time, believe that things are
not knowable of themselves, although they are certain
that every physical or psychical phenomenon belongs
to the same order, that is, to motion.   But whoever
believes in motion must believe in a substratum of
matter.   And as it is not shown that psychical phenomenon consists of anything save motion, it is
contradictory to state that the base common to both
phenomena is not knowable, since this raises the purely
physical phenomenon to the grade of the other.   Neither
is it just to consider with the simple perception of sense
the method where one cause, interpenetrating with
other forces, produces a phenomenon, because such a
notion is reached only by way of the concepts.   These
contain the essence of things and make clear the manner
in which the various elements mingle and act in order
to effect the result.   In studying the reactions between
the body and spirit we do not meet any greater difficulty

than is found in the physical studies themselves. Suppose, says Lotze, that we wish to have complete knowledge of a mechanism, we begin by taking apart its most minute parts and then by looking at their coördinance and transmission of motion. But to what do the coördinance and the transmission regarded by themselves tend? In what does the coördinance consist? If it is in the forces of attraction, how are such forces put in play? How do they excite a certain action in the bodies? What is the impulse and how does it originate? What is transmission of motion and how does one body by moving communicate the same motion to another? To all these questions we cannot reply; and so we must admit frankly that man is ignorant of these things, and not imagine illusory solutions. Lotze calls this prudent manner of conduct in researches about physico-psychical mechanisms the theory of occasion. Proceeding under this theory, there is no sudden impediment, because physiological psychology can appropriate to itself the results of the excellent studies in psychological physiology which show constantly new relations and proportions between the explication of the organs and the psychical activities. Finally we must reflect that matter is not the object of sensible perception but is (as Stuart Mill defines it) the permanent possibility of sensation. Is not the possible in itself ideal? Here materialism is converted into idealism, and Mill agrees with Berkeley. In truth, the conception of matter is not the model proof of objectivity that it is said to be, arising, as it does, from a long and difficult mental elaboration, which includes external causes as they appear to it and not as they are in themselves. Extrinsic agents exist for us as they are felt and thought. Wherefore, materialism does not derive what is subjective from what is objective, for example, sensation from the stimuli, but receives sensation from sensation, thought from thought, and does not escape from the *idem* from *idem* (as Spaventa observes in his book on " Kant e L'Empirismo").

§ 52. *Spencer's Unknowable.* With this much on the factors of the correspondence between the body and spirit as a premise, we must see in what form such an harmonic life is realized and manifested. Many are inclined to believe that the law of evolution, imperative in the physical world, in which the entities form an uninterrupted progressive series, governs also in this life. Spencer is regarded by all as the philosopher of evolution. His theory, as gathered from his " First Principles " and " Principles of Psychology," can be briefly sketched: Philosophy unifies knowledge, but the unification cannot be perfect because there will always remain something absolutely unknowable. The external and internal world constitute two orders of change, whose principles we cannot know. What can be known of external change depends upon the elementary conditions of knowledge. The ideas about the relations between the states of knowledge are not the real similarities or differences of things, and therefore cannot be called real from this aspect. But they are real from another point of view since they continue in the consciousness which cannot change or destroy them. Something, therefore, that is conditionally or absolutely determined, should correspond to them. There must be an underlying force in all changes. The conception of the persistence of force contains that of the indestructibility of matter and of the continuity of motion. Every new manifestation of force is the equivalent of another that disappears; the quantity of matter and of motion remains unaltered throughout the changes. The concentration of matter implies the dissipation of motion and the

absorption of motion produces the diffusion of matter.
In other words, the parts go closer in losing motion, and
separate in acquiring it. In concentration, matter
integrates; in diffusion, it dissolves. In all distribution
of matter and motion there is a process of continuous integration and dissolution. If there is evolution, it is a
passage from what is indistinct to what is distinct,
from the homogeneous to the heterogeneous. Evolution is
inorganic, organic and super-organic. The evolution of life
is a never-ending adaptation of internal to external relations, of the living being to the place and surroundings;
an adaption which is at first direct and homogeneous and
afterwards indirect and heterogeneous. Homogeneous
adaption takes place through a simple external means
not very dissimilar in essence and force from the conscious acts of living beings; heterogeneous adaption is
shown in changeable, complicated, and diverse circumstances. Evolution connotes an increase of attributes,
functions, and organs. It is increasing multiplicity and
at the same time is the cause of a greater coördination and agreement of parts. Psychical life is a process
of continual differentiation and integration and, in relation to circumstances, is adaption through association. It is a process of continual differentiation and
integration, because in all phenomena of thought, there
should be a unity of composition; in a word the form and
process of knowledge should remain the same. Now a
form of knowledge is not evolved except through a
change of state. Whatever change takes place is noted
only in relation to the anterior similar or dissimilar
changes. As long as this relation does not become clear
through a sufficient repetition of similar or diverse
change, the knowledge of it is obscure. It is an adaptation through association, in that the intellect should
rule the series of its internal modification in order to

harmonize with external series, with co-existence, and with the sequences of things.

§ 53. *The Doctrine of Cosmic Evolution.* Starting out with the ideas of Spencer, the doctrines of cosmic evolution, as understood by the greater number of recent interpreters and as illustrated by Anguilli in "La Filosofia e la Scuola," can be briefly outlined. The doctrine includes the questions of being and growth and is of universal application. Everything is derived from matter and force, which is motion, as is matter itself. Evolution is always the passage from the homogeneous to the heterogeneous, from the indistinct to the distinct, with a progressive specification of parts, organs, and functions, and with an increasing agreement between them. It is accomplished by epigenesis, that is, the new parts do not unite with the old, as new formations, but develop from them as transformations. From the conjunction of the simple elements arise phenomena with properties not contained in the elements. From a higher aggregation of albuminoid substances, which combine variously with some minerals, is derived the protoplasm, a ductile transparent substance rather unstable and rich in active properties. It is easily affected by the action of its surroundings and reacts energetically against them. This faculty of reaction is irritability, which shapes into sensibility, a habit of reaction with greater facility and promptness, and is connected with motion. Irritability and mobility are inseparable in life from nutrition and procreation. The protoplasm, besides the power of reaction, has another power in the faculty of preserving as a molecular disposition the effects of the sudden changes that it has undergone. In other words, it has memory or the reproductive functions. Sensibility, mobility, and memory are found in every phenomenon of life and constitute the primitive elements of mental phenomena. Thus, the question of the origin of mind is the same as the origin of life. The idea of life is distinguished from the idea of organization because life is a product of the aggregation of matter and organization is a product of the development of life. Before the most simple form of organization, there existed a mass of slimy, amorphous substance, without apparent division, monera, bathybius, etc.; the monera contained all the essential activities of life. From the unformed monera come the individualized monera with signs of organization, then comes the cellule, the first morphological organic union. The morphological evolution of the cellule is epitomized by every higher organism which remakes in its course the stages covered by the organism that preceded it in the scale of life. The embryonic process has its rationale in the evolution of the species to which it is referable and of which it outlines the aspects and processes.

§ 54. *Environment and Heredity.* Gradual and progressive transformation, adds Anguilli, is completed by environment and heredity; environment corresponds to nutrition, heredity to reproduction. Nutrition is the increase of the living substance where, through favorable aggroupment of means in its external surroundings, it can gather in the evolutionary state more than it loses. Advantageous variation depends upon the abundance of nutritious means and not upon disadvantageous circumstances. Before a struggle with its rivals, an organized entity should gain its position against exterior agents. It should acquire the property which renders it fit to survive. From the processes of reproduction and the circumstances of generation come other variations. The generated unities can separate or can remain united to sustain better the attack of external circumstances. The living entity multiplies; it develops

new complications, and evolution brings about a division
of physiological labor. With the law of division of
physiological labor, is bound the other of association,
which is a means for the preservation or perfection of
existence, a potent factor in biological evolution. And
here we must note too, that the principle of the struggle
for life and that of choice or selection are applicable to
the parts of the organism, to the molecules, cellules,
tissues, and organs. The properties acquired in such an
internal struggle make conditions favorable for the
external struggles of the organism. Adaptation becomes
higher as beings capable of a larger imagination and of a
more provident intellect are found. Progressive and
selective variability is, without doubt, greater in the
being in whom the mental faculties prevail. The law of
association can also be considered in relation to an organism which becomes more complex or in relation to other
organisms. The first form of internal association tends
to volume (as in the infusoria). Then association is
seen in compositive individuals bound together by the
internal communication (as in the reptilia), and by
progressive transformation in the beings, it develops
into the groups of organs in the vertebrate animals,
which are marked with a greater nervous and mental
centralization. The condition of development of complex organisms is the formation of sensibility, and social
consciousness, together with a principle of coördination
in their movements.

§ 55. *Criticism, of Spencer's Evolution.* The theory
of Spencer is not entirely empirical, as many believe,
because the supreme principle of the external and
internal world of the two orders of change is unknowable and transcendental, and is therefore without
the confines of experience. It does not come from the
mystery which the positivists find in metaphysical doc-

trine, because this absolute principle is not knowable and the rationale of its manifestation cannot be known. How is it possible to say what a thing is, if it has no relation to knowledge? If a thing is *per se* unknowable, it does not exist for the mind. It is nothing. Spencer analyzed the data of experience and came to the ultimate elements, to ideas which resisted analysis, and were irreducible, before which he had to stop. These ultimate elements are space and time (as formal conditions), matter, force, and motion. Universal analytical truths are connected with these; the indestructibility of matter, the conservation of energy, the transformation of forces, the continuity of motion and the like. He then with such elements as the basis, reconstructed the cosmos, through the laws of evolution which imply integration and differentiation. The ultimate elements were conceived of by the English philosopher as manifestations of a principle which does not know itself. Now if this principle is unknowable, it cannot be manifested. Only what can be known, can be shown and revealed. It is useless to state that the ultimate elements, matter, force, motion, are knowable if they depend upon an unknowable power. Spencer admits that it is not possible to know reality, except as it appears to us and as it is present in the mind. And yet he raises the unknowable to a principle of itself. Spencer is not consistent, and this is true from another point of view as well, because first he said that things are as they are shown to the mind, and then that the latter in its self-adaptjon governs the series of modifications in conformity to objective coexistence and the real sequence of things. He did not have an exact conception of evolution, which is defined in his book chiefly in a quantitive aspect. The increase of extension in space and time, division and subdivision, the increase in

comprehension and complexity are only forms or methods
of quantity. Evolution is not only a motion of increase
of division and coördination, but is a process of an increasing and always more perfect qualification. If
this conception is accepted, the number, variety, and
intermingling are no longer exclusive factors in the
value of things. It is true that Spencer shows that
evolution is constant differentiation, but he does not
make clear enough what the Germans call the qualitative
momentus, in which a constantly higher heterogeneity
is not thought to be explicable with simple changes of
quantity or combinations of an inferior order; in other
words, not measurable by simple physical forces.

§ 56. *Evolution is not Mathematical.* Experience and
scientific reasoning teach that matter is one, that
it has an atomic constitution and is indestructible.
They teach, furthermore, that force in its external
and mechanical aspect is the movement of matter
itself and that, therefore, matter and force are one;
that matter and force do not create or destroy one
another; that matter must·have possessed from the
beginning a quantity of motion not subject to increase or
diminution. From this, it follows that the conception
of the persistence of force is identified with that of the
continuity of motion. But they do not teach us that
evolution lies in the whole and not the parts, nor do
they tell us that there is a direct transformation of every
kind of force. Every evolution demands a precedent
dissolution or dissipation, and therefore there must be a
continual circulation of matter and force. It has been
well said by Masci that a rectilinear evolutionary
process, that is, the evolution of the whole, would be in
contradiction to the principle of the conservation of
energy, since it would necessarily include a continual
increase of energy. If direct transformation of the

physico-chemical forces is proved, we cannot say the same of the physico-chemical forces in relation to the vital forces. Experience does not show this kind of a transformation, nor does it authorize us to conclude in favor of the thesis which upholds the transformation of nervous force into mental force. The fact shown is only this, that psychological variations correspond to the physiological manifestation of the organism. The simple parallelism is not indicative of transformation because it can be derived from the union of diverse elements, which are reciprocal conditions, or from a kind of bilateral existence of the same energy. Neither does experience and reason force us to hold that everything is reducible to matter and motion, and that every formation is resolved in the last analysis into its different distribution. The existence of the products of evolution, which have properties not contained in their components, is undeniable. Lewes distinguishes resultant facts which should be referred integrally to their cause, and emergent facts which cannot be referred to them, because they contain new qualities not included in the elements from which they are derived. Life, for example, presupposes a physico-chemical combination, but that is not the only cause, and, therefore, life is an emergent fact, like mind which presupposes life but cannot explain it. If, therefore, there are true emergent facts, if evolution proceeds through heterogeneous generation, the new products cannot be created by mere mechanical causes from the various distributions of matter and motion, but must be born from intimate energies. Recourse cannot be had to the conception of an energy innate in the substratum, in order to make the principle of causality clear and to show the truth of emergent or heterogeneous facts.

§ 57. *Mechanical Evolution.* Mechanical evolution explains all reality by foreign elements and properties. Its idea of force as a movement of matter and an extrinsic movement attests its incompleteness and absurdity. Within its own confines, the mind cannot understand either the highest products of volition, which contain something new and not reducible to mechanical elements, or even the direction of forces, which is observed in a gradual ascent from the forms of the kingdom of nature to that of the spirit. The facts of the cosmic order cannot be reconciled with mere mechanics, because in that case everything would be the effect of external and casual combinations of motion. Pure mechanics and causality are logically one and are in absolute antithesis to the direction of forces and coördination. The conception of a causality or permanent accidentality, the presupposition of mechanical transformism, is a contradiction in terms, because true chance is always dissimilarity, difference, and variety, admitting the infinite indeterminateness of nature in her productive activities. A chance which is always repeated is no longer chance; it is its opposite;— mind, as Vico would say. Reality has not only external and mechanical properties but originally possesses other internal powers and subjective and dynamic qualities. Through evolution, it is continually raised, assuming more complicated, heterogeneous, and perfect forms. But even from its lowest origin, it has shown two kinds of qualities. The external characteristics predominated at the beginning and it is only later that final supremacy of the internal qualities has been assumed. At first, reality, though appearing with both kinds of properties, assumed forms more natural than spiritual; now the opposite is true. The internal property, at first, is simple energy enclosed in the atom, which is not identified with receptivity, nor related to motion communicated from without. It is at first a power of modifying relations by the use of means within its grasp, nor is it vital and psychical as Masci, the author of an efficient criticism of mechanical transformism, has pointed out. Such energy, nevertheless, is the first and weakest form of reaction that emphasizes, rather confusedly, the nature of the subject. Afterwards, the internal property gains more control, develops more, becomes more active, responds better to stimuli, succeeds in modifying the relations by the actions of means within its grasp, and advances by degrees to the sensibility of an animal and the knowledge of a man. Knowledge is not, however, the effect of sensibility. Sensibility is not derived from irritability and the latter is not formed from the elements of inanimate nature. Each of these facts is constituted from qualities that are not found in the precedent form. It is heterogeneous, and depends upon a particular and new attainment of the energy intrinsic in the material substratum, not explicable with the simple conceptions of matter and force as attributes extrinsic to the body. From this point of view, it is not true that the problem of the origin of the mind is identical with that of the origin of life, although the mind is not possible within the limits of experience without sensibility, and sensibility is not possible without irritability, mobility, nutrition, reproduction, and so on. The phenomena of life do not appear without an organic synthesis of the material elements, although it may be confused, indistinct, and rudimental, and do not exist before it. Sensibility is always connected with some kind of an animal structure, and does not develop prior to it. Under this principle of intrinsic energy to which the phenomena, not resolvable into matter and motion, are reduced, evolution comprehends reality, understood in its integrity.

§ 58. *Habit.* The theory of evolution in general, as explained by the Darwinists, has a distinctly mechanical character.   Lamarck states that the active principle of transformation in animals is the environment which modifies the manner of living and creates new habits and needs.   It is capable of changing the substances of nutrition and the structure of organs.   Darwin starts out with the superiority which is obtained by organized entities by the accidental acquirement of advantageous qualities in the vital competition or struggle for life.   Malthus raised this intuition to the dignity of an economico-demography; and later it has proved true in biology. Habit fixes this quality, heredity transmits and consolidates it; and natural selection is attained by the origin of new species.   For Lamarck, variation is established little by little in the course of existence; for Darwin, it appears even from birth or during embryonic life and is not reliant upon heredity.   It is extended by Spencer to the intellectual life and by others to personal characteristics.   It is corrected to avoid the intrinsic defect of its childish development, which led to the hypothesis of the "tabula rasa" of the old empiricists and materialists. But this well worked out correction does not exclude the hypothesis, because hereditary predeterminations resolved into their primal elements and, considered at the moment when they are fixed upon the life and spirit, are only characteristics imported from without.   The spirit especially, before receiving such impress from external circumstances, before habits and hereditary transmission have affected it, is a blank, unfigured slate.   It, at that moment, has only receptivity; later it acquires spontaneity which arises from the accumulation and reinvigoration of the impress given.   From this it follows that the theory cannot be freed from the representation of the living being as passive and of the spirit as a mere echo of the world which surrounds it and to which it adapts itself.   Yet the spirit lives a life which has need of corporeal excitements and is active and develops according to its own laws. It is true, nevertheless, that habit introduces into life a method that heredity can transfer and increase without an original disposition. Habit is a particular attainment of a living being acquired by the frequent repetition of the same actions or by the prolongation of a single act. Aristotle observes that some men contract with a single impression a habit more complete than others contract upon frequent repetition. Habit produces the great result of making the past live again in the present and future, by diminishing gradually the force necessary to an act and increasing the energy and facility of the power to do it. With this understood, it is not hard to see that habit, arising in some manner from repetition and continuity, is composed of many movements of which the first is the germ that begins the series and is shown in the second. The second movement has its reason in the first; the latter must be derived from some other cause besides the habit, therefore it is primal and new. Although the first movement is simply accidental, yet the life and spirit move; if they move, it signifies that they can move themselves. They have a natural habit of motion. Plants and animals respond to an external excitement. They are, therefore, excitable and have a natural disposition to excitement. On the other hand, habit is not a creative power; it is the original energy, the same nature grown, developed, and reinforced.

§ 59. *Heredity.* What has just been said about habit can refer as well to heredity, because in repetition, each act inherits something from its precedent and transmits it, slightly increased, to a subsequent act. Habit is an heredity circumscribed by the confines of the life of an individual. Heredity is a habit which passes from generation to generation. Like habit, it is connected with the laws of

evolution, giving the qualities fixed by repetition or prolongation of acts by the ancestors to the descendants.
If evolution was not followed by heredity every new
modification would disappear at the death of the individual. And if there was heredity and no evolution, the
entities would be always identical and there would be no
change in the world. Like habit, heredity has no
creative power but is a faculty of growth, or consolidation
and perfection. In fact, disease, wealth, and nobility,
in that they can go back to a remote age, presuppose a
first individual who was the victim of his own constitution and external circumstances, a head of a house that
knew how, by merit or force, to acquire a title and
amass wealth. In this way he led to dispositions which
are not the children of individual or hereditary customs
but are the product of accident free from any connection
with nature. The accidental cannot be understood,
when we abstract the character of the being in which it
is found. It is an anomalous variation but not a contradiction of the nature of the being. It is an anomaly
in respect to ordinary methods and derived characteristics but not in respect to essential characteristics.
We must, therefore, place by heredity the idiosyncrasy
which explains it, as a generation of idiots or epileptics
results in an idiot or epileptic descended from parents and
grandparents who were of sound mind and body. But
even if heredity is not a creative force, its importance, as
a means of transmission, is very great because the limbs,
trunk, head, features, form, volume, and irregularity of
the skeleton, proportions of the cranium, thorax, pelvis,
and spine, the quality of the system of circulation, of
the digestive, muscular, and nervous systems, the size
and form of the circumvolutions of the brain, the
abundance and scarcity of blood, the degree of fecundity,
the length of life, the voice, and the organic diseases pass

from father to son with great frequency. Neither can one fail to recognize that psychological heredity transmits the instincts; the modalities of the senses, memory, imagination, various habits, sentiments, and emotions, individual and national characteristics and finally hallucinations, monomanias, dementias, and paralyses. So physiological like psychological heredity is now immediate and direct, and now mediate. In the last case, there is a phenomenon of atavism which is not conceivable without presupposing the latent state of hereditary germs.

§ 60. *Mechanics do not fully Explain Evolution.* The laws of evolution cannot be understood in all grades through mechanics alone, as the believers in the genealogical theory maintain. The victory of mechanics produces a diminution of force because if the quicker motion conquers the slower it follows that the quicker becomes relatively slower. This does not happen in the intellectual, moral, and esthetic relations, in which the stronger, that is the most ingenious and clever, the best and most perfect character by its conquest gains and does not lose in bounty, beauty, and cleverness. Experience shows that criticism makes the mind acute and generates new ideas; the ethical will, by facing evil, is tempered and strengthened. The insufficiency of mechanics and the need of theology not abstract and extrinsic to life but concrete and objective, is proved by one of the chief principles of the Darwinian theory, — the theory of the opportune adaptation of the entity. In reality, the advantageous variations of adaptation are only means to obtain the safety of the entity. It is not accurate, therefore, to say that Darwinism, by itself, considered in all its power, is the negation of finality, that it is "finis finis," as Spaventa called it in "La Legge del Piu Forte." Advantageous variations are not pure and simple changes, because they signify amelioration and progress.   The concepts of variability, heredity, cause, and law are not enough to explain this increasing perfection.   To explain the discernment of the best (which is natural selection) we need a conception of an impulse towards an end.   The struggle is seen, it develops in the senses, but the selective choice or foresight is supersensitive.   It is neither visible nor tangible, because it includes the end.   The struggle, the separation of descendants, their association to better resist environment, the more abundant nutrition of life without struggle, are means of selection.   And here we must notice that the internal property of matter or intrinsic energy of the atom, of which we have spoken before,[1] is fundamentally the initial and obscure tendency of the lower grades of existence.   Later it becomes the plastic power of functions that are modeled in organs adapted to their regular and full development and finally raised to the rational will power of man.   Without this internal energy, or tendency, the progressive order from the natural forms to the spiritual would not be intelligible. It has been said and certainly sufficiently proved, that the laws express the tendency of phenomena to develop in constant determinate relations, upon which the cosmic regularity depends.   The error of the metaphysicians did not consist in recognizing this tendency in human beings, but in conceiving it to be a truly human finality like that of consciousness and will.   The tendency is the germ of the immanent and objective theology shown in modern empiricism, although the moderns openly disagree with the search for ends called metempiricism by Lewes, who denies their existence.

§ 61. *As yet, the Evolution of the Social Organization is Inexplicable.*   The mechanical theory of evolution does

[1] Cf. § 57 *ante.*

not take sufficient account of the fact that man enters into the struggle of life not only with his organic faculties, but with a complexity of intellectual and moral forces capable of transforming the exterior world. It is true that man is the son of earth, as the mythologists say. It is true that he is made of water, air, and dust; and that the harmony between the earth's forms, the flora and fauna, are reflected in the phenomena of the other fauna, humanity. But none can doubt the action of man, who succeeds in modifying most noticeably the surface of the world by stripping it of its forests and reclothing it with new plants at his pleasure, by piercing mountains and joining seas. This control of man over nature, in place of the action of nature on man, which developed to a large extent in primitive times, is important, because on the one hand it is the beginning of civilization and the growing series of the victories of intelligence, will, and power over external agents, and on the other because it serves to show (as Lampertico pointed out) that messology, or the science of the relation of beings to the surroundings in which they live, from one aspect materializes man and from another spiritualizes the exterior world. Furthermore, we must remember that the great organism of human society, if not those of particular political and national societies, has eternal life. It is always acquiring more new forces as it extends and deepens the connective tissue represented by the innumerable accumulations of experience which excite psychical activities and functions not before developed; on the other hand, the natural organism of the individual begins in infancy, and proceeding toward adolescence, youth, and maturity, is exhausted in old age and disappears. Individuals arise and disappear, but human society goes on forever and the history of the life of our race does not end. Evolution, therefore, has a different meaning when it is studied in relation to this great organism.   Spencer himself distinguishes the inorganic from the organic and super-organic evolution, although he admits that inorganic matter is not confusable with life, and that the latter is not one with the ethical and social organism.   It is certain that science has not reached the point of surprising the life that lies outside of matter, that is, the transformation of inorganic matter into an organized body, neither has it yet been able to show how the ego and the spiritual life of the human race are derived from the combinations of atoms.   Two great modern naturalists stop before the continuity of molecular motion in the phenomena of life and consciousness.   One is Virchow and the other Tyndall.

§ 62. *Historical Review of the Theories of Evolutions.* We may here recall that the theory of evolution has its roots in the ideas of Aristotle, Leibnitz, Vico, and Hegel. Aristotle conceived of the spirit as action or ἐντελεχία, and the body as power or matter; for him the nutritive, motor, sensatory, and intellectual spirits produced the various grades of life, where nutrition, motion, the senses, and mind are respectively predominant, and form the concrete development of the ἐντελεχία.   The spirits or faculties are placed so that the lower and the less complicated have the possibility of the higher and are contained and at the same time governed by the latter. Leibnitz regarded the spirit as a monad.   The monad completes an intrinsic evolution, in which the universe is contracted (as Bruno poetically says) by the representative power of each monad.   Extension, having its roots in the obscurity of the monad, is a phenomenon of the latter.   Vico understood that true principles become real through evolution; things first being evolved from them and ultimately terminating in them.   The nature of things, he said, is nothing but their birth.   The spirit, for him, changes from sense and imagination to fully developed reason; whence the evolution of the three historical ages.   Neither can it be doubted that from the Logos to nature and from nature to spirit is, for Hegel, a complete evolution.   In this his followers and all his adversaries agree, although the latter say that it is a question of purely dialectic and subjective evolution.

CHAPTER V

COROLLARIES OF THESE THEORETICAL PRESUPPOSITIONS

THE THEORY OF EVOLUTION AND PSYCHOLOGY. — FUNDAMEN-
TAL SENTIMENT AND THE SENSATIONS. — CONSCIOUSNESS AND
ITS ORIGIN. — SENSIBLE AND COGNITIVE REPRESENTATIONS. —
THOUGHT AND THE CATEGORIES. — COGNITION ACCORDING TO
OBJECTIVE EMPIRICISM. — CRITICISM OF THAT THEORY.

§ 63. *The Spirit as a Monad.* The person presupposes
psychological life in its highest grade; the spirit, purely
sensitive, united to the body cannot at once assume
the position and title of a person. The theory of
evolution, applied to the spirit, strictly understood
in the fullness of its activity, completes and amends
a fundamental notion of ancient psychology and removes a great difficulty. Ancient psychology defined
the spirit as a simple substance and went no further,
while the physicists base their theories on atoms or
monads, from whose combination bodies are derived.
Now how can the psychological monad be distinguished
from the physical? The conception of a simple substance is not enough to explain fully the spirit and determine its full development. We must consider the spirit
not merely as a monad, but as action and energy shown
in the rich development of its attitudes and capacities,
because its true essence lies in action and growth, as
experience teaches us. The great difficulty which evolution removes lies in the vexed question of the relation of
the spirit to its capacities. Gallupi thinks that external

and internal sensibility, analysis, synthesis, imagination, desire, and will are original, diverse, and irreducible qualities of the spirit. Cousin, Rosmini, and Lotze seem to have the same opinion. Lotze writes that there are many possibilities in the specific nature of the spirit which can contain original diverse characteristics as easily as the matter composing the earth can be variable. Such possibilities are realized under the influence of external impressions. On the other hand, Condillac, Herbart, Spencer, and Bain believe that the capacities are only quantitative differences. Condillac states that all the powers are transformations of sense — thus thought (and here he agrees with Campanella) can be called rare and pure sense. Herbart does not believe in original differences in the capacities, nor in moments of development, but regards the differences as states of the spirit growing out of representation. Representation is the conservative act of the spirit disturbed by impressions. The spirit is one of those simple " reals," not relative, but existing of itself, which Herbart thought out to solve the contradictions in the world of phenomena. If it is thus self-sufficient and has no need of contacts; if contacts do not alter its being and are accidental, it is not true that representation and the capacities are reducible to external states and are subject in their combinations to the laws of mechanics. The teaching of Spencer and Bain, that sentiment, emotion, and will are methods of adaptation and association, does not differ much from this theory. In the judgment of the most famous English psychologists of to-day, the law of association, illustrated by Hobbes, Hume, and Hartley, is the equivalent in psychology of the law of attraction in the physical world.

§ 64. *Spirit is not Divisible, Qualitatively or Quantitatively.* These beliefs do not harmonize the unity of the spirit with its concreteness or multiplicity of capacities. In fact, those who believe that the capacities are mere qualitative and original difference implicitly deny the identity of the spirit, since they can only conceive of such differences as characteristics, elements, and parts.   In qualitative difference each spirit is not a whole entity, but a part of an entity.   In it an entity is divided and variously distributed, each part having its own content. Now experience proves that the spirit is a single indivisible force.   When it begins its life from the senses, it does not lack representative virtue, mind, and will; and when it is self-revealed in reason, it does not cease to be sense and representation.   In both cases, there is only the prevalence of one particular form over the others.   They who think that the capacities are qualitative differences, if they do not deny the identity of the soul, at least do not explain its various development, because between sense, representation, and intellect there is difference apart from the abstract relation of more or less.   In intellect there is sense, but it is sense resolved in a new and diverse manner of the spirit which cannot be shown by signs of addition or multiplication.   Granted that the capacities are quantitative differences, and therefore extraneous determinations of the spirit, it follows by this theory that continuous and profound psychological phenomena (a never-ending qualification) cannot be explained.   Therefore, some say that the contrary theory, which we have denied, is true, and that the capacities must be original differences, notwithstanding the arguments to the contrary just sent forth.   But the truth is that they are not quantitative nor qualitative differences alone, but moments of development; various changes of the spirit in its progressive movement can be seen in both quality and quantity.   The spirit is a unit differing within itself; it is a great energy and power which

assumes diverse and opposite forms, because it is both
sense and reason, instinct and will, and is shown as
necessary and free, as moral and immoral, as just and
unjust, as impious and good.   These forms so interpenetrate that the lower are contained and resolved in the
higher; so representation has within itself sensation as
matter.   Thought, in its turn, comprehends and raises
to its own level the data of representation.   The stages
of nature are not similar to the forms of the spirit, because the former are separate entities.   Mineral, vegetable, animal, and human stages, are self-sustaining,
although the vegetable presupposes the mineral, and the
animal succeeds the vegetable, and man develops after
all of them, which are, nevertheless, the terms of evolution.

§ 65. *Spirit and the Senses.*   The spirit has knowledge and will.   It is a theoretical and practical process.   Aristotle says that spirit joins with sense,
appetite, knowledge, and action.   The psychological
disposition of the spirit as sense, or as the cognitive
principle, is the nervous system which transmits
impressions; the muscular system serves the spirit
as appetite or volitive principle, in which there is a
contraction when an impression is transmitted to the
nerves.   Sense is first indeterminate because it does not
know anything but life or its presence in the whole organism and lacks special organs.   It is intimately connected
with some of the nerves and, therefore, grasps the general
conditions of the body, such as oppression, weariness,
vivacity, heat, and cold, inasmuch as they refer to the
economy of life.   This property or indeterminate sense
of self is called vital by Zimmerman, while by Drobisch
it is referred to as the barometric sense.   Rosmini calls
it fundamental, because it is found in all of the sensations,
which are its methods.   Who can hear any sound or see
any sight without feeling himself alive?   Bain and some

modern psychologists are forced to recognize it under the name of organic life, something having a continual and optional action and capable of noting the state of the muscles, nerves, circulation, respiration, and digestion. The primary, indeterminate sense becomes determinate and is specialized in the muscular, tactile, auditory, visual, olfactory, and gustatory sensations. The muscular sensations are connected with the condition of the muscles and teach us the different degrees of tension in the organs in motion, and the measure of their force. They consist of the pleasure or pain growing out of the exercise of the organs themselves and always have regard to motion. They are elementary and enter into every kind of sensation, because it is not possible to feel without motion. They differ from the tactiles because the latter presuppose contact with external stimuli. Bain connects them with a spontaneous and primitive activity which comes from within and is not a reaction against external stimuli. He states that the brain not only obeys impulses but is gifted with spontaneous action, and that a nervous influence, transmitted through the motor nerves and exciting the muscles, is a product or automatic method of the brain itself under the organic stimuli of nutrition. Bain furnishes proof of his statements, and Stuart Mill praises him for having bridged a large gap in the psychology of association. This lacuna was the denial of a primitive energy within ourselves which is not the echo of the external world. Certainly it is not possible to derive sensation from impression, because the former is in the appreciation of the latter, as we have said above, and because in feeling, there is always an original spontaneity which transforms the action of the stimuli, limits their force, and sometimes is not influenced by them, leaving them, as it were, standing apart. Such energy is psycho-physical — of this there can be no doubt. In fact, the proper character of psychic activity is that which, excited by stimuli, produces a new fact whose causes, from a point of view of quantity or quality, are not found in the external world. Psychic activity, consequently, is not comparable to an overflow because of superabundance, and it is what completes the transformation of the stimuli when they have done their part towards the psycho-physical process. All these sensations — muscular, tactile, auditory, visual, olfactory, and gustatory — can either be united with the vital sense or not; if they are united with it, they increase its force; if they are not united, they impede its development. In the first case, the sensation is pleasant; in the second, disagreeable; pleasure and pain give the tone to our sensations.

§ 66. *Consciousness.* Let the sensations be external, that is, caused by stimuli operating outside the body; let them consist of pleasure or pain, and they will always partake of the nature of sense which cannot get beyond the individual as its terminal, and which always concentrates in a particular and temporary affection of a sense without being able to distinguish it from sensation in general. Sensation is always an indistinct whole of actively sensible beginning and passively felt cause. If distinction appears, sense is resolved and gives place to consciousness which alone is fitted to distinguish subject from object and to refer the latter to the former. The cause becomes the object, a *quid* placed before subject when consciousness is shown. Psychical activity arises, stimulated by its own sensitive acts, above the combinations of sensation and is not exhausted in them. The first form of consciousness is a bare feeling of difference in the subject which is conscious of itself through a sense terminus and a reference of the object to the subject that is called sensible but which must not be confused with pure sense indistinct in itself. In this grade of psychical activity lies the first product of the mind in that the matter gathered by our sensitive impressions is formed by the faculty and converted from a sensitive cause into an understood object. Knowledge, therefore, is derived from something distinct from itself, which is not simple impression or sensation, because its object is not transferred from without into the spirit but consists of an intellectual formation. Its possibility lies in some *a priori* original conditions, as Kant said. The necessity of a spontaneous and original psychological principle in the explanation of the fact of cognition has not escaped the great empiricists. Campanella thinks that knowledge of external things, called "addita," must rest on "cognitio abdita," that is, on the certainty of being, power, will, and knowledge. Locke disagrees with the innatism of Descartes but admits innate attitudes and natural constituent capacities of the spirit. Spencer recognizes an hereditary active preformation in the mind, and that mind is not really explicable without it, because habit is not formed and transmitted to descendants. It has been shown by not a few psychologists that consciousness cannot be an association of states, for these states must either be considered as belonging to the entities whose states they are, and in such a case the result is a sum and not a unit, or they must be regarded as convergent in their action towards a point without themselves, and then the reason and manner of the convergence would have to be understood and the point of convergence known. On such a hypothesis, there would be a complex state, which could not be a state proper, because it would lack the necessary unity. For the phenomenists and pure associationists, the ego is not a reality but a complexity of states bound together in various relations. Neither can consciousness be the function of any point of the brain because matter is of itself complex and cannot be conceived of as a unit nor can the sum of things be so considered, — granted that it can be conceived of at all. Lacking the point to which the forces are applied, consciousness cannot be assimilated to the single result of concurrent forces or to the electric current generated by action and reaction of several substances, because it, too, is composed of the particles of a fluid. Consciousness studied in its essence and in its primitive simplicity as an act of distinction or reference is not born from the sentiment of the organism or synthesis or from association and necessity. Ribot thinks that the ego, the sum of the actual states of consciousness, is in its continuity of time the product of memory, depending fundamentally upon the complexes of sensations provided by all the parts of the body. Consciousness in his mind changes by reason of the rapid or slow variations of such sentiment, hence cases of the successive formation of the ego, of the disintegration of the ego into different egos, the origin of the pathological phenomena of double consciousness. Some speak of a new state of the brain cells which have the virtue of making a diverse ego appear, but Ribot and others, (writes Masci, in his book "Coscienza, Volonta, e Liberta,") do not agree that their theories can be applied to formed, developed, concrete, and individual consciousness and not to the original form of consciousness. Certainly the sense of self, of synthesis, always supplies new material or content to consciousness, which, however mute, is together with memory the foundation of personal identity expressed in "ego qui quondam." Without doubt the concrete individual ego has a history. It presupposes a long and complicated succession of states which imply association, memory, and mutations of sensibility. The simple act of distinction and reference, however, does not emanate from impression or sense and is independent of memory and the recognition of the sense termini. For memory itself presupposes the unity of knowledge and the act of reference, because recollection is not possible without reference. Consciousness in its elementary form is empty; it is the visive internal centre to which psychical phenomena belong and through which they are recognizable and appear through comparison.

§ 67. *Representation.* When an impression and physical cause are withdrawn the sensation does not disappear but is preserved in the mind and can be reproduced. Reproduced sensation is representation. It is known that similar representations are based on a single representation. The contrary are elided and the different ones form groups. Elision is the retirement of the weaker representation to the back of the mind, from which it comes forth when it is reinforced by a new one either like it or opposed to it, but coexistent in space or time. Representations are evidently forces, and we should not be surprised that they are subject to the laws of mechanics. Representation is derivative as the reproduction of a sensation, and so representative consciousness or the second form of consciousness, in which the external object is the image of something with given properties, is derivative, although the object is a simple existing *quid* and nothing else for sensible consciousness, the most elementary and poorest of consciousnesses. Psychical activity is shown in this field with the power of directing the force of our representations, a proof that reproduction is not voluntary. It controls when the mind separates the psychological associations from representations founded on extrinsic and accidental combinations, and gives them their logical relation. Abstraction is the act of separation or isolation of a characteristic of a common quality from several particular representations. Thus, the common image or abstract universal is formed, of which we have spoken before.[1] Language is intimately connected with the image or common representation, which is intermediate between the singleness of the sensation and the true and effective universality of the ideas. A word is a phantastic universal or representation, because the sound of which it consists is made to indicate a given property of something, a property which recalls to the mind the whole thing with its other characteristics. Grimm, Curtius, Steinthal, and Max Müller give this definition and agree in recognizing the representative virtue of words. By means of words, a picture of the ever changing nature of objects is attained. The mind can thus rise from the sphere of representation to that of thought. The conversion of the image into a concept is quite easy when the image is not absolutely fugitive, but is connected with a sound. The predominance of the original activity of the mind arises in the structure of a language, because conjunctions, prepositions, and adverbs express relations that are not born of impressions or representations, as nouns and verbs, but constitute the formal and categorical element of language.

§ 68. *Thought*. Thought emerges from representation. Knowledge advances and becomes intellectual. By going deep and plunging its searching look into things, it conceives necessity and universality. The object of knowledge and mind is universality. No longer phantastic, imaginative, and shifting, but that in which the essence is understood, the universal is the combination of all the qualities and condition of phenomena, without which phenomena could not exist. There is still progress in

[1] *Cf.* § 32, *ante.*

this form, because the object is not the bare *quid*, of which the existence alone is known, nor the thing with ever changing properties. The intellectual, as well as the perceptive or representative knowledge, is derivative. Originally, in all its phases, there was only the difference between subject and object, a distinction which did not lie in impression and sensation. In such a state, the synthetic activity of the spirit gained theoretically its highest development, since the knowable object was understood, and since representation cannot show necessity and universality; it deals with contingent or particular objects. There are logical conceptions to which no sensible or representative matter corresponds: for example, substance and cause. It has been pointed out, therefore, that all their value lies in their form alone and that they can be likened to algebraic signs which do not express quantity, but its function. It is not possible, says Locke, to obtain the conception of substance from experience, because we conceive only the methods; substance is a mere abstract idea, a collection of methods. Reality, Hume holds, shows facts joined and not necessarily connected. The conception of cause can only be formed through habit. Locke and Hume are right in showing that the two categories of substance and cause cannot arise from experience, but they are wrong in exchanging substance, which is an object thought of as an intrinsic mass of qualities, for a simple collection, and what is habitual for what is logically necessary. Bain has recourse to instinct as defined by the Scotch school, an inexplicable and mysterious principle, as a basis for causality. These categories of purely logical concepts are not innate, not beautiful and formed in the mind, but are original and constitute the active foundation, the systems of the functions of the mind itself, which, stimulated by impression, produces and functionizes according to its conditions and laws and makes a first acquirement without which no other acquirement is possible. The cognitive act, if not impression or passion transferred by the stimulus of the mind, is a primitive acquirement, the conversion of sensation into an understood object, the comprehension of the object and the formation of experience as cognition.

§ 69. *Origin of Mind according to the Positivists.* Some positivists say that it is an error to presuppose an always constant organization of mind, and not to admit that necessity or universality can be derived from experience. They criticize Kant, recognized by them as the forerunner of scientific metaphysics, for these two opinions, and hold that the *a priori* forms are explicable by the supra-individual factor of experience itself. This factor is not logical activity or the original synthetic activity, but is found in the more recondite history of psychics and human culture. The apperceptive function of thought, according to them, belongs to the knowledge of civil man, because in primitive experience the logical factor is given by a simple process of organizing the evidence of the senses. The dualism of the ego and non-ego is not original. It is a gradual formation that the child learns. The ego is nothing more than a whole by coalization. The generative elements of experience, says Angiulli in the book cited,[1] are found in events anterior to the distinction of the ego and non-ego, that is, in the sphere of unconscious experience and mentality. The problem of the origin of mind is that of the origin of life. The first element of experience is the reaction of the organic substance under stimuli. This reaction or irritability is fundamentally inseparable from sensibility and motion. Irritability,

---

[1] "La Filosofia e la Scuola," cit. § 53 *ante.*

sensibility, and mobility are intimately connected with nutrition and reproduction. The law of nutrition is adaptation and that of reproduction is heredity. They say that mind is the capacity of an organism to learn through experience, so that adaptation to external relation becomes gradually selective. The second element is the power of organic matter to preserve the effects of sudden change in the form of molecular dispositions. Sensation is not an element of the mind unless associated with precedent states. It has a power of assimilation, distinction, a kind of unconscious judgment. This assimilative something is connected by the nerve groups; it is established by the experience of the race and generated by the same nerve organs in the earliest adaptations of animal life. The third element of experience is attention, which has the virtue of transforming sensation into perception, consciousness into autoconsciousness, the image into the ideal.

§ 70. *Variation Depends on the Stimuli.* Following Angiulli, who is the most lucid interpreter of the doctrine in question, the method of nutrition is psychological, that of memory is psychical, and that which governs the assimilation of external excitements is nervo-psychical. This is the energy of cerebral centres with a directive and inhibitive motion by which the mental acts are shown to us as the effects of an internal, not external, activity. It is the result of hereditary accumulations which, if not very numerous, give the mind a greater power of modifying and correcting existing phenomena. The mental faculties are formed by the aggregation of the residuals of experience which interact to create organs, functions, and capacities. The capacities produced by association differ, nevertheless, in quality, because we see even in the sphere of natural entities such a result in the combination of several elements having properties different from those of the single components, as Lewes has shown. Experience is an evolution in which the products are constantly different from their components. Psychological elements are mutable unities and presuppose in their development, especially in the phase of their abstraction, collective and historical experience. The necessity and universality of knowledge are based on the equivalence of a fact to the sum of its factors. The impossibility or inconceivability of the contrary has always had its base in real or possible experience. We must explain everything by the energy of the stimuli, because the differences in the forces and qualities of entities are the first causes of the differences in the structure and property of our senses. The eye sees light because it is a product of light. There exists nothing in an object of itself, because what appears is the real. In the subjective order, the thing of itself, the ego, is the physiological function, the manifestation of cosmic forces. Fact, law, and cause are three aspects of the whole. Fact is the sum of conditions, law is the fact regarded in its growth, and cause is the fact considered in its conditions. The principle of cause is that of the persistence and transformation of forces. Things are only syntheses of properties. Knowledge of things is, therefore, real; relative in its realization, absolute as a whole. One cannot speak of relative cognition without admitting absolute cognition.

§ 71. *Dependence of Variance in Stimuli is Contrary to Modern Thought*. It is evident that the above theory is a form of purely objective empiricism moving on the principle that it is the *res* which gives the essence. What is internal is constituted by what lies without; everything is a derivative of the external. Yet by reason of its origin modern empiricism should have a different character from the ancient because it, together with the principle of idealism, is born from the principle of subjectivity. There can be no more doubt that modern philosophy is informed on such a principle in every direction, than that ancient philosophy looked always to natural or ideal objectivity. Natural objectivity was dominant before Socrates; the philosophers sought truth in the natural elements.[1] From Socrates on, truth was placed in concepts and ideas regarded as objects. Modern empiricism is not simply impressionism as Spaventa shows, because, although he admits with Campenella a "cognito abdita," he recognizes with Locke certain natural attitudes of the subject, and conceives with Condillac of sensation as an act of internal energy, and follows the *a priori* of the Helmholtzian laws of causality with the logical and appetitive activity of Wundt, and with the synthetic activity of Riehl's earlier works. On the other hand, Cartesian idealism and transcendental idealism prove clearly the dominance of' subjectivity.

§ 72. *Criticism of the Positivist Theory of Knowledge.* The theory set forth in the last paragraph confuses experience, which is knowledge, complete cognition, apperception, and certainty with feeling and living and even with simple organic irritability, thus reducing it to a mere impression. It denatures consciousness, because it speaks of an unconscious experience, discernment, and judgment. An unconscious experience is not an experience or a full cognition, but a knowledge which does not know; an unconscious discernment is not an act which distinguishes object and subject and refers the latter to the former. It is not a judgment. Experience, comprehension, discernment, and judgment always presuppose consciousness, but can be unaccompanied by reflection. There are primitive

[1] *Cf.* Intro. p. 1.

and spontaneous judgments, and there are secondary and
reflective judgments. Primitive judgments contain the
act of distinction and reference in which lies consciousness; the secondary are the children of reflection which
necessarily implies the act of which we speak. All judgments are conscious, but all are not reflective. We
must not confuse reflection with simple consciousness,
otherwise we will fall into error. Only in the mechanism of reproduction can we allow unconscious conceptions and judgments in the sense of already formed
acts of consciousness, which have fallen into the obscure background of the mind and lie there with a
tendency to come forward upon any of those occasions
of necessity which are tested in psychology. There is an
unconscious psychicality which embraces sensitive and
instinctive phenomena, and those of revivication which
form the indistinct substratum of the intellectual spirit
of Aristotle. But we should not confuse experience as
an act of preservation of sensation with an understood object as a form of knowledge. Experience
alone can be one with conscious psychicality. Now the
theory above indicated carries the internal acts of man
into the animal and attributes those of the animal to
man; and, always retrogressive, it comes to the physical
properties of matter, the *a priori* of positivism, and
reaches the limits of materialism.

§ 73. *Knowledge is Subjective.* Spaventa sounds a
grave warning in his posthumous work " Esperienza
e Metafisica," that in all this genealogical theory,
knowledge is considered as an effect of some kind,
as a phenomenon among phenomena; while it is
the condition of all phenomena, their principle, in
fact, it is phenomenality itself. If the world of phenomena, that is, the real and relative world, is that of
representations, one cannot find the origin of knowledge

which is representation, because to find the origin of it means to go back to a phenomenon from which it is derived. And phenomena are representation, from which it follows that knowledge and representation are not derivatives, but are presuppositions if one wishes to derive them from phenomena, and presuppositions also, even if one derives them from phenomena or from combinations of physical and sensible elements. Things of themselves are not phenomena; they are transcendental and not knowable, the combinations of elements which are natural realities and not representations or simple facts of sense, and cannot produce representation. Thought and knowledge, experience, perception, and certainty become inexplicable in the hypothesis of an absolute posteriorism. From this arises the new objective empiricism which regards experience and even irritability as a kind of basis for external stimuli, as a reaction of the subject which develops its nature and constitution. *Volens nolens*, modern empiricism should be informed on the principle of subjectivity, from which it tries to separate. Knowledge and experience are double in appearance but are fundamentally one, because the thing is present, apparent to the ego, and would not be able to be present and appear to the ego, if the ego was not apparent to itself. Nothing appears to me if I do not appear to myself. In sensation, I do not feel anything if I do not feel myself; in knowledge I know nothing if I do not know myself in what I know. I do not know without being present with my nature in the object of my knowledge. From this, it is seen that the ego is not without sensation, and that it cannot exist after sensation disappears, because I feel nothing if I do not feel myself. Thought is the same; if it is not original, it cannot develop. The *a priori* here is the priority of myself, the apperceptive

unity of original synthesis, and the energy which reduces the multiplicity of impressions to a single point.
This *a priori* is in every form of knowledge, even the most
elementary and poor. It belongs to man in that he has
experience and knowledge, in that it is certain and does
not belong to civil man alone, as the empiricists hold.
The accumulation of successive experiences upon which
they insist, the hereditary *a priori*, is possible exclusively
through such an originality of the ego, the basis of
Kantism. Such accumulation constitutes the concreteness, the richness of knowledge, but knowledge has always
that double appearance which is single in fact, that
original distinction between subject and object about
which we have spoken.[1] The object is not the end of
sensation, it is the product of thought; it is born from
the conversion of the sensation into understanding.
Reality, objectivity, and truth are not found in blind
unformed sensation, but in the sphere of knowledge.
If reality lay in fleeting, variable, and contradictory
sensation, we would have to give up the search for truth.

§ 74. *Knowledge is "a Priori."* It has been stated
that experience is evolution in which the products are
dissimilar from the nature of the components,[2] without
reflecting that by such a statement one denies the universal principle of the causal equation. The effect, the
knowledge, would be conceived of as something absolutely
different from cause, that is, from the combination of
elements of natural reality and the acts of the senses.
The effect cannot be conceived of as something absolutely different from the cause, because there would be
no connection between them. It would not be an effect.
Neither can it be regarded as absolutely identical with
the cause, because it would be only the cause repeated,

[1] *Cf.* § 66 *ante.*
[2] *Cf.* § 53 *ante.*

and in this way, too, there would be no result. Causality
is not abstract difference or abstract identity, but both
together, an *a priori* synthesis. If experience is admitted
to be the result of the sum of the indicated combination,
the heterogeneity of the result can be reconciled with the
continuity of the elements only by explaining in some
manner how thought is contained in what is not thought,
how light emerges from blackness, how the logical connection, necessity, and universality are created by
mechanical combination, by physiological and psycho-
logic association, by contingency and particularity. The
necessary connection of the elements and factors of things,
and the impossibility of the contrary shown by every real
and possible experience are not derived from the aggregation of the residues of experience. Certainly these
conceptions presuppose empirical data, but they are not
formed without the original activity of thought, which is
the base of knowledge. Full and true knowledge of a
thing is had when the mind understands its necessity.
Necessity understood is the very absoluteness of knowledge to which some positivists to-day are tending.
Necessity and absoluteness exceed the confines of
sensible data of the experimental method and of
aposteriorism.

§ 75. *Noumenon is Knowable through Phenomenon.*
It is objected that the reality of knowledge must fail
if it is admitted that knowledge expresses the nature of
the knower and is therefore subjective and relative. If
the essence of things depends upon our representation,
things are what they appear to us, — they become phenomena. In other words, the thing is lost in its representation, and the theory of Berkeley is reinstated.
Is it not better to follow the path shown by Comte, and
sink representation in the object? The objection arises
from a false conception of knowledge which puts it in the

vision of the object considered. Knowledge does not lie in seeing an object which is without us, but in transforming what the sense conveys to the understanding; it is the projection and distinction of the object produced by the mind. The existence of things, objectivity, and reality, are one with their image in the mind. Things are true only in cognition, and what is supposed to be their existence before and without cognition is not their true essence; it is nothing. A thing of itself without relation to knowledge, a thing which can never stimulate the subject and appear, cannot be said to exist. It is right to speak of a thing of itself in that it is knowable, that is, that it can appear to the mind, even if it does not appear and does not make itself known. This kind of thing of itself, which Kant even admits, makes the perpetual possibility of phenomena, sensation, representation, and knowledge. It is the thing transcendental in itself, not simply empirical existence or appearance, nor mere ultra-empirical existence which, from its nature, takes all reality from the object. The mistake of Spencer lies in the conception of a thing by itself without referring it to the mind. His absolute unknowable is gnostical, add some positivists, because it is a thing of itself without any relation to the mind and therefore has no reason of existence. In this, it is like the religious, mythical absolutes, and the metaphysical absolute (if self-sufficient and self-ruled), for they become transcendental principles. These positivists recognize three kinds of absolutes. The methodological (or system of the ultimate concepts of the sciences), the cosmic absolute (or the world as a whole), and the objective absolute (or the perpetual possibility of sensation and representation). They recognize the absolute in a certain sense, they admit metaphysics, but only if scientific and experimental; and here the hated and abhorred metaphysics rise again to aid positivism itself in its critical phases. Certainly the existence of a real and intimate supreme principle cannot be denied when philosophy is sought to explain the general scheme of the world. There are some who wish to find this principle in a series of laws always more comprehensive and universal, and there are some who seek it in a series of forces or causes, or of ends and in the mind. Denying the possibility of knowledge of the absolute, some say that the ultimate law and end cannot be known. By regarding only the series of law, one does not see the cause; by limiting the attention to a series of forces or causes, one cannot see the end. The absolute, should include in itself law, cause, and mind, if it is a true absolute. Spaventa says that ultimate law is cause, ultimate cause is end, and ultimate end is mind. He cites Bruno on this subject to the effect that "the pursuit of the absolute" is to be made by "motion not physical but metaphysical going round by the steps of perfection and coming" thus "to the infinite centre." By an indefinite direct line one will never reach the absolute.

CHAPTER VI

PRACTICAL FOUNDATIONS OF THE DEDUCTIVE IDEA OF LAW. — DEVELOPMENT AND DIVISION

INSTINCT, DESIRE, AND WILL. — CAPRICE AND MORAL FREEDOM. — THE CONSTANCY OF HUMAN ACTS AS SHOWN BY STATISTICS. — END OF MAN AND HAPPINESS. — HUMAN HAPPINESS AND THE LAW. — THE IMPERATIVE, PROHIBITIVE, AND PERMISSIVE FORMS OF LAW. — LAW AS A PRINCIPLE OF COERCION OR COEXISTENCE AND OF HARMONY. — THE RATIONAL TRI-DIVISION OF LAW. — THE DIVISION OF GAIUS.

§ 76. *Other Attributes of the Mind.* The mind has not only knowledge but appetition, desire, and will. It is a theoretical and practical process. The muscular system is physiologically fitted for the practical process. A muscular contraction or reflexive action follows every impression transmitted by the nerves, and, furthermore, it is not the simple mechanical effect of the blow received, but has its form and measure in the excitement of the organs. The impression is not sensation and the reflexive action is not appetite. Appetite is a state of psychical activity, in that it is a tendency towards pleasure and aversion to pain. Reflexive action is a physiological movement and is not to be confused with a tendency. The appetite in its turn transforms the stimuli and, considered in its indeterminateness, is the same vital and fundamental sense and the same sensitivity in motion of which Rosmini speaks. It is sensation become practical activity.

§ 77. *Instinct.* The first concrete and particular appearance of appetite is instinct, a tendency unconscious of its ends and means. Its end is the attainment of what is best for the satisfaction of the needs without precedent experience. Many biologists and psychologists derive instinct from the adaptation of animals to their environment begun through necessity and persisted in through useful experience and later become a hereditary and organic custom of the species. It is certain that in adaptation generally, however large the part allowed genealogical theories, we always need a nature in the plant and animal capable of being influenced by external circumstances. Now this is presupposed by custom and heredity; it is resolved into an intimate and original force, and in our case into a preëxisting tendency to persevere in pleasure and to avoid pain,—an animal property. The hypothesis of a "tabula rasa" is to-day abandoned by the empiricists themselves.

§ 78. *Desire.* The second state in which appetite is developed is desire, a tendency towards a representation which attracts the mind. In desire there is a knowledge of the end but the choice of means is lacking, because the relation between the end and the means is learnt, not by representation, but from an already experimented association of our internal states and external objects through reflection. So love, differing from passion, is a secondary form of appetite presupposing representation. Love is a lasting, purposeful, objective appetite; passion is equally a derivative state because it is referable to sentiment, but it is a momentary desire or sudden attack and is not associated with calculation and has no thought of the object which has excited it. On the contrary, love implies an end tenaciously sought with constancy of purpose. It always looks to the object, and is like the

river that gradually overflows its banks and forms a
new path for itself, says Kant, while passion is like the
water that suddenly breaks a dyke and inundates the
land.   Love is an attribute of man, a maxim of conduct, an end tenaciously sought.   Passion is common to
animals, a sudden motion of feeling.

§ 79. *Will.* The third and highest state of appetite is
will, which is considered by Aristotle because it partakes of
reason as a derivative power, originating in appetite itself.
In will or rational appetite are found, according to him,
the determination of ends and choice of means.   There
is a common element in the inferior and superior appetitive faculties, that is, in instinct, desire, and will.   This
is spontaneity, a principle that is in us and not without
us.   Now in instinct the end is immediately before us;
it is not joined by knowledge.   In will, on the other
hand, the end is mediate.   It is meditated upon and reflected about and is established sometimes as a necessary
and universal determination of conduct.   The end is
necessary and universal, if it is the supreme and true
human end.   Aristotle emphasizes this conception as
Fiorentino points out in "Lezioni di Filosofia," that
there is no deliberation about the supreme end, but that
there is deliberation about the means which are in our
power, that is, about those things which originate in
us.   Spencer confuses physiological conditions with
psychical activity in regarding the will as a more complicated and slower reflexive action.   In reflexive action
there is an impression which is followed by a muscular
contraction; in instinct there is found a complexity of
impressions coördinated by heredity and organic custom
with a sum of muscular contractions; in will, several psychical states are connected through a stimulus and enter
into a struggle; the one that prevails is said to be the one
wished for.   Instinctive action must be immediate by

the effect of automatic association, and voluntary action mediate and often slow because there is a struggle between the different series of representation. As impression is not sensation, thus, as we have said before,[1] reflexive action is not a tendency, nor is it inclination, aversion, or appetite. Evolution is not only a progress of quantity but a progress of more perfect qualification. According to Spencer, between reflexive action and will there is exclusively a quantitative difference of more or less complexity, and a mechanical difference of more or less speed. On the other hand, if the conflict of internal states is governed by laws of mechanical association one could never explain the fact (attested by experience as Aristotle pointed out) that the deliberation about the means is restricted to those that are within our power to adopt, and does not extend to other things which do not lie within our power.

§ 80. *Character.* A simple tendency is the immediate rebound of pleasant or painful sensation and is not accompanied by knowledge. Desire or appetite, properly so called, contains an attempt to recall a psychical state, that is, a tendency with knowledge, but knowledge in mere appetition is the spectator of an energy which has all its being in the exciting object from which it takes its name. In this state of practical activity there is knowledge, but deliberation is lacking; impulse and emotion predominate. In will, on the other hand, knowledge is active as reflection and reason capable of arresting an impulse and of generalizing and submitting the objects of desire to a judgment of practical objective experience. It differs from emotion. Will, observes Masci, begins always as an act of inhibition because it arrests, elides, and converts the force of impulse into ideation, but reaches fulfillment in an inverse process, by the transfor-

[1] *Cf.* § 65 *ante.*

mation of ideation into impulse, becoming action. In this lies the difference between involuntary and voluntary intention. The first depends upon the force of representation and the sentiment which it excites. The second is derived from reason because representation is not of itself strong enough, its vigor being diminished by the act of inhibition. Ribot, in "Les Maladies de la Personalité," regards will from the three points of view: as the power of impulse, distinguished from the anterior activities, because it is an ideomotive force; as the power of inhibition, in which it stops motion either by the creation of contrary impulses or by restraining the emotions, through fear; and as the form of individual reaction expressing the intimate nature of the subject. The principle cause of volition is not a conflict of motives, but character. If this were not true, the men richer in ideas would be the more irresolute. Character is the psychical revelation of the organs and is partly original and partly derivative. Now this theory is identical with Spencer's because it is founded on the principle of evolution and considers the voluntary phenomena as cases of the incoherence between excitement and action. But it includes an important correction of the doctrine of the English philosopher, — the recognition of the necessity of a practical subject who chooses and from whom volition emanates; an essentially active fact which becomes passive if you conceive of it, as Spencer did, as a result of a conflict of motives. A phenomenon so various and complex as will cannot be explained by the conception of a simple incoherence. For, thus, the greater incoherence would make the greatest resoluteness out of the greatest irresoluteness. In spite of the need of activity revealed by Ribot, his will as a power of inhibition is passive, because it is a consequence of fear. True active voluntary inhibition controls and arrests an impulse not through a prevalent emotion, but through the dictates of knowledge and the development of reason. In substance, Ribot confuses simple appetition with will and then tries to form character independent of the latter. Pathological experience, every day contributing valuable data to the study of psychology, shows us that where knowledge is lacking or is simply a spectator, there can be no will; and that will decreases in the same degree that knowledge is suspended or inactive. Voluntary action is destroyed by lack of the power to convert the force of impulse into the force of ideation, and by transforming it into impulse. Examples of the first kind of impotency are found in all the cases of irresistible impulse, unconscious as the impulses of epilepsy and hysteria, or conscious as the rare tendencies to incendiarism, homicide, and theft. The most specific case of impotency of the second kind is aboulia, in which the mental faculties are sane, the mechanism of motion intact, and yet the will of those attacked by this malady cannot reach a determination except under intense pain.

§ 81. *Chance must be a Result of Causality.* Will is not the license of indifference or the power of the absolute initiation of a series of acts. It is not determined without motives. The principle of causality demands a continuous series of antecedents and consequents and applies the conception that similar causes and identical conditions produce similar results. The license of indifference breaks the causal chain. It is an element of discontinuity. It does not presuppose any antecedents and is resolved into the absurd notion of the possibility of several identical causes productive of dissimilar results. To admit that the infinite progression of causes and results should stop at a *causa sui* does not mean the recognition that the latter is determinate. The *causa sui* may be internal and extrinsic necessity.

The fact of change does not in any way, even partially, show an absolute beginning because the energies are preserved and persist, merely undergoing a transformation. The heterogeneity of results does not show an indifferent power but rather the complexity of conditions and causes which give it birth. The license of indifference is casual and accidental will and because chance, philosophically regarded, has a cause, casual will must have one. Chance is not opposed to the laws of causality but expresses a coincidence of facts whose casual series set apart can be considered as independent. This is the doctrine of the incidence of the series accepted by many philosophers and explained by Windelband in "Die Lehren vom Zufall." He writes that chance cannot be possible, if growth forms a single chain in which the links are necessarily joined. But, in fact, we see a great number of threads developed which touch, interlace, and cut into one another to form that marvelous tissue which is called world progress. The points at which threads touch, and where new threads constantly unite with them, show us two facts that coincide in time and space without having the relation of cause and effect. Reasons are not lacking, according to Tocco's "Il Concetto del Caso in Aristotele," for holding that such was approximately the opinion of the Stagirite. Aristotle did not deny that every result must have its cause, but held that the chain of causes is interrupted by foreign events that are the product of distinct causes and have no relation of causality with the first series. The number of the causes of these accidentals are indeterminate because the number of threads that can affect or come into the causal chain of a series is indeterminable. Now if coincidence is a fact, like every other fact, it should have a reason for existence. Coincidences, therefore, cannot be removed from the jurisdiction of the laws of causality, and neither can the casual will. It is repugnant to the mind to admit an empty and indeterminate activity, a power of willing and not willing, a will that wills itself. A profound observation of Leibnitz is widely known; man does not will to will, but wills to do, for if he wills to will he would will the will to will, and so on forever. Knowledge cannot give evidence of a power beyond the scope of action or of a mere possibility. Such a possibility is inferred only through ratiocination. Knowledge in its simplicity embraces the subject and will, but the relation between will and motive constitutes a deduction. Knowledge gives evidence only that if there is a will to do a thing the thing can be done, and goes no further. In a great number of cases, it shows us the motives; and if sometimes it is not able to show them, that does not mean that the motives are lacking. Advice, prayers, threats, laws, promises, and agreements all act as motives, and the desire to show one's own power over strong motives or the opportunity and necessity of decision when there is perplexity are often motives. The belief in license arises from the fact that the cause-motive is a thought not followed immediately by action and that the action does not appear as equivalent to the intensity of the cause; whence a certain incoherence, that is believed to be absolute independence. On the other hand, it is easy to disregard feeble desire or the fleeting and weak solicitations on the part of the object and accept an indeterminate power of the license of indifference, which is fundamentally an immoral principle because a will indifferent to motives is a will of itself indifferent to good and evil.

§ 82. *Motive. Definition of Character.* The will presupposes a cause, or at least a motive. The external cause modified by its excitability of the organism on which it exercises its actions, determines the will. It becomes motive when it has been represented by the mind, in which case it has its virtue *qua* motive, that is, not by what it is but by what it is represented to be, that is, its reproduction in the mind. Psychical activity begins with the transformation of causes into motives. Every man forms his motives for himself since each represents differently the external stimuli of which he increases or decreases the energy. At first, there is only isolated action; then there arises in the subject a certain facility of renewing such action which, reacting strongly, is called propensity. Propensity springs from habit in one or more parts of the sphere of action and thus characteristic lineaments and traits are created. If characteristic traits are coördinated and subordinated to a supreme will there is character. Whence it follows that the activity of the mind, besides converting cause into motive, raises motive to the importance of a law, forms habit, and is the organic principle of all the coördinate and subordinate volitions. Character differs from nature, temperament, and idiosyncrasy, although such terms are not foreign to it. Nature depends upon the variable conditions of the organic systems and upon the prevalence of one over other, for example, upon the prevalence of the muscular system. Temperament is the result of different dispositions of receptivity and nervous spontaneity. Idiosyncrasy is reducible to congenital sympathy, antipathy, and apathy. The character is formed; nature and temperament exist from birth. Character appears in youth, the others belong to every age. Character cannot be voluntarily formed. In fact, there are many individuals without character, although all have characteristic traits. Nature, temperament, and idiosyncrasy are common to all. Character presupposes spontaneity. The other terms presuppose

necessity.   In character, all the natural elements dependent upon the organism are found as well as the influences
of external circumstances of both a physical and moral
nature.   There is much that is derived from our activity
that merely coöperates, or acts to transform or create
new power.   The conception of motive is not contradictory to that of free will, not synonymous with casual
will or license, since motive demands an act of intrinsic
conversion or full approval by the mind.   Such an act
is a valuating judgment of the practical worth of the
cause, and the more it is extended and lengthened so
much more does responsibility increase.   But what
emanates from our activity, which coöperates, transforms, and creates, is the action of an entity not necessitated to act, but which has nevertheless motives for
prompt action.   On one hand, freedom, or free will, is
presented as a power of diverse and contrary parts under
which the conversion of cause into motive and the creation
of rules of conduct and the formation of habit can or
cannot take place.   On the other hand, motives are not
lacking.   In other words, it is necessary to keep the
notion of the necessitating force of motive and volition
entirely distinct and not to confuse appetition with will
and above all not to fall into indeterminism.   If the
force of motive is one with that of will, there is necessity
and not freedom, and if appetition is controlled by
impulse there is no will.   Holding that the subject
increases and diminishes the force of motive without
reason is to admit indeterminate and empty power.
Certainly, the will does not determine an action without
a motive, but the motive of a voluntary act is not converted by itself into action, as Masci tells us, but is an
idea and thought, a valuing judgment.   Ideas have the
least impulse and move by the causal energy of the subjcet,
hence the semblance of choice between several reasons

which are without impulsive force and indicate different possibilities.   Volition is the act of that energy accumulated by reflection, judgment, and abstract ideation, and is accompanied by a feeling of effort or tendency which a latent activity, overcoming obstacles and expanding, has for self-realization.   The subject has not necessarily acquired this energy since it is formed together with the habit of will in periods of reflection or in the train of practical tendencies in the state of independence of impulse derived from the power of knowledge.   Energy is constituted little by little by that freedom which is not a lack of motive but an autonomy of deliberation. The subject is capable of predetermining its volitions and preparing them from afar, increasing and not diminishing its freedom, because the single acts, that work together to give the constant direction of the will, are autonomous.   The greater coherence and, therefore, the greater force of character is accompanied by a greater imputability, so that if the prevalence of impulse is not a natural phenomenon and a consequence of nature, voluntarily acquired responsibility increases because action is not so much the result of a momentary volition as the product of a predeterminate and fixed will.

§ 83. *Chance and Statistics*.   The subject of the regularity and constancy of moral facts which are the result of the general permanent conditions of the social organism gives this problem still another aspect.   It raises the question whether moral statistics can harmonize the conception of the free will of man with that of the general laws by which in every year of a determinate period of the life of a people there is the same number of crimes similar in complexity, in kind, and even in method of execution, and the same proportion between the acquittals and convictions, and the same number of illegitimate births.   We must reflect that the regularity of moral facts is neither absolute nor equal to the immobility of external forces but is relative and comprehends social and historical causes capable of modification and susceptive of reform. Neither is it the constancy of tellurgical and climatological conditions that forces man and society, particularly in civilization, to contribute in a given proportion to the balance of crime, but it is the great complexity of unaltered, intellectual, moral, and economic conditions which brings about approximately the same number of crimes in a given period. We are very far from constructing in the moral order those characters of true stability and generality that exist in the physical order. Such characters are easier found in matters that have important physical and physiological elements, that is, in the statistical doctrine of population and in anthropometry. The school of Quetelet, with its mechanical and astronomic tendencies, attempts to explain the constancy of moral phenomena by relying more upon external than internal relations, teaching that the necessity of such phenomena is to be found in the complexity, while the difference, the individual note, and freedom exist in the men who compose the social essence. Drobisch in "Die Moralische Statistik und die Menschliche Willensfreiheit" proceeds in an inverse way and shows that the constancy of moral statistics is not a fact, although it is a product of causes capable of change; that the average man represents the relation between those who do something and others who do not; that the habit of doing something from the point of view of statistics depends upon the nature of man in general and of the race, and upon the social conditions and the character of the individual in particular. Habit produces or does not produce an act depending upon the force of the occasion of impulse, the degrees of resistance derived from the predominance of reason and culture. With a change in such conditions the constancy expressed by the average would fail. Moral statistics cannot answer the question of free will, he adds, because it is not suited to the examination of psychological motives of action although it can explain the proportions of action. Oettingen in "Moral Statistik" treats of social ethics on an empirical basis of this kind of statistics and starts out with the conception of man as a free and responsible being bound to society by infinite relations. Oettingen sees in the regularity of social facts an immediate providential control. In this, he agrees with Suessmilch, differing from Quetelet who believes only in natural and physical law. But he does not admit the religious predestination of the old theologians or the mere license of the philosophers, but accepts the principle of Lotze that freedom of will without a motive is absurd. He believes that the more the moral life of the individual interpenetrates that of society, the more the consciousness of responsible existence will increase. But Drobisch and the others are right in denying the competency of moral statistics on this subject. The question of free will is not properly an object of statistics because it is referable to human activity which is considered by the entire group of moral sciences. Whereever the action of man is found, the essentially physiological problem of freedom arises. It is as old as philosophy and theology. Moral statistics study reality, the determined extrinsic act of the will, as a unit, and not as the possibility of the will, the subject of psychology. Moral statistics can only deny license which is without motive, because in human acts, impulses and motives always arise, but it cannot deny free will. Those who appeal to statistics to disprove free will, base the internal necessity of determination on the simple uniform-

ity shown by the average, going from the complex result
to the individual fact, while it is not right to confuse the
extrinsic conditions of phenomena with the phenomena
themselves.   They think that the relative constancy of
the result excludes an indefinite variety of combination of the free elements and so the constancy is greater,
observed Cournot in "Exposition de la Theorie des
Chances et des Probabilités," when the elements have
freedom of position and independent movement, because, in that case, compensation between the possible
individual variations becomes fuller and more perfect.
It is necessary above all to define the nature of like
elements to come to a conclusion, and the definition
is not within the sphere of the social sciences and
statistics.

§ 84.   *The Summum Bonum.*   Will is rational appetite
and tends as such to the end of man.   The end of man
is his well-being, or happiness, says Aristotle, in which,
since man is a spiritual and organic subject, is included
well-doing and well-living, duty and pleasure.   The
true human good in which lies the supreme end of
conduct demands the subordination of sentiment, passion, and interest to reason.   So conceived, the good
is not confused with the mind freed from passion of
the Stoic, with the spirit hostile to the world of the
early Christians, or with the abstract formal will of
Kant, which is only autonomous when it wills *per se* and
proudly distances every alliance with the inclinations
of the senses; nor is it reducible to the mere pleasure of
the Epicureans or the interest of the Utilitarians.
Starting out with the idea of good which most conforms
to human nature, the sentiments and appetites are not
contradictory to moral will, but on the other hand,
constitute its concreteness.   According to Bruno and
Spinoza, the good is properly a transformation of pas-

sionate movements into rational tendencies. The will is effectively autonomous; it contains the sums of our sentiments, emotions, and interests, and subjects them to the control of the mind. On this condition only is moral liberty obtained, which is realized by virtue or the habit of doing the good. Aristotle makes virtue consist in a measure of reason and in custom with advice and deliberation, equally far from the excesses of too much or too little, that is from hyperbole and ellipsis. He says that it does not lie in passion, capacity, science, or art. Passion is the sudden excitement of sentiment depending largely upon the organic state or temperament and really deserving neither blame nor praise. A capacity is given by nature, while virtue is acquired. Science teaches us good and evil but virtue is the practice of the good. Art shows us the external part of action but virtue puts a value on the intent. Virtue, he adds, does not come from nature, that is, it is not a capacity; nor is it without nature, but it should include all of man and should not be placed in a particular part, even in the most noble part of his being. Happiness, the good, the supreme end, or virtue presuppose autarchy, that is, the condition of self-sufficient man. He is not happy; he does not attain his ends or the good; and he does not become truly virtuous, when that sufficiency is lacking. Autarchy is gained in society, in communion of life, sentiment, and in discussion, common ideas, and language. Man naturally tends to this and can be called the political animal. Furthermore, says the Stagirite, every common good keeps men bound together and urges them towards social life. From this it can be inferred that ethics are a part of politics, and that happiness and virtue are not possible without social life. We moderns express the same idea by saying that morality and the subordination of interest to reason do not appear with-

out language, culture, custom, and education, which
imply the existence of society.   The mind develops by
the aid of language, teaching, and culture, and the will
is effectively free when educated for the good.   Man,
from a simple individual, develops into a moral subject
and person in civil communities, where he acquires a
full knowledge of himself and concrete independence.
So, in ethics, the primal activity of the mind is seen
because moral necessity is intrinsic in the idea of good
and cannot be the effect of organic need, custom, and
sentiment.   Moral necessity is the human end freely
conceived.   It is the mediate and reflected end of which
there is no trace in instinct and which can be born only
from the depths of the spirit as practical knowledge.
Nature gives us life and a tendency to preserve it.   She
adds happiness as a purpose and shows us the advantages
of society, but the ethical necessity of these ends and
their universality are productions of thought, which gives
form to this sensible matter.   It is true that organic
need, custom, and moral sentiment are antecedent, but
such things are not sufficient for the genetic explanation
of the conception of morality.   It is certain that man
begins by following selfish and social impulses and
later he becomes accustomed to act so that his knowledge
is in accord with the knowledge of his fellow-beings
about that which it is well for him to do for the benefit
of his existence and of that of the others, approving and
disapproving actions according to some variable criterion
at first imposed upon him, but later transformed by him
into a universal principle, and changed by habit into a
duty; so that he is wont to act as he should because he
has discovered the ethical necessity of the tendency to
live and of the social sentiments and civil community
as Fiorentino said in the book cited.[1]

[1] "Lezioni di Filosofia," cit. § **79,** *ante.*

§ 85. *Morals and Law are Part of Ethics*. Human good, which is the unity of right doing and right living or the subordination of the appetites and interests to reason, presupposing as it does the common life, is an object of ethics. Ethics, understood in this broad sense, contain the universal determination and the supreme principles of will and action. Morals and law are parts of ethics because the good can be developed largely in the intimacy of the relations of knowledge, and can, on the other hand, be well shown in the external relations between man and man, and man and things. In the first case, the mind, says Vico, should act against cupidity and construct ethical virtue or the sphere of morals in order to preserve and increase its empire. In the second, the mind becomes measure or proportion in which it is necessary to divide the utilities equally among men, and such is the idea of law. The matter of law is utility; the form or the measure is born from the depth of the mind. At this point, there reappears in the highest degree the original, synthetic activity of the spirit, which is found in feeling, representation, thought, and appetite, and which is the base of man's personality. The conception of Hegel is identical with that of Vico because the conformity of the subjective to the objective will, which is the ethical act or freedom for Hegel, as Spaventa showed in "Studi sull' Etica di Hegel," is externally revealed as law or else internally explained as the origin of morals. Law is the kingdom of external liberty; morals are internal liberty. In this way, the idea of law is found deductively starting from the double series of theoretical and practical principles. Such principles are essentially philosophical and connect the philosophy of law with philosophy in general. They are the foundations of science which show the supreme rationale of justice understood in its proper sense.

A juristic philosophy, independent of the two orders of mother-ideas emphasized in this and the preceding chapters, would not be a philosophy. It would be at most a formal introduction to the study of positive law. It is useful to keep constantly in mind that the philosophy of law is, and necessarily must be, part of philosophy, no matter how great a development of particular studies it necessitates.

§ 86. *Positive Law is Mandatory and Inhibitive.* Now the measure or proportion of utilities, which is law, imposes commands and prohibitions upon men. Through commands it prescribes what should be done so that the proportion may be obtained; through prohibitions it determines what it is necessary to abstain from doing in order to attain the proportion. The juristic imperative is in both positive and negative. It demands respect from man, allowing him what is his and prohibiting him from offense. The proportion of utilities cannot be effected without the idea of individual and social man and the principle of personality. Between the command and prohibition lies the zone of the permissible, recognized by the exclusion, command, and prohibition, and which does not consequently need a formula of rational law. The possibility of a "lex permissa" is found in positive law, which removes a prohibition and allows a "jus singulare," or allows an action in cases of doubtful legal right. The sentence of Modestinus, therefore, "Legis virtus est imperare vetare permittere," is referable to positive law and but to a limited extent to philosophical law. When law commands or prohibits in the last analysis, it merely assigns to a person the determinate quality or quantity of rights with which he can attain his essential ends. It establishes the "suum necessarium" of the person. What the law neither commands nor prohibits is the complexity of conditions and advantages not necessary to man. Such complexity forms the sphere of the "suum non necessarium." From this it follows that action is a question of duty if it is connected with a law that commands or prohibits, and whoever finds himself in the ethico-juristical necessity of fulfilling it, can have a reasonable expectation of not being disturbed in carrying out his obligation. It is in this sense of law as the norm that the first juristic duty is derived, and later comes law as a faculty or power. But action is purely facultative if it is considered in relation to legal permission. Under this aspect, therefore, law has its origin in the power of doing something perhaps not juristically obligatory but merely convenient, and then comes the duty or the necessity of respecting another's rights. It can be easily understood that he who thinks it convenient to do something should not offend the laws of ethics, of which law is a part. Neither is it difficult to understand that this theory refers to juristic duty and law as a *facultas agendi*, and not to moral duty, which is always based on the supposed justice in the object and has no correlative in the rights of others. If it has, it becomes juristic. It is possible that an act juristically facultative is morally obligatory, because we can point out that in such a hypothesis it is a question of the precedence of moral and not juristic duty. It follows as a consequence of what we have said, that law in the subjective sense is not all reducible to the permissive, as Rosmini and Seydel in his "Ethik" thought. The first defines it as the faculty of doing what is pleasant, protected by moral laws, provided it does not hurt another. But often a right is the legitimate claim to do what is necessary for human nature. In the series of the higher relations, the connection between juristic rights and duties is more rigorous. In it, it is seen that a faculty belongs to a person to exactly the extent that he has a duty to fulfill it. The exercise of a public function, for example, constitutes the right of authority, but it is first a duty. Secondly, as the series of relations descends and approaches the sphere of the permissible, the connection becomes less stringent and finally disappears. The individual has certain rights of a family nature which do not presuppose precedent juristic duties, although they can be connected with moral duties.

§ 87. *Law is Coercive and Harmonious.* If law is the good which can be realized in the external relations between man and man, and man and things, it is logically inferable that it contains potential coercion, and that it is the principle of coexistence and harmony of life. The exteriority of the relations implies action; both render physical and psychological coercion possible; that is, physical force and intimidation. Coercion is the means for enforcing the law against recalcitrant wills. It is the victorious manifestation of the law. Force, put in the service of the law, loses its blind and brutal attributes, and develops into an ethical power. The spectacle of the triumph of justice through coercion can in no wise be likened to a spectacle of natural forces set loose, because it is the ethical power ruling in the world of free essence, as Schelling says, before which the very activities of nature give way. It is customary to picture justice with scales and a sword. The scales without the sword are powerless; the sword without the scales are violence. It can be shown that law is the principle of coexistence and harmony by reflecting that if each is given his own, there can be no lasting motive for discord and war. The friendship of the parts of the great social whole is to be preserved by realizing the proportion of advantages. Moral well-being is the only basis of constant friendship. Justice is the true

magnet in civil life.   Aristotle reached the same conclusion starting with another idea, that of the impossibility
of picturing virtue without the common life.   He speaks
of the individual virtues; for example, temperance,
bravery, and prudence; but in these he sees merely a
commingling of appetites and reason.   According to him,
justice contains all the other virtues and is the chief
fundamental of ethics, because it shows more clearly
than the others the demands of common life.   Everyone
can be brave, prudent, and temperate if he take no care
for his fellows, but on the other hand nobody can be
just, except in society.   Now society is derived from
need, because the individual is not self-sufficient; need
is conducive to reciprocity of service and to the exchange
of acts and things.   Inter-exchange demands equality,
and this equality is justice in its original form.   Common
life, therefore, the essential condition of virtue and morality, cannot be sustained without justice, which, however,
is but complete virtue.   Rosmini tries to eliminate from
the definition of law the conception of society and even
that of real coexistence, but he cannot get away from the
notion of a possible coexistence, so intrinsic is the union
of the idea of the coexistence of men with justice.
"Let us hold," he said, "that the idea of law would
exist if there were but a single individual of the human
species"; then he goes on to consider him in a hypothetical relation with other possible individuals.   Without doubt, possible coexistence is a supreme abstraction
beyond which we cannot go without renouncing all
attempts to understand law.   But the ideas of moral
well-being, virtue, and law presuppose common life,
understood in its integrity; that is, civil community and
real coexistence in which alone self-knowledge and true
liberty, with their innumerable physical, intellectual, and
moral subsidiaries, accumulated by the collective activ-

ity, are acquired.   In other words, concrete and active
common life is necessary for the development of ethics.
Rosmini puts aside the conception of possible coexistence, and has recourse to that of society and real coexistence in his definition of the law as the personal
activity or the activity of the subject, master of his
acts, because this mastery over one's acts is only developed in full self-knowledge and freedom.

§ 88. *Law is Subject to Evolution.*   To conceive of law
as the principle of coexistence and harmony of life is
equivalent to regarding it as an organic principle and,
therefore, to subjecting it to the general laws of evolution which all organisms obey.   Evolution means the
development of new attributes and the increasing division
of functions together with a progressive autonomy of
parts, a complication of forms always more distinct and
coherent with more perfect qualifications.   Law follows
evolution because it comprehends an always increasing
number of relations, that in time become better distinguished, at first formed by sense, then by phantasy,
and finally by reason.   Law grows progressive and
struggles to conquer the resistance which it meets in
its path; " Jus autum majorum gentium," says Vico,
"est jus privatæ violentiæ"; which has attended the
existence of the struggle in law from its very beginning.
To Ihering we owe a theory about the struggles of law
that is not without importance.   "Law," he writes,
"is like Saturn who devours his own children, because it
creates and then destroys statutes, institutious, and interests."   It looks to preserve its actual form by force
reinforcing itself against civil wrong and crime.   So the
manifestations of the law, as norms, do not escape
the struggle, because habit is not established without
conquering obstacles.   Jurisprudence advances among
the disparities of beliefs and the contradiction of decrees;

and the statutes of our day can well be considered the result of parliamentary battles. Ihering stops to consider the struggle for rights subjectively understood. The struggle for rights should be inspired by the feeling of wounded personality, and not by economic interest alone, about which it is reasonable to compromise, unless there is a wound to the personality. In the defense of one's rights, all the ethical conditions of life take part and, therefore, the struggle constitutes a duty on the part of the person towards himself. The struggle is also a duty of the individual towards society, by keeping whole and safe, by his resistance, the vigor of the law, and hindering it from becoming ineffectual. The State has its most ample source of strength in the sane and vigorous juristic sentiment of individuals, because only those who have had the courage to struggle bravely for their rights and the protection of their personality, are in a position to feel the sentiments of patriotism or take an active part in the civil concerns when the national dignity is offended.

§ 89. *The Laws of Evolution Show the Course of the Development of Law.* The laws of evolution, to which law is subject, give us the principle or criterion of its logical division, and it seems indubitable that the first forms of law must have been the most simple and abstract, that is, the least complicated. They included the relations of private law, since members of the social order strive for the attainment of their particular ends by means of voluntary acts. Less simple and abstract are the relations of public law which embrace the relations arising from the realization of universal ends through an ordered power, in which the individuals take part as citizens and not as private men. And still more complex are the forms of international law which presuppose the coexistence of countries and the great principle of the humanity of nations, of which Vico wrote. The evolution of law is parallel and to a certain extent identical with that of personality, (for it first is singular, then collective and political, and finally international,) since the idea of personality is the essential principle of law.

§ 90. *Distinction between Private and Public Law.* As to the distinction between private and public law we must say that outside of the criterion of the nature of their respective ends and means, alluded to in the last paragraph, first pointed by Ahrens and later by Del Giudice in "Enciclopedia Juridica," there is no other acceptable criterion because it can only lie either in the subject of the relation or the means of its enforcement. If the difference lies in the individual or political subject, the logical consequence is that moral entities, at whose head is the State, would not be able in any way to enter private law, while in many cases they are in conventional relations with individuals and act as private subjects as far as their peculiar nature will allow them. If it lies in the action, and the relation protected by a private action is private, and the relation protected by a public action is public, we have a very extrinsic criterion, that is, the method of giving the law strength that would not be in itself private or public before thinking out the means of effectuating it. The particular and universal ends which we have emphasized are not foreign to the Roman definition of private and public law, the former founded on private, the latter on public utility. Private or general, the utility is always included by the principle of the purpose or the teleological criterion which rules in the human world. It is not possible to reduce the scope of private law to a reasonable control over a true and proper utility, because public law has the same object. The right, which is obtained by a proportionate equali-

zation or the imposition of a tax, looks to a true utility
as well as a right of property, legal servitude or obligation. The utility, which is the exclusive matter of
private law, has essentially to do with rights of a financial value. It gives the special characteristic to the
juristic relation whether the subject is a private person,
a moral entity, or a State. The right of a citizen, for
example, to the restitution of tax unjustly paid, is
private, as is the right of the State to have the price of
something that is sold or leased, because in both cases
it is a question of a utility of financial value. The
electoral right, liberty of conscience, and the right of
the State to demand tribute are not private rights and
do not include financial utilities, but are advantages or
utilities in a broad sense. This is the theory of Gabba,
who points out that the error of believing that private
rights are derived only from voluntary and contractual
acts. It is born of such acts, but it has its origin as well
in unilateral licit and illicit acts and even in public law.
Harm once done, even if extra-contractual, there is generated in him who suffers it a private right; the obligation of indemnity, which binds the State in the case of
appropriation for public utilities, is correlative with the
private or financial right of him who is deprived of his
goods.

§ 91. *Individual and Social Man are Intimately Inter-
penetrant.* Certain it is that in private law the particular
will is dominant, whence its sphere lies within the bounds
of the "jus voluntarium," but it should not be believed
that the "utilitas singulorum" is exclusive and egoistical,
because man lives in society, and consequently his will
is limited by the general will and his interest is tempered
by the interest of all. On the contrary, the general will
is imperative in public law. It is a "jus cogens" and not
susceptible to modifications through particular agree-

ments. The maxim, "Jure suo uti nemo cogitur," is applicable to private law. In public law, on the other hand, the principle that he who has a faculty to exercise is in duty bound to use it, is rigorous. The two maxims, however, are not in all cases exact because in private law, for example, there is guardianship, which is a social office, "munus publicum," and in public law there is no obligation to exercise of the right of suffrage. In fact, there are no mathematically fixed boundaries between private and public law, since the development of law includes all men, the individual, and society. The private person in the concrete is inseparable from the collective person.

§ 92. *Law is Historical.* There are various opinions about the methods of sequence in private and public law. Stoerk notes that the method in the two branches of law cannot be separated from the nature of the mind of the legislator and from a coördination of ideas through the categorical characteristics of subject, object, and acquisition, exercise, and loss of rights. In private law, however, the formal element, the generalizing activity and methodical process which consists in connecting juristic principles with human nature prevails, since the private relations are very simple and typical. In public law, on the other hand, the historical element has a large development; variability is dominant and, therefore, the systematization of the logico-dogmatical element is less important than the search for facts, and takes secondary place. Laband writes that the method of civil law is strong in maxims and that they have less importance in public law. We must first give a preliminary explanation to the conceptions of civil law, because it is necessary to eliminate from it all the specific elements and traits peculiar to private law. Now, looking closely at the two opinions and putting aside the notions that are exclusively referable to positive law and its technical construction, we must remember that law, be it private, public, or international, is always a human idea, that is, an ideal principle which develops in history, and that it does not consist in a mere logical construction. We must look upon it as a real and living formation. It is always based on human nature, in that it is explained in all the wealth of its attitudes and forms throughout the lives of nations which constitute the panorama of history. It is not possible, therefore, to dissociate the rational from the historical element in the treatment of law. If, in private law, the generalizing activity is more developed and the formal part is more worked out, that does not mean that this branch of law is not an historical formation, but only that the relations of which it takes account are not as complex and variable as those of public law. If we admit that the relations of private law are less complex and variable, the prevalence of the formal element should cause us no surprise. On the other hand, public law presupposes more elevated, comprehensive, immutable relations, and it is, therefore, evident that the formal element and the generalizing activity should be less marked, although such relations are also based on the common principle of human nature. If the relations of public law are more elevated and contain new elements, the simple conceptions of private law have not much weight in public law. Their expurgation should follow the movement of real evolution by being definite and complete. In other words, there should be a transformation. Their expurgation is thus the subtraction of what has lost its value and the addition of something that is new. Civil law has been active in such a work and has been profoundly altered.

§ 93. *The Five Categories of Private Law.* The law of evolution is observable in the categories of relations understood in indicated general forms. Every juristic relation demands a subject and an object. Man is the subject, the person, the subject of rights and duties. By the necessity of his nature he is urged to bend external things to his will, and to bind himself to his fellows in order to establish a reciprocal and continual interchange of necessary and useful objects. By his nature, too, he is fitted to realize his personality in the family which in its development gives place to inheritance. From this it follows that there are five categories in private law: the law of personality, the property law, the law of obligation, the law of family, and the law of inheritance. It is evident that the idea of inheritance is founded on that of the family, which in its turn is founded on the idea of an activity developing over things or in inter-personal relations; an activity which is referable to the principle of the person in himself, the beginning and base of every system of juristic relations.

§ 94. *Civil and Commercial Law.* Private law is civil and commercial. Commercial law is a form of private law that is properly connected with right of obligation, because its relations comprehend particular objects and means derived from the will of individuals in harmony with collective ends. Commercial law is needed because of the principles of civil life and special rules of trade to give facility, promptness, and security in commercial relations. It is special and not exceptional or privileged, applying to all acts of trade and to all merchants.

§ 95. *Public Law.* The family is the cellule of the State, the high and perfect human communion. Now we will first show the fundamental structure of the State and then its functions, its administration, or that action which more especially is taken over by the executive power and the government. It is the duty of the State to enforce the law against every act tending to violate its precepts. It is likewise its duty to determine the procedure, to declare the law in the interest of two contending parties, and to punish its infringement in the interest of society. From this it can be seen that the categories of public law, in the wide sense, are constitutional, administrative, penal, and judicial or procedural law. In a strict sense, public law contains the constitution and administration of the State. The law of procedure presupposes private law, public law, and penal law and is, therefore, the most complex. Penal law presupposes the organization of the State and all the statutes whose violation it regards. Administrative law is to constitutional law as function is to structure; but the most simple relations of public law are constitutional. This does not mean that no regard is paid to functions in constitutional theories. There are functions in such theories, but they are political. When it is said that constitutional law has for its object the structure of the State, while the administrative regards its functions, the structure is not excluded from the administration, but in a general way the constitutional law is made predominant statically, while administrative law is more dynamic.

§ 96. *International Law.* In general, international law controls interstate relations, or the relations between the citizens of one State and those of another, dividing itself thus into public and private law. Public international law embraces the categories of international persons, their possessions, obligations, and actions. The right of action is one with the right of war which includes the subjects of debate between States and the methods of eliminating and resolving them, together with the rights of neutrality and peace. At this point, we may notice the progress from what is less complex to that which is more complex, because war presupposes the normal condition of peace, the existence of rights of property and obligation between different States founded upon their personality. Private international law follows logically public international law, because the relations of individuals belonging to different nations are based on the highest principles of the common natures of the peoples,· their coexistence and solidarity. It cannot be believed that private international law should exist prior to public international law for the same reasons which prove the antecedence of private law to public law. Yet we cannot admit the similarity of international private law with private law in an absolute sense; that is, allow international private law to antedate national public law. Private law is essentially domestic. It is enacted by the legislators of each State, while international private law is foreign. One is actuated by the general will of the people; the other demands the express or tacit consent of another people for its application. Private law varies with diverse national consciousness; private international law tends to establish identical norms for the decision of contests about the applicability of statutes or laws foreign to the nation.

§ 97. *The Tri-division of Gaius and Justinian.* A last observation on the tri-division of private law made by Gaius and emphasized by Justinian: "Omne jus quo utimur vel ad personas vel ad res vel ad actiones pertinet." It has been many times pointed out that this is of no rational value, because it is not based upon the essential character of juridical relations and has the vice of including the family relations in the personal rights, inheritance in the property rights, and procedure in the law of actions. The tri-division, however, has no small historical value in relation to the legal divisions of the sources antedating the Institutes. The First Table of the Decemvirs has a certain number of rules of procedure, "De in jus vocando." The Pretorian Edicts begin with a title on the same subject, " De actione danda." The Digest begins with some general propositions of law and then furnishes the nomenclature and description of divers imperial officers with jurisdiction, coming thus 'to the fourth title of the second book with the same subject as the first table of the decemvirs, " De in jus vocando." As can be seen the sources begin where the tri-division of Gaius and Justinian ends. Maine in his book already mentioned[1] pursues the similarities between these and the monuments of primitive law and shows the great similarity on this point, because the "Lex Salica" begins speaking of citations and exhibits in a court of justice. The Irish law is marked by the extraordinarily large part devoted to procedure whose principle is the original act of giving jurisdiction through agreement, by transcribing it before a judge. The codes of Manu and Nerada speak first of the judges and procedure and only later of law and the matters which can be the subject of litigation. It cannot be doubted that in the beginning the constitution of the judicature and procedure were things of capital importance, because it was necessary to establish custom in order to bring men to obedience and to form the fibres of a legal sense. The idea of punishment and the judge had great effect upon the consciousness of peoples at the dawn of civilization. When the habit of obedience was once formed, the control of law established, the social company gotten together, the mind developed, the idea of punishment and the judge became addictions,

[1] *Cf.* "Early Law and Customs," cit. § 39.

as Bentham would say, to the paragon of juridical relations *per se*, a great sustainer of substantive law.   The
tri-division of Gaius represents this second phase and
shows an idealistic progress over the old legal order.

CHAPTER VII

CRITICAL ANALYSIS OF THE PRINCIPAL DEFINITIONS OF THE LAW

THE DOCTRINES THAT GIVE PREFERENCE TO THE SENSIBLE
CONTENT OF LAW: HOBBES, SPINOZA, ROUSSEAU, STUART MILL
AND SPENCER. — THE DOCTRINES THAT CONSIDER LAW AS AN
ABSTRACT RATIONAL FORM: KANT, FICHTE, AND HERBART. —
THE DEFINITIONS OF KRAUSE AND OF TRENDELENBURG. — THE
TRUTH OF THE DOCTRINES EXAMINED.

§ 98.   *Two Kinds of Definitions.*   The principal physiological definitions of law have reference either to its
sensible content or its rational form.   Among the first
we must place the definitions of Hobbes, Spinoza,
Rousseau, the utilitarians, and the positivists; among
the second, those of Kant and Herbart.[1]   All these
definitions show but one factor characteristic of the
idea of the law fully understood.

§ 99.   *Hobbes's Definition of the Law.*   Hobbes, following Bacon, states that there can be nothing except
matter and motion; and that thought is exchangeable
with feeling; and that the phenomena of our internal
economy are explicable by the laws of association.
His ethical concept, developed in "De Cive" and "The
Leviathan," relies upon the tendency of self-preservation
as the basis of the duties of justice, gratitude, and
piety; by the fulfillment of which duties the general
struggle of man against man is avoided.   In the state
of nature, when everyone had a right to everything, and

[1] *Cf.* § 111 *infra.*

therefore there was a general struggle of man against man, force was the method of decision. In this state there were no duties because there was no certainty of reciprocity. Limitless fear, the tendency to self-preservation, and the need for the protection of honor, forced man to a fundamental agreement out of which arose an absolute power to determine the honest and just, which was later given sanction through religious beliefs. Law, therefore, according to Hobbes, is not in itself an ethical principle but an external means, like ethics, for the termination of the terrible war in which all men were engaged. In the last analysis, it brings back the thought of Thrasimachus, who reduced justice to the power of the strongest without understanding its true value or moral nature. Plato opposed Thrasimachus and showed that power *per se* is brought into play to defend the weak, giving as an example the power of the doctor over his patient and the captain over those who are on his ship. Although the theory of Hobbes shows a certain high character in emphasizing the protection of honor, yet it establishes the predominance of instinct aided by calculation in ethics, and derives law from the mind oppressed by passion, endeavoring to build up a legal union through the blind influences of weakness or fear. Surely law should not be weak, — mere scales without the sword. It should have force; which does not lead us to believe that its essence is cowardly intimidation. Hobbes deserves credit, however, for having put in evidence the side of law which refers to the protection of the ethical and social elements of human nature.

§ 100. *Spinoza's Definition of Law.* The definition of Spinoza, given in his "Ethica Ordine Geometrico Demonstrata," and the "Tractatus Theologico-Politicus," approaches on one side very closely to Hobbes's theory. Thought and extension are unified by Spinoza in one indifferent and active point in substance, as the "causa sui;" he holds that all develops in these two infinite attributes and distinguishes them from the universe or "natura naturata," whose particular objects are simple methods and objects of imagination. Substance is God. Substance is absolute and cannot be determined by anything except itself and is, therefore, free. God alone is free, and not man, who does not exist through the exclusive necessity of his nature, but is a method and as such is limited and determined by other methods. Man is a natural force with the illusion of freedom. Passion, desire, and appetite rule his actions. Law is not born of reason, but of appetite. Law is the power of the nature of man, — a force similar to that by which everything exists and perseveres in its existence. The power of nature is the same as the law of nature. God can do everything and has right over everything. In the human struggle, growing out of the passions, the power of one man is neutralized by that of another and in this way is annulled, and there is no security. The union arises from the need of saving one's own power which increases in the union itself as the right increases. The State, the greatest union, appears omnipotent and tends to guarantee secure coexistence. So in this theory law is not an ethical principle but grows out of the tendency of self-preservation acting through force, mechanical causality, and natural power, aided by agreement. Here, too, the State is an absolute empire with the object of ending the struggle of men divided by cupidity and passion. Natural power, as such, cannot be law, although it can accompany it in its development and render it efficacious, especially if aided by agreement. Law gains strength in its concreteness when realized in a union, "vis unita fortior," but Spinoza, although self-contradictory, gives some conceptions which correct the doctrine before emphasized and fully conform to the truth. It is only just to give them and to notice them as De Tullio did in "Il Concetto del Diritto Secondo Spinoza," because they represent precious germs of truth. If, on one hand, Spinoza denies the freedom of man, on the other he is constrained to admit it, because man is body and mind, and as mind is not destructible, participating in ,the eternity of substance, referring all things to God, and thinking them in Him. He is capable of controlling his passions, desires, and appetites, and approaches nearer to God the more he extends his control over them and raises and purifies his will. At this point man attains his end; his "acquiescentia" and his will are free as those of God. "Hinc sequitur quod Deus quatenus seipsum amat homines amat et consequenter quod amor Dei erga homines et mentis erga Deum amor intellectualis unum et idem est." The same conception of the freedom of the soul and of its union with God is developed by Bruno in "Eroici Furori." Law, in this new phase of Spinoza's thought, is not a natural and mechanical power but a "potentia" by which man approaches his rational end, which end is attainable in the common life and the State, which is a communion founded on reason. "Animorum unio concipi nulla ratione posset nisi civitas id ipsum maxime intendat quod sana ratio omnibus hominibus utile esse docet." Spinoza adds, "finis ergo rei publicæ revera libertas est."

§ 101. *Rousseau's Definition of Law.* Rousseau, in "Le Contrat Social," starts out with the principle of inalienable liberty. With such a principle he resolves the problem of finding a kind of political union in which freedom is not alienable and each man in obeying the State obeys himself with a complete and reciprocal renunciation of all individual rights in favor of the community; whence the general will to which the will of all or the particular wills are subjected by free agreement, and the inalienable, indivisible, and non-representative sovereignty are formed.   The general will manifested by the majority of votes is the source of law, and therefore law is reducible to the decision of the majority.   Now the general will of Rousseau not being intrinsically connected with reason, the supreme ethical idea becomes license or the pleasure of the mob, very different from that constant measure or proportion of advantages, founded on the moral nature of man, which is law.   Under this aspect, Rousseau's definition has to do with the sensible content of the law.   What is true in this definition is that the "reipublicæ sponsio," as the Romans say, when they declare the conception of the law or the will of the greater number, is the concrete and effective expression of the law in the life of the people.

§ 102.   *The   Utilitarian   Definition   of   Law.*   The Sophists, Eudoxus, Epicurus, Helvetius, Bentham, and Stuart Mill are the greatest representatives of utilitarianism.   They try to find moral truths and justice in pleasure and pain and to reach the general interest by starting out with particular interests.   Hobbes and Locke showed the same tendencies although they are not usually cited as utilitarian philosophers.   It is to Stuart Mill that we owe a truly scientific exposition of this system which he adopted.   He denies in his book "Utilitarianism" that morality is based on rational and *a priori* elements, and follows the empirical and inductive theory, based on the sense of pleasure.   When this is generalized, it constitutes the idea of utility; the only object which experience adds to conduct is happiness, or an existence free from pain and rich in enjoyments both qualitatively and quantitatively. The proof of the quality of enjoyments and the measure of their quantity are found in the preference given by those who, through opportunity and their own aptitude, are best furnished with means of comparison. Happiness is the true and only good. Virtue itself is first desired as a means of happiness and then is desired on its own account, in the same way that man begins by doing a kindness to his fellow-being for recompense but later goes on through habit. Complete happiness, however, cannot be attained except by the accord of private and public interest. Individual utility cannot be developed largely or securely without the aid of one's fellow-beings, without the help of all. General utility is the condition necessary for the development of the private utility, and is at the same time its protection. From this comes the distinction of good and bad actions, depending on whether they promote or oppose the happiness of all. This knowledge grows gradually, and in the same way moral sentiment makes its appearance, whose elements are the instinctive desire to live in harmony with one's fellow-beings, the conception of human solidarity and of the impossibility of an egoistic state, the habit of coöperation with others, and the influence of civilization. In civilization are found the principle of obligation and the basis of natural law. The idea of utility is not contradictory to that of justice, but the latter is part of the first. The etymology of the word justice, "jussum," shows that the genesis of such a notion is legislative prescription. The idea of a legal constitution precedes the idea of the just, whose content is the most stringent and imperative utility. It is true, therefore, that all cases of justice are cases of utility, but that the most impellent of them are those that are derived from the needs of man. The idea of justice includes three ideas, those of a certain conventionality of action, of law which punishes unconventional actions, and of a right given and protected by law to certain persons with a penalty for its violation. To this idea of justice, there corresponds a complex sentiment, the resultant of the impulse of self-defense and the tendency to sympathy. The first impulse gives rise to resentment for an offence offered us, the second causes a resentment for offences offered to others. We want the offender himself to suffer the harm that he has caused. Such sentiments, together with the three ideas, determine the penal restrictions of actions not conforming to general and particular utility.

§ 103. *Criticism of Stuart Mill's Definition.* The radical vice of this theory consists in deriving in logic everything by induction and in ethics everything from custom. It is well known that induction does not explain the necessity or universality of theoretical principles, and that habit is always a mechanical and unconscious conjunction of acts and cannot be productive of duty or ethical necessity. The pursuit of virtue for itself, disinterestedness and sacrifice, are in Stuart Mill's mind the result of mental habits. An obligation is the result of the continuous and energetic association of all the elements that compose moral sentiment. The accord between one's own advantage and that of another and of all, is the result of the same cause. The exclusive principle of ethics is the internal association of mental states, unaccompanied by intrinsic bonds of reason and regulated only by tendency to pleasure and aversion to pain. In fact, such spiritual enjoyments, as knowledge, freedom, and independence, are not desired for their substantial advantage but for their emotional force and likelihood of increasing one's pleasures. It seems that the preference of such advantages is for Stuart Mill a question of taste, which can be decided only by persons who have special experience in all kinds of enjoyment.   We may note that mental activities, cultivated for the enjoyment which they bring, can be corrupted because one is led to think too much, since thought brings pleasure.   It is necessary, however, to remember that Mill says clearly in places that the reason of the preference lies in the idea or sentiment of human dignity; that all men are able to appreciate and value these advantages, if they think. By such a confession, Mill leaves his system and shows an incoherence in introducing a principle superior to empirical eudemonism.   But Mill's thought wavers on this point, and even the value of the idea of human dignity and higher advantages depends upon the quality of sentiment; and this happens in the majority of cases; therefore the incoherence is not permanent. For Mill, the accord between private and general utility is not a fact, as Bentham thought, but a need created by an association of internal states, the basis of a progressive mental habit.   The obligation of seeking the good of all, together with one's own good, has no other base, and consequently moral and rational necessity are exchanged for psychological necessity.   But the problem of the passage from one's own good to that of another remains still unsolved, because pleasure, from which, by generalization, the idea of utility arises, is a state belonging absolutely to the person who feels it.   Pleasure is unstable and most variable, subject to indefinite modifications of the nervous system and of the fundamental senses.   One man's pleasure is not another's, and the same pleasure enjoyed repeatedly by the same subject is not identical.   In this way there is no passage from egoism to altruism.   Neither is it true that the whole appetitive nature of man is concentrated in pleasure alone and the original selfish tendencies, for instinct is an activity not preceded by pleasure when it first appears, and the inclination to live and re-live in others through love was never lacking to man. Law is the child of positive statutes and penalties for Mill, although its content emphasizes a superior principle. Imperative utility should in the last analysis be recognized by reason, because only the latter is competent to fix the "suum necessarium." But in the system of Mill the most stringent utility is valued by the quantity and degree of feeling and is the result of experiment and positive calculation on the part of the legislator. Of the two elementary and natural sentiments which compose justice, neither contains the exact measure or proportion, which constitutes law. The selfish impulse to render ill for ill is certainly not moral, neither is sympathy based on a constant and equal criterion varying in degree according to the relations of its subject with the person offended.

§ 104. *Utilitarianism is the Material of Law.* With all these vices, utilitarianism contains part of the truth, because utility, if not the principle, is certainly the content or matter of law, as the Italian school of philsophers and jurists have always taught. The Roman jurisconsults stated that "utilitas" is the substratum of the "jus civile," and the "jus publicum" is distinguished from the "jus privatum" because in the first the "publica utilitas" is important and in the second the "utilitas singulorum," but "utilitas" according to Pedius it only "bona occasio juris," since the base of the law is the "natura rerum," the "natura hominis," and the "naturalis ratio." Among the Romans, law, although conceived in this manner more practical than speculative, preserved a certain ethical character in all its phases, which was derived from the conception of the "æquum bonum, equitas, bona fides, boni mores," and on the nature of some of the institutions, such as that of the "prætura" and "censura morum." The scholiasts say that law should develop the "bonum" of "utile commune." In Bruno's mind, it should be lightened by the divine sun of truth and should tend towards the useful. Vico considers law as a proportion of utility. Romagnosi, agreeing with the Genovesi, Spedalieri, and Lampredi, defines law as a system of utility in conformity with moral order. Rosmini looks upon it as a eudemonistic faculty protected by moral laws.

§ 105. *Maine's Criticism of Utilitarianism.* Maine disagrees with the historical theory of Bentham according to which the different societies modified their laws in conformity to their changed ideas of general utility, because utility is a potent but not the only cause of change, which is effected by the influence of new ideas and sentiments which are distinct from utilitarian conceptions and tendencies. The criticism of Maine that new ideas and sentiment are referable always to a new form of understanding and conception of utility is true, and bears consideration and the light of a strong examination. Certainly all men and societies desire the good, and if the good is wanted by itself and confused with the useful, there would be no method of distinguishing and recognizing that special system called utilitarianism. Utilitarianism is a kind of hedonism. It understands the good only or principally in its sensible aspect and measures it by the quality and quantity of the consequence produced by its effectuation. Maine disagrees, on other grounds, with the utilitarianism of Bentham as an ethico-juristic system, and believes that its adoption in the realm of legislation implies no necessity to receive it in that of morals; that one can be utilitarian in legislation and non-utilitarian in morals, contradiction or no contradiction. But here Bentham is right and Maine is wrong. Nevertheless, it can be observed that the non-utilitarian in ethics is obliged in the study of law by the very nature of the object of his attention to regard utility as the material and the "bona occasio juris."

§ 106. *Spencer's Evolution.* Spencer in "The Data of Ethics" admits with Bentham and Stuart Mill that the end of conduct is happiness or utility, but does not follow their method. The method of these two philosophers is inductive. But Spencer points out that the norms of conduct will never be scientific if we cannot learn by deduction the method and reason why one fact is the necessary derivative of another. Experience teaches that some actions bring good and others evil, and indicates the norms of action, but it tells nothing about the method or reason for this derivation. We must start from a principle upon which we can base all the facts of the physical and moral life of man and all living beings. This principle is the persistency of force. Every being tends to preserve its share of force and to react against the elements of disturbance. The capacity of beings to assemble and get enjoyment grows in direct ratio to their capacity of self-adaptation to external circumstances. The adaptation is, however, the law of conduct. The end of all the acts of sensate beings is the conservation of their individual and racial life and coexistence. Conduct cannot be perfect in respect to the first two ends if it is not so in respect to the third, which represents the mutual aid of one's fellow-beings. Only in the human race is the harmony of these three ends fully developed, and so the accord between the individual and the general good is an unavoidable consequence of biological laws. Man and his conduct are the last product of many adaptations

between internal and external forces. No one can marvel
at it when he thinks how closely ethical and physical laws
are bound together. From impressions are born sensations
and reflexive actions; the sensations are pleasant or
painful, and man as a sensate being tends to prolong
the duration of the former and stop the latter. It was
found pleasant to live together, so the great utility of
it was discovered. The social inclination was formed,
and through long custom and heredity it was trans-
muted into an instinct. From the social instinct
come all the emotions known under the general
name of sympathy. Sympathy is agreement and
coöperation which renders the greatest development
of individual existence possible. From such an impulse arise actions which demand complex representation, while actions born of selfishness have immediate
objects; that is, the enjoyment of present pleasure and
the shunning of imminent ills, and, therefore, presuppose
simple representation. To the series of selfish motives
dependent upon social conditions, such as the fear of
revenge, law, or public opinion, there comes another
order of motives consisting in the consequences of actions
not accidental or extrinsic but natural: for example,
grief, shame, the harm of one's neighbor, his well-
being, without regard to one's own utility. The complexity of these motives of growth, habit, and heredity
constitutes the moral sentiment which is free of the
motives which are founded on a kind of authority.
Sympathy increases the more we see the pleasures of
our fellow-beings and the more society changes from
warlike to industrial. In the first ages society was preoccupied with its own existence and took only secondary care of the development of the individual, so busy
was it in the war and struggle for self-preservation.
Later it became industrial, since its life was less threat-

ened and its existence assured; and it now has for its immediate purpose the protection of individual activities in the diverse spheres of labor.   Thus human conduct ends by being governed by an egoistical altruism.

§ 107.   *Criticism of Spencer's Theory.*   The first observation which occurs to the student of Spencer's theories is that inductive or deductive utilitarianism is substantially the same, showing, that is, a prevalence of the inclination of the senses over reason contrary to the intrinsic order and real value of beings.   If it meets the approval of many, it is because it conforms more with what men are wont to be than with what they should be.   The simple appetitive tendency to the pursuit of pleasure and avoidance of pain can never, through habit, heredity, or in general by the greatest variable adaptation, be changed into moral law and obligation. In the first place, all these factors lack the character of necessity and universality of ethical law and obligation; characteristics which mere reflection cannot give and which are not found by the mind in searching the depth of its essence.   Association and adaptation do not lead us out of the sphere of psychological mental necessity.   And so in Spencer's system we can note what we have already pointed out in the theory of Mill:[1] that the obligation depends upon the greater efficiency of emotions, more complex and more representative; that is, on the quality of sentiment. Adaptation of itself cannot be the supreme law of human conduct, because, though it is true that morality is developed in the common life and should feel its influences, it is none the less true that it remains morality and is governed by the principles of the good as shown by reason, which furnishes the measure within which the individual advantage can be reconciled with general

[1] *Cf.* § 103 *ante.*

utility, considering the special conditions of the individual and society. The limits, however, cannot be fixed entirely by circumstances; neither can they be entirely external. The doctrine of adaptation is not capable of developing the real ethical initiative which foreruns the ages and emphasizes higher ideals to be effected, because it has a political character and proclaims conduct good which tends to another's happiness in a measure compatible with the individual interest in the given social conditions. Neither does it solve the problem of the change of pleasure into general utility, because pleasure preserves always its selfish and exclusive character, which cannot be tempered or modified except by a higher principle. Spencer renders the accord between the two antagonistic poles of private and public interest objective, and transforms the interweaving of the three ends of the preservation of the individual, the development of the species, and coexistence, into a natural law of life. But he does not succeed by this in creating the ethical necessity which is the only production of thought. In order to attain the idea of duty and right the reason must advance and develop, and it cannot be converted or debased into a calculation of utility dependent upon the tendency of the senses. All the utilitarians, modern positivists, and materialists place the foundation of law in the fact of life, in the organic demand of the species and the social instinct, and do not succeed, therefore, in giving a true explanation of its principle. Nobody doubts that the needs of life, as well as the useful, are a matter of morals and law, and that social instinct, common belief, habit, and heredity, which form the great connective tissue of civil existence, are the conditions of justice and virtue. The question is of the form of these elements and their principles, which are not found outside of reason. The ancients talked about a primal law intended for the satisfaction of the immediate needs of life, for self-preservation, the union of man and woman, procreation, and the support of children. In the primal law, that is, that of the "antecedents of nature," according to the Stoics, man wishes his own existence, as Vico says. They emphasize, however, a "secondary or derivative law," the same as "consequents of nature" of the Stoics, in which reason was the controlling faculty and man desires knowledge, as Vico says. Whence this part of natural law (it is the Neapolitan philosopher whom we quote) is more immediate and rules the first, giving it its firmness. In this distinction, we can see again the Aristotelean difference between what is first in respect to us and what is first in nature. Sense is first in respect to us, and reason in respect to nature. Now we must find the principle, the fundamental, which is first *per se*.

§ 108. *Spencer's Sub-human Justice.* Spencer has developed his ethico-juristic conception in a recent book, "Justice." Following his theory of connecting moral laws with the most general laws of the cosmos, and of rendering ethics more deductive, he begins by speaking of a morality of animals and a sub-human justice. Moral and human conduct is a part of conduct in general, that is, of the sum total of the acts of various beings which are adapted to their own purposes. Among animals, the more perfect conduct tends to a longer, more ample and complete life, and is connected with the two principles which insure the continuance of the species. The first is the natural protection of offspring not able to take care of themselves. The second is that the adult himself should realize all the advantages and disadvantages of his acts. Sub-human justice means that every individual is subject to the consequences of his nature and con-

dition. It advances as organization progresses. The
primal law for all being is that of the relationship
between conduct and its consequences. Then comes
the other law (fundamentally the same) of common
life, since it prescribes limitations. The second law
orders that the acts through which an individual
seeks advantages and avoids disadvantages should be
limited by the necessity of leaving the way free to
similar acts on the part of his associates. There is
a third law which restricts the application of the first
and in certain circumstances sacrifices the individual
for the species. Human justice is the development of
sub-human justice. Fundamentally and essentially both
are of the same nature, parts of a whole. In general,
justice is characterized by self-subordination to the
bonds of relationship, of social limitations, and of the
health of the species or community. Among the social
sentiments, which are the product of evolution, is found
the sentiment of justice. Justice is the extirpation
of selfish sentiments which arise when an animal
resists the restrictions put upon the acts of his spontaneous life, and can become the object of altruistic
sentiments which presuppose the more or less ample
development of sympathy and are connected more
properly with the régime of voluntary coöperation.
But before the development of the true altruistic sentiment of justice there are sentiments "pro-altruistic"
that constitute the conditions of its development and
contain its germs; for example, the fear of retaliation,
hate, revenge, and pain. The sentiment of justice
cannot fail to have a close relation with the idea of justice which is its criterion. Such an idea has two elements,
one positive and one negative. The first is freedom,
which creates inequality, because every individual
should be treated unequally if he has a different degree

of merit; the negative element is the limitation of the sphere of everyone's activity, by which every individual is considered as the equal of every other. The fundamental principles of law, which are entirely included by the idea of justice, are not fruits of induction, but are *a priori* truths — experience inherited from hundreds of generations. Empirical utilitarianism exaggerates the force of induction and cannot grasp any of its primal ideas, which it is forced to presuppose. The idea of the sum total of happiness to which individual and collective man should tend, and that of the equal rights of all to happiness, are not deductive but *a priori*. Positive laws are made on these principles of justice.

§ 109. *Criticism of Spencer's Sub-human Justice.* Spencer's "Justice" does not alter his theories as contained in "The Data of Ethics." Consequently the criticisms apply equally to both books. If obligations cannot be born of appetitive tendency, habit, heredity, or psychological association, it surely cannot be derived from animality. A moral animal is not conceivable, because an animal does not understand an obligation with its necessity.and universality, which are born only of reason. It is the reason of man, furnished with knowledge and free will, that recognizes the coördination of individuals and the necessities of life, conceived even by Spencer as the substratum of morals and law. Obligation is the very necessity of things known, valued, and desired by man. What is called the duty of the animal is nonsense, because the animal has no true knowledge or free will. By this loose expression the organic demand or the effect of habit and domestication is often described. There is no sub-human justice, because justice is a virtue. It is a habit of realizing, through knowledge and free will, the rational law of the proportion of advantages belonging to human nature considered *per se* and in its methods of individualization, regarded in individual, social, and collective forms. Obligation and justice are facts brought out in evolution and do not effectively appear before man and human social life. Both, as emergent and not resultant facts, are specific products; they have their own characters and principles, which only in an abstract and indeterminate manner can be reduced to the common characters and universal laws of the cosmos. The egoistic and altruistic sentiments of justice are founded on human nature as the two elements of the idea of justice, which are freedom and the reciprocal limitations of personal activities, are founded on it. The feeling of an animal impeded in the development of its energies, and the indignation of a man deprived of his, are different. Different is the altruistic sentiment of species and the sentiment which arises from the knowledge of the identity of nature between men and the bonds of union; that is, the coöperation of intellects and wills. Explicable freedom is certainly a principle distinct and more elevated than animal energy, than sense of self and spontaneity. The restrictions or limitations on the life of members of an animal species are not at all like the system of bonds inherent in human existence. Spencer makes the mistake of confusing facts and ideas which belong to different orders of evolution because he cannot see the specific differentiation of the evolutionary movement. He confuses organic demands, blind and fatal tendencies of nature, and strictly natural adaptation, with duties, virtues, and purely human facts. The characters and potentialities of human nature are placed by him in the anterior grades of evolution. He compares the instinctive protection of offspring and the conduct of the adult animal, gifted with foresight, with the intelligent love for one's descendants raised to a duty, and with freedom, the source of responsibility.   We can observe here that abuse of analogy and arbitrary anticipation of elements and attitudes which we have noted on the subject of the explanation of knowledge.[1]   Finally we must point out that Spencer goes back to the definition of law given by Kant.   He says that the coincidence of his thought with Kant's is entirely due to chance.   In 1850, when he wrote "Social Statics," he did not know of Kant's book on the principle of law, whose existence he discovered many years after.   The only real difference between Kant and Spencer is this: Kant does not look, in his desire to define law, beyond the abstract conception of the human world, while Spencer discovers a moral animal and a sub-human justice.   Kant could in no wise recognize this projection of ethics, as we shall see later on.[2]

§ 110.   *Reason is a Result of Evolution.*   There can be no doubt that morals presuppose biology and association.   Association raises the powers of life and becomes the immediate condition of a fact of a higher order; that is, of historical development.   History is the life of the human race.   It is the evolution of the nature of man in that it leads thought, the great dynamic factor in the world of nations.   Now adaptation to existent social conditions is not all of ethics, even for the positivists, who recognize historical progress and a tendency to come nearer to the idea of the perfection of human life.   Ethics for them are a practical science which seeks not only the laws of moral facts but determines the best means of modifying them in order to attain a perfection not yet existing.   This renovative and perfective work of ethics represents emancipation from nature and from the control of existing facts,

[1] *Cf.* § 28 *ante.*
[2] *Cf.* § 111 *infra.*

as Angiulli points out. It makes for freedom. Mechanical necessity and chance take away all moral value from
our actions. In the very conception of a scientific determinism is included the power of inherent variation.
Such a power is at first natural and then is transformed
into conscious activity directed towards an end in the
progress of social life. As historical experiences and the
influences of culture increase, the power of changing
the motive of actions by valuing the present state in
respect to an ideal future increases both in the individual and in society. And here is the real root of
freedom. But freedom is not fully understood without
cognitive activity and reflection, which constitute and
increase the proper energy of the subject in moments of
impulse. Freedom is based on reason which is explained
by the accumulation of historical experiences but which
is not their simple result or sum.

§ 111. *Kant's Definition of Law.* Kant's definition
of law is one of those which refer to the abstract rational form, as we have said before,[1] and we will
now add, those of his follower Fichte, and of Herbart,
belong to this class. Kant points out that knowledge
is a complex fact, a resultant of sensible and intellectual
elements, and that it must be considered in its integrity
and not in one of its parts, as Locke and Leibnitz have
regarded it. Locke desires to solve the problem of
knowledge keeping but one part, sense, in view. Leibnitz, on the other hand, bases all his theory on the
other factor of mind. Knowledge, or experience, is possible according to Kant by means of simple concepts
applicable to empirical intuitions. These concepts are
not innate, beautiful and made, but constitute original
functions of the mind, and are cognitive activity of
our spirit. They are called categories, and are not born

[1] *Cf.* § 98 *ante.*

from experience because they are the strongholds in which phenomena are collected; that is, things as they appear to us. They are the functions not of concrete and empirical knowledge, which continually changes, but of always identical transcendental knowledge; that is, of the "I think." Experience, therefore, presupposes the categories, which render thought possible. If such is the nature of experience, the mind does not know things in themselves, as noumena, but as they appear; that is, as phenomena. Kant, in his "Kritik der Reinen Vernunft," attacks the problem of knowledge which is reducible to two primal elements, sensation and *a priori* functions. In his "Kritik der Praktischen Vernunft" he attacks the problem of morality which lies in the two termini of the promptings of the senses and in moral law. He, above all, casts aside all the practical principles which make the motive of ethical determination lie in matter. In conformity with these practical principles, the value of moral actions is measured by their consequences, and by a calculation of their result. The only motive of will is pleasure, and the basis of ethics is purely empirical. The heteronomic systems which deduce origins from such principles (for example, hedonism and utilitarianism) cannot explain moral, necessary, and universal law because founded on empirical terms which of their nature are accidental and particular. Thus a heteronomic system is always constructed when a rational element is raised to a principle (for example, when happiness, in its broad sense and in harmony with the higher faculties of man, is made a principle), because an action is fulfilled for an extrinsic eudemonistic reason or an empirical motive, and virtue becomes the result of a maxim of practical prudence. True morality, for Kant, demands a will that is self-ruling by purely formal laws. Will can give laws to itself because it is free and independent of the determining causes in the world of the senses. The property which the will has to give itself laws, separating itself from extrinsic objects, is autonomy. Autonomous will, the indispensable condition of morality, is that which is determined by itself at every point, which is self-sufficient and does not look to foreign objects. Law, therefore, is born of the will and at the same time it alone immediately determines the will, because it is pure form. Moral principles, according to Kant, notes Chiappelli, in "Sul Carattere Formale del Principio Etico," should be a common law valid for all rational natures. It should be universal and necessary as well and have an imperative character, not hypothetically imperative based upon the convenience of actions to their ends and consequences, but categorically and absolutely so. Law lies in what will has determined, not for an external end but with regard to the harmony and utility of which the law consists. Law must be unconditionally obeyed, but in knowledge categories have no value unless they are applied to intuition. The ego would not be blind without categories, not vain without intuitions. Kant unifies these two terms, and places the possibility of cognition regarded as a whole in the principle of the original synthetic unity of the intuitions and categories, of sense and intellect. In the moral field, the two terms are absolutely contrary. They do not agree, and form has value without being applied to empirical data. Hence the lack of harmony between practical and theoretical reason. Cognition is essentially phenomenal and relative. It does not touch things in themselves. Free will alone urges us towards the noumenon, the supra-sensible reality which is not known as an object and cannot be brought into existence in the practical order. By such a method there arise, as

postulates of practical reason, that is, as the demands
of moral consciousness but not as knowledge, the three
concepts of freedom, the immortality of the soul, and
of God.   Pure reason contains some antinomies which
destroy their theoretical value.   Having premised these
considerations, we can say that Kant deserves great
credit for having determined the ethical principle in its
greatest purity, and for having given duty an uncondi-
tional and absolute value.   Kant's ethics are constructive
and imperative, differing from the ethics of the ancients,
which were realistic and descriptive, founded on external
elements of nature and custom.

§ 112.   *Kantian Ethics*.   The ethics of Kant are
abstract and formal because moral law, duty, and
the autonomy of will lack concrete content.   Man
is not only reason but sense and appetite as well, yet in
the doctrines of Kant he is looked upon entirely as
reason which proudly throws off all allegiance to every
inclination of sense.   In fact, will is autonomous when
it does not remain indeterminate but enters the lists
against desire, passion, and interests to conquer and
transform them to reason.   True autonomy is the result of the active energy of the will and does not consist in simple abstraction.   Aristotelean eudemonism
and Kantian formalism are logically connected in the idea
of the perfection of human nature.   Eudemonism gives
us the content, and the imperative category, the form.
Happiness in such a conciliation is not the empirical
principle of ethics argued against by Kant but the consequence of the necessity of subjecting instinct and interest to reason.   It is not true that all systems which give
a content to moral principles are founded on pleasure
and are reducible to egoism.   Human nature tends
towards its end.   The end is the good, the perfection
of man.   The end of man is his perfection or good,

and therefore law consists in his subordination of the
elements of sense to reason. This subordination once
realized, we have eudemon, happiness. Pleasure is the
necessary complement of perfect human activity and not
the motive of will. The idea of the end is derived from
the essential character of human nature, and therefore
is obligatory and constitutes the imperative category,
whose concreteness is shown by Kant when he says that
rational nature must be considered as ultimate and not
medial. The categorical imperative of Kant, containing the formal ethical principle, is of no avail. It decrees
that a right of action is convertible with law and can serve
as a rule of conduct in all times and places, but it does
not indicate what should be done. Every right of action
gives rise to a universal maxim, but from this it does not
follow that the action is moral. And if the maxim was
made universal, the action would not longer be possible,
and it is evident that a recourse would have to be had
to a calculation of the consequences, which is impractical.
Law, for example, prohibits a breach of promise; but
no promise would be possible if this law became a universal maxim. Kant himself argues in this manner
without reflecting that he looks to the consequence
of the act, which he should not do according to
his premise. Certainly universality is an essential mark
of the ethical principle, but does it constitute all its
origin or substance?

§ 113. *Kant's Morals are Abstract.* The abstraction
of the theory is seen as well under another aspect
studied by Chiappelli in the book cited.[1] Kant
bases all morality upon pure will understood in
itself and does not emphasize in the slightest its
concrete derivation. Aristotle, on the other hand,
understood that the end, the good and happiness, pre-

[1] *Cf.* "Sul Carattere Formale del Principio Etico," cit. § 111.

supposes autarchy which is obtained only in the common life and he, therefore, together with the other Greek philosophers, concluded that ethics were part of politics. According to him, morality is not possible without the interpenetration of individual consciousness with society. Kant, however, departs from this condition and stays within the confines of the subject itself, without regard to its concrete position. Aristotelean thought is to-day revived by the doctrine of evolution, based on the conception of ethics as part of politics, and tries to explain morality as a natural formation due to a coming together of natural, spiritual, hereditary, historical, and social causes. Evolutionary ethics gets its data from moral consciousness, explains the concrete genesis of moral facts, but cannot solve the problem of morality. The apriority of moral laws is very different from apriority in biology, history, or heredity. Moral law is necessary and universal, and as such cannot be the result of experience. But as the apriority of the forms of intuitions and categories of the mind do not exclude the formation of empirical knowledge, so the evolutionary and ethical explanation of the concrete and historical genesis of morality reduced to the proportions of a doctrine, or their data about moral consciousness, can be accepted as the complement of the theory of the possibility of the ethical act and of the nature of the moral principle lying in the purpose of man.

§ 114. *Kant's Idea of Law is Abstract.* The idea of law is formal in the theory of Kant. Law, for him, is the sum of the conditions of coexistence — of the will of everyone with the will of all through a universal law of freedom. But of what this sum and this universal law consist in their concreteness is not told by Kant. Law becomes thus a purely abstract principle, that takes no account of the real

historical relations of the order of things. Rosmini
makes four observations about the Kantian theory of
law.   The first is: Whoever wishes law to consist in the
possibility of the coexistence of persons does not make
enough of the element of the rectitude of action.   There
could be an action wrong under the laws of nature promotive of coexistence, to which no one would have a
right since there is no faculty for doing evil.   The second
can be formulated as follows: Even when all the sum
of the illicit actions would effectively destroy coexistence they would not be illicit only on that account.
The failure to detract from coexistence is not the con-
stitutive part of the rectitude of actions and law but is
the sign of it, the very mark of universality.   It is the
"principium cognoscendi," not the "principium essendi."
The third is: Universality is equivocal and needs interpretation, because it is either absolute universality, in which
case, however licit the act, if done by all men, it
would destroy coexistence; for example, if everybody undertook to make shoes, who would remain to
cultivate the earth? — or it is relative to the circumstances of the man in question, and no iniquitous action
would destroy coexistence although it were permitted
to all men in the same circumstances, because the
condition would never be renewed.   Finally, and this is
the fourth observation: It cannot be said that if any
action is clearly licit and not harmful to coexistence
that it should, therefore, be left free to all men; a requisite
condition for it to constitute a right.   A father can
hinder the most licit actions of a son through his paternal
rights, though those actions, become universal, would not
destroy existence.   These actions of the son cannot, however, be called, in relation to the father, true rights.
Logically, coexistence and limitation of freedom are the
results of the realization of the rational measure or

proportion of advantages, but do not form its essence. For Kant, the State has no other mission than to regulate the coexistence of freedom, and looks only to acts of protection; that is, to law and police. It nevertheless represents, for the German philosopher, a necessity of reason because though born, it is true, of contract, it is not arbitrary, since man acquires true liberty, equality, and independence in the State, as he says. This conception contains in itself the germ of the correction of the theory and assigns to the State the restricted finality of mere protection of persons and goods. Likewise, looking deeply into the formal categorical imperative itself, we find traces of something positive, or the principle of the will as the supreme and absolute purpose which demands respect for the person and liberty for all.

§ 115. *Fichte's Definition of Law.* The idea of law under the aspect of conditionality is developed still more in the school of Kant by the work of Fichte in "Grundlage des Naturrechts." He states that the ego should recognize itself as free essence; that is, should limit its liberty by the conception of another's liberty. The juridical relation is that which extends between two rational beings by which each limits his freedom through the notion of the freedom of the other on condition that the other limits his. Formalism is here manifest because it always remains to be determined of what the positive and supreme principle consists from which the law as a possibility of the limitation of free essence is derived. The very imperative of Fichte's "Be Free" is formal, since freedom is formal. Moral action, which for Kant is based on conformity to necessary and universal law, is derived for Fichte by the action of the ego through conviction, and succeeds through a reciprocal enthusiasm and excitement in so working. But Fichte does not say in what this conviction lies, or rather he does not indicate its content, because it becomes a condition of morality. According to Kant, juridical freedom is from its birth limited by universal freedom; for Fichte it has its origin in the individual real existence of the ego and lies in the right of the rational being to advance as the only cause in the world of the senses, and is of itself as unlimited as the coercive faculty which adheres to it. If it was not that one ego must admit another, it would attribute to itself unlimited power, and therefore would spontaneously moderate its own power when it limited the power of others by its own.   In the rational being, there is love of duty for duty's sake, a love of self and of one's co-citizens *per se*.   One is called a tendency and is absolutely obligatory, and the other is called a power and has not the same character because it is reducible to unlimited freedom, which excludes every law.   Such subjectivism and ethical relativism is a direct consequence of Fichte's system.

§ 116. *Herbart's Definition.*   Herbart states that philosophy is nothing but an elaboration of the concepts.   Philosophy is divided into logic, metaphysics, and æsthetics.   Logic works for the formal clearness of the concept and pays no attention to their content. Metaphysics, for its part, is occupied with the content, and clears the concepts of the contradictions in which they are involved, makes them whole, and gives them their justification.   Æsthetics include the series of concepts and judgments that are referable to particular states of mind, to pleasure and pain. Between theoretical and æsthetic judgments there is this difference: that the first give the cognition of things and look to their value, and the second do not consider the value and are limited to showing their pleasure and pain.   Many of the æsthetic judgments

are made by ethical judgments which approve or dis-
approve of actions. Ethics entering into æsthetics
cannot understand any imperative because an imperative always implies a duty to do or to abstain from doing
something. Morality is therefore a formal concept and
cannot be reduced to an imperative, as Kant taught, but
is reducible to five practical model ideas; the idea of
freedom (the accord of the will with its own motives),
the idea of perfection (the harmony between the
extension and intension of our volitive activity), the
idea of benevolence (the agreement between one's own
will and the wills of others), the idea of law (the harmony of several wills in respect to an object for the
prevention of a contest), and the idea of equity (the
accord between merit arid recompense). If all these
forms of accord are present, there will be an ethical judgment of approval, and if not there will be one of disapproval. Such models act also as motives. From
the five practical ideas come five social ideas: from the
idea of perfection comes the system of education, from
benevolence the administrative system, from law comes
the juristic system, from equity the system of retribution. Now it is evident that the doctrine of Herbart,
shown in his "Allgemeine Praktische Philosophie," is
founded on the most exaggerated and absolute formalism excluding every substantial content from the ethical
principle. Ethics are deprived of the duty of action.
They lack nomology and exist only in the sphere of æsthetics or sensibility and formal harmony. Without doubt,
law with its prescriptions tends to prevent and eliminate
disagreements and struggles. But it cannot be reduced
to a simple norm for their avoidance, because it is an
energy which passes from one phase to another and tends
to maintain a determinate figure and meet the obstacles
in its path. Law has not a true æsthetic character

apart from the struggle which is its life. True beauty
does not arise from adherent elements, but from the
depth of the soul, from effort and activity. Accord
and harmony are abstract forms of law, or rather the
consequence of its realization, like, in that, to coexistence, but they cannot possibly constitute its principle.
Law, struggling and conquering opposition, establishes
peace, and the peace which succeeds the war against
injustice on the one hand increases the force of law
itself, which becomes a power more to be feared, and on
the other confers upon it greater splendor and beauty.

§ 117. *The Definitions of Krause and Ahrens.* In
the definitions given by Krause in "Abriss des Systems
der Philosophie des Rechts oder des Naturrechts,"
and by Ahrens in "Naturrecht oder Philosophie des
Rechts," the principal defect lies in including all the
essence of law in the single conception of conditionality.
In fact, Krause and Ahrens, defining law as the organic
complexity of free conditions for the harmonious fulfillment of the destiny of man, show but one aspect, the conditional, and degrade law to the point of representing
it as a simple collection of means. Certainly, law offers
man the conditions of life and development, and protects his advantages, but it must also be considered as
the realization of the principle of good, and therefore
under the higher aspect as a participant in uncondi-
tionality. Geyer in "Geschichte und der System der
Rechtsphilosophie in Grundzügen" thinks that Trendelenburg's definition is like the definition of Krause
when the former says that law is the complexity of the
universal determinations of action, which render possible the preservation and perfection of human society
in the form of an ethical whole and its particular parts.
Geyer is right if these universal determinations of action
are understood as conditions necessary for its realiza-

tion, as Trendelenburg himself says, followed by Ulrici in "Das Naturrecht"; that is, that it is ethical in dealing with national law, with the power proper to an organic whole.   But, if this interpretation is accepted, law would lose its very substance and be reduced to a means for the realization of ethics, and what is purely ethical would be the ethical branch of law.   Thus its coercive power would implicitly be denied, because force is repugnant in the sphere of pure morals.   If, therefore, the complexity of universal determinations of action can be thought of as the system of external freedom, the definition of Trendelenburg is the same as the conception of Hegel that we have given before.[1]   In truth the thought of Trendelenburg of the specific essence of law is not precise and is capable of a double interpretation.

§ 118. *Law is an Ethical Principle.*   All the definitions examined contain, as shown by their criticism, part of the truth.   Law is an ethical principle and has intrinsic form and material content.   Reason is the form as shown by Plato, Aristotle, Stoics, Roman philosophers and jurisconsults, Saint Thomas, Dante, Grotius, Vico, Hegel, Rosmini, and Trendelenburg.   The matter is the need of life, the demand of species, utility; — elements shown clearly by the modern materialists and positivists, by Epicurus, Bentham, and Stuart Mill.   Law presupposes common life with language, custom, and heredity as has been especially shown by Aristotle, Mill, the Darwinists and Spencer. In its realization, it gets its value from force of which Thrasimachus speaks and from the physical and psychological coercion of Hobbes, and becomes the united force of all or the power of union, as Spinoza teaches. Law is manifested concretely by the will of the major-

[1] *Cf.* Intro. p. 68, *ante*.

ity according to Rousseau.   It results in the limitation
of freedom upon which Kant and Fichte base their
definitions and the harmony of Herbart, after the
struggles which Vico and Ihering describe.   Finally
law, since it is a higher ethical principle, offers and
protects the conditions necessary for the life of man
and his perfection, as Krause and Ahrens thought.

CHAPTER VIII

LAW, MORALS, AND SOCIAL SCIENCE

LAW AS AN ETHICAL STUDY. — THE RELATION BETWEEN
MORALS AND LAW IN HISTORY. — CRITICISM OF THE CON-
FUSION AND SEPARATION OF THE TWO TERMS. — THE COM-
MON BASES AND REAL DIFFERENCE. — ETHICAL AND SOCIAL
LIFE. — ViCO, SUESSMILCH, AND THE PHYSIOCRATIC FORERUN-
NERS OF SOCIAL SCIENCE. — COMTE'S SOCIOLOGY AND THE
VARIOUS MOVEMENTS. — SPENCER'S SOCIOLOGY. — SOCIOLOGY
AS THE PHILOSOPHY OF THE SOCIAL SCIENCES. — THE ANALO-
GIES BETWEEN SOCIETY AND ORGANISM. — THE RELATIONS
BETWEEN LAW AND THE SOCIAL SCIENCES.

§ 119. *Positive Law is Allied with Morals, the Social
Sciences, Economics, and Politics.* After we have
determined the idea of the law in an inductive, deductive, and critical manner, we must show the connection
of rational law with morals, the social sciences, economics, politics, and positive law. Law is above all an
ethical study and therefore it is best to begin with an
examination of its relations with ethics in general and
with morals in particular.

§ 120. *Morals and Law Originally One.* There
was necessary in primitive days an all-powerful, extended, single, indivisible force which contained all the
activities of man within certain limits and established
customs, and enforced obedience and normal action or
the fibre of legality, as Bagehot expressed it. These
were the days of the Polyphemi, of which Vico speaks.
In them, spiritual and moral were indistinguishable from

juristic and legal punishments; the mind, still in its childish state, was confused and was not in a position to analyze and abstract.   Centuries of unchanging uniformity, monotony, confusion, and slavery always precede those of variety, analysis, and freedom.   It is useless, therefore, to search in those ages for the traces of law distinct from morals.   The confusion of the two terms lasted even into the classical age, in which the spirit was emancipated from the yoke of nature and was given new life through art and speculative thought. In fact, the laws of the Greek States not only controlled the external activity of the citizens, but tended to inter-penetrate with their intimate will, not separating motive from action.   For example, justice according to Plato consists principally in internal acts; Aristotle calls only those men just who desire and realize what is just. In Greece there is no word to signify law, because it is resolved in the universal concept of justice.

§ 121.   *Morals and Law Distinguished by the Romans.* The Roman philosophers and jurisconsults distin-guished morals from law, but the distinction was not always precise and clear, neither had it the force of an explicitly declared speculative principle.   It appears from their distinction that the "bonum," defined by Seneca as "quod ad se impetum animi secundum naturam movet," became external in two forms in the "bonum quod honestum est" and the "bonum quod æquum est." Following the philosophers more particularly than the jurisconsults it can be stated as Cicero said, "honestum est summum bonum," and that it is *per se* voluntary because "nihil honestum quod ab invito quod a coacto fit," as Seneca pointed out; and that it develops in the sphere of intimate consciousness as well as in that of action.   The jurisconsults, however, recognized moral facts and distinguished them, as Capuano points out in his "Primi del Diritto Romano." Moral facts are those which depend upon purely individual ends, such as the good or bad administration of one's affairs according to whether one acts moderately or without due thought. They are referable to acts of liberality incapable of coercion and to "cognitatio" for which no one is punished and to acts upon which no pecuniary value can be placed, such as freedom. The grounds of distinction according to the jurisconsults is the spontaneity of the moral act and the necessity of the juristic act. It is written in the sources of law: "Sicuti voluntatis et officii magis quam necessitatis est commodare, ita modum comodati finemque præscribere eius est qui beneficium tribuit. Cum autem id fecit (id est postquam commodavit) tunc finem præscribere et retro agere atque intempestive usum commodatæ rei auferri non officium tantum impedit sed et suscepta obligatio inter dandum accipiendumque: geritur enim negotium: et ideo invicem propositæ sunt actiones ut apparent quod principio beneficii ac nudæ voluntatis fuerat converti in mutuas præstationes actionesque civiles." The "bonum æquum" is founded on the "naturalis ratio" and is derived from the "bonum" and "honestum" because, as Papianus says, "facta quæ lædunt pietatem existimationem verecundiam nostram et ut generaliter dixeram contra bonas mores fiunt nec facere nos posse credendum est." This derivation is taken from Cicero's and Ulpian's definition and from the three "præcepta juris." Cicero wrote that "justitia est habitus animi communi utilitate confirmata suam quique tribuens dignitatem," and Ulpian stated that justice is the habit of the mind "constans ac perpetua voluntas jus suum quique tribuens." Of the three general principles of law or "præcepta juris," the first or the "honeste vivere" represents the moral basis of law; the second, that is, "neminem lædere," is the formula of the negative legal duties; while the third or "jus suum quique tribuere" regards the positive legal duties, as Morianus points out. Ulpian adds that the jurisconsults are called the priests of justice because they teach men to be good and just. The three concepts of "sapientia," "prudentia," and "jurisprudentia" emphasize the connection between the "bonum æquum," the "bonum" and "honestum." But this does not imply the identity of the three terms. "Sapientia" is the knowledge of all good, human and divine. It is the "scientia divinarum atque humanarum rerum" of the Stoics, philosophers, and jurisconsults. "Prudentia" is the knowledge of the "bonum honestum." "It is," thought Cicero, "rerum bonarum et malarum, neutrumque scientia." "Jurisprudentia" is the knowledge of the "bonum æquum, est justi atque injusti scientia," founded on the "notitia divinarum atque humanarum rerum." The "bonum æquum" is connected with utility. It is "constitutum hominum causa." It admits of coercion, for, as is written in the sources, "Sanctio legum certam poenam irrogatiis qui præcepto legis non obtemperaverint." It is developed in external action and not in the intent; "nec consilium habuisse noceat nisi et factum secutum fuerit." The distinction between morals and law is proved as well by the sentence of Paulus: "Non omne quod licet honestum est;" and by the Institutes, "condictio ob turpem vel injustam causam."

§ 122. *Distinction between Morals and Law Disappeared in the Middle Ages.* In the Middle Ages this distinction does not appear, because the Church subjected the most intimate part of man and acted as the conscience of the State, which lost its ancient and classical signification and was forced to live as the body of the Church. The latter pretended to

scrutinize men's souls and embraced in the Holy
Inquisition the coercive means of civil authority. Sin
was converted into crime; — the great sin of heresy
became the greatest crime to be stamped out by the most
efficacious prevention and the most energetic and
exemplary repression. Exorbitant claims, however, provoked a reaction, and the principle of liberty of conscience appeared at first in Italy and afterwards in other
countries. Bruno taught that acts or deeds should not
be punished, which did not affect the peace of the
State. Later, Grotius emphasized a strict and perfect
right comprehensive of power, property, and the permissibility of demanding what is due, and an imperfect
right which connotes virtue, liberality, and reward.
He did not distinguish law from morals in so many words
since he reduced both terms to a kind of law, but it cannot
be denied that this broad conception of the two terms
in the qualifications of an imperfect and perfect law are
the germs of a specific differentiation. Puffendorf, the
author of "Elementa Jurisprudentiæ Universalis," "De
Jure Naturæ et Gentium," and "De Officio Hominis et
Civis," retarded the progress of philosophy in sub-
ordinating internal duties to theory and external duties
to natural law. Leibnitz, in his celebrated treatise
"Nova Methodus Discendæ Jurisprudentiæ," corrected
the error and took the internal duties away from theological control and replaced them in moral philosophy. Thomasius, in "Fundamenta Juris Naturæ et
Gentium," really separated the imperfect and incoercible
duties which are referable to the internal peace of mind
from perfect and coercible duties which keep the
external peace. Kant conceived the unity of morals
and law in his metaphysics of customs, as a science which
comprehends the principles of ethical and juristic notions,
but attained knowledge of their absolute separation

when he wrote that morals have to do with internal acts and intentions, and can command in their own way what law commands, while law which has to do with external acts has nothing to do with intentions, and cannot enforce moral precepts. Moral legislation has its motive in the absolute idea of duty; juristic legislation demands only the conformity of action to an established norm. Fichte adds that law would go on existing if nobody had a good intention; that physical force alone would give law a right to existence.

§ 123. *The Confusion and Separation of Law and Morals are Both Wrong.* Confusion and separation represent two excesses: confusion is the mark of primitive times or the epoch of immobility; separation is the product of modern dispersive analysis. Intention cannot be the same as action, pure will as act. Internal freedom ("bonum quod honestum est") cannot be the same as external freedom ("bonum quod æquum est") because the interiority of a thing differs from its exteriority. Thus the confusion of morals and law renders all morality coercible and places a value upon the intent of itself and not upon its result and action in the field of juristic relations. On the contrary, separation destroys the natural bonds between the terms and removes them absolutely from their original synthesis. In intent and act, in will and work, in internal and external freedom, there is man with his ethical action. Neither in the "bonum quod honestum est" nor in "bonum quod æquum" alone lies the whole principle of the "bonum." Separation cannot be admitted, because under the negative and prohibitive precepts of law and the statutes, the spirit of morality is active, working for the attainment of the high ends of education, now establishing chastity and moderation of custom and now rejuvenating the soul and spirit, as

Trendelenburg says. The matrimonial laws which prohibit marriages under certain conditions and those which
forbid military trials, show the two ends indicated. It is
not true that law takes no account of intent, because it
considers it in contracts, wills, constitutions, and crimes.
Law does not consider the intent except as it is shown by
the act and does not contemplate it of itself as morals
do. It is not possible for the State and statutes to
exist long if they are threatened by general hatred.
The truth is that morals and law cannot be confused or
separated but only distinguished with due recognition
to their common origin, which is found in the universal
practical philosophy of the ancients or in ethics making
for the realization of the ends of man, for his well-
being in its amplest extent. The ethical act, the reality
of the human end and good result from the process
which subordinates the inclination of the senses,
interests, and utility to the sovereign control of reason,
as we have said.[1] Such was the universal justice of the
philosophers, which is not now morals and now law but
rather their primitive unity. Platonic justice coördi-
nates the particular virtues and assigns its field to each
faculty. The universal justice of Aristotle is the whole
of virtue. Law, in the broad sense given it by Grotius,
embraces morals and law. And the force of the true
in human reason which struggles against cupidity and
weighs the different utilities is, for Vico, the principle
of the two studies. Hegel admits law in the general
sense growing out of the confusion of the subjective and
objective will and comprehensive of the two terms.
Romagnosi speaks of law in the same sense; that is,
as the norm, which moderates human acts, derived
from the real and necessary nature of things. Rosmini
regards juristic justice as a part of universal justice.

Cf. § 85 *ante.*

We have observed before[1] that if the process of subordination comes to a preference in internal consciousness and is seen in the sphere of intention *per se*, we have
morals; and if, on the other hand, it has to do with
external relation between man and man or man and
things, we have law properly so called.   Morals and laws
are two branches of ethics, are two methods of effecting
the human end, or that of ethical reality.   Whence it
follows that morals are not complete entirely in the consciousness but are shown in action, because they are
always an ethical reality and as a reality cannot fail to
have an external side.   On the other hand, law is not
reducible to a wholly external and pharisaical practice
without any basis or intention because it, too, is ethical
reality and therefore essentially implies a certain intent.
The ethical act, the conformity of the subjective and
objective will, and the subordination of the elements
of sense to reason cannot be absolutely internal or absolutely external because they are the effect of the whole of
man and the development of all good in general.   The
internity and externity represent only the prevalence
of the intention or action in the development of this
principle.   Morals comprehend action but consist principally of intent.   Law is extended over the intent but
is particularly occupied with the act. Since they are
branches of ethics, they cannot be contradictory in their
origin, nor can either be entirely abstracted from
action or intention.

§ 124. *Separation and Contradiction of Morals and
Law.* Some believe that there is a separation and sometimes a contradiction between morals and law.   A man,
for example, can legally break a promise which morally
he is bound to keep.   The creditor can cruelly pursue
his action against the unfortunate and guiltless debtor

[1]*Cf. § 122 ante.*

and put his family out into the street, though that is immoral. Everyone can dissipate his own estate and lead a dissolute life, but morals prohibit dissipation and dissoluteness. The debtor can with bad grace pay what he owes the creditor; the act is legal but immoral. All these examples, however, prove only one thing; that morals and law have two different spheres and are separate but uncontradictory studies. It is true that whoever breaks his promise is guilty of an offense against morality and possibly none against law, but on the other hand whoever fulfills it observes morality and is guilty of no offense against law. If there was a true contradiction, as Cavagnari showed in "Corso Moderno di Filosofia del Diritto," respect paid to morality might — though it is not certain — be an offense against law. In the case of a fundamental right there is no contradiction, because the law is essentially permissive. There would be a real contradiction if the creditor was made by the law to sue his unfortunate debtor. Man has a right to freedom in private conduct and can dispose of his goods as he desires, saving always a respect for the opinions of others and the limitations of a social and political order. He has, therefore, no right to dissipation and dissoluteness but a right not to be interfered with in the exercise of his power of disposition and conduct of life. So in the hypothesis of the observance of law without a good intent there is no contradiction, because there is an act ethically perfect performed to all appearances as if the good intent accompanied the legal act. If sometimes the intent is discordant with the act, that depends upon the distinction between the two realms and sciences, but if there were contradictions the coincidence of the two terms in a single act would not be possible. Rosmini taught that the so-called immoral rights are relatively and not absolutely immoral. In other words,

law is immoral whenever it does not forbid an irrational
or wrongful act, whenever it permits an act presuming
it to be honest because of the impossibility of proof,
and whenever it does not forbid an immoral act because
of underlying fundamental right.

§ 125. *Rosmini Does Not Clearly Understand the
Difference between Morals and Law.* If, on one hand,
Rosmini eliminates the possibility of the true contradiction between morals and law, on the other
hand he is not always exact in his conception of
these two terms. He reduces the sphere of the law
to that of the licit, as we have shown before,[1] and
does not give his attention to the juristical duty
which is the natural antecedent of the "facultas agendi."
In treating of the essential ends of personality, law commands or prohibits, but primarily there is a duty of
doing or not doing what the law commands or prohibits, and this duty is juristic and there is a legitimate
right not to be hindered in the fulfillment of the duty.
According to Rosmini's conception, the field of law is not
as large as it should be, and consequently he is not on
the road to fix correctly the boundaries of the two
sciences. Furthermore, Rosmini places the specific
difference between morals in the eudemonological content of law, as if the general good, as an ethical object,
did not comprehend happiness interpenetrated with
reason. The good is derived from the subordination
of the elements of sense to reason. Ethics contain
eudemonology and are not modelled upon an abstract,
formal, and empty principle like that of Kant. In morals,
the eudemonological content is referable more to the
internal sentiments of the mind; in law it has more
regard for extrinsic utility; but this does not mean
that the useful is foreign to morals or that pleasure or

[1] *Cf.* § 124 *ante.*

displeasure is foreign to law.   It is only a question of the prevalence of one or the other elements.

§ 126. *The Theory that the Useful, Just, and Honest are Three Aspects of the Good.* Carle in his "Vita del Diritto" writes that the useful, just, and honest are three aspects of the good. The useful corresponds to the senses of man by the bonds which it has with matter, from which he gets his means of sustinence. The just is connected with the social nature of man and is coercive, thus rendering civil community possible. The honest is that side of the good which is most intimately connected with the spiritual and moral part of the human being, and his growth towards perfection. The honest is incoercible and is realized through the development of freedom, becoming a desire and aspiration of the finite towards the infinite. The useful is the matter of the just ; the honest constitutes its form. In this theory, morals have no real eudemonological content because the idea of the honest does not comprehend the useful and conservative. The honest is absolute, ideal, *a priori*, an object of deduction. The useful is relative, sensible, *a posteriori*, an object of induction. And yet moral good should have a material, sensible basis, which is had in pleasure and the useful in the broad sense. The perfecting of man is not possible without conservation that has an ethical meaning, and therefore should be regarded by morals. The honest, as well as the just, is a human idea and determinable through deduction and induction. Morals have their relative side as has law, and both are parts of the science which is, according to Vico, philosophy and history. The difference between law and morals in this theory is fundamentally the same as Rosmini points out, because law is born of the union of the useful and honest, while morals take nothing from the useful.

§ 127. *Increase in the Field of Law.* As time goes on, the objects and relations subject to law increase in number and grow more intricate and complicated. Law governs objects which were first in the jurisdiction of morals. In our day, for example, habitual drunkenness and cruelty to animals are punished, while such acts in the past fell under the control of morals. This does not show that law is little by little absorbing morals but means that in its self-explication, it subordinates those relations to itself which are rationally within its sphere. It is not law which is gaining ground to the injury of morals, but it is merely taking possession of all its estate. On the other hand, the more the sphere of law increases and extends, the greater becomes that of morals, which is also governed by the laws of evolution. The internal freedom and autonomy of moral subjects are more developed as the intimate ethical relations multiply and develop. Here it is that the character of the person is concretely shown and, at the same time, the great difficulties of the slow formation of his nature and temperament appear. External and internal liberty are developed as sentiments grow higher, and ideas come nearer the true, the good, and the just. Man's power is bounded only by his will, and his will by his knowledge. Buckle and Spencer do not agree in this. Buckle taught in his "History of Civilization in England" that ideas alone are obedient to the laws of progress and that moral sentiments and will are stationary. Spencer states that knowledge does not determine conduct because man himself acts in contradiction to what he has learnt, and that on the contrary action and habit depend on sentiment. But the theory of Buckle paralyzes the spirit-making movement of thought, and a subsequent change of will impossible, as if the will was not thought, mind, and practical reason.

Buckle is in the position of him who admits the entire action of the nerves of sense and yet denies the reflexive phenomena and the transformation of sensation into movement or tendency. He has fallen into this error because he based his argument too much on the fact that reflection remains identical or changes but little in the moral world, and has not put a true valuation on what new change there is. Without doubt, the most important elements of the cosmos and of human nature change little in relation to the other elements, but there change has more value. The head of the organism changes little in comparison with the arms and legs, but when change takes place it is greater in importance. The mind changes more than the will which represents the essence of the person, but a change of will is more important to human life. And this is what is true in Buckle's often erroneous theory, as shown by the continuous variability of customs and sentiments. Spencer disagrees with Buckle's chief idea with arguments that really confirm it. To say that the mind does not determine conduct, because man often acts in contradiction to what he has learned, is to apply a wrong test, because in such cases the ideas are always the guides of action. The ideas are old (opinions born of sentiments, passions, and interests of another historical period) but in the end they are always ideas or guides of conduct. It cannot be denied that ideas of themselves are often weak and inefficient, and that strength and vitality come from the passionate reason or impulse. But the impulse would be blind and casual if it were not directed to its purpose by the mind which is active through sentiment. Stuart Mill writes that to hold the above thesis is equivalent to stating that a boat reaches its destination by the force of the steam and not by that of the fire. The stimulus of sense or impulse is like the steam while the intellect can be likened to the fire.

§ 128. *Ethics are a Social Science.* It has been shown that ethics are active in a social and political life understood in a broad sense.[1] This is the thought of the Greek philosophers and especially of Aristotle; among the moderns, Hegel teaches that the effective ethical spirit presupposes not only the bare conformity of the act to the law of good but demands conviction in the good itself, of itself, and for itself, because there can be respect for law without such a conviction and there can be such a conviction without respect for law. This conviction, however, should not be shown in a subjective, accidental, and fugitive manner but substantially, necessarily, and stably; that is, in ethical habit, custom, the common course of events and the Ethos. The Ethos is the community of minds; it is a conscious and free state and should not, therefore, be considered as a simple substance or indifferent unity of individuals, but as a subject, spirit, or person. As soon as the community appears as the result or effect of the aggregation of individuals, it is present immediately in the form of a cause by which the individuals themselves adhere to the union, since the community cannot be regarded as a simple substance, but must be regarded as a subject or person; and it follows that the individuals are not reducible to mere method, to pure accident. The subject is at first family (a union based on sentiment), it becomes civil society (a unit of relations and individual or domestic interests), and finally it becomes the State, the community in which reason is all-supreme.

§ 129. *Vico Believed in a Social Science.* Now common life or society, in which ethics are realized,

[1] *Cf.* § 123 *ante.*

is the object of a particular science in our day. The conception of a social science was not foreign to the mind of Vico, though he declared in the "Scienza Nuova" that he wished to consider God as provident in moral and political affairs; that is, in civil customs; and that he believed such a theory possible because this civil world is made by man, wherefore its principles can be found, as they should be, within the modification of the human mind itself. According to the Neapolitan philosopher, knowledge and action in God are the same thing; and man partakes of the divine nature. The difference between man and God is that man has made this world, according to his principles, without knowing it, and even in the belief of doing exactly the contrary. It is the benevolent wisdom of Providence who has used man's natural customs and from their particular and restricted inter-est has brought forth such ample results adapted to the preservation of the human race. Men wished to avail themselves of bestial lust and to scatter their seed, but the result of their attempt was the chastity of marriage, whence came the family; the patriarchs wished to exercise unlimited paternal control over their clients, and cities grew up; the nobles wished to abuse their freedom as lords over the masses and fell into the slavery of law, which has resulted in popular liberty. What did all this was mind, because men accomplished it with intelligence. It was not Fate, because they did it through election. It was not Chance, because they have progressed through continuous action. The Providence of Vico is not an arbitrary and transcendental principle upon which it is not possible to found a science, but is present in custom. It is eternal reason and does not act upon man in immediate, incomprehensible, and miraculous ways. It creates everything through natural cus-

tom and works always for the elevation of human nature,
and constantly increases the wealth of its developments.
Vico, in describing the action of Providence, lays emphasis upon the intimate laws of man's nature and mind.
This description renders clearer still the generous truth
that the civil world is surely made by men, and that
therefore they can understand the science of it.

§ 130. *The Beginning of Sociology.* Suessmilch and
the physiocrats recognize more or less the possibility
of a social science. Suessmilch was the first to discover a fixed order in the quantity of social facts,
such as births, marriages, and deaths. This order
is intrinsic in the facts although it has a providential character. And here we see a providence
that works through man with ordinary means, one
that cannot be called an entirely transcendental principle for certainly the providence of Oettingen, who is
of the school of Suessmilch, is not transcendental.
Mercier de la Rivière and Dupont de Nemours
speak of a natural order of society, especially
when they show the intimate relation between
economic and other social phenomena. But the
credit for having clearly and precisely distinguished sociology from the other sciences and for giving it its right conception belongs to August Comte,
the head and founder of the positivist school. Sociology
is, in his mind, the final science, which is immediately
founded on biology. It is divided into social statics
and dynamics. Statics is the theory of relations, and
dynamics of progress. Simple biology in the conception of the Comtian school, as developed by Littré in
"La Science au Point de Vue Philosophique," can hardly
explain the more or less marvelous associations of certain inferior animals and the phenomena of gregarious-
ness among the higher animals, and cannot at all explain

social and historical evolution depending upon the faculty which the common life has of creating groups of things which can and must be learned. Such a faculty is expressed in traditions, monuments, and writings, and can be considered in four successive stages: in that of need; in that of relations of man to family, society, and the natural forces by which he is dominated; in that of poetry and art; and in the last, of abstract knowledge. The creation of an inheritance of knowledge is purely sociological, Littré points out, and there is nothing in biology which can take its place. Custom and heredity can aid social evolution but cannot create or direct it. Quetelet regards sociology as a social physics. Spencer in the book we have cited,[1] Schäffle in "Bau und Leben des Socialen Körpers," Lazzarus and Steinthal in "Zeitschrift für Völkerpsychologie und Sprachwissenschaft," look upon it as a social physiology and psychology. Buckle, Lubbock, and Tyler in his "Primitive Culture," whom Bagehot follows, see in such a science a natural history of humanity from the primitive savage state to the later phases of civilization. Letourneau in his "La Sociologie d'après l'Ethnologie" bases it on ethnography. De Roberty approaches Comte and Littré in his "Fragments de Philosophie Positive et de Sociologie Contemporaine." The legitimacy of a psychology of peoples or society has no place in the discussion, because many psychological phenomena found in life and history are not explicable by the activity and attitudes of the individual psyche and are illustrated only through the principle of a social or national psyche. Vico pictures this psyche as a live and not a blind form, since chance has not diverted or fate forced men from their primitive natural course, in which they availed themselves of the suitable

[1] *Cf.* "Justice," cit. § 109 *ante*.

and ready material to make their republics in which they were active both in mind and body. The ready materials were suitable religions, suitable languages, lands, names of people and things, suitable arms and, therefore, suitable empires, suitable masters and laws, and with these suitable elements there were real freemen, and because of the real freemen true republics or States were constituted.

§ 131. *Spencer is the Great Sociologist.* Spencer is the philosopher who has finally presented the largest and fullest work on sociology, the study of the reciprocal relation between the human units and their aggregate, of which he shows the structure, growth, development, and functions. The common action of men, which is the origin of society, depends upon the general character of human nature and upon characters peculiar to the different races and individuals. Social science has obstacles of three kinds, — objective, subjective, and mixed. The objective difficulties arise from the great complexity of social phenomena, their indefinite number, and their great diffusion in time and space. The subjective difficulties are derived either from the intelligence of the observer, as from his automorphical inclinations, or from a disposition to contribute facts conforming to his ideas and feelings and from a lack of large comprehension, or else arise from sensibilities, as hate, love, or impatience. Those of the third class are caused by the different positions in which the observer is found, whence arise prejudices of patriotism, class, party, or creed; partizanship, which Spencer analyzes accurately in "The Study of Sociology." Super-organic or social evolution, Spencer states in "The Principles of Sociology," is determined partly by external circumstances and partly by the nature of the units in the humane aggregate. The extrinsic factors are climate, the conformation of the land, its composition, and the flora and fauna.   The intrinsic factors are referable to the constitution, sentiments, and intelligence of the men composing the society.   In primitive times, the extrinsic factors were predominant; in civilization the contrary is true.   Besides the original extrinsic and intrinsic factors we must recognize secondary or derivative factors, the products of the social evolution itself, such as increase in population, reciprocal influences of various social bodies, and philological, scientific, juridical, and political progress.   Sociology is the most complex of all sciences and presupposes all of them, more particularly the studies most closely related to it, psychology and biology, because psychological and physiological facts arise immediately in society.   It can be gathered, by analogy from the individual organism, that society is an organic being. The social aggregate grows as all vital bodies grow; its progressive increase in volume is accompanied by complications of structure and a greater division of functions together with a more extensive and accurate coördination.   Anyone can prove these statements by comparing the structure and coördination of the offices of primitive society with the constitution and development of functions in a progressive society.   Society is composed of vital elements; that is, of human individuals, as the living body is the union of other vital individualities. The globules which move in the blood and the epithelian cellules which detach from the animal and continue to live in water are proof of this.   Society remains while individuals appear and disappear and institutions, even, vanish; as the organism remains while the blood, the skin, and the cellules are continually renewed.   Society has three main attributes, the productive, the regulative, and the distributive.   The productive or digestive is essentially industrial and changes the raw material into alimentary substances. The regulative gives society its relation to the external world and other aggregates and serves for defense and protection. The distributive is represented by the means of exchange and transportation and connects the first attribute with the second, as the animal has an internal apparatus for alimentary substances and external apparatus, which puts it into communication with what is foreign to it, and a vascular apparatus, whose duty it is to connect the two. The productive and regulative apparatus, and in general the internal and external apparatus, are closely connected and reinforce one another but are more distinguished as we ascend in the animal and human scale. The same is true of the distributive which develops only when the complication and distinction of the two others is full and complete. Society, as all individual organisms, is subject to the laws of the struggle for life and of competition in its amplest sense.

§ 132. *Sociology is the Social Philosophy.* It has been pointed out that sociology, understood as a science which studies the social organism in all its elements and forms, showing its structure, development, and functions, is a kind of encyclopedia which absorbs the various social studies and cannot be the object of research or meditation for a single mind. Sociology is not possible, says Vanni in his "Prime Linee di un Programma Critico di Sociologia," unless it is understood as the philosophy of the social sciences, a general doctrine comprehensive of the first principles of the social sciences systematized with respect to individuality and the particular competence of each unit, and with a due recognition of the fruitful law of a scientific division of labor. The study of the diverse forms of the social fact belongs to social studies. Sociology is the pursuit of fundamental and supreme laws that have to do with the structure, function, equilibrium, movement, and development of the social organism conceived in its integrity; the particular social sciences are limited to the order of phenomena which concerns each, investigating only the laws adherent thereto, and are not obliged to elaborate a general theory of society, which is the exclusive duty of sociology, as Stuart Mill pointed out.   The social sciences have the same relation to sociology that all the particular branches of knowledge have to philosophy, which is the search for supreme principles and the connecting point of the mother-ideas.   Spencer and Schäffle have said nothing about this, Comte is more preoccupied with sociology than with the social studies, but Stuart Mill and, among the Italians, Vanni have seen this relationship. Sociology as a philosophical theory is called upon to apply cosmic laws to the phenomena of common life by determining their modality in relation to proper forms and character.   Society is an ethical organism that develops in history.   It is an ethical organism because the whole and its elements are conscious and free persons, existing as reciprocal ends and means.   It develops in history because its life is the evolution of human nature. Society is not a mere biological and physiological product, and its progress, therefore, does not consist simply in a complexity of organic and psychic variations.   It is an ethico-historical production, and an emergent and not a resultant fact, and its movement and progress are synonymous to civilization; that is, to the predominance of the spiritual over the natural factors in human reality. Social progress is more than the super-organic evolution of Spencer; it is development in time; it is historical dynamism.   From this it can be seen that society cannot be explained by biology and psychology. The proper quality of the social being, as an ethico-historical organism, is beyond the competence of these two sciences. We must remember that new forms in evolution, on one hand, include the precedent forms, but, on the other, present a specifically higher character. The abstract doctrine of identity and of a single force cannot give a satisfactory explanation, because by these only the quantitative and not the true qualitative differences are shown. The progress of their growth and their constantly more perfect qualifications in more complex forms still remain obscure.

§ 133. *Sociology Must Regard the Aggregate and the Units.* If we admit the analogy, shown by Spencer, between society and an organism, we are forced to conclude that it is a living entity in the true sense of the word, but we must not forget that society is a whole, an ethical organism. Man in the abstract, to use the Platonic phrase, is the result of the intimate union of human elements of definite persons who are ultimate in themselves. In the ethical community, the individuals are collected and united and reciprocally strengthened (Trendelenburg says), while the whole is organized in its parts and is divided in the individuals. The idea of strengthening includes the increase of the energy of the individual through the individual for his particular ends; that of organization implies the realization of universal thought and purpose through the whole. The strengthening and organization should proceed with conservation. A strengthening in contradiction to organization is the predominance of selfish and destructive interest; an organization hostile to strengthening means sacrifice of the parts. If society is an ethical organism, the analogy and application of physical and physiological laws should be received within the limits and under the control that we have pointed out before[1]

[1] *Cf.* § 61 *ante.*

in relation to the laws of evolution. We do not deny the existence of a social physics or physiology, but we mean that both enter into ethics and cannot be otherwise considered. The same can be said of all those chapters of sociology that are based on biological studies, as can be seen from the work of Schäffle and others.

§ 134. *Law is a Part of Sociology.* Now the relation between the human units and their aggregate, the structure, development, and functions of the latter, have a juristic aspect in that they refer to the action of the individual and of the aggregate itself and realize externally the law of good. Law in such a case is, as it is in all cases, the proportion or norm and protection. On one hand, it is the principle through which the assignment of their due is made to the social elements and the whole. On the other hand, it prevents, by its guardianship, the development of life of the part and the aggregate from being disturbed. The ethical organism demands singular and collective activity or human action and is, therefore, subject to the rules of law, the right measure of strength and organization. Philosophy of law is, therefore, the study of the highest principles of the social organism, contemplated especially in respect to human activity. It is not possible to effect the proportion allowed by reason, which is law, and to apply it to the phenomena of common life without knowing the intimate structure, functions, and laws of the development of society. Neither can it be denied that justice enters in the composition of the social elements and forces, although it may be a secondary and derivative factor. Justice is such a factor in the sense that the ethical principle appears after the elements of sense but, nevertheless, has more intrinsic value.

§ 135. *Sociology is More than a Philosophy of Law.*
Ardigo in "Morale dei Positivisti" and "Sociologia"
considers the natural formation of justice as the mark of
the social organism. Justice, for him, is the specific
force of such an organism and is explained in conformity
with social ideas, based on the nature of man who
wishes to act freely in accordance with the dictates of
reason. From this point of view, sociology itself is
reduced to the philosophy of law.   But without wishing
to admit such an identification, it cannot be denied that
the bonds between the two sciences are intimate and
substantial, since one presupposes the other. Philosophy of law, conceived as a genetico-evolutionary doctrine, as a theory based on the human idea of law,
must study all social elements which enter into the natural
formation of the juridical fact and its idea. The juridical
fact is essentially a social fact since law is not possible
out of society.   It is the chief social fact looked at from a
particular point of view, from that of the external relation
between man and man and man and things, in which
the human good is realized in conformity with the laws
of proportion and the principles of protection. If this
is the nature of the juridical fact, it is clear that the
philosophy of law as the pursuit of the knowledge of
such a fact and as a practical science tending towards
perfection, cannot disregard the social elements and
ideality that the civil community works for, of which
Ardigo speaks. The profound belief of Vico about the
two sources of natural law and his analysis of the necessity and utility of social life is again in point. Law is
born and developed in society. It is transformed by
society and works always for the attainment of the
ideal which human knowledge indicates. Sociology, or
the science which systematizes the fundamental ideas
of separate social studies, cannot for its part contem-

plate the social organism in its integrity without storing away the supreme principles of law. The philosophy of the social sciences and the general theory of society presuppose the philosophy of law, because without law, society is incomprehensible.

CHAPTER IX

LAW, SOCIAL ECONOMY, AND POLITICS

THE SOCIAL-ECONOMIC REGULATIONS AND THE ANCIENT
AND MODERN PHILOSOPHERS OF LAW. — ETHICS, SOCIOLOGY
BASED ON BIOLOGY, POLITICS, AND HISTORY AS HYPOTHESES
OF ECONOMICS. — THE CHARACTER OF THE ECONOMIC FACT. —
THE RELATIONS OF LAW AND ECONOMICS. — THE CONCEPT
OF POLITICS. — POLITICS, THE SOCIAL SCIENCES, ETHICS, AND
LAW. — THE FULL MEANING OF THE STATE.

§ 136. *The Beginning of the Study of Economics.*
Grotius, Vico, and Kant did not study the social-economic order in its relation to the supreme rationale
of law. It can be said in general that the first writers on
natural law paid exclusive attention to the essential
rights of the person, and did not attend to the nature
of the things over which human activity extends. The
science of economics was not born in those days, but
was only about to make its appearance. Wolff alone,
in his "Jus Naturæ Methodo Scientifico Tractatum,"
speaks of business, immigration, population, and men-
dicity. After him, the next philosopher who treated
in a masterly manner the relation between our study
and social economy was Romagnosi, who changed the
most certain economic principles into arguments of
rigorous and indispensable law and of natural and necessary duty. In his mind, economic perfection began with
agricultural life demanding individual and stable property, tending to procure through the equality of law larger
and more equitable diffusion of pleasure. Its base is

the conception of commercial liberty, which is "axiomatic," as he says, "in public and private law," the equal distribution of taxes and class separation, its result the diffusion of social value over the greatest number or the acquisition of the capacity of production. The State has the power of intervening in personal affairs which lead to the gradual destruction of the many to the advantage of the few.

§ 137. *The Early German Economic Philosophers are Forgotten.* Hegel, Trendelenburg, and Ahrens considered the economic order of society in relation to rational law. Hegel speaks of public wealth, labor, social classes, the price of merchandise, pauperism, immigration, and the control of corporations. Trendelenburg treats of agrarian and forestry laws, of the law of the arts and of commerce, of exchange, insurance, wealth, and population. Ahrens studies the economic aspect of every philosophico-juristical theory. The new German economists, however, no longer have recourse to Hegel and Trendelenburg. They cite Ahrens with great consideration to show the connection between economics and the modern philosophy of law. The socialists alone sometimes remember the name of Hegel. The chief reason for this is found in the widely different nature of their writings. In the books of Hegel and Trendelenburg, philosophy is the prevailing factor; those of Ahrens abound in details; and the speculative elements have not a large development. Hegel and Trendelenburg are not jurists in the true sense of the word. Ahrens is more jurist than philosopher. Yet there is a second reason. The two philosophers have been condemned as metaphysicians by the positivists, who have a large following among those who like an easy philosophy. After the condemnation, no one cares to see whether their ethical, juristic, and economic ideas conform to the actual movement of

the studies about wealth or not.   Ahrens, on the contrary, has been able expressly to adhere to this movement, thanks to which whatever little metaphysics is
attached to his doctrine is condoned.

§ 138.   *Ahrens' Theory of Economics.*   The adherence
of Ahrens to the recent movement of economic science
is clear.   Economics, this author writes, are an ethical
science that is governed by the principle of the
good, which man should attain by his own forces
aided by those of nature.   Man is the subject and
end of wealth; man is individual and social and therefore economics tend to express the law which guides
individual and collective action in production, exchange,
distribution, and consumption of wealth.   Economic
laws are not identical with physical laws because the
moral and social laws of which the first are part refer
to man, the free being.   Ahrens disagrees with the
theories of Kant, Smith, Bastiat, and Buckle about
the office of the State, because it appears to him
abstract and negative; and he shows that this great
personality is constructed not only for the security of
persons, and goods and chattels, but for culture and
civilization.   The State, according to Ahrens, should
remove the difficulties in the way of the full development of the actions of individuals; should even help
in a direct positive way.

§ 139.   *Hegel's Economics.*   Reading Hegel's "Grundlinien der Philosophie des Rechts," it seems at first
that he accepts the conception of the absolute and
fatal coincidence of private and general interests
and likens the economic to simple natural laws.
In fact, he says, that except for the family, the
moral world presents itself as a complexity of atoms
because the common interest in domestic society is
resolved into many particular interests, which, how-

ever, can be reduced to unity in that they aid and help one another spontaneously. There is in the antagonism of the individual interests a complexity of universal and necessary relations. In this, there appears something similar to the grandeur of the planetary system in which the eye perceives only irregular movements while scientific research determines them with accuracy. When we consider the theory of Hegel concerning the community and civil society, we must change our judgment, because economic laws are for him social and civil, and reducible to ethical laws. Civil society is the form of the ethical spirit, according to Hegel. Economic laws are moral laws but regard the vegetation of political bodies, as they say to-day, or the sum total of things destined for the satisfaction of needs. This is certainly ethics, but natural ethics, which are very close to social statics and not very far from biology. This is clear because it is not contradictory to speak of ethical laws and emphasize at the same time their unknowability and spontaneity. The natural spirit, as such, has the characteristics of a spirit. For Hegel, the State has not only the office of protecting persons and chattels, but tends as well to rule the moral world and to realize the ends of culture and happiness without destroying the principle of individuality which is shown in the free exercise of a business, profession, and of activities in general. Trendelenburg distinguishes two kinds of theories, the natural, economic theory, and the political in the old sense of the word. The first, founded by Adam Smith, has its origin in the energy which takes its impulse from the physical and moral needs of the individual. It recognizes no other value than the price of merchandise, and looks upon the State as only a protector. The second holds that the value of individual activity depends upon the internal object of the State, which represents the ethical whole and must preserve the elements of culture and education from the harms of the variable and illusory price of merchandise. Both theories are insufficient, unilateral, and exclusive, because the first regards economic value and the second political principles alone. We must have recourse to a higher doctrine which will conciliate the extreme theories. Such a doctrine gets its name from the ethical organism, in which the part lives the life of the whole, but has its own personality. The part is the individual and the whole is man in the abstract, in the form of a people. Trendelenburg refuses to accept the idea of the State formed under the influence of individualism, and considers it as a high personality destined to develop all the human powers.

§ 140. *Economics were Considered Without Ethical Content.* We may note that the great number of writers until a few years ago thought economics a science entirely separate from ethics, politics, and history. According to these philosophers, whose leader was Pellegrino Rossi, one can and should pay attention to the principles of this study only in the application of the economic theory in the empirical spheres of art and not in the field of the pure science of wealth. To-day opinions are changed; the politico-social school speaks of the ethical principle of economics; the positivists reduce it to a chapter in sociology founded on biology and theories of evolution; and the historical school wishes to change it into a science of facts. Opposed to these three innovating schools there are a number of economists who defend the old conceptions with vigor. Do the three schools respect the independence of economics with their doctrine and their method? Or is this independence better preserved by the followers of the classical school? Certainly, economics are the science of wealth which depends, however, on the element of human nature and physical, biological, social, and political conditions, and in general upon historical factors. Economics must, therefore, be based on a complexity of agents and show the latter's influence on wealth, but should not study them especially and by themselves and draw their nature from them, because this would be usurping the office of the other sciences. To the economist, such causes represent merely a series of presuppositions. If ethics, sociology founded on biology, politics, and history are considered only as presuppositions, the autonomy of the science of economics is in no wise injured, because autonomy does not mean isolation. But if these studies are confused with economics in such a way as to make the latter a civil ethics, a true sociology or political science, a branch of natural history or even of technology, economic history or statistics, the independence of the science of economics is denied. This point should be developed fully because, although it is not a proper subject for the philosophy of law, still it serves in the formation of an adequate conception of an important science which has multifold intimate connections with the law.

§ 141. *Economics Have an Ethical Content.* Economics have for their object wealth. Wealth is referable to the activity of man, and therefore political economy is essentially a practical science. Now the most practical science is ethics, which considers the law of work in respect to its natural end, which is the good or the perfection of the person. From this it follows that economics are part of ethics understood in the broadest and most universal sense. In the conception of wealth is included the conception of human nature, its ends, and perfection. In reality, wealth is chattels or things which satisfy our needs and can be exchanged

or are objects of work. It is evident that wealth is not
conceivable without the act of man, without his activity
creative or productive of the means of satisfaction,
and without such means, consisting of objects capable
of exchange. But our needs, activity, and objects
cannot be understood without their relation to the ends
of human nature and their reciprocal coördination and
subordination, because the ends constitute a true host
in which each occupies his position that deserves the
exercise of the power of man which is applicable thereto.
In the fulfillment of these ends, thus bound together, in
the satisfaction of the tendencies of sense and mind
lies happiness which contains pleasure and duty, and
represents the state of perfection. Aristotelean well-
being, or happiness, is human well-being, the object
of ethics, and wealth or economic prosperity is part of
it. In wealth there is human well-being in respect to
useful and exchangeable things. At this point, we meet
the ethical principle of economics, which one cannot
disregard and from which one cannot escape without
denying the common basis of all practical or moral
studies. Neither does this principle lead to the confusion of such studies, because it expresses only their
proximate nature and nothing more. If economics
accomplish the human good in wealth, morals, properly
so called, contemplate it in the intimacy of consciousness, and law considers it as a measure or proportion of advantages, and is a guaranty of the external
relations between man and man. Now all these sciences
are derivatives of ethics, the true universal practical
philosophy. Starting out with this principle, we see how
far from true is the doctrine of Rossi, who saw no
bond of causality between wealth, prosperity, and moral
perfection, and on the other hand, how true is that of
Minghetti, who knows that happiness cannot be unac-

companied by duty and that economics, the eudemonological science, cannot be separated from ethics, to which,
however, it should be subordinated.   Sometimes it
happens that relations not ethical become economic
as in the case of the anxious pursuit of immoral objects,
but this is the consequence of pathological conditions
and of perverted minds and customs.   The objects of
nature are in such cases inverted, and the economic
phenomenon follows its own laws under the impulse
given it by man.   But if this impulse were always or
more generally opposed to ethics, economics would be
turned from their object and would no longer be a
truly human science.   Economics cannot be indifferent
to good and evil because man is the subject, to whose
nature good and evil are certainly not indifferent.   All
facts which raise and develop our powers cannot fail
to exert an influence over wealth.   If wealth presupposes
human nature, economics should not be altogether
founded upon the tendency to personal interest but
should take account (although to a subordinate degree)
of other individual and social tendencies, which affect
wealth.   Among the individual instincts differing from
that of interest, the sentiments growing out of a knowledge of dignity or decorum, and from the need of freedom
and independence, can be distinguished.   Among the
social sentiments we should place family affection,
patriotism, and religion.

§ 142. *Politics are Ethical.* Ethics are completed
in politics according to the Greek philosophers. As
a matter of fact, the good cannot be obtained except
in a community in which man acquires knowledge
of himself and what surrounds him by instruction
or culture, and where he can through education
direct his will towards the ends of reason. The common life or civil society is the *conditio sine qua non*

of true and concrete virtue (the object of morals) and of proportion of goods between men, and of the principle of protection in which lies the law. It is, furthermore, the presupposition of economics, a part of ethics in general. Economics have to do with wealth which demands exchange of goods, which in its turn demands trade and the common life. Production is not developed without coöperation and division of labor, two facts essentially social. The circulation and distribution of wealth cannot be thought of except in society. On the other hand, free economic activity would be a mere abstraction without the complexity of social department of safety, health, and education. Sociability furnishes a constantly increasing intellectual light, new combinations and powers to the individual, because it carries on a victorious struggle with nature and deprives her of the advantage of strength. It completes the deficient action of individuals and sometimes through its coercive branches promotes agreements to which the particular and general interests would tend too late. In this last case, the existence of society is not a presupposition of economics, but their principle and properly the principle which is applicable to state control in industrial undertakings. But with this exception, generally speaking, there is no doubt that the nature of the laws which govern the social organism are not within the powers of the economist and do not belong to economics. They are a presupposition for him even if economics are considered as a branch of sociology. Economics are a part of ethics, and should be developed within the confines of the latter science, but that is no reason why all of ethics should be confused with economics. For the sociological economist, sociology is a presupposition, as the mother science is a presupposition for the derivative science.

§ 143. *Economics are Biological.* Economics are the branch of ethics which is intimately connected with biology and more distantly connected with the other natural sciences. The first connection between economics and biology is Aristotle's natural κτῆσις that is, the spontaneous appropriative activity, common alike to animals and men, which develops over the objects necessary and useful to the existence of the individual in the social body. For Aristotle, the abundance of these things constitutes wealth, whence it is that his "Ctetics" is put in his "Economics." The Stoics, Cicero, Pliny, Celsus, Albertus Magnus, Thomas Aquinas, and Nifo admit and in places illustrate the fact of the common ownership of such activities by men and beasts. Later the physiocratic school studied fully the correlation between the physical, social, and economic orders extending the conception of the natural laws. Gioja showed in a confused way the relations of similarity between the economic functions of beasts and the economic facts of man, pointing out the causes of differences. After Gioja, among the Italians, Cognetti de Martiis collected and put in order all the scattered studies on the economic functions of animals and wrote an essay about the types of economic fact in inferior races and primitive civilizations; and by the aid of such research tried to establish the initial data of economic sociology, laying emphasis upon the criteria of Ingram. He believed that the office of economics consists in finding the forms and determining the laws of the appropriative activity in all its evolution from zoölogical rudiments to the highest progress in the life of human species. He looks to economics to show that the conscious adaptation of utilities and needs is first made by the natural organs, then by the aid of tools, and finally by exchange capable of transforming goods into money; and we know the intimate connection between the economic function of beasts and the economic fact of man so thoroughly illustrated by the positive school, but we do not admit that the duty of pursuing all the evolution of the appropriative activity from animals to man is incumbent upon the economist. The economist should occupy himself only with the economic functions of man, and presuppose those of animals, the object of biology, only stating the connection between one and the other.   It is true that a new product of evolution takes its origin from precedent forms, but it is likewise true that where there is a specific difference it cannot be the same.   The new product in such a case should be studied by itself in its own particular elements and differentiating qualities.   In economics, the appropriative activity of biology is transformed and acquires a new meaning.   The needs, energy, and utility of economic functions in the life of beasts are not the needs, activity, and advantages of the economic function of man.   The needs of man are not exclusively physical but intellectual and moral as well, not purely individual and collective but personal and social.   The physical needs of man are much modified by the influence of mind, and produce various and progressive tastes.   Mind is touched with a universality and does not feel bound to a single impression of the moment although it proceeds from knowledge of the particular.   Morality is created by the force of will capable of arresting the force of impulse and determining it according to reason.   The need of the individual, as such, is not the same as the need of the individual person, neither are the needs of coexistence those of society.   We know that a person is more than a simple individual as society is more than coexistence. Furthermore, the activity of man directed by mind

develops thought continuously subject to the forces
of nature and is essentially personal in concrete and
abstract man.   The advantages are not simple utilities or satisfactions of blind and indistinct tendencies,
but corporeal and incorporeal wealth, merchandise, or
objects of exchange, which distinguish the society of man
from the mutuality of animals.   The ethical end or the
conception of the perfection of the person of which we
have spoken before[1] is apparent in all the elements of
the economic fact.   For the economists such characteristics of the fact constitute merely presuppositions.   He
must recognize them but need not develop them in detail.
Their development and demonstration belong to other
moral studies, as the explanation of the appropriative
function in its first steps belongs to the natural sciences.

§ 144.   *Another Connecting Link between Economics and
Biology.*   A second connection between economics and
biology is found in the theory of population, because this
contains physiological and social elements and is connected, therefore, with two orders of conditions and
causes of differing efficiencies.   There are statistical and
economic theories of population.   The statistical theory
studies population by itself in its intrinsic elements and
explains the law upon which its actual methods of
existence or states of development depend.   The economic theory regards population in relation to the means
of subsistence, and was formulated by Malthus.   The
two theories are connected, since one cannot fully
treat of the state and movement of population
without considering social and economic causes, or the
relation between existence and subsistence without knowing the reasons and manner of demographic movements.
At present there is a tendency to assign a special and
distinct post to the entire study of population.   This

[1] *Cf.* § 84 *ante.*

new study has been variously treated, under many
names, from a social or biological point of view, but
the economic theory of population is directly bound up
with economics. We must not forget that man is the
subject of economics, and that his capacity for multiplication cannot be foreign to the social order of wealth.
No one is ignorant of the fact that Darwin and Spencer
have converted the Malthusian theory of population
into a universal law of organic nature. Malthus sees
a deep and general cause of poverty in the excess of population over the disposable means of support, from which
has sprung up a fierce struggle. Before this cause
he stops, as Messedaglia points out. Darwin and
Spencer consider the inequality and struggle as facts,
in which can be discovered the dawn of progress
and glimpses of nature itself, and reach a conclusion
of the perfection of the species, or at least its slow
and gradual transformation. With this premise, it is
clear that the economist should consider population
more from the social than the biological point of view.
He is not called upon to develop a law of organic nature,
but to show its applicability to man and especially its
limits and control. The universal law is for him only a
presupposition. The economist, for example, considers
as his biological premise the doctrine of Spencer on
population in general, and turns to study especially
the laws of human population, as they influence wealth.
Certainly all organisms, vegetable or animal, are exposed
to destructive and conservative forces which are so
composed that the prevalence of one provokes the reaction of the other. If a species is extraordinarily increased, it always happens that a predominance of
destructive forces will follow; such as a scarcity of
food, a restriction of space, or struggles with hostile
species. On the other hand, it cannot be denied that

the force of preservation develops in an inverse ratio to the generative force, and that where the greatest fecundity is found, there is the least force of self-preservation in the generant. The more complex and distinct in itself the organism, and the higher the being in the scale of life, the less is its coefficient of multiplication. Now, in economics, this biological doctrine is not gone over again, but a regard is had to a specific new limit and a conscious and voluntary adaptation to a preventative re-equaliberation, as Vanni calls it in his "Saggi sulla Teoria Sociologica della Popolazione." This re-equaliberation, no longer organic, that Spencer makes the mistake of disregarding, is foresight, the moral restraint of Malthus, the ethical principle of population. This principle, understood in its entire efficiency, serves to rectify the Malthusian doctrine, of which it is the base, showing the rationale of a fact not rare in times of civilization; that is, an increase in population inferior to the increase in the means of subsistence. We know that Malthus states that a corresponding increase of population should follow of necessity every increase of means. This principle is not contrary to the natural and historical laws which deny the possibility of progress that comes from the predominance of those better adapted for the struggle of life; which struggle is the result of the multiplication of mankind beyond the means and limits of subsistence. Furthermore, the struggle does not cease in the increasing development of civilization, neither does the predominance of the more fit decrease. But the struggle changes its aspect; one does not fight any more only for the preservation of life but for every kind of human advantage. The struggle is no longer the savage war for existence of primitive days. It is changed into competition and the pursuit of all the advantages of a more progressive life, in which forewarned is forearmed.

§ 145. *Economics are Historical.* Economics presuppose the laws of human nature. Now human nature is not a quiescence without development, but is urged on by a constant, continuous, and progressive internal movement, due to which it becomes, step by step, what it should be, and approximates its own ideal. This movement is the very life of the human race or history. Economics presuppose also the laws of society which is an organism which moves and fulfills an evolution determined by extrinsic circumstances, such as climate, topography, and by intrinsic factors of a physiological, intellectual, and moral nature, and by factors produced by the same evolution called by Spencer derivative, such as the increase in population, juristic and political progress, and the increase of culture. Since human nature and society move in history, the economic activity of man cannot be subtracted from the laws of progress by which it is divided constantly into multiple functions and acts that have an intimate correlation between themselves. It extends to a great number of things and becomes more intelligent, free, and potent, aided by artificial means of every kind. The science which studies these activities cannot forget the two golden "dignities" of Vico; one, that the nature of things is nothing else than their birth in certain times and in certain manners, and the other, that the study should begin when the matters of which it treats begin. The beginning to which he refers is the human and not the biological. This is the object of the Neapolitan philosopher's severe analysis of the necessity of social life. Hence, economics presuppose history. To state that history is a presupposition of economics does not in the least mean to reduce the science of wealth to economic history and statistics, to change it into a mere description of facts, or at most to convert it into a kind of philosophical discourse about the phases of economic reality. Economics, conceived in this way, would no longer be a science or a research of universal laws or typical forms; they would become only an empirical collection of concrete individual phenomena. Reduced to a philosophical discourse about the historical phases of wealth, economics could no longer examine intrinsic elements and would be confused with part of the philosophy of history. Now history is a presupposition of economics in the sense that induction, from social or historical facts, is not foreign to history. But it is its beginning and complement, without prejudice to the proper right of deduction, and does not imply the abandonment of universal laws and typical forms. Furthermore, it does not exclude the true or the ideal principle merely because it begins with the certain or the real, for mind proceeds from the particular to the universal. The ideal truth is immanent in fact although it does not appear in it and is not confusable with it. What should be is recognized in what has been and is; the type is seen in the variety and what is eternal is seen in the temporal, to borrow a phrase from Vico. On one hand, it is not reasonable to sacrifice law or duty to phenomena *per se* contradictory; on the other hand, it is absurd to wander in the empty and transcendental ideals of abstract and formal thought which have no relation to life. In this case, what has been and is does not count in comparison with the immovable universals and rigid types.

§ 146. *Economics Constitute the Condition not the Cause of Society.* The economic fact is not original, but derived, as we have seen,[1] from physio-psychical and historical elements and external forces. It is not predominant

[1] *Cf.* § 141 *et. seq., ante.*

in the sense that social life is a function of economics. It is not true that all social facts are born of the economic facts and that morals, religion, law, politics, and science are its effects.   This is the thesis of Marx, Gumplowicz, Loria, and others who forget that the simplest social fact has its origin in many causes and that once produced, reacts on such causes and is capable of modifying them.   Heretofore, we have several times laid emphasis upon the great complexity of social phenomena, the result of conditions of every sort; physical, intellectual, moral, juridical, political, religious, and historical.   In the cosmopolitanism of interest, for example, promoted by free trade or hindered by the reappearance of protection, we see the ethical conception of the brotherhood of man.   This shows that a Christian or pagan economics is always possible although it is absurd to think of a Buddhist geometry or a Mohammedan algebra.   Where cosmopolitanism exists, it is evident that it must exert an influence and modify the very causes by which it is formed, and therefore it can be stated that the ethical conception of brotherhood is not the same as it was at first.   After the development of such a fact the conception indicated acquires new elements, and assumes a more concrete and sensible form.   If, from one aspect, the economic fact presupposes the totality of social causes from which it springs; from another point of view, it is the condition for the development of facts belonging to a higher order.   It is true that the energy of mind, will, and imagination would not be had if the organic forces, especially those of the stomach, were lacking.   If the needs of life had not been more or less satisfied, scientific research, for example, would never have arisen.   A determinate manner of distribution of wealth is the presupposition of some juridical and political institutions.   But, as the

stomach is not the cause of the inspirations of genius
or of the strong resolutions of character or of the more
spiritual emotions, so the economic fact is the mere
condition and not the determining principle of social
life and civilization.   This principle is mind or thought.
If there is a predominating social factor, it should not
be sought in the lower forms of evolution, but in
the higher, where there is found a principle that
is conditioned on the whole series of precedent forms
and nevertheless exerts an influence, modifies each of
them, and gives them a greater meaning and value.   Only
mind is capable of doing this.   It appeared last and
has need of all the other grades of the series, though it
transforms and re-creates them upon its appearance.
The criterion for the consideration of the social fact is
always restricted to a unilateral method; the entire
social fact cannot be considered except with economic
elements.   Human life and history are not understood
in this narrow theory.

§ 147.   *Law is Economic.*   A great part of the content of law is economic matter, because law is the
measure, the proportion of advantages, utilities, and
wealth.   It cannot fail to refer to advantages, but
it does not necessarily refer to wealth and utilities in
the strict sense.   There are ethico-juridical relations
which have nothing to do with wealth, interest, and
utility as objects and which cannot be given a material valuation.   Here lies the error of the German writers
(for example Dankwardt, and Böhm Bawerk[1]) who wish
to reconstruct the science of law on the exclusive basis
of economic life.   Minghetti, in his work "Dell' Economia
Pubblica e delle sue Attinenze colla Morale e con il
Diritto," points out that the ancient philosophers had

[1] "Recht und Verhältnisse von Standpunkte in Volkwartshaftlich
Gütenlehre."

an idea of a cosmic order founded on proportion and wished to make it the type for the moral and civil order. The "ne quid nimis" of the Delphic oracle, the doctrine of numbers of Pythagoras, the dialectics of Plato, the Aristotelean mediety, the "servare proportionem" of Cicero all denote how these philosophers placed this conception at the base of science and art, which, raised to the dignity of a dogma and connected with the idea of Providence, holds its own in the doctrine of the Fathers of the Church and the great writers of the Middle Ages, among whom Dante made law consist in proportion. Modern experimental science finds the law of proportion in the great movements of celestial bodies or in the most minute combinations of chemical attraction. This law, too, should be considered in a general study of history and in the various parts of all civil sciences. The greatest production, the best distribution, the best trade, the most commodious consumption, and the best coördination of all these factors are obtained through the laws of proportion. To maintain the proportion between land, capital, and labor, we need science, diligence, and the habit of sober, hard work. To maintain the proportion between population and the means of existence, we need forethought and wealth. To maintain it between production and the division of wealth, domestic and foreign commerce, cash and credit, we need accurate judgment of offer and demand, truth, and faith; and to maintain it between supply and demand we need the true valuation of goods, temperance, and abstinence. In all these things justice and the respect of another's rights are presupposed in a well-ordered and honest civil community. Starting out with Minghetti's conception, it is evident that law is a proportion which contains another proportion in itself. There is no doubt that law is in

Minghetti's mind a proportion of goods, because he thinks the idea of proportion dominates the cosmos, in that it is the object of the physical and moral sciences. Economic proportion cannot be realized without justice; that is, on one hand the measure of mine and thine and on the other a principle of protection. Law is the norm and guaranty of the reciprocal enforcement of individual activities and of the organization of the ethical whole in respect to every external advantage, social utility, and perfection, and therefore in regard to the production, movement, division, and consumption of wealth. But wealth is not the only matter of law, but every form of human well-being realized or realizable in external relations between man and man and man and things. The economic content of law is revealed in its three divisions. In private law it is shown in property, and its methods of acquisition, in contract, the family relations, and inheritance; in public law, in the relations between prosperity and wealth of citizens, and in political and administrative government. And in international law, the humanity of nations and justice between peoples, is capable of a future development and consideration as a consequence of a strict economical calculation, as Antonio Scialoia said. No jurist of these latter days can be ignorant of or fail to take into consideration the laws of economics, because they control a large part of the objects of law and of legislation.

§ 148. *Definition of Politics.* Politics, according to the ancients, contain all the science of the State. Plato considers philosophy the royal art and says that politics lies midway between the theoretical and practical studies; and that the politician is a man of science. Aristotle includes in politics all the teachings which have to do with the State. In our own day

Mohl in "Encyclopädie der Staatswissenschaften," Bluntschli in "Die Lehre vom Unternem Staats," and Holtzendorff in "Die Principien der Politik," restrict its conception and agree in considering it the science of the ends of the State and of the proper means to attain them. Holtzendorff determines his thought with marked precision, stating that politics are not occupied with the administration of justice, which is the object of the juristic sciences. Among the Italians, Rosmini defines politics in the same way; that such a study should advance social ends and explain the means which the government has in its power in relation to these ends, and the most convenient method of using them.

§ 149. *Politics are a Practical Social Science.* The subject-matter of politics refers to a single aspect of the social fact, the one that regards the finality of civil life ordered by the State and the more convenient means to obtain it. Politics are a special science distinct from sociology which, as a philosophical study, considers fundamental laws and includes them in the more general laws of social organization. From these laws it takes the directive principle of the action of the State, that assumes imperative forms which become practical norms. It can be accurately stated, therefore, that politics are not part of sociology, but a practical social science based on the results of the general theory of society. It can be shown by the important conclusions of Rosmini, which cannot be overlooked, that politics are not part of sociology. Rosmini believes that civil society is a body tending towards a destination, and divides the political rules according to whether they regard the end towards which the social body should move, the laws of its movement, or its forces. We must recall briefly the classes of rules, stated in his

"Filosofia della Politica."   The rules, treated from the point of view of the result, first can be formulated as follows: Let the government be careful to maintain and develop the prevalent force on which the existence of society depends; the second urges the government so to act that prosperity will produce the proper welfare upon which man relies, because contented citizens are tranquil and quiet. The prevalent force is the result of the complexity of all the physical, intellectual, and moral forces.   These latter impress their characteristics upon the physical and intellectual forces and constitute its unity and give it its character.   In every society there are four epochs: in the first, existence is given to society and it is therefore concerned with the substance and not the accidentals; in the second, the age of the fulness of social life, the accidentals are considered without losing sight of the substance; in the third, regard is had to the accidentals and not to the substance, whence a decay; in the fourth, the accidentals of the accidentals are thought of and the substance of society is forgotten, and all its accidental features are thought true and efficient.   This is the epoch in which civil society is subject to great upheavals and turbulent explosions, and can easily fall into ruin.   The prevalent force or the substance of society in one age can consist of physical force, in another of prudence and astuteness, and finally of the principles of justice.   The rules, decreed by the nature of social bodies, can be outlined in this formula; that the politics which bring civil society nearest to its natural and regular construction are good, and those which separate it from its nature are bad.   The natural construction is the result of an equilibrium between population and wealth, wealth and power, civil power and material force, civil and military power and science, science and virtue.   The

rule which grows out of the consideration of the laws
of movement (hinted at but not sufficiently developed
by Vico, because of the lack of diverse social transformations of various peoples), can be reduced to the
following: The political means, that are in harmony
with the laws of natural movement of civil society, are
good; the others, contrary to its nature, are bad. As
to satisfaction, society first tends to existence, then to
power, wealth, and pleasure. True satisfaction lies in
virtue and justice. The progress of good is one thing,
and progress in general is another, as there is a difference
between progress and movement which consists of a step
forward or back, ahead or across, or a mixed kind of
progress, the head turned over the shoulders. We
must clearly distinguish the movement of humanity
in its intellectual development and in the corresponding external forms of society, from the moral and eude-
monistical movement. The last rule, shown by the
study of the direct and indirect forces of society, can
be put in this proposition; the political means that
with the least expense and trouble effect the greatest
social good are the best. The physical, intellectual,
and moral forces of a society of a determined period in
their reciprocal influence and relation with the social
whole can be worked out in proper proportion on an
exact scale with politico-moral statistics.

§ 150. *Politics are Moral.* The political purposes
and means cannot be immoral because they are connected with the supreme principle of human welfare.
There is not nor can there be contradiction between
moral laws and the true utilities or permanent interests
of the individual or collective person. The State is
an ethical organism, and therefore, its efficacious work
should not be opposed to the principles of the honest
and just, which are not rigid formulæ, but which par-

take of the certain and which are developed in life among the vicissitudes of opportunities, becoming always more varied in the different spheres of human activity according to race, age, and place. Politics, like law, are not separate from ethics nor can they be confused, but are simply distinct. If we believe that politics are separate from law, we are governed by two prejudices: by retaining the belief that the art of government has for its object power and the accumulation of material means of control, the selfish utility of the State, the destruction or ruin of other nations; and by confusing public with private morals. The first is a denial of the true finalities of the State and of the conception of the moral and juridical communion of peoples, whose humanity is developing step by step if they are adaptable to progress. The second is discordant with the nature of the ethical principle, in that it is applicable differently in different spheres and acquires in each a new significance. The individual, for example, can sacrifice his life, but the State must preserve its life. Murder, assault, the destruction of property, slander, and highway robbery are serious crimes if committed by individuals. In war such acts are permissible for the State, and the State is allowed the power of profiting by illegal or immoral acts; the reception of deserters and the use of spies are acts of this category. A statesman can profit by evil; that is, by avarice, selfishness, vanity, or simplicity. The evil act, however, should be offered and then can be taken advantage of, but must not be sought by an honest politician. The art of government or politics, as an art, is not the same as the practice of deceit or bad faith or acts of violence, because it realizes among the various social contingencies the principles of a science which is distinct from ethics, but not substantially opposed thereto. The art of politics makes statesmen able to recognize the laws of human nature and society, to understand and take in situations at a glance, to measure the proximate and distant results of an act, develop the reciprocal influences of the forces of the State and civil community, and get the greatest profit out of every occasion by adapting his conduct to the indefinite variability of events in order to obtain his end and the ideal he has set before himself. So politics have their part in the ideal, because they are a practical study and tend to the perfection of activity and are, in that, like ethics. True politics are not a materialistic, immoral, brutal art, nor a poetic, imaginative, sentimental study, but include high ethical and social objects to be attained by the most opportune, convenient, and efficacious means. All politics, says Schleiermacher, lie in the efficiency of action. Now the efficiency of action contains elements of two kinds; elements which have to do with the finality, and elements which stand in relation to efficiency. The finality alone is abstraction and mere exigency; the efficiency alone manifests a causal series of facts, forces related and dependent, by which everything which already exists is developed, but nothing more.

§ 151. *Politics Include Statesmanship.* Politics, Bluntschli writes, are the science of the State in that it is alive, and public law is the science of the State in that it exists. Politics are occupied with the ends and means of the State. Public law establishes its legal coördination. It is clear, from this definition, that politics should be in accord with the constitution, otherwise a deep and irrational contradiction is introduced into the life of the State. This is true only in the abstract, because in fact a constitution outgrows its usefulness and becomes an antiquated and rigid form.   In this case, politics should not be stopped by such a form.   Politics, the science of the State in that it lives, tend in such a case to promote the recognition of law *in fieri*, that incites the collective consciousness, and tends to usurp the old law and develops more fully the sources of unwritten law to fulfill and reënforce the written law.   A constitution, statute, or ordinance is the effect of the given position of things in a certain state of society at a certain time and has no reason to exist when the position of things is changed and when the state of society is different.   For politics, a constitution, statute, or ordinance are so many means, and as such cannot be perpetual forms.   It is not right to sacrifice the freedom of generations and the interests of life to the vain and irrational ideas of the past.   But aside from this variation and again considering politics and public law of themselves, it cannot be denied that in both studies there is the whole essence of the State, conceived of not only as a high union for objects of law and culture, but also in the form of a civil community founded on the division of classes of individuals having common physical, economic, intellectual, moral, and religious interests.   The word "State" has two meanings, one broad and one narrow.   In the first sense, a State contains civil society; in the second it is as distinct from society as the simple community of interest is distinct from the political community, which is, nevertheless, a personality.   The conception of civil society contains all the collective formations which are found between the individual and the State; or rather between the family and the State.   The definition given by Mohl, Bluntschli, Stein, and Gneist refers to society thus understood in its strict and proper sense.   Even Hegel looks upon civil society as a community of interests bound together, spontaneously aiding one another, distinct from the family and from the State, and occupying a place between them. When society is thought of as an organism of collective formations and intermediate centres, it connotes a great variety of groups or classes which tend to diverse objects of life and represent common interests. These objects may be physical, economic, intellectual, moral, or religious, according to the means of satisfaction. All are developed separately and even can be in a state of struggle among themselves, but they tend always to interpenetrate and harmonize since they are derived from the activities of man, which are not of their own essence antagonistic. Over such a community of the interests of life rises the State, which is the juridical personality of a people; man in the abstract forms man in the particular of a nation. The State realizes law which comprehends all human nature that develops in social relations. The State can be called the juristic form of the civil union. Furthermore, it is the natural moderator in the struggle of the interests and classes. Hence the difference between the social, political, and juristic sciences; the first have for their immediate object society understood in the broad and proper sense, the second have to do with State, and the third with law. The social sciences indirectly consider the State because it is inseparable from society; the political sciences consider society. We know that the juristic sciences, although they have law as their immediate object, cannot get along without social and political studies. Politics without public law would lack concrete forms and institutions; public law without politics would be a casual juristic organism; that is, a legal asset not based on knowledge of the finality of the State and the means at its disposal. The real and living State arises from the concrete fusion of politics and public law.   The idea of the State becomes philosophical (a human idea, as Vico would say), when it comprehends the State, in that it lives and exists, and when it is a result of elements that are referable to the certain understood in its generality, and to the true regarded in its highest rationale.   The State thus conceived is the proper object of the philosophy of law, which reforms its unity, divided into politics and public law, and determines its value and places it in relation with the other fundamental notions which form the system of the most universal juristic ideas.

CHAPTER X

RATIONAL AND POSITIVE LAW. SOURCES AND APPLICATION

THE DISTINCTION BETWEEN RATIONAL AND POSITIVE LAW
IN THEIR NATURE AND IN HISTORY. — HABIT AND PRIMITIVE
CUSTOM. — JURISPRUDENCE AND ITS OFFICE. — LEGISLATION
AND THE CODES. — THE EFFICACY OF STATUTES IN SPACE. —
THE EFFICACY OF STATUTES IN TIME. — THE DIVERSE THEO-
RIES OF RETROACTIVITY.

§ 152. *The Difference Between Rational and Positive
Law.* It has been shown that law is composed of the true
and the certain. It is idea and reality, it is a principle
of reason which develops in the stages of life adapting
itself to the particular condition of the people according
to time and place. Law as an intelligible principle
does not fully develop in the historical forms in which
it is realized, since they do not equal its content, whence
the eternal striving for progress that governs institutions and laws, urging them to ends more universal and
more in accord with reason. Rational law is based
immediately on the true, and is universal. The true is
developed in the certain, in which lies its proof, when
it is generalized and historical, not considered and
studied in its several parts. Positive law, on the other
hand, is based immediately on the certain, and has a
particular character, since it is the elaboration of popular
or national consciousness. The certain is not foreign
to the true — it is its extrinsification. And therefore
ideal elements are found in positive law, as historical ele-

ments are found in rational law. The certain of positive law, a detached fragment of the idea of law, is a part of reality, and is not identical with what is part of philosophy, that is, with reality in general. We must not forget that philosophy endeavors to explain not this or that reality, but the reality of knowledge *per se*.

§ 153. *The Belief in a Rational Law.* We have pointed out before[1] that the Greek philosophers before Aristotle had advanced to a conception of a law superior to the positive laws. Aristotle showed the distinction between natural and positive justice. In his mind, the just *per se* was a universal measure, contradistinguished from positive justice or that of the State. The latter can be the mere determination of the statutes or founded on nature; and hence the difference between legal and natural justice. We have shown that, in Cicero's mind, the "jus naturale" depends on the "recta ratio," and the "jus civile" is connected with the "ratio civilis." Cicero distinguishes the "jus gentium" from the "jus naturæ," considering the former as a form of positive law common to all peoples and thinking that in it lies the principle of the "recta ratio." All the interpreters of Cicero's thought, however, do not agree on this. The Romans at first recognized only their own law, the "jus civile." Later they found, through their many relations with other peoples, that there was something identical in all laws, and conceived of a general positive law, a "jus gentium quo gentes humanæ utuntur." In progress of time and with development of the mind, the jurisconsults based the origin of the "jus gentium" in the "naturalis ratio," and defined it "jus quod naturalis ratio inter omnes homines constituit." Later still they generalized further and came to the conclusion of the existence of a law more

[1] *Cf.* § 44 *ante.*

ample and constant than the "jus gentium," that is, a "jus naturale." Ulpian defines this "quod natura omnia animalia docuit," and Cervidius Scævola and Paulus as "id quod semper æquum et bonum est." The Stoic influence that controlled the idea of antecedents and consequents of nature[1] is reached in this definition.

§ 154. *Origins of Different Kinds of Law.* St. Thomas distinguishes positive law, "lex humana," from the "lex naturalis" and "lex æterna." The first is "quædam ab hominibus inventa" and should be part of the "lex naturalis," which in its turn is part of the "lex æterna," "ratio in Deo existens," "ratio æternæ sapientæ," identical with the "voluntas Dei." Now such a distinction shows an advance on the philosophical theories of the Middle Ages, in which natural law is based entirely upon divine will as shown in the revealed word. Filomusi-Guelfi, in his "Concetto del Diritto Positivo," shows clearly that natural law began to lose its theological character and to be more intimately connected law in the days of the Renaissance and Reformation. The attempts of Melancthon, Oldendorp, Hemmings, and Winkler, show the new phase. Grotius denied that the Scriptures are the source of natural law and admits the possibility of the existence of law even in the case of the non-existence of God. Natural law is derived from right reason to insure a tranquil society; civil law emanates from the common will of men. So Hobbes recognized natural law, "dictamen rectæ rationis," which imposes peace and is a guaranty, and positive law, the effect of the sovereign will which harmonizes with natural law in keeping the peace. Positive law for the rest is in antithesis to natural law regarded as the original law of the state of nature and fear.

[1] *Cf.* § 107 *ante.*

§ 155. *Rational and Positive Law Compared.* Puf-fendorf finds the fundamental rationale of law in divine command and makes science take a backward step here as well as in the discussion of the relation between morals and law. St. Thomas and Wolff both believe that natural law is based on human nature and 'that positive law arises from will or agreement; that the first is given by reason and the latter enacted by the State. Filomusi-Guelfi shows the germ of distinction in the doctrine of Rousseau, because the principle of inalienable liberty is the law of nature, and the will of the people is the principle of positive law. There is no doubt at all in Kant's mind, because he strictly separates rational law (the complexity of norms which create external legislation) from positive law (the collection of statutes which exist as such, and which depend upon the will of the legislature governed by reason). Fichte sees the realization of natural law in positive or historical law. Schelling starts out with the principle of reason as the identity of the ideal and the real, which he reaches by a simple intuition without a dialectic process. He places the same difference between the two terms that there is in his system between the ideal and the real, both being originally the same. In his mind, positive law is the necessary form of natural law. Hegel shows that rational law is based on universal principles,while positive law is determined by the national characteristics, religion, and degree of civilization of the people. Positive law is not contradictory of rational law, which by degrees appears in it. Hegel is wrong only in saying that the positive law stands in relation to rational as the Pandects stand to the Institutes. The simile is bad, because the Pandects and Institutes are both treatises of positive law, the one full, and the other restricted to the use of the schools.

§ 156. *Distinction Between Rational and Positive Law among the Positivists.* The distinction between rational and positive law is recognized in positivism in diverse forms. Spencer, in "The Man Versus the State," admits a natural law based on the uniform and constant conditions of existence. He is bitterly criticized by other positivist philosophers for departing from historical truth and contradicting the laws of change and the relativity of cognition, and considering man only as he is shown by biology. There are writers who say that this conception of Spencer is a relic of his early theory contained in his "Social Statics," according to which morals and law are based on the realization of the divine idea. God foreordains the happiness of man, which is obtained by the observation of the inflexible laws of existence. These express a connection between cause and effect, between conduct and result, and determine necessarily what is good or evil, just or unjust. If the exercise of faculties is indispensable to human happiness, the duty on one hand and the right on the other to exercise them are derived from it. These are the very words of Vanni, who gives a résumé of the Spencerian doctrine, and says at the same time that such an absolute ethical system cannot take account of actual imperfections, and therefore represents the law of ideal humanity; and that eliminating the theological and teleological conceptions, there remains in the later theories of the English philosopher the idea of an intrinsic reason in morals and law due to the conditions of existence, and of a law not created by the State but growing out of relations established by nature. This idea is clearly developed in Spencer's last book, "Justice," we may add. Spencer says in its preface that he wishes to explain justice first, abstracting every presupposition belonging to a supernatural order. He distinguishes positive law, the work of the State, from natural or potential law, corresponding to social ideality, absolutely true and just.   This kind of law, he says, has its base in the nature of man, who wills freely according to the dictates of reason.   Vanni accepts the conception of a law founded on the indispensable conditions of existence and the constitution of things, and says that it is the true part of the old theory of natural law.

§ 157. *Custom is the First Source of Positive Law.* The first and chief source of positive law is custom, which presupposes the juristic sentiment of people and certain external, constant, and general acts by which it is shown.   Ulpian says, "Mores sunt tacitus consensus populi longa consuetudine inveteratus."   A need arises in society and demands a legal recognition.   At the beginning, its satisfaction is obtained through transitory and isolated acts, and then a general conviction of the necessity of this satisfaction grows.   The acts are repeated with uniformity and constancy by the greater number of the members of the community. This leads to the appearance of the "diuturni mores consensus utentium comprobati," of the customary or unwritten law, which has its expression in custom. The factors of struggle and adaptation enter in such a process, but its character of immediateness is beyond controversy, because the process is entirely intuitive and irreflexive and needs no special organ of the State. Sometimes, this irreflexive and unconscious process has its beginning in a conscious act of a single individual, imitated by others.   Who is ignorant of the influence of the example of Lucius Lentulus, Augustus, and Labio on the Roman law concerning codicils?   Is it not often true that a local dialect forced on or chosen by a people becomes a national language?   Does not a type or individual characteristic, strongly emphasized and in a position of attraction, become a model for all in an age where the spirit of imitation is strong? With this premise, the statement of the Glossators may be very far from true that holds that the essence of custom lies in the action itself as well as the theory; of Puchta,[1] that bases it entirely on general conviction, and of Savigny, in his "System des Heutigen Römischen Rechts." Custom involves necessarily the two conceptions of the conviction and the constant and general use which have the mutual relation of a basic principle and an external expression. It can be easily understood that it must contain as positive law the true. In other words it must be "rationabilis" and must in progressive times be recognized as law in order to have an obligatory force.

§ 158. *Primitive Custom Differs from General Custom.* But custom, so conceived, is particular and is already a distinct legal form, and as such is posterior to the primitive custom imposed by a single, indivisible, and absolute power (of which Bagehot speaks), which tended to form the tissues of legality, reducing, as Vico said, the inhuman and wild Poliphemi to obedience. Before legal customs and norms, before religious decrees, there were customs and norms of another kind, appertaining to the government of ceremonies, according to Spencer. Maine points out in his "Ancient Law" that the Homeric Themis is divine, inspiring the sentences of the gods and kings; that the succession of these sentences, similar in similar cases, created custom; and that in Homer the word νόμος is not found, nor is there any conception of a god, the author of a code. He cites some observations of Grote which seem new; — that in the beginning heroic royalty prevailed of divine right, then an aristocracy, religious in the Orient, military and civil in the Occident; and that the aristocracy exercised a

[1] Das Gewohnheitsrecht.

monopoly in the interpretation of law, and began thus
a customary law. Leist, in "Graeco-Italische Rechts-
geschichte," thinks that positive religious decrees preceded the formation of custom. Pantaleoni, in "Saggio
Intorno ad una Quistione di Diritto Preistorico," severely
criticizes the theories of Maine in respect to Homer,
but he thinks that there is no doubt that the opinion
of the English writer can be applied to a more remote
and ante-Homeric period. Here it may be well to point
out that Maine, who was the first to write that the repetition of the judgments of the patriarch-kings created
custom, later gives us to understand that such judgments are on the other hand the result of custom. He
says nothing, however, as to the origin of this custom
or the method of its formation, since he studied a phase
of relatively advanced evolution which contained the
patriarchal society and did not go back to the beginning. Maine considered an already formed law; he
cleared away the confusion between this and other social
forces, especially religion, but he started out from the
time in which legal custom appears. Now, it is not
possible to go back to the first origins of law without
a generic custom which the greater part of the recent
writers consider as the result of imposition, after which,
when the legal tissue has been built up and strengthened,
other particular customs, distinct among themselves,
such as purely legal customs, spontaneously come into
existence. Certainly, the observation of the customary norm is not possible unless man has first acquired
the habit of obedience to some norm. Primitive man
was not in the least disposed to submission to a precept,
except under a rigorously coercive discipline. The
observations of Grote, repeated by Maine, are old and
are found in Vico's works, whose ideas on the divine
prerogatives of the primitive age are known. Vico

said that customs existed as examples before the laws, which are universal; that the laws of the Twelve Tables are preceded by the customs of the Fathers. He says further that the penalty inflicted on Horatius is an example of the custom of the ancients; and that the governments of the oligarchs were ruled by custom, the custody and inalterability of the customs of the ancients being the base of this régime. The law of this epoch is a hidden mystery. Maine is right in pointing out that in primitive times the recognition of a social authority was not necessary for the existence of custom. Law is shown spontaneously in custom, and no one disputes its validity of form or demands its recognition on the part of the State in such an age. An extensive development of mind and a profound analysis of fact is needed before the conception of the necessity of the recognition of this source of the law on the part of the State is felt. Such a conception is the fruit of pure reflection in the ages of reason. But if originally there were no such recognition, and if custom had its worth by its own force without having need of an authority to decree it, later it was explicated, made certain, and strengthened, losing the elements foreign to it by the work of special bodies of magistrates, and of those learned in the law, who formulated and applied it. In Rome the College of Pontifices, learned in the law, and the prætor interpreted the law. At the beginning the poets who stood by the side of the Indian and Greek kings, inspiring their decisions, were the depositories of these customs. After the days of the College, the jurisconsults came with the mission of clearing, developing, and purifying the first and obscure source of law.

§ 159. *Custom Loses Importance, as the Statutes Multiply.* In historical times, with natural reason fully developed, custom which represents mere juristic intuition cannot have its old extent and former efficacy. When reflection about universal principles dominates, and the organization of public power is developed, custom cannot have the force of annulling the laws, as it had in Rome. To-day the precept of the jurisconsult is no longer true; "Quare rectissine etiam illud receptum est ut legas non solum suffragio legislatoris sed etiam tactio consensu omnium per desuetudinem abrogantur." Custom has entirely lost its control in criminal law, because no penalty can be inflicted without a statute, and has preserved only the part of it that is essentially voluntary in civil law. It has a marked development in international law in which codification has been lacking, and in commercial law in which codification has had to assume a very general character in order not to hinder the indefinite and constantly changing combinations of the life of trade and exchange, and to keep the different people together through common and useful customs favoring the cosmopolitanism of mercantile interests.

§ 160. *Learned Research is the Second Source of Law.* The second source of positive law is doctrine or jurisprudence, which represents scientific reflection on the statutes and general convictions shown by customs. It is considered, however, as the immediate and supplementary form of customary and legislative law. Its action in respect to law is first practical and is shown in the "usus fori" or "rerum perpetuo similiter judicatarum auctoritas": and then becomes theoretical through exegesis and systemization. Jurisprudence tends to interpretate the living law, to supplement it with equity, and to show the necessity or convenience of accepting new principles. Interpretation means the understanding and reproduction with proper knowledge of the thought of the legislator. If all the laws should be understood, we have to interpret not only the obscure laws, as

Borrelli says, but even those that are clear. It is customary in the schools to distinguish interpretation by its elements of efficiency and origin. In regard to its elements, interpretation is literal, logical, historical, and systematic, depending upon whether it has to do with the word the *mens legis*, with conditions of the time and organic complexity of the legislative disposition; as to efficiency it is declaratory, extensive, and restrictive; as to origin it is judicial, scientific, and legislative, depending upon whether it is made by the judge, the interpreters, or the legislator. Donnello calls these divisions popular; Savigny calls them strange. They point out that all interpretation is a free act of the intellect, of a learned and declaratory character, and uses the four elements indicated, which are only means and not species or forms. The modern codes decree that the judge can never refuse to apply a law alleging its obscurity as a pretext, but must attribute to it a meaning in accordance with the literal meaning of the words and the intention of the legislature, and when he cannot decide the case with a precise legal disposition he can have recourse to other dispositions of similar cases. When the case remains at all doubtful it should be decided according to the general principles of law. Such principles are not those of abstract natural or rational law, but rather those of the philosophy of positive law, a part, however, of philosophy of law in general. Thus, the science of law and its philosophy become sources of law, and form, together with customs and statutes, the juridical inheritance of a people.

§ 161. *Jurisprudence is Distinct from Custom.* Thus much understood, it is clear that Bluhme, in "Encyclopädie Jurische," is wrong in regarding jurisprudence only as a reflexive form of customary law; and that Stahl in "Philosophie des Rechts," Marezzoll in "Lehrbuch

der Institutes des Römischen Rechts," and Bruns in
"Encyclopädie der Rechtswissenschaft," are wrong in
denying that it is a source of law. Even historically
this statement is not exact because there have been
instances in which some rules have had practical efficiency through the work of science. Warnkönig in the
"Encyclopädie" and Savigny point out that analogical
interpretation is not a kind of extensive interpretation
because the former fills a gap and the latter extends
the sense of the law. Interpretation by analogy is
allowed through the conception that the judge cannot
refuse to apply the law, and not through strict principles of interpretation. In analogy, a conclusion is reached
by coördinating one thing to another, where if they
were coördinate the rule of the first case would not be
general but special, as in exceptions and as in the case
of the "jus singulare." Besides interpretation, jurisprudence supplements law by equity, which is not in the
least opposed to law. Equity, Aristotle taught, is better
justice, differing from legal justice and correcting it. It
is the law itself in opposition to its literal and narrow
form. Cicero says "jus civili est æquitas." Celsus defines
the science of law as "ars boni et æqui;" so the sentence
of Paulus, that natural law consists in "id quod semper
bonum ac æquum est." It is the constant thought of
the Roman jurisconsults that the "legitimum" lay in
the word and in the letter of the law. "Verba et literæ
legis" should be based on the "æquum." Beyond the
"æquum" there is the "rigor juris," the "jus durum
summum callidum," the "angustissima formula," and
the "summa crux." The "æquitas" is "jus benginum,
temporatum, naturalis justitia, ratio humanitatis." All
the history of Roman law shows this progressive movement from the "legitimum" to the "bonum," in which
"fictiones" forms of analogy, capable of modifying the

substance of law, without altering its appearance, play
no small part. Finally, jurisprudence expresses its
desire of reform, the result of a long and attentive
critical practical examination of the legal institutions,
and encourages legislative changes and new codifications.

§ 162. *Statutes are the Third Source of Positive Law.*
The third source of positive law, independent like
custom, and not supplementary like jurisprudence, more
certain and general than either and at the same time
reflexive, is the statutes. These are the expression of
the sovereign will of the State, or people formed in a
State, and are reducible to a "communis reipublicæ
sponsio," to a "commune præceptum" according to the
Roman definition. A statute is an independent source
because the direct and formal effect of the supreme social
authority, and is reflexive because it is the result of the
meditation of the legislators and jurisconsults. It is
more certain and general than custom and jurisprudence because it is a fixed and abstract formula intelligible to all and withdrawn from the interpretation
of the judges and the discussions of the scientific
schools. It is connected with jurisprudence, in its
learned preparation and development, and with custom,
which at the beginning furnishes the material, although
later it is formed more on a scientific basis. It is
not born of rocks and trees, as Plato points out, but
it presupposes a number of natural and historical
conditions which constitute its bases in fact. At this
point, it is useful to point out that the definition of
a statute as the expression of the sovereign will of the
State can lead to error, and that it is necessary to
avoid every possible error about the relations of a
statute. The English analytical school, represented by
Bentham and Austin, says that the notion of law, as
a statute, is inseparable from that of sovereign power

and its coercive force; these ideas are found in the above definition of a statute. Maine disagrees with the analytical school and thinks that the definition is exact if it refers to an advanced state of civilization and therefore to a mature juridical system, but that it is inexact if applied to the earlier stages. In primitive times, law was not the product of a legislative organ but lay in the complexity of venerated customs. Their obligatoriness did not depend upon the coercive force of sovereign power, but grew out of public opinion and religious beliefs. We have said before[1] that Maine did not see that the authority of power, coercion, and obligation were preëxistent in an indistinct form in generic custom, from which various customs developed, among which was the distinct juristic custom. Generic custom embraced all the norms which were resolved into authoritative traditions, respected for themselves. Authority is given by custom, and the obligation of its observation is connected with the fear of offending the will of dead ancestors, whose spirits influence human acts. This general fear is a coercive force, and is dominant in conduct regulated by general opinion. The three conceptions, included in the notion of the statutes, do not develop all at once in an epoch of reflection, but have their antecedents in the most remote times from which, therefore, according to Vico, the study should begin because the thing began then.

§ 163. *Statutes are not Mere Growths.* As to the relation between the statutes and environment, we must remember that it can be exaggerated in the sense that the formation of law and of statutes is looked upon as the natural unconscious and slow product of things that move of themselves without force or struggle. Neither should an excessive action

[1] *Cf.* § 158 *ante.*

be attributed to spontaneity. Vico taught that the human world is developed through modifications of mind. Consequently, it is necessary to attribute a large part to the factor of reflection.   Now, it is generally admitted that the historical school is inclined to this exaggeration, a fact manifest in the theory of Charles Comte, the author of "Traité de Legislation," and in the doctrines of many positivists, disposed to look upon legislators as kinds of copyists or secretaries of their times and registrars of customs, and upon legislation as natural history. If this were true, science would have only the duty of describing facts and not of giving advice, since the statutes would be the real powers, the relations of nature, of which Montesquieu speaks, which determine the methods of the existence and development of a people; it would be useless to go to the legislator and it would be vain to hope anything from him.   Without doubt these theories are partially true, in that environment influences man and in primitive times subjected him, and in that nature determines man and gives him his characteristics, and makes him similar, but does not make him identical (as Gioberti says).   It is clear that the statutes should conform to the conditions of space and time and the customs of the people. About this there can be no question, but then comes the moment in which man reacts and takes his revenge by dominating them in his turn, modifying and transforming their elements and forces, and beginning the course of civilization.   In such a moment, reflection or mind is prevalent and human liberty begins, and a second cycle in creation from man to nature opens; — the first is from nature to man; — two cycles visible in the life of the individual who epitomizes the life of the species.   In law, nature enters with all its influence on man but man also enters with his reflection and free transforming activity. Statutes, as the work of man, succeed within certain confines in producing modifications; environment and experience prove this. As the sources of positive law increase and are higher, we see less of the subjection of man to nature. And as legislative law is explicated, the power of the statutes to modify the environment increases, because science prevails and with science, freedom. We have said that the doctrines pointed out are not speculatively true because development implies force, whose idea is not complete without the notion of obstacles to conquer. Neither are they historically true because law has run its course between cruel contrasts and struggles. Such doctrines are also dangerous because they lead men to inertia, teaching that things fulfill themselves with little or no coöperation on their part.

§ 164. *Laws should be Clear, Precise, and Indubitable.* Statutes, says Trendelenburg, should be stated in serious and dignified language since they are ethical will, that is, superior to the passions. They should be brief and calm (since they are potent will), and as intelligible to all as common speech. The expression of the social will should be precise and incisive. Precision of conception is limited by precision of definition. In the sciences definitions show the boundaries of the conceptions. In law they are something more, and determine the limits and legal relations, and represent a true creative force. The ancient maxim, "Omnis definitio in jure civili est periculosa parum enim est ut non subverti possit," shows the difficulty which there is in comprehending the changeable relations of life in a clear and precise conception, but one cannot deny the necessity of exact definitions, custodians of the certainty of law, kept within the borders of legal determination. The definitions of law are sometimes, therefore, nominally declaratory, and sometimes are creative; there are not lacking kinds in which all the essence of concept is not contained, but only an element or some characteristic sign of it.

§ 16§. *Codes.* As statutes multiply the need of compilation is felt. They may be private or public, made according to chronological order or according to subject-matter. After the compilation, a higher need is felt, that of the code which is the systemization or organization of juridical institutions and laws. A compilation embraces many laws which remain distinct; a codification contains a single statute extending over the greater part of the field of law. It is error to believe that codes are suggested for political ends and not for scientific reasons, because their necessity is confused with the profound demand of systemization in the sphere of cognition, and is shown in times of fully developed scientific reflection. This does not prevent codification helping the education of a people and consolidating their unity. The modern idea of codification, which made its appearance in the XVIIIth Century, became then a general and powerful desire of civil nations, because the mind felt the need of synthesis, because of the great confusion in the law, which entailed great inequalities. Not the least cause of codifications has been the school of Grotius with its idea of a natural universal law to which positive law should be as far as possible assimilated. Leibnitz pointed out the necessity of codification (shown in Germany by the followers of Wolff). In Prussia, an eternal territorial law based on reason was wanted. In Austria there was a demand for an equal and stable law which would have regard to the universal law of reason. In those days it was generally believed that the Roman law was the "ratio scripta" or "jus naturale" realized. The French Code rested on the firm ground of natural law and on the virgin soil of the Republic. The Franco-Prussian War revived patriotic sentiment and gave Thibaut a desire for a common German Code. Savigny was opposed to this because he, with his school, considered codification as the petrification of the law and the cause of the prevalence of conceptions not based on historical sources, and as an incentive for mediocre commentaries. All agree in admitting that if a code had been made in Germany at the beginning of the last century, the law could not have obtained the broad scientific development which it has to-day. Savigny was right in speaking of the probable dangers of codification for Germany at the time the motion was made. But is he right in speaking of codes in general? Savigny does not absolutely exclude codification, because in some of his later writings after the publication of "Vom Beruf Unser Zeit für Gesetzgebung und Rechtswissenschaft," he says that there can be cases in which codification is not to be condemned. But it cannot be denied that outside of such rare cases he is the enemy of codification, which has the merit of being the highest synthesis of laws of the age of reason, and cannot be called a crystalization of the law, because its parts can be constantly amended according to results of experience, or it can be entirely reënacted, as we have seen done in our own day. To-day there is an effort to base codes on life and the historical conditions of society. These are not formulated in an endeavor to find in reality the only principles of reason. The ancient conception of the "jus naturale" is no longer dominant after law has been conceived of as the human idea. Modern science proceeds on the history of human ideas. It consists in the systemization of ideas according to facts. It prepares codes and makes them show the real state of human relations, preventing the introduction therein

of imaginary or purely subjective notions.   Neither is
it tenable to hold that the scientific explication of
codified law, understood in its integrity, is a subject
of exclusively mediocre exegesis.

§ 166.   *Law in Relation to Space.*   That ideal principle, that is, the proportion or measure of things of
which law consists as realized in the life and consciousness of peoples, demands coexistence and succession, space and time.   But if space and time are
two conditions of the development of law, without
which law would be a pure and abstract logical idea,
they are certainly not its causes.   Law is always a principle superior to the conceptions of coexistence and
succession.   To make law the same as space is to confuse the person with the place in which he resides, and
with nature, which is the matter and means of human
activity.   To make law the same as time means to
exchange its essence for a transitory form and to make
injustice sometimes legitimate.   Space, as Pepere writes
in "Encyklopädie der Rechtswissenschaft," has two
relations with law.   From one point of view it appears
to us as a territory or extent in which law as positive
enactments has control.   If positive law is the expression
of popular consciousness and of the will of the State,
the organ of the law, it can be inferred that it is territorial, and extends as far as the supreme power of the
State itself throughout the whole domain; but this idea
of the territoriality of the statutes is not applicable
when private relations are found that have been caused
by foreign laws, in which case the "lex originis" and not
the "lex loci" governs, as is seen particularly in cases of
private international law.   From another aspect, space
can be considered as the material over which the energy
of the person can extend to attain his ends, and here we
see the connection between the natural sciences and law,

which assumes different and various features or attitudes according to the nature of the natural object to
which it refers.

§ 167. *Law in Relation to Time. Retroactivity.* The
discussion of the relation between law and time brings
up the grave question of retroactivity. Does the law
govern only the future or does it also regard the past?
The most philosophical doctrine on this subject is that
of Lassalle in his work "System der Erworbenen Rechts,"
clarified and amplified among the Italians by Gabba
in his "Teoria della Retroattivita delle Leggi." Lassalle
teaches that a new law cannot affect acquired rights
because they are derived from acts fulfilled under the
protection of the old laws. To admit retroactivity in
such a case would be to offend the principle of respect due
human individual liberty. Now this conception was
developed, long before Lassalle, by Trendelenburg, who
wrote that formal or recognized law is the basis of liberty,
and that acquired rights are under its protection. The
formal law of the statutes and the acquired rights of
individuals sustain and help one another. But a new
law, Lassalle goes on, is retroactive in regard to the
individual independent of his acts, if it looks to the
person himself or his qualities. This is true whether
the qualities depend immediately on natural law or on
positive and social law, or are contemplated by the new
law in a correct or incorrect manner. For example,
a law doing away with slavery and vassalage is applicable
to the past because it regards the personality of man
denied by such institutions. There can be no true acquired right in a faculty given by positive law in open
contradiction to natural law. Gabba accepts the doctrine of Lassalle, but enlarges and amends it until it has
a marked individualistic character. According to the
Italian, the acquired rights comprehend any permissible

act capable of financial valuation, exercised over an object which is capable of becoming part of the estate. Lassalle saw only the permissibility of the act and omitted the other requirements. But it is not true that an acquired right arises exclusively from the act and will of an individual person, because it can also arise directly or indirectly from the law. In Gabba's mind, every right is an acquired right, which is the resultant of an act, legal when done, although the occasion giving it value has not occurred before the passing of the new law, provided that the right by the terms of law of the time when it was done could have a financial value. Acquired acts are of three kinds. The first are consequences of the will of man, which intends to create a given right by the acquisition of a "res nullius" or by agreement with another. Acts of the second class are also voluntary but do not contain the proposition of originating a right, but if given by the law, the right arrives "ope legis" as in the case of crimes, or even more clearly in "obligationes ex delicto." The acts of the third class are involuntary or fortuitous; from them the right arises "ope legis," as in alluvion. If we admit these reasonable modifications of Gabba because they are based on a more detailed examination of the subject, the doctrine of Lassalle and its amendments can be epitomized as follows: A law is not retroactive if it affects the voluntary or involuntary acts of an individual or facts done which could give or create an acquired right according to the law of the date in which they are done. The reason of the non-retroactivity, in this case, lies in the principle of cause and effect; the acts and facts indicated should be governed by the law of the time in which they are begun or completed. Here the cause is not the time, but the control of the law by which these facts and acts are governed. If it is a question of person-

ality, of a new and higher conception of man and his
substantial attributes, the new law is retroactive, because
an individual cannot hinder the ascending course of
the law by his will or objection. A new and more
rational declaration of the idea of man and his faculties must be able to change the social state and attain
full realization. Two juristic conceptions of the person and his fundamental powers in the same society and
time are absurd and contradictory.

§ 168. *False Rules of Retroactivity.* The other doctrines concerning retroactivity have a scientific and
speculative value inferior to Lassalle's, as Gabba shows.
There are some that make retroactivity depend upon
the words of the legislature, and in doubtful cases the
presumption is in favor of retroactivity. This is no
rational criterion, but a canon of construction. We
are concerned with the principle which the legislature
should follow in extending the action of a new law to the
past or in limiting it to the future. The maxim of the
applicability of a new law, because it is better, to the consequence of prior acts should at least be limited in respect
to acquired rights. Many believe that a law should be
retroactive if of a public order or prohibitive nature
without reflecting that it is not possible to establish
rigorously the boundaries of public order and of social
interest in contradistinction to private interest. This
criterion is not definite because the respect of acquired
rights is a matter of social interest and public order.
Neither is exact, because a new criminal law, which
is of a public nature, is not always retroactive. It is
clear that this conception of a law of public nature enters
in the more complex idea of retroactivity, which corresponds to the demands of society, as the idea of private
order is connected with that of acquired rights and non-
retroactivity, which satisfies the demands of the indi-

vidual. Science, however, seeks a higher principle, a supreme and ultimate reason that is definite and fixed. The writers who say that prohibitive laws are retroactive because the prohibitive character brings with it necessarily retroactivity, and thence deduce a rule, are not far from the conception of public order. Savigny distinguished laws that have to do with the acquisitions of rights or the allowance of a faculty to an individual from laws which refer to the existence or non-existence of rights and the recognition of an institute. New laws of the first class cannot destroy acquired rights, as the new law affects capacity of action; those of the second class are retroactive, for example, a law abolishing feuds. It has been pointed out that this distinction rests on an abstract and unstable category entering into both camps, because the same law looked upon from the point of view of the individual appears as a law of acquisition, and from the point of view of the object is the law governing existence of a right. The existence or non-existence of a right, the legal recognition of an institution is very much similar to the public order and the social interest of which we have just spoken.

§ 169. *Retroactive Criminal Law. Compensation.* Law has nothing to do with simple hopes or expectation when the title has not become irrevocable. Nor has it to do with mere powers granted by the statutes, until the fact on which they are based has happened. If this fact has happened there is a true acquired right, and the new law does not affect it. In criminal law it is not accurate to speak of the acquired right of a criminal. What belongs to the criminal can never be of financial value to him. In general, it can only be allowed as a "suum" of the criminal without acquiring the significance of a "jus quæsitum." Nevertheless, the maxim that the most lenient laws are those which are applied whether they are anterior or subsequent has an equitable value. Equity has constant control in the field of transitory law, in which it is well to examine the excuses of the contending parties, those of the individual with his acquired right, and of society with its reasons of general well-being and progress. The claim of society fundamentally is not the need of the majority or of those who profit from the change of law. It is equitable, Trendelenburg writes, that all who demand the change and are benefited by it should give some indemnity for the damage inflicted upon the victims of the law. If it is a question of simple personal rights, for example, the suppression of a class privilege or patronage, there is no room for damages, because to give gold for honor is dishonorable; but if it is a question of property, a change of law should not take away without labor and without a certain contribution on its part from him who has gained something. In other words there should not be an acquisition. The English government is most praiseworthy in that, in abolishing slavery in the Colonies, it gave an indemnity to the slave-holders and obliged the freed negroes to work for a certain time as servants of their old masters.

BOOK II

PRIVATE LAW

CHAPTER I

THE INDIVIDUAL AND HIS RIGHTS

THE PERSON. — ESSENTIAL OR INHERENT RIGHTS AND ACCI-
DENTAL OR ACQUIRED RIGHTS. — THE PRINCIPLE OF RIGHTS. —
THE RIGHT TO PHYSICAL AND MORAL LIFE. — THE RIGHT
TO FREEDOM. — THE RIGHT TO EQUALITY, SOCIETY, AND
HEALTH. — THE RIGHT TO WORK.

§ 170. *Juristic Man the Subject of Rights and Duties.*
The personal unit is the subject of rights and duties
in the strict juristic sense.   The personal unit is man in
his quality of an organism endowed with sense, cognition, and free will.   If his sense is controlled by definite
and transfigured knowledge, if his will is practical
reason, it can be truly said: "Persona est, cujus aliqua
voluntas est."   But man, the simple potentiality of individual will, or the autonomous determination of the
ego, is not the actual subject of rights and duties, for
though each individual is part of man in the universal,
yet he differs from him in the act of cognition, a precept
of law, because the individual juristic unit begins to have
his own life and functions.   Yet abstract and concrete
man are of the same essence; the former has the power
to effect acts.   And action is necessary; it is the second
element in man, the individual subject of rights and
duties.   It is a kind of investiture, not a part of personality, but a civil consecration.

§ 171. *Society a Necessity.* This investiture is easily given recognition, when one sees that the individual becomes the true ethical subject and unit in society, and that without society there can be only the beginning and elements of an ethical being. This being develops into man, acquiring freedom from the dominion of the senses through knowledge and education. The presence of language, education, and discipline presupposes a society. On this hypothesis is based Aristotle's theory of the ultimate destiny of man, of his autarchy and the relation between ethics and politics; from this doctrine the modern philosophers have not departed. Vico, in "De Uno Universi Juris Principio et Fine Uno," defines character or "auctoritas" as the principal resultant of the interpenetration of power, freedom, and control. If power, he says, connotes the wise distribution of property, and freedom consists of its moderate use, and the control is the strength of mind which governs power, one cannot doubt that the "auctoritas" presupposes civilization, because wisdom, moderation, and strength do not manifest themselves without language, culture, and education. Kant holds that the State is contractual, but asserts that the individual acquires in it freedom and independence. Hegel believes that the community is the ethical substance or spirit and that the individual is but a simple manifestation or form of that substance, although man is an end for himself which develops and advances within it. From his point of view, the community and the individual are reciprocal cause and effect, because the community is the force which holds the units together, keeping them to their original character, while the individuals by their separate acts try to change. Trendelenburg says that an individual without the ethical whole or society is an impossible conception, and that the idea of man is always that of a community inclusive of the individual. In psychology, as it is conceived by Comte, statics concern biology, dynamics the mind, and are the source of historical development, but not of biological change. It is evident that the individual in Comte's mind becomes an efficient unit only because he is a factor in an entirety which develops by historical steps.

§ 172. *Two Prerequisites: their Appearance in History.* The juristic person is fundamentally the same ego as the human unit to the extent that he takes part in life or in the sphere of external relations. But there are two prerequisites essential to his existence, will and social consciousness. Let us begin our consideration of the philosophy of law from the time when these two requisites first appear. As early as the period of the family communities, and in the ages of the "gens" or village communities, that is, before the birth of civilization, we find these two elements more or less imperfectly portrayed. The juristic person, therefore, does not necessarily exist only in civilization. In a state of civilization his development is greater and more complex, and he finds conditions better suited to his life and advancement, but he had his place in the antecedent stages. When we say that he cannot exist except in civil community, we by no means say that he had no existence in the earlier state of the social aggregation, but merely assert that he cannot be efficient without a society, though it be primitive, and that only in historical times has he developed his efficiency to the full. The definition, "Persona est homo statu civili præditus," does not mean that man's advance depends upon a civil state or civilization, but means that there is no man without a relation to rights, which the law and State recognize. This possession of rights is civil capacity.

It is quite true that the principle of the juristic person is
manifest in different ways varying with the organic
structure of society, its sentiments, traditions, and
beliefs, and with the flora and fauna; but in all its
different manifestations, the two elements, will and the
civil investiture, which we mentioned,[1] are always
present. These elements are two formal conditions of
man whatever his particular or concrete character.

§ 173. *Absolute Rights and Relative Duties.* The
individual has rights when considered absolutely, or
as an end, and duties when considered relatively or
as a factor in the whole or ethical organism, of which
Trendelenburg speaks. The individual is medial, not
because he is the equivalent of an object, but because he
is a force and conscious factor of humanity or the ethical
whole, to which he should be subordinate. This idea
apparently is in Rosmini's mind when he speaks of
generation as the origin of paternal rights and says that
the son is medial, in an ethical or personal sense, to the
pleasure and happiness which his parents can obtain
through him, and that he is ultimate or absolute considered from his own point of view. The son in his relative
quality has duties and in his ultimate quality has rights.
But the individual is an end for himself; and we must
consider him as such when he desires to be free in the
fulfillment of his duty or in the enjoyment of proper and
expedient, if not obligatory, actions. He is medial when
he must do or not do something, because under those conditions he is the instrument for the realization of ethical
principles and the idea of humanity. We must observe
that the ethical organ does not live merely the life of the
whole, but has its own life and being and its own character differing in this from a simple natural organ.
In natural organisms of a high grade, the part has its

[1] *Cf.* § 170 *ante.*

own life and a certain independence. But the life of
the part is quite inferior to that of man in respect to the
ethical whole. The individual is a unit, which the part
of the natural organism is not.

§ 174. *Inherent and Acquired Rights*. The rights of
the individual are inherent or essential and acquired
or accidental. The essential or inherent rights are
not the powers derived from the "antecedents of
nature" of the Stoics or primary rights intended
merely for the conservation or propagation of the race,
although they are founded immediately upon the common and abstract nature of man, conceived in the
integrity of its essential parts. The acquired rights
have their origin in the concrete and individual nature
of man, not regarded exclusively in relation to the intellectual and moral elements; that is, not under the aspect
of the "consequents of nature" or secondary rights.
The essential rights express the true, the acquired show
the certain; the first are elementary forces, the second
represent development and realization. Rosmini writes
that there is one primal and essential right, that of the
person, and that then there are rights growing out of its
exercise in a mediate or immediate manner. The connection between the activities and the personal essence
was either given to man by nature with his first existence or is formed by the exercise of his activities. If
united and proper to the personal essence (through the
nature of man), they constitute the natural and inherent
rights; but if appropriate to the exercise of his activities and his natural rights, they are called acquired.
We cannot have an acquired right without a natural
right, and in general we cannot acquire a new right
without a precedent right. To acquire a certain activity it is necessary to act, and in order to act one must
have the necessary power, and therefore one must have

the right to that power to rely upon in acquiring the new activity or right. Thus the sphere of rights can be extended as far as the activities can be developed. In other words you can acquire the rights of which you have the germs.

§ 175. *The More Development, the Greater Rights.* A man's rights multiply as his opportunities and capacities develop. The more perfect the man, the more progressive the community; the more civilized the nation, the richer he is in rights. As time goes on, the inherent rights assume through the realization of acquired rights new forms and manifestations. These, through evolution, grow and separate more and more, and have more modifications and enter into a greater number of correlations, so that the inherent rights no longer appear as capacities given and immutable, but as activities or powers of human nature which lie more in the realm of action than existence, marked by the most detailed and energetic unity and the most extended and indefinite variety.

§ 176. *Qualitative and Quantitative Distinction Between the Capacities of the Spirit.* These activities, being capacities of the spirit, are not subject to mere qualitative or quantitative distinction in the individual. In qualitative difference there is not the whole entity but something of the entity which is divided and distributed in different ways, and therefore each difference is a factoral part, and is circumscribed. But since the spirit is not divisible, but a unit (being wholly a complex capacity), so the person is a unit and complete in all his natural and inherent rights. Hence the conception of the capacity and inherent rights as subject to qualitative distinction is opposed to the theory of the unity of the person and spirit. Neither can these rights be measured quantitatively, because between them there is not merely the relation of more or less, and because they do not exist in terms foreign to the person. The right to life, for example, does not differ from the right to truth or freedom by a sign of addition or multiplication, and cannot exist without its subject. We know that quantity is a foreign measure of determination because one can augment or diminish without a qualitative difference. Whence it follows that the theory that capacities and inherent rights are subject to quantitative distinctions, even if it does not deny the unity of spirit and man, does not look towards his development. In conclusion, inherent rights are capacities of the spirit; different forms, therefore, of an ample and potent energy in constant progressive motion, interpenetrating and resolving one in another, the lower in the higher. This energy, which is seen in the richest development of its methods, attitudes, and forces, is mind in psychology, is the person in ethics.

§ 177. *The Person as the Source and Origin of Rights.* The source of the logical derivation of essential or inherent rights can only be in the person, all of whose rights are activities or powers. But we must understand that we have not used the word person in an integral sense, but meaning rather the abstract or ethical man, of which he is a part. For it is not logical to speak of absolute rights without considering relative duties. Trendelenburg has correctly said that inherent rights represent a series of postulates, guaranteeing to the individual conditions suited to his development. Whoever invokes these inherent rights should first recognize the ethical whole in which alone they are possible and efficient. The idea of these rights is inseparable from the end, which both the individual and the community should strive to attain. This end is the full realization of the human essence. But the person so conceived, more than the rights themselves, should be considered as the principle and form of inherent rights. And when we speak incorrectly of the rights of personality we do not mean special and different rights but the common centre of rights, the human power itself. The criterion or general character of a right, which distinguishes it from the activity subject to it, is, according to Rosmini, property or ownership in its broadest sense, indicating what is connected with a man physico-morally, or acquired by him; that is, brought within his ownership. In this meaning, property makes a sphere around the individual, whose centre is the individual, in which sphere no one can intervene because no one can deprive another of what is his.

§ 178. *The Development of Rights.* And to show the nature of the chief inherent rights, let us follow the Italian philosophers, unsurpassed in this respect. Every power is an activity, ungrown and in embryo, but having a tendency to open and fulfill its nature in acts suitable thereto. At first feeling tends to the repetition of known sensations, then it makes for the attainment of known results, and tends to happiness. Foresight leads to the discovery of truth. Will makes for the love of known pleasures, and tends to virtue. These three tendencies to happiness, truth, and virtue, which are one with the powers of sensibility, cognitions, and will, are as well inherent rights as the powers from which they grow. If the capacities are intermingled and resolved one in another according to the laws of development and evolution, and if fulfillment presupposes truth and happiness, it is clear that the inherent right to fulfillment brings with it truth and happiness; and that the right to truth comprehends that to happiness. With-

out confusing the inherent rights with the "antecedents
of nature," but extending them also to the "consequents,"
we can agree with Vico that rights, when referring to the
"consequents," give the regulations, which show the
certain, and that the necessity creates the "antecedents."
We must, however, always keep in mind that in dealing
with the "antecedents" we are dealing with the lower
side of human nature, and that the "consequents" show
the rational or voluntary part.

§ 179. *Subsidiary Inherent Rights.* The individual
ought to realize his ideas, and accomplish his ends by
the attainment of happiness, truth, and virtue, and therefore he is the subject of other inherent rights, that is, of
rights to physical and moral life, to freedom, equality,
social existence, to assistance and work. Ahrens deserves the credit of having made a comprehensive
study of these rights.

§ 180. *The Right to Life.* Without doubt the first
in importance among them is the right to life, which
begins with man, "in fieri," with the embryo or unborn
child. For either of these is a potential person, and
as such is inviolable and has rights. And yet the rights
of an unborn child are not fully recognized by some
codes; for example, the French and Italian, which
base the right of inheritance upon birth. Such a condition is not just because the capacity of rights should
depend upon existence and not upon the possibility of
life. Man lives regardless of what his prospect of continued life is, and while man lives his rights should not
be lacking. Besides, this condition has given rise to much
doubt in the minds of the learned and, as Savigny points
out, is contrary to criminal law, which protects the life of
an unborn child. In practice, many inconveniences
occasioned by this erroneous principle are avoided by
the presumption that a child "en ventre sa mere" is alive.

§ 181. *The Right to Life Does not Comprehend a Right to Suicide.* Suicide is a crime because self-preservation is a duty of man. This duty is both moral and juristic. There is no controversy on the question of the moral duty because there can be no condition of life to which the idea of happiness is not attached. Those philosophers err who recognize a possibility of human existence irreconcilable with ethics, because the deepest grief and greatest disgrace cannot justify a man in the disregard of his duties and exempt him from the attainment of his proper ends. The knowledge of duty fulfilled is a comfort in suffering and trouble and gives the despairing man a feeling of tranquility and courage. There still is, however, the juristic duty that a man, as far as his acts are concerned and in his external relations, shall act in concordance with the community and other men in matters of general concern. Whence it follows, that the community which, together with law, has the duty of guaranteeing his actions, can punish whomsoever wishes to destroy a man, even if that man be himself. The right to life is as inalienable as human nature, which cannot develop except through life, which is the condition of the existence of all rights and duties. Neither can we say that it is inalienable only as an essential of social existence, because an inherent right is *per se* essential as a part of personality. The inviolability and inalienability of such a right are not consequences of mutable social necessity or personal interest in the State, but are concomitant with the incarnation of the human principle in the individual. The teaching which we combat is only the remnant of the Greek theory about the relation of the individual to the State; that man is but a fraction of an all-absorbing unit. This theory rests on the power of the natural organism over its parts and not on the rights of the ethical organism or whole limited by the character of its component parts. It is true that man has no juristic relation with himself; but in the above instance, the relation lies between the individual and the ethical whole or community, in which relation there develops a duty of the person to realize the ideal of man in matters relating to acts which affect either his fellows or physical objects subject to their possession. Not only every man, but also his children, wife, parents, brothers, and other men have a right to his life, as we have said.[1] The community, therefore, has also a right to preservation of his life. The analogy given by Beccaria, between the right of self-destruction and emigration, is not well taken, because the former destroys the man while the latter only transfers him from one place to another. One's native land is not a prison, and the State allows citizens to withdraw; but the State cannot permit a man to perish. This duty is not a derivative of national or political relations, but of universal human existence.

§ 182. *The Philosophical Relation of Suicide and Law.* No inference that criminality is lacking can be drawn from the failure to punish a suicide. He is not punished because social justice cannot take the culprit. It is neither human nor civilized to insult his corpse or his memory, nor is it just to inflict the penalty upon his descendants and heirs by a confiscation of his estate. The State can, however, punish the tentative suicide (because the above reasoning does not apply), if it thinks it wise to place a penalty on the attempt and not to treat it with absolute contempt. For a statute is not sufficient to stop the hand of him who no longer feels the natural instinct of self-preservation, but will only make him take all necessary precautions that his hand shall not fail. But if civilized society is in a truly pro-

---

[1] *Cf.* §§ 179, 180 *ante.*

gressive movement, and happiness in life is attainable for the majority; if the State makes life easier by the aid of well-developed, educational discipline, and law is not considered as a tyrannical and foreign master, legal prohibition, with such factors as these, will accomplish the best results. With the moral education of the individual extended and invigorated, the causes of this sad act will diminish; and the knowledge that the meditated act is criminal and dishonorable will act as a sufficient restraint over many to whose mind comes the thought of leaving this world on account of some sorrow suffered or feared. While these conditions are unattained and causes for suicide continue to increase, there will be some men who have not sufficient physical bravery to take their own life or undergo the penalty in case of a failure, and others who will hesitate, because of the disgrace attached to the act. But it is clear that in both these cases the voice of instinct is not spent, and the suicidal intent is badly formed and therefore can be rendered nugatory by a statute. Furthermore, it is a logical deduction from the above rule that it is criminal to help the consummation of the suicidal act. The maxim, "Volenti non fit injuria," is only applicable to alienable private rights and does not apply to those whose disregard, as Berner says in "Lehrbuch der Deutsche Strafrechts," violates a duty. The power to renounce one's rights is limited by the rights of others.

§ 183. *The Right to Freedom from Bodily Harm; and Self-Defense.* The inherent right to physical life comprehends the right to safety and health, and to self-defense. Mere life is not all: one must live in free enjoyment of the qualities and the organs which nature has so generously bestowed on man in order that he may attain his ultimate end. This is admittedly true.

No one has a right to self-mutilation. "Nemo memb-
rorum suorum dominus esse videtur" was prescribed
by the earliest law. Whoever mutilates and destroys
or otherwise affects another's body or health, even
though the person injured has given his consent, is
guilty of an offense against the human personality and
law. The innkeeper who encourages drunkenness deserves punishment for injuring the health of his fellow-
beings. On the same ground, statutes have been
passed limiting the working hours of women and children. The right to self-defense allows recourse to
force, when there is no opportunity to invoke the
arm of social justice for the protection of one's own
rights or those of another threatened with an unjust
attack. This is the private protection derived from
"auctoritas monastica," of which Vico speaks. It is,
therefore, descended from the solitary man or from
the State, in which he could not invoke the protection
of the law to repel an unjust attack. Vico thinks, on
this account, that man was originally a solitary being,
and that he can kill an unjust assailant in self-defense
because justice is on his side and against the aggressor.
Self-defense is inherent in every right, allowing the use
of power in the exercise of it. Rosmini goes further
and says that this use of force is a function of every right.
This doctrine recognizes that the human personality is an
inviolable centre of rights and that man can make full
use of force in their exercise. Since man is furnished
with intellectual and physical powers, he has the right
to use them in the maintenance of his rights. The harm,
which necessarily is inflicted upon the assailant, is justified by the general rule of justice, that a voluntary wrong-
doer must bear the penalty inflicted by the wronged
man, who becomes the instrument of justice. There are
two prerequisites to the exercise of the right of self-

defense, — the injustice of the attack and the presence of
danger.   The injustice of the attack must be considered
by itself with due regard to the character of the assailant
who, for example, may be mad, but his lack of reason
does not take away the right of self-defense.   The
danger must be real, but not inevitable in an absolute
sense, because the right of self-defense cannot be strictly
construed form the point of view of the man attacked,
who is without fault.   Girardi correctly says in his
work, "La Difensa Legittima," that one need not scrutinize this right too closely.

§ 184.   *Self-defense is Limited by Circumstances.*
Self-defense cannot be limited by conditions which
are inconsistent with the dignity of the man attacked;
for example, flight; or which require a cool calculation
of the most suitable means of avoiding the attack and
lessening its brunt at a moment when the instinct of self-
preservation is aroused and when the brain is confused.
The right of self-defense in its fullest extent, as a derivative of "auctoritas monastica," gives protection both to
life, safety, honor, freedom, and even personalty and
property, the projection of the personality.   Grotius
and Rosmini agree to this fully on abstract grounds,
one in the name of full justice, and the other because
of his conception of private property.   But public feeling is against them, and does not lend countenance to
death-dealing in defense of rights or property of little
value.   It is certain that the use of force is an attribute
of a right, and the possessor of goods can have recourse
thereto to prevent their injury or destruction, but equity
forbids him to inflict a great injury to avoid a little harm
which can be easily remedied.   It must be understood,
however, that if to preserve property, one runs a risk of life
through the attack, then no matter how petty the thing,
one can always kill the assailant.   The right of self-

defense belongs not only to the man attacked but to
his relatives, friends, and in fact everyone can defend
the innocent party, since all men are bound together by
a natural bond that each one must help his neighbor.
With the right to life there is another right of necessity
or "jus æquivocum," which is only an agreement to
waive punishment, as Kant says.   It is when a starving
man commits theft to save his life.

§ 185.   *The Right to Honor and Good Name.*   The inherent right to moral life connotes honor and good
name.   A person is presumed honorable, and therefore should be treated as just and honorable until the
contrary is proved.   Reputation is not limited by life,
but comes into the world before the individual, and lasts
after his death.   The heirs have the right to defend the
deceased's reputation and memory because of the inviolability of his character, whose moral existence
extends beyond the tomb.   Punishment cannot be infamous because man has always a personality in the
juristic and ethical sense, and can always wash away
the stains of dishonor acquired by the commission of
evil deeds.   Disgrace, a consequence of a man's acts,
is the effect of public opinion, and cannot be inflicted by
statutes nor rationally be enacted in a law.   The "exceptio
veritatis," or proof, cannot be reached by attributing acts
to a person, for they by their nature belong to the sphere
of autonomous will or to exclusive valuation of the
man.   Neither can it be reached by referring an unjust
act to an individual, thus giving him a dishonorable
qualification, because it is not possible to give a definition relying upon one fact. The "exceptio veritatis" can
be accepted under facts prosecutable under social authority *ex officio*; that is, in crimes affecting the rights of
all and producing social harm.   It is important to society
to discover crimes and to pursue criminals because it

must reinstate the violated justice and look to the general safety.

§ 186. *Dueling.* With the question of honor comes the question of dueling, a method of justice unknown to classical antiquity, when the State wrapped the individual in on every side, but appearing in the barbaric Middle Ages when the State was powerless and highhanded individualism was strong, in whose eyes honor and bravery were confused. Dueling is an absurd custom because to accept a challenge and win a duel are acts which can constitute the proof of bravery or skill at arms, but which can be no proof of morality, justice, or honor. An injury to these is only remedied through the intrinsic justice of the public conscience. A duel, it is said, in Chauveau and Helie's "Théorie du Code Pénal," is a violation of the holy law written in every heart, "Thou shall commit no murder." Not only does morality forbid it, but society is alarmed by it and with reason, because it is a substitution of individual in place of social justice. To avenge an injury disturbs society. The belief in the justice of revenge undermines the conscience. It is an offense against the public peace. A duel, therefore, is criminal for three reasons: because it is an attempt against the life or body of a man, because it is against public peace, because it represents an irrational predominance of the "vis privata." The consent of the duelists does not do away with the crime because the maxim "Volenti non fit injuria," as we have observed before,[1] does not apply to the inalienable rights. It is not logically possible to let a duel go unpunished and inflict the severest penalty upon a homicide committed in anger and under provocation. Whoever, in a moment of anger, kills a man has his brain beclouded and his mind confused. The duelist who

[1] *Cf.* § 182 *ante.*

kills or wounds does so in a state of relative calm since several days have passed since the insult. According to some, dueling exists because of the not unfounded conviction of the insufficient care of honor taken by the statutes. But often duels grow from causes, as the lie given, an act of disrespect, or some petty rivalry, which have not the slightest characteristic of a crime. Any increase in the penalty for such offenses in order to avoid duels would be most unjust because the penalty should be commeasurable to the intrinsic value of the criminal act. Neither by such a remedy would the desired end be attained by the legislature, as Carrara says in his "Programma," because the consideration of the severity of the penalty, which the insult entails, does not affect duelists. The insult itself is the cause. They believe it a mark of bravery and virtue to demand satisfaction with their own hands. Penal law should punish dueling for the reasons given above and to protest against erring public opinion. But it is impossible for it to destroy the practice. The eradication of this barbarous custom depends in the first place upon a change of public conscience, which will correct its error, and secondarily upon statutes which can only indirectly take the glory from the physical bravery of the duelists and the honor from this kind of fighting. Perhaps the multiplication and reconstruction of courts with jurisdiction according to class and rank, permitting the consideration of some questions of honor which arise from acts which are not criminal, would tend to overthrow it.

§ 187. *The Right to Freedom.* Granted a right to life, immediately the right to freedom arises. What mass is to our bodies, freedom is to the person, because the person has his distinct ethical essence in free will. Under its general aspect, the inherent right to freedom is confused with the right of personality and

is not a special or distinct right but the human right
above all others, as Spencer says. Conceived in
its special and distinct sense, it assumes various
forms, because there are freedoms of intellect, morality, religion, economics, civics, and politics. Intellectual freedom has for its object truth and beauty. It
concerns science, art, and education. Moral freedom
is the autonomy of will, by which the motives of judgment and conduct are freed from all coercion and enter
untrammelled into the realm of juristic valuation,
evincing themselves in actions which have relation to
others' rights. Freedom of conscience (including, as it
does, freedom of worship), making human existence and
action one, is not, as it is generally defined, the internal
and absolute power of the individual to think as he pleases
in matters of religion, because man, by nature a social
being, is relative, not absolute. True and full freedom
of conscience, or of election in matters of belief, is
developed in society by the agreement of the majority of the individual consciences in a given belief,
and a common and identical discipline and cult.
Industrial freedom is synonymous with competition in
the production of goods. It is the freedom to make
what one wants, how, where, when, and in 'whose company one wants. Civil freedom consists in the undisturbed exercise of private rights, while political freedom
is the participation of the citizens in the control of the
public affairs.

§ 188. *Equity and Socialistic Equality.* Spedalieri
and Romagnosi teach that freedom in the individual
causes equality, and therefore the inherent corresponding right. Men, whether units or citizens, are all
equal. Equality, growing out of abstract personality,
consists in the possession of the rights essential to
the individual; that is, inherent rights or theoretical

and ultimate powers, as Romagnosi (who follows Vico) calls them, confining them to ownership, freedom, and safety. This abstract equality is purely formal; that is, equality before the law. But the manifestation of freedom in individuals is marked by a natural variety in quality, quantity, and modality. It appears in individual and primarily diverse forms because individuality is as primal as the identity of human nature; whence comes the concrete inequality which governs the acquired rights and practical powers of Romagnosi. Formal equality is above the concrete inequality and takes precedence of it. Thus a man cannot take from another a part of his immense property, for the same reason that the second, who may have many possessions, cannot take part of the small possessions of the first. An inherent right or ultimate power, becoming by realization an acquired right or practical power, clothes itself in an infinite number of forms due to the various nature of the objects over which it is exercised and the different physico-moral constitutions of its subjects. The socialists disregard the medial action of practical power, in which lie all the processes of individuality, and consider only the ultimate, indeterminate power of ownership equal in all, and its agents in the external world common in themselves. They do not perceive the actual and positive bond between the individual and the object; they deny the right of private property and believe in the collective ownership of instruments of labor. As is easily seen, absolute equality and collectivism can only exist in abstract Utopias.

§ 189. *The Right to Associate.* Man is free and essentially social, whence the inherent right to associate. Even among animals there is a kind of social intercourse, wonderful in its forms in certain species, but directly and immediately connected with their physical needs, remaining always instinctive, and never passing beyond the limits of simple aggregation. Human society, on the other hand, develops through reflexion and free will, and is most complex. It appears with most particularity in the companies and partnerships, which demand the coöperation of many wills for one object, a knowledge and a will to coöperate, and a union of many wills for the common object. The companies and partnerships so distinct from aggregations owe their origin entirely to the right of association, and while they are in part necessary they are in part free and eventual. The right to society takes in all the ends of life applying to art, literature, science, economics, morality, religion, and politics. It assumes always new and complex. forms and grows more and more free from the element of instinct. We can see that if the association or partnership does not look to one or more common interest or advantage or the utility of its members, according to what is right and just, but tends to the destruction of the principles of the civil constitution or organism of public power, whose existence is required by the rights of all, it should not be recognized or tolerated.

§ 190. *The Right to Aid.* Individual man is not self-sufficient, but tends to autarchy and full self-realization in all possible ways. He has an inherent right, as part of the ethical whole, to assistance, and this right is complementary and subsidiary to his nature, presupposing self-help and deficient personal power. This right can be upheld as a necessary condition of life independent of the will or as the result of a primordial state of freedom; in the first case he has the right to social assistance because society is an indispensable and natural state, in the second, through contract and quasi-contract.

§ 191. *The State and its Evolution.* When the State
and the people were antagonistic, and the State was
considered as a means for individual ends, the political
ideal lay in the constant diminution of action by the
political power. And it was held that the activity of
the individual in the course of civilization would
almost entirely take its place except in the maintenance of public safety and protection. But if the
State is an organism, it cannot escape from evolution,
which causes a constantly increasing complexity of
relations, functions, and powers, as has been shown before. The State, in the progress of time, has, on one
side, lost many functions which implied a denial of the
principle of personality and individual initiative, but,
on the other hand, it has acquired a large number of new
powers intended to help, aid, and protect in a thousand
ways the growing affairs of the individual. The more
the modern State develops, the more it tries in every
way to help individual activity, once aroused; but its
aid is not given in inverse but in direct ratio to
individual effort. Spencer and Wagner are both wrong
in their defense of two opposite theories. One thinks
that the action of the State diminishes in ages of civilization, while the other thinks that it increases to the
great danger of individual energy and initiative. Experience shows that neither of these theories is true,
because the number of the functions of the State increases and the public expenses are enormously aug-
mented, while at the same time there is a great increase
in social wealth. The first two facts discredit Spencer's
opinion; the third is opposed to Wagner's. We may
further observe that Spencer contradicts himself because
he recognizes the State as an organism, and, although the
great master of the doctrine of evolution, applies it only
to the individual and not to the State. For certainly

he is not making the State subject to evolution when he
says that the individual, with progress, becomes more
active, as it were, gains new powers; and the State loses
those that it had and could still have in relation to society,
and retains merely its juridical and negative duties.

§ 192. *The Right to Work, Distinguished from the
Right to Work of the Socialists.* The individual, free,
social, and assisted by the community, accomplishes
his objects and has a last inherent right, that is, to
work, consisting of freedom to exercise his forces
and attributes in the production of goods and
wealth. The State for its part, to quote Romagnosi,
is confined to giving the people social worth, that is
to say, to making men skilled in different kinds of production, and to awakening their productive powers by
instructions and education. This right to work, however, must not be confused with that other right to
work announced by the socialists, in which the individual
can normally go to the State and obtain from it the objects and the means for the exercise of his business.
This right cannot be recognized, because the State
exists with the object of protection, education, and
happiness, and not to constitute or keep alive any
especial kind of business. The modern State particularly feels a certain repugnance to assuming functions
which have a comparatively economic character. It has
sold its lands and no longer exercises any industries
along the line of private effort, and gets its greatest
revenue from the customs. And if it enters into
economic affairs, it is only because private effort is not
made, or not made with sufficient vigor, or else to destroy
the harmful effects of a monopoly or give financial en-
couragement. The State does not take the place of the
individual in business, but protects him and helps him
make his efforts availing. The right to assistance is

complementary and subsidiary and presumes the principle of self-help and personal initiative, as we have said
above.[1]   Thornton, in his book on "Labor," asks why
the rich have any duty to save from starvation in any
way at all those who come into the world without act
of theirs.   Has the world been given to humanity on
condition that it feed all its inhabitants?   Or has part of
humanity been deprived of the means necessary to life?
If the first is true, the condition imposed is not just,
because the population would rapidly surpass the means
of subsistence; one must remember the Malthusian
theory that population tends to increase with greater
rapidity under the best industrial conditions than the
means of subsistence.   But to put aside at once any discussion about the geometric progression of population
and the arithmetical progression of the means of subsistence, there is no doubt that propagation is too easy for
existence to be without a struggle.   If we answer the
second question in the affirmative, one should return to
the disinherited all that would have been their share
if the land had not been allotted.   In this case, they
would need the fragments from the tables of the rich to
pay the equivalent, because land is of little value without work.   If we recognize, therefore, this right to work,
capital would diminish to a marked degree, because the
State, become purveyor of labor, would take through
duties and customs the savings of the citizens to a great
extent.   Besides, the State would always need to have
ready the material for work in all the industries of mind
and hand.   The sloth of laborers, sure of their wage,
would be the practical consequence of the establishment
of this so-called right.

§ 193.   *The Correlation of Rights and Duties.*   So far
we have defined the individual in the juristical sense

[1] *Cf.* § 190 *ante.*

as the subject of rights and duties, and we have
seen that the individual is man and that man is the
personal unit.   The two conceptions are interchangeable
because equipotent in the philosophy of law and, for
that matter, in positive law.   Full civil capacity embraces the enjoyment or possession of rights and their
exercise, that is, the capacity of the right and its use.
The enjoyment can be without the exercise, but the
exercise presupposes the enjoyment.   We understand
that civil capacity is full or limited, depending upon
whether the intelligence and will of the person is perfectly or imperfectly developed.   This limitation has
to do with the exercise and not with the possession,
because there is no person without rights, although
he may not know of their existence; as, for example, a
baby or an embryo.   But it is certain that he has not
duties if he is ignorant of them.   This is not true of
rights, because a man merits respect because he is man,
without his knowledge of the respect that is due him.
It is sufficient if the duty of respect be known to them
who should exercise it.   The individual begins by having
rights and not duties through his lack of knowledge of
the latter.   And thus there is not a correlation of rights
and duties in the same individual though there is between
different individuals.   The civil capacity, of which we
speak here, differs from political capacity inasmuch as
it is more complex and makes for ends more ethical and
general, and therefore needs for its exercises new conditions and attitudes, besides those requisite in the exercise of private rights.   The limitations of civil capacity
are determined by the interest of the persons who are
subject thereto; the limitations of political capacity
from the conception of the welfare of the State.

CHAPTER II

THE HISTORICAL CONCEPTION OF INHERENT RIGHTS

THE RIGHTS OF MAN IN THE STATE OF NATURE. — THE STATE OF NATURE ACCORDING TO THE PHILOSOPHERS OF THE XVIII CENTURY CONSIDERED IN CONNECTION WITH THE NATURAL STATE OF THE ROMAN JURISCONSULTS AND THE GREEK PHILOSOPHERS. — THE THEORY OF KNOWLEDGE, AND THE METHODS OF CONCEIVING THE ESSENTIAL RIGHTS OF THE PERSON. — THE INHERENT RIGHTS OF MODERN PHILOSOPHY. — THE REGIMES OF STATUS AND CONTRACT.

§ 194. *With Abstract Thought Comes Self-realization.* The individual, at first absorbed in the ancient State, then bound down by imperial and ecclesiastical power and later by absolute monarchy, begins to take action, and acquires with the passage of time full knowledge of his power. With the development of abstract thought he sees his own possibilities. He tries to escape from the historical bonds which are opposed to his individuality. He imagines a primitive and extra-social state of existence, and calls it the beginning and end of the moral world, and so he acquires all those abstract ideas which caused the French Revolution.

§ 195. *Man's Powers in a State of Nature.* It is clear that to cause such a movement, inherent rights must be conceived as the powers of man in a state of nature. Hobbes admits an original right of everybody to everything in such a state, which was a cause of general warfare. Locke recognizes in it a law comprehensive of the right to life, freedom, and property, and a certain power of punishment over the individual. Rousseau regards it as a primitive condition typical of the life of humanity, but one not found at the present day, which allowed full and positive exercise of freedom, equality, and independence. According to this doctrine, the mind in the primitive epoch could grasp the idea of the essential and universal rights of the individual; that is, the object of the social contract. The constitutional agreement of a civil community or State towards man's inherent rights could then be formulated. As we have said before, Rousseau, believing in the principle of inalienable freedom, resolved the problem by finding a kind of political union in which freedom was not lost, but each citizen in obeying the State obeyed himself, with a full and reciprocal renunciation of all individual rights to the community.[1]

§ 196. *The Doctrine of the Natural Goodness of Man.* The philosophy of the XVIIIth Century believed in the natural goodness of man, his original unlimited freedom, and a primal law of nature. It taught that social acts are governed by laws of nature, which lead men to happiness, if the vices of existing institutions did not interfere. Rousseau says that everything is good as it comes from the hands of nature; Turgot holds that man is good by nature; and Quesnay founds the physiocratic doctrine on that of the reign of nature, and believes in the restoration of the empire of natural law through the abolition of all artificial and arbitrary ordinances that impede its development. Adam Smith adheres to these principles in "The Wealth of Nations," and says that the obstacles will disappear with the establishment of a simple system of natural freedom. His followers never grow tired of repeating with the physiocrats

[1] *Cf.* § 101 *ante.*

the doctrine of leaving all to nature — of conforming to God's will.   Economic optimism reached finally its most splendid expression in the necessary and inevitable harmonies of Bastiat.

§ 197.   *The State of Nature is Found in the Earliest Writings.*   The doctrine of original perfection and the state of nature is connected with the oldest traditions of a Golden Age, anterior to society, and has in Italy its historical antecedent in the treatise of Girolamo Vida on "Dignita della Republica," published in 1556, and in the work of Giovanni Bonifazio, "La Republica delle Api," edited in 1627.   Vida begins the "apologia" of the state of nature and criticizes society, saying that Theseus, who changed Attica from a pastoral state to one of civilization, was the author of a public calamity.   Bonifazio describes the customs of the inhabitants of an imaginary island of the Pacific, who follow their own will in a state of nature, without statutes or codes, without popes, priests or monks, the men worshiping the sun and the women the moon.

§ 198.   *The Jurisconsults' Belief in a Golden Age.* Roman jurisconsults of the classical age, under the influence of Stoic philosophy, speak also, though very vaguely, of a primeval state of nature and of a remote antiquity in which natural law had the force of statutes. It is written in the Institutes: "Palam est autem vetustius esse naturale jus, quod cum ipso genere humano rerum prodidit: civilia enim jura tum esse cœperunt, cum et civitates condi et magistratus creari et leges scribi cœperunt."   But we must observe that with the Greeks the word nature signified primarily the physical world as a manifestation of a single principle, and only later was used to indicate the moral world, governed by general and simple laws; therefore, to live according to nature meant to live normally with one's kind.   The juris-

consults, imbued with the Greek idea of a state of nature
and believing it to be a primitive order of life, taught
that freedom and equality are natural rights; to cite.
the Institutes: "Jure enim naturali omnes homines ab
initio liberi nascebantur. Quod ad jus naturale attinet,
omnes homines æquales sunt."

§ 199. *The Difference between the Belief of the Jurisconsults and the Physiocrats.* Yet we must admit the
Roman jurisconsults, in recognizing the reign or state
of nature, differed not a little from the greater number
of the authorities of our own times, because they did
not emphasize, as the latter, conditions which were
extra-social or of savage isolation, but meant by the
reign of nature a primitive State ruled by simple and
harmonious laws. There is a profound and general
belief among the jurisconsults in a "societas gentium"
or "generis humani" as the product of nature. The
quotation cited above,[1] besides others, proves it, and
Gaius says, "Juris enim gentium est societas, quam
inire omnes homines naturali ratione possunt." Satur-
ninus also, "Natura hominum est communis"; and
Florentinus adds, "Inter nos cognationem quamdam
natura constituit." Cicero welcomes the Stoic idea,
"Hominum causa homines esse generatos," and accepts
the other belief, which he expresses in many ways;
"Mundum autem esse quasi communem urbem et
civitatem hominum et deorum." Seneca writes, "Natura
amorem indidit mutuum et sociabiles fecit." Over the
minds of the jurisconsults, the Epicurean theory (though
reproduced by Lucretius, Horace, Vitruvius, and in places
by Vergil and even Cicero) did not exercise a great
influence. This theory teaches that men in the beginning
live "more ferarum" as a "mutum et turbe pecus,"
struggling among themselves, "pugnantes unguibus et

[1] *Cf.* § 198 *ante.*

pugnis propter glandem et cubilia," ignorant, without marital or paternal relations, with no moral sense. In such a primitive period fear, utility, and blind chance were the beginning of society, according to the followers of Epicurus. Furthermore, the ancient philosophers and jurisconsults do not deny the present control of natural law but think that positive law must gradually become like it, while our philosophers do not see its existence in actual reality and wish radical and immediate transformations in society to realize their fantastic types.

§ 200. *The Early Greeks Believed in the Connection of Natural and Positive Law.* The conception of a primitive order of nature among the Greeks is older than Stoic philosophy and belongs to the Sophists, according to the statements of Chiappelli. The idea of nature was the beginning of speculative thought before the time of the Sophists, and is the base of ethics in the first phase. Prodicus of Chios and Hippias of Elis placed nature above positive law and therefore in opposition to it. According to these two Sophists, the honest and just have roots in nature from which the positive law has far departed. We must return to a state of nature if we wish the rule of justice. Other Sophists, to quote Chiappelli, believed the contrary and placed positive law above nature, regarding it as the purification of the undeveloped and savage state of nature, or as an artificial convention and superimposed fiction. This is the position of Protagoras, the idea of King Νόμος, and the destructive theory of the later Sophists. According to Hippias, the unwritten laws of nature enter into all legislation because they are a divine work, while positive laws are various and contradictory, being the offspring of accidental agreements of men. Statutes often do violence to nature and create inequalities between fellow-beings. The typical human life can only be found in primitive conditions and not in civil life. We must not marvel at such beliefs if we consider slavery as an institution contrary to nature introduced by positive law. A Sophist, a disciple of Gorgias, Alcidama by name, taught that the gods gave freedom to all, and that nature never introduced slavery. Aristotle referred to the fact that many believed slavery wrong and combated that opinion. Later a tendency contrary to the movement instituted by Hippias grew up among the Sophists tending to destroy the moral reason of nature and to sustain in its place civil custom and convention. Gorgias showed that the state of nature must either be variable or constant; if variable it cannot be the ethical norm, if constant it can only be the beginning of civilization. And he adds that we cannot be sure that it ever existed and further that, if we can have definite knowledge of it, its reinstatement in the changed conditions of society is impossible. Protagoras compares the natural state to that in which man has neither education, statutes, courts nor the force which urges him to excellence; saying that men in such a state are savages resembling the famous Chorus of Misanthropes of the poet Pherecrates. In his mind excellence is attainable in civil life by education. The State decrees the norms of moral life by its statutes; therefore the honest and just are determined through them by public opinion. Justice is a reality, not because a gift of nature, but because the result of a higher power, that is, of a political agreement. Such is, in a few words, the signification of King Νόμος. From these opposite principles of Hippias and Protagoras, the Sophists, Callicles, and Thrasi- machus come to the apotheosis of individual sovereignty, despotism, and anarchy. Callicles argues as follows: that if a state is not a convention contrary to the laws of nature, and if in nature might is right, he infers that the just is what he who has the might wishes and makes it. In society the majority rules the stronger individuals, who await an opportunity to rebel and free themselves from this state of impotence by overthrowing the constituted order from its base. Thrasimachus departs from the conceptions of Protagoras, and shows that if there is justice in the statutes of the State, inasmuch as these are rules imposed by the stronger, justice is only utility; that is, the interest of the stronger. Thus the two schools of the Sophists, one teaching the supremacy of nature over law and the other teaching the supremacy of law over nature, lead to the same result; that is, despotism and social dissolution.

§ 201. *The Golden Age an Impossibility, as Shown by the Historical Trend of Government.* Admitting a primitive order of nature ruled by this "jus naturale," and from this the growth of freedom and equality of all, we must conclude that the mind of a man in the initial ages could not conceive of the notion of "jura innata," or essential and universal powers. It would discredit the evolution of the human mind, which from the consideration of phenomena goes on to that of the essence, from the particular to the universal, and from the prompting of the senses or instinct to the attainment of freedom. And we fall into the error of generalizing from the present and transferring it with aid of fancy into the distant past. Natural man is also social man, but the social conscience is undeveloped in him. He is not rational and good as the philosophers of the last century imagined him, but selfish, without a sense of evil, and impatient of restraint. In the first grade of society everything belongs to the strength. Violence is the measure of right. Whoever is better armed and possesses an organically stronger constitution conquers and kills him who is less prepared for the struggle of existence, as is shown by the life of plants and animals. Civilization is the emancipation of man from the yoke of foreign influences, and freedom from the wild state, pictured by Epicurus and Hobbes, who believed, however, in a condition of solitude to which society has succeeded as an artificial creation. Society progresses and extends as man grows further away from the primitive world. The idea of a "jus naturale," common to our entire species and fitted to the principles of a "naturalis ratio," in which the essence of man is found, could not have a place in our mind, if we first had not thought out and compared the many similarities and likenesses among the diverse laws of different peoples.   Neither can there be any doubt that the conception of the constitution of society and the State, through contract, exceeds the force of the rude primitive intellect and is modern, because the predominance of contracts in all relations of ethical life show the most extended and exaggerated affirmation of the principle of individual freedom.   Now the law of primitive times was not founded on the individual but on the tribal or family community, and made rather a "jus cogens" than "voluntarium," disciplining men to the control of power or will.

§ 202. *The Development of Reason.*   It is a fact that the mind at first tries to explain the relation of phenomena superficially and arbitrarily, trusting to the fallacious testimony of the senses, not going beyond the sphere of purely assertive and simple judgments. Judgments, in this stage of intellectual development, are assertive (inasmuch as they are founded entirely upon our intuition) and simple (because they grow from sensation). As the mind progresses, judgment becomes problematic, because the mind is not satisfied with primitive conceptions external, rough and not conforming to fact; and consequently it begins to be bothered by that fecund doubt which is the father of science. A thing can be thus and so from problematical judgment, so we search for particular judgments and thus discover that not all things of a given kind have a certain quality, but only some of them. Then the intellect succeeds in comprehending the essential elements of phenomena, and from hypothetical judgment attains the apodictic or universal, which, being universal, is therefore necessary and certain. It appears to us that the theory of cognition, contained in Hegel's "Phänomonologie des Geistes," best explains both the doctrine of the evolution of ethical relations in general, and of individual rights in particular, because it is applicable to all forms of knowledge, both in its theoretical and practical aspects. There may well be knowledge born in a moment of action and after simple theoretical cognition of which we must take account if we wish to resolve the problem of knowledge in its integrity. But the "Phänomonologie" begins with the most elementary and lowest form of knowledge, that is, from the knowledge which has but one object, and is not certain of anything except of the existence of something distinct from itself, whose nature and name it is ignorant of. In representation, the second stage, knowledge knows that the object is such and such an external thing with such and such qualities. In the mind, therefore, knowledge has within itself intelligence, a universality with its inherent and essential attributes, one and indivisible. The purpose of knowledge, therefore, is always distinction and correlation. So the ego is fundamentally the consciousness of consciousness or auto-consciousness, because the object has the same form. So the ego is identical with the object, but that it does not recognize this is the cause of immediate or appetitive auto-consciousness. If the ego and the object were not identical it could not have this desire, which is for its own essence, to which it is attracted. And if it knew of the identity this desire would cease to exist, being satisfied by practical knowledge of the object. When the object is not another ego in which the subject can see and find itself, but is a thing which is consumed in the act of satisfaction, the knowledge of this identity of subject and object is not attained. If one ego be placed before another, at first it denies and excludes the other, as each has a different sense, knowledge, will, and body. Because of this exclusion there is a struggle between the two auto-consciousnesses, — a struggle of life and death, in which each ego has a body. The struggle is mortal, but after the death of one auto-consciousness the other does not discover itself in the one which is dead: preservation of life is necessary for recognition. Later the victorious auto-consciousness grants existence to its victim and makes it its subject, whence arises a new relation between the two units, — that of master and servant. The ego, become master, no longer sees in the servant an enemy, but takes thought for its protection, and later, through habit, considers it as a part of itself; the servant ego fears and obeys its master and thus loses sight of itself. It works for the master and makes its own circles of interest include that of the other unit; hence, "Timor domini est initum spientiæ et libertatis;" and is the groundwork of the discipline which conquers natural freedom and fits man to control himself and others. It is useful to observe with Spaventa, in his "Principi di Filosofia," that the servant ego of the "Phänomonologie" is appetitive auto-consciousness; that the ego in which appetition alone is aroused has neither theoretical nor practical reason; and that the servitude is not a constraint on a free ego, but is merely the education of man about to become free. Freedom and

equality succeed slavery.   The form of mind has within
itself the form of auto-consciousness, a perfect identity
always distinct in itself between the subject and object,
— the beginning of logic.

§ 203.   *Vico's Sketch of the History of Human Development.*   History shows that from fear and slavery came
freedom.   Vico teaches that civil peace and human freedom consisted in keeping within bonds the motives of
desire, which made their appearance in the world as the
effects of frightful superstition.   With the first thunderbolts after the flood, men of gigantic nature were panic-
stricken and lost their pride and ferocity, and became
subject to a superior force, hiding themselves in the caves
of the mountains, whither they dragged women, whom
they held prisoners, keeping them always in their company throughout their lives.   This gave origin to the
first human marriages with definite wives, children, and
fathers, and therefore created the family.   Of a proud
and fierce nature, they ruled with a Cyclopean hand over
their children and wives.   And, upon the growth of the
cities, men thus prepared were already disposed to civil
control.   Providence ordained some economic republics
of monarchical form under the Patriarchs, who were the
strongest in sex, age, and virtue, and who, in the state
of nature or in the family age, had formed the first
communities, owning their own land, harvesting, hunting,
and effecting a family government over their servants.
But men, after a long period, blinded by the force of
their own evil deeds, which had resulted in an infamous
promiscuity of chattels and wives, grew shameless and
wicked; and driven to a life of violence by the strife born
of this infamous license, they again sought refuge with
the Patriarchs, who received them into their protection as
retainers.   Now, is not the dependence on the Patriarchs
of the retainers, deep-dyed with sensuous cupidity,

fundamentally identical with the dependence of the appetitive or servant auto-consciousness or on the free and
master auto-consciousness?   Is not this dependence the
source of freedom?   The retainers, under the discipline
of the Patriarchs, little by little became pious, wise, and
virtuous, and the Cyclopean realms became civil and free
states.   Bagehot, who applies the Darwinian theory to
political life and formation of national character, admits
that centuries of stagnation, monotony, and slavery
preceded the times of progress, variety, and freedom, and
are a preparative necessity.

§ 204.   *The Struggle for Individual Freedom.* From this
premise, it follows that inherent, essential, and universal
rights must be conceived as originally acquired, accidental, and particular powers of the individual.   In other
words, those natural rights first appeared as acquired
powers in an accidental manner, as faculties introduced
by a causation deep in the moral or religious ideas of
certain social classes or by a new positive justice, and
developed in the struggle to conform to the conditions
of existence.   Afterwards, such faculties, having the advantage of showing a higher degree of rational growth,
remained victorious in their struggle against the institutions which retarded their development, and, strengthened by custom and heredity, became original, necessary,
and common rights, after human nature had recognized
her own essence in them.   The history of the right of
personality, although not a special and separate right,
but the source of every faculty, brings us face to face
with all the phases of the "jura innata."   For centuries
the individual was the subject of acquired rights, particular and accidental, because all men were not born
free and those who were became so in a certain sense
through determinate deeds or acts, and so a complete
or incomplete right of personality came and went by

chance. For the slaves who represented the greater part of the human race were not persons. They acquired the "status libertatis" or incomplete personality by "manumissio," and only got full individuality with the possession of the "status libertatis civitatis et familiæ." Freedom came and went by chance, which governed even the position of the individual not born of a slave mother, but of free parents in marriage, or at least of a free mother. The chances of war and captivity caused the loss of personality, and the "postliminium," which depended on chance, revived it. Terrible, long, and bloody were the struggles undergone and suffered from the beginning against diverse and tenacious forms of slavery, in the effort to extend personality to an always increasing number of individuals, and to complete it in those already called free subjects. The result of this struggle has been a series of victories obtained one by one. And with long custom and heredity, the common consciousness has attained a conception of essential and universal rights. Recently enough has come the declaration of the rights of man, for even since the French Revolution there are found in the codes of European nations steps towards the denial of the right of personality. It is only during the past few years that freedom is not among us a cloak for the protection of usury. And but lately has the senseless and barbarous right of the "jus albinatus" developed into its softened and useful forms of a system of reciprocity among most nations. In Italy there is wise legislation by which a foreigner, because he is a man, is permitted the enjoyment of civil rights.

§ 205. *Subsidiary Inherent Rights in the Struggle for Development.* The other inherent rights to physical and moral life, freedom, and equality are contained in the greater right of personality, even imperfectly thought of. At the beginning, these faculties were acquired, accidental, and particular, as the germ from which they sprang; that is, the human unit, which was disregarded as we have seen by the ancient State, the arbiter of his life and death. By chance, he was born free or slave, and slaves had no right to life, limb, or good name. Freemen had rights if their nation had not retained compulsory military service or if the father was not given the "jus necis." For a long time, it was not a crime to kill a child. The right to physical and moral life, therefore, was always accidental, here acquired with freedom, and there with citizenship, belonging to some and not to all. In respect to freedom we should recall with Hegel that in the Orient the despot alone was free, and that in the ancient world, freedom was restricted to a portion of humanity and had at bottom a political character and was always freedom in or through the State. Such was the equality which, denied by the law of caste, was given only to citizens. From citizenship in an ideal state, Aristotle says, farmers and artizans should be excluded, because excellence is not compatible with manual labor. The conditions of excellence, and here we mean political excellence, are leisure, and therefore the true components of the city are judges, warriors, priests, and counselors. The right to freedom and equality became essential and common attributes with the appearance of the inherent right to physical and moral life; that is, when the conception of the personal unit, after many struggles, became that of man.

§ 206. *Rights not Distinct Abstractions, but Components of Life.* The intellectual modern philosopher no longer looks upon inherent rights from an abstract point of view as powers of the individual in a supposed state of isolation without correlation to duties, but connects them, and reproduces, under new and more rational forms, the classical doctrine of the relation of ethics and politics. Our juristic philosophy objects to formal abstractions for another reason, and treats inherent rights always in relation to the acquired rights, a relation based on the ideal innate in nature, life, and history. If law is a human idea, if it is true and certain, it must include all elements, essential and accidental, universal and particular, primal and acquired. The mind begins by considering it from casual, particular, acquired, or temporary aspects and afterwards comes to the contemplation of its necessary, universal, primal, or eternal characteristics. Vico, therefore, finds fault with the principles of natural law and with Grotius, Selden, and Puffendorf for having begun the teaching of its theories, not from the time in which the *gens* began, but from the time when natural reason was first fully developed. The criticism of Vico is contrary to the teachings of Kant, Rousseau, all the representatives of the abstract movement of natural law, many ancient philosophers, and the Roman jurisconsults, because they generalize from their time and believe all that belongs to the human ego is primal. Neither can modern thought be based on an hypothesis of the state of nature, so contrary to the conception and history of man, whose development, intellectual, physical, and moral, is not possible without society. The idea of contract as the origin of the State and of society is not primitive, as we have said.[1] Contract that has for its object the exchange of utilities can exist or not exist; law and the State must exist. The contract which would establish a State presupposes the same State to execute and enforce it. Examine with critical attention the French Declaration of the Rights of Man, made in 1789 by the Constituent Assembly, and you will find all the abstract belief in natural law bound up in it. It speaks of rights

[1] *Cf.* § 197 *ante.*

anterior to society, and supposes that the natural man
was born with these rights; makes no mention of any
duties, but admits the anarchical right of resistance, and
confuses the will of the majority with law, enacting
the principles of Rousseau. The English Bill of Rights
of 1689, and the American Declaration of Independence
do not lend countenance to such ideas, but sanction historical rights and follow the feelings, traditions, and customs of their framers. The American Declaration of
Independence, however, drawn up a century later than
the English Act, shows in its Preamble some influence of
the dominant philosophical theories of the XVIIIth Century, though these do not alter its concrete, historical
character.

§ 207. *Italian Philosophers are Opposed to the Doctrine
of a State of Nature.* In Italy Genovesi, the author of
"Diceosina," is opposed to the existence of a state of
nature and cannot imagine natural and acquired
rights without civil society, because man strives for
happiness, for which law is instrumental, and happiness is only attainable in the equilibrium between
individual cupidity and the social sense, an equilibrium obtainable only by law, which protects rights
and remedies their violations. Spedalieri in his book
"I Diritti dell 'Uomo," even better than Genovesi,
before the abstract movement was so well developed
either in doctrine or practice, made a careful study of the
state of nature and showed clearly that it had never existed and that a state of society is necessary to the full
corporeal and spiritual development of man. He discards
the doctrine of contract as the base of all obligation, because there are obligations derived from natural facts,
from necessity, the synonym of reason, and not from
agreement, and he enumerates the natural rights of
man as those which look to life, development, and prop-

erty, and freedom to act concerning these three rights, freedom of thought, and the use of force in self-defense. He adds, also, the right to the aid of one's fellows, which is but a limited right, except in cases of extreme necessity. Natural rights, according to him, owe their origin and use to the social state, and can only by a fiction exist in a state of solitude.

§ 208. *An Equivocation, the Confusion of Status and Contract.* Before we reach the end of this chapter, we must state an equivocation. Maine has said that the progress of law consists in the change of régime from status to contract. The status is necessary, superimposed, coercive, and can well be considered as the necessary effect of the principle of community of primitive times. Spencer enunciates this theory when he affirms that progress consists in the advance from a system of obligatory or military coöperation to one that is industrial or voluntary. Fouillée, with the same premise, places the specific differences of social phenomena in degree of freedom of consent. The equivocation lies in confusing two distinct conceptions, the conception of individual freedom and that of contract, as the source of all ethico-juridical relations. Without doubt, the emancipation of the individual from the ancient yoke is a sign of progress, but it does not mean that the moral world depends upon his will and is his arbitrary creation. There are many relations and institutions not in the least dependent upon the wills of the parties, as matrimony, or the State. These are not voluntary in the sense that they are made or dissolved at will, though such relations or institutions are made by the agreement of individuals in the sense that they can marry or not, or enjoy one political form or another. The ability to contract is not the source of law which is partly above the individual, and unaffected by his contracts, although it demands the acknowledgment and voluntary obedience of the individual because he is a factor of the ethical whole. The ability to contract, therefore, is not the mark of the social fact, in all its integrity in human times, and *a fortiori* was not so for the same reason in the past, which was dominated by the rigorous régime of status.

CHAPTER III

INCORPOREAL PERSONS

THE SCOPE OF INCORPOREAL PERSONS. — THE THEORIES OF
FICTION AND OF EQUIVALENCY. — THE THEORY THAT LOOKS
UPON THE INCORPOREAL PERSON AS A VEHICLE. — THE
THEORY OF THE COMPLEXITY OF RIGHTS "SUI JURIS." — THE
IDEAS OF THE GERMAN PUBLICISTS. — THE REAL SUBJECT IN
A CORPORATION OR FOUNDATION. — THE RIGHTS OF THE IN-
CORPOREAL PERSONS AND THE "JUS CONFIRMANDI" OF THE
STATE. — THEORY OF GIORGI.

§ 209. *Are Incorporeal Persons Fictional or Real?*
Incorporeal or collective persons are the subject of
civil rights and public duties.   Instituted, as they are, for
purposes distinct from those of individuals, in extent and
length of life they exceed the latter's power.   Is the
incorporeal person a fiction or a reality?   This question
is studied more by students of Roman and modern civil
law than by philosophers of law.   Accurate and profound thoughts on this theme, however, are not lacking
in the works of Vico, Hegel, Rosmini, and Trendelenburg, as we shall see, but they do not contain a true
philosophico-juristic theory.   Ahrens has felt the need
of such a theory, although he has not shown whether he
thinks incorporeal persons are fictions or personifications
by the State, and does not proceed in a philosophical
manner, because he starts out with a presupposition.

§ 210. *Different Theories about Incorporeal Persons.*
Many jurists cannot believe in the real existence of
incorporeal persons, because they think that reality

connotes only the individual or corporeal person, per-
ceptible to the senses.   They are governed by the same
principle as the Ionic philosophers and the Sophists; —
that reality lies only in natural and phenomenal objects.
These jurists are in accord with the phenomenalists and
conceptionalists of the Middle Ages, since they admit the
reality only of the individual and consider the universal
as a name or as a simple abstract conception without
real existence.   In this they differ from the positivists
of to-day, who state that the conception of objects was
not less real than the sensations in which they originated,
and who have no scruple in regarding incorporeal persons
as existent among true organic entities.   Perhaps the positivists go too far in making the ethical organism the full
equivalent of the physical, but there is no doubt that they
look upon them as real persons.   At present the position of the jurists resembles that of the great masters
of the orthodox economic school, who denied that
immaterial products had a real value.   But the jurists
are less logical than the economists because they recognize
"res incorporales" and admit at least the personal reality
of the State, because this cannot be held to be a fiction.
Savigny, for example, who does not believe that juridical
persons are real, says that the State is the corporeal form
of a spiritual unit.   Those economists who teach that
immaterial products have no real value follow the theory
to its logical conclusion that real value lies only in the
"res corporales" and do not go out of the sphere of
mechanism when they talk about the supreme incorporeal
personality, the State.   We must remember that the
classical school of political economy looks upon the State
simply as the means for the protection of the life and
goods of the associated individuals, or at least as a
mechanical aid for the attainment of human ends, to
quote Romagnosi, and never as a person with attributes
of its own.

§ 211. *A Contradiction. Rights without Subjects.* The jurists who doubt the reality of the incorporeal person must solve the great contradiction between the rule of law, which requires a subject for a right, and the incontestable fact of some combinations of capacities, which would in their theory be without true subjects. Many of them try to eliminate the contradiction by calling the reality a fictitious and artificial subject, others by so transforming and amplifying the idea of law as to create the possibility of a right without a subject.   All of them construct, then, the doctrine of the juridical person with the gift of the senses and with the mere abstract virtue of thought, because, inasmuch as the subject is artificial to that extent, the unions of rights without a subject are abstractions.   They cannot be otherwise if reality lies exclusively in material objects.

§ 212. *Non-existence of Incorporeal Persons a Logical Impossibility.* Puchta in his "Vorlesungen über das Heutige Romische Recht," Savigny in his "System des Heutigen Römischen Rechts," and Unger in his "System der Oestreichischen Almeinen Rechts," teach that incorporeal persons are useful fictions of positive law, or ideal subjects created by the State. This theory falls into the contradiction which it tries to avoid; for, on one hand, there cannot be a right without a subject, and man alone is the subject of rights; on the other, there are combinations of rights without real subjects. Fictions and personifications will not do, because, by imagining the subject or creating the person, we recognize that there is none, while there must necessarily be one. So, when the theory under consideration is given the most favorable interpretation, and we say that the juridical person is imaginary or artificial only in respect to private law, while it is existent and undeniable in the spiritual community, as universality, and a subject of public rights, the contradiction is not avoided, because the collective person of public law is always in private law a fictitious individual created by law, and the imaginary subject of rights of ownership.   Private law cannot consider any other subject than a real person. Furthermore, while under this theory man alone is the subject of rights, its champions must finally admit that rights can act upon a subject which is not a natural human being.   An incorporeal person, according to the jurisconsults, is not a *de facto* subject, and therefore does not enter into the domain of fiction in its proper signification.   By means of a fiction, an act is shown in connection with another act juridically regulated, and is given the same relation to law as its model has.   Two real subjects are necessary to a fiction; but in this case there is only one, — the separate, corporeal person.

§ 213.   *The "Quid Simile" Theory of the Incorporeal Person.*   Randa in his book "Der Besitz nach Oestreichischen Rechts," Böhlau in his work on the subject of law, Bruns in his article in the "Encyklopädie" of Holtzendorff try to escape the contradiction of the theory of personification by saying that the attributes not belonging to individuals should not be attributed to artificial and fictional subjects, although they should be equal, in the eyes of the law, to the individuals themselves.   Here there is no fictional person, but a "quid simile" of a person, which exercises its functions and has its place, "personæ vice fungitur."   But the three writers cited above do not in the least answer the question; they allege the fact that they must prove, that is, the existence of property and rights not belonging to any physical subject, as if they had a subject. Nor is the much feared contradiction avoided by the conception of property without an owner, because this

destroys the well-known principle that there can be
no right without a subject. And further, it remains
to be shown what is the "quid" which has the attributes of a person without being a person. Evidently
here the function is confused with the fiction, which is
the object of such abhorrence.

§ 214. *Ihering's Theory of Individuals as Subject
of Rights.* Ihering, in his "Geist des Römischen
Rechts," fights the theory of personification and
assimilation and prepares the way for the champions
of the existence of private rights without a subject,
denying that there are things which do not belong to
individuals and alleging that the juridical person is not
the subject of rights but a simulacrum, a simple mask,
an empty form, an exterior shape invented for convenience and created as a means of mediation. The
juridical person is the technical means of developing
juristic relations between the members of a corporation, or those interested in it, and strangers; the true
subject is man, the efficient subject of rights, he who
enjoys them. In a corporation or association, the subjects are those who enjoy the advantages derived from
the moral being. The abstract entity does not enjoy
them; it cannot have, therefore, any interest, scope,
or rights. Ihering confuses facts and rights. It is one
thing to see who has a right, or rather who enjoys it,
and another to discover the subject of the right itself.
Certainly a man can enjoy the advantages growing
out of wealth, without being the owner and disposer
thereof. The citizens of a commonwealth and the sick
are not the owners of the capital of the community
or of the hospital, although they reap the benefits. In
a word, it is always necessary to distinguish the material enjoyment from the ideal enjoyment, the possession from the ownership of rights, since one can have

the first without the second; but Ihering does not get away completely from the idea of personification, since his juridical person needs an apparent subject or mask. He founds his theory (which he believes concrete and based upon the strictest realism) on an abstraction, regarding the elements entirely by themselves and separate from their natural centre of adhesion.

§ 215. *The Doctrine of Rights without a Subject.* Windscheid and Brinz, in their "Lehrbuch des Pandekten," and Bekker, in his study of the subject of rights, go further than Ihering and combat the well-established principle that rights, not belonging to individuals, must have a subject. The idea of law, they say with Demelius, in "Die Rechtsfiktion," is abstract in dealing with facts and particular institutions; if the existence of a combination of rights without a subject is a fact, we must conclude that the idea of law should comprehend such a fact and contain the possibility of rights without a subject. Windscheid defines a right as an impersonal capacity of will, which only needs a subject in its exercise to become real. Brinz distinguishes wealth belonging to a person and that devoted to a purpose, laying stress on the fact and leaving the fiction once for all. Bekker denies that the will is the subject; in his mind, the name or title is that which confers upon a man the free disposition of a right; for example, the name blacksmith gives a man a blacksmith's rights. To this theory the thought is opposed at once that law is not reducible to a simple mental aggregation of determinate properties separated from the facts. There is in such a theory, as in every other universal conception, a series of necessary elements and relations which simple experience cannot furnish because they are by nature contingent and particular. The hypothetical basis of this theory, therefore, is erroneous, and equally

erroneous are the conceptions which arise from it. The
definition of a right, given by Windscheid, is not correct,
because a capacity of will is an adherent right and
impersonal only in the sense that it can be attributed
to this or that man, but not in the sense that it can
separate itself absolutely from its subject and become
a capacity of will, a power without a subject, to exercise this by a conception without content. The argument of analogy from the case of a child has no weight,
because children are potentially able to will. If, in
this case, the characteristics are found, the substance
is certainly not lacking, but the impersonal capacity to will does not exist, and therefore it must represent what is non-existent. Neither has the opinion of
Brinz a better foundation, because the idea of property rights *sui juris*, independent and existent, implies
either personification of them or the object from which
they are devolved. The essential characteristic of property is its dependence on man. It consists in the
sum of the means necessary and useful for the attainment of personal development. This theory is an
abstraction which leads on one side to the elevation of
the inanimate, to the status of a juridical subject, and on
the other, debases man to the inanimate. An end cannot
be self-attaining, arising from property without a subject,
or without referring to one in a manner not accidental,
and therefore it is not true that there can be rights
without a subject. Bekker proceeds along the road of
indefinite personification of animate and inanimate
objects, and clearly confuses the uncertain subject of a
right with its object. The title of blacksmith can belong
to one or another individual, but cannot lack a subject.
Nor do the successive possessors of an office, for example,
a king, form a juridical person, as Kant and Windscheid
say, because the office or the crown have no will; the

true subject of the rights in that case is the State. Even the right of inheritance is not a juridical person, for the possessor or subject is not lacking, but only uncertain. Here we must remember that the right of the heir, who enters, is considered as beginning at the moment of the death of the "de cuius." Neither does the appointment of a trustee show the presence of a juridical person, because a trustee can be appointed for an absent heir.

§ 216. *Wealth Cannot be Subjective.* The followers of the doctrine of which we speak confess sometimes that a right cannot be without a subject because a right is subjective, but allege that it is not absurd to admit of corporate or associate property rights without subjects because they are a simple collection and objective union. They add that this property, as a subject, is not a mere collection of things but the sum of them made one, organized, and raised to an autonomous unity by virtue of its purpose or the unifying will which dominates it, with the approval of the State. But property objectively is a part, an element, and not unified totality. Above all we must remember that there is not the slightest deviation from the principle of the doctrine recognizing that there is no right without a subject, for this is founded entirely upon the opposite conception. In the second place, we must observe that property looked upon as an organized totality cannot be looked upon as a subject of the unifying principle or central organic force, which is purpose or will. Purpose and will rule and shape the totality, reduce it to a true unity, and therefore the subject should be found in such factors. Things are things and form objectivity; purpose and will by their natures belong to the subjective sphere. Purpose is the limit of the will and is essentially connected with it.   Purpose can be defined in terms of will, consequently the subject can be found in the capacity of will.   Purpose cannot be attained without will, and on the other hand, the subject can only be will if it organizes the totality of things with regard to man and makes it a unit.   Property cannot be conceived without a person to whom it belongs, without a will to which it can be united and by which it is animated. Property is a personal attribute of the individual, and a person can never be an attribute of property.

§ 217.   *Incorporeal Persons are Existent.*   The jurists, who do not believe in the real existence only of sensible and simple objects, are disposed to believe, as is logical, in the reality of incorporeal persons.   The general conviction of a real personality in the State, which is seldom considered a fictitious entity, the knowledge that the theories just described cannot be applied to public law, the ideas of philosophers about the State itself have contributed not a little to the awakening and full development of this belief. Vico wrote that as from the aggregation of bodies called "comitia" with "coeundo" and "comeundo" has come the body of the republic, thus from the unity of wills has been found their mind, more gracefully defined by Papinian as the "communis reipublicæ sponsio," or the general will of all citizens to have equal rights.   The mind of this will is civil authority, reason, and architectural justice.   From this mind and spirit is derived civil power, which makes the person of the republic, whose life is public health, which comprehends the lives of all individuals.   The great Neapolitan philosopher, to whom we have referred, spoke of the national soul as a live and not a blind form.   Veggasi is right in saying, as many others have also said, that the conception of the existence of incorporeal persons, and

especially of the real personality of the State, owes its
origin to the doctrine of Bluntschli in his book "Deutsches
Privatrecht." In Germany, too, Schelling, before Blunt-
schi, raised the standard of ethical ontology, and Hegel
regarded the State as a system of the moral world, as
an auto-conscious substance, founding it on the reality
of the universal will, which is the sum of individual
wills, a reality very different from that of the Herbartian Thilo. But at first we must notice that the founder
of the historical school, Savigny, had recognized the
actual existence of the greatest of incorporeal persons,
the State, in spite of his theory of personification. After
Schelling, Hegel, and Savigny, Trendelenburg revived
the Greek political conception, harmonizing it with the
principles of modern times, and came to the same conclusion, that is, to the recognition of the State as a
true unit, an ethical organism, as abstract man in the
particular form of a people. In Italy philosophers
of law, even before Bluntschli, admitted the existence
of incorporeal persons in treating of the State and society.
Romagnosi often spoke of the State as a perfect and
vital interpenetration of the individual intellects,
wills, and powers. And Rosmini, without distinguishing society from a moral person, distinguished the
internal and invisible part, which forms the spirit of
society itself, and the external visible part, which
constitutes its mass. Society is real and vital, and
because real and vital is the concurrence of the wills,
which are its foundation.

§ 218. *A New Will, the Resultant of the Union of Two
Wills.* Baron, Beseler, Lasson, and not a few others
in Germany agree with Bluntschli on the existence of incorporeal persons; they look upon the State and moral
entities as real organisms, efficient subjects of public
rights; but of their personality in private law, that is, of

their civil capacity, they either do not speak or else, following Savigny, make it a mere fiction, or perhaps a presupposition. Zitelmann, in his book "Begriff und Wesen der Sogenanten Juristischen Personen," states a full theory applicable to private and public law. He essentially conforms to philosophical principles, although he does not speak accurately, and uses not a few metaphors and similes. He starts with the principle of personal will, in which rights are inherent, and admits the reality of this principle in juridical persons as well as in individuals. By being subject of rights, the juridical person acquires a potential or actual capacity to will; that is, personality, which should be recognized by the State. The result, therefore, is that the personality of the entity is not a creation of the statutes, as some believe, but of the union of many wills considered, not in their integrity but in their reference to a definite purpose, creating a new, general, and efficient will, which is the natural basis of a corporation. Here happens what is always observed, to quote Zitelmann; that is, that when two forces are associated by a unifying third, the two forces lose their individual existence and form a new force with the common properties of its components. In law there is the example of the "universitas bonorum," which has its power as a unity distinct from the separate elements composing it.

§ 219. *This New Force is a Higher Form of Evolution.* We can add to what our author says, that if the corporation is an intimate concurrence of many wills for a given end, and if it is a totality or ethical organism, it is, in a certain aspect, more real than the individuals, because it possesses greater complexity of parts and represents a higher form of evolution. Without human life and the various social nuclei, the individual is an abstraction. Mass and, therefore, true reality, are found in organic compositions, in communities, in the centre of the union of parts whose existence have their signification through the existence of the whole. Nevertheless, the parts of the ethical organism are free and individual entities, and besides being subordinate participants in the life of the whole, have their own lives and appropriate ends. An association is a special ethical organism consisting of an entity entirely distinct from the individuals and bringing about results which are of an immediate advantage to it. The unity is not an abstract entity incapable of enjoyment, as Ihering thinks, but is a real and single power which arises from the profound interpenetration of many wills.

§ 220. *A Corporation Must be an Organism.* Zitelmann does not and cannot show clearly the real personality of a corporation unless it is an ethical organism derived from the interpenetration of the component wills. Its essence lies in the irrevocable act, and in the recognition by the State by which a juridical subject consecrates some of its capacities or all its wealth to a definite purpose. They err who think that the union or association of many persons to follow one another in succession for the attainment of an end is an ethical organism, for, though such persons in their quality of agents have more power than as individuals, they do not constitute the more substantial elements of the institution. A priest, for example, is not, in respect to the benefice which he enjoys, a member of an organic series of priests, his predecessors and possible successors, established by a determined act of the Church and having a quality of subjection to rights, but he is simply agent, a method by which the person can exist. The idea of association is spontaneously connected with that of the founder whose act the association is, and therefore the necessity arises to distinguish in our definition this similarity, and to lay emphasis upon the secondary or perhaps accidental elements. The act of foundation is the very will of the founder become objective, concrete, and irrevocable, developing along its own lines, and is the subject of rights contained in the institution itself, and therefore the natural origin of the personality that the State recognizes. But this will, although separated from the person and become objective, is fundamentally subjective and personal. It is an act distinct from the power, though not conceivable without it, suitable to give form, quality, and coördination to the association. The determinate will in such form has nothing in common with the impersonal will of Windscheid, who distinguishes the subject only by the exercise of its rights, and not by its essence. Neither should it be confused with the purpose without subject, the conception of Brinz, because the purpose for which the powers are given is subsequent to the will of the founder, and is the termination of the volitive act of the person, and presupposes the will, and the volitive subject which renders objective an act suitable to the end desired. Here there is a case of the decomposition of the empirical ego, of the ego consisting of successive growth; in other words, the integration of concrete subjectivity. The empirical ego can be distinguished from diverse particular egos. This is possible under normal and pathological conditions. There were two egos in Manlius Torquatus, when he said to his son, "As your father, I praise you, but as your captain, I am going to condemn you to death." Psychologically, a plurality of persons is possible in the same subject; and juridically, an individual can have even more personalities. This is the reason why it is not a self-contradiction to raise the act of will or the will in respect to a single and fixed purpose to the grade of a subject or individual. In conclusion we can say that if the institution is not made an ethical organism by incorporation, it at least comprehends the same principle and personality, and therefore the capacity to will.   In corporations the subject is the new and single will which is born from the interpenetration of many wills; in unincorporated associations the subject is the will become objective by the act of the same will of the founder.   There are some institutions that are equinumerant to the wills although the latter are resolved in them.   Here comes a peculiar difference between a corporation and an association.

§ 221.   *Incorporation.*   The theory stated is deduced as a corollary from what we have already said, from a fundamental principle of the philosophy of law; the person consists really in the capacity to will.   Now this capacity is found both in corporations and associations.   In the former, it is one with the new and distinct unity growing from the interpenetration of many wills; in the second, it is the same as the will of the founder become objective in a single purpose.   The incorporeal person is raised to the equal of the juridical and civil subject by the State after its social advantages are recognized, and has property rights and sometimes political rights and powers of guardianship. It has rights of property, "jura in re aliena," rights of possession, contract, and testamentary succession.   It lacks, however, a right to delegate, and is in a condition analogous to that of a minor, hence its representative government.   The State does not create but only registers incorporeal persons, because legal authorization deals with the preëxistent personality of the moral body; that is, of the capacity to will.   Where this is lacking, there cannot be any grounds for authorization.   Creation is synonymous to existence of the fictitious person or personification, and is as absurd as either of them.

In fact, it amounts to the same thing. It is strange that Savigny teaches that juridical persons have not their origin and end in the State, while they have, in his mind, an artificial existence. If juridical persons are fictitious or artificial, it is not possible to deny that they owe their existence and dissolution to positive law. The State registers not only the existence of incorporeal persons, but first examines the question of the social utility to be derived from the institution of the moral entity, and then recognizes and raises it to the state of a simple subject, watching and controlling it. The law of the State is a "jus confirmandi," and if it is to be called a "jus constituendi," the notion of creations must be abandoned and only that of an elevation of an initial person to a juristic person relied on. We understand that the State has the powers of taking away from moral entities already constituted the capacity that it has given them when their existence is no longer justified or when they run contrary to the ends of civilization and social utility.

§ 222. *Incorporation Does not Affect Question of Reality of Association.* Giorgi, in "La Dottrina delle Persone Giuridiche," has severely criticized the opinions of various writers on this subject, expressing a theory of his own that completes to his satisfaction those of Bluntschli, Baron, Lasson, and Beseler. He accepts the way in which they consider the State and collective entities, but considers it defective as to associations. According to Giorgi, associations have substantially the same real essence as corporations, that is, an existent collectivity, and therefore cannot be reduced to a fictitious personality. This conception had been developed by Fisichella, in his book "Sulla Realta delle Persone Giuridiche," as Giorgi frankly confesses. The whole reasoning in aid of this thesis can be outlined thus: The wealth of an association comes from the people; it is intended for the accomplishment of general duties, and is given to the people as its true owner. The assignment to a board of managers of a separate fund, department, or particular branch gives it a single and autonomous being but does not change the subject. It multiplies only juristically and administratively the collective personality, in other words the people, with the meaning either of the whole political aggregate or its subdivisions by local boundaries for administrative reasons. Two methods can be followed by the sovereign power for the satisfaction of social needs; it can provide directly with a simple and undivided exchequer, or it can dismember this in many parts, conferring on each an autonomous individuality, and make it proportionate to the needs for the attainment of this or that other end, hence moral entities and associations.

§ 223. *More Contradictions in Distinguishing Corporations and Associations.* The doctrine stated is in contradiction to the principle with which the author started out. To his mind it is ridiculous and metaphoric to assimilate society to an organism: for example, such expressions as "the social organ," "the social body," "the social will," "the social or national soul." Society is the mere aggregation of individuals, a simple collectivity, which cannot be conceived as an entity or organic unit. Giorgi declares specifically that society is nothing but a collective entity and indirect means for the satisfaction of individual interests, and therefore must fall in line with the atomic theory. But if society is not a spirit or consciousness and will, and if it is a collective entity and nothing else, how can it have its own exclusive, so called, public rights? How can Giorgi agree with the ideas of the German writers on public law who regard the State as an organism, if he says

in so many words that this belief is an untrue and
ridiculous metaphor? Giorgi states that man alone being
capable of duties, he is, therefore, the only possible
subject of rights, which presuppose duties, which in
their turn demand consciousness, will, and responsibility.
The human community has not a psyche, and therefore
cannot have duties nor rights of any kind whatsoever,
exclusively its own. Further, we should observe that
Bluntschli, Baron, Beseler, Lasson, and the others tend
to make the principle of public law the base of the juristical personality of moral entities, and therefore are reso-
lute in their denial that commercial associations founded
for private gain are juridical persons, excluding every
entity which has a private character. The same cannot
be said of Giorgi, who says that he bases his reasoning
on the principles of these writers, and yet holds with
ponderous arguments that the commercial associations
are true juridical persons.

§ 224. *The Members Cannot be the Subject of Corporate
or Associate Rights, Giorgi's Theory.* According to Giorgi,
the subjectivity of corporations and associations lies in
the existent collectivity. Fixing our attention for a
moment on this collectivity as the subject of the
rights of corporations, we must remember that it is
not intended in the sense that Bolze and Ihering
use it; according to Giorgi himself, collectivity cannot be considered as plurality in order that we may
attribute to individuals the rights of the juridical person,
and no longer need to recognize that subject separate
from them. This would be making a juridical person.
Neither can we understand it as essentially one with its
separate members, even though they have interests in it
and enjoy it, because it is one thing to define the subject
of rights and another to determine the question of the
enjoyment of the advantages connected with it. If

collectivity cannot be defined in one way or the other, we must abandon once for all the instrumental point of view, and consider the community as an organic unity, and come to the theory of Zitelmann, at least in its essential particulars. Collectivity, however, as an organic unity, is not simple collectivity, but something more than that. It is the single will which arises from the interpenetration of individual wills, of which we have spoken before.[1] This will is a new vital and distinct principle very different from the unity which an arithmetical formula expresses. The common will has nothing to do with the $7+5=12$, and therefore with Zitelmann's erroneous example, but Giorgi does not believe in this theory of will, which is inconsistent with the operation of nature, he says, in separating the will from the individual, and in making will the essential in law, and man but a "quid superfluum." But this theory, to tell the truth, is not inconsistent and does not presuppose the separate existence of will. In ethics and law man is considered only as will and not as a simple theoretical mind or phantasy. Mind and phantasy are activities which ethics and law regard only in so much as they are comprehended in will. Is it not possible that both of them enter into practical reason? Reason is called practical when it has for its object the welfare which is the end of will. Will is not accessory in those sciences but is essential, even as man, the subject of will, is essential. If the conception of will without man is impossible, equally impossible is that of man without will. On this account, we have not subscribed to Windscheid's theory of the impersonal will, and have said that a capacity of will without a volitive subject is an impossible conception. If a corporation is an organic and not an instrumental unit, the subject of the rights must be found in

[1] *Cf.* § 221 *ante.*

the fusion of individual wills, in a single general will. Social man is possible to the extent that he admits of that fusion. Both in the particular and general will is found all human nature considered as the subject of ethics. It is not true, therefore, that under the theory of the will man takes the part of a "quid superfluum."

§ 225. *Giorgi's Theory Criticized.* In associations the will is not separated from man in the true sense of the word because it is derived from the founder and conserves his character and continues his personality in a particular form. In the act of association there is a relation not belonging to the will of the man, and this relation, become permanent, is the base of that multifold personality which a man can assume in the eyes of the law corresponding to the plurality of the empirical ego admitted in psychology, as we have said before.[1] The will of the founder is an empirical ego, a derivative personality, more than a mere transitory act of the mind. In law there is no contradiction in the existence of various personalities in a human individual, although there be but one substantial personality, as in psychology the formation of various empirical consciousnesses does not include the necessity of an original and primitive act of distinction between the ego and non-ego. With this premise let us examine the theory of Giorgi, which makes the subject of the rights of the association the entire human community, the people as formed by the State. To us it seems that his theory is not tenable, because it has the same vice as the repudiated doctrine of Ihering. Giorgi also confuses law with fact, because, though associations are useful to society and their institution of important social interest, it does not follow that society should be their subject. The poor and

[1] *Cf.* § 220 *ante.*

the sick get many advantages from charitable institutions, and yet they are not owners of the endowments. Logically from this premise every individual right in the last analysis should belong to the State, because from every right society gets some advantage. Every individual right in a certain aspect is a social interest and therefore should be given to the State; a "reductio ad absurdum."

§ 226. *The Basis of the Criticism of Giorgi's Theory.* Giorgi made the mistake of considering associations only in regard to their object and in paying no attention to their origin and the right of those who founded them. The error of his theory becomes luminous when one tries to apply it to juridical persons which have a purpose of markedly private interest. The fact that the State has a right to authorize and destroy moral entities on the ground of social order, does not show that they are departments of the State and are not separate from it. Giorgi confuses a division of administrative control with the formation of a new entity, as Bonelli observes in his work, "Di una Nuova Teorica della Personalita Giuridica." Now to subdivide the administration and departments of association into many branches, and to confer upon one part juridical personality, are two different things. A private individual divides his administration into many branches with separate treasurers and agents. In such case, however, there is not an equal number of juridical persons. The juridical personality arises when the portion of the "corpus" thus separated becomes juridically independent of the rest, so that all the juristic relations into which it enters concern it alone. The juridical person is an autonomous unit entirely separate from any other unit. As long as a department, Bonelli says, destined for some public service, continues to be in the control of the State, no new personality appears, and such division has an exclusively administrative value. To make a department a juridical person signifies that in regard to private law it no longer belongs to the State. There must be a true and real change of owners made, and the new relations will have the new and not the old owner for their subject. Giorgi does not see that if the old subject remains the new one cannot be born. The existence of the old and the new subject at the same time is impossible.

CHAPTER IV

PROPERTY AND THE METHODS OF ACQUIRING IT

PROPERTY AND ITS RATIONAL BASIS. — DOCTRINES DEALING WITH THIS BASIS. — LIMITATIONS AND CONTROL OF PROPERTY. — ORIGINAL AND DERIVATIVE METHODS OF ACQUISITION.

§ 227. *Fundamental Bases of Rights of Property.* Man must attain his ultimate end, and therefore he expands his activity and binds and subjects to himself external things and makes agreements with other men for the reciprocal preservation of necessary and useful objects. From the expansion of his personal activity are derived property and personal rights; the first having to do with the relations between man and things and referring mediately to other persons inasmuch as they have a duty to respect these rights and sometimes a power to limit them, the second dealing with the relations between man and man and acting only indirectly on things, containing all obligations reducible to an agreement or promise. This distinction of rights is not opposed, as can be seen, to the principle that a person is the conscious subject of a right. Furthermore, the union of property and personal rights constitutes the estate which is the total of the extrinsic material and spiritual property created by a person for himself. Property rights comprehend property and one's rights over the possessions of others; personal rights are concerned with obligations of an economic or financial value. Whence it follows that the estate is composed of all these elements, some corporeal and some incorporeal.

§ 228. *The Greatest Property Rights.* Property is the greatest right, the "plena potestas in re." It is a general if not absolute power over objects, and at least it comprehends the greatest number of rights, including possession, acquisition, enjoyment, and disposition. Enjoyment implies the possession and use of the fruits; disposition embraces transformation and alienation. Fundamentally property is nothing more or less than freedom applied to things, as freedom in the last analysis can be reduced to self-ownership. These two conceptions interpenetrate and are convertible because property is the dress and investiture of individuals and is as inviolable as the person. Hegel says that a person has his external existence in property. Through property it comes about that things have no other signification than to create the reality or manifestation of free will. Trendelenburg looks upon property as a victory of mind over matter, as the instrument of the person. Things, in the power of man, become animated means for the purposes which they may serve, and, ceasing to be impersonal, represent the determination of will. In property we extend the conception of an organ to external things, and we feel ourselves in it, as in our own members. Rosmini asserts that the common character of all property is due to the connection of an object with the personal principle. The connection is duplicate, both physical and moral. He further says that the concrete connection has in the suitability of its occupancy for the attainment of some end, and that the moral connection is shown by the act of intellect by which we conceive a thing as useful to us, free and such as can be occupied, and by the act of will which

attempts to take it juridically and sets in motion the
forces suitable to take and keep it.   Concrete connection comes from the nature of the subject, which
seeks its own good in things.   Moral connection
comes from the nature of the object, which seems open
and free to occupancy.   Concrete connection is the
material of the right; the form lies in the moral connection
with the loss of which one loses the right itself, as the
jurisconsults have shown when they said "possessio
animo et corpore adquiritur."   Rosmini, Trendelenburg,
Cousin, and Thiers all agree in admitting two kinds
of property, one natural and the other acquired.   Man
has a primal property in his person and   powers.
The "mine" here is primal and original property, the
root and model of all others.   From it all the others are
derived, and are simple applications and developments
of it.   Our body belongs to us only as the home and
instrument of our personality, and is our next most
closely connected property.   Man has a second property,
less closely bound to his existence but not less legitimate, in the products of his powers.

§ 229.   *Philosophy of Property.*   Property is the
expression of a practical synthetic judgment *a priori.*
We know that Kant was the first to admit in theoretical philosophy the synthetic *a priori* judgment in which
the subject is an intuition or sensual element, and the
predicate is a category or an element pure, intelligible,
and original, not, therefore, a derivative of experience
or the outside world, but of the intrinsic activity of
the intellect or mind.   It is not the unity of two
conceptions, but of an intuition and a category, and
makes the conception because the subject, a sensual
element, is transfigured and made intellectual in the
act of uniting with the predicate.   A category is not
an innate idea immutable and in the mind from the

first, but a method or function, and thus is the original *a priori* element derived from the depths of the mind. Now property expresses a practical synthetic judgment *a priori* in as far as the thing or eudemonological term is reduced to a personal predicate. "Meum," "teum," and "suum" are predicates of this kind which show the activity of the person and the substance of the will. A person is original since it is not an external production and does not come from without, but at the same time is not at the beginning all that it should be, and is less than its full conception. However, it attains this conception through its energy, which develops in society. And here we see that the act of appropriation of the mind begins before the practical synthetic judgment *a priori*. It shows in theoretical judgment because to judge is to reduce the variety of objects presented to the unity of knowledge. It is to know, comprehend, and cognize what it feels, and to make it a property of the mind. The act of appropriation and theoretical judgment has only a cognitive value, while in a practical judgment it has an ethical significance.

§ 230. *History of Property — the Theory of Grotius.* Diverse are the opinions about the rational basis of property. Grotius states that private property, succeeding to the "communio bonorum primæva," descends from the occupancy and partition of land. Occupancy presupposes a tacit agreement, and partition an express contract. In his opinion private property is based upon the consensus of the components of society. In the beginning property was common to all the human species, and later to a people or family. When through determinate forces private ownership came into existence, there was no division of the common possessions, and by general consent each man kept what he had. The theory of Grotius confuses the rational basis of property with its

historical origin.   The basis of the property right must
be an idea, a principle and not simply a fact, as occupancy or partition.   Express consent is a fact, and so
also is tacit consent.   Locke, in his "Treatise on Civil
Government," the physiocrats, Adam Smith, and Stuart
Mill in "The Principles of Political Economy," and
many economists state that property rights owe their
origin to work.   According to Locke (the originator of
this theory) every individual has originally the duty
and right to work, and, as a means for the fulfillment of
his duty and the exercise of his right, has the power
of occupancy.   The theory of the English philosopher
makes property come into existence only after work
has been applied, yet bases it on work, as a right to
exercise suitable activity, and therefore gives rise to
property at the moment in which he uses such a right
through occupancy.   But work understood in this sense
is as inviolable as personal activity with which it is
confused.   In fact the true basis of property is the
person.   If applied work is conceived as the cause of
private property, private property cannot be justified,
because we must show first that there is a right to
occupy things to make them the object of work.   Work
is the method of acquisition, which demands a prior
justification of property.   Hobbes, Montesquieu in
his "L'Esprit des Lois," Bentham, and Charles Comte
make positive law the base of property without bother-
ing themselves whether positive law, in its recognition of
private property, conforms or not to reason and justice.

§ 231.   *Kant's Theory of Property.*   Kant thinks that
property cannot depend upon the isolated act of the
individual, such as occupancy or transformation.   Property lies not only in physical possession, but in intellectual possession, because the "mine" by right is,
according to that philosopher, so inherent in me that

its use by another without my consent harms me even when I have not the physical possession of it. Every external object can become somebody's; otherwise things would be of no use, and there would be an opposition between the appetitive capacities of free will and freedom, determined by reason, which demands property. To conceive of an object as under my power, not in the sense of mere physical possession, demands intellectual possession. In general, juristic propositions, as "dictamina rationis," are *a priori* in Kant's mind. The proposition of an *a priori* right is analytical or explicative of the physical possession, because he who takes something from me restricts my freedom and violates a juristic axiom, and then affects the rights of my person. But the above proposition of the possibility of intellectual possession, despite the want of physical detention, is synthetic, as the thing is not in my hands, and is *a priori* in that it establishes the necessity of a possession of right without possession. The right of individual possession lies in the original common property in land, and in the *a priori* general will, allowing such common ownership. Land cannot be free by nature originally, otherwise it would have in itself a quality which would place it above all possession. Freedom of land could only arise by agreement among those who had a right to its service, and nevertheless forbade the use of it among themselves, in which case the land would be theirs. Prehistoric common possession cannot be the notion of individual possession, otherwise free objects would be free of themselves, and should be regarded as "res nulius" by right, — an absurd proposition. Kant cannot conceive a "res nullius" in property, but supposes that it must be "res communis." For common property excludes individual property, as is noted by Tullio in "Il Diritto di Proprieta nella Dottrina di Kant." If

I wish certain external things to be mine, it is necessary that in the same act, I, of right, recognize the obligation of all to respect private property. Such an obligation is contained in the very conception of the right of possession. The only will suitable to enforce this obligation and to protect the "meum" and "teum" is the general will of society. In a state of society possession is not provisional as in the state of nature, but is permanent. The State itself, a product of reason, enforces the relations into which men enter, but does not create their necessity. A civil constitution, writes Kant, is merely a law by which each one is assured of his own. A State does not create or determine property. Now all this theory, while it is based upon the principle of individual personality and puts in evidence the social element of property, is capable of being generalized where it touches the propositions about intellectual possessions and of furnishing the philosophical reason of private ownership, because the practical synthetic judgment *a priori* is not the only proposition which enunciates the possibility of intellectual possession, but every proposition as well that is concerned with the fundamentals of property, as we have said before.

§ 232. *Fichte's Theory of Property.* Fichte constructs his doctrine with the elements of Kant's theories, but he exaggerates the significance of the social element. He believes that it is necessary to distinguish three kinds of contracts binding individuals together, as Filomusi-Guelfi says in the "Enciclopedia Juridica." These consist of the contract of property, the contract of defense, and the contract of union. By the first an individual possesses something, and demands that others do not claim it, obliging them to respect his possession so that he will respect theirs. By the second each one promises to help the other defend his property, if the other promises to do the same for him. The force of defense is established because individuals form part of the State through an agreement of union which guarantees the other two contracts. The individual has an original right to be a causal unit in the objective world, and therefore by the contract of property there is assigned to him a portion as the sphere for his activities, provided that he respects the freedom of others and promises the inviolability of their spheres of action. Freedom and activity are not possible without life. Freedom once guaranteed, life must be guaranteed; an absolute and inalienable property of man is the right to life. In that is found the ultimate object of the use of things. When a man cannot live by his work, there is not left to him anything which is really his, and the contract as regards him is void. Everyone must give conditions of life to those who lack them if he wishes to be helped in turn; whence, eleemosynary institutions. In the above theory ownership is identified with the personal principle, but the conceptions of contract and of the right to life and work, place an intrinsic limit on this same ownership, which is the logical premise of socialism. This premise is that every man has an inherent right to a part of the external world as his property; that there is a natural right of property which the State should recognize and protect. It is only necessary to be a man to have this right as sacred and inviolable as freedom or personality. It is the State's duty to put each one in possession of the property to which his need and capacity give him a right. To the doctrine of Fichte, and to the principle now stated, Laveleye agrees in his book, "De la Proprieté et ses Formes Primitives." We must observe that Fichte and Laveleye confuse two very diverse conceptions, the conception of guaranty that the State should give to the development of the equal capacity of all towards ownership, and that of the duty imposed upon the State of procuring property for every individual. We cannot doubt that every man, as such, has an essential right to exercise his activity over objects within his sphere by the use of means necessary for the attainment of his purposes. The State should give each man conditions suitable to carry out that right or tendency towards acquisition eliminating possible obstacles, and, in fact, aiding him. But since an individual has initiative power he should act himself, carrying out the series of particular acts by which the things may become his. His inherent right or theoretical power of property should take the form of an acquired right or practical power. The first is an abstract power without the second, referring more to the essence than the individuality of man. It is the simple right that all have to property. The second is a concrete and individual power, and is the true property right which looks to acquisition. The acquisition of property in the concrete is for the individual and not for the State, which is called upon to recognize, guarantee, and to protect the activity of the citizens, but not to substitute its actions for theirs. The State must hold safe the principle of formal or juristic equality, but since it owes the greatest respect to human liberty, which develops with the indefinite quantity of various original and acquired powers, it cannot decree material equality.

§ 233. *Property a Right of Man in the Abstract.* The individual is a part of society and should be limited in his control of material objects. Individual rights presuppose always an ethical whole, in which there are conditions of development, protection, and control. The individual derives the stability of will over concrete objects from the ethical whole, that is, from the laws governing the disposition of property.

Trendelenburg notes that the right to property belongs
to man in the abstract, who confirms and limits it.
The doctrine of Kant about the two kinds of possession
began to affirm speculatively the necessity of a criticism
of the other doctrines, which based property upon the
isolated act of the individual.   Vico has clearly seen that
control is the very law of the existence of private property, as Cocchia shows in his book, "I Limiti della Proprietà."   He distinguished the occasion of private ownership, that is, the motive of its historical appearance,
from its cause or rational basis.   Private property, like
freedom, has its base in human nature itself.   In ownership there are, according to the Neapolitan philosopher,
the "cupiditas" or interweaving of egoistical senses, and
the "vis veri," the "ratio," the ethical law.   Ownership
is "prudens utilitatum destinatio, hoc est destinatio facta
ratione non cupiditate suadente, gignit dominium."   In
other words, in regulating ownership we must be guided
not only by what is useful for the individual, but by the
community's needs as well, following the dictates of
civil prudence.   Vico said that there is a civil control,
which is exercised over the possessions of the citizens,
superior to every private right.   This control is the
limiting social reason, and not eminent domain, which
makes the State the owner of all property.   Romagnosi
speaks of a natural ownership, distinguishing it from
one purely civil, but using the words in an entirely
different sense.   Natural ownership is synonymous with
an absolutely egoistical use and would be possible in
a state of nature, while civil ownership is had in a
society, and necessitates the tempering of an individual's
right with necessity and social utility.   In a state of
nature powers are always controlled, and the legislator
should observe that law, based on real relations.   If
the legislator place a limitation on private rights he

does not order a sacrifice, because such limitation is necessary to the attainment of security and other benefits which the individual obtains from society. The chief requirement of positive law is that it equalizes between individuals their power to be useful to themselves through equality and security of common freedom. The tempering of their egoistic freedom harmonizes; does not weaken, but reënforces; does not take away the powers of private use, but rather makes it greater and surer. Whoever obeys the laws of the community obeys necessity and himself; whence it follows that this control does not lessen individual ownership, and that natural control is not changed, but subdued. Rosmini expresses the same theory when he distinguishes between property and the right of property. Considering only the relations between persons and things, property can be conceived of in an unlimited way, but looking upon property as a right, it should be subordinate to practical justice; and so a man can be forced to give up something of little or no use to himself, which is harmful to others, or an obstacle to their welfare.

§234. *Code Definitions of Property Considered.* The definition of property given by the French and Italian Codes recognizes in so many words the conception of control and limitation. Property, according to these codes, is the right to enjoy and use things in the most absolute way as long as you do not make a use of them forbidden by the laws or ordinances. Rosmini finds the limitation in the last part of the definition. What is the object of laws and ordinances, he says, if they do not forbid individuals making use of their property in a way injurious to others or the Commonwealth? Do they not thus show that they have no right to use their property so? The legislatures in fact do

show that there is a feeling that property, as a right, has
limitations, even if they do not state this categorically.
Perhaps it would have been better if the conception of
limitation had been expressed in the definition so that
the idea of absolute enjoyment and disposition could
not be reconciled with the prohibition of certain uses,
and if it had not been necessary to emphasize the notion
of property as a general power given over inanimate
objects; but we must remember that the French legislature had in view the making of a solemn proclamation
of the individual rights of property to supplant the then
doctrines, — that such rights lay in positive law.
Examples of limitations are condemnations for public
use, legal servitudes, and forced coöperation. By condemnation the owner is forced to give his property to
society but receives reimbursement. Without condemnation for public use, observes Rossi, there would
not be any improvements, — streets, canals, harbors,
or monuments. There would also be no means of
gaining profit in many countries from the generous
treasures of nature or of getting the precious metals to the
industrial and commercial world. Condemnation often
increases the value of property, as in the case of the
construction of a railroad. If the railroad were not
built the land and houses near the appropriated land
would suffer, not getting the value which they acquire
from the railroad. Servitudes established by law look
to a double end, both to public and private benefit.
Military service is of the first kind; forced concession
of water to lands that can profit by it, ways of necessity, aqueducts, and party-walls are servitudes of
the second class. Obligatory coöperation is certainly
an important limitation of property, in which the
subordination of private property to public use is
allowed and enforced. By condemnation the private

property is ceded to the State, which puts it to a use that the citizen could not; by servitudes the State forces the owner to let it make use of his property.

§ 235. *Necessary Restrictions on Property.* The theory of the necessary restrictions on property, about which Lomonaco has recently written in a monograph, "I Temperamenti della Proprietà Prediale," is a contradiction given by the legislature to optimism and settled harmony of the economic school. The simple and normal compatibility of private interest and public use, presupposed by Adam Smith, Malthus, Ricardo, Say, and Rossi, is transformed by the work of Bastiat into an irresistible harmony. An individual, Bastiat says, finds in selfish interests the stimuli to action, but at the same time is subject to a providential law forcing him to work for the good of all, while he works freely for himself. There is no doubt that a man can err and violate the law, but it is none the less true that sorrow follows error, pain follows vice, and punishment follows wrong. From this it is plain that discord is accidental and transitory and harmony essential and permanent. The free course of nature is not impeded; it gives human power free scope for expansion, and thus we have the higher orders. The State intervenes when the use of force is legitimate, that is, if a right is trampled under foot, but for the most part it recognizes the fullest freedom. But this immutable and universal harmony, imagined by Bastiat, does not exist in the physical world, because the cosmic system is always altered and modified by perturbing forces, which affect the flora, fauna, seas, and continents. Harmony, in Bastiat's mind, is the social order or human welfare that develops into acts without the intervention of the State, which need not take part, and without true individual freedom, on which he

so much insists, for it cannot in any way hinder the
development of the harmony. Certainly there is no freedom here in its real sense since he pays no attention
to the effect of stubbornness, obstinacy, and wronghead-
edness in ethical relations (for example, in economics).
And at the same time he asserts that the certain consequences of error, vice, and wrong are sorrow, pain, and
punishment. That is contradicted by experience which
teaches that an individual following his interest, even
if he does not know or cognize it, is led spontaneously
to the point of coincidence of his good and the general
welfare. To Cairns, and before him to Minghetti, we
owe a just and clear criticism of the optimism of Bastiat.

§ 236. *Equality of Inherent Rights Gives no Right to
Equal Property.* Man has an inherent right to use
his activity over external things for the attainment
of his objects. But a belief in this conception does
not indicate a title to property common to all men
whose inherent rights are equal. A particular fact
intervenes, which takes away the abstract similarity
and gives birth to a juristic power over the things;
acquired property makes its appearance. Now this
concrete fact is acquisition, in which we can distinguish four grades or four successive rights according
to the analysis of Rosmini. There comes first, as cause
and origin of all other rights, a natural right, which is
the right to legitimate action which does not violate
another's property. This right when exercised produces the same action that, fulfilled, becomes something
adherent to us, a part of us and our right as long as it
lasts. If the action be such that it can bind an external
object to ourselves while we enjoy the right of action,
we enjoy as well the right of joining to us an external
thing and of making it our own. The action completed,
we have joined something to ourselves and have ampli-

fied our power to work, and the right of all these actions is ours. The methods of acquisition are partly original and partly derivative; the first do not demand the agreement of the will of others, the second presuppose it. The original rights are appropriation, accession, confusion, and prescription; the derivatives are agreement and inheritance.

§ 237. *Appropriation.* Appropriation is the taking possession of a vacant external object with the intention, recognizable by others, of having its exclusive use. There are three requisites, — a thing which can be possessed, the taking of possession, and the sign of such taking recognizable by others. The thing must be subject to appropriation, must be external, otherwise it is not an object of acquired property, to which appropriation refers, but is the subject of natural property. It must be susceptible to the physical acts necessary for the physico-moral bond to realize the idea of property or of the union of the thing and the person. It must be free, because appropriation cannot be subversive of the rights of others. The taking of possession is composed of the moral act or will to have and to keep the object, and the physical or the subjection of it to the power of the person. If the first is lacking there is simple detention; if the latter is lacking there is a mere intent. The token shows to men that the object is part of our estate. We cannot say that the right to property is formed when other men do not know what is taken and what not. We must always distinguish the token from the physical link; the former only presupposes the existence of the latter, as a token always presupposes the thing itself. There are four means of appropriation, — simple occupancy, hunting, fishing, and finding, — which in their turn comprehend three conditions, — that of an object unacquired, of a "res pro derelicto," and of things lost, found, and not reclaimed within the time established by the statutes, after suitable means of publication have been used. Appropriation is bounded by limits both of juristic and physical rules. The limits of the juristic order are fixed by quality and quantity. Qualitatively, of course, appropriation cannot extend to those things which, being immense and inexhaustible, are in negative union only with mankind, although a relative small portion of them can be occupied. It is limited quantitatively because we cannot exercise our activity on whatever free things we believe suitable to the attainment of our ends to the point where our acquisition becomes destructive or harmful to another personality. The limits depending upon the physical order are such that man can occupy all those things which he can reduce to his power in such a manner that others may know of his right to them.

§ 238. *Accession.* Accession is a special method of acquisition and denotes the act by which an object losing its individuality is united and incorporated in our property without being transformed or confused with it. With this understood, the acquisition of the property in fruits and in the young of animals can be seen not to be an example of accession, since their existence is begun with separation, which is opposed to accession, which consists of union and incorporation. In this case, as in others similar to it, there is the exercise of the right of property, and the increase is governed by the "jure domini." Neither does specification, confusion, and mixture enter into the sphere of accession because in that case there are not objects which transform and unite. On this point the Austrian and Italian Codes have followed a rational conception departing from Roman law and the French Code in their recognition of accession as a simple development of property, and in their

extension of its bounds to comprehend the acquisition
of nature's increase, specification, confusion, and mixture. Accession is caused either by nature or by the
act of man. There are examples of accession by nature
in alluvium, in "avulsium," in "alveus relictus," in the
"insula in flumine nata;" of accession by the act of man
in "inædeficatio," "plantatio" and "satio," "scriptura,"
"pictura" and all other forms of "adjunctio." A kind of
mixed accession is also sometimes spoken of, which is
brought about by nature and art together. This is proved
by the example of agriculture. But we must take care
that in artificial accession we do not lose sight of the
element or forces of nature, as we need the latter in many
kinds of productions. From this it follows that the
examples of mixed accession, that is, "satio" and "plantatio," belong to artificial accession or that derived from
the act of man.

§ 239. *Alteration.* Invention and prescription are
the other two original methods. Alteration is an act
by which a thing is transformed in such a manner
as to make it "nova species." To some it seems
existence depends upon form, and the "nova species"
therefore should be attributed to him who has produced it, while to others it seems that the material
was more necessary and the "nova species" should
belong to its owner. The jurisconsults' "eriscundi" distinguish two cases; if the new species could be reduced
to its primitive form it should belong to the owner of
the material; if the new thing could not be reduced it
must belong to him who made it, upon payment by
the owner of the price of the material. Modern legislation, believing in the reality of work and the principles
of equity, enacts that if a person has taken material
that does not belong to him to form something new
whether the material can or cannot be returned to its

original form, the owner of the material has the right to the thing formed from it reimbursing the laborer for his work. When, however, the work has been such as to greatly increase the value of the material taken, the labor expended is considered as of more value, and the worker has the right to retain the thing upon which he has worked, paying to the owner of the material the price thereof.

§ 240. *Prescription.* Prescription is not an infamous power created by positive law to decrease litigation, but is an institution conforming to reason, because in property there should be action of the person, and failure to act for a long time entails the extinction of the public recognition which binds the person and thing. Now recognition and connection diminish for the old owner as they develop, strengthen, and increase for the possessor. The conception of necessity of the will of the person therefore, active or visible in some manner in the object is the true foundation of prescription. Prescription is the method of acquisition "sui generis," yet not absolutely independent, because it serves to supplement a bad title or the lack of title on the part of the possessor.

§ 241. *Derivative Methods of Acquiring Property; Agreement and Inheritance.* The derivative methods are agreement and inheritance; contract is the accord of two or more wills over a juridical object of economic value. In agreement the essential by which property changes hands is consent, which is the meeting of the minds of the parties. The Roman law demanded "traditio" for such a change, but modern law requires fewer physical conditions, as expressed by the phrase, "consensus parit proprietaten." The principle is just because the real cause of the transfer does not lie in the material act of delivery, which is the token, but in the "consensus in idem placitum." In the interest of

the third parties, however, to whom it is of great importance to know changes of title, it has been established that title passes by writing. Inheritance is administrative and testamentary; in respect to extent total in administration, and partial in testamentary descent.

§ 242. *Difference between the Philosophy and the Law of Property.* In the "modus acquirendi" we find immediately the "titulus" of the positive law, and mediately that of the rational law. In the eyes of the lawyer legality of title lies only in contract, will, prescription, and occupancy; that is, the methods of acquisition which are right recognized by law as the source of the right. The philosopher wishes to search out the inherent right, considering the facts and recognizing the title on them, and then the "modus acquirendi" in the method. The "modus acquirendi" is the term between the inherent and acquired right. A lawyer must prove the act which is the acquired right with its approximate cause which is the method of acquisition; the philosopher wishes to go further and to find the ultimate cause that is part of the person and is natural rights.

CHAPTER V

THE HISTORY OF PROPERTY AND OF METHODS OF ITS ACQUISITION

THE ACQUISITIVE ACTIVITY OF ANIMALS AND MAN. — THE
HISTORY OF PROPERTY AND THE HISTORY OF PERSONALITY. —
COLLECTIVE PROPERTY. — THE FAMILY COMMUNITY. — CHRIS-
TIANITY AND THE WORTH OF THE INDIVIDUAL. — FEUDALISM.
— THE REFORMATION AND NATURAL LAW. — COMPLETE INDI-
VIDUALIZATION, AND THE CONTROL OF PRIVATE PROPERTY.
— THE METHODS OF PRIMITIVE ACQUISITION. — THE DIVISION
OF PROPERTY. — PRESCRIPTION, EQUITY, AND CIVIL PROCEDURE.

§ 243. *Tendency to Acquisition an Instinct.* Aristotle speaks of the natural κτῆσις that is, of the spontaneous activity, which looks to the procuring of nourishment, common alike to animals and man, and which seeks
the things necessary and useful to the existence of the
individual and the social body. An abundance of such
things, according to the Stagirite, constitutes wealth, and
therefore his "Ctetics" are part of his "Economics,"
which are based on the science of life. The human activity, which looks to the procuring of food, is a development
of the same property in animals but it is determined differently by the complexes of his qualities, which distinguish the human species from all others. There is no doubt
of such a development if mind itself presupposes, comprehends, and is superior to nature; if thought lies
apart from sensibility and reason, contains and raises
sense as well as thought, making the development and
grasp of mind more perfect. The analogy between phy-

siology and economics, so much in vogue to-day, is true
if we understand it in its wide sense, because economics,
the science of things destined to the satisfaction of
necessities, contain the theory of social vegetation.
Carried to an extreme it leads to a grave error, since economics on the one hand enter into social statics (very
near the animal kingdom) and, on the other, the same
statics receive an impulse from dynamics which depend
upon the elements of the highest forces of human nature
and include historical development. The economic activity of man cannot be separated from thought and free
will since no entity can act independently of its nature.
The consequence is that economic laws are not absolutely
the equal of philosophical laws because they do not depend, as the latter, upon thought and will.

§ 244. *Property an Attribute of Man.* In the economic functions of animals there are two coördinate
actions, the moving or transforming of the material,
and the action or movement of the special organs which
perform the above operation and tend to effect the purpose. This coördination gives evidence of the presence
of an ultimate end and is the clearest proof of the
necessity of teleology, not abstract and transcendental
but concrete and objective. The difference between an
organism and a mechanism lies properly in this: that in
the organism the end is ever present, and is brought
about by activity; in the mechanism it is extrinsic. In
this coördination of two actions, however, the perfecting
influences of a well-developed mental energy are lacking
in animals, as well as the constant volitive variations
of methods; so that an animal is not an efficient worker
nor can he increase the complexity or specialization of
his labor by adapting himself always to more convenient
and progressive methods. An animal ceases to advance
at some stage of economic life because its organism

(especially in relation to psychic activity) does not allow
it to pass the bounds within which its acquisitive functions are confined by nature. In animals such functions
are always limited to the sphere of instinct and the
mechanical associations of desire and satisfaction, and
lead to the temporary possession of the object; in man
mind, which desires everything, and the principle of its
autonomy control such functions, and they make for
ownership and property. Only mind can dominate
nature and comprehend it in theory and practice. This
is an attribute of man alone. No one has yet dared to
say that individuality furnished with sensibility and
spontaneous motion, that is, sensibility in motion, can
be the equal of the individuality capable of enunciating
the duo-syllabic ego, which is the sign of the separation
of man and brute. An animal can join itself to an
object by a physical bond and can grieve for it if he
is deprived of it, but he is not able to create the moral
bond, which distinguishes property from possession.

§ 245. *The Right of Property Subject to Evolution.*
The history of property is in the last analysis the history of human nature, because property is freedom
applied to things, as freedom is nothing but ownership
of self. Wheresoever one is found there is the other;
and where ownership is violated, there personality is
violated and vice versa. In all manifestations of human
activity progress (as in the case of the universal evolution of entities) is the divergence from the simple to the
complex, from formless homogeneity to varied heterogeneity, accompanied by the greatest similarity and
profoundest correlations of parts and by a constantly
increasing perfection of attributes. The ancient philosophers expressed this conception by saying that from
the one and from the whole, before the existence
of any sub-divisions of the great unit, there came a

division and separation of the parts, which tend to develop into one distinct and concrete unit or whole developed to its fullness, an harmonic synthesis very different from the original and embryonic synthesis. At first the human community was one in which the individual was only a part and instrument, then he developed concrete individuality, trying to free himself from society, and tends to reach a rational harmony between his particular determination and the social.

§ 246. *Origin and Development of Property.* Property goes through the same phases; being at first collective, it becomes individual and egoistic, and finally tends to take its place in society and the State. In the primitive and infantile development of law it is not possible to distinguish a "jus personarum" from a "jus rerum" because the childlike mind, confusing and not distinguishing, established rules substantially identical for both. The distinction began in the days of Rome, in which a notable development of juristical thought took place. Maine, in "Ancient Law," criticizes the doctrine which recognizes individual occupancy as the method by which the "res nullius" of the primitive world became private property in the historical world. This criticism is well founded. He gives two reasons for not believing in the doctrine which was then generally acknowledged. In the first place, individual appropriation presupposes the very fact of property and the extension of it to a great number of useful objects. For it is clear that, when possession is taken of a "res nullius" (a thing which has no owner), society allows the possessor to become its owner because it presumes that everything useful should be in the exclusive possession of somebody and should be of use to its possessor, who has the right of property over it. In the second place, individual appropriation is a fact essentially dependent on the will and action of an individual. And it is shown that primitive law is based on the community and not on the individual. This is proved by the fact that at first we find collective property acquired by appropriation in mass and not individual property. The collective property of our remote ancestors is not the effect of a sense of justice or an instinctive affirmation of the natural rights of man and the conception of equality, as Laveleye pretends in his work "De la Propriété et ses Formes Primitive."[1] It is the consequence of two necessities (Belot notes this, too, in dealing with the same subject), one a natural development, the other a product of the social state. In primitive times the greatest part of the earth's surface was neither cultivated nor cultivatable by the then imperfect methods of farming. The number of inhabitants, therefore, in a given district, could not be great. The division of such land which had no value was useless; and, furthermore, to cultivate it in separate lots was impossible. The only purpose to which it could be put was that of a common pasture. The first divisions were made later by the agrarian communities. These were the offspring of economic thought existing as they did at great cost and labor in the cultivation of arid lands. The land was assigned every year by lot, because of the necessity (when the science of fertilization was unknown) of letting the part which had been cultivated over lie fallow for several years, so the annual distribution of shares by lot was not unjust because all the land was of the same value. The state of society demanded the adoption of such a régime at that time for common defense, because they were forced to form groups to preserve themselves from destruction. The history of the colony of Nantucket (a sandy island of

[1] Cf. § 232 ante.

North America inhabited since 1671 by members of a small dissenting church persecuted by the Puritans of Massachusetts), where the system of the agrarian communities has been the rule, shows the physical and economic situation which produced such a régime. Their history teaches us that the cause of collective property is not the sentiment of justice, but the impossibility of permanent allotment of lands of little value which cannot yield consecutive harvests in any other way that necessitates such a régime.

§ 247. *Property in Greece.* It can no longer be doubted that in India, before the system of caste, property was collective. God gave the land to men for their enjoyment simply. They had no existence apart from the life of the tribe or family. When caste was introduced, the Brahmans considered that God had given the land, which they allowed others to use. Among the Hebrews the earth was the Lord's and men were strangers on it, to whom He gave it as to tenants. Moses allotted the land in perpetuity to certain groups. Alienation could only be temporary. The debts of the Israelites were remitted every seven years, and every forty years property gone out of the tribe or family must gratuitously be returned to its ancient division. According to Heinnecius in "Elementa Juris Naturæ et Gentium," Puchta in "Cursus des Institutionen," Mommsen in his "Römische Geschichte," and even according to Laveleye in the book we have cited,[1] and Viollet in his study of primitive property, the ancient people of Greece and Italy also passed through the stage of communism. To sustain the opinion of Mommsen we can cite among the Germans Niebhur, Arnold, and Bachofen, and in Italy Pantaleoni and Burtagnolli. Lange, in his "Handbuch der Römischen Altertümer,"

[1] *Cf.* "De la Propriété et ses Formes Primitive," cit. §§ 232 and 246 *ante*.

and Fustel de Coulanges, in his "La Cité Antique," are
to the contrary.

§ 248. *State Ownership of Land in Greece.* In Greece
land was considered the property of the State, the
citizens having an interest subordinate to the general
right; and from this conception came the frequent divisions of land and the constant legal interference with
property. Laveleye shows that Sparta at the time
when she appeared in history had already come out
of the régime of primitive communism and had probably
reached that of collective control of the "gens." The
constitutional element of society was the γένος, a kind
of group of families reunited by the tradition of a common origin, together with an inalienable estate. Sparta
possessed a vast domain including forests and mountains,
whose rent paid for the public banquets. Plutarch,
in his life of Lycurgus, says that at the birth of every
child the elders of the tribe assigned him one of the
nine hundred lots belonging to the city, representing the
common land which was the family estate. The sale
of land was forbidden; its bequest prohibited. Custom permitted a citizen to use the horses, dogs, and
utensils of any man who did not wish to use them. In
Athens Solon placed property under heavy limitations,
probably the vestiges of primitive communism. He
enacted that the sale of a property entailed the loss
of citizenship. He imposed a progressive tax. The
State treasury gave a dowry to poor girls and furnished
grain to the needy and paid the expenses of the senators.

§ 249. *Property in Rome.* In Rome the earliest private property was personal and not real, probably consisting of slaves and cattle. The ancient "mancipatio,"
the general form of sale, applied primarily to things
which the vendee could take in his hands. Land was
common, called "ager publicus." It became greatly

increased by successive conquests. The farmstead of remoter days ("heredium") was little more than the enclosure of the Germans, containing about an acre. With the Romans as with the Greeks, the ass and the ox were mediums of exchange and units of value. Now it is not possible to admit that while the land was individual property cattle were a means of exchange, because the wherewithal to feed them could not be found. If the ox and the ass were receivable in payment, the greater part of the land must have been common pasturage. There was, however, in Italy and Greece, a tradition of a Golden Age in which private property was not thought of. As it agrees with the economic history of humanity, this tradition should not be considered mere poetic fiction. Diodorus Siculus narrates that the Greeks of the Liparus lived with common property in the land. Aristotle wrote that there remained some trace of ancient communism of land in Tarentum even in his day. Porphyry and Jamblichus (in writing the life of Pythagoras), say that in Magna Græcia there were two thousand people who established a political state under the Pythagorian régime of the community of wealth. Trusting to the statement of Porphyry, it seems possible to conclude that some of the Italian cities of the Middle Ages arose in like manner. Is it not possible that with the name and exploits of Pythagoras there were mixed some historical traditions of the community of wealth in Magna Græcia? Another argument can be based on the many institutions of public banquets scattered throughout Italy and Greece, and on the constant allusions of ancient writers to an ancient division of land and on the necessity of the consent of the whole social body for the sale of land to a foreigner, a consent necessary in Turin and Greece. As to Rome this necessity took the general form of the

"cessio in jure,"—full testimony of the absolute ownership of the State.   Lastly the primitive prohibition on
the alienation of land (certainly introduced from Greek
law, and probably from Italian custom), the absence of
testamentary power at the time of which we speak, and
later the exclusion of women from the inheritance
(because upon marrying they would have transferred
part of their property to another family) constitute
new evidence to confirm the opinions of Mommsen
and the others.

   § 250. *Common Ownership of Land Exists in Many
Countries*.   In some provinces of India, about the fourth
century before Christ, the land was cultivated in common with a division of the fruits at harvest.   To-day the
Indian villages still possess as undivided property in the
forests and uncultivated land; the arable land is no
longer common.   In China there were, in primitive times,
communities which assigned a convenient part of the
land, but the remainder was entrusted to those who
could cultivate it.   But about two and a half centuries
before Christ, the families of the cultivators divided
the arable land among themselves according to the number of noses; a tenth part was cultivated for the profit
of the State.   To-day the emperor is the principal landowner of the Empire.   Diodorus speaks of an agrarian
community living on the coast of Arabia who rewarded
their members according to the merits of each, assigning
to the better farmer the greater part of the harvest.
Among the Germans there was the "mark," or common
territory of the clan, of which a small extent was the
object of private occupancy during the year.   But the
hereditary property included only the house and its
enclosure.   Analogous to the "mark" is the "bland-el-
djemaa" of the Arabs.   The Gauls had separate farms
and individual estates, assigned each year, however, by

the magistrates among the clans or family living together. In Egypt, in the time of Pharaoh, the land belonged to the sovereign. The Mussulman laws have preserved the same principle. Among the aborigines of America the same system of collective property prevailed.

§ 251. *Examples Still Extant of Primitive Property among Uncivilized People.* There are still some examples of primitive property among uncivilized people which serve to make us better understand it, because one of the qualities of our mind is, as Vico says, that men cannot obtain a full idea of distant and but slightly known things, yet present and known examples will make the object clearer. In Russia the land does not belong to the crown or to the nobles, but is the undivided property of the community or "mir." The community is the owner of the soil and the individuals have only the temporary use of it. There is no private ownerhsip of land except the ground upon which the house is built and the garden annexed to it. These are hereditary. They divide the land among themselves, coming together in an assembly for the purpose. In Java the owner of the soil is God, and consequently his representative upon earth, or the sovereign, the "dessa" or community, has the use of the soil and distributes it yearly among its members. Private and hereditary property in Java extends to the house and enclosure, as among the Romans, Germans, and Russians. In the Island of Pelew the individual is the owner of his personalty, of his house and boat; the king is the owner of the land and gives its use to his subjects. In the Caroline Islands there is a régime of relative community. Land in central Africa belongs to the community or the head who represents it. Among the native Americans, the land intended for hunting and fishing belongs to the tribe. In Peru property is governed by a system of patriarchical and authoritative communism. In Mexico there was a feudal régime founded on the ultimate ownership of the emperor. Cattle are more or less common property among the nomadic pastoral Mongols. And habits of communism are extensive and deep-rooted among the Tartar tribes in Mongolian Asia. The system of communism is still in full force among the aboriginal tribes of India. In certain provinces of Spain, Altmarck, in all ancient Scandinavia, Denmark, and Jutland, among the ancient Bretons and Afghans, in Wallachia and several other regions we find village communities.

§ 252. *Examples from Ancient Europe.* In primitive Switzerland the "allmenden" or communal property included the forest, grazing, and cultivated land. To have a right to a share in its enjoyment, it was necessary above everything else to be a resident of the commune, to have the right of political citizenship, and also to be descended from a family which had enjoyed such rights from time immemorial, or at least for a century. The "allmende" was found before the "mark" in southern Germany, and consisted of the common property in woods, meadows, and cultivated lands, the usufruct of which went to the individuals of the family. In Amsterdam the common land of the clan or "mark" was observed. Cognate institutions are the "almaenning" of Sweden, the "aldmindiger" of Norway, and the "township" of Scotland, which recognized the common property in the soil, its distribution in certain portions, and private property in the house and enclosure. The communal estates of Belgium and France reproduce in varied forms and fragmentary ways the types of collective property in the soil. These consist of land occupied by an association of citizens free from private appropriation and dedicated to the general needs of the association or the particular needs of the associates. The communal property, writes Venezian in his book "Reliquie della Proprietà Collettiva in Italia," goes back to the very first state of the group of the family or tribe which instituted agriculture in place of pasturing. Pastoral communities, with the meadows given over to alternate enjoyment under certain periodical distributions of land, with the forests and the communal lands, indicated by such names, over which the private citizens had special rights, give evidence of the survival of archaic property. This can be seen to-day in parts of Portugal and in not a few places in Spain and Italy, as shown by latter-day studies. Among the Italians there are still in the "marches" institutions very similar to the collective property of Switzerland, that is, the "allmende." These are called "communanze," "universita," "consorzi di famiglia," belonging to the "marches" and existing even before the Roman Age as Valenti proved in "La Proprietà Collettiva nell' Appennino Marchigiano." In Fruilia and the ancient Duchy of Modena we can still find extensive traces of archaic property in communal goods. And in general throughout the peninsula there are traces of ancient servitudes of fishing, selling sod, sowing, and taking firewood from the property of the community and the citizens. According to some there are traces as well of "usi civici" of the Southern provinces. In regard to these "usi civici" in several of the provinces of Italy, we should note that they are exercisible not only over property of the nature of crown lands but also over all private property called allodial or "burgensatische." The property belonging to the crown was of various kinds; in fact in mediæval Italy imperial crown lands were granted as feuds which became either feudal domains or ecclesiastical or communal (so-called public) property. All these different domains were subject to the "usi civici," which constituted an inalienable and indefeasible right if they were granted by the sovereign power; whence it could be said "nec per regem tolli possunt." Much erudite inquiry has been spent upon the historical formation of these domains in which an estate in the fullness of private control, by the influence of Roman law, was subjected "pro bono publico" to a great number of rights designed to provide the citizens with the "necessaria vitæ subsidia." The Neapolitan jurists were of the unanimous opinion that these domains were "jure naturæ," subject to the civic uses "ne cives vitam inertem ducerent et ne fama perirent." It seems clear that Neapolitan estates of this kind were created by the abandonment of private property at the time of the fall of the Roman Empire; so they can be considered more as a return to the ancient commune than a relic of Rome.

§ 253. *Polynesia Shows an Exception to the Rule.* In Melanesia and Polynesia we find individual property in land though they are hardly out of the state of tribal community. In Australia, New Caledonia, at Viti and Tahiti, there is not a sufficient development of civilized conditions to justify the appearance of private property, since the social state is still in its infancy. Nevertheless this kind of property has arisen, making a notable exception to the rule of the primitive world. The rule of common ownership is applicable to land and not to personalty or the house and enclosure in which the individual character of the person is first shown. But it cannot be applied to land when there is no game in the place occupied by the tribe, which necessitates pursuit over great distances, but where reptiles, the lava of insects, fish, and roots are in abundance. In this case there is no need of a large expanse of common territory because there is no hunting, but it is more expedient to keep the individual in his part of the land without freeing it from the eminent domain of the tribe, exercised by the head, as in the countries before mentioned. The inapplicability of the rule cannot be said to be absolute on account of the eminent domain. As long as man lives by the chase, by fishing and gathering wild fruit, he considers the object taken or produced by his own hands as his own and has no thought of the appropriation of the soil. Property in land limited to the space covered by the flock of the tribe makes its first appearance in the pastoral régime. The idea of individual property in the soil does not appear even in the agricultural régime; the property is still in the tribe; the arable lands, meadows, and forests are cultivated in common. Later the cultivated land is divided into parts by lot among the families who give individuals the temporary use of it, but the whole preserving its character of collective property of the tribe, to which it returns from time to time to be redivided. The parts, as time goes on, remain in the hands of different patriarchal groups who occupy the same land again and again. Thus the system of common possession and periodic division falls into disuse; the land becomes the hereditary and inalienable estate of the family. When repeated fertilization and advance in agriculture has made a richer soil, it can be easily understood that land is left fallow for a very short time. The assignments are at first made by each group for three years, in which the cultivator works on the land, improves it, and leaves the mark of his activity on it, but it becomes always more difficult to separate the various groups from their territory, and periodic distribution begins to be made every six, nine, or ten years. Less and less frequent become the new divisions and greater the injustice of taking land which has increased in value through the application of labor and capital from those who labored on it. In this we see the economic motive for the end of the periodic division of land. In all this advance the law of evolution is active, because there is an increasing division or specification, all tending from the unformed homogeneity of the tribe to the marked heterogeneity of the family. The heads of the latter cannot dispose by will of the hereditary portion, for that always belongs to the family, but they are owners of their saving and of what they made by the labor of their hands. Women are excluded from ownership of land because it otherwise through marriage would constantly be transferred from one family to another. They can have dowry from the private property. In some aristocratic forms of the family community there are family trusts; in others the control is given to the eldest. In them the possessor and the "primogenitus" are regarded as having the use of the inalienable and indivisible property of the family.

§ 254. *Ancient Family Communities.* The family communities date back to the Indians and Semites. The associated family in India was a large corporation of relatives maintained to an indefinite number of generations having as its object the communal methods of support, the cultivation of land, and the preservation of the cult. It had for its chief the "primogenitus" of the eldest branch, or if he was not of sufficient ability, some elected relative. The chief was not the "paterfamilias" or "dominus," but simply the administrative head. Cæsar in speaking of the Germans said that none owned land, but the head or magistrate distributed it every year among the families, "cognationes hominum, qui una coierunt." Among the Germans there was a "condominium in solidum" in the family growing out of the active and passive unity of relations (as is shown in the obligation of "faida" or "vendetta," and in that of paying tax or "wehrgeld" due to all the relatives of the victim). This unity is still clearer shown with the "mundium" and the hereditary possession on which the maxim is founded: the dead enfeoff the living. All the relatives were owners, and therefore there was some community of possession. When the "munduald" died, those who had been under his power either became heads of the house or remained subjects of the new "munduald," to whom there was an instantaneous transmission of the goods under the "mundium." The members of such a community elected a chief who governed the family with the advice of its members and exercised an executive power. By the side of the "mayor" or master there was a "mayorissa," also elected, who took care of the domestic economy. The Irish "sept," a kind of corporation of relatives of an industrial and agricultural nature, whose existence depended on the occupancy of the land, was very like the associate family of India. No component of the "sept" could alienate his hereditary part except in urgent necessity and with the consent of all, but he could dispose of the capital gained by labor. This is the rule in the Indian and Russian communities. The absolute control of the tenant in "rundale" in Ireland gave emphasis to the "mark," because a section of country was occupied by family groups, the arable land was divided and changed possession by temporary assignment, and the pasture was common. A like mode of tenure is observable among the Highlanders in Scotland. In Ireland the hereditary farm was governed by the rules of "gavelkind," by which upon the death of the owner of a farm, which was part of the "sept," the head made a new division of all the lands of the corporation, adding to the shares of the different families the inheritable property of the descendant. Such institutions tended to keep relative equality among the associate owners as long as periodical division was kept up. In Slavonia, Croatia, Servia, the Coastal States, Bosnia, Bulgaria, Dalmatia, and Herzegovina, we can still find that form of community called by the Germans "hauskomunion," and by the Slavs "zadruga" or "druzina." The chief of Slavs, the "gospodar" or "starchina," chosen by the members of the community, has the executive power, although the legislative power belongs to the community itself; he is the guardian of minors, and represents the family in the courts and before foreigners. He is assisted by a woman, also elected, whose duty is the direction of household affairs. The family is a civil person; its estate is indivisible. There is, therefore, no inheritance of real estate, yet personalty is inheritable because each of the members of the family is allowed to get together his own herd. Sons have a right to a part of the products of the land, not through heredity, but because of a personal right or of participation in the work upon the common property. The right to dispose of land by sale or will is not allowed as long as any member of the family is alive. A daughter can receive her dowry but has no right to claim part of the real estate. Even in Italy there are traces of this kind of tenure which have combined (as Jacini says) with the system of leasing for a share of the crop. The associations of this kind in northern Italy, especially in Lombardy, are composed of four or five families living together in a house situated on a large estate. They recognize the authority of a "reggitore" and "massara." The "reggitore" sells, buys, and invests the savings and directs the work with the advice of the associates; the domestic cares are given over to the "massara." And here we should mention the two institutions of the "homestead" and "höferecht." The first, begun in

Texas in 1839 and then extended to most of the States in the Union, is a law that forbids creditors from sequestering the farmstead of the family, on which the family has actually established its home, for it is the home which the law protects. It is necessary that there be an inhabited house on the land granted. The other institution of "höferecht" (a German and Austrian institution) takes from the hereditary assets a part of the land called the family inheritance, which pass in their entirety to a privileged heir. Both institutions consequently propose to preserve a part of the domestic property, declared such by the head of the family and recognized as such by the law and by outsiders, and to insure the permanence of the family.

§ 255. *Disbelief in the Theory of the Priority of Collective Property.* Belot wishes to show (especially against Laveleye) that private ownership of land preceded the collective. He thinks that property has not descended from the tribe to the family and from the family to the individual, but that the family is a union of individuals and the tribe a union of families. Collective property is only the extension of individual property to a family more or less large. The father of the family, as the head or absolute king, was originally the owner of the house and enclosure. This property was necessary to the defense of the family and the preservation of the domestic religion. The "gens" and the village (a growth of the family) possessed a common property presupposing the original individual property of the ancestor. We can see in the Island of Nantucket that twenty-seven colonists began to distribute among themselves the land necessary for the construction of their houses and the formation of enclosures, and have kept in common only the pasture and cultivated land. Such is the system that must have been in vigor in primitive times.   The collective property of agricultural associations of the Middle Ages was created by grants of individual property.   The agrarian communities of Russia originated in concessions by the nobility; consequently the community of the serfs inhabiting a village is subsequent to private property.   Now the opinion of Belot is opposed to the law of evolution as it refers to property and family.   Nor is it based on solid arguments.   Aucoc in "Caractère Collectif des Premières Propriétés Immobilières" notes that the examples given by Belot are of a date long after the primitive ages when private control of land was established in its entirety, nearly contemporaneous with the agrarian communities of which he speaks.   Belot did not examine the origin of the agricultural communities of the Middle Ages or distinguish the association of the serfs, to escape the death tax, from the association of free men.   Probably he would have found a different origin of collective property in the two kinds of communities if he had distinguished them clearly.   Without doubt he makes clear that the colonists of Nantucket did not invent the constitution of private and collective property in their island, but reproduced the old Scotch custom of "lauder," which has an extremely archaic form according to Maine. Such a custom, according to Maine and Belot, is the type of the most ancient uses of Germanic property and culture. But it is difficult to admit that the Germans have not passed, in a remote age, through a nomadic state before reaching the condition in which Tacitus found them, who spoke of their neighbors without arms, horses, houses, or agriculture.   How had these people and the Germans passed from the nomadic state?   If Belot had studied the phases of property among the Arab tribes of Algeria, the transition would have been clear.   Some of the Arab tribes are still in a nomadic state, covering great distances with their herds.   Others are nomads only, within a limited space, and are occupied both with cattle and the cultivation of the soil, but live in tents and have no fixed habitation.   Other tribes, near cities, know of the advance in agricultural methods in culti- vation and irrigation.   They have permanent houses, and in these tribes, side by side with the public domains, there are the "melk" and "arch" lands.   The first are pri- vate property and have a family character, for a member of the family can annul their sale, reimbursing a foreign purchaser.   In the second, which form the greater part, for a long time the tribe has had a simple right of enjoy- ment.   These facts have the double advantage of being contemporaneous and of existing in a society which has remained in an almost primitive condition, and show how people pass from the nomadic to the sedentary state, and how the property of the tribe is transferred little by little to the family and the individual.

§ 256. *Christianity Developed Individuality.* Chris- tianity shows the value of the individual, the image of God, and recommends work, the source of produc- tion, and sacrifice which is the origin of thrift and of that universal brotherhood economically realized through the universality of interests. It is true that at first Christian teaching preferred poverty and a life of charity; it is true that it looked upon wealth as the means to the fulfillment of beneficence and charity, tending towards the spontaneous community of goods: but we cannot fail to recognize that the new religion did not have many followers in a world which was still pagan, and for that reason at first abhorred all that could offend its purity by any connection with the worldly pleasures and sensual inclinations of the pre- ceding age. At this time Christianity opposed to the law of the flesh that of the spirit, to worldly wisdom

superhuman virtue, to the terrestrial city the ⌐ ⌐
God, and social fraternity and spontaneous common
ownership to the egoism of the Roman landowner with
his "plena potestas in re" and his quality of "moderator
et arbiter." This abhorrence began to disappear through
the contact of the new opposite terms, by which the
world was Christianized and the Christian religion was
made even too mundane. Barbarian individualism contributed not a little to this transformation and to the
development of personality made sacred by the religion
of Christ preventing, as Guizot says, society after the
orgy of pagan egoism from losing itself through the
ascetic spirit of communism in the depth of a limitless
abnegation.

§ 257. *The Feudal System was Individualistic.* The
feudal system, derived from the subordination of public office, of territorial jurisdiction and seigniority to
the category of private law, that is, to the laws of
property, family, and inheritance, was the emanation
of the personal principle. The grantee of land had
control over it; the control was at first temporary, then
hereditary, and ultimately acquired the character of a
family possession which could be transferred and transmitted with the rights of alienation and subinfeudation.
First in the feudal system are the figures of the grantor
and grantee, and therefore the right of private property
connoting jurisdiction. In this entered all the social
elements, even the more spiritual, and from this the
worldliness of the religious idea was increased through
the temporalities of the Church, now grown into a complete and powerful hierarchy. The feudal system was a
vast hierarchy which undertook to correct the erring
existence of the people of Europe and to give it a fixed
order and develop individual energy in their estates and
castles reinvigorating the bonds and ties of the family.

This hierarchy was strong enough to establish a chain of limitations on the power of princes and monarchs, although it denied the principles of liberty and equality. Vico teaches that the feudal system was a reflux and that there is an eternal law of feuds. To many the idea has seemed false because advances and reflexes destroy history (that does not presuppose simple continuity, but mutability) and do not show the proper and true character of acts and institutions. Certain it is that the feudal system, as organized in the Middle Ages, was never seen before and will never be seen again. The feudal system, understood in its entirety and in its historical development, is not a reflex, though its primary elements can be found in the earliest antiquity, especially among the customs of the primitive Aryans. In this aspect Vico is right. Its idea appears as a great intuition which has hardly shown all its richness in our days when it commences to be developed by analysis and with the aid of erudition in comparative and critical history. Maine, among all the moderns, has come nearest to the Neapolitan philosopher (whom he does not quote and of whom perhaps he was ignorant). The feudal system according to the English writer had its beginning in Roman emphyteusis, in the limitrophic camps,[1] in patronage and the primitive customs reintroduced into Europe by the Germans. The great patricians possessed large estates cultivated by bands of slaves directed by other slaves or freemen. Such a system was harmful to the interests of Italian municipalities, whose representatives, often changing, were not in a position to take care of the cultivation of extensive domains. The municipalities began, therefore, to make perpetual grants of land to free cultivators who must pay a fixed rent and fulfill certain conditions. The

[1] *Vide*, Maine, Ancient Law, 10th Ed., p. 309.

example was followed by private owners and the grantees became subject to a right almost equal to that of ownership. Thus the bands of slaves were transformed into groups of colonists or rural serfs who owed the patron a portion of the crops produced. In the great forests along the Rhine and the Danube there were limitrophic camps[1] occupied by Roman veterans who held them from the State by emphyteusis with the duty of responding to military calls. Patronage relied on gratitude, respect, and aid, which really are duties of a vassal towards his lord.

§ 258. *Feuds Come from the Village Communities.* Among the Germanic customs and institutions, the division of society into compact groups of families and classes is notable. The family is administrated by the eldest member or one elected in his stead. The classes are governed by a member of the dominant family. Tacitus observed that among the Germans the chief received from the king cattle and grain as a recompense. The companions of a chief lived with him and received a horse and their weapons, as is the rule to-day at the court of a Kaffir chief in South Africa. The chiefs were rich in cattle, perhaps on account of their military operations, but they did not have sufficient pasturage. On the other hand, the people lacked capital to apply to the cultivation of the land; whence the necessity of taking cattle from the chief and of becoming his man and of rendering him services and homage besides paying rent. The scarcity of capital makes us understand why in remote antiquity everything depended on the oligarchs. In Athens the people were slaves to debt. In Rome the plebeians were heavily bound to the patricians. In Germany the influence of the equites, borne witness to by Cæsar, grew with the quantity of

[1] *Vide*, Maine, Ancient Law, 10th Ed., p. 309.

debtors. In such an unfortunate state, there is, however, an eternal law of re-accommodation that was one of the causes of the feudal system.   The very word "feud" is derived from an ancient gothic word "fihu" or "fiu," meaning cattle, the chief source of wealth in primitive times.   The bull was sacred in India and a "res mancipi" in Rome; the word capital comes from "caput" and means horned beasts counted by heads.   When the population multiplied and conquests grew enormously, gifts of land took the place of the assignment of cattle or gifts of arms, and therefore the idea, associated at first with personal grants, continued probably to refer to land. Originally a feud related more to the State than to owner- ship.   The lord was the βασιλεῦs, the king; the freed men formed the γερουσία, the senate or counsel; the vil- lains represented the mass of the people who had under them the slaves.   The seigniorial court was the ancient assembly of the village which was concerned chiefly with the administration of justice.   Other questions of general interest were discussed under the presidence of the lord and peers of the manor. The villains were pres- ent as a crowd at the deliberations.   The tribute at first had the character of a tax and took the place of the ancient subsidies paid by the administration of the little village communities.   The overlord answered for the feud and was the administrator and governor. The land belonged to him only in part and he received the rent from the lords of different rank.   Immedi- ately under him came free lords who rendered him mili- tary and honorable service and were obliged to follow him in war.   The greater part of the soil was occupied by the villains who owed the lord every kind of service and could not abandon their land or inheritance without his consent.   The law in theory gave the lord the prop- erty in the villains' personalty.   The whole organism reproduced in its fundamentals the type of village community although modified in not a few parts. The chief difference between the feud and such a community consists in the substitution of private authority for common power. What the lord could do, that could be done by the head of the village and the council of the elders. The chief and elders were responsible to the community but the lord succeeded in being the owner of the soil.

§ 259. *The Personal Principle Reinstated by the Reformation was Again Destroyed.* The Reformation destroyed the ecclesiastical hierarchy and allowed the direct reconciliation of man and God and the interpretation of the divine word by the individual, and went back to the rights of the spiritual personality. The enemy of the intermediary and the hierarch and inspired by the principle of individual personality, the Reformation opposed the hierarchical system of ownership. In this opposition it was aided by Roman law which did not recognize other title to land than that derived from the free disposition of the owner. Feudalism had made the king the supreme lord; the jurists appealed to the traditions of imperial Roman law exaggerating the signification of royal power and changing it into the eminent domain of the prince in order to destroy feudal bonds. Later, in another struggle between the despotism of the king and the ancient régime, the eminent domain was given to the nation. Property was placed upon the basis of the personal principle, and in confirmation of such a principle proclaimed by the French Revolution, it was regulated by a civil code. This principle, brought to light by the Reformation, demonstrated by natural law and shown by study of Roman law with respect to real rights, was emphasized by industrial labor which created personal property. The limitations of the "fidei commissus" and of primogeniture disappeared. We can no longer find the trace of eminent domain; the right to hunt over the estate of the peasants has been destroyed; the rules about cultivation and harvest have been done away with; and the abolition of the rights of use, pasture, woodbote, the last vestiges of the primitive communism, have begun. Privileges are becoming rarer. Estates are divided. The right of the co-heir to demand partition is recognized. Hereditary equality in personalty and realty is enforced. Land is democratic. Legislation, however, has not yet completed the work and does not apply democratic principles to all kinds of property, to goods, for example, though of less importance than land in the doctrine of the physiocratic school, according to which agriculture alone furnishes a net product and all the other industries are unproductive. Personalty brings men closer together, cements their union, promotes fraternity and close relations, feeds those who cannot gain their living from the soil, and is a protection for the individual, who can remove from the vexatious or absorbing action of the State by emigrating with his goods and chattels. On the contrary, ownership of land binds a man to the soil, obliges him to apply his activities to it, gives him a house and isolates him, and is a sign of subjection and obedience. Goods and chattels, connected in the most immediate and sensible way with the individual, were at first tangible, such as weapons, clothes, and other utensils. They preceded property in the soil and were well developed among the Germans who, proud of individual autonomy, favored their circulation with the maxim that possession is nine points in the law. This maxim means that voluntary delivery of a thing made by one who is not its owner to another in good faith gives him property in it.   The free cities showed in history great progress in art, manufacture, and commerce, and therefore a notable increase in personal property, to which the return of the Crusaders loaded with merchandise and precious objects (and cured of all illusion of finding their divinity in a sepulchre) contributed largely.   A century thereafter this kind of property was immensely increased by the progress of production aided by development in mechanics and freedom of work.   It constitutes a highly variable and, as it were, a capricious kind of wealth, observes Rossi, and tends to become the most important.   Despite the irregularities of their movement, goods and chattels were raised to a high level and will be raised higher still.   A strenuous and prudent organization of industry, commerce, transportation, and credit is what our social state demands.   Like the results of all of the revolutions, these facts have in themselves both good and ill; a prosperous future if the publicists, economists, and legislatures fix their attention on them, one of incalculable misfortune if they neglect them.

§ 260. *Modern Individualism.* The evolution of property is connected with complete individualization which, left to itself and deprived of the necessary modifying influence, leads to an orgy of selfishness and consequently to the savage destruction of poverty. When the individual becomes the beginning and end of everything, the State becomes small and is only a means of defense of the individual and his belongings. As in the ancient world society absorbed the individual, so to a certain extent in modern times the individual has absorbed society.   Individualism, however, in our day, has described a parabola and is almost exhausted.   A new theory, which has gained ground in political doctrines, makes for the harmony of the ancient notion of

the social community with the principle of personal freedom.   The doctrine regards the community, and therefore the family and the State, as ethical organisms, the
one within the other, in which the parts live the life of
the whole but have also their own value and personality
as well.   Man in the abstract and concrete, in virtue of
such a doctrine, becomes cause and effect, reciprocal
means and end; the individual, the family, and the
State in their medial quality have duties, in their ultimate quality have rights.   It is clear that this conception once accepted, atomism should be disregarded even
in the sphere of property.   The defeat of atomism does
not mean the negation of individual personality, because
the period is beginning in which, having developed and
tried to withdraw from society, it re-enters, takes its
place, and recognizes its subordination to the organism
as a whole.   True evolution, we must repeat, is not
only individualization, but growing correlation, so that
property remaining individual should not be egoistic,
but should obey social aims in a system of rational
limitations conforming to the historical condition of the
people.   One-sided and erroneous are the ideals of the
individualist and the socialist, for one sees only in evolution the abstract tendency to progressive particularity
and the other loses sight of the diverse aspects of this
progress in the material world and only notices the
object of the whole and organic correlation of the parts.

    § 261.   *Primitive Means of the Acquisition of Property.*
The means of acquisition in primitive society were
very difficult and complex because the relations established were not between individuals but between organized social bodies, between the diverse communities
existing in the midst of the tribe.   An individual in that
age did not acquire rights and duties by himself, but
as the head of a society or family.   The methods of

acquisition, since the mind lived in sensations and images, lay in ceremonies, rites, and symbols, and demanded the presence of a great number of witnesses. The inherent difficulties were overcome one by one. Maine shows the methods with truth and precision. The first method of conquering this difficulty was the division of property into categories. The goods of a higher category were those first known; those afterwards learnt were in a lower category. Those of higher category were acquired with difficult and solemn methods. They were the "res mancipi," to which the "mancipatio" applied. The others of the lower category, the "res nec mancipi," were transferred by the natural and easy method of "traditio." The methods for the acquisition of property of the second category were facile and suitable, and consequently they were soon extended to goods of the higher category. At the time of Justinian "traditio" was enough to pass property in the "res mancipi." Here we must destroy an illusion of the later Roman jurisconsults, who generalized from their own time and believed that "traditio" was older than "mancipatio," while in fact the "traditio" only dominated after the "mancipatio" had lost its force. Gaius says, "Quarundam rerum dominium nanciscimur jure gentium quod ratione naturali inter omnes homines peræque servatur quarundum jure civili. Et quia antiquius jus gentium cum ipso genere humano proditum est, opus est ut de hoc prius referendum sit." Besides the distinction of goods by categories or kinds, there was another means of distinction of later origin. In India the father could alienate inherited goods only with the assent of his sons, but could freely dispose of goods acquired through his own industry. In Rome a son had free disposition of money earned in the army. Among the Germans, free and allodial land was difficult of aliena-

tion.   To allodial land succeeded feudal land, and then
there only remained the distinction between land and
goods recognized by Roman law, although of not
so much importance as the distinction between "res
corporales" and "res incorporales."   In the Middle Ages
land was thought more of than goods, which acquired
thus great importance and the laws referring to it
tended to become absorbing because wealth was converted into personalty.

   § 262.   *Modern Distinction of Land and Goods.*   Modern legislation considers the division of land and
goods as fundamental, but we must inquire if this
is admitted by rational laws.   Zacharia thinks that it
lies entirely in positive law because he conceives rational
law within the boundaries of subjective rationalism,
which deduces everything from the category of thought
separating it from the exteriority.   Such confines being
overcome, and starting with the principles of natural
law founded on objective rationalism, we come to a
different conclusion because the object is what urges
the faculty to act and in the object the act terminates and
is quiet, as Rosmini says.   Every right is a power over
an object which determines its bounds according to its
nature.   The nature of the object is the basis of the
diversity of rights, as the natural differences of men
constitute the base of the differences of persons.   Puchta
teaches that in all external things law singles out what
they have in common, their essence, which is subject
to law.   The right over a thing itself is the same
whether it treats of land, animals, plants, or anything
whatsoever.   But this natural diversity was not foreign
to law that makes a difference between land and
goods, between rural and urban property, between
wild and domestic animals, etc.   The question arises,
when the speculative suggestion is raised, whether the

modern division is primary or secondary, fundamental
or not.   Rational law, it must be admitted, prefers the
Roman classification of objects into corporeal and
incorporeal, because both land and goods are corporeal.   The Roman classification is objective as well
as the modern, and at the same time it has the advantage
of being logically primary, apart from any discussion
as to the practical or jurisprudential value of the one
or the other.   It places material things, real or personal,
on one side, and on the other the rights which are also
useful and permutable external objects of financial
value.   The ambiguity arises in confusing what is
incorporeal with what is intrinsic to the mind or person.
Now what is incorporeal is not intrinsic or inseparable
from the ego.   A patent right, for example, is certainly
incorporeal but extrinsic; it is part of one's estate and
can be the object of exchange.

   § 263. *Other Means for Rendering Acquisition More
Easy.*   Other means of conquering the inherent difficulty in the methods of primitive acquisition are found
in prescription, equity, and civil procedure.   Prescription
offers the advantage of curing with years the defects of
a title of acquisition and of reuniting the possession and
property.   Equity and the courts produce later another
important advantage.   The owner "jure quiritium" could
take advantage of the "rei vindicatio" to defend his possession.   The proceeding was formal, long, and solemn;
and with time the need of a summary procedure was
felt and the defense of possession was allowed through the
"interdictum," which originally referred to the "habere
in bonis."   The purity of procedure thus was hurt, but
society gained thereby a quick and easy means of protection.   The "in jure cessio," a kind of fictitious sale
similar to the lease and release of the common law,
offered greater facility in transfer because the old owner

did not defend against the action of sale brought by the vendee and the judge "addicebat rem." Finally we must note that methods of transfer of property in the primitive period were public because the land belonged to the tribe, the village community, or family, — collective and strongly organic entities. Even when the land belonged to an individual, society reserved important rights (and among these the power of authorizing alienation) because it always wanted to keep foreigners from the native soil. The ancient "mancipatio" bears witness to the original publicity of acquisition. Public, too, was the alienation of allodial lands. After centuries, the principle of publicity reappears and obtains again to greater extent for a different reason; that is, for the protection of the rights of third parties.

CHAPTER VI

PREDIAL PROPERTY IN THE SOIL

COLLECTIVE OWNERSHIP OF LAND. — WAGNER'S THEORY OF
THE OWNERSHIP OF MANUFACTORIES. — SPENCER'S THEORY ON
THE OWNERSHIP OF LAND. — PRIVATE OWNERSHIP OF LAND
AND RENT. — THE DOCTRINES OF HENRY GEORGE AND OF
LORIA AS TO LAND.

§ 264. *Collective Ownership Disappears upon the Development of Work.* The less civilized people who have not a well developed conception of the right of property allow private ownership of weapons, clothes, and ornaments, because work confers on these objects a value apart from that of the raw material. Tribes that live by the chase recognize, as a general rule, that the property in animals belongs to him who has killed or wounded them. In the life of semi-nomadic races, property in the soil is collective, but the products are given to the cultivators. When civilization begins, the principle of private property, as the result of man's acts, becomes more marked and extended. The application of communism to the products of the activity of the group or individual is contrary to the most elementary ideas of justice.

§ 265. *Ownership of Land Subject to Same Rational Law as Goods.* There are some writers who think that all the economic and juristic reasons for private property in goods have no value in regard to land. These writers belong to the school of territorial collectivism and are not of one accord among themselves, some denying individual property in houses, others limiting the application of their theory to land. Wagner, for example, is not in favor of private property in houses, and exchanges the conception of control of property by the State for that of absorption. He starts out with the principle that private property is a loan entrusted by the State to individual administration, and that when rents go up the State has the right of re-appropriation. Between urban and rural property there are, according to Wagner, two important differences; a city house once built, the owner does not expend any labor and for many years is put to no expense, while the countryman must expend labor and capital every year. The exceptional gain received by the householder when there is an excessive crowding of people into a determinate space is much greater than that of the owner of the richest soil. Wagner is right in making these two differences; he is wrong only in considering private property as a loan to the citizens by the State, denying the right of the individual, who makes his impress on the object and makes it a projection of himself. The State can and even should limit this right, but not absorb it, for in absorbing it, it does not recognize the human essence in the individual and degrades him to the position of a simple instrumentality. It is true that capital is the moving factor in urban property, but capital is the work of yesterday, as work is the capital of to-morrow, and in capital there is the activity of man; and as a product of such activity it should be respected. The State, in cases of an exaggerated increase in rent, can lessen the taxes or in a thousand ways urge the erection of new buildings, can even erect them itself, and above all has the power of appropriation, if necessary, but appropriation should never be as general as the property, and should not be connected with the erroneous idea of a

loan by the State.   Here we should be careful not to
confuse two very different things, that is, unjust monopoly with the possession of things incapable of indefinite
multiplication.   The first is an artificial and unreasonable restriction of the freedom of production and should
be destroyed; the second is in no wise connected with
true monopoly because it furnishes a return dependent
upon the change in value, and not upon individual will.
It is clear that the normal value of property capable of
free and indefinite multiplication is shown by the cost
of production, because, if the product brings more than
it costs, competition will reduce the price in a gradual
and progressive manner, and if the cost of production
is more than its value, the supply will decrease, because
no one will do business at a loss.   But the normal value
of goods of limited quantity such as houses and land is
determined by the combination of supply and demand;
these two are not capable of indefinite increase.   This
kind of property ordinarily brings more and sometimes
much more than its value, if the cost of production
expresses its true minimum value, as in the hypothesis
discussed by Wagner.   We cannot say, however, that
their possession has a fictitious value in order to
destroy it by a forced appropriation, inasmuch as it is
the result of the legitimate connection, physical and
moral, of individuals with free or legally acquired objects.
In other words, there is no contradiction between the
conception of private property and that of the limiting
laws of nature, as we will see in the next paragraph.

§ 266.   *Spencer's Collectivism.*   Spencer, in his "Social
Statics," says that private ownership of land is
unjust.   Given a species of beings, he says, who have
equal right to enjoy the full scope of their tendencies, given a world made for the satisfaction of their
needs, it is easily deducible that each of these beings

has a right to enjoy the good things of the world. If each is free to do what he wishes, provided that he does not offend another's freedom, each is free to take natural gifts for the satisfaction of his needs, provided always that he respects the same rights in his fellows. The converse of the proposition is clearly that no one can use land so as to impede an equal use on the part of others. Justice, therefore (concludes Spencer), does not recognize individual property in the soil. If we admit that a portion of land can be the domain of one man, the other portions can be occupied under a similar title and so the whole face of the globe would fall into the hands of some individuals. The rest of mankind would live by the toleration or good grace of the exclusive proprietors. The arguments of Spencer, identical in the main with those of all the writers who believe in territorial and complete collectivism, are reducible to Fichte's proposition and contain the same error. It is undeniable that all men have an inherent right to property and that things are made for all. There can be no doubt that it is the duty of society and the State to recognize and protect the full play of such essential rights in a human being. But this inherent right of property is simply potential, and so should be realized and transformed into the right of property. Every man has the right to take advantage of natural gifts, physical forces, and the soil, but no one has a particular right over the external world unless he has applied his activity to it. If he has not made something, if he has not acted and thereby taken away the abstract equality and created a reason for special juristic privilege, the State should not act for him and create a reason for a privilege, because the inherent rights of man become acquired by the act of the individual himself, whose power and faculty are in question. An individual can exercise his natural right of property by applying his action to the soil or in the sphere of manufacture, industry, or commerce. The State is only obliged to insure him conditions for the development of individual activity, and is in no wise called upon to help him by giving him the wherewithal. We must not forget that land is of limited quantity and that at one time it was not sufficient for all, and that the means of existence are not won from it alone, but from the arts, industries, and commerce as well. Spencer finally contradicts himself because he says that industrialism promotes the development of private property and that common property in the soil is destined to reappear when industrialism shall have reached the height of its development. How is this possible, if industrialism, opposed to the military system, signifies progressive differentiation and the presence of individuality, contract, and voluntary coöperation? Spencer, seeing the contradiction, writes that industrialism has not actually reached its definite position, and that we will have another phase in which private property in land will disappear. As there have been centuries in which the property of one man in another was admitted, which right with the advance in civilization was denied, so in the future, when industrialism has received broader development, private property in land will cease. But in his last book, "Justice," he has no longer the same strong faith, although he says that he is still convinced that the human aggregation is the owner of the soil. He believes military systems have been a constant cause of the loss of personal liberty, the introduction of slavery, and even the destruction of collective property. He adds that side by side with the decline of the military belief and with the development of industrialism, he sees personal liberty grow stronger and stronger, and that we will soon be forced to a partition of land. If land should again become common, justice would demand indemnification for the actual private possessors. These possessors are not all descendants of the first occupiers and usurpers, but many of them have gained possession through derivative methods of acquisition, and at the same time not a few members of the proletariat are descended from the original usurpers. Society has a right to have the land back again as it was in the primitive state, but cannot appropriate what the possessors have expended throughout centuries in labor and capital for ploughing, improving, and cultivating. We would have to pay enormous sums in such indemnity and in the end we would undergo a loss paying more in indemnity than the value of the land. To this indemnity we should enter also the sum spent by the landowners for the assistance of the masses, for this sum represents a part of the product of the so-called private land. The re-transference of land to society would produce a state of affairs perhaps worse than the actual state through the control of "bossism," and the administration by the State, the worst form from an economic aspect. Spencer concludes that a more profound examination of the arguments induces him to adopt the opinion that it is better to maintain private property in land, merely subjecting it to the sovereignty of the State. This change of front on the part of the English philosopher is very noteworthy.

§ 267. *Private Property is Economic.* Once admitted that private property is based on the personal principle, economic sciences bring out its useful side. The useful, it is well to remember, is no stranger to law because it constitutes the material therefor. The distribution of wealth has for its base (and its only base) the right of property referring interest, profit, and rent to property in the capital and land, showing the connection between capital and labor. If there were not individual and stable property, there would be very much less stimulus to production and accumulation, because man would not feel the fervor of work when he was not sure of enjoying its fruits and of leaving them to those who after his death would continue his personality. It is incontestable that agriculture presupposes exclusive possession of land, at least from the time of planting to that of harvest, as it is not presumable that any man would sow so that another might reap. The alternation of crops, so necessary to the productivity of fields (to which it restores strength), is an object of "ars longa," requiring long possession. The most active cultivator must invest large sums to make but little profit. This is not possible without certainty of the future. It is not possible for any power to determine the point in which the return from land becomes usurious because in farming, as in life, to-day is a continuation of yesterday, and the beginning of to-morrow, and there is a cycle of production recommencing with each new accumulation of capital. Exclusive and continuous possession of the soil is the first law of civilization and heredity, and is a form of the connective tissue in the social organism, as Lampertico observes in his book, "La Proprietà." With the establishment of private property we cannot fail to have increased production; with the increased quantity of wealth the State acquires a great economic impulse, and is enabled thus to better and more fully take care of the social welfare. Private property in favor of consumers allows the competition of producers which would be non-existent or restricted under a collective system.

§ 268. *Socialistic Communism.* Socialists of a few years since said that property in land was the usurpation of the rights of the chase, pasturage, and harvest; those of to-day repeat the same accusation under a different form, maintaining that land, minerals, and wild beasts cannot belong to anyone because they are not the result of human labor. This is very true as long as the things have no real value, as long as the handiwork of man does not appear in them, as long as he does not place the stamp of his individuality upon them, but when such an impress is made, then value is created and property cannot fail to arise. To produce is not to create, and even Marx, in his work "Das Kapital," cites lengthily from Verri to show that all the phenomena of the universe do not give us the conception of the creation but only that of modification of matter, and that man can only unite and separate natural elements. Now the so-called usurpation of the first occupant does not take away but gives land to others, because it takes less space for a family to live by agriculture than by hunting and nomadic pasturing. The collectivists maintain that in the system of private ownership of land humanity is rendered tributary to a few privileged persons and they wish, for the benefit of humanity, the collective forces and machinery reserved for the profit of the laboring classes. But it appears to us that there is not a shadow of tribute where the products are exchanged for products, because tribute is a value without an equivalent. But industrial products are exchanged for agricultural products of equal value and consequently there can be no tribute. To hold, therefore, that the collective forces and machinery should belong exclusively to the laboring class is only to confess destructive tendencies and biassed hopes while one is declaiming for humanity, society, collectivism, etc.

§ 269. *Rent Arises from the Work Expended on the Land.* Socialists are opposed to private property, basing their arguments on the rent, due to the owner of the land not dependent upon labor and capital. If this

surplus is a gift from God it should be gratuitous,
they say, and cannot be the object of individual appropriation.   Property in this aspect is robbery, and rent a
monopoly.   Not a few economists, with Bastiat at their
head, wishing to make the cause of property threatened by
such an attack secure, resolutely denied the right to rent,
and taught that the coöperation of the natural forces of
land is gratuitous and should remain gratuitous in the
system of property, because it does not enter into the
price which the consumer pays the owner.   He receives
with the payment what he has invested in capital and
labor in the land and nothing further.   The socialists
and economists have not reflected that goods acquire an
economic character only when they are part of a limited
quantity.   The true sources of wealth are those which
satisfy needs and are exchangeable and alienable.   Alien-
ability demands that the thing be external to the grantor,
acquirable by man and of limited quantity, because if
they were inseparable from the person and if the man
could not possess them, exchange would be impossible;
thus also if their number were such that everyone could
have them at any time without labor.   The law of limitation, illustrated by Cossa in "Elementi di Economia"
and his memoirs, arises more or less in all branches of production, because natural forces are not distributed equally
but differ in quality and quantity, and also because of the
abundance and scarcity of capital and labor; the relation
between fixed and circulating capital, between manual
and intellectual labor, determine an industry by their
variances.   When one speaks of goods capable of an
indefinite increase one does not disregard the law of
limitation, because these goods are only relatively
unlimited, in comparison with others of a more limited
quantity.   The products of manufacture, capable of
multiplication quicker than crops, belong to the first

category, although their multiplication meets its limit in water, air, coal, or wind.   From the divers combinations of qualities and quantities of these limits arises the fluctuation of prices in general and of rent in particular. Rent can be seen more clearly in the property of arable land and of factories, because these show more clearly the law of limitation.   It can be seen constantly where there is an oversupply not due to capital and labor but to the coexistence of productions of the same kind, which demand varying expenditure in production.   The most expensive production, where the cheaper cannot meet the demand, shows the average value.   Rent is the surplus of the producer on whom the least expense of production falls.   It is derived from natural and artificial elements.   These latter can be incorporated in the object, for example, in the soil, in such a way as not to constitute a distinct capital.   The situation, the richness and fertility of the soil are natural elements, but the hand of man and work of civilization are not foreign to it, because the situation depends on the means of communication, the richness of the soil is renewed by science, and fertility is increased by labor.   The owner's labor in such a case may have lost its individuality and been incorporated in the soil.   Rent, not entirely an effect of the forces of nature or conditions dependent upon the action of man, represents a handicap but is very analogous to that which the basic nature of man carries from birth and receives from education.   He who will not consider the natural differences between man and man, and is biased by their identity, will find the phenomenon of rent unjust.   Pasini, cited by Lampertico, says that there is always one man who has the greater capital or a better site, with the capacity of carrying on a work more advantageously. Under the economic juristic aspect, property in capital and labor and property in land are the same.   The

cultivator who carries out a more limited plan and has
a more limited capital and therefore obtains less results
cannot say that the cultivator, furnished with capital for
more advantageous exploitation, should be debited with
the difference. Rent is not unjust on another score;
it is a surcharge which is reduced to a compensation
through past and future changes of the productive fund.
It is a kind of insurance; not reciprocal, not that of the
State, but of the owner towards himself. Rent is reduced with the increase of production which, as we have
already seen, is effected by the system of private property.
Private ownership is not the cause of rent, which
varies with the cost of production, but accompanies it
and makes it an attribute of the owner alone; and so, if
there were no private property, rent would not be lacking to satisfy the needs of the population which would
require an equally expensive cultivation.

§ 270. *Henry George's Theory*. In order to study
the theme of private property in land under the economic aspect, let us for a moment study two recent and
important theories, the theory of Henry George and that
of Loria. The concrete and real character of social acts
should not be disregarded by the philosophy of law,
— facts whose economic structure is a natural presupposition of the juristic relations and civil institutions.
Henry George, the representative of scientific American
socialism, confuses the control of private property,
which preserves it intact, with its absorption, in his book
"Progress and Poverty." He asks why poverty is
greatest where the progress is greatest? Why, with the
increase of productive ability, wages tend to minimum?
Modern political economy, as he calls the classic doctrine, answers that wages, being determined by the
number of laborers and the proportion of capital to pay
that labor, decreases because the number of laborers

increases in greater proportion than the augmentation of capital. Such a solution, says Henry George, depends upon two erroneous theories, — on the theory of wages and that of Malthus. It is not true that wages are paid by capital, but they grow out of productive labor. It is not the employer who precedes the labor, but the labor that precedes the employer. If every laborer makes the fund from which he receives his wage, wages could not diminish with the number of laborers, provided that the efficiency increases with the number of laborers. The more laborers there are, the higher should be the wages, all things being equal. Statistics prove that the higher nations are not those in which nature is more prodigal, but the nations which are marked by a more productive labor, and that with the increase of population there is a corresponding increase in the medial production of wealth. The cause of the decrease of wages and the increase in poverty, according to the more progressive philosophers, is not to be found in the law of production but in that of distribution. Rent does not represent in any way an aid given to production, but merely the power of assuring to the owner a part of the results of production. The law of the phenomenon of rent is found in the theory of Ricardo, which Henry George formulates in a broader manner. Property (he says) in a natural agent of production will give the power of appropriation of so much of the wealth produced by the labor and capital thereto applied as exceeds the return from the same amount of labor and capital expended, less productive in occupations, to which it could be freely applied. Thus the interest of the manufacturer and the wages of the laborers are determined by the limits of cultivation. Rent increases as the limit of cultivation is approached, and decreases as the limit is increased. Interest and wages are lowered when the limit of cultivation is approached, and increase as it goes up.   The movement of rent is progressive while that of wages and interest which vanish is not.   Rent sometimes is increased through the increase of population, through the progress of art and commerce, and through speculation.   Rent takes, therefore, what wages and interest lose; both depend not on the product of labor and capital, but on what remains above the rent. In other words, wages and interest depend on what production there could be without the payment of rent, that is, of the poorest of cultivated lands.   Whatever, therefore, be the increase in productive power, if the rent increases *pari passu*, wages and interest cannot increase, and the owners grow rich and all the others grow poor.   The only remedy for the evil is the confiscation of rent through a single tax which would absorb it all.   The confiscation of rent is a remedy instrumental to clearing the way for the final remedy of the nationalization of the soil and the recognition of the equal right of all to the collective possession of land.   This, in a few words, is the doctrine of Henry George.

§ 271.   *Criticism of Henry George's Doctrine.*   This doctrine is founded in a great part on facts which do not exist.   It has no base in reality.   It is not in the least true (as has been observed by Rae in his book, "Contemporary Socialism") that with progress the poor become poorer and increase in number.   Wherever there is civilization and progress, there the number of poor decreases and charity is largely developed, the means of tenure of life increase and also the duration of human existence.   If in the great cities the poorer class seems numerous, the same is also true throughout the country districts; it is natural that in those places where immense wealth and luxury exist the poor should appear poorer than they really are.   The true sign of increasing poverty is shown by restriction of the number of things necessary to life and increased difficulty in obtaining them.   Experience shows that in times of economic progress the number of needs which we cannot renounce grows, and that there is a facility for obtaining them even when there are not exceptional conditions.   The laborer of to-day is accustomed to have many things that a hundred years ago it was madness for him to hope for.   This changed tenure of life through the effects of civilization is taken into consideration in his wages; for it is not true that wages have decreased; in fact, they have been increased as a result of increased demands in all branches.   If we make a comparison with fifty years ago we will see the actual increase in wages, even though we remember the changed value of merchandise and money.   If there is not a general decrease in wages, the persistent poverty alleged by Henry George is lacking.   He should, too, consider all the other causes of poverty, — lack of foresight, alcoholism, consumption, accidents, sickness, and death.   It is not true that the decrease in wages is produced by the constant increase in rent which absorbs automatically the greater part of the social income, because we cannot say that the agrarian wages are increased wherever there has been an increase in rent.   Statistics show that rent bears no greater proportion to-day to national wealth and agricultural production than formerly, and wages are not in a less proportion.   The theory which Henry George champions in place of the already abandoned theory of the origin of wages is erroneous, since it is not true that wages are always drawn from the production itself and that the laborer precedes the employer.   In fact, it happens in the majority of cases that the value given by the worker in exchange for the wages is not a true exchange for the commercial employer, until after the product is sold. Sometimes years pass in which the employer receives nothing from the product over which he has expended much for raw material and wages. The other theory of Henry George about population is equally false because founded on the untrue hypothesis of the unlimited productive capacity of the earth. There is no relation of cause and effect between the increase of rent and the decrease of wages. Rent and wages ordinarily have the same favorable and unfavorable conditions. We can even say that with the increase of rent the profits and wages increase, and with its decrease they fall away. This absorption of an always increasing quota of the social income by rent is imaginary, for rent has a tendency to increase with the increase of population that urges men to cultivate the less fertile land, cannot be a truly absorbent power because of the great technical advance of agriculture which increases the fertility and natural forces of the soil. Furthermore, the greater part of modern wealth is not in the hands of the landowners, neither is it increased exclusively by the existence of rent. Industry and commerce are without doubt potent causes in its extraordinary actual development.

§ 272. *Agricultural Land is not a Gift of God.* Henry George cannot consider that class which to-day holds the greatest part of social wealth an influential factor, that is, the capitalists and contractors to whom the interest and profits belong. He calls wages profits and tries to place the latter under the laws of wages while they are really regulated by different laws, often opposed thereto. Who can fail to see the difference between them? According to Ricardo, first wages and interest are paid and then one takes out the rent, which is the over-profit, and represents what remains by the above process. Henry George, on the other hand, says that wages and profits are determined by the rent while that presupposes the prevalence of labor or capital. According to Ricardo, notes Rae, rent in no wise affects the price of bread; its increase is not a cause of high prices but rather it is the high price of bread which increases rent. The price of bread does not depend upon the will of the owner of the land, but is derived from the increase of population and the decrease of the harvests. Henry George is governed by absurd ideas, since he believes that the increase of population results in an increased offer of food stuffs for sale, and that there cannot be a constant decrease in the harvest because the material is unlimited. This would be contrary to the laws of limitation of production, and shows a confusion of the eternity of material with the unlimited productive capacity of the earth. Material is eternal, but its capacity is limited. The two conceptions logically are not exclusive. Henry George thinks that where there exists an abundance of unappropriated land, there rent will be low and wages high, because none will wish to work over anything to obtain less than he can get from land which he can himself purchase for a trifle. But admitting that such a faculty of choice can exist and influence the wages paid by employers to their workmen, there is no doubt that wages would increase to the detriment of property. In such an hypothesis, it is not possible to think that the profits would increase, because the contradiction would not permit it. We know, according to Henry George, where there is an abundance of free land, rent is low, and wages and interest considered by him as a natural and legitimate increment of capital are high, but we must not forget that he tries always to place these diverse terms under the same law in order to oppose them to rent. The proposed remedy by the confiscation of rent through a single tax is not practical, because it is given

to no one to separate in the productive farm the elements
of rent from those of labor and capital.   The nationalization of the soil cannot render land more productive, to
argue from the economic conditions of those American
States which own a large part of their cultivated
soil, in relation to the system of private property
in the other States.   There is, perhaps, not as much
or as widely extended poverty in those States which
have still vast territories at their disposition.   Henry
George does not deny this fact, but tries to explain
it.   The mistake in which he falls with many other
writers consists in regarding agricultural land as a
gift of God, forgetting that land only attains its value
when man applies his own activity thereto in ploughing,
fertilizing, cultivating, and making it a productive agent.
Cultivated land is as much the true production of man
as anything else in which the action of the individual
can be seen.   It is strange that Henry George recognizes
private property in everything else, even in factories
which in the great centres give a greater return than the
farms, but denies private property in land which is not
a gift of God, except in the sense that an artificial
product is so given.   He proposes control of property
in land equivalent to absorbing it, because he wishes
to confiscate rent.   This confiscation of rent is intended to pave the way for the nationalization of the
soil, a confiscation of private property.   Land can become
an object of property as anything else, and can take its
part as an organ, projection, or investiture of the person.
It differs from other things because it is more subject to
the laws of natural limitation and does not enter into
the category of goods which can be indefinitely increased.
Its greatest productive capacity presupposes as a necessary condition the system of private property.   At this
point social economy joins forces with law, which should

control private property in land in such a manner as to obtain from it the greatest good for the individual and society.

§ 273. *Loria's Theory.* Loria, in his book "La Terra ed il Sistema Sociale," gathers together all the theories of the economic system into three principal groups; for some of them base economic phenomena on man, others deduce them from a technical system, and still others from the conditions of external nature or more generally from land. The theory which connects the economic phenomena with man is the dogma of orthodox science. It affirms that the rule of such phenomena is the necessary and immutable product of the very nature of man, and the personal interest which never far departs therefrom. Now this doctrine cannot explain the diversity of historical relations in the different ages and the marvelous evolution of social forms, because the personal interest is immutable throughout all times and is unaffected by the modifying action of history. The theories of the second group consider social relations as a product of the dominant technical system, and are divided into socialistic and commercial theories. The first make the system of production and the series of special economic relations which govern all the acts of life and society correspond to a given state of productive instrumentality. But the evolution of productive methods makes a radical change in the technical instrumentality, and renders the antecedent system of production and economics impossible. Then the antiquated economic form is destroyed by a social revolution and supplanted by one more suited to the new phase of productive instrumentality. This has occurred four times, to which as many forms of economic relations correspond,— Asiatic, ancient, feudal, and the middle class economics. The constant progress of productive instrumentality will soon render this economic form impossible and will substitute a more perfect one, consisting in the collective property of land and means of production. The second theory of this group connects the economic relations with conditions of exchange and the commercial constitution. There is no choice between these two doctrines of the second group because the socialist does not see that technical instrumentality itself must have a cause and must depend on some precedent element and that this, also imperfect, must be connected with the new superior economic form. The socialistic theory does not show the reason why, in the period of undeveloped instrumentality, there should be slavery, and in the period of machinery, wages instead of collective property. The commercial theory does not consider that the conditions of exchange are derivative facts,— the consequences of the economic system and not true causes.

§ 274. *The Conclusions of Loria.* The primary element and first cause of social relations is land, according to Loria. Land as the productive element is the first cause of economic facts, distinguished from the technical instrumentality which is a derivative phenomenon, and is the moving cause distinguished from the personal interest which is immutable in its structure and intensity. Land is the basis of the economic system. It is the supreme principle of political economy, which is a mere natural deduction from the analysis of land and property. The theory of land comprehends the law of laws because it considers the social organisms substantially diverse, which succeed one another in history, and shows the first reason for the various historical laws which have ruled those organisms. This supreme law is the law of motion with the continually changing conditions of occupancy and productivity for its object, and not man, crystalized in the immutability of his character and tendencies. The analysis of property in land can be stated in its general results in the very words of Loria: When land is free and when every man can and hardly wants to occupy a portion of it and to expend labor and capital on his own account, property will be impossible, because there will be no worker disposed to expend his efforts for the benefit of a capitalist. If the productivity of the land is increased, the producers will have no need of associating and limiting their own independence, so that the economic form necessary will be the isolation of independent producers; if, however, the productivity of the land is decreased, the producers are disposed to associate to increase the productivity of their labor and under such conditions, therefore, the economic form necessary is either the close association of producers, who work together dividing the property into equal parts, or the associations of producers and simple workers with the division of products into equal parts. In any case the division of society into a class of capitalists who are not laborers, and of laborers who are not capitalists, is not possible if the land is free, because it is impossible to gain profit for a capitalist who does not work. The formation of this kind of profit is only obtained by the violent suppression of free land, where the population is scarce and cannot occupy all the land. But with the constant increase of population, and with all the land cultivated, the workman loses at once that option which is his greatest protection against the usurpation of capital and is obliged to abandon to the capitalist the greatest part of the produce. At this point comes the profit not less violent, but automatic, due to the appropriation of land which takes the option from the proletariat. The basis of capitalistic property is always the suppression of the free land, and the exclusion of the workman from the land. Free land, on the other hand, is the destruction of capitalistic property. By the increasing demand of a progressive population economic bonds, founded on predial property, become intolerable, and therefore free land must be reëstablished, or rather the free property of the farm must be established, recognizing in every man the right to occupy as much of the earth's surface as he can cultivate with his labor. On the basis of free property in land the association of capitalists and workers will be made and the social equilibrium will result.

§ 275. *The Criticism of Loria's Theory.* The criticism which Loria makes of the different theories is not accurate, neither does his doctrine appear to us true. How can he combat the theory which places human nature at the base of social and economic relations, if society be man in the abstract and if wealth, the object of political economy, is due to the work of man and presupposes his needs, ends, and activities brought to bear upon the production of the means of satisfaction? The conception of wealth is absolutely inseparable from that of individual and social man. The conception of man comprehends human essence, not as a quiescent principle, but as urged on by an internal motion always continuous and progressive, by which human nature by degrees reaches its ideal. This motion, which is one with the action of external facts, constitutes history; human nature cannot be understood without the history in which it develops, not ever losing its fundamental characteristics, which contradistinguish it specifically. In spite of the diversity of the historical relations of different ages and the marvelous evolution in social forms, man will always be man, and have tendencies more or less individualistic and impulses, now weak and now strong, towards sympathy for his fellows. The sense of self and of society are essential forms of human nature which will never disappear, although they are shown in various guises and new forms in different periods, and combine in constantly different ways. The history of man is the history of these changes; human evolution is their development. It is not accurate to say that the personal interest is immutable and unaffected by the modifying action of history, for it follows the vicissitudes of feeling and the development of tendencies which, from a blind and primitive egoism, develop into one that is altruistic, as Spencer says. Individuality is not destroyed but modified, and therefore it is not absurd to admit the persistence of some elements which express immediately its characteristics. Political economy and law, growing out of human nature, must consider personal interest power. Political economy should be founded principally upon the personal interest without forgetting other individual tendencies and the social tendencies which exert an influence upon wealth, as we have before said.[1] Private law should be founded essentially upon the idea of individual personality recognizing, however, the natural bonds which it has with society.   But it cannot be altogether controlled by the social idea, for in that case it would cease to be private. Socialism alone would suppress individuality in economics and law, losing sight of human nature.   It is not logical to look upon the tendencies to personal interest as immutable, for the collective interest can be conceived of as having the same character. Admitted that immutability means the permanence of necessary marks by which one thing is distinguished from another, we must conclude that social interest is likewise immutable, preserving always, as it does, its own nature and having at all times the general good as its object.

[1] *Cf.* §§ 140, 141, *ante.*

As to the criticism which Loria makes of the two theories of the second group, and especially of socialism, we should observe that the first principle of this system is not really placed in the technical instrumentality. Socialism has revealed and even exaggerated the connection between technical instrumentality and the form of economic relations. It will not see that an imperfect technical instrumentality can be associated with a superior economic form, and it will not closely examine the reason why, in the period of undeveloped instrumentalities, there should have existed slavery, and wages; but it is not right to deny that socialism is based on the idea of a technical system and that it sought its base in human nature. Socialism in all its phases has proceeded from the conception of man in the abstract and has always been hostile to individual liberty. It has considered human nature abstractly, that is, from the side of original capacities which are equal in all men, and from its theoretical and final powers (so called by Romagnosi), and has not understood fully enough the value of the acquired faculties and practical powers derived from different characters of individuals or from diverse activities. These practical powers become by action the final powers and represent a full process of individualization in which all the native and artificial modality of the individual arise as well as the differences growing out of objective diversity. Socialism considers merely the equal capacities of man and the common agents of a sensible world, forgetting entirely the medial term of practical powers, and therefore would substitute the collective possession of the means of production in place of private property.

§ 276. *Man is the Origin of Economic Relations.* Land cannot be the real beginning of economic relations, as Loria thinks, without inverting the factors of production and the premises of the science of wealth. Capital and natural forces are instrumentalities of production, the one derivative, the other original; but both presuppose man. Without man there would be no capital and no land as a productive element. It would have a physical existence merely and not economic. Man is not a mere coefficient of production, but its subject, its first cause and limitation. Land cannot become the moving cause save to the extent that man works upon it and gives it value. Its evolution is not physical, but economic; it moves as work modifies it and renders it always more powerful for the satisfaction of human needs. It is not true that of the three premises of classical economy,—the personal interest, the instinct of procreation, and the limitation of the extent and productivity of the earth,—the first two are constant and land alone variable, developing in a series of the digressive steps. But personal interest changes according to its various combinations with altruistic sentiment and general interest. The instinct of procreation is more or less modified by foreign obstacles and by the development of intellectual faculties. If the constancy of personal interest and of the instinct of procreation means that man always desires his own good and tends to multiply, there is reason also to retain the constancy of the third premise because the limitation of the extent and productivity of the earth will never fail. Natural law forbids it.[1] The mutual conditions of the occupancy and fecundity of the earth depend on man and do not constitute a supreme principle. The same conception of the freedom of land, on which Loria is so insistent, includes essentially the relation of man as an individual and in society. Land is free; but in respect to whom? Demonstrated that the theory of the earth as the first

[1] *Cf.* § 144 *ante.*

cause of economic relations is false, it follows that it cannot be the origin of the more complex social facts. If this theory is not sufficient to explain the facts which regard wealth, how can it explain social evolution? That the economic factor in sociology is not absolutely predominant will appear clearly in the discussion of industrial property.[1]

§ 277. *A Contradiction in Loria's Theory.* Loria's theory of free land contains a blending of two conceptions, for it appears on the one hand that he denies entirely predial property, the origin and basis of capitalistic and unproductive property, and on the other hand he accepts the right of every man to occupy the extent of cultivated ground which he can cultivate in that free property in land, which the State must protect. We cannot clearly see whether, after private property in land is denied and ownership is attributed to the community, the usufruct will be the right of every man, or whether there will remain a remnant of predial property, a right to the amount of land necessary for each man to obtain the means of sustenance by labor. In both cases the theory is not new and is confused with collectivism, or that form of socialism which is the consequence of the conception of property in land as the right of all, realized by work. It does not disagree with either doctrine on the question of State intervention, because that can be based either on the total appropriation of the land or on the limitation of its control according to the needs of human beings and the labor of each. So in the hypothesis of free land (or of free property in the land, as Loria says) there is the phenomenon of rent or of surplus, because there will always be a difference in the cost of cultivation. To whom will the rent belong? Will the State confiscate it by a tax which the grantee

[1] *Cf.* § 293 *et seq.*, *post.*

must pay, or will it go to the benefit of the labor-owner
or to the association? We understand that if the rent
goes to the benefit of the possessor or the association of
capital or of capital and labor, the principle, contrary
to that of free land, of land necessary to every man or
of land as the gift of God is implicitly admitted.   This
contrary principle is the exclusive appropriation of the
common natural forces not derived from labor or capital.
If land is every man's, if it is not a creation of man, if
it should be free, how then can an individual or an
association take a surplus from that which is the gift of
God?   How can the appropriation of the rent be justified, if the basis of free property in cultivated land is
labor from which the rent does not come?   Loria says
that in the system in which everyone can and hardly
wants to occupy his piece of land and expend his labor
and capital thereon, property is not possible which
absorbs a great part of the product to the harm of the
workman; that is, capitalistic property.   The workman
will have a beneficial power of choice between the
possession of his own land and labor on that of another.
So Henry George puts forward the hypothesis of the
abundance of free farms and speaks of this alternative
offered to the workmen believing that in such circumstances the rent will go down and the wages will go up.
But despite Henry George, we can say that the alternative is not one of the best for the workmen because
capital is necessary to give value to land and it takes
time to reap its fruits.   The observation can likewise
be applied to the theory of Loria which on this point
is not essentially different from that of Henry George.
It is manifest that capitalistic property by Loria means
the same as by Karl Marx; that it is not the fruit of
work.   According to Marx, property in land and in
all instrumentalities of production generates capitalistic

property, and therefore in his mind the suppression of this kind of property includes not only land but the means of production, as we will see in a following chapter.

CHAPTER VII

PROPERTY IN FORESTS AND MINES

THE FUNCTIONS OF THE FORESTS. — RIGHT OF DEFORESTA-
TION. — ITS RESTRAINT AND THE REASONS THEREFOR. — MINING
PROPERTY AND THE PHASES OF THE INDUSTRY. — CRITICISMS
OF ARGUMENTS IN FAVOR OF THE OWNER OF THE SOIL. — THE
DOCTRINE THAT ATTRIBUTES THE ORE TO THE DISCOVERER.

§ 278. *Forests and Mines are not Land.* Law is
not an abstract formula but a concrete principle.
It is constituted and developed in life, assuming
various and diverse attitudes according to the nature
of the object to which it refers. If land should not be
confused with minerals and forests, it is evident that
the law applicable to property in land should not be
applied to the latter.

§ 279. *The Advantages of Forests.* With this
premise, let us briefly state the particular functions
of a forest, which are four in number. In the first
place, a forest furnishes wood for civil and military
constructions and for the daily uses of the arts. It
prevents landslides, avalanches, snowslides, and the
washing away of the vegetable earth, and avoids the
evaporation of the rain water. It protects the soil
from the rays of the sun and keeps ample deposits of
water, moderates the wind, and keeps the air more
pure. Besides, we must consider that in the lumber
industry, labor and capital play a small part in comparison to the amount invested in agriculture. A
forest is fertilized by fallen leaves and it is perennial.

It seems as if nature wished to protect herself against the arbitrary disposition of man.

§ 280. *Should There be Public Control of Forests?* Now the special character and functions of forests are more or less admitted by the representatives of all the possible systems of forestry regulation, that is, by those who are in favor of absolute freedom and by those who are champions of control, general and constant or partial and changeable in certain cases. The former are firmly persuaded that the harmony of the social interests and the interests of the owners of the forest will be the natural effect of the free development of the activity which is aimed at the production of a valuable asset, and that therefore the State should not interfere. There does not seem to be any doubt that these are actuated by the general presupposition that economic order is reducible to a spontaneous unconscious and instinctive coincidence of private interests for the good of all. But such a presupposition is erroneous, as we have shown above.[1] Human interests are not blind, natural forces, subject to shocks, perturbations, and changes, but are ethical forces little dependent upon freedom, the effective principle of history. This implies the influence of nature on mind, but still consists properly in a progressive series of victories always more important and decisive of mind over nature. In such a process of emancipation, freedom shows, to adopt the phrase of Vico, its divine essence or birth.

§ 281. *Restraint is Necessary in the Present State of Development.* In the argument of which we are speaking, the profit of the owner is evidently opposed to common interest. Let us take a society which has need of the permanence of its woodland because of the physical conditions of the country. The owner

[1] *Cf.* § 272 *ante.*

of this woodland in obedience to the general need
should willingly restrict himself to cutting down a
few dead and dying trees and to repairing the damage done by wind and snow. And if the wood is
capable of a large lumber production he and his
heirs should *sponte suâ* calmly await the slow
rebuilding of their capital, always insecure, waiting
from sixty to a hundred and twenty years for the development of a tree of fair size when an unforeseen
accident can destroy a huge amount of lumber. A
private citizen thus would be constrained to renounce
a quicker and greater return from his capital and in
place thereof undergo many burdens from which little
advantage comes to himself. Is it possible to imagine
all this? Are we by any chance in the happy times of
the normal conversion of self-interest into the heroics
or altruism, of which the followers of Comte speak?
Do we not need more artificial chains, or if there is a
reason for not wanting them, do we not need an economic
order founded on nature and, let us add, on "natura
medicatrice"? Can we disregard so openly the character and tendencies of human individuality?

§ 282. *Restraint is Bad, but Often Necessary.* Beccaria writes, in his celebrated lectures known under
the title of "Elementi di Economia Publica," that
the control of an industry should be free and the
divers interests left to themselves and their natural
development, by which they tend to reach a union
and equilibrium; but he adds that coercive and legislative discipline is necessary when we see that a private
interest will not or will only too late join with the public
interest, and where the discovery of fraud is slow and
remote. Moving from this principle and understanding
the discord of interests in the forest question, he becomes
the ardent champion of control, and fights the danger-

ous freedom of destruction.   This liberty is also combatted by Mengotti and Romagnosi.   Mengotti holds
that the law should forbid not only criminal actions
but those which are imprudent and foolish, and by which
others are harmed and ruined.   How can it be right
to set fire to one's own house, if the probable consequence of that act is burning the next house or the whole
city?   And if one cannot consent to leprosy, plague, and
hydrophobia being found in the public street, or an
owner of a property establishing a rope or rice factory
next door, it is right to forbid the owner of a forest
from destroying it or unsodding his land on steep mountain sides to his own advantage.   Romagnosi also does
not think that the principle of non-intervention, either
active or passive, should apply to avalanches and
snowslides, thinking that private love of gain should
be controlled for the good of the community through
the intervention of public authority.   If you make
rules, he says, for canals, which are the property of
individuals, so that the streets be not flooded and ruined,
can you not with greater reason make rules against
landslides in mountainous countries which ruin at one
sweep the whole territory and subject it to destructive
floods?

§ 283. *The Restraint Should be Conservative.* Public
control should not be determined by hypothetical
reasons or unproven opinions, but should be based
on facts fully demonstrated as dangerous to society,
since it is a question of limiting the free ownership of an individual.   Since the restraint depends upon
these facts, it is necessary that it be established to
hinder the damage which ordinarily comes in the course
of floods to agriculture, husbandry, geographical or
territorial stability by deforestation or unsodding.
That the forests contribute to the permanence and regu-

larity of the springs, so useful to agriculture and husbandry, no one *sanæ mentis* can deny.   Neither is there
anyone who can doubt the influence of the forest on
geographical permanence.   Humboldt says that the trees
act on the abundance of the springs, not, as was believed
for a long time, by a particular attraction for the vapors
in the air, but because they protect the soil from the
direct action of the sun and diminish the evaporation
of rain water.   One of the results of the destruction of
forests is that the beds of rivers are dry during part
of the year, and turn into torrents when the great
seasonal rains fall on the heights.   When the grass and
roots disappear on the heights of the mountains, when the
moss is dried up, the rains, no longer retained in their
courses, sweep over the drenched fields and cause sudden
floods which devastate the countryside.   The destruction of the woods, the absence of permanent springs,
and the frequency of torrents are three phenomena
closely connected.   Marsh notes, in his book "Man and
Nature," that with the disappearance of the forests the
precipitation becomes irregular, and snow and spring
rains, no longer absorbed by a porous, spongy, vegetable
soil, scour the frozen surface and then pour through the
valleys towards the sea in place of saturating a portion
of retentive earth and giving it a supply of dampness
for the perennial springs.   The earth, stripped of its
carpet of leaves, is crumbled and powdered by the plough,
since it is deprived of the small fibrous roots which hold
it together.   It is dried up and turned to dust by the
sun and wind.   The face of the earth is no longer a sponge
but dust; and the deluges, which the waters of heaven
pour on it, are precipitated along the slopes carrying in
suspension great quantities of earthy particles which
increase the mechanical force and erosive action of the
current.   This quantity, reinforced by the sand and

pebbles of the landslides, fills the beds of the streams, forcing them into new channels and obstructing their outlets.   The little streams, lacking their primary and regular supply and deprived of the protective shadows of the woods, evaporate during the summer and change into devastating torrents in the autumn and spring. From such causes there is a constant destruction of the highlands and a marked raising of the bottoms of the rivers and lakes.   Reclus, after observing that a thick wood is the best protection against all kinds of snowslides, notices that mankind disappears where the woods disappear; the axe of the woodsman no less than the sword of the conqueror has destroyed and decimated entire peoples.

§ 284. *Italian Writers Believe in the Control of Forest Lands.*   The necessity of control to preserve the springs and territorial substance is fully shown by Italian writers. Mengotti,[1] for example, says that when nature is not overcome, due to the imprudence of man, it reclothes itself of its own free will with a covering of various leafy plants on the heights, spurs, and flanks of the mountains.   This is surely the most efficacious means which it can adopt for retarding and arresting rain and snow, so that they cannot be precipitated all at once into the valleys, producing instantaneous and headlong rivers. A great forest holds an immense quantity of water with its roots and stumps, its bark, branches, leaves, and with all those marvelous means with which plants are furnished.   The density of the leaves, the cones of the pines and the fir, the endless number of branches increasing in size from the top of the trees downwards from tier to tier and from storey to storey, the roughness of the thick bark itself sometimes supplied with scales, the crevices, the gummy and sticky sap all are suited

[1] *Cf.* § 279 *ante.*

to put obstacles in the way of the flow of the water. Stoppani thinks that landslides are caused exclusively by subterraneous infiltration and circulation of water. Now woods in the first place hold together the loose earth by the intersection of their roots, in the second place the rain water is delayed in falling directly to the ground, which it cannot do except slowly through such a filter. In the other case it is natural that erosion gains power. Messadaglia has learnt some of the unbelievable effects of deforestation through the observation and concrete study of corresponding localities. Such, according to circumstances, are the washing away of water-sheds, the suppression of springs, the formation of torrents, the alteration in the course of the torrential rains, and the rising of the river-beds. If it is a question of stating the effects in determinate localities, you must understand that one must give attentive consideration to the place itself and the difficult comparison of it with other places in similar and different conditions, and with its prior state. Then from such a starting place one should enlarge the argument by the sum of meteoric and hydrographic conditions in an extended territory. The question becomes at the root very intricate, depending upon various local conditions. The solution in such hypotheses is not fully ascertainable and much less can it be raised to a general doctrine. Thus it is not possible to determine positively the influence of forests on the quantity and annual division of the rainfall without taking into account the proximity of vast evaporating basins and the degree of temperature, the prevailing winds, and the typographic structure of the surface of the earth. It may also be possible that the influence of the woods is affected by other factors. As to the action of forest vegetation on the division of the rain-water for the year or in general from one period to another, it is necessary to look at other determining causes, such as the temperature, winds, cosmic order of the soil, and difference in geographical latitude. As to the velocity of the flow, the condition of the soil, whether it be wooded or bare, is a ruling factor; the woods modify the absorption and decrease the speed of streams, especially along the water-sheds, to a relatively greater extent, the steeper the incline. In conclusion the geometric action of the forests, that is, their influence on the quantity and regulation of the rains, is only modifying, secondary, and particular in respect to those other causes which are called primary and general, because they have relation to the fundamental condition of the rain. Stronger and sometimes decisive is the action of the forest in regard to infiltration, although here too we must be on our guard against statements too universal and absolute.

§ 285. *The Regulation of Control is Difficult.* Admitted that for purposes of the regularity and conservation of the streams and of the territorial conformation, control should be established over forests situated on mountain sides, it is a question if it should be imposed and have the same extent and same general form for meteorological and hygienic reasons in woods situated on plains. Humboldt believes that the forests operate as refrigerators defending, as we have said,[1] the earth from the raging heat of the sun, increasing growth of the grass, and increasing with the multiplication of leaves such growths as are burnt up by the sun. Arago affirms that forests can in certain cases make the climate more mild, and in others produce a contrary effect. Gay-Lussac thinks that we cannot be positive about the real influence of woods on the climate of a country and that such a question is complicated and seems impossible or at

[1] *Cf.* § 381 *ante.*

least most difficult of solution. Boussingault observes that in Central America, in the same latitude, at the same height above sea level, and under conditions geographically identical, the forests cool invariably the climate. Becqueral cites that fact and explains it as Boussingault did, teaching that the vast influence of forests on the climate depends on their extent, the height and nature of the trees, the power of evaporation possessed by the leaves, their facility in heating or cooling, and the inherent qualities of the physical state of the soil and sub-soil. Forests form a defense, he adds, against low winds; such a defense is naturally proportionate to the height of the trees. We can point out that the wet air, containing miasmata, loses them in crossing a forest. Rigaud de Lille shows that there are certain regions in Italy where the interposition of the defense of the trees keeps fevers away, while the uncovered parts remain exposed to the infection. Marsh, in his remarks, of great weight as always, about the effect of deforestation in relation to meteorology, does not fail to state the great uncertainty that there is, but adds that hailstorms, almost always united with electric disturbances, seem to be of greater frequency and intensity in definite relation to the decrease of the forests. In such a diversity of opinions, which in particular cases may all be true, Messadaglia reaches the sensible conclusion that we should consider the question of the thermometric influence of forests from a scientific point of view *sub judice*. It is true that Arago, Gay-Lussac, Becqueral, and Marsh are, as we have seen, very far from an absolute and certain solution. As long as there is any doubt, the wise legislator cannot create a general and fixed control, on account of the influence of heat and cold, but should bring it about by a series of examinations of the particular regional conditions. He should conduct it in such a case as he has conducted it in respect to the rice fields. He should, that is, leave a large margin to the variable element of locality, where the control cannot be special and changeable, if he wishes to accomplish his purpose.

§ 286. *Control Should Not be Industrial.* Not a few believe that the control of forest land is necessary, no matter where it is situated, for the protection of the lumber industry. Now this view has had weight in the laws from the XVIIth Century onwards and seems to have maintained itself in our days by the increasing danger of the failure of wood for heating and building as a consequence of the great deforestation. But we do not think that the control founded on motives of industrial protection is just. As we are open adversaries of unbridled free will, we declare ourselves hostile to excessive State control. We wish the State to interfere only where it is manifest that individuals, working on their own account, would disregard the correlation of interests, which assures the long existence of society. Now this condition does not exist and cannot exist in relation to the production of lumber, because competition and freedom, applied to an industry, are the only means of obtaining the greatest production. Society will need lumber, and the business sense of the private citizen will supply this need by a sufficient and appropriate cultivation of the forests. The price of forest products increases from day to day and constitutes a growing impulse to forest industries besides being a guaranty of a settled business. It is true that the movements of the lumber market are not general and do not always follow the same direction and depend often upon local and changeable conditions, but it is none the less true that there is a notable increase in the price of forest products. To-day the woodland is markedly decreased in almost all parts of the world, and therefore its cultivation for exportation cannot fail to be lucrative, although sometimes the great expense of transportation and the competition of other countries reduce the gains not a little. It is, however, useful to observe that the control of forests on plains once taken away, the expense of transportation of wood is not in the last analysis as grave a difficulty as it would be if the wood had to descend from a mountain side. Let us imagine that with the system of personal interest and of freedom there can still be a certain lack of lumber. Can there not, for example, be introduced in the workshops materials which will take the place of wood, as anthracite, lignite, or peat, whose use could be made practical with but little expense and a few practical lessons? Neither can it be opposed to such ideas that it is not possible to satisfy great national interest, as the public marine service, railroads, and telegraphs, because abolishing the servitude of the "martellata," the modern States rendered inalienable a part of their forests and thus destined it to civil and military uses. It is sometimes affirmed that such reservations are not sufficient in certain occasions in the life of people, but it is not thinkable that the remaining private woods, be they within or without the national territory, cannot more or less supply the hypothetical lack.

§ 287. *Control, Based on Physical Harm, Does not Entail Indemnity.* If it is true that the State, as Beccaria teaches, should act in cases in which it is seen that the private interests will never or will too late harmonize with the public interest, it is necessary to conclude that control based on the consideration of economic order has no other logical reason for existence. The constant and great provision of forest material, of which Marco Balbi, a member of the Venetian Senate, speaks, should limit forest property only to prevent the harm resulting from deforestation to water courses, industries, agriculture, to geographic conformation, and in certain places to the health of the population. Every other limitation being unnecessary would be a violation of individual freedom in its relation to things. The necessary and rational limitations can be composed without any obligation of indemnity because it does not hinder the owner's use thereof but merely forbids its abuse, as a damage to the rights and interests of others. The control is purely negative, created to hinder the owner acting in a way harmful to society on his own land situated on mountain sides by deforestation or unsodding and in such terms of fact the conception of indemnity does not correspond to any principle of law.

§ 288. *Special Conditions of Mining Require Special Laws.* It is indubitably true that mining law, founded on the particular nature of this kind of extractive industry, should follow in the phases and be modified according to the development of the industry itself. When mines were merely holes in the soil, the property in them was considered as part of estate in the land, but when the mineral needed deep caves, a network of tunnels, pits, and galleries, it became little by little a property distinct from that of the super-soil. At first, when the industry was not progressive, the Roman law gave the mineral to the owner of the land; then when there had been some development, especially in the marble quarries, in the time of Constantine, it allowed the extraction of marble from another's territory.

§ 289. *History of Mining Law.* In the age after the fall of the Empire there arose clearly the same tendency in the industry as in its law. There was an epoch in which the industry was elementary and entirely superficial. In such an epoch, the right of the owner of the land controlled absolutely. When the industry began to demand large capital, the owner of the land recognized the freedom of the mine, keeping the power not only to control its development but also the right of entrance and supervision. Later these rights belonged to the feudal lord; the owner of the surface had his moiety in the output of the mine besides certain other quota and proportion at the mine's mouth. Regal power was substituted in the place of the power of the lord; the mine was truly part of the regalia; the State, which had eminent domain over the entire territory, granted out the use of the mine and directed its working and placed an impost on it. The owner of the land in this period had the same rights which he enjoyed through feudal legislation. Then the industry was transformed, the modern mine, a subterraneous world in which a whole population of laborers is employed, was born; the freedom of the mine began. The right to a mine was attributed to the discoverer and contractor, with the obligation of holding the owner of the land safe from harm. A State can no longer exercise royal prerogatives; it does not take part in mining as formerly, but determines by laws and positive recognition the rights of those who are interested therein, and intervenes to protect morals, policy, justice, and civilization in its exploitation. From such fugitive remarks on the historical development of mining and its law, the notion of the emancipation of mineral products from the soil is clear. Now we must see if such a tendency, which has been developing throughout history, conforms to reason.

§ 290. *Objections to the Emancipation of Mineral Property.* The followers of the system which attributes the mineral to the owner of the soil object in the first place that the area covered by the subsoil is a simple geometrical surface; that the tillable land, which is not limited to the first strata of vegetable earth, belongs to the agriculturists, and that the mineral is part of the cultivatable soil. The answer to this objection is not difficult. The surface is not separated from the subsoil, and is not a plane with length and breadth but no depth. When we speak of the surface, we mean as much of the subsoil as can be useful to the owner and can become material for his practical interest. We admit the impossibility of separating absolutely the surface and the subsoil, but it does not appear legally impossible that one man should be the owner of the surface and the first soil and another the owner of the cavities of the second crust. Such a state of affairs can be brought about by contract or will, also by the statutory regulation which recognizes in the owner of the soil the control of the mineral. On the other hand, we must remember that the limits of the surface are not always those of the minerals because the latter, according to the testimony of geologists, are irregular and peculiar in extent, with innumerable ramifications of veins. And science in its turn contributes always more to the separation of mineral property from the control of the soil, as becomes evident from the various methods used in ancient and modern mining: the ancient was shallow, and the modern sometimes very deep. They oppose in the second place the distinction of the two domains, on the ground that no one has a right to enter the land of another and that the owner of the land gets his mineral by the right of occupancy. As to the first part of such an objection we can note that the right of entering into the land of another for such work and discovery could be caused by a legal servitude established with equitable compensation in favor of the owner of the soil. There are, however, cases in which the search and discovery could be made without having to enter the land, but rather by exploring from one's own land under the other's at a depth, for example, of a thousand feet. As to the second part we can point out that the primitive or derivative methods of acquisition presuppose always knowledge and will. A mode of acquisition is a method of "posse" and that power demands "velle" which in turn demands the "nosse." How, therefore, can the owner of the land occupy in a true sense of the word a mine which he does not know of? There is no rational possibility of the control of the unknown or the undefined.

§ 291. *Title to Minerals is Not by Accession.* Opponents of the system of separation allege then the right of accession as determined by the modern laws, that is, in its widest sense, and the doctrine of treasure trove to aid the owner of the soil. As to the theory of accession, it takes no intelligence to see that the mineral is not a fruit; it is not something self-perpetuating. Neither is it found, as far as the use of the soil is concerned — a relation that every accession must have with its principal. We can also see that the value of the mineral much exceeds that of the land, and so it is very permissible to doubt if the soil be the principal. In respect to the theory of treasure trove, we must point out that we can draw no strong analogy to the question of minerals here, because the treasure is personalty and the mineral is not, and because the division into equal parts of the property in the treasure is ordered by the statute only when it be found by chance, but the mineral can be discovered and usually is discovered not by chance, but by virtue of constant study and patient experiment.

§ 292. *Title to Minerals Cannot be Proved by Roman "Fictiones."* Many invoke the authority of the Roman Law, according to which the scholiasts say that the owner of the soil is the owner of a column of air to heaven and of a column of earth to "infernus," but such statements are a hyperbole invented by Gino da Pistoia and have no foundation in the sources of Roman law, which teaches different limitations of the property right in regard to what is above and below the soil. Justinian, for example, says that the owner of a building cannot so build as to prevent the wind reaching the thrashing floor of his neighbor. A copper mine found in land after its sale belonged to the finder. "Neminem nec vendere nec excipere quod non sit et lapidicinas nullas esse nisi quæ appareant et cædantur," Labeo taught. Ulpian wrote on the subject of usufruct: "Inde est quæsitum, an lapidicinas vel cretifodinas vel aredifodinas ipse instituere possit? Et puto etiam ipsum instituere posse si non agri partem necessarium huic rei occupaturus est. Proinde venas quoque lapidicinarum et huiusmodi metallorum inquirere poterit. Ergo et auri et argenti et sulpheris et æris et ferri et cæterorum fodinas vel quas paterfamilias instituit exercere poterit vel ipse instituere si nihil agricolturæ nocebat." Constantine admitted the free right to quarry marble, and there was recognized by the other emperors a right to a tenth in favor of the owner of the soil. In other words the miner could give indemnity for harm and not recognize the right of the owner of the surface. Rights for the Roman jurisconsults extended only so far as they were useful; when the utility was lacking the right ended. I can force my neighbor to cut the branches of his tree which extend over my land from a height of more than fifteen feet. I can use my right if, in sinking the well in my land, I interrupt a water course which supplies my neighbor, but I cannot tap this course at my pleasure and waste the water. The owner can follow the vein of metal

from his land and acquire property in it "jure occupa-
tionis," but not because of his property in the soil.

§ 293.   *Property in the Air.*   There can be no
doubt that atmospheric space like the soil and subsoil is an object of private property, because the use
and enjoyment of the soil would not be possible
unless the owner had the right to enjoy the space
above.   It is quite impossible to say that atmospheric
space is not substantial, is not a thing, and does not,
therefore, constitute material for property, because it is
a form of concrete space and as such has objective
reality which is useful and valuable.   And it is inexact
to consider the atmosphere as a common object not susceptible to private ownership, because common objects
are incapable of exclusive ownership in their totality, but
not in their parts.   The sea is a common object and yet
it is reducible to property in the parts near the shore.

§ 294.   *Property should be Limited by Practical Interest.*
Neither is it true that the subsoil, not lending itself
to common use, is a "res communis."   It can rather be
regarded as a "res nullius," and as such is capable of
ownership.   The general principle is this: Property in
the air and the subsoil is one with the property of the soil.
Whoever acquires the property in the soil acquires it in
the atmosphere above and the earth beneath.   There
is no need of a special occupancy for either.   But
property in the atmosphere and the subsoil is limited as
any other property by the needs of social coexistence
and the activity and the general interests of man.
Private ownership should work for the good of law
and is justified by that idea.   This is not attained
when a claim is exorbitant, or contains elements of
power not necessary for its exercise, or does not accord
with the conception of the wise distribution of goods
and rational moderation therein, which Vico teaches.

This shows the social limit of private property, which is the activity developing as a practical interest of another human subject. The activity of man cannot be separated from the good, the useful, and the advantageous, as these things cannot be understood without the activity of which they are the terms. Ihering declares clearly the practical interest of the owner of the soil in the column of air and subsoil. His practical interest in the column of air is that no one shall take away from him the air, light, or rain, hinder him from building, or make him give up his position on his land on account of pestilential odors, smoke, and dust, but he has no right to stop birds or balloons passing through the aerial space. The Roman jurisconsults, who had an exquisite sense of the realities of life, never exaggerated the right of the owner and maintained it on the base of practical interests of which they had an admirable intuition. Practical interest is the limit also of the owner's right in the subsoil, and therefore he has no right to hinder another from gaining from the subsoil without harm to himself any utility profitable to him. Such utility is not referable to the actual continual and ordinary purpose of the land, to its cultivation or regular use, and is without the sphere of the practical interest of its owner. It is not reasonable to consider that the possibility of a different enjoyment is a practical interest, arguing from the present state of technical and industrial means, because in such an hypothesis the discoverer would only rarely have the right to the minerals which, in the greater number of cases, can be enjoyed by the owner of the soil if he takes advantage of existing scientific and technical means. In practical interests, thus defined, it is not the cause of the discoverer which needs a broad interpretation, but rather that of the owner of the soil. There is a strong presump-

tion that it is more just to give the former the ownership
of the mine.   The mineral discovered cannot belong to
the owner of the soil, either by the theory of labor or
personality.   According to the theory of labor the
property should be placed where the individual activity
lies and the owner of the soil who has not been active
cannot be the owner of the mine. It has been the activity of the discoverer, and to him the mineral should belong.
Starting out with the conception of individual personality which develops in things and stamps on them its
mark, making them its own, the same conclusion is
reached, because the discoverer and not the owner of
the soil has been active in the mine.

§ 295. *Economics Favor the Freedom of the Mine.*
As to the economic reasons in aid of the present
thesis one must see that Dunoyer, in his book "De la
Liberté du Travail," contradicts himself when he looks
upon mining as an industry separate and distinct
from agriculture and then attibutes it to the owner
of the soil.   Sella, a competent authority, shows that the
cultivation of the mine demands a strict unity of conception, and therefore the mine cannot be divided like
land.   The mining industry encounters many financial difficulties in making deep tunnels where the property is much scattered.   With the increase of depth the
expenses increase; therefore from the larger mines,
conducted with intelligence and economy, there are not
as large returns as are offered by ordinary industries.
Let there be added that the pretension of the owner of the
soil to an aliquot share of the mineral lessens the depth
of the mine and has no regard for the future.   Besides,
experience proves that the pretension of the owners of
the soil to be representatives of the State, the presumption that their wealth is more staple, their small love of
progress and their fear of destroying the productivity

of the soil hinder the development of the mineral
industry in countries in which the system of the independence of mines is not recognized. Neither can we
hope that the greater part of these troubles would
disappear with the association of the mine owners,
because such associations meet great practical difficulties, and it is inexpedient to create difficult conditions,
trusting to conquering them through the genius and
ability of individuals. From such ideas, which correspond to the real state of affairs and the special conditions of the development of the industry, comes the action
of the State at the present day. A State should remove
the obstacles to the industry, should promote the discovery of minerals, should aid the industry by geographical descriptions, should create statutes to prohibit
the present generation from taking all the mineral, should
govern the employment of women and children in mines,
should establish school regulations, should limit the working day of laborers of this class, should enforce precautions of safety and hygiene to avoid the deleterious
action of gases and explosions, should promote charitable and pensioning societies among the workmen, and
should facilitate the transportation of mineral products.
But it should not do more than protect the industry
and make technical rules. It should decide questions
of property in mines, but with the object of such
decision it should not create a property but merely
recognize and define it, as the decree of inheritance of
the Austrian Code recognizes and defines a preëxisting
law.

CHAPER VIII

INDUSTRIAL PROPERTY

THE MERCHANDISE OF LABOR AND ITS PRICE. — WORK AS
PROPERTY. — UNIONS AND STRIKES. — THE INDUSTRIAL JURY. —
THE OWERSHIP OF CAPITAL AND PROPERTY. — COLLECTIVISM
AND MUTUALISM. — THE THEORY OF MARX. — CRITICISM OF COL-
LECTIVISM AND OF THE THEORY OF MARX. — TRUSTS.

§ 296. *Industrial Property is Important.* Industrial
property arises in manufacturing industries. It finds
its justification in the chief base of property, that
is, in the principle of personality. It deserves a special
study not only because of the great importance it has
acquired in modern times but because it is made the
object of grave objections and criticisms which fundamentally are aimed at private ownership in general.
Here, as in similar discussions, it is necessary to remember not a few difficult economic theories in order
to understand and examine the facts juristically. Law
is always a proportion, a rule, a measure which attaches
diversely according to the nature of the object to which
it is applied. The matter in our case is essentially
economic.

§ 297. *Fundamentally the Interests of Capital and
Labor are One.* A manufacturing industry presupposes
labor and its instruments. The instruments of labor
are primitive and derivative; the primitive are natural
forces, the derivative are comprehended by capital.
Between labor and capital there is not and cannot be
an original and natural opposition, because the former

is the capital of to-morrow, and the latter is the labor of yesterday, as we have said more than once.[1]   In the abstract, therefore, labor which robs capital robs itself, and if labor is the father of capital, capital in its turn nurtures labor and becomes its patron and guide. In concrete, the interest of him who demands labor is to acquire it at the lowest price, and the interest of him who offers it is to sell it as dear as he can. There occurs, therefore, the same struggle as can be seen in every active exchange between consumer and producer, since one wants the lowest and the other the highest price.   Furthermore, the conditions of exchange can be good for one contracting party and bad for the other.   What causes the greatest harm to labor depends not upon the egoism of the capitalists but upon the poverty of the workman who, with a large family to support, saves little or nothing.   The competition of those who offer labor reduces the price, and the decrease in wages exerts a sinister influence on the conditions of the workman.   But the price of labor differs from other sales in this: that the vendor of labor is bound to his goods while the vendor of other objects is separated from them.   Whence it follows that the price of labor touches the workman directly, in that it restricts him if it decreases, and extends his needs if it goes up.   It diminishes or promotes the development of his life and morals.   In this sense alone the workman is bound to his property in labor. He does not become a means or a part of the personality of the master, as was the ancient belief.   Furthermore, the workman, at least as an individual without coalition, cannot in crises withdraw the offer of labor in order to keep the price up, because if he does not work he dies of hunger.   On the other hand the ordinary

[1] *Cf.* § 262 *ante.*

vendor in such an event lessens, suspends, and abandons production without suffering therefrom.

§ 298. *Labor is Merchandise.* Some writers on this subject do not admit that labor is an object of exchange, alleging that it is an agent of production consisting of human activity, and not a product susceptible of accumulation. They hold that the hiring of labor lacks the character of a true contract because the workman is forced to sell his labor if he does not wish to starve, while the capitalist is free to employ the workman or not. They have not considered that the conception of an agent or factor of production in general is not repugnant to that of an object of exchange. In fact, both the capital and the agent or factor of production are merchandise. Labor is not properly a part of man but is the exercise of his activity over the forces of nature regulated by the laws of least resistance, the universal tendency of entities to accomplish the greatest result with the least expense. Man is not the instrument or coefficient of production, but the subject and end. Nature is the object and labor a living bond between man and the outside world. Labor as the activity of the person is not really merchandise. It becomes such, not in its potentiality and internal extent, but as it develops and manifests itself in separate operations and definite ends. Not the entire personal activity, confusable with the person and inalienable, becomes merchandise by the partial and temporary exercise thereof. In this meaning labor has a value of exchange. It is reducible to money and becomes part of one's estate. Neither is labor, in one sense, alone incapable of accumulation, because there are objects which are in the same condition; for example, a fresh egg or a strawberry, to which nobody denies the character of merchandise. It is true that a capitalist is free not to ask for the work, but only on condition that he does

not employ his capital; if he wishes to make profits
from his wealth he must have workmen; — only the
capitalist can wait and take his leisure better than the
workman.

§ 299. *Price of Labor is Twofold, the Current and
Natural.* The price of labor is twofold, current and
average. The current is determined by the offer and demand; the average is a point toward which the oscilla-
tions of the other tend, and represents the tenor of life,
that is, the sum of satisfactions, among which is the
accumulation of capital to which the working class is
habituated and which it does not think it can renounce
without degradation. The tenor of life grows with time
and comprehends new advantages which at first the
workman did not think it possible to attain. The
current wage tends to become the average, not being
able to mount too high because of competition. Neither
can it descend below the absolutely necessary wage,
because the workman would not have means to live.
But it is not right to believe that an increase of
workmen necessarily produces a reduction of wages because such an increase can well be coincident with a
rapid development of the industry, in which case there
occurs the phenomenon of an increase of workmen and
wages. On the other hand it is undeniable that with
economic and civil progress the efficiency of moral restraints which lead to foresight and in which the intellectual faculties are predominant, whose development is not
in direct ratio to the power of generation, is more emphasized. Statistics show that in the more progressive nation
there is also more wealth, greater population, and higher
prices. It is true that the price of goods has increased but
it is not less true that wages are higher than they were in
the past. The famous "iron-bound" law of wages by
which these tend to diminish to the simple expense of

production of labor is not as iron-bound as Lassalle and the later socialists say. The measure of prices is bound up with the measure of production and the measure of wages depends on the demand for work and the demand for work depends upon the quantity of capital. The quantity of capital depending on the accumulated production of goods and the demand for them, the quantity of production has its origin in the medial productivity of labor. With increased production the wages should go up and not down. The "iron-bound" law is such no longer in the face of the present organization of unions, which not only prevent the reduction of wages but even demand that the workman be given the greatest amount possible in the given economic situation. We must not forget that the increased production is of greatest interest both to the employer and the workman. The first must understand that good wages sustain the physical forces and awake intellectual qualities in the workmen, resulting in better labor. The second should remember that to limit the production entails great harm upon them, since with a decrease in the demand for work wages go down. On the other hand, if the work is more productive, that is, more intense and rapid, production increases and the demand for labor goes up. On the other hand, the working day, becoming more intense, cannot fail to be shortened. The increase in wages and the subsequent amelioration of the conditions of the workmen are notably accompanied by a general and marked increase in production. The associations of workmen effectively aid the raising of wages and are most useful when production is tending to increase. When production is not increasing an increase in wages is not possible, because there is a minimum profit beyond which the capitalistic employer will not go. In these cases the unions do not gain their object and do grave harm to the interests

of the workmen. And here, too, it is well to note that
the demand for a product is not always directly in proportion to the demand for labor, as in the case where the
product is already made and in that of the ceasing or de-
creasing of the demand for some luxury and the beginning or increase in the demand for some other. In this
last hypothesis capital leaves one industry and takes up
another, and one cannot say *a priori* whether work
is increased or not.

§ 300. *There is a Property in Labor.* Work from
a juristic aspect is always property. It is a primitive property, if considered in its potentiality as
the activity of a man tending to the production of
wealth, because a person is master of himself and his
capacities and relations. It is an acquired property in
the exercise of his acts in that it makes something of
a different nature from that of other salable articles.
Work has its title in the principle of the inviolability of
the person and his possessions; the contract for work
merits respect as every other contract in which the use
of property is brought into play. For if it is in good faith
and without breach of the freedom of contract, it is
valid. The economic law of supply and demand, which
determines the current price of labor, and the approach
of this to the average price show in the abstract; then
there is full knowledge and freedom of exchange, the
principle of justice. Justice means proportion, equality,
equation, — a conception found in the economic laws
regarded in their ideality. In fact, the demand shows
the utility of a thing. The offer represents the power
of acquisition, and the point at which the two combine
is their centre of balance, their equality and equation.
We can see such a point in respect to labor. In
the case of a large offer of workmen, there is not a
bare living and the satisfaction of the most urgent needs

which they want, but all the needs of life always
tend to increase. Of this, Turgot and even Ricardo
have, in their day, given a clear notion. Labor is always
property in every form of remunerative system, even
in the simplest division of products of hunting and
fishing by lot. Then come wages, the true transaction
between the workmen, who desire safety and immediate
pay, and the capitalist, who desires his time free. The
system of wages has two defects. It is founded on a
time system and is not payment according to the
quantity and quality of the labor. Thus it divides the
workman and the investor. Work, according to amount
done, possible in cases of uniform operation and of
divisible products, stimulates the activity of the workmen to the advantage of the business. It is the most
perfect plan, but is applicable with little difficulty only
in those industries where the work has a great importance
in comparison with the fixed capital. The law should
recognize all the conditions and then should help and
promote the most suitable remunerative system.

§ 301. *Unions are Based on the Property Right in
Labor.* From the conception of property in work we
come logically to the right of the workmen to unite in a
pacific manner not harmful to the freedom of others and
to act in concert in order to increase their wages. Strikes
and coalitions of workmen form a kind of rarification
of labor because the workmen, trusting to the common
right of association, withdraw the supply at once and,
stopping the sale in detail, await the time when this
course shall have raised their wages. The workmen in
this instance do what every merchant does to sell his
goods at the highest price to those who have need of
them. The "International Association of Workmen"
recognizes that strikes are contrary to economic principles, increasing the antagonism between capital and

labor, but believes that during the existent organization of society they are opportune means to save the pay of the workmen from the effect of the tyranny of capital and to incite the indigent classes to reform the laws and social institutions. We should remember that the "International" has a plan of new birth, attainable through the famous social liquidation, which cannot be obtained without inspiring the proletariat with hatred against society; to be attained by raising agitations, suffering, and misery, the fatal and only consequence of strikes. In this the coalitions, whether they be "trades-unions" or "gewerkvereine," differ from the "International," because the unions have ordinarily no philosophic or economic program of regeneration. Although they struggle against capital, it is not to destroy it and substitute artificial combinations, but merely to ameliorate the conditions of the workmen. The means possessed by the unions, without breach of law, are only mutual help and coalition, the first defensive and the second offensive.

§ 302. *History of Unions.* A strike is one of the results of the unions. A union cannot be found in classical antiquity except as a commercial monopoly, because, all labor being slave labor, wages took no part in the arts and industries. But in the Middle Ages when labor began to be emancipated, then there arose a possibility of industrial coalitions, to which the penalty of the Roman law for commercial monopolies was applied, which made an industry a part of the State and took away the determination of prices and wages from the decision of the individuals. Then a new age dawned, and together with the abolition of apprenticeship came the freedom of labor, which ceased to be a governmental possession and became a natural right. Freedom of labor entailed the juristic recognition of the union which could no longer be considered as criminal. But the French Revolution was afraid of every kind of association because it feared to see the guilds and old privileges reëstablished. It did not, therefore, look upon coalition as a right. From that time on the crime of which we speak was not based upon the usurpation of a public power, but on the union or coalition. This fear, however, disappeared entirely in the course of years and was changed to trust and confidence, because the State on the one hand at last understood that the progress of time had rendered the reinstatement of guilds impossible, and on the other, turned the spirit of association to its great advantage. This conception has eliminated the act we are discussing from the category of crimes in almost all the civilized nations.

§ 303.   *Unions are Legal.* A union is not illegal, because the act of temporary association of many people is not criminal in itself; neither can the right to use such means to raise the rate of wages be illegal.   In order to hold the contrary it would be necessary to show that every coalition, however temporary, is against the law and that there is no property in labor, which would imply a complete denial of all modern civil progress.   But, say the enemies of the freedom of union, the true foundation of such a crime does not consist in its elements studied apart, but in their sum and consequence, which can be reduced generally to moral duress, the disturbance of the laws of offer and demand, and public disorder.   It is curious that among those who reason thus is Proudhon, who affirms that a union is an association for violence against social liberty and is a violation of the economic protection of the State.   The alleged duress, however, intended as a limitation of another's rights, does not exist, as there is nothing forbidden to the employer that is allowed the operatives. Liberty is complete when by the side of the coalition of laborers we can place that of the masters. In this case we can see a true equality of rights. To the other objection we cannot say that free coalition disturbs the regular flux and reflux, offer and demand, for this is not true, as we will see. The workmen's leagues operate either on population or capital to bring about a raise in wages. If they operate on population they should try to restrain the offer of work; but this is not practicable without threats, violence, or fraud, and on this score is within the rigor of the law. The trades unions and the "Sessions of the International" give us examples of such excesses. If these leagues influence invested capital, which can be increased without stopping or retarding the development of industry, they do not break the law of prices, which tend to approximate distributive justice. But the conditions of the workmen always affect the circulating capital, promoting an increase in wages by the increased prices of other things. In this case the increase of wages falls upon the consumer and the economic law is in no ways broken, because cheapness is desirable when it grows from a less expenditure of force and not from a stint of wages. Furthermore, if in the determination of prices there are other causes, separate from the principle of supply and demand, a coalition can gain control of them; an example of such causes foreign to supply and demand is custom. We must note that when the workmen's league does not gain its object, the law of offer and demand is not altered, but resists its unreasonable claim, as Del Guidice said in his book, "Coalizioni Industriali."

§ 304. *Unions cannot be Forbidden because of their Tendency to Illegal Acts.* As to disorder, let us recognize that strikes too often produce fatal consequences for all, especially if wide in extent and long in duration. It is only necessary to read the description of some strikes in England, especially one of those which was followed by a "lockout," to feel a deep abhorrence of them. But confessing the damage derivative from strikes, we must consider whether a union can be declared illegal on the single ground of its possible harm. It appears to us that the question when put in such terms is easily answered, because it is clear that the penalty must always refer to a violation of law, which does not exist in the workmen's league itself, as we have briefly shown. Neither can we continue to call a strike, unaccompanied by violence, a breach of the peace, but must reserve this (as the criminal lawyers teach us) for threats and violence. If intimidation accompanies a strike and entails the use of force against those who will not strike or against the employers, the criminal law should be invoked. Every workman who is guilty of fraud should also be punished. But to our way of thinking molestation and obstacles, without the characteristics of real violence, which are used as a kind of indirect force, should not be punishable, since it is not possible to determine such facts accurately, and since it can thus render the freedom of coalition illusory. Penal action should always be taken by the government to avoid a state of intimidation which often accompanies a contest between manufacturers and their employees, who are sure of impunity from violence because of their great numbers. Law should also deprive of legal effect any penal clause enacted between an employer and his workmen to assure the observance of agreements of a union, because everybody has the right to leave an association when he believes it contrary to his interest.

§ 305. *Industrial Jurisprudence.* Freedom of association is intimately connected with industrial jurisprudence. There is no reason why employers and
operatives should not have their disputes decided
by technical judges and not by the regular courts,
which are bound by unavoidably slow rules of procedure and the habit of strictly legal criticism. The
disputes are often due to mistakes or momentary exas-
peration; whence it follows that they can be amicably
settled by a committee. It can constitute a court of
special jurisdiction, it can exercise a summary and
executive jurisdiction in causes which are brought
before it by the consent of the parties without affecting
the jurisdiction of the regular courts, or it can act
with only advisory powers, leaving a right of appeal
to the regular judiciary.

§ 306. *Divisions of Industrial Jurisdiction.* The committee may be elected by the workmen and the
employers, but it should be presided over by a dis-
interested person, possibly chosen by the government.
It is a good plan to elect the workmen's representative
by the employers and the employers' representative
by the workmen in order to establish a closer relation
between the two classes. It is necessary, however,
to distinguish the character of the disputes, as it may
relate to the execution of a contract already concluded
between the employer and his workmen, or to objects
and conditions of an economic and not juristic character. Arbitration and mediation are more suited for
the settlement of the former than the latter. A judgment
is always unfair and tyrannical which, with jurisdiction only over a particular subject-matter, imposes general conditions which demand the fullest
knowledge of the circumstances. The principle of liberty
of work and capital is fundamentally denied by this

kind of judgment, which is equivalent to the legal determination of prices, wages, and interests, and suffers from
the same defects. Industrial arbitration will undergo
a large development in the future if approved by the
larger associations of workmen, and recognized by the
statutes. In this case the committee has great authority,
because their office of settling controversies of an economic
nature is the effect of common confidence and trust. Here
is the substantial difference between the "Prudhommes"
of France, who conciliate and define particular controversies, and the English Courts of Chancery, that
conciliate and define questions of common interest.

§ 307. *Profit is Like Rent.* Profit is the remuneration of capital as wages are the compensation of
mechanical labor. Profit is the part which belongs to
him who invests in an industry, carried on at his risk,
a capital that is his or that he has borrowed. It is
the rent of the capitalistic employer. Wages and
interest are determined by precedent agreements; not
so the profit. Workmen and lenders of the money cannot be forced to make restitution of their wages or
interest. An employer, when the undertaking fails,
cannot break his contracts with third parties, alleging
a right to remuneration for his capital. Profit is also
a property because it is the price of the work of him
who founds and directs a business. It pays him for the
sacrifice of his savings and is a compensation for his
risk. In it we find the effect of the action of the person
over animated things, by which ownership is created.
Profit is current or average. The first is determined
by the laws of supply and demand of the capitalistic
employers; the second is the sufficient payment for the
labor and risks of those who have rendered the carrying on
of the industry possible by the investment of their money.
Interest and profit are justified by the principle of social

utility. Rae says that interest is just because capital is socially useful and because the owner of capital in applying it to productive purposes renders society a service, the value of which is measurable by its social utility. The service which the capitalist renders to production is as indispensable as that rendered by the workmen; the justice of interest is based on the solid foundation on which the justice of wages is based. Workmen cannot produce by labor alone without materials and instruments precisely as the capitalist cannot produce without labor. And capitalists have need of a recompense which will induce them to save precisely as workmen have need of it in order to come to a resolution to work. The employer exercises a social function inasmuch as he unites and directs the elements of production, thereby satisfying the needs of the consumer. He offers means for work, he creates relations with foreign countries, he foresees all the events which can occur to hinder production, and he provides for them in time. His services to society are invaluable. What could the State do in his place? In public administration the spirit of enterprise and the keen interest to economize are lacking. Capitalists are more adventurous and more economic directors than public officials. With public control the numbers of parasites and intermediary agents against whom the socialists fight would be manifoldly increased. The production would be less and slower, the saving would greatly diminish, because no one makes self-sacrifices on another's behalf.

§ 308. *The Socialists and Private Property.* Modern socialists attack private property in capital vigorously and think its profits criminal and unjust. Among them Marx distinguishes himself particularly, because he has made the most powerful and coherent criticism of capital. Lassalle differs from Marx in his economic principles, considering the question as it concerns the conditions in Germany, while Marx treats the discussion from a higher, that is, from an international point of view. Marx and Lassalle differ greatly from the French socialists, for example, Proudhon and Blanc, not falling into those superficial abstract theories of imaginary idealism so slightly reinforced by scientific discovery. German socialism is eminently logical, based upon the latest analysis of facts and doctrine, and armed by all the means of erudition and modern science. Marx belongs to the Hegelian Left and follows Feuerbach, who transforms absolute idealism into humanism, eliminating every transcendental principle and all the fantastic projections of the human essence. The humanism of Feuerbach is materialistic because man, who is the beginning of everything, is nothing in his essence but body. Principles are gods and must follow man's destiny, allowing him absolute freedom, since they are his creations. The dissolution of theology into anthropology is united in the sphere of thought with the transformation of monarchy into democracy in the field of politics. The State should be humanized; it is a means for the well-being of everyone. There is nothing above man, neither superhuman beings nor consecrated persons, nor is there a person who is more than man or one who is less. Humanism cannot lend itself to collectivism because only social man is the true human essence, and the individual must bow before him, as Rae notes. Marx regards humanism as the beginning of the political and industrial reorganization which will be attained when the universal proletariat becomes an irresistible force. Lassalle, too, is Hegelian, and is disposed like Marx to recognize the law of natural historical evolution of which the French Utopists have not the slightest notion.

§ 309. *The Old Theory of Socialism.* The theory of Marx, with which we are now concerned, is closely connected with collectivism and mutualism. The collectivists and mutualists say that in the same manner as in the natural world inorganic matter (mechanical, physical, or chemical) is the determinate base of organic matter (vegetable, animal, or cerebral), so in the social world which used to be regarded as the last cognitive step of the material world, the development of economic questions has always been and continues to be a determinate base for all systems of philosophy, religion, sociology, and politics. According to them, society to-day is divided into two classes: the one is that of the oppressors, who live like Sybarites, having rights and not duties; the other is formed of the oppressed, of the miserable proletariat, destined to constant labor without recompense or legitimate hope of it, surrounded only by restraints, called, for politeness, duties. The revolutions of a century ago have substituted the power of gold for the power of chivalry, and for the old feudal aristocracy the new, but not less iniquitous oppression of the middle class. We must destroy the tyranny of capital and guarantee the triumph of labor, an end unobtainable without the universal union of agricultural and industrial associations, which union will undertake to fight the existing slavery, whose stronghold is matrimony and law. It will proclaim anarchy and reconstruct the society on two new foundations, — collective property in the instruments of labor, and the absolute and general equivalence of functions. Arable land, forests, quarries, mines, canals, ships, railroads, telegraphs, factories, and mills will be subject to a collective control because instruments of economic activity. The equivalence of functions will be brought into existence with the exchange of the products regulated by the cost and the value of the material needed for their production, because services, being equivalent, must necessarily be gratuitous. There will be no difference in profit between one producer and another, and the principle of one for all and all for one will be the rule. But in order to attain the accomplishment of the social liquidation there will have to be many unions and grave and extensive strikes over the abolition of national character, which will lead to the universal unity of workmen. On the other hand, obligatory free education, complete and common for both sexes, is intended to promote the equality of nature between individuals. Such was the program of the socialist of a year or so ago.

§ 310. *The Socialists' Theory of To-day.* Schäffle, in a book of to-day, "Die Quintessenz der Socialmus," shows the secondary differences between school and school and party and party. Everyone knows that in the bosom of socialism itself there are discordant varieties as in every other system. The object of the whole socialistic movement is the fundamental transformation of the actual social economy. The mother idea is collective property in place of private property in all means of production; that is, farms, forests, factories, and mills. The other principal objects are the social organization of labor in place of the capitalistic community, the creation of corporate organism and a social direction of production, the public division of common labor on the base of collective property in the materials of social work, a redivision of products of every kind among the laborers with regard to the quantity and value of each one's activity. According to this idealistic theory, the producers would be laborers and not capitalists, because the capital would become collective and the producers would work using the means belonging to society, and there would

be no more employers and employees, but rather pro-
fessional workers with equal duties towards society,
their paymaster.   In consequence, there would be no
more private income in the form of surplus values, but
instead remunerations due exclusively to labor measured
by quantity and quality. Those who render society
services of the greatest utility, such as judges, those employed in public service, professors, artists, and thinkers,
would receive a part of the national production in proportion to the function of their work. The means
necessary to each kind of production would be determined by a directive committee.   Social industry would
be regulated by such determination of public organisms.
The occasional decrease or excess of products would
demand a reserve in anticipation thereof or a deposit
in social storehouses.

§ 311.   *Karl Marx.* In his book "Das Kapital,"
Marx starts out with economic principles of the most
abstract economists. Galiani said that work is the
only cause which gives value to anything, that value
is measured by the expenditure of work, and that
by its duration the value of a product is equal to
the food consumed by the workmen during the time
of production. Beccaria says that value is measured by work. Later Adam Smith and Ricardo admitted that the sole source and measure of value is
work.   Locke and almost all the economists have placed
the origin of property in labor. Bastiat shows that
service is interchangeable with service. Now Marx presupposes all these conceptions of the orthodox economic
school as undeniably true, and sees the consequences
with the greatest logic. The fundamental postulate
on which his system is based is: In every sale there is
a value of use and exchange. The value of use regards
the needs which the product is destined to satisfy; the

value of exchange corresponds to the interchange of products, to their power of acquisition. In primitive society the value of use prevails; in a society which has advanced to the basis of a division of labor the value of exchange predominates. Labor creates the value of exchange, which, however, contains also some value of use. The labor or use of human force, which accompanies the consumption of nervous, muscular, and cerebral substance, is what is common to all value, and is the measure of value of exchange. Labor, the creator of value, is what is socially necessary and what society must pay for. With such notions Marx carries out the theories of Adam Smith and Ricardo. If the steam spinning jenny produces in the same number of hours thirty times as much silk as a weaver, he must work a month to make the silk which will only have the value of one day's labor. Labor is measured easily in terms of labor by its length, and therefore if the space of time is equal in two occupations it should have an equal reward. But to whom by right does this value of exchange belong? He who produces and sells wants his recompense. He claims that by his industry he has created a real excess of value. The real excess of value is the effect of labor for it has the virtue of creating a value of exchange greater than the object alone has. Capital does not create value; the factory reproduces the value it destroys; a machine produces no value, but transmits its own by labor to objects which it makes. If there was not a real excess of value generated by labor no one would take the trouble to work. But that which for the independent workmen is a constant source of new value gives no reward to the wage-earner. His property in his labor is stolen from him. The capitalist makes his value out of his employees, paying for the labor the simple expenses of production, which are less than its utility. The capitalist gives the workmen the price of their useful forces, whose value is determined by its intensity and function and is equal to the cost of the food necessary for the life of the laborers and their families, and he takes all the surplus value. He gains six hours out of the twelve hours of the workmen's labor, for they should work only six hours to earn wages sufficient for their support. The workmen sell their energy for a Mexican dollar in order to produce a continuous work of six hours, and for such a price give labor for twelve hours. In this lies the secret of the extraordinary increase in capital, with the injustice and tyranny from which society cannot escape except by the abolition of private property and the creation of a collectivism, based on the division of labor.

§ 312. *Communism is a Mark of the Existence of Extremely Different Classes.* Communism and socialism are always born from the appearance of extreme opulence and poverty, from the failure of a large middle class, from the wide gulf between capital and labor, by which it appears easy to get rich in inverse ratio to personal merit, from the alteration in feelings of justice caused by continual revolutions, and from the claims of lower classes aroused by democratic constitutions. Roscher, in "System der Finanzwissenschaft," shows that the prevalence of communism and socialism in the times of Greek decadence, of corruption in the Roman Republic in the periods of reform, and even to-day, is the result of such conditions. It is necessary, therefore, to scan closely the particular characters of the Utopias of our times, to reflect on the great knowledge of rights attained by an incomplete study and on the rapidity of propaganda to-day. And, on the other hand, we must also remember that the forbidden and tyrannical guilds have not separated the interest of the worker from that of the employer, however much they have been the cause of the infinite evils of to-day and the slowness of the development of trade. Here labor has prevailed, depending more upon the excellence of the art than on fortune, being advanced from disciple to the grade of master. A corporation given a free foot for the benefit of human beings, great production results and two distinct classes appear, one furnishing the means of production, that is, the capital, the other deprived sometimes of necessities even and deep in want. It is natural that such a noticeable difference between the two classes should cause jealousies and finally bring about a reaction more or less violent. Such reaction is the origin of modern socialism, whose errors are explicable as all similar errors as due to the unsatisfied needs of humanity.

§ 313. *Modern Collectivism Considers Economics the Base of Civilization.* The principle with which the modern collectivists are inspired is not true because they confuse the conception of the simple condition of development with the more complex conception of a determinate base or incentive. Let us recognize with Littré and with the others that economic well-being is the necessary condition for scientific religious and political progress, but not that it is the motive of such progress, which is thought, that has been busy, in history passing from mute times to the mythical age, and from the days of the heroes to the time in which the mind considers everything for itself. Certainly the stomach is an indispensable organ, a prerequisite of mental and spiritual feelings, but it is not the cause of the sublime flights of genius or deeds of heroism. That the spirit is the motive power of the economy of peoples and States is proved by considering the influence of knowledge, faith, and politics on labor. Science is

substituting the activity of nature for the labor of man
more and more, and celebrates, therefore, every day
the discoveries of important processes; numerous
victories of mind over matter. Christian faith revealed
the principle of individual personality which, together
with the conception of society, is clearly the foundation
of economic science. Now there is no doubt that for
the greater number of collectivists and socialists, if not
for all of them (for there are some of them Christians),
Buddhism, in which every activity is absorbed and
everyone is annulled, should be placed before Christianity. Did not the celebrated Bakunim in his letter
written to Massini at the instigation of the Central
Committee of London say, accepting the accusation of
atheism and materialism, that we are poor individuals
who, like waves, rise to be quickly scattered in the
immense ocean of collective life? Finally we must
reflect that political liberty, taking root in the customs
of a people and extending its sphere, cannot fail to
generate economic liberty, although the development of
one is not contemporaneous with that of the other, as
we have seen by the recent experiences of the American
and French laws. We must remember that America,
which has a democratic form of government, has adopted
protection in foreign commerce, and that France of
the Second Empire, if it was liberal in commerce, was
autocratic in politics.

§ 314. *Capital and Labor are Not Fundamentally
Antagonistic.* The war to the knife begun against
capital in the name of the disinherited cause of labor
is absurd, because originally capital and labor were
one. And it is obvious that with the multiplication
of capital, labor is increased, and with the diminution
of the former the latter is destroyed. On the other
hand the grave evil produced by the present system

of the distribution of wealth, by which the employers
grow richer and richer while the workmen continue to
live in poverty, can be eliminated by the diffusion of
the capital and property. Let this be made in such
a way that the workmen be trained to become possessors of the capital, and the question of pauperism
will have begun its journey towards a distant solution.
The coöperative method aims at this purpose in various
ways but within clear limits, and is animadverted against
by the collectivists, who say that coöperation is the
mother of petty tyrannies and false sympathies, and is
worse than the present capitalism. Coöperation, they
say, creates a new class with one foot in the camp of
the middle class and the other in that of the proletariat.
But the coöperative system in industrial enterprises
has not had a fair trial. There are certainly great
benefits to be drawn from the system of participation, — a system which is still in its infancy. There are
methods of making the acquisition of property easy, to
which one must add those which increase the opportunity
of industrial investments for the working classes, through
facilities, means of credit, saving, and insurance suited
to their means. The advantages of a larger extension of
the sane and efficacious incorporation of unions or helping
societies, with the object of disproving the statement
that the workman, if he does not wish to starve, is always
obliged to yield to the demands of the employer, are too
important to be denied. The sums deposited in saving
funds, collected by unions, and wasted for drink and in
poor domestic economy show that not a few workmen
possess the means with which to begin their own emancipation, if a good opportunity were offered them of using
their money to advantage in productive enterprises, as
Rae points out. There is, too, the experiment of reform
by wise social legislation which makes for the improve-

ment and emancipation of the lower classes. These reforms reduce the cost of living and look to the increase of productive capacity, the conservation of the workmen's physical forces, and to fostering such foresight as is possible in these classes. They are based always on the principle that the State's mission is to complete, aid, and save the deficient activity of the individual without, however, substituting its initiative for theirs. Its duty is always to guard the liberty of the weak. The crises and vicissitudes of labor can be foreseen by a good system of insurance which is also the subject of social legislation.

§ 315. *Present System is Not so Black as it is Painted.* The socialists exaggerate the evils of the present industrial system when they affirm that it constantly produces tremendous crises, with perpetual excess of the laboring population, by the rapidity of technical transformation and the headlong changes in commercial relations. Experience has shown that machinery has employed more hands than it has rendered idle and that with increased production the demand for labor has increased likewise. Commercial and financial crises are more frequent now, but on the other hand they are less grave and violent, especially in those nations that enjoy free trade, than those of the past century. The danger of rash and pure speculation can always be reduced by the organization of good offices of statistics, which the socialists reasonably and opportunely demand. The greater extension of private property and the development of personal liberty are the two great factors in modern progress. Nor has it been shown by any advocate of socialism that private property has not increased and accelerated production. It is impossible to maintain seriously that the administration of the State is more interested and acute than private enterprise and that the lessened responsibility of the workman, sure of his position and future, can produce better results. Lassalle declares that if socialism does not increase production it is not economically justifiable (this is certainly true), and there is reason to believe that the nature of socialism is such that it can ever bring about the result desired by Lassalle and the economists, who with one voice say that the preferable system is that under which personalty, realty, and wealth in general give the largest product and nourish the greatest number of men. This has always been one of private property which contains the most powerful incentive and gives the greatest energy to production. Neither has it been shown that socialism would be favorable to the other factor in progress, that is, to the principle of individual liberty, but it has been proved that rather the contrary would result, should the socialistic industrial policy become active and develop the authority of public administration, to which the entire duty of directing and organizing collective labor would be entrusted. Schäffle, a socialist, writes that the definite victory or defeat of socialism depends upon the possibility of an agreement between the organization of production and individualistic principles. If such an agreement cannot be made socialism will be defeated. Socialism, he says, will conquer only by admitting that each individual should take part in the labor for his own private interests as actively as he does in the present system, by recognizing that each man should suffer the penalty of his fault or neglect and should be graded according to his merit, and by directing the numerous forces of labor in such a way as to render it more productive, not by force, but through personal interests. Schäffle adds that he is convinced that socialism can so harmonize with liberty, but he confesses that now it does not show the necessary guaranties for bringing about such an agreement.

And in fact it seems to us that socialism will never be able to offer such guaranties, if its essence is what Schäffle has described. How can socialism ever be conciliated with the principle of personal liberty if it is founded on the substitution of collective for private property, the organization of production, the public division of labor, and the distribution of collective products of all kinds among the laborers? Socialism for its love of equality sacrifices liberty, the source of difference and inequality. One word in conclusion: if socialism is correctly defined by Schäffle it becomes essentially irreconcilable with the principle of individual personality. If it is something else, let us be told what manner of thing it is and of what it consists, and we will see how it can be in accord with this principle.

§ 316. *Socialism and Progress.* Socialists and collectivists base much on a vague and indefinite notion of progress, which is motion. Movement, says Galileo, cannot be without a substance, without the inheritance in its subject, whence it is that motion is always determined by the nature of the subject moved. With this warning it is clear that progress cannot be understood except as regulated by the things which progress, nor can we grasp an historical movement of man which does not take into consideration the greater sentiments and rational impulses of man which influence him. Aristotle stated that there are two causes which urge men to desire, — the sense of ownership and the feeling of affection, — and that without property neither life nor a good life is possible. The progress of modern collectivists is of such a kind, because it draws away from religion and nationality and the principle of individualism which it considers a barbarous and egoistical notion. To deny God and religion because the one is worshiped and the other invoked by the whole official

world, officers, aristocracy, and all the privileged classes,
by bondholders and business men, politicians high and
low, by all State officials, policemen, and street cleaners,
by priests and clergy, and dissenters, is the same (Maz-
zini said in his letter to the Italians against the "International") as to deny the air because it is full of the
deadly germs of disease. True faith should not be
eschewed because much of the worship accorded God
is hypocritical. The thought, then, of substituting a
general autonomy for the nation is a reminiscence
of the infantile life of the people who developed from
a state of communism into nations. Eliminating
nationality, one cannot easily reach that spirit of
general fraternity in the various social aggregations
towards which all projects of reform are aimed and
all efforts of the socialists directed. The theoretical
and practical mind does not come to the greater
universals except by passing through a series of lesser universals. Socialism, placing itself in the sphere
of the more ample universals and conquering the national phase, faces the fact that one people would be the
owners of the land in which nature has accumulated its
gifts, and another would be kept in barren region.   Is
not land the common inheritance of humanity?   Is not
occupation as unjust between one people and another as
between man and man?   Do not violence and fraud
enter into the acquisitions by nations as well as in those
of private persons?

§ 317. *Society is Not a Natural Organism.* The
conception of the ethical organism is in itself concrete because it contains the social person or the whole,
while the part must be considered as a conscious subject.
Such conception is born in a time of maturity and represents the harmony between two opposite elements for
a long time in enmity, the one political, and the other

individual. At first the State was predominant and the individual had no value in himself. Then he prevailed and the State, reduced to a conventional reality, became a simple means for safeguarding the individual. Now collectivism and mutualism take a retrograde step, bringing back the old pagan idea of the absorbing community, the perfect image of a natural organism in which a part is a simple means having no individuality. The old idea is advanced by modern socialists clothed in forms more industrial than political, presenting itself to their eyes as the natural distributer of labor, which innovation is understood without difficulty when we remember that for the followers of the system in discussion economics are the determining base of scientific, religious, and political development. In such system the freedom of the individual is conceived of in an abstract and general manner, that is, without his natural differences entirely independent of the matter to which it refers. But freedom so generalized and isolated cannot be upheld, cannot fail to impede the logical deduction of the famous *de facto* equality (if in the moral sphere surely in the economic) of the absurd collective ownership of the instruments of labor and of the not less erroneous absolute and universal equivalence of functions.

§ 318. *Criticism of Marx's Theory.* The principal error of Marx depends upon the theories of Galiani, Adam Smith, and Ricardo, — that value depends only on work. Utility is a factor as well. To produce a given temperature in winter, we have to use more coal than in summer, and if the quantity of labor is the same in the two seasons, the money value of coal in the winter is higher. In a day's hunting, says Laveleye, in his book "Socialisme Contemporaine," the force and duration of the work are equal in killing a doe and a fox, but the first will furnish nourishment for five days, while the latter will only be sufficient for one, whence it follows that the doe with the greater utility is worth more than the fox. That utility is an undeniable element of value is shown in Marx's own theory of work socially necessary. The weaver, for example, can make in a month the quantity of silk that a steam weaver makes in a day. The buyer will give the workman who has labored for a month the price which he would pay the owner of the steam weaver, because he pays the laborer not for the force used in a month, but for the service rendered, and he pays him in proportion to the utility produced. Galiani saw these two factors of value and calls them rarity and utility, meaning by rarity that which we moderns call power of acquisition. He exaggerated the efficacy of both, because he admits value should develop in perfect proportion with rarity and utility. Now it is not true that the price of products (which is their value in money) increases step by step as the demand increases (which corresponds to utility) and diminishes step by step as the offer increases (that corresponds to rarity), because the price is influenced in various ways according to the diversity of products, sentiments, judgments, desires, and fears. Marx has not followed Galiani in this doctrine but has accepted its conceptions in treating of average value, reducing one the measure of value of exchange to labor, and has therefore fallen into error. Products cost not only the labor which is spent on them, but also the conduct of the person who either abstains from the unproductive use of wealth at his disposition, or deliberately prefers results more distant to immediate results. We have seen that the theory of Galiani, Adam Smith, Ricardo, and Marx cannot be applied to many important economic phenomena. A general rise of wages is the result of the value of the product, into which labor enters in great proportion, in relation to capital; in such a case there is increase of value not preceded by any augmentation of the quantity of labor necessary to production. If the principle of Marx were true the products which demand a longer and more burdensome work would have the greater value. This, however, is not true in reality. In fact the opposite is often true. A porter is paid less than a teacher, and yet the porter works a greater number of hours in a much more burdensome employment. A minister of state gets more than a teacher, and yet he has more time for preparation and training. It is not the length of the work nor the time spent in preparation which causes the difference in reward, but it is the different social utility of the service. Admitting the principle of Marx, we cannot account for the existence of industries in which there is a fixed capital. These should give a profit less than that of other industries which have a capital made almost entirely of wages, since the value increases in direct ratio to the quantity of labor expended. But experience shows that this is not always true. A capitalist does not give the workmen all the value of the product since he must pay interest on his capital and rent on his land, and since he must receive a profit from his activity, sacrifices, and for the risks which he runs. If the workmen were capitalists then things would go differently and there would be no reason for quarrels and lawsuits, but there has always been and there will continue to be a claim on part of the workmen's time in favor of him who gives the things necessary to production, because rent is natural and interest is an indispensable and not irrational fact. Suppose, says Von Sybel, that a manufacturer, during normal conditions in which the other contractors paid wages of a dollar, one fine day paid two dollars. This, according to Marx, would be right, because the manufacturer would have justly paid for twelve hours' work. But now a manufacturer desires to redouble the wages because he has seen a propitious change in his prospects and does not want to lose his workmen. In this hypothesis, if the possibility comes true, the manufacturer would be enriched not through the work of his men but by his intelligence and the outcome of events. Surplus value is almost a consequence of such intelligence and of the variations of price. Marx is wrong in recognizing an excessive and absorbing importance in mechanical labor, and in considering the instrument as the motive power and giving it the appearance of a parasite, while he himself writes that the capitalists make production possible by coördinating and directing its forces. He falls also into another error because he believes that wages are simply what serves to keep the workman alive, an error we will criticize in the next paragraph.

§ 319. *Marx's Presuppositions are Untrue.* The theory of Marx is founded on hypotheses accepted by his followers as facts already demonstrated and about which there can be no doubt, but these hypotheses are questionable enough because they do not correspond to reality. The first hypothesis lies in considering that a day's work includes twelve hours, while it appears in certain recent official reports that it is ten hours and in some industries is restricted to nine or even to eight. The second hypothesis, even further from the truth, is that a workman gains always in six hours' work enough for the support of himself and his family. The third represents the workman as resigned not to gain more than is strictly necessary, being disposed to give twelve hours' work to the contractor who only pays him for six. We need only state such suppositions to see that they are arbitrary.

§ 320. *Property in both Capital and Labor.* From this long analysis it appears that property in capital and profit is equally as legitimate as that of work and its recompense. Property in capital and freedom of association and industry come from the right of the employers to unite and agree among themselves. The union of manufacturers not accompanied by fraud, threats, or violence is not criminal, as likewise the coalition and strikes of workmen are legal. In our day, besides the coalition of workmen for the question of wages, there are associations to limit production and keep up the prices. Such a coalition has come to be called "kartell" in Germany, "cartel" or "syndicate" in France, a "ring" or "trust" in England, and a "pool" or "corner" in America. They are of various types, depending upon whether they regulate the quantity of production in a given time for every participant, or whether they fix a minimum price of a product to be observed by every member of the union, assign a given radius of sale, or distribute the production among the members of the trust in such a way that none has a want or superfluity of commissions. All these kinds are legitimate consequences of the property in capital and of free association and they do not in the least presuppose fraud or violence. Cannot the producer of his own will limit his production and make agreements with other producers about the price and place where he will sell, that is, enter into a league or fusion of commercial societies? There is here the exercise of the right similar to that which the workmen have to form their union, and the State cannot fail to recognize it if it wishes to be just to all. There will be harm done the consumer in such cases, since he is obliged to pay more for his product, but he must remember that such trusts prevent the ruin of important national industries, and that therefore they are helpful to the workmen. If the workman as a consumer loses to a certain extent, he gains as a producer.

CHAPTER IX

COMMERCIAL PROPERTY.—THE RIGHT OF AN AUTHOR OR INVENTOR

THE CONCEPTION OF COMMERCIAL PROPERTY. — FREEDOM OF
EXCHANGE. — COMPETITION. — PRIMITIVE NOTION OF TRADE.—
THE RIGHT OF THE AUTHOR BEFORE AND AFTER THE INVEN-
TION OF PRINTING: ITS BASIS AND ITS CHARACTER.—THE
RIGHT OF THE INVENTOR.

§ 321. *Definition of Commercial Property.* Commercial property is the child of commercial industry. It
is of its nature a go-between, because with trade, exchange, and transportation, it makes the relations
easy between producers and consumers, based on their
purpose of money-making and their chances of gain
and risk of loss. Commerce is domestic and foreign,
depending upon whether it is complete within a country
or not. It is distributive as far as it consists in the
purchase and sale, wholesale or retail, of things acquired
for sale. It concerns transportation and storage if it
brings to the consumers of one place the products of
distant countries or saves for days of want objects
bought in times of abundance. It includes all alienable
goods of any kind which are material for commercial
speculation. In this category are all forms of personalty,
chattels, money and checks, and other incorporeal things
such as the credit and the good-will of a business. Realty
also can be included if it is an object of speculation. In
all cases, the goods by becoming commercial, acquire
a new value, which must belong to him who adds his

labor to that of the producer and to him who invests and risks his capital. Commerce frees the producer and consumer of the work of coming directly together. It saves them no little loss of time, anticipates capital, provides transportation, preserves the products, runs the risk of not selling, for one cause or another, and acts as intermediary. Commercial property, therefore, is justified by the same principle of personality which is the foundation of all kinds of ownership.

§ 322. *Freedom of Trade.* Admit the right of property and the freedom of labor, and the logical consequence is freedom of trade or competition. Clearly the owner of anything has the right to exchange and re-exchange it as best he can so long as he has full control over it. If an individual can choose his trade or profession and exercise one or more, work with whom he pleases, how he pleases, and when it seems best to him, others are surely free to follow identical lines and compete. Romagnosi is right in saying that exchange is an undeniable principle of private and public law; that this is a principle of private law is without question. It is thus placed with the right of property and shows in a very clear manner as its logical effect. Turgot, before Romagnosi, discovered and stated this truth. Free trade is a principle of modern public law because it is founded on the territorial division of labor among the nations, avoiding the wasting of their productive forces. It is the cause of an increase and perfection of products, whose price it lowers. It encourages competition, increases knowledge, multiplies the relations between men, makes the more distant interests safe, and is a sign of peace and brotherhood. It is necessary, however, not to stop with such abstract considerations; we must study it concretely. The pure, extreme theory of free trade is set forth in the manuals of political economy and is not listened to by new writers because it supposes as true in fact two conceptions which are not always so, and confuses simple abstract tendencies with reality. This theory starts out with two premises, — the unity and cosmopolitanism of merchandise, without keeping in mind the events which can affect the simple elements which compete in the world's commerce, and the hypothesis that the workmen are the owners. Universal welfare can sometimes be obtained with the ruin of one or more nations, but these nations have the right and duty of providing for their own safety, especially if they have in themselves initial conditions for the favorable development of some industries which could destroy foreign competition. On the other hand, if free trade helps the workers in their character of consumers it can harm them deeply as workmen. The loss will be felt by them in a noticeable manner because ordinarily they are not owners and do not enjoy the advantage of free trade in proportion to the damage, which can, in certain cases, be done to them by its adoption. We must, therefore, temper this principle with the particular condition of the national industry, and proceed slowly. Commercial treaties, easily revoked, better than general tariffs, make for the establishment of control and the gradual adoption of the principle, leaving to consular conventions the care of realizing the freedom of commerce in respect to the exercise of an industry, profession, or foreign trade. This freedom once recognized, it is clear that we should condemn the old grants of monopolies to trading companies, the old regulations, and all that which stopped free circulation, such as the provincial customhouses, toll-gates, prices fixed by law, etc.

§ 323. *Right to Compete.* The competition of an individual is always a right although it does harm to others who follow the same trade.   It is an undeniable maxim of law that no one can do another harm by exercising his own rational or legal powers.   The law of the right of competition, therefore, does not and must not bring harm.   At that point there arises a duty of indemnification because there occurs a private wrong which, under the form of a legal right, is harmful to a proprietary interest.   In such a case the private wrong assumes the general name of unfair competition, as the lawyers say.   Competition is fair and recognized if anyone uses the legitimate means at his disposal to attract a greater number of customers.   It becomes unfair if he resorts to mislabeling or adulteration.   Various are the ways and means of unfair competition.   There is the public crying down through pamphlets and prospectuses of the other's goods, the taking of another's name, reputation, sign, or trade-mark.   All of these represent persuasive force exercised by merchants on customers. There are also cases of unfair competition by the breach of a contractual relation by which one man obligates himself not to compete with another, or the violation of trade secrets obtained by a workman of the factory where he has learned them.   These kinds of unfair competition are methods harming the credit and reputation, the "achalandage" of the French and Belgium writers, which has great economic value, and constitutes a true commercial property in that it is alienable and the material of money making.   Names, signs, and trade-marks are referable to the "achalandage," representing the worth of the manufacturer and merchant, and form a distinct commercial and industrial property.

§ 324.   *History of Commercial Law.*   We cannot fail to be struck with wonder when we compare the modern notion of commerce and commercial prop-

erty with the primitive forms outlined by Cognetti
De Martis in his "Forme Primitive nell' Evoluzione
Economica." From the stories of trustworthy ex-
plorers, we find that there are savage peoples who
lack a conception of exchange, in that they take
what is offered them and do not understand that they
should give anything in return. Primitive man, like a
child, desires everything and tries to grab what pleases
him, because he is selfish and controlled by strong
impulses. And it is only after a long period of development that he can accustom himself to a system
of exchange. At the beginning of such a system, the
selfishness and rapacity of the savage is transformed into
bad faith and trickery. The fact that foreign traders are
considered enemies increases this bad faith. Exchange
is first silent, taking place in neutral land where the
contractors without seeing or speaking to each other
come, go, place, increase, and diminish the merchandise
and thus determine the "quid pro quo." Then appoint-
ments are made and continuous and permanent markets
in which custom controls are constituted in neutral
lands. The authority of the chiefs is absolute over the
contractors. After the market comes the phase of
peddling merchants and that of caravans, to which
succeed naval expeditions and commercial enterprises
such as were tried and carried out by the Phœnicians.
The Greeks and Romans despised work, which they
left to the slaves, believing leisure was the condition
of life for a citizen who took part in the government of
the Commonwealth. The arts even were condemned by
Zenophon, Plato, Aristotle, and Cicero. The Greeks
and Romans for the same reason abhorred trade and
tried, at least at the beginning, to withdraw the State
from the influence of foreign commerce. This tendency
is shown by the habits and customs predominant in

primitive times.   In fact, foreign commerce alters
custom and the law of the fathers and influential
men, and seems to destroy society from its very base.
In those times commercial law was not separate from
the civil.   The ancient civil law, like the Roman, contained some rules for commercial affairs, and regulated
commercial property.   Then came the first primitive
legislative synthesis.   In the Middle Ages the old
statutes were given new significance and new commercial forms were created.   For example, limited
partnerships and cheques were invented, and bills of
exchange, partnerships, contracts, and the law of
agency were enlarged and defined.   At first these
relations, which later became statutory, were ruled
by custom.   They were a subject of profound study
by the school of Stræcha, Casaregis, and Anzaldo.
Codification made its first appearance in France with
the "Ordinance Generale" of 1673, and with the Marine
Orders of 1681.   New commercial codes and new special
laws, taking account of the great development of personal
property in all its phases and of the limited commerciability of realty, extended and reinforced the protection of
the property which was derived from the "commutatio
mercium," and were based on the conception of the freedom of commercial combination and exchange.   Modern
legislation before the recent return to the older plan
was almost entirely freed from those prejudices which
lent weight to the system of the balance of trade,
protection, the colonial system, the granting of monopolies.   There was a tendency to become uniform in commercial more than in any other part of law, because the
interests of trade are confused and interlaced in a
manner that prohibits the national factor.

§ 325.   *The Right of Invention or Discovery.*   Coming
to the right of an author or inventor, we must remem-

ber first that before the invention of printing an
author had no financial interest distinct from that of
the owner of the product, and therefore there was no
need for a special legal protection, as Del Giudice says
in "Enciclopedia." The difficulties of the reproduction
of a manuscript were great, and the trade in books was
small. With the introduction of printing reproduction
became easy and the trade in books was greatly increased, consequently a special protection appeared
that from the first controlled the privilege of re-editing
and reprinting. In the XVIIIth Century all privileges
struggled for existence, and among them that of copy-
right. As there are no particular rules on this subject in the Roman law or statutes, recourse had to
be had to the common base of all rights of property.
The right of an author or inventor is the right of literary, artistic, and industrial property; thus it is held
in the works of philosophers,—Diderot, Fichte, Hegel,
and Schopenhauer,—and of the jurists and by the French
statutes. Certainly, in books, works of art, discoveries of new combinations and new industrial processes,
we must recognize an element which is general and an
element which is particular. The first lies in the ideas,
in the truths which belong to every man; every author
or inventor assimilates thoughts accumulated throughout centuries which form the collective patrimony
of the human mind. The second consists in the research and intellectual activity of him who makes a
new elaboration of general ideas, creating a form which
before had no existence. This form may be expressed in
print, in silk, in marble, in design, in sound, in a combination or process, and marks the true boundaries of
the right of him who has devoted his labor to it. It is
just that society admit and protect the new labor,
recognizing the right of an author or inventor, but this

right should not prejudice the interest of humanity because the more it progresses the more the new ideas and new discoveries, by being diffused, become means at the disposal of all those who wish to profit thereby.

§ 326. *Such a Right is Economic.* It is objected that law should not forcibly create openings for men who try to sell their books and inventions upon conditions of their own. Once a book or invention is sold, the purchaser has full right over it and the vendor has no right to exercise any restraints. But, upon reflection, such considerations cannot have much weight, as in fact they are only weighty with ordinary producers who may be unfortunate in not selling their property, but who in such a case at least retain possession of it. This is not true of authors and inventors who can be dispossessed by the first printing press or manufactory. We can observe that in the industrial products the value lies entirely in the object made, and therefore the common protection given to property is sufficient, while in the spiritual production the material is a simple sign of ideas and of little value, so that the protection of the property in the material is not a sufficient protection. A special protection is needed. Society, therefore, must assure the author the exclusive right of reproduction and sale and the inventor the exclusive use of his invention. It is not true that when one sells a copy of a book the buyer can reprint it on his own account, because this would be contrary to the rights of the author and would make his own that special utility of value which belongs to another without doing anything to gain it. With the purchase of a book one acquires no other right than that to read, study, lend, and give it away, obtain from it all possible intellectual profit, and even burn it if one wants.

§ 327. *Inventions are Property Rights.* The right of an author or inventor cannot be strictly a right of property because property is by its nature perpetual and hereditary, while these rights are not of such a character. Besides, society cannot consent to books and inventions remaining in the possession of heirs who may be ignorant, selfish, and always quarreling with those who improve the original work. It must give works of the intellect free circulation when the necessary time of the exclusive right has passed, during which the author or inventor can gain sufficient recompense for his labor. The conversion of the right of an author or inventor into property, on one hand, causes a confusion accompanied by frequent litigations between the inventor and the man who has or thinks he has improved a process or machine, and, on the other hand, causes a kind of oppression of humanity by the selfishness of the heirs. It is clearly irrational that ownership which effectuates the laws of well-being (as Vico has told us) should produce disorder and injustice and render human life stationary by opposing intellectual progress. Neither is the right of an author or inventor to be regarded in the aspect of personal right, because it is at bottom a direct relation between a man and things, between the author or inventor and the book or invention, both products of individual activity. In the right of an author or inventor the personal element is subordinate to the economic element, and this subordination is the cause of its transferability by acts "inter vivos" or by will. The subordination of the personal to the economic element shows that the industrial or literary work is considered as an economic interest, as a financial value, and not as an important spiritual product giving glory and fame. The right of an author or inventor includes the profit which he can get from his intellectual

labor incorporated in a given form, and does not embrace
the incorporeal property which is represented by the
reputation of the author or discoverer of a truth, law, or
phenomenon, which is not guarded by law and exists
only in the opinion of the erudite.   This incorporeal
property can be the matter of literary, scientific, and technical discussion, but is never the object of legal action
except in the case of plagiarism, and is distinct from the
right of an author or inventor.   If this property, purely
moral, is confused with the right of reproduction and
sale, it is necessary to remember that it ends when such
a right ends, and therefore needs no special recognition.
It is said that this subordination is not true because
the economic element cannot exist in scientific and
literary works, but this is not a question of fact, but
of right.   It is sufficient that there be a possibility of
economic interest or profit in order that the right of
an author should be guarded, and nothing further is
necessary for legal recognition.   The true reason of the
transferability of the right of an author lies in its
economic and financial character, because purely personal rights cannot be transferred.   Eliminating the
two hypotheses that it is a property or personal right,
there still remains the possibility that it has the nature
and form of a property right analogous to that of a
usufruct.   With the usufruct there is a just proportion
between the merit of work (into which not a few elements of human activity enter) and the recompense
which does not constitute an obstacle to the diffusion of
ideas and the propagation of the invention. The usufruct
harmonizes equally the undeniable right of the author
or inventor with the evident needs of society without
sacrificing one to the other. We understand that it
can be given by law to the heirs who represent the personality of the author during the remainder of his

period of enjoyment of it. But the usufruct, you say, supposes property and cannot pass to heirs. The reply is not difficult since it is a property which is closely connected with the community, and besides, such a right is a usufruct "sui generis," because though it is of short duration it can pass for a certain number of years to the heirs.

§ 328. *Patents.* Inventions are generally protected by patents, an English institution which gives an inventor a right to the exclusive use of his discovery for a certain number of years. A patent ordinarily does not insure the reality or the utility of the invention, since the State cannot enter into technical discussions, and merely guards the right founded on the supposed nature of the invention. Not a few objections are raised against this institution; it is said that the patent harms the inventor because of its short duration, that it is a cause of frequent litigations which harm all business, though ignorance will not admit it. Without doubt the inconveniences shown are true, but then there has not been found in industrial law a better means of protecting the inventor's right. Everyone knows that there is good and bad in everything; the object is to obtain the predominance of the former, since it is impossible entirely to eliminate evils. It is useful to remember that the abuse of patent rights is one of those examples of unfair competition of which we have spoken.[1] The rights of an author or inventor exclude by their very nature any competition which, in their case, becomes a private tort or wrong, capable of a monetary valuation.

[1] *Cf.* § 320 *ante.*

CHAPTER X

SUNDRY PROPERTY RIGHTS

CLASSIFICATION OF RIGHTS OVER THE PROPERTY OF OTHERS.—
SERVITUDES AND THEIR KINDS. — THE METHODS IN WHICH
SERVITUDES ARE CREATED, EXERCISED, AND EXTINGUISHED.—
EMPHYTEUSIS. — THE SUPER-SOIL. — PLEDGE AND MORTGAGE. —
THE CHARACTER OF LIENS.

§ 329. *Personal and Property Rights.* Property
rights are relations direct and immediate between
persons and things.   They can be reduced to two main
categories; to "plena potestas in re" and to "jura
in re aliena."   The rights over another's property
are not a dismemberment of the complex right of property but limitations placed upon its exercise, because
property is always a power complete and full over its
object and would not be such if its elements could be
separated from one another.   In this case the division
would not be a quantitative variation, of no importance
in itself, but a change of quality, for the essence of
ownership is control of all the attributes.   The "jura in
re aliena" have their justification in the diverse uses and
utilities of things by which they become advantageous
to men whom they affect, and although they are property of a particular individual and to society generally.
These rights, inasmuch as they are direct relations between
persons and things, assume logically the character of independent rights of themselves, like "plena potestas," and
are very different from those limits and bonds which contractual rights place on ownership.   Whoever acquires
right of this last kind (for example, a lease) exercises par-

524 SUNDRY PROPERTY RIGHTS

tial rights of property conferred upon him in the name of
the owner, because personal rights are immediate relations between one individual and another. The difference
can be explained by the different nature of property and
personal rights and the separation of property rights
from their subjects by virtue of which they stand
alone. In this way we can conclude that the Roman
maxim, "Servitus in faciendo consistere non potest," is
not exclusively applicable to servitudes alone but can be
applied to any "jus in re aliena." In the first place,
every "jus in re aliena" subjects another's property to
the special and restricted power of him who is the subject of the right independently of any claim through the
owner. The latter would be held to the "facere" if the
relationship from which grows the "jus in re aliena"
was personal and did not refer to the property itself.
The "facere" is the object of a contract right but is
repugnant to a property right. The special property
rights either look to the enjoyment or protection of a
right. Servitude, emphyteusis, and the right to light
and air are of the first kind; pawn and mortgage are of
the second.

§ 330. *Servitudes in General.* A servitude is the most
ancient of the particular property rights. It was at one
time the only one. It can be considered in an active
or passive sense as it tends to increase or diminish the
property. In the active sense, that is, from the point
of view of the person or thing in whose favor it is
established, it is a right over another's property, by
virtue of which the owner of the latter is held bound
in regard to a person or estate to tolerate or not to
do that which as owner he could do. In a passive sense,
that is, from the point of view of the thing involved,
it is a burden imposed on land to the advantage of another person or land. From this definition we can see

the first division of servitude into personal and real or
predial, according to whether the object of its establishment is a person or a thing. In respect to the object, all
servitudes personal or predial are essentially real rights
because they fall on things or land, never on persons.
The dominant tenement in a real servitude cannot be
regarded as a juridical person, as nothing which lacks
will can be the subject of rights. In the dominant tenement there is a right which can be exercised by any
future possessor of it, but no subject. Metaphor is
not reality; the representation of a thing is not its concept. Personal servitudes, on the other hand, are different
in many aspects from the predial. These do not suppose
a tenement but are attached to a person, and therefore are
not perpetual like the real, whose duration is the duration of the two tenements, and they can fall on personal
property while the predial can only fall upon land. The
usufruct of clothes and of money is an example of the
personal servitude over personal property.

§ 331. *Personal Servitudes.* The personal servitudes
are three: usufruct, use, and "habitatio."[1] "Usufruc-
tus est jus alienis rebus utendi, fruendi salva rerum
substantia." The owner of the usufruct should enjoy
the thing as a good father, as the owner should enjoy
it, saving his substance as well in matter as form.
The preservation of one's substance is not the same
as the preservation of value, because the termination
of value does not touch the essence but expresses
the measure of exchange or the power of acquisition
of another's goods. The owner of a usufruct has the
right to the "uti" and the "frui." He can make use
of the object and take its fruits and enjoy them to the

---

[1] Usufruct is the right of enjoyment of an object and its products.
"Usus, ' or user, is the right to as much of the natural product of something as the user needs to sustain life. "Habitatio" is the right to
use a house as a dwelling.

full satisfaction of his personal and domestic needs. He has also the right of granting title to a third person both gratuitously and for a consideration.   The law establishes between the owner of the usufruct and the owner of the object such relations as guarantee the latter complete enjoyment during the usufruct and keep his interest from doing any possible harm to the property and to the future enjoyment when the usufruct will become one with the property. From the simple conception of the usufruct it can be inferred that it could not strictly be exercised over destructible objects. The Roman law of imperial times had recourse to an analogy and constituted for such things a "quasi-usus-fructus," which was very similar to pawn because the owner of the usufruct of perishable objects acquires property in them and has only the obligation of the restoring the "tantundem" at the end of the usufruct. And yet it cannot be strictly said that the "quasi-usus-fruct" constitutes a right of credit and is not a property right.   When the "quasi-ususfruct" begins the "res" is "aliena" and becomes the property of the owner of the usufruct through the exercise of his right.   The right of enjoyment of destructible things, therefore, is not a mere right of credit but is that of an owner by the "tantundem."   From the usufruct we must distinguish the use which according to modern codes is a usufruct limited to the needs of its owner and his family, and the "habitatio," which is the use of a house. Going back to the sources of Roman law, the conception of a use is given a reasonable determination because by rule it contains only the "uti" and not the "frui."   If the thing is useful without its fruits, the owner of the use must use it (as it is written in the early law) without appropriating the fruits; but if the thing is not useful without its fruits, the owner of the use can gather them for his individual and domestic needs. A use cannot be leased or sold since it might be changed and extended to the harm of the owner of the property.

§ 332. *Predial Servitudes.* Predial servitudes (which are the primitive forms) were anciently divided into rural and urban because of the great difference of the needs of the country and the city; consequently there was a division made of servitudes into those relating to fields and buildings. And we can say, although not a few servitudes are applicable to both the country and city, there are in all ages servitudes which look principally (if not exclusively) to the needs of agriculture and servitudes of a distinctly urban character. The rights of water and ways are of the first kind; those of support, party-walls, and light belong ordinarily to the second. The servitudes are distinguished as positive or negative depending upon whether they are permissive or prohibitive; as continuous or discontinuous depending upon whether or not they demand in their exercise an act of man; into apparent and non-apparent depending upon whether they can be seen or not with the eye. This distinction has no practical importance, as we commonly say, but it is bound up with the principles of the methods of acquisition and exercise of the servitudes, which must conform to their nature. A "jus in re" is without doubt classed with the "dominium" and "jura in re aliena;" the "dominium" concerns the "res corporales," through the intimate and individual inter-penetration of the "plena potestas" with the "res"; the "servitutes" on the other hand, are concerned with the "res incorporales." The "possessio," a relation between persons and things, is logically connected with the property rights, and therefore can be extended to the servitudes which are "res incorporales." We will see now the consequences of this. In the first place predial servitudes can be derived from law or the act of man. Law establishes them for purposes of public and private utility; the legal servitudes are increased with time through the evolution of individuals and society. A party-wall, according to the Roman law, was only created by private contract, but now it is brought about by statute. The Roman law allowed a right of way only to get to the sepulchre of one's ancestors; modern law allows it for cultivation and the convenient use of one's land. An aqueduct was recognized in Rome as a servitude because of its necessity. It has been introduced in our times because the interests of the agriculturists and industrialists should not be made to depend upon the selfishness of the landowner. The Roman law gave the owner of a tenement the right to dig wells, even tapping the water supply of his neighbor, and did not decree specific distances between the wells of different owners. Modern law, however, establishes a distance, which can be increased when necessity demands it (the judicial authority fixes the increase) in order not to harm other land, springs, and preëxisting canals and aqueducts. In all these examples we can clearly see that constantly more control is exercised over property for social objects, and its selfish use is forbidden without harm to its individuality. Still more triumph will yet be accorded those principles of economic law, of which Romagnosi has been the systemic standard-bearer.

§ 333. *Servitudes Derivative from Acts.* The predial servitudes derivative from the act of man, if continuous and apparent, can be acquired with title, or by the designation of the pater-familias,[1] or prescription; but if discontinuous and non-apparent, with title alone. Is

[1] Where an owner of two farms creates a servitude, which springs up upon alienation to two different owners, there is a "designatio."

this an arbitrary disposition of positive law or is it consonant with rational law? Admitting by the light of reason that servitudes are capable of possession (or "quasi-possessio," as the Roman jurisconsults say,) and that continued and uninterrupted possession, if certain and public, gives a prescriptive right; we must conclude that the methods of acquisition established by positive law are consequences of a rational principle. And in truth, in the continuous and apparent servitudes there is certain and public possession, and therefore the possibility of acquisition by prescription. The designation of a pater-familias presupposes a single owner of two neighboring farms who makes one subservient to the other. Since both of them belong to him there is no servitude, but the servitude springs up when the farms belong to different men. Only continuous and apparent servitude can be shown by a "designatio" or result therefrom. A "designatio" could not have the power of establishing discontinuous and non-apparent servitudes. Such servitudes cannot be acquired by prescription or by the designation of the pater-familias, as they lack the requisites of legitimate possession. The methods of exercise of a servitude are governed in the same way as their acquisition. If they originated by a grant, it determines their exercise; if they arise by designation or prescription, we must remember the state of things left by the single owner and have recourse to the maxim, "tantum præscriptum, quantum possessum." Predial servitudes are extinguished by merger, by the change of the state of the dominant or servient tenement so that the former can no longer make use of it, by the renunciation of the owner of the dominant tenement, by the joining of boundaries, and by prescription. Prescription cannot bring about all the servitudes but has the power of extinguishing all of them, because society has an interest in the complete freedom of property. Property, freed from burdens and dependent upon a single will, is quicker to use, and therefore more productive.

§ 334. *Servitudes of Constructions.* The right of construction in modern times cannot be understood more accurately or in a manner conforming more to reality than it was by the Romans. According to the Roman law, the rigorous maxim, "Superficies cedit solo," was in force, and it was not possible to determine exactly the right of construction, which is really only shown as ownership by the erection of a building. The owner of such a right, though he had in fact the rights of an owner by pretorian equity, was not considered as such, but was looked upon rather as the subject of a "jus in re aliena." Getting down to the reality of things, whosoever acquires the right of building over the land of another does not wish in the least to make the owner of the building the owner of the soil. The latter is the owner of the subsoil, but can well limit the extension of his right over the super-soil and allow another to build and be the owner of the construction erected over land which continues to be his. There is no legal impossibility in this case that is reconcilable with the presumption of the civil code that any building, crop, or work over or above the soil shall be regarded as made by the owner at his expense and belonging to him as long as the contrary is not shown and as long as it is not shown that another has acquired the "jus superficiei," by paying the owner of the soil for it. In looking at the relation between the two owners, there is no doubt that the right to build over the land of another and to hold this right against any possessor is real. It cannot be a right of property when the building is lacking, as Lucci says in his book "Natura del Diritto di Superficie." But in considering the relations between the owner of the building and the right, the right is proprietary and has peculiar characteristics. Coviello, in his monograph "Della Superficie," notes that such property is not limited by itself but by the object to which it is applied. Such property in a building cannot be confused with the property in a house. The owner of a house or of any kind of an estate is the owner of what is above it and below it as far as his practical interest extends. The owner of the right has only property in the light and air,—what is "super faciem soli." We must understand that the right goes with the ownership of the land and therefore must be determined in the measure given by a necessity of having the construction on the soil or of using that already existing, and everything which exceeds this necessity exceeds the sphere of rights of its owner. Also in the hypothesis of a temporary and destructible right the owner of the right is the owner of any construction. The buildings of private citizens on public land, by concession from the government, are revocable property, the land always remaining public. Tombs and sepulchral monuments have a similar nature but are constructions belonging to individuals on public soil. The individuals have the right to take away the statues, demolish the chapels or monuments, and put them in a new cemetery. The right of a railroad, states Coviello, is a true right of property. The soil is public, but the company enjoys the exclusive right of erecting stations, warehouses, houses, depots, tracks, and all that constitutes its outfit. The same can be said of tramways, boxes in theatres, or pews in church.

§ 335. *Emphyteusis.* Besides the servitudes there is another particular property right giving a right of use; that is emphyteusis. This, with its many powers, is nearer than the other "jura in re aliena" to owner-

ship. It is the right to use a thing, take its fruits,
and grant it by will or deed, but with the two obligations to pay the grantor of the estate an annual
rent and not to let the land deteriorate. When the
emphyteuta fails in these obligations there is a reversion of the estate to the grantor. The constitution
of Zeno gives a special and distinct character to emphyteusis, solving the questions of whether it was a lease or a
transfer and recognizing the right derived from it as a
"jus in re aliena." The school of commentators sees in
emphyteusis a division of "dominium," and gives the
grantor the "directum" and the grantee the "utile."
Reasonably this division cannot be admitted because
in emphyteusis there are two wills, one of which
exercises on the estate an effective and almost complete
control, the other of which is abstract, more distant
from the object, and is shown only by the exaction of a
nominal rent and by the reversion upon deterioration.
The first will is really that of an owner because it is shown
with almost complete powers of property. The second
is that of a man who simply has a right over something.
The property of the grantee is controlled by his resolution to fulfill his two obligations; the right of the grantor
is more of a right of credit and assùmes the semblance of
a real right "sui generis." In Germany emphyteusis is
considered as a kind of divided property; in France it was
so connected with the feudal system that the Code did
not speak of it. The Italian Civil Code recognizes it but
establishes a right of redemption in favor of the grantee;
and this is in accord with economic principles, with
which emphyteusis should not run counter because it is
useful in those cases where we find a large extent of uncultivated land. The owner, in such a case, can get no
profit from his estate either by a transfer or long term
lease, but through emphyteusis he can obtain a certain

sum of money in rent. On the other hand the emphyteuta by careful work can have a good profit, and by taking advantage of the exemption laws acquire definite and irrevocable property.

§ 336. *Pledge and Mortgage.*[1] Pledge and mortgage are "jura in re aliena," which guarantee a debt. The obligations of the person are placed upon their present and future chattels because such are the projection of the person himself. The goods of the debtor are the common guaranties of his creditors and their value is divided among them ratably, unless some creditor has a legitimate cause for preference. In spite of a generic pledge, the debtor can dispose of his goods in whatever way he wants, but this right is limited by bad faith and the consequent removal of goods in fraud of creditors. Some do not wish to run any risk, and therefore get a pledge in strict form by which the object passes into their hands, but without becoming part of their estate or object of their enjoyment. The right of the pledgee lies in the eventual receipt and appropriation of the value and price of the object pledged. It is not a "jus in re aliena." Differing from them, it does not give a partial property over the object or any right of enjoyment. The creditor cannot dispose of the pledge upon failure of payment without an order of court, to the appraised value, or that it be sold at auction. A "pactum commissorium," which authorizes the creditor to take the pledge and dispose of it without the conditions established by law, is a nullity because it is the result of a dishonest calculation founded on the stress of circumstances and the illusions of the debtor, and because it changes a right to the value of something into a future right of property. At one time the word "pignus" in Rome

[1] Mortgage is here used to translate the Italian "ipotica," the civil "hypotheca."

534 SUNDRY PROPERTY RIGHTS

had a broad signification and took in all the kinds of securities given to a creditor, the pledge of realty and personalty, antichresis, which gives the profits of the pledge in lieu of interests, mortgage, which had a strict and determined meaning and which applied to personalty. The Austrian Code uses it as a general word comprehending the pledge, properly so called, and mortgage, and yet it distinguishes the two institutions. The French Code includes antichresis in pledge, thus differing from the Roman law by which realty or personalty could be given in pledge without making an antichresis. The latter consisted in an agreement added to the contract of pledge, giving the creditor a right to enjoy the property, taking the fruits instead of interest. Antichresis was originally a reciprocal loan and not a pledge, and created no privilege over the object or property rights against third parties. The French Code looks upon antichresis as the pledge of realty, but does not give the privilege to the anticredical creditor and thus falls into a clear contradiction. If the Roman law did not admit this privilege, it was consistent because it did not include antichresis in pawn. The Italian Code shows better than the other codes the nature of the three institutions which, in truth, are methods of security, although not all of them give place to property rights. It assigns different legal features to the three institutions and speaks of them separately without the use of the definite article.

§ 337. *Antichresis. Pledge and Mortgage. Recording.* Pledge and mortgage are property right of guarantee, one implying the possession of personalty and the other applying the case of realty. Antichresis is a contract apart, by which the creditor takes the fruits of the debtor's realty, with the duty of applying them to the payment of interest and capital loaned, and creates a personal right. It is just and proper to restrict the effects of the contract of antichresis to the parties, because the law furnishes a creditor means of arming himself against the bad faith of a debtor by the property right of mortgage. Social economy cannot greatly favor antichresis; the interest of the creditor is to get the greatest amount of fruit from the estate and to expend on it the least that he can. It is enough that the debtor gives the creditor the right of getting the fruit without conferring preferences upon him. We may add that antichresis is apt, especially if it is for a loan of long duration, to cover usury because of the uncertainty of the amount of the fruits, and the usury would not be affected by the only restraint that is in force to-day, that is, publicity. This is the reason why both the canon and Austrian law do not recognize antichresis and the granting of the usufruct of a pledged estate. If the creditor is not put in possession of the pledge he will only have a personal action against the debtor to obtain it. But he will have no property right, because a property right supposes a direct relation between the person and thing, which is lacking here. Tradition in pledge is like the recording in mortgage; and we can note that tradition can be actual or symbolic, as in the cases of the pledge of commercial property. Mortgage is defined in the earliest writings, as it is defined in modern law, but the Roman system made almost exclusively for the interest of the mortgagee and had a particular regard for the owner of the first mortgage, while the law of to-day is based upon the two financial principles of publicity and certainty. Publicity is gained by "transcriptio" and recording: a "transcriptio" is applicable to the transferable titles of realty and is a right that does not destroy or affect its disposition; recording regards the mortgage. Recording is a kind of public tradition, which the Romans did not have because they

laid emphasis on physical tradition. Publicity, therefore, is in the interest of the third parties, who
should know who is the owner of an estate and what
encumbrances there are upon it. Through recording,
third parties can know of the mortgages and can defi-
nitely determine the value of the mortgaged property.
Certainty has to do only with debts, and is duplicate in
the sense that a mortgage can be certain in that it
falls on determinate goods and is for a determinate sum.
The object of this is to warn third parties so that they
will not be misled as to the financial condition of the
debtor, and so that the inconvenience of the opposite
system, deplored for so long a time, and so harmful to
the development of credit, may no longer be possible.

§ 338. *Vessels.* The question has been raised
whether a ship can be pledged or mortgaged.[1] Various have been the opinions, diverse the legal definitions. Really, a ship by her nature should be
placed among personalty, and as personal have the
Roman law and the Italian school considered her,
unlike some of the laws of the Middle Ages. A ship,
however, is a kind of personalty "sui generis," so
the statutes, realizing her particular importance and
wishing to protest and promote maritime credit, are
forced to subject her to the same conditions as are necessary in conveyances of realty, to assign her to a definite
district, and to remove her from the jurisdiction of personalty and its maxim that possession is nine-tenths of
the law. If a ship is regarded as a simple chattel and can
be pawned, although remaining in the control of the
debtor for his use, a formality representing the transfer
of possession is necessary, that is, the appointment of
the trustee; but if we consider a ship a kind of personalty
"sui generis," which must be considered from certain

[1] *Cf.* § 337 *ante.*

legal points of view as realty because of the necessity of
not depriving the debtor of his possession as well as of the
accidental nature of the formality of appointing a trustee, it is more reasonable to allow a mortgage, as the
French law has done.

§ 339. *Liens.* Another method "sui generis" of
guaranteeing credit is the "jus retentionis" or lien.
This is the legal authority given to the possessor of
something who is the creditor of another by either
a property or personal right, to continue in possession of the debtor's property until his demand, based
on the thing obtained, has been satisfied. There is
a full definition given by Guarracino in his book
"Il Diritto di Ritenzione." The "jus retentionis" in
its strict and proper sense presupposes a recognition of
another's right over the object, and looks only to the
guaranteeing of the payment of a debt in its regard, and
therefore does not extend to cases in which the object
is kept through the failure to satisfy a debt, and more
particularly to those cases which give the "exceptio non
adimpleti contractus." Neither should this right be
confused with contractual possession, which is part of
pawn or antichresis, for it can be established independently of these contracts. The "jus retentionis" is a special accessory right which differs fundamentally from all
other property rights or obligations. It is not like the
"jus in re aliena" because it does not give rise to any use
or enjoyment, as the servitudes and emphyteusis do, and
because the object on which it is exercised and its price
are not applied to the satisfaction of the debt, as in pawn
and mortgage. On the other hand it is not a personal
right because the creditor does not claim that the object
is owed him by the other party, through a "vinculum
juris" existing between them. It can be a relation of
obligation, Guarracino says, but in a different sense, that

is, for the benefit of the debtor, since he can claim to have the assignment or restitution of the object by a personal right which is contractual. The "jus retentionis," admitted more or less by all legislation, is based on natural equity which will not allow the claim for assignment to be satisfied thus depriving the assignor of the payment of a debt due in the same transaction. It would not be right to alter the equality between the parties to the possible harm and no little trouble of him who has suffered expense for another's property.

CHAPTER XI

POSSESSION

THE NATURE OF POSSESSION. — ITS HISTORICAL ORIGIN. — ITS
DEVELOPMENT IN LEGISLATION. — CRITICAL EXPOSITION OF THE
DIFFERENT ABSOLUTE AND RELATIVE THEORIES. — ITS RATIONAL
BASIS. — CRITICISM OF IHERING'S THEORY OF THE WILL TO
POSSESS.

§ 340. *Possession is not Property.* The "jus possidendi" is one thing, and the "jus possessionis" another.
The first is the consequence of a right of property, its
more immediate actualization; the second, distinct and
different from the "plena potestas," forms a separate
and different institution. In early law we find this
separation, because there it is said "separata esse debet
possessio a proprietate" and "nec possessio et proprietas misceri debent," since there was nothing in
common between the two institutions: "nihil comune
habet proprietas cum possessione." The earliest sources
of Roman law declare that possession is a distinct right
and the material of a special institution, when they
affirm, "possessor hoc ipso quod possessor est plus juris
habet quam ille qui non possidet."

§ 341. *Possession is a Right.* The "jus possessionis"
or legal possession, is a direct relation between a person
and thing and therefore is a "jus in re," a property
right. But it is not like the other rights, as Bruns says
in his work, "Besitzklagen des Römischen und Heutigen Rechts." It has a special character and is a relative
right because the will of the person to control objects

is not exercised over objects without an owner and does not become absolute ownership, but must yield before the higher right when the latter is shown. Legal possession is composed of two elements, — a chattel with a *de facto* right over it, and the intent of keeping the chattel and working therewith. The phrase, "Corporalis possessio corpore rem attingere corpore in fundo esse," indicates the first element. The phrase, "Animus rem sibi habendi animus possidendi animus domini," refers to the second. The chattel and the *de facto* power over it must join in the person in such a way as to give rise to knowledge of the possibility of enjoying the thing or of exercising the power. This condition, shown by Savigny in "Recht des Besitzes," and admitted by Bruns and Windscheid, has more to do with the continuation of possession than with its beginning, because at the moment of acquisition it needs a positive effective activity, through which new relation between the person and thing is brought about. And in the continuation of possession, too, the knowledge must not be confused with the "vis inertia," but should be practical and active. It should appear in a partial exercise of the *de facto* power. The intention of keeping and using the thing is a specific mark of possession and is the concept by which it is distinguished from mere detention. The detainer has no intent to keep the thing for himself or his own advantage; he has possession in the name of another and is not the possessor, but the agent, of him in whose name he keeps it. The possessor does not lose his right of possession when he does not exercise his power in a direct manner, but through another, who exercises it for him and in his name. If possession is an immediate relation between a person and thing, it cannot be extended to obligations and family rights (as Bruns would wish) but must be limited within the sphere of property rights. Yet not all property rights are capable of possession, but only those which are based on a continuous and known use, as emphyteusis and usufruct, the continuous and apparent servitudes; and therefore the right of mortgage which is a property right is not susceptible of possession, because it would be extinguished by its use, that is, by the sale of the land. From this it can be inferred that possession is of two forms, depending upon whether it is applicable to chattels or rights. The possession of the thing corresponds to the exercise of the right of property; the possession of a right corresponds to the exercise of a "jus in re" that has the qualities that we have shown.[1] The "quasi-possessio," as Bruns teaches, is a regular form of the simple notion of possession and is not anomalous or exceptional, as was believed by Savigny, Thibaut (in his "System der Pandekten"), Windscheid, and others.

§ 342. *The History of Possession.* The historical origin of possession is obscure and has been the subject of much controversy. If it is a relative property right, as we have said before,[2] it cannot arise where individual property is lacking. Possession is a direct relation between a person and thing and yields only in the face of a property right, which must be proved in order to conquer and overcome it. The very notion of possession presupposes the existence of private property. Filomusi-Guelfi cites a law of Locros, attributed to Zaleucos, and a place in Aristotle, to show that the need of an independent defense of possession gave rise sometimes to a process of property. The Locrian law, preserved for us by Polybius, protected the possession of a chattel in controversy for a certain time without

[1] *Cf.* § 326 *ante.*
[2] *Cf.* § 338 *ante.*

hindrance, "nec vi," until a legal decision was rendered, as is equitable. Aristotle says that it is a rule of justice to give preference to the possessor until the decision is rendered. Even in Rome, according to Puchta, the institution was invoked when there was an uncertainty about the possession in the case of a sale, and it was also used to solve the question until a final decision on the property, which made the possession exist *per se* and apart from the property. Niehbuhr, in his "Römische Geschichte," and Savigny say that the protection of possession is connected with the "ager publicus." The citizens had only the enjoyment of this "ager," and felt the need of a means of protecting this right which was not included by the laws of private property. This means of protection was the pretorian edict, at first applicable only to the "ager vectigalis," then, on account of its great utility, it was extended to private property. Sciajola, in his "Commento alla Procetura Sarda," admits with Puchta that the provisions for possession have been preliminary, but he does not believe that they have been the origin of possession but that it is a derivative of the "ager publicus." Van Wetter disagrees from Puchta, and tries to prove that the tests on which the latter relies show only that there was need of an injunction until the question of possession, which was a question of ownership, was settled. Contrary to the belief of Niehbuhr and Savigny is the fact that in the earliest law there are no illusions to possessory injunctions over the "ager publicus," which was protected by a special injunction "de loco publico fruendo." Ihering tries to show that the cause and purpose of the possessory injunctions are found in the necessity of the preliminary action for ownership, but Savigny had already noticed this necessity in the "vindieiæ" and in "manus concertæ." Bruns, in his work "Das Recht des Besitzes im Mittelalte und in der Gegenwart," showed

clearly that these injunctions were for the protection
of the right of possession.

§ 343. *Possession in Roman Law.* If it is true
that the nature of things is nothing but their birth
at definite times and with definite characteristics,
as Vico taught, the modern doctrine of possession,
like every other doctrine, cannot be understood without
tracing its first elements. These are found by studying the laws of Rome and the common and canon law.
This Milone did not do in his study "Possesso delle Cose
e dei Diritti." Roman law divided possession into three
kinds, the "naturalis possessio," or simple detention; the
"possessio," enriched by work; and the "civilis possessio,"
founded on a just title, good faith, and leading to title by
prescription. In the early law books it is said "possessio
animo et corpore constat." It seems that the "animus
possidendi" includes the "animus domini" or the possession with title to the property or possession with any
other title, as Van Wetter and Milone show. This intent
is lacking in the agent who keeps the object for another.
It is lacking also to the factor, bailee, and pledgee who
have possession by contract and not by any property
rights. The "juris quasi-possessio" embraces the cases
of personal and real servitudes. The Roman law treated
as a possessor the pawnee-creditor or him who took in
emphyteusis, the owner of the right in the air, and the
bailee only when the parties to the bailment allowed him
possession to break the prescriptive right, and him who
has the object by virtue of a "precarium." Rationally, of
these five cases of "possessio" only three are regular, that
is, the first three which have to do with property rights;
but the last two, those of bailment and "precarium,"
constitute an anomaly in the philosophy of law because
they are without the sphere of the "jura in re." We
know that the means of defense of possession were

peculiar, some of them like the interdicts, and some were general actions like the "condictiones."

§ 344. *Possession in Modern Law.* The three kinds of law, the canon, common, and feudal, applied the right of possession to new property rights in the form of offices, dignities, immunities, and taxes. It clearly is not rational to confuse public functions with private rights. But the application of the right of possession to these functions, considered as "jura in re" while they rightly cannot be such, was not illogical and contradictory. The canon law made no innovation besides this extension of the "unde vi" of the Romans through the "actio spolii" which applied it to new kinds of chattels, and to personalty. The common law followed the maxim already cited;[1] the hand should make the hand safe, and therefore held that the voluntary tradition of a thing made by one who was not its owner to a third party in good faith should pass the property to the latter. To overcome the severity of such a rule they had to have recourse to an equitable action, which, however, could not be used against innocent third parties. The French law accepted this maxim and amplified it, not permitting the right to pursue a thing which had not been stolen or lost. There was, therefore, no possessory action for such things, but the principle was absolute, that possession as far as personalty was concerned was as good as title. This was necessary to increase facility in trade and was allowed only because of universality of personalty, less by "sapit quid immobile" than by the "universitas." The ancient French law allowed a "complainte" for the disturbance of possession, and a "reintegrande" for theft: the first presupposes the Roman condition of legal possession for a year and a day before the infringement; the second does not demand

[1] *Cf.* § 226 *ante.*

possession for a year and a day, and according to the
Scholiasts could be availed of even by detainers. Is it
rational that the condition of a year and a day should be
brought down from the Roman law? Does it conform to
principle to accord the action of the "spoilatio" even to
detainers? We may notice first of all that the Roman
year of prescription did not regard the acquisition of the
right but the duration of the interdiction, although in
certain cases the Roman law required the exercise of the
right, within the year which preceded the interdiction, that
was based on acts done in that time or on acts affecting
personalty destined to pass freely from hand to hand; as
in the case of the "interdictum de itinere privato" which
required thirty days for exercise, and in the "utrubi" which
presupposed possession "majori parti anni." The possession of a year and a day (the "saisine" of the French law)
is connected with the German "gewere." The "gewere
recht" depends upon possession for a year and a day without interruption by the counter claimant, and is based upon
his silence. It dispossesses a possessor only by the proof
of an adverse acquisition of possession, but it does not dis-
pense with an oath on the justice of his possession. The
"saisine" was originally the same as the "gewere" because
they were acquired in the same way, that is, by entering
into possession and by inheritance, and were equivalent
to a possession based on enjoyment; but "saisine" had one
advantage that "gewere" could not give. Because getting
free of its feudal element and of the title of investure, it
was based on the conception of an abandonment, as
shown by silence for a year and a day, and also on the
conception of the presumption of property. Thus possession is transformed into a provisional property and
becomes a presumption in French law, changing the
method of its protection from that allowed by Roman
or canon law. Possession is no longer viewed *per se*, but

in relation to property. It changes its fundamentals, though maintaining the ancient methods of defense. The "saisine" shows, therefore, the deviation from Roman principles as well as from those of reason, by which possession was an institution independent and separate from ownership, as Viti has clearly shown in his "Commento Sistematico del Codice di Procedura Civile." It is not right to allow a detainer to have recourse to the action for theft (regarding it only as a remedy against violence) since it is essentially possessory, as may be seen from its historical origin which (an extension of the "unde vi") presupposes legal possession. Yet the detainers' right to the action of spoliation cannot be denied if we only allow two kinds of possession, legal and natural, as the French writers have done. Civil possession would have all the necessary conditions, and the natural would have none of them. And hence it is clear that civil possession would be confused with detention, and consequently we must allow detainers an action for theft. But we must not forget that logically there cannot possibly be less than three kinds of possession, — detention, civil possession, and prescriptive possession. Between detention and civil possession the difference lies in the intent to keep the thing. Prescriptive possession is ordinarily characterized by a good title and good faith, but sometimes it has no need of such elements and need show only the marks of publicity, undisturbed continuity, etc. The action for theft, if we accept this definition, can only be given to him who has legal possession.

§ 345. *Possession in Rational Law. Relative Theories.* But let us consider the philosophical base of the institution. The theories are various, but can be divided, as Ihering says, into relative and absolute, depending upon whether they treat it as having a principle within or without. The first relative theory is that of Savigny;

that the violation of the right of possession is the violation of the person, and that therefore the injunctions are
analogous to "actiones ex delicto." Cavallari, in his "In-
stitutiones Juris Romani," wrote that the action for the
right of possession was established to avoid fights between citizens. Rudorf, in his appendix to Savigny and
Serafini in his "Instituzioni," repeats that an attack upon
possession is a breach of public peace. Thibaut states
that the protection of the right of possession is based on
the presumption of law in favor of the "statu quo."
Ahrens makes the basis of possession the maxim, "Quilibet
præsumitur bonus et justus donec probetur contrarium."
Gans, in "System der Römischen Civilrechts," and
Trendelenburg consider that possession indicates property. Romagnosi and Zacharia, in "Handbuch des
Französischen Civilrechts," Mühlenbruch in "Doctrina
Pandectarum," Troplong and De Crescenzio in "Sistema del Diritto Civile Romano," teach that the base
of possession is the presumption of property. Ihering
looks upon possession as the advance guard of property;
that the protection of the right of possession is as necessary as protection of the right of property.

§ 346. *Absolute Theories of Possession.* Among the
absolute theories the earliest is that of Gans, which
was followed by the others of Puchta, Molitor, Bruns,
and Randa. Gans thinks that the right to a thing
through particular will and universal will or law is
property, while to have it only by your particular will
is possession; the particular will is a substantial something and should have a protection at law. Puchta
and Walter add that possession is a right, and that
it is referable to the person himself. Molitor gives
the characteristics of possession, saying that a fact
without a will behind it remains in the category of
facts and does not take its place among rights, and that

the will, a common factor of right, brings about the
"jus possessionis," based on the "animus possidendi."
Bruns thinks that the protection of possession is founded
on the thought that man, through the single fact of his
personality, has control over things. When his will
to own by taking possession of the object becomes
effective control of anything without an owner, it establishes an absolute right or right of property; but when
it concerns things not without an owner, it brings into
existence a right which yields only upon the proof of
property. The control of the possessor, until the moment
this proof is made, cannot be disturbed, and therefore
"possessor hoc ipso quod possessor est plus juris habet
quam ille qui non possidet." Randa writes that the
will when realized objectively, even if unjustified, must
have a right to appear as defendant in a court of law.

§ 347. *Criticism of Absolute and Relative Theories of
Possession.* After deep reflection and a thorough examination of all the absolute and relative theories, it is
right to infer that in all of them there will be found one
identical fundamental conception, although it may be developed in different manners, that is, the inviolability
of the individual person in connection with his things.
Let us first compare the relative theory of Savigny with
the absolute doctrine of Gans, and after an accurate critical analysis the common principle will appear, as Pepere
has shown. It is true that Savigny contradicts Gans
because the latter does not see how particular will, sometimes unjust, can develop into a right. It is true, too,
that Gans contradicts Savigny by saying that the right
of possession cannot owe its origin to its violation
because its violation presupposes the right. Yet it is
undeniable that Savigny thinks the ultimate rationale
of the possession lies in the intimate relation between the
possessor and the things possessed; wherefore, in the vio-

lation of the fact of possession, though perhaps it is not a right, as he says, there is a tortious change of the personal position which can be remedied by the restoration of the prior conditions which the violation has affected. The conception of the inviolability of the person is found in the doctrine of these two philosophers, with this difference: that in Savigny it assumes a negative form, while with Gans it is positive, very similar to the celebrated theory of Kant about the philosophic and rational nature of possession. To the same conception we can reduce, too, the theories of public peace and of the presumption that everyone is held good and honest until the contrary is proven, because the base of public peace is respect of the human personality, individual and collective. And in all men the elements of a rational and free nature are found in their highest development. The doctrine which makes possession a presumption of property and the bulwark of ownership is reducible in the last analysis to the same conception, that is, of property as the projection of the inviolable person. Neither can it be argued that such a principle is the origin of all rights, and therefore cannot be the specific base of the right of possession, because the jurist philosopher should first of all look to see if possession is a simple fact and one which can be a right. It is not possible to begin this research without having recourse to the early authorities and to the supreme criterion of rights, that is, the principle of personality. On the other hand this principle is the specific base of the absolute control of things without an owner or the relative right in things which have an owner, as long as his rights are not clearly shown. This explanation of Bruns is not really contradictory to the theory of Gans, which also gives a specific base, because the absolute right or full control is the effect of the realization

of the particular will recognized as a will to control by
society and the law; and the relative right which gives
rise to possession is derived, too, from the individual
will, protected, too, like the general will, but as absolute
control, except on the proof of a further right. The
theory of Gans cannot be interpreted otherwise if you
wish to give it a serious consideration. Speaking of
the universal will only in relation to property and not
in relation to possession, one would not know how to
give the latter any protection.

§ 348. *Possession is a Right.* One can see how far
from true was the affirmation of Grotius: "Possessoria
judicia juris civilis sunt." Ruggieri, in his work "Il
Possesso," reproduces this belief, holding that the protection of possession does not arise from its nature, from
its absolute virtue, but directly from positive law in
consideration of its external relations, which are of
great convenience; that it is best to keep things as they
are (in doubtful cases) and leave the possessor in possession. Possession is a fact that is protected by inter-
dict and creates a prescriptive right for external reason
of convenience and discretion. All that we have said
before is the most direct criticism of this manner of
looking upon the institution in which the author has
skillfully made use of the early Roman authorities.

§ 349. *Intent is Necessary to Possession.* Ihering,
in a recent work "Der Besitzwille," has expressed a new
objective doctrine about the "animus domini" contradicting the subjective doctrines of Savigny, but he
has not changed his basic ideas on possession. In conformity with the principles as developed by him, he has
studied this state of fact which has legal consequences.
Savigny regards intent as an essential requisite of
legitimate possession, but Ihering says that possession
is a fact. It is necessary to guard its exteriority, the

"corpus," and when this element is proved, that is, the "corporalis possessio," the "animus" which is included therein is proved as well. According to him, the objective fact is enough to prove legal possession. This argument can show the impossibility of legitimate possession in an absolute sense because the thing is external, or in a relative sense because there is a "causa possidendi" which excludes it. The principle that possession has to do only with the objective fact cannot be shaken unless it is determined by positive law that there is simple detention, unless physical possession is impossible, or unless some special circumstance is proved. Now apart from the question of the proof of the intent it is clear that Ihering thinks that it is essential, and shows the difference between detention and possession. He will look to circumstances to prove that the intent cannot be shown by the presence of a special "causa possidendi," but this does not mean that the intent is not an essential condition. The intent exists for Ihering either in the "corporalis possessio" or a presumption. In substance the law accords the possessory action only to him who has this intent in fact or by presumption. Ihering himself says that the opinion which bases legal possession not on the actual and concrete will of the individual, but on a presumptive will, that is, on the will which the possessor ought to have, is the same as the objective doctrine, distinguishing detention from possession by the "causa possidendi." But if the "causa possidendi" is what causes the difference between physical and legal possession, it is clear that legal possession cannot be admitted except in cases in which the presumptive will is shown. The simple "possessio corporalis" is no true indication of legitimate possession. It is an equivocal fact, because it may or may not be accompanied by the intent which the possessor ought to have. How can we presume, therefore, the intent or presumptive will from the fact of the "corpus"? Ihering does not solve this difficulty. Neither does he agree that it is only positive law which allows true possession on the failure of intent or impossibility of subjecting the object to corporal possession. From this point of view his theory is in accord with those of Grotius and Ruggieri.

CHAPTER XII

OBLIGATIONS

OBLIGATIONS.—THEIR ORIGIN.—THE SOURCES OF OBLIGATION —THEIR VARIOUS KINDS AND FORMS.—THE DIFFERENT FORMS AND THEIR DISTINCTION.

§ 350. *Definition of Obligation.* One's wealth does not consist only of property rights but includes also personal rights, that is, obligations. A personal right is a "jus ad rem, jus ad rem consequendam," and therefore consists of "res incorporalis, quæ tangi non potest," while a property right is a "jus in re," and refers to "res corporalis, quæ tangi potest." An obligation has been defined as a legal bond by which one is held to do or give something. This has a different meaning when it is applied to property rights or to the other free rights of a person. The right of obligation, however, from this point of view, is an extension of the property right. An obligation, as an element of one's estate, is the obligation which looks principally to one's material interests, or, as the saying goes, has a financial significance. The jurisconsults, laying stress upon the cause of such obligations, said, "Ea enim in obligatione consistere quæ pecunia lui præstarique possunt." The obligation called by Stahl and Ahrens ethico-juristic, for example, conjugal fidelity, has a basis entirely moral and is superior to human caprice and does not enter at all into one's estate, being without financial value of its own. The rational principle, which distinguishes an ethico-juristic obligation from one which has a monetary value, is the limited nature of man, "unus homo, nullus homo"; man should act with other men in order to attain his end.   The idea of man is always the idea of a specie. Through such relations he becomes self-sufficient and acquires the autarchy of which Aristotle speaks.   The tendency to development urges individuals to a reciprocal exchange.   By this every man increases his strength, and in the increase of the strength of individuals lies the increase of the force of the social whole.

§ 351. *Prerequisites of an Obligation.* An obligation supposes at least two persons: an obligor and obligee; that is, creditor and debtor.   The right to be created is a direct relation between one person and another and therefore is not binding except upon the parties to it.   The obligation does not imply a power over the person of the obligee, but a temporary limitation of his liberty in certain respects.   This conception is expressed in the early books as follows: "Obligationum substantia non in eo consistit ut aliquod corpus nostrum aut servitutem nostram faciat sed ut alium nobis obstrigat ad dandum aliquid vel faciendum vel præstandum." The object must be possible in a physical, moral, and legal aspect; in other words, the obligation must conform to the laws of nature and freedom.   When anyone undertakes to do or to give what he is physically incapable of doing or giving, the contract is illegal.   The contracting parties break the natural law of freedom.   They break the law of freedom if they promise to do acts contrary to morality or subversive of law, because freedom is acquired with truth and justice; without them there is no liberty, but caprice and license. The object of an obligation, as value, which enters into the estate, must be reducible to money.   The breach of an obligation entails a penalty in damages capable of pecuniary estimation.   Damages include the real diminution of the estate and the gain which has been lost ("Damnum emergens et lucrum cessans"), and the penalty includes also "omne quod interest," being co-extensive with the harm done. The theory of damage is applicable directly to financial obligations and approximately to obligations of another kind, like those growing out of bodily harm or dishonorable conduct. Bruns has observed that in acts which harm the organic or moral activity of man it is not possible to create an indemnity to overcome the harmful effects, but it is not out of place to allow pecuniary indemnity for the creation of the means of a new activity or different enjoyment. Let us recognize, with Ihering and Windscheid, that the judicial protection should be extended to ideal interests, and that the conception of interest should be full and relative, including the necessities of every class of life, varying according to the time, place and race, as Ihering says: "Let us not deny that money, besides acting as a penalty, can often be a certain satisfaction, and that from the action for damages and from the money satisfaction accorded in some cases of tort it is not right to argue that the object of the obligation is commercial; but let us state merely that the obligation capable of affecting one's estate is ordinarily susceptible of a direct pecuniary appraisement, although sometimes the value of the object in question could not be exactly stated in money, since sentimental feelings of the individual cannot be weighed. But if an exact valuation is lacking we can always put an indirect or approximate pecuniary appraisement on it, which will represent a penalty and a satisfaction or help in ethico-juristic obligations without pretending to express their object in money, and will be part of the estate though the obligation had nothing to do with it." In a word, an obligation generally cannot be conceived of without a *quid pro quo*, that is, without an end in view, and the consideration is the same as the immediate or intrinsic end, independent of the internal and subjective motives, as we will see forthwith.

§ 352. *Five Sources of Obligation.* Obligations, according to modern jurists, are derived from five sources,— contract, quasi-contract, tort and quasi-tort, and the statutes. The Roman jurisconsults recognized only four: "Obligationes aut ex contractu nascuntur aut ex maleficio, aut proprio quodam jure, ex variis causarum figuris." The "variæ figuræ causarum" are described in the Roman books as "quasi ex contractu, quasi ex maleficio." The philosophy of law can reduce these sources to two, — to human will and natural juristic order,— because all obligations (except the contractual) are not assumed freely but are imposed directly or indirectly by the law of reason, as we will see. In truth, quasi-contract results from the legitimate act of a man who becomes bound to another without a definite agreement. Quasi-contract is distinguished from tort because it is caused by an act and by contract originating in the will of one of the parties. Examples of quasi-contract are the acceptance of a bill, the payment of a debt of a third person, and the "communio incidens." The base is the average will of man which law presumes, and of which Lassalle speaks, or the presumed consent, that is in harmony with the principles of equity. In the acceptance for honor of a bill there is no contradiction in speaking of a quasi-contract; one can suppose the consent of the "dominus negotii." As it is logical to infer that the man who wishes the end wishes the means, there is an implied duty to reimburse. Rosmini looks upon this form and nomenclature as absurd, not being able to conceive of a mean between contract and non-contract. He believes that in such form the law im-

agines a consent and that there is in fact none, and that
by the principles of equity he explains obligations based
on defective agreements as quasi-contracts. But he
does not agree that the common presupposition of
obligations is will: this conception eliminates at once
all objection and shows that there is not a true "fictio
juris" where the just will of human nature is found. He
does not understand the average will of man, which he
confuses with the changeable and concrete will of the
individual, when he says that presumptive consent is
uncertain and cannot produce certain rights and obligations because the "dominus negotii" is sometimes incapable of consenting through madness or infancy. The
average will conforms to reason. It is the will which
a man should have in the conduct of life. It is "sanæ
mentis." Such a will is always certain and could be
found in the fool, if not being a fool he were sane, or
in the child if he was not such, but was an adult. No
other kind of will can be raised to a principle of law,
that is, a manifestation of reason. It is clear that the
obligation in quasi-contract comes directly from the
presumption of the consent, from the will, and indirectly from the statutes which are based thereon.

§ 353. *Obligations Sounding in Tort.* From the conception of a natural juristic order come, too, the obligations which are the consequence of fraud or negligence.
The order infringed, the law broken, there arises a
necessity of restoration, which is had through penalties
and reimbursement for the harm done. A tort is the
result of fraud or harm. Negligence is a kind of quasi-
tort, being an infraction of due diligence ("debitum
diligentiæ") which has caused some damage. Negligence differs from accident because in the former case
that has not been foreseen which could be foreseen,
but with an accident the unforeseen was unforeseeable.

Tort and quasi-tort in modern times produce first a penalty and then the duty to compensate. When the private penalties of Roman law, by which the defendant could pay the plaintiff a sum of money, were abolished and the principle that a penalty is a demand of social justice and a system of public law was installed, the principal obligations dependent upon tort and quasi-tort were no longer part of private law, as with the Romans, but there was only the accessory obligation (called Nicoline, after the Roman family of that name) which looks to the interests damaged. From the natural juristic order, however, there arise directly some obligations of a monetary order. It is not true that all the obligations originating in statutes belong to public law because statutes can establish obligations for the interest of private utility, and declare rights which can be acquired in the strict sense of the word.

§ 354. *Divisions of Obligations with regard to their Subject and Object.* Obligations, to no longer consider their origin (from which point of view they are voluntary and involuntary), are divided into various kinds according to their subject and object, the tie created and the legal action that protects it. The subject can be a single debtor and a single creditor, or several debtors and one creditor, or *vice versa*, or several debtors and several creditors. Obligators from this point of view, and especially in the case of the number of subjects, are either (*pro rata*) several or (*in solidum*) joint. In several obligations the debtors and the creditors have reciprocal rights and duties. It is not one, however, but is divided into as many parts as there are parties to its obligation. The joint obligation is one unity essentially subjective by which each of the debtors has the right of demanding full performance by the creditors, and each one of the creditors must perform the entire obligation for the debtor or debtors. The Roman law made a difference between the "obligatio corporalis" and the "obligatio in solidum" because in the first there is a common obligation, while in the second there are several persons held to the performance of the entire duty imposed upon each of them. If in the first the creditor pays, he frees his co-creditors acting in the cause of all and cannot claim a right of contribution as in the joint obligation; and if an obligation becomes absolute by a judgment against one, all his fellow contractors are free, something which does not occur in a joint obligation. A distinction somewhat analogous is made by the jurists who follow the theories of Molineo, and who say that there are joint and joint and several obligations. The first are based on an explicit agreement and on a presumed contract with the parties "ad servandam et perpetuandam obligationem"; the second arise from a fact or statute and do not presume the agreement. The result common to both kinds is the "deberi in totum," but the prescription by a debtor or creditor in the joint obligation is a defense for all, and a plea of abatement against one obligation is good against all, while this is not true of an imperfect joint obligation. The different results depend upon the reciprocal agreement between the parties presumed in the case of a perfect joint obligation but not permitted in the imperfect one.

§ 355. *Subdivisions of Obligations as they regard Objects.* As to the object, obligations can be divisible, indivisible, alternative, and potential. An obligation is divisible if the promise is capable of being divided naturally or legally; it is indivisible if the thing or act is not susceptible of division (as a promise to give a horse), or if, though capable of division, the parties have not so considered it (as the contract to build a house). Indivisibility is an objective unity and is enforced against the heirs. In this it differs from jointness, which is extinguished when the subjects to which it belongs are destroyed. The writers who follow Molineo are wont to construct an obligation perfectly indivisible and an obligation imperfectly indivisible. The former arises from nature and agreement and has in consequence the "deberi pro parte sed in totum." It should be "pro parte" because the parties do not constitute a single unity, as in the joint obligation, and nevertheless should be one "ratione rei et facti." On demand against one of the creditors a good defense should bind all the debtors in the perfect indivisible obligation, since no debtor can preserve his part of the right without preserving that of his fellows. The imperfect indivisibility is established "ob incongruitatem solutionis," that is, to avoid the harm which would be caused by a divided payment; and exists only between the heirs of the obligee and not among the heirs of the obligor, which proves that there cannot be a full "individuum solutionis," as Pothier believes. Here the single payment alone is not divided because its division would do harm. The agreement is alternative if there are several distinct things of which the obligee must necessarily only do one, and he has the election. In the potential agreement the objects are not in the consideration and the obligee can at his pleasure do what he wants.

§ 356. *Kinds of Vincula in Obligations.* As to their obligations, agreements are simple, conditional, modal, and penal. Simple agreements are without any provisions as to the means. A condition implies a future or uncertain event upon which the obligation depends. Conditions are various according to the quality of the event, the effect which they produce, and the manner in which they are shown. In respect to the quality of event conditions are affirmative if its happening is necessary to the contract, negative if it is necessary to the contract that it should not happen, potential when the event depends upon the will of the obligor or obligee, casual if it depends upon chance, mixed when it depends partly upon the will of the third party and partly upon chance. Of course, they can be possible or impossible physically, morally, and legally. An agreement is not binding which depends upon a mere potential condition, that is, from the "si voluero" of the obligee, or upon some insignificant act of his that is confusible with a "si voluero"; for example, "I will give you a hundred dollars if you look me in the face." Ageements are void which are based upon a condition that is impossible from any of the three points of view, but the agreement is valid if it is based upon a condition of not doing an impossible thing, because the condition must be fulfilled. A negative immoral condition is admitted because the law cannot disregard the promise of an advantage, accepted to induce the other party not to do harm. An affirmative immoral condition, if casual, should be recognized as legal as to the obligee, since it depends upon the act of the third party and is for him the same as any other event. As to the result, the conditions are suspensive or revocatory if an acquisition of a right or the carrying out of the obligation depends thereon. The first keeps the obligation in suspense until the fulfillment of the condition. When the event happens the obligation is considered not as placed upon some condition, but as originating from the contract. If the event does not happen the duty is considered as never having existed. The second does not hold over the execution of the obligation, but upon the happening of the event the obligation is considered as not having existed at all, and the obligor must return what he has received. In respect to the forms of conditions they are express, tacit, or implied. If the end of the contract depends upon a future and certain event it does not affect the obligation, but merely retards its execution. A penal clause is a kind of antecedent liquidation of damages. It is used when the contractor wishes to insure the fulfillment of the contract and promises something in case of failure or delay. The penal clause is an accessory, and therefore the nullity of the contract involves the nullity of the clause itself.

§ 357. *Obligations in Civil and Natural Law.* As to actions, obligations are classified as civil and natural. Civil obligations are, of course, founded on natural law, (on which positive law is moulded,) as well as the natural obligations, and are fully recognized by the statutes which give a right of action. Natural obligations are founded also on civil law, which recognizes them without giving them full effect, and protects them only by way of exceptions when their immediate origin is rational law. Natural obligations differ from moral duties ("officia") which obtain their strength only from morals. These, from the viewpoint of positive law, are incomplete obligations, not absolutely inefficacious, born of the need of recognizing in certain relations legal purposes and reasonable restraints, but which cannot be given, for many causes of social interest, a right of action. In natural obligation we can recognize the "vinculum æquitatis" and "debere natura," as the old Roman law said, and the execution of the promise is regarded not as an act of moral justice, but as the fulfillment of a legal duty of a "debitum naturale." It excludes, therefore, the recovery of what has been paid. There is no possibility of restitution in cases of filial ingratitude or pride. Certainly this "vinculum æquitatis," which is a "vinculum juris" in the philosophy of law, would be extortion if not kept within confines of a determinate nature by positive law. Personality itself, in order to be the effective subject of rights and duties, has need, as we have seen,[1] of a civil investiture.   There is no need of wonder if such a recognition is given to the "obligatio naturalis," which does not signify that there is no other base for the obligations than that of civil law.   Rational law has no practical effect without the recognition of the statutes, but this does not mean that law and personality are creations of the statutes.   Natural obligations have a foundation beyond positive law in the sense that they are derived from the "recta ratio," which is shown in our civil statutes, but which nevertheless does not arise from them.   This indicates a superior source, but one not absolutely extrinsic and transcendent, because natural law is developed in positive law and is connected with it as the true interpenetrates with the certain.   From another aspect the "obligatio naturalis" lies in positive law.   It is founded on the statutes because it can have more value as an exception.   Windscheid thinks that it represents the inorganic part of the legal system, and he is right from an historical point of view.   The ancient "jus civile" was restricted, narrow, and ironbound, taking no account of many relations which were really juristic. Little by little these relations, regulated at first by the "jus gentium" or the "jus naturale," became part of the "jus civile."   The statement by Windscheid, considered in itself, is not the rule, because the incompleteness of the "obligatio naturalis" depends upon its own purpose and nature.   We can say that its perfection consists in its defective origin by which it cannot be equal to the "obligatio civilis."

§ 358. *Extinguishment.* (a) *Payment.* Obligations are extinguished in ten ways: The first is the payment defined in the strict sense as "præistatio eius quod in obligatione est."   The statutes, to promote the in-

[1] Cf. § 170 *ante*.

terests of trade and render redress easy against the debtor, who paid in order to be free of the contract, have introduced subrogation, consisting in a fictitious settlement by which a debt extinguished by the payment of a third party is considered as existing to the latter's advantage, who can use all the rights growing out of the contract to recover what he has paid.

(b) *Novation.* The second way of extinguishing a contract is a novation. "Novatio est prioris debiti in aliam obligationem transfusio atque translatio." Novation can be subjective if it concerns the subject of an agreement, objective if it concerns its object. Subjective novation takes place when a new contractor is substituted for the old towards whom the creditor is free, or when a new creditor is substituted for the former one who is freed. In the first case, the consent of the creditor of the former debtor and of the new debtor are needed. It is different from the extinguishment of a debt which needs only the consent of the granting creditor and the grantee, and produces no novation. In the second case there can be the *delegation* or *appropriation.* Delegation needs the consent of the obligor of the new and old obligee, while appropriation needs only the consent of the debtor and new creditor. The principle that governs the requirement of consent in respect to persons in novation is always placed in the protection of the reasonable interests of the parties who could be harmed by the change. Objective novation is where a new object is substituted for the old object and contract, changing the modality of the contract.

(c) *Release.* The third form of extinguishment is a release of the promise or gratuitous abandonment of it. It is really a gift, and therefore needs mutual consent.

(d) *Substitution.* The fourth form of extinguishment is substitution. "Debiti et crediti inter se contributio."

The promises should be of the same kind because "aliud pro alio invito creditore salvi nequit," and should be liquidated and mature; that is, the certainty of the "quantum et an debeatur" should not be lacking and should not be dependent upon conditions or events. Substitution (the utility of which was discovered by Pomponius: "Interest nostra potius non solvere quam solutum repetere") acquires in modern times the greatest importance, and becomes in large cities the most important method of extinguishment. Civilized people go through three stages; at first they adopt a metallic coinage, then a mixed coinage, and when they have fully developed, they limit the issue of notes and adopt a system of extensive credit. Luzzatti has correctly compared the economy of circulation in its last phase to a pyramid whose ample base is of metal, and whose apex is of bank notes, while the whole body of the edifice is built of commercial paper, deposits, and substitutions. The tendency of bank notes to economize metallic coinage is not so great as that possessed by other kinds of credit, especially through the system of substitution, represented by the circulation of checks assigned in the form of orders to pay either by a "clearing house" or house of exchange. Patterson, Bagehot, and Pelgrave show by statistics the law of English trade in which through bank notes substitution takes the place of credit. The sum issued by the Clearing House in 1844 did not surpass forty times the total of the paper issued. In 1872 it was a hundred and thirty times as great. And yet England and the United States were at one time countries run mad with paper money.

(e) *Confusion.* The fifth method of extinguishment is confusion in one person of the two qualities that are mutually destructive; that is, the quality of debtor and creditor.

(f) *Destruction.* The destruction of the thing which is owed or an event which renders the fulfillment of the contract impossible without fault on the part of the debtor, an event such as would absolutely destroy the object, is the sixth manner of extinguishment. This destruction is not extended to contract with objects of a general nature because "genera numquam pereunt." This sixth method is based upon the failure of the object of the contract.

(g) *Rescission.* The seventh method is annulment or rescission. Annulment is produced by an inherent vice in the contract. Rescission depends upon breach. The obligation is gone in the case of annulment. Rescission can result in the avoidance of the obligation or its continuance with the payment of the part due.

(h) *Fulfillment.* The eighth method is the fulfillment.

(i) *Prescription.* The ninth lies in prescription.

(j) *Death of Debtor.* The tenth and last is the death of the debtor with the obligation unfulfilled, where he was bound to do or not to do something in a relation established on personal considerations. In agreements of giving, the death of the debtor is not a cause of extinguishment, because the thing can be given as well by his heirs. With the death of a man all those relations end which are joined in a most intimate manner to him, but those relations continue which are financial.

CHAPTER XIII

CONTRACT AND ITS FORMS

THE NOTION OF CONTRACT. — ITS PHASES AND BASIS. — ESSEN-
TIAL REQUISITES. — VICES OF CONSENT AND SOME RECENT
THEORIES. — THE INTERPRETATION OF CONTRACTS. — THEIR
CLASSIFICATION; AND THE DOCTRINES OF KANT AND TREN-
DELENBURG.

§ 359. *Ethical Origin of Contract.* Contract arises
from voluntary obligation and comprehends all the part
of private law that is called from it "jus voluntarium."
A contract is clearly connected with ownership because
the will of the owner is the untrammelled disposer of
the object and can keep or give it away or can provide
for his successor by an agreement. The agreement is
made by the free will and consists in the exchange of
the utilities of life. Its rationale is found in the limitations of human nature and in the tendency to autarchy,
as we have said before.[1] This proves once more that
the ethical relations of a higher order, although not
foreign to the will, cannot be ultimately explained
through contract, because the latter has in it a factor
of caprice and accident and is influenced by utility.

§ 360. *Definition of Contract.* A contract according
to the Roman jurisconsults is "duorum vel plurium in
idem placitum consensus." We must note, however, that
two people can agree theoretically and still there will be
no contract. Hence it follows that the addition by
Heineccius to the Roman definition is good, that is, "de
re danda vel facienda vel præstanda." Modern writers

[1] *Cf.* § 347 *ante.*

define a contract as the agreement of two or more persons for a legal purpose that has a financial value. Among these, Rosmini looks upon a contract as an agreement and legal effect of the corresponding acts of two persons, one of whom, the owner of a right, voluntarily frees himself from the legal chain (with or without conditions) so that the other may become owner of it if he wishes; and the other makes an efficient acceptance, fulfills the conditions, if any, and appropriates the right. A contract, therefore, is an accepted promise; a promise without acceptance is the desire to give, to do or not to do something. A promise according to the Roman law is "pollicitatio." "Pactum est duorum consensus atque conventio, pollicitatio vero solius offerentis promissum." In three cases the "pollicitatio" is enough to obligate the promisor because of the particular favor given by the statutes to certain institutions, that is, when the promise creates a dowry ("dos") or is in favor of a municipality to obtain an office or for some religious purpose, such as an offering to God.

§ 361.   *History of Contract.*   In primitive times contract did not and could not have the importance which it has to-day.   Primitive law was essentially imperative because it had to coerce men into obedience to the statutes towards which they were most hostile.   For this purpose it needed a strong hand.   Centuries of slavery preceded through historical necessity the centuries of liberty and personal initiative.   The community, not the individual, was the base of legal government in primitive times.   The individual did not create rights and duties of himself but rather as the head of a tribe, village community, or family.   Contracts were binding between the heads of particular communities.   They were not easy of creation, being surrounded by many formalities, because the mind was deep dyed with sensations and fancies which took the place of reality, as we have said before.[1] Formality and ceremony, absolute necessities, had the greatest importance because they gave strength to the promise or showed the absence of consent. Good faith had but little power, says Maine, for in the Homeric poems the deceitful cunning of Ulysses is praised as fully as the gallantry of Achilles. If bad faith is victor in our day, we must remember the indefinite extent and immense complexity of modern social relations and the increase of objects and opportunities for it.

§ 362. *Historical Phases of Contracts.* Maine also shows clearly the three phases of contract, that is, the phase in which the contractual idea was confused with the transfer of title, that of the separation of contract from pacts, and the other of the absorption of contracts in agreement. The Romans at first called a contract a "nexum" and the "nexum" involved the "jura in re" and was the means of transferring property. Subsequently the "nexum" referred to contract only, while the "mancipatio" was applied to ownership. The same development affected the "nexum" and the "patria potestas," which originally included in its authority the son, wife, and property and then was restricted to its narrow use of "mancipium" and "manus." When contract was separated from the transfer of ownership it was looked upon as a pact accompanied by an obligation and was distinguished from a mere pact which had no obligation. After the unity of initial vagueness there came the antithesis of development. Of the four kinds of contracts in Roman law, the eldest was the verbal, of which the "stipulatio" is typical, consisting in a question by him who could accept a promise, and the answer. Written contracts appeared later, made by writing the sum

---

[1] *Cf.* § 268 *ante.*

due into an account book, and of still later date were real contracts, in which the execution of one part for equitable reason imposed the duty of fulfillment of the other.   Last came the consensual forms: pledge, partnership, sale, and lease.   The consensual contracts were "jure gentium" and developed when Roman commerce became general and regular.   The Roman jurisconsults nevertheless believed that this kind of contract was primitive, governed by the belief in the historical precedence of the "jus naturæ et gentium" before discussed.[1]   Let us here observe that what is more spiritual and universal cannot appear at the beginning but at the end, as is proved by the eternal history of men and people.   In the third period, the pact absorbed the contract by the progress of the "jus naturæ."   Pacts were entitled to an equitable action which supposed a consideration but did not have the form of contract, and the "obligatio naturalis" was recognized and protected as an exception.   In the Middle Ages the Roman conception of the third period became more explicit and the difference between pact and contract disappeared, especially by the application of the law of the "Longobardi," through which arose the "actio de nudis pactis."   Tacitus had already said of the Germans, "vir bonus solis verbis obligatur."   Every agreement added to a contract "in continenti aut ex intervallo" gave a right of action.   A strictly legal contract was not clearly distinguished from an equitable one.   All contracts were thought to be of good faith and it was universally admitted that fraud or deceit vitiated them.

§ 363. *Duty of Keeping Contracts.* The duty of keeping a contract is not only moral but legal. Its breach is a breach of good faith and is harmful to acquired interests and rights. The promisee gives

[1] *Cf.* § 153 *ante.*

up his property and transfers it into the power of
the promisor and has a right, therefore, to the fulfillment of the latter's obligations, through mutuality.
And the promisor has the right to the promised objects
which have already become his by the meeting of the
two wills.   The old authorities said that if the promisor
retracted his promise he would wish to join to himself
something legally belonging to another, and the promisee
who wished to rescind would subject the promisor to
a new acquisition in spite of himself; in both cases there
would be clear injustice.   Now when Fichte states that
the obligation for fulfilling a contract arises when
one party begins to act under it, he follows the untrue
theory that executory obligation is exclusively moral
and not legal.   Fundamentally, the obligatory force of
contract lies in the pre-agreement of the parties controlled by the rules of equity and justice.   Schlossmann,
in "Der Vertrag," argues against this that this force
is not a derivative of will because the promisor might
not intend to be bound as in obligations in which the
words do not correspond to the true will of the obligee.
For example, he who contracts as a joke is bound, if his
declaration makes the obligor believe that it is a serious
proposition to do or to give.   So is he who contracts with
a mental reservation or signs papers prepared by others
without reading them.   Schlossmann has not considered
that by the meeting of the minds in the contract there
is formed a common will which is law between the
parties.   The promissor cannot destroy the will to be
bound because it needs mutual agreement to destroy
the chain which has been forged.   If some obligations
in conventional matters are created simply by statute,
which represents the principle of justice and equity,
and are not voluntary (although they arise on occasions
of a voluntary act either deceitful or fraudulent) we can-

not on this account deny that the other obligations owe
their origin and force to the wills of the parties.   In the
examples given by Schlossmann there is an obligation
through the imprudence or bad faith of the promisor
or subscriber: "Nemo ex sua culpa beneficium trahere
debet; factum quique suum non adversario nocere
debet."   On the other hand, there is the maxim, "Male-
tiis non est indulgendum."   The belief which we have
emphasized is closely connected with the broader but
inaccurate theory on the subject of juridical acts,
many of which are contractual.   We know that such
acts are a manifestation of will with the object of
making, changing, or destroying a legal relation; now
it is stated that the legal effects of the act of man do not
depend upon private will, but upon the statutes.   An
act of man is a fact, to which the statutes, without considering the intent, and therefore without regard to
the legality or illegality of the purpose, attribute certain
definite consequences.   There is something true in this
doctrine in that the statutes recognize and regulate legal
consequences and acts of men, according to a criterion
of natural causality and social efficiency.   But the statutes do not create legal consequences, as they do not
create either will power or the acts resulting therefrom;
their proper scope being limited to recognition and punishment.   In life, individual acts and purposes are developed which the law recognizes and regulates, and some
acts and purposes are accomplished which the law
forbids, whence the unavoidable difference between legal
consequences and illegal acts.   In regulating such consequences, the law, influenced always by their natural causality and social efficiency, allows some wished for by the
parties, prohibits some, and further adds others.   Law
tends through regulations to realize the will of man, but in
some cases the effect foreseen is not legally possible.   The

bequest of the usufruct of perishable things, for example, cannot be strictly allowed in the Roman law, therefore the owner of the usufruct was given property in the things themselves, but he was obliged to give bond for restitution of it or its equivalent, therefore there were legal effects of which the grantor had no knowledge and which were not especially wished for by him.

§ 364. *Essentials of Contracts.* The duty to keep one's contract depends upon four essential requisites, that is, upon capacity of will, free consent, the possibility of carrying out the promise, and the consideration. The contractor should be a person who has the effective use of his reason and can legitimately carry out his intentions, therefore lunatics, drunkards, minors, and in general those who must subject their will to the will of others, have not the right or capacity to contract. The consent must be determinate, that is, it must be an act of firm intention to alienate or acquire. It must necessarily be uniform in both parties, otherwise the "idem placitum" would not exist, and there would be no mutuality. This demands the contemporaneous meeting of the minds of the parties. Conversely, if diverse desires are shown, there is no true consent, as in the example in which one answers negatively to an offer and later changes his mind and accepts; in this hypothesis it cannot be known whether he who has made the offer still holds open his proposition, and a second answer must be received before there is a contract. Through ratification a consent made *post factum* has the strength of a contemporaneous promise. A ratification has such an effect naturally and not through any positive institution, as can be seen from analysis. Consent either express or tacit must be clear. Admitting that the consent must be determinate, uniform, reciprocal, contemporaneous, and clear, according to the analysis of Rosmini and Ptolemy, yet if it is not free it has no legal effect. Consent is free when the activity of man, by which it is effective, works without obstacles, for example, mistake, fraud, or duress, to impede its exercise. Here the word free has a very broad and generic sense.

§ 365. *Offer and Acceptance.* The requisite of contemporaneous consent gives rise to the question of when the contract is perfected, when offer and acceptance cannot take place simultaneously. Are such contracts made from the moment of acceptance or when the notice of acceptance is brought to the offerer? Let us follow out the theory that the contract is binding from the time in which the acceptance is made known to the offerer. The consent is the meeting of two minds or the agreement in the "idem placitum." This meeting is not blind temporal coincidence, but rather their interpenetration not possible without conscious effort. The minds unite only in the consciousnesses of the persons who wish to make them unite, and manifest this desire by definite acts. If, when they are in the same place, words spoken and understood by the contractors give rise to an obligation, a letter or telegram of acceptance must be received by the offeror, if he is absent, because there is an "obligatio mittentis seu scribendis." Suppose, in the case of people contracting face to face, that the offerer was physically incapable of understanding the answer or the words of the offeree, it is evident that the contract would not be complete until such an understanding was brought about. So, if the offerer has not received notice of acceptance, there can only be a "propositum" without an obligation. A letter or telegram from the offerer are always inanimate things and cannot be considered as agents to receive and acknowledge the acceptance. We cannot allow a contract to exist where one of the contractors does not know of the acceptance of the other, and therefore has no knowledge of his own obligations. Offer and acceptance are necessary to a contract, and they should be governed by the same rules. The offer creates an obligation when it is known and accepted by him to whom it is addressed; the acceptance is binding only after it has been brought to the knowledge of the offerer. There is no need for introducing a different rule for the two parties, binding the offerer from the very beginning and letting the offeree have free foot as to acceptance or refusal. Justice is preserved in the system which we have defended because the offeror can revoke his offer as long as the offeree knows nothing of it, and the offeree can withdraw his acceptance until it has reached the offerer. As soon as the notice of acceptance has reached the offerer, however, the two minds have met and interpenetrated and the contract is made, because the two minds have met and fused and there is no reason to give another notice to the offeree, thus going on in an endless chain. Under the principle that the contract is made when the acceptance is known by the offeror, we must make some exceptions commanded by reason and by the nature of things themselves. In the first place, it is understood that this rule is not applicable where the offeror has expressed or implied that he would assume the obligations before hearing. Theory teaches us that in unilateral promises or contracts we must presume such an intent. In contracts of pledge or deposit,[1] the sending of the object, its receipt and retention, without refusal, imply its acceptance. This is not the case,

[1] The words used by our author as examples of contracts for goods are "mutuo," "commodato," "pegno," and "deposito." A mutuum is a loan of consumable goods which the borrower can use and return in kind. A commodatum is where there is a loan for use by the borrower who is to return the same goods. A pegno is a common law pledge. A deposit is where an object is loaned for custody and care, but the custody is the more important.

however, in some consensual contracts, bailments for work, and agencies,[1] though the contractor to whom the offer is made immediately carries out his part. This principle is not applicable in certain urgent transactions of business life through force of custom. Contracts made over the telephone are not made between people at a distance, because the contractors are in direct means of communication in spite of the distance between them. The presence of the contractors should not be understood in an absolute manner implying that they should see each other and study one another mutually from head to foot, because it is enough that their minds be in accord while making the contract.

§ 366. *Fraud and Mistake.* Mistake is a false belief about the contract into which a contractor falls of his own accord; fraud is mistake caused by the other's trickery or deceit. Fraud, the old authorities teach, differs from mistake only in the source from which it is derived, but is fundamentally the same as mistake, both being reducible to an untrue belief. If the mistake is about the substance of the object or an accidental quality considered as essential by the parties, or about the person without whom contractor would not have been entered into the contract, the contract is void under the old Roman maxim, "Non videntur qui errant consentire." Mistake about an accidental quality (not considered as essential by the parties) does not render the contract void, but gives rise to indemnity for the difference between the terms of the contract and the contract as carried out, for nobody can enrich himself to the harm of another. Fraud practised by one of the contractors

---

[1] The words used in the original text are "mandato" and "commissione." A mandate is the same as a deposit except that the care is more important than the custody. A commission is a common law agency.

or by a third person with his knowledge, if it is such
as to induce the contract, is an even stronger reason
for its invalidity, because its enforcement would be a
manifest injustice. The contractor who is a victim of
cunning can demand the nullification of the contract and
reimbursement for any damage suffered. The fraudulent contractor cannot do this, otherwise both would
be placed in the same legal position with an evident un-
balancing of the scales of proportion, which is the law.

§ 367. *Duress.* Duress can be either physical or
moral: the former makes a man submit like a
machine, and excludes all meeting of the minds because the license of him who uses duress is absolutely
dominant; the second can be exerted by depriving
the victim of the use of his mind and free will, thus
rendering him incapable of giving a valid consent.
If the fear is not such as to destroy the intelligent
use of the mind and free will, the consent must be
considered as valid, but in this case there is injustice
on the part of him who desires to enforce the contract, and the other contractor should be allowed to
rescind or proceed with the contract. The fear must
be real, "non metus vani hominis," and must be such
as would induce a reasonable man to enter the contract.
The severe Roman law gave no remedy to him who made
a contract under force or violence.   Later, the pretorian
equity allowed a tempering control under the "exceptio
quod metus causa." It is clear that a statute should use
great precaution and assume the medial way, that is,
should not favor the abuse of moral influence or encourage moral cowardice.

§ 368. *Contract is the Meeting of the Minds.* It
may be useful to develop a little more at length the
above conception of error, fraud, and duress. There
are some German jurists, as Schlossmann, Bähr, and

others, who base the validity of contract entirely on the
words of the contractors and deny that the State can
exercise a right of nullification, in the first place, because
the declared will is not understood to produce of itself a
juristic change, but rather visible or audible signs by
which the other is persuaded of the existence of a will to
make the indicated change. Windscheid, in the "Archiv
für Civilistische Praxis," disagrees with these jurists
and shows with little difficulty that the declarations of
the parties of their intention becomes external and comprehensive. It would be strange if the parties, in entering
into relations with each other, only produce sound waves
or come together only in such a way as to perceive light
waves in place of understanding one another and of
agreeing and creating rights and duties.   It is clear they
can move, speak, or write, but their movement, words, or
gestures are means or signs of their thought and will,
through which the transmission of rights is made and
understood. Bähr says that a contractor who has fallen
into a mistake knows that the other must be governed
by his words, and therefore consents to their apparent
meaning.   He treats good faith and the importance of
trade with such consideration that he would obligate him whose signature has been gotten by fraud.
He adds that everyone in certain cases (as in that of
a mental reservation) admits the efficacy of statements
which do not conform to the will. Bähr has not considered that a contractor who is a victim of mistake has not
intended to make the declaration different from the one
in his mind, which conforms to his real will, and intends
that the other contractor should be governed by what
he supposes his statement has been, and does not consent in the least to the appearance of what he says. Good
faith and commercial interests should not be made to
prevail against the law which (in order to protect the

interest of the bona fide debtor or endorsee) does not recognize the liability of him in whose name a receipt or a commercial paper has been forged. The rational principle that a grantee cannot have greater rights than his grantor is not logically reconcilable with the theory advanced. The grantee in good faith has not greater rights than the guilty or forging grantor; that is, he has no right and consequently the appearance has no weight. In law, a mental reservation has no effect because it is a purely internal and unexpressed volition. Thus it can be looked upon as an example of the "idem esse et non esse," for it is impossible that the will should be self-contradictory. A declaration is an act of will. It is the will made sensible in determinate form and it cannot be coexistent with a mental reservation which negatives the act.

§ 369. *Void and Voidable Contracts.* The French jurists divide legal mistakes into mistakes which do not give rise to consent, called "ostative," and into those which destroy it. The Roman jurisconsults saw a logical difference in the error *in corpore*, subsisting in the mistake of one thing for another, and the error *in substantia*, which was a mistake of the material of the contractual object. Both mistakes brought about the annulment of the contract according to the statement of Ulpian: "Ego me fundum emere putarem cornelianum, tu mihi vendere sepronianum putastis, quia in corpore dissensimus,—emptio nulla est. Inde quæritur si ipso corpore non erratur, sed in substantia error sit, ut puto si acetum pro vino vendat, æs pro auro, vel plumbum pro argento nullam esse venditionem puto quotiens in materia erratur." In both cases there is an "aliud pro alio." The error *in corpore* corresponds to the "ostative" mistake of the French, and the error *in substantia* to the mistake which destroys consent. In the philosophy of law, a distinction which has only a logical or intellectual value has no weight, because the two kinds of mistake are always reducible to an essential mistake, one concerning the object of the contract, about which the parties have exercised their wills or without which they would not have been in accord, that is, upon the substance of the thing, not understood of itself and objectively, but as it was thought of by the wills of the contractors. There can be no doubt that such an error voids consent, the effect of knowledge and free will, and that it therefore voids the contract. And the nature of essential mistake cannot fail to be of such effect, be it excusable or not, since the consent is lacking; but the inexcusableness of the mistake gives the other party the stronger right to claim damages. We have said[1] that fraud and mistake differ only in the source from which they arise and the fundamental basis of both of them is the false belief. To have fraud, we need the false belief brought about in the mind of one by the deceit or trickery of the other, and in civil law we need nothing more. It is based on the intention and possibility of harm, because fraud produces the same consequences as mistake, with which it is confusable.

§ 370. *Extent of Duress.* In regard to duress one should consider the inexactness of Schliemann's doctrine, which starts with the conception that duress is not really a voluntary act but forces a declaration which does not agree with the internal will. In Schliemann's mind, there is no consent in this case, and the contract is void. Now this doctrine would be applicable to the two cases of "vis absoluta," in which one becomes the mechanical instrument in the hands of him who uses duress, and of the "vis compulsiva," which can momentarily take away knowledge and freedom. In such cases there is an external similarity to will, but will and

[1] *Cf.* § 362 *ante.*

consent are in fact lacking. If the fear is not such as to over-shadow the mind and to destroy absolutely the normal will, consent cannot be said to be lacking, and yet the contract can be avoided because freedom is hindered in its exercise by injustice, from which no right can arise. In such a case the principle of the failure of consent is not applicable, but that of the unjust limitation of another's freedom.

§ 371. *Contract Must be Possible.* The possibility of carrying out the agreement is of three kinds, physical, moral, and legal, as we have said before.[1] As the first kind of possibility we must remember the old saying, "Ad impossibilia nemo tenetur." Law connotes the idea of well-being and consequently we must remember the dictum of the jurisconsult: "Generaliter novimus turpes stipulationes nullius esse momenti." So in the early Roman law books, we read on the subject of conditions not allowed in a will, "Quæ facta lædunt pietatem existimationem, verecundiam nostram, et contra bonas mores sunt, nec facere nos posse credendum est." Whatever contract has for its object an immoral action or a transgression of a duty is void, because if ethics do not include all of law, they contain a great part of it. The legal possibility of carrying out the agreement presupposes an alienable right and a person who can dispose of it. Essential personal rights cannot be alienated or transferred because they are the person himself, one and incommunicable, — property in the true sense of the word. We can add, says Rosmini, that in order to transmit a right, we must be able to loose the chains by which it is bound to us, but a person can never break the bonds of his own personal rights because he cannot will self-destruction or annulment. The same can be said of the complex exercise of the personal powers or the perpetual

[1] *Cf.* § 350 *ante.*

exercise of one of them, because their loss would always mean the end of personality.   Only the resultants of the personal powers — and but temporarily — are capable of transmission.   On the same principle we see that one cannot promise another's right, although he consent to it, to obtain some advantage for the promisor.   A failure of performance gives rise to indemnity, that is always due, notwithstanding the refusal of the third party, if the promise has been made absolutely.

§ 372.   *Consideration.*   Consideration ("causa") is an essential requisite to the validity of a contract and of obligations in general because of the relation of cause and effect.   There is no juristic bond or constraint upon him who is held to his promise to give or to do without a reason, which is always the immediate determinating cause, and as such cannot remain without the law, although it need not be expressed in the contract.   In law, the consideration is the relation between promises.   In a bilateral contract, the consideration is one promise regarded in its relation to the other.   In contracts of beneficence, the consideration for one contractor lies in the beneficence itself, and for the other, in the act.   It is said — and with truth — that the consideration differs from the object in this; that in the consideration the promise is regarded relatively, and in the object it is regarded absolutely.   The consideration must be *bonæ fidei*, because legal relations cannot be based on falsity or immorality.   This requisite serves to show whether or not there is trickery.   It cannot, as Rosmini says, be held as an obstacle to the trading of honest men, because they work with honest motives and have no repugnance to show their motives.   The law should not hesitate between the two evils of not punishing trickery and deceit or of wounding the susceptibility of some honest people in peculiar positions; so much better is it for the latter to suffer the inconvenience. But the minor ill can be avoided, as, in fact, it is avoided, when the law follows the maxim that the consideration is presumed and therefore there is no need to show it.   In fact, in those countries in which there is such a requisite as in France and Italy, there is no talk of reform on this point, and there seems to be no necessity to follow the example of the Austrian legislation in the contrary rule.

§ 373.   *Rules of Interpretation of Contracts.*   In pursuing the subject of contracts in general a step further, we must say a word about the rules of interpretation and their fundamental divisions.   The object of the rules of interpretation of contracts is to get at the understanding of the intention of the parties.   Now the first rule (like the others) is based on the knowledge of the Roman jurisconsults, the logicians and geometricians of law: "In conventionibus contrahentium voluntatem, potiusquam verba spectari placuit."   If the intention of the contractors is not clear, the meaning of the words may be gathered from the context.   When the meaning is obscure even then, a court must interpret them.   "Incivile est nisi tota lege perspecta, una aliqua eius particula proposita, judicare vel respondere."   If the meaning cannot be determined by the court, the object of the contractors must be considered; "Iniquium est perimi pacto id de quo cogitatum non docetur."   If the object is obscure, then this rule may explain the contract: "Semper in stipulationibus et in veteris contractibus id sequimur quod actum est, erit consequens ut id sequamur, quod in regione in qua actum est frequentitur.   Quid ergo si neque regionis mos apparent quia varius fuit?   Ad id quod minimum est, redigenda summa est."   Ptolemy adds (and there is no doubt that he is correct) a further rule: If in the indicated ways the clear intent of the contract cannot be found, one should give the words the sense in which they have some reasonable effect: "Quoties in stipulationibus ambigua oratio est, commodissimum est, in accipi quo res, qua de agitur, in tuto sit."

§ 374. *Division of Contracts.* A philosophical division of contracts was first made by Kant, who has been followed by many writers, among whom the most distinguished are Hegel and Ahrens. It is founded on the substance of the contracts themselves and develops with a "principium divisionis," which is not foreign and arbitrary, as those generally followed by legislators. Every contract, according to Kant, has for its object either a unilateral (gratuitous contract) or a bilateral advantage (the contract with consideration), or is a guaranty. The gratuitous contracts include deposits, pledges, bailments, loans for use[1], and gifts. The contract with consideration includes exchanges and leases. Exchange in its most general sense is divided into exchange, properly so called, sales, and loans for use; leases include contracts of hiring, mandates,[1] which implies the substitution of one place or name for another. If it merely means the substitution of place and not of name, it has the commercial notion which results in a contract with consideration. The contract of guaranty has three forms, pledge, "fideicommissus," and the giving of security. This classification of Kant, although it has a speculative value, is useless because it does not contain such important contracts, as, for example, that of partnership; it is also erroneous in that part in which it confuses a lease.

§ 375. *Trendelenburg's Division of Contracts.* Less incomplete but equally dialectic in substance is the division of Trendelenburg, which does not consider the contracts of guaranty as a third kind, but ac-

[1] *Cf.* § 365 *ante.*

cording to their nature adds them to gratuitous contracts and those with consideration. According to their form contracts are (this philosopher teaches) verbal, written, and implied. The simplest form is where the agreement is expressed with words which become precise and solemn formulas or symbols. A written contract can acquire great force through judicial classification. In implied contracts, the agreement is shown by acts and deeds. The tacit contract presumes always a manifestation, no matter how slight the agreement by words or acts, and appertains, therefore, to one or the other of the above categories. As to content, Trendelenburg goes on, contracts have for their object an increase of force or the removal of an uncertainty of rights. The former are generally either a gift, exchange, or partnership, and form a continuous and progressive series, raising the relations from a unilateral to a bilateral, and then to a communion of things through a complicated business arrangement for common gain. It is clear that promise and counter promise are of a lower order than an agreement to carry on a business in common. Contracts of gift are unilateral and beneficent because there is an obligation upon only one of the parties. They regard either the donation of a property, utility, or right, constituting "donatio," properly so called, or the gift of the use of something (a bailment), or the gift of gratuitous services (a deposit or mandate). Contracts of exchange are bilateral and not gratuitous because there are mutual obligations on both parties. The principal kind of contracts of exchange can be called exchange proper, the gift of merchandise for merchandise, buying and selling, or the exchange of merchandise for money, the exchange of things or of work (the use of properties or of forces as well corporeal as spiritual because both are representative of value), and loans (the use of money exchanged for money). Among the bilateral contracts we must place insurance contracts because the parties impose upon themselves reciprocal obligation under given conditions. The partnership contract not limited to single acts and counter acts is naturally more general, since it looks to a common purpose to be obtained by many common acts. These contracts differ among themselves, because the obligation can either create an entity distinct from the partners or not. A settlement ("transactio") defines uncertain rights by reciprocal renouncements and concessions between the parties, and shows a separation and not a voluntary increase of strength, therefore it interrupts the continuous and progressive series.

§ 376. *Trendelenburg's Division is Exhaustive.* In the above classification, the principal kinds of contracts are considered, though it is true that emphyteusis and leases find no place there, but it cannot be denied that these two are bilateral contracts and are easily reducible to the conception of exchange or of trading in its widest sense. Emphyteusis is the lease of a farm "in perpetuum," or for a term under an obligation for an annual payment in money or in kind. The leases and loans are the exchange of real estate or the payment of money (which the grantor cannot demand back) for a rent or annual payment in kind or otherwise. All the other bilateral contracts which look to an exchange (resolvable in the "do ut des," the "do ut facias," the "facio ut des," or the "facio ut facias") can figure in the classification of Trendelenburg. It is true that Trendelenburg does not numerate contracts of guaranty, but he speaks of pledge and bond. Such contracts can be reducible to "fidei-commissum," pledge, and mortgage. The division of Trendelenburg is like that of Kant, but has an inferior dialectic value. Trendelenburg himself confesses that in the principal series of contracts making for an increase of strength, there is a progress from the unilateral to the bilateral, and from the latter to the common will of a partnership. The progressive advance is stopped by the contract of settlement, which represents a separation of forces. After further reflection, however, upon Trendelenburg's division, we must see that the settlement separates in the sense that it defines uncertain rights and, in proceeding to their definition, results in an increased strength. Confused, uncertain, and unlimited rights are apparent but inefficient; true strength begins with limitations, distinctions, and certainty. A settlement eliminates obstacles, avoids losses, determines the rights or acquired powers of the person, who feels more freedom and self-assurance and finds satisfaction and pleasure in the contract. We know that a feeling of pleasure is brought about by an increase of power and that fatigue or pain is caused by their deficiency. A settlement is a kind of bilateral contract based on mutuality and exchange and as such must be placed before that of the partnership and after the unilateral contracts. The series of principal contracts becomes thus continuous and progressive. All the contracts, therefore, considered in respect to their contents, look to an increase of force in due conformity to their origin. Besides, we must not forget that they are bound with the impulse towards autarchy. With this addendum the classification of Trendelenburg seems full and philosophical.

CHAPTER XIV

FREEDOM OF CONTRACT AND THE CONTRACT OF LABOR

FREEDOM OF CONTRACT, ITS LIMITS AND ITS GUARANTY. — THE
SOCIAL MISSION OF PRIVATE LAW. — THE EQUALITY OF THE
PARTIES IN THE CONTRACT OF LABOR. — THE SYSTEMS THAT
REGULATE THE LIABILITY OF THE EMPLOYER FOR INDUSTRIAL
ACCIDENTS.

§ 377. *Freedom of Contract should Not be License.*
Now let us pass to the examination of the nature of
some special contracts which have given rise in our time
to not a few difficult trials and discussions in the economic-
juristic sphere. A contract is the most definite expression
of the "jus voluntarium" and freedom of the individual. If
the individual is free and can dispose of the things which
belong to him in the ways that he finds most convenient,
it is a logical inference that he has free rein to place himself in relations with his fellows by the promise of objects
or useful services. Law should respect the freedom of
contract up to the point where it becomes license and
takes a position opposed to the principles of reason, morality, justice, and the true interests of society which is
composed of individuals. As we have seen, the conception
of freedom of contract (a consequence of property and of
the freedom of man) is limited by other conceptions of a
higher order found in the very human nature, which make
for the happiness and necessities of the great ethical
whole represented by social life. It is not only the right
of contract which is thus limited, but the rights of
property, family, and inheritance. Private law, in fact,

must be subordinate. Hence it follows that private law is in the last analysis the "jus voluntarium." It is clear, however, that individual will is more dominant in private than in public law, and that in private law it is more dominant in property and in contract than in the family relations. But no one has seriously contended that in the sphere of contract, the limitations placed by the higher order should not be observed. With the progress of time, the freedom of individuals develops and grows larger, taking possession of all the domain which belongs to it, and substituting itself for illegitimate coercive control. But at the same time there is born a larger comprehension and a more real and concrete meaning of duties which demand conditions possible for their existence and their work.

§ 378. *Freedom of Contract should be Protected by Law.* So the reasonable limits of freedom grow, while freedom itself increases and gains strength, ceasing to be a name and becoming a reality. By this we do not mean to say that nature changes. Heretofore, it has shown itself in its true aspect when the statutes allowed it suitable conditions and gave it real guaranties of development. The new age reclaims not an abstract and nominal freedom but a freedom that is concrete and real. The statutes establishing conditions and guaranties are not based on questions of organization, that is, on the attainment of a general purpose through the whole, but provide within the marked boundaries of their jurisdictions for the protection of existing freedom. The protection should not be understood merely as the purpose or effect of the agreement of two wills but should be considered as a guaranty of the contractual freedom of one party in respect to the freedom of the other. A reform of positive modern contractual law is only justifiable under two heads; in the name of the increasing correlation of conditions shown in the great increase of specialization and individualization, and for the increase of the actual conditions of freedom. The social mission of all private law, of which Gierke writes, is not possible except in the train of these two general conceptions, because private law is formed on the principle of the freedom of individuals always limited and controlled by the higher order of social liberty. If this principle fails, and if the collective will as a "jus cogens" is put in its place, the series of relations by which the individuals hope to obtain particular objects, by means which they themselves choose, will be entirely destroyed. Socialism in private law is its destruction, because there is no private law where the individual personally has not free play. Neither can there be a private code of law made to help the poor classes against the overweaning power of the middle class, as appears to be the idea of Menger in Germany and of Salvioli in Italy. This kind of law made into a code would be essentially privileged class legislation. It could have no place in a mind free from prejudices, and would be injustice and not law. "Cuique suum" is the slogan of justice, and therefore a civil code for the poor classes cannot be allowed, especially when the equality of all citizens is proclaimed in public law. It is not presumable that the poor, declared capable of participating in public life, are at the same time inexperienced men, innocent creatures who fall victims to the greed of the rich in almost every relation of civil life. Such a code tends to sacrifice freedom to material equality among men. Now there is no need to confuse these two distinct conceptions,—of effective freedom and material equality. The statutes should place the individual in a state where he can really and usefully exercise his freedom without giving him the property of others and the product of their industry.

§ 379. *Freedom of Contract is not Absolute.* Contractual freedom is never considered as an absolute principle, but as limited by motives of morality, public order, or social equity in codes which are truly individualistic. There are many examples of equitable control: the action of rescission in cases of breach of contract; the avoidance of a contract of redemption after more than five years from the sale; of agreements for interest in agency and antichresis; certain prohibitions in contracts relating to shipments of cattle, by which the common carrier obligates himself to bear more than a moiety of the loss of beasts through chance and without his fault, or to share to a greater extent in the loss than in the gain. The legal prohibitions in all these cases tend to protect freedom itself against dangers which threaten it in certain conditions of life. A clause in a lease, by which a farmer, who waives his right to be relieved of rent because of accidents foreseen and unforeseen, must pay the rent even if he receives nothing from the property, and the renunciation of remuneration for improvements made by a lessee in cases of failure where he has to return the property, could be made void for the same reason. Gianturco, in his book "L'Individualismo ed il Socialismo nel Diritto Contrattuale," shows that these two prohibitions would have in reality the same object as those already recognized, which we have mentioned above.

§ 380. *Economic Duress in the Contract of Labor.* Everyone recognizes the serious omissions of the law on the subject of contracts for labor. This important contract, the object of bitter criticism, is still governed by a few rules derived in part from Roman law inapplicable to the new conditions of modern times. Certainly, the contractors in a hiring contract or a contract for labor are not in a state of equality, because on one side there is the employer with plenty of capital who can decrease or suspend work and, on the other, there is the operative who, as vendor of labor, cannot rest from his trade, withdraw his offer in crises, or wait, but who must work for wages which will keep him alive but which need not permit him any gain.   The one is often stubborn in his pride; the other struggles to avoid starvation.   Even if the wages are relatively high and he can enjoy a decent manner of life, the employer is always the stronger.   Hence the necessity of equalizing as far as possible the conditions of the parties to a contract for labor, not by attributing to the operative what is not his, not by reducing the rights of capital and of him who unites and directs the elements of production, not by the establishment of reasonable wages through decrees of public authorities, but by protecting the freedom of the operative and giving him opportunities of development.   Among such means, we can count, for example, the prohibition of wage paying in kind or in a system of "truck" by which the wage is decimated, and by the determination of reciprocal rules and duties of employer and operative in case of an omission from the contract.   If a house or some real estate is rented with an omission in the terms, the laws provide and establish the length of the lease by a presumption; but if the labor of a thousand operatives is contracted for without the aforesaid clause, the laws are mute and the contract runs *ad libitum*.   Another means is the limitation of the penalties which the employers can impose.   The laws about the employment of children and women, Sunday rest, accidents, employees' insurance, and industrial regulations have a distinct influence on labor and represent a series of equitable limitations.

§ 381.   *Employer's Liability must be Increased.*   The principle of the employer's liability for negligence in cases of industrial accidents which exists to-day according to existing law, must be amplified.   On the operative, hurt in an accident, is laid the burden of proving the negligence of the employer. The employer should be obliged — at least to a certain extent — to indemnify the operative for injuries which are really the trade risks, received by chance. The employer is the head of the industry, and as such takes all the profits and advantages, while the workman labors in the interest of the master, and receives a fixed wage. It is only just that the employer, because the gains are his, should bear the consequences of injuries inseparable from the exercise of that branch of production. No one should be enriched through harm or injury to the others who work for him. We should note the maxim: "Qui habet commoda ferre debet onera." These accidental injuries differ from unavoidable accidents, which are inherent in the business. Unavoidable accidents are foreign to the management of the business and are beyond the provisions for the ordinary course of events. We can easily see that in the cases which are not connected with the management of the business, there can be no liability on the part of employer, whether you consider him as the author of the injury or whether you consider him as the head of the business; neither can he be held responsible for the negligence of the operative who, of his own free will, has placed himself in a position to receive the harm which affects other persons and the capital as well as himself. There is no doubt that such increase of liability should be regulated by law, which could not be waived by agreement. Such a system does not shift the burden of proof, because it is right that the employer who alleges the contributory negligence of the operative or the unavoidable accident as a ground for escaping liability should be made to prove it.

§ 382. *Shifting of Burden of Proof will not Answer the Problem of Employer's Liability.* There is a system which hopes to realize the principles of equity by a. simple shifting of the burden of proof without disturbing existing statutes, which hold the employer liable for accidents only when his negligence has been shown. By the shifting of the burden of proof, this negligence is presumed, and the employer must show that he is not in fault. But this is in derogation of common law, founded on the maxim that he who makes an allegation must prove it, and that the author must prove his act as the man bound by a covenant must prove the exception which sets him free. And further, this derogation is not just because the proof is not easy for the employer, since the operative in the factory is in a state of continuous activity. Fusinato, in his monograph "Gl 'Infortuni del Lavoro," observed that this presumption of negligence on the part of the employer does not conform to reality, giving statistics to show that the majority of industrial accidents are caused by chance or facts whose cause it is not possible to establish. The state of the locality and materials is often so changed by the accident as to become irrecognizable. The men who could testify about the negligence are either dead or in a condition in which they cannot testify, if they are not parties to the action themselves. In these circumstances the employer cannot get evidence. (Of course, it is true under the existing rule that the workman, after the lapse of months without means, and deserted by his fellow-workmen through fear of a loss of employment, is in the same predicament.) It is clear that no presumption of negligence should be allowed against the employer only because he is rich, and it is not just to presume the master negligent since the operative was engaged in the business and therefore was in no wise like a passenger on a railroad. Fundamentally, the system of shifting the burden of proof modifies the present law by saddling the employer with the injuries not only of his own negligence but with those of unknown cause.

§ 383. *Employer's Liability is not Contractual.* Besides the system of shifting the burden of proof, there is one which bases the liability of the master in cases of accident on the contract itself, by which he is bound to provide all the necessary precaution to protect the operative. This contract creates relations of dependence and subordination on the part of the operative to which the duty of guaranteeing protection on the part of the master corresponds. It is not the negligence, say the upholders of this system, that causes the liability, but the agreement. The operative must only show the contract in the case of an accident; the master must prove that he was not in fault. Now we must show that, admitting the fundamental idea of this system, the master is bound by the contract to make all provisions necessary for the protection of the life and health of his operatives; but that is the extent of his duty. If such provisions have been made and followed, but nevertheless the accident happens, the master is not responsible and is not bound to give indemnity for the accident of unknown origin. From the contractual nature of the master's obligation, there is brought about no shifting of the burden of proof, because the contract is not for the rent of a man but for his work, which cannot be considered as a machine that, leased, must be returned after use as it was or with compensation for wear and tear. There is neither obligation nor demand to restore the person of the operative, but he wishes payment and looks to the contract as evidence of his right. In lease, transportation, and bailment, the real author of the contract demands the object and he who is bound proves the event which frees him from responsibility, but in contracts for work, in cases of accidents, the person is not demanded back.

§ 384. *Employer's Liability Question can be Settled by Obligatory Insurance.* Accepting the principle on which for equitable reasons the system of full liability is based, there is no serious objection to not enforcing the obligatory accident insurance of operatives by the employer, since he takes all the profit of the industry, and therefore must bear the consequences of chance events or trade risks. The law has the power to force those engaged in a trade to insure the payment of an indemnity of a definite amount to the operative killed or wounded as the result of an accident occurring in the course of the work. If the accident happens through the malice or negligence of the employer, the operative is entitled not only to the indemnity insurance, but to the necessary sum to compensate for the damage, under the rule of common law. It is clear that no indemnity is due the operative for his malice or negligence, or for unavoidable accidents. Through the insurance, the risks are divided among a great number, and thus when the accident happens the masters are not obliged to disburse large sums and have lawsuits with their employees. The system of liability creates a state of war between the employees and employers; insurance institutes a reign of peace. Obligatory insurance implies a new element in cost of production bringing about an increase in price of the objects falling chiefly on the consumer and somewhat upon the producers themselves. On this point, we must have no illusions. And the law, in determining the measure of damages to be paid by the employers for insurance, should take accurate thought of the real conditions of the production and the industries of the country. It is necessary above all to see if the obligation can be placed at all and within what limits in a particular situation. There is not much foundation for the fear that obligatory insurance will make the employers negligent in adopting provisions and precautions for the employment of labor, because the insurance companies are none too willing to pay indemnity and make payment only when there can be no doubt that there has been no contributory negligence of the master contributing, as Ferraris has shown in his book on this theme.

§ 385. *Laws of Employer's Liability should be Both Preventive and Remedial.* The laws should not be limited to the reparation of damage but should also take forethought to prevent it, establishing the general rule on which special regulation could be based, imposing necessary precautions in regard to the health and life of operatives and to prevent accidents. Twofold, therefore, is the duty of the laws: to foresee and prevent the accident, and to insure reparation and help when the injury has happened.

CHAPTER XV

USURY

INTEREST AND ITS LIMITATIONS. — FREEDOM OF INTEREST. —
USURY AND ITS METHODS. — USURY AS A FORM OF CIVIL WRONG
AND THE METHODS OF FIGHTING IT. — USURY AS A CRIME. —
CRITICISM OF THE THEORY OF STEIN. — THE SPECIAL FEATURES
OF THE CRIME OF USURY. — LAW AND LIFE.

§ 386. *Interest is Legitimate.* Interest is profit gained
by lending others capital; it has been regarded from
a biased point of view and has been held in ill-repute
for historical causes and through moral, philosophical,
and religious prejudices. The severity of the Twelve
Tables, which has been depicted in "The Merchant
of Venice," has not been the ultimate reason for the
abhorrent discredit with which it has been regarded.
Loans to the rich for objects of luxury and dissipation,
and those to the poor to obtain money, especially in
the time of barbarian devastations, and the precepts of
charity in the Old and New Testaments which prescribed succor for the poor and forbade interest, have
had much influence on the minds of the people and the
legislature. To the impulses of sentiment, to the voice of
fraternal love is added scientific authority represented
by the celebrated reasoning of Aristotle on the natural
unproductiveness of money, which was accepted by the
jurisconsults who first taught "usuræ vicem fructum
pertinent," but ended by affirming that "usura fructu
non est," since it was not derived "ex ipso corpore,"
but from the money itself.

§ 387. *Recognition of the Legitimacy of Interest.* The more complex needs of life, the growth of trade, the increase of commerce, and the gradual development from an economy of nature to economy of finance brought about the legal recognition of pawn-shops, state offices, as well as that growing out of the loans of traders in business There was introduced a kind of justification of interest, not of its own virtue, but as a compensation for the non-user of capital through the conception of "damnum emergens" and "lucrum cessans." Legal interest on a judgment was not looked upon with the same dread. Kings sold to the Hebrews and Lombards the monopoly in the State of lending money at high interest, but were always ready to confiscate their goods at every popular demonstration against usurers, thus making a double profit.

§ 388. *Interest fully Recognized at Law.* Finally the exception became the rule and interest was allowed in an age in which the object of lending was not to preserve or consume money, but to invest it as capital; thus the seed is distinguished from the fruit. The seed value is the value which money has as merchandise, that is, the expense of coinage; the second is bound up with the use of money as capital. This distinction teaches that the justification of interest does not lie only in the amount of capital. The discovery of a mine, for example, can lessen the price of money and at the same time interest can increase through the insufficiency of capital. In our day, the conception of physical fecundity is distinct from that of economic productivity, and therefore we can see that money, although it is not fecund physically, is economically productive. Interest (the civil fruit) is justified by the undeniable principles of economico-juristic reason because it is the compensation for the use of another's capital. It is also the price of risk. The return of the capital is a direct consequence of the respect due to individual property. About this there can be no doubt.

§ 389. *Usury can be Legally Forbidden.* But if the interest is allowed in such an age, one so nearly our own, usury was forbidden. In other words, high interest was not allowed. A limit was placed upon the interest rate. Limiting laws, inspired by the spirit of charity, are aimed against a high interest which worries and harasses the largest and unhappiest class of debtors and represents an age in which communication between men was difficult and when there were great differences among the laws of different nations. But when the interest rate is limited, capital, too, suffers a limitation which should not be placed thereon. It is deprived of its full scope and has not that self-governing characteristic of to-day when, by virtue of credit, capital can almost be separated from its owner. With the increase of communications and the decrease of contrasts between the laws of nations, with the development of trade and the increase in quantity and mobility of capital, it is no longer possible to enforce laws of limitations (now abandoned by the greater number of progressive governments). A new principle seems to be making its appearance generally. And though hardly clear as yet, it is on the way to relegate to the limbo of the other sophistries the conception of the limitation of the interest. True and complete freedom becomes a fact with the freedom of exchange and commerce. Money is merchandise as much as any chattel and should not be subjected to a law of maximum. The jurists of the old school defended the alleged right of limitation by the State by holding that the chattel in coins was a special property since money was the means of exchange. If the State, they said, establishes the denominations in value and gives the legal quality of a means of exchange to money, it can restrict its use without thereby hindering the chattel of which the coin is made, being the subject of barter and sale. They did not understand the nature of money and the State's duty of coinage, and they made no distinction between creation and certification. Though the State coins, it does not create the value of money which is intrinsic and preëxistent. It merely certifies the quality and weight in order to give it recognition as a universal means of exchange. It could not abandon coinage to private competition because the law of Gresham would be immediately manifest, that is, that bad money is more apt to circulate than good, and drives the good from circulation. These are the only reasons for statutory enactments in this regard. There is no creative virtue in the State, and therefore the reasoning of these jurists does not apply. Neither can we say that it is possible to fix *a priori* the maximum of interest because the fruits of money are essentially most changeable, being ruled in every case by the correlation of many facts, among which we must notice the length of the loan, the security, and the quality and quantity of the risk.

§ 390. *Abrogation of Legal Interest Laws.* With the abrogation of the limiting laws in many modern countries, usury has remained free and unpunished by their codes. It has become more extensive and immoral, until it is the terrible plague of all times and places. Its extension and deep corruption are explained by the developments to which economic life is subject. Evolution means a growing quantity of exchangeable goods, a progressive development of credit, an enormous development of needs, and great progress in intelligence. Evolution is confused with modern civilization, which,

though it is seen under the economic aspects just mentioned, does not in general make for great progress and
morality.   It is a fact that the mentality goes rapidly
forward while morality remains the same or varies very
little.   Briefly; the more new forms that economic life
includes, the more complicated it becomes, the greater
needs and desires it causes, and the more intimate relations it gives rise to; just so much more will usury become rampant, acquiring new attractions, new material
and a greater sphere, and at the same time will become
more cautious and deceptive.   Now public opinion, which
has in every age and every country demanded a defense
against usury, is in a terrible dilemma due to the contradiction between the impunity of usury and the great
progress of this frightful plague.

§ 391. *Interest is Economic.* Is the contradiction
so generally deplored real? Does usury besides being
immoral offend the law? At this point it is necessary
to remember that the substance of law is eudemonological and in a great part economic. Now economics
teach that a loan should entail a profit. If the debtor
does not invest the capital lent and cannot receive
interest and principal from the investment, he loses by
his loan. Willing or unwilling, a debt always entails a
dependence of the debtor on the creditor, but he can
easily acquire the means of liberation and change his
position, if he is intelligent enough to profit by the
use of the loan. It is clear that a loan is capable of
such beneficial results only when it is real, and not
fictitious. Rational law holds there can be no debt
without a corresponding value given (unless we want
to call some obligations of indemnity, decreed by
law, by such a name). From this principle comes the
origin of some "actiones" or "condictiones," as the "condictio sine causa," "causa data," "causa non secuta,"

"actio de in rem verso," "exceptio non numeratæ pecuniæ," and the "læsio enormis." All these actions presuppose the failure or inadequacy of the value received. Law must always be based on the nature of things and on the reality of economic relations. If it is not so based it is no longer law, but rather the direct opposite of law, wrong; neither can it be said that this conception of law is foreign to reason, which should be its essence, because the nature of things and the reality of relationship are connoted by "recta ratio."

§ 392. *Methods of Usury.* Usury may be an isolated act or it may be a habit of profiting from the folly, inexperience, necessity, or enthusiasm of the debtor, raising a small and reasonable obligation to a large loan, by making new agreements more stringent and for a shorter term according to his financial condition. The usurious creditor grows rich on the large rate of interest, and upon the repayment of the loan, without investing an equal sum, he increases his capital. He gains a wage through the work of the debtor who can never free himself from this slavery created in the name of liberty, as Stein has said. The creditor, by high interest, receives more than the capital lent, while he forced the debtor to continue to borrow from him in order to pay the interest; from one hundred dollars given on interest at a given time he receives twenty dollars as annual interest and perhaps a thousand dollars' capital after three or four years. This is usury of interest alone and nothing else, but there is also a usury of capital because a money-lender realizes on the debtor's personal property, capital, friendship, and affections, which in moments of coercion can have a monetary value. A money-lender, after receiving a high and scandalous interest two or three times the capital lent, makes a further gain at the expense of honest creditors because he

alone is in a position to know and choose the day best
for a bailment or levy, obtaining thus an advantage by
his bad faith.

§ 393. *Two Kinds of Usury, Simple and Seductive.*
Usury can be simple or it can be underhand and
seductive. Even when usury is simple and the debt
is not provoked by a thousand different schemes, it is
always a debt without a corresponding loan, or a debt
enormously disproportionate to the loan, prohibiting
the accumulation of the capital, absorbing income and
possessions, destroying liberty and financial independence,
and affecting the honor of the men in its toils. For
even simple usury begins with a malevolent study of
the powers, character, and situation of the debtor and
involves the slow destruction of his wealth. With the
aid of a high interest rate, with the constant increase
of capital, with the advantage of bad faith, it receives three or four times the value of the loan, as
does the deceptive usury. It uses the same means of
pressure and threats as the latter. At first, it affects
a tenderness for the poor debtor, until it has him
well within its grasp, then it shows him a hardened
visage and finally adopts its true colors. Usury excludes kindness as kindness excludes usury; without
a certain brutality, without a certain animal ferocity,
one cannot become a usurer. Any kind of usury
is a close and ferocious calculation. The marks of
usury are generally the same in the case of simple or
hidden usury; in both, a loan is made presumably out
of kindness by third parties who are in secret accord
with the usurer for a short term upon an assignment
of wages, a pledge, a sale of chattels or crops in the
ground, or of products before harvest. Stein points
out that usury to-day always seems to tend towards
hidden usury and to adopt all the forms and activities

of its true nature. It extends from the cities to the villages and the countryside; the reason of this phenomenon must be found in that evolution of modern economic lie that we have spoken of above.[1]

§ 394. *Usury not to be Confused with High Interest.* If usury consists in a debt without a corresponding loan, it is clear that it has no relation to the interest rate which is the effect merely of risk and scarcity of capital. A loan where the risk is great is not usury, though usury is always a loan without security. In the first, there is a real loan and a commercial activity and calculation of interest in the enterprise. In the second, there is a debt without a loan and no activity on the part of the creditor but a keen awaiting for the ruin of the debtor. High interest has been correctly likened by Stein to a doctor who makes high charges, and usury is like a wild beast on the field of financial activity. From this it follows that the legislator who wants to destroy usury should not take up the old method of limiting the interest rate, because freedom of interest is the consequence of true economic and legal principles. A great part of the criticism of the usury laws, that we hear to-day, is aimed more at these laws of limitation than at any particular civil or penal law against usury itself.

§ 395. *Usury can be Stopped: It is a Question of Price.* From what has already been said we can readily infer that both simple and seductive usury are illegal, for the law should be founded on the reality of economic relations. There seems no doubt that such an offense is a civil injury against which principal means of defense *in jure* is the "condictio indebiti" or the "exceptio non numeratæ pecuniæ." The special action and defense, especially at the time of the payment, strike usury

[1] *Cf.* § 386 *ante.*

at a vital point.   We can easily see that the law
must allow presumptions, and parol, and circumstantial
evidence, if it wishes to make good these means of
defense.   And in this case, harmful results too may
be brought upon the *bona fide* creditor.   The change
in the system of evidence would be great; we must
frankly confess it.   The practical question always remains, which can receive different answers according
to the different moral conditions of nations: Is it wise
to change such a system with the possible harm to
credit in order to punish usury in particular cases, or is it
better to let usury alone in order not to alter the rules
of evidence or disturb the public confidence?   We may
as well admit that no system in this world can be
perfect and free from abuse.   At one moment trickery
enjoys the protection given to honesty, and escapes
under the protection of the law, and now honesty is
wounded by the provisions adopted against dishonesty.
Here, as in other branches of the social and juristic
sciences, it is well to see on which side the scale
inclines, in other words, what proportion the advantages bear towards the evils, and be governed thereby.   When statutes allow such means of defense for
the debtor, they cannot deny them to honest creditors,
otherwise the usurers would make their money answer
for the usurious loan.   The final immoral and unjust
privilege of the usurer, that is, the preference growing out of a bailment would fail, were usury proved.
There is no use in introducing bankruptcy again
(proposed by Stein, with the intention of depriving
the usurer of a method of grave extortion) in which
all the creditors join and the debtor is deprived of his
goods which are given to a trustee, because bankruptcy
which deprives the miserable debtor in good faith through
the hardness of personal coercion has no excuse for exist-

ence to-day, when imprisonment for debt is abolished. The exemption of salaries and pensions is another civil remedy against usury. Let us disregard the other remedies of Stein, which include the invalidity of a sale of crops before harvest and the prohibition of recognition of a second board or lodging bill when the first is not satisfied. The invalidity of the sale of products before harvest can well be included among the means of nullifying usurious contracts and is logical, but it is harmful to the freedom of the trade. And harmful, too, to freedom of credit is the prohibition against the validity of a second lodging bill when the first is not satisfied, though this is frequently the first step in usury in some countries.

§ 396. *Is Usury a Crime?* Now we come to the question: Is usury only a form of civil injury or can it be considered as a crime? The modern school of penal law, writes Carrara, which has placed at the base of coercive legislation the solemn principle that no human act can be punished if not immoral or destructive of rights, is not aggressive in protecting society. Usury measured by this criterion should not be made a crime, because the payment of exorbitant interest is freely consented to, and there is no right to overthrow or punish what everyone is free to do or not. Without wishing to go into the fundamentals of punishment it appears to us that the doctrine of social security considered by itself is not opposed to the criminality of usury, because the harm which usury does to society in hindering the collection and development of capital is great and renders more artificial and more cruelly dishonest the attempts of bad faith and destroys the economic freedom and independence of individuals, as we have said before.[1] There is no freedom of consent when the

[1] *Cf.* § 389 *ante.*

debtor through inexperience or necessity of life is forced
to accept an outrageous agreement.   It seems that
it was true yesterday as it is to-day that the plague of
usury brings panic to the minds of the people, who demand penalties against usury.   All laborers and farmers,
the military and the clericals, landowners and nobles,
fear usury and with good reason.   It is necessary to
recognize that the fear in all these classes is the effect
of daily sad experiences.   Usury is not a negligible factor
in the increase of suicide, and usury inflicted upon the
proletarian fosters a savage hate of capital and becomes
a true social danger.

§ 397.   *Stein's Distinction of the Two Kinds of Usury.*
Stein had tried to prove that if a creditor of whom a
debtor borrows of his own free will takes a disproportionate gain from the disorder of the latter's finances,
poverty, prodigality, or lack of foresight, he is guilty
of an act of simple usury which falls under the jurisdiction of civil law.   If, however, a creditor in any way promotes a debt maliciously to his own advantage and the
disorder in the finances of the debtor, he is guilty of the
crime of usury which is a kind of extortion.   Usury
threatens and forces the victim into a state of financial
ruin in order to obtain an unjust advantage.   Usury
is extortion with the intent of getting an acknowledgment of a debt owed without a corresponding loan,
by making short terms and threatening exposures in
case of failure of payment and taking advantage of
the social position of the debtor.   To us it seems, as
it seemed to Andreani in "Delle Leggi Contro L'Usura,"
that the distinction of Stein is without foundation,
because usury of any kind involves fraud and injury.
Even simple usury includes trickery, because it presupposes the desire of obtaining an illegal profit from the
exceptional position of a debtor who is forced to assume

a debt without a corresponding loan, or one out of all proportion to the loan, consenting through inexperience, necessity, or enthusiasm, and subscribing an unfortunate agreement to his own moral and financial perdition; it is a Satanic agreement of which either folly or necessity is the occasion. The dishonesty of receiving profit from a fictitious loan is an essential and criminal element, and the ruin of the debtor is the consequence. We can affirm that the characteristics of extortion are not foreign to simple usury, if we follow the penal definition of Stein. There is extortion when threats of a future misfortune are made for gain, and the victim is forced to give something at once, or when he is threatened with an immediate misfortune to obtain a promise. Extortion is aimed at, gaining an undue profit through threats of great injury. In this sense the usurer can be guilty of extortion whether the debtor borrows of his own free will or whether the usurer artfully provokes a debt and creates the causes of his financial embarrassment. A creditor in simple usury, to get money, threatens futile ills and forces the debtor to give something in pawn or to offer it for sale, or threatens actual evils, coercing him by threats, bankruptcy, etc., to obtain new promises and new and more exorbitant gains. Even if he does not urge a debtor to contract the debt, he wishes to gain undue advantages from debts without loans. He induces great and unjust fears by reasonable but untrue statements. Simple usury cannot be reduced to a simple tort, to legal fraud as in the case of close bargains or the exaggeration of the value of an object for sale, or even of a lie unaccompanied by trickery. There is always something more than this, because in no case can there be any agreement between good faith and the usurer. A tortfeasor acts in good faith, but a usurer always acts in bad faith.

Often the creditor in simple usury, even when he has not created the financial disorder of the debtor, has to no small extent increased it, hastening the ruin which he has foreseen from the moment when the debtor first came to him. In usury, which instigates and seduces, the premeditation of the debtor's ruin begins with the picking out of a victim who is at that time in no relation to him and whom he proposes to entice by his perverted art.

§ 398. *Usury Lies in the Debt without Consideration; Fraud and Extortion are Accidental.* There are some who look upon usury as a crime only when it is connected with fraud, which presupposes an act intended to deceive and the attainment of illicit gains injurious to another. According to them, those forms of usury only are criminal in which the usurers adopt artifices to protect themselves with the cloak of civil law intended to prohibit illicit gains. This is the theory of the Tuscan Penal Code which punishes cases of usury clothed or marked by fraud, for example, swindling, where the debtor declares that he has received so much money, while in fact he has only received a certain part of it, the rest having been given in worthless securities, although it was agreed that they should have a stated value. Above we have proved that usury has always the elements of a crime, trickery, and injury. It is distinguished from civil injury whether it be simple or instigating, and seductive whether it is accompanied or unaccompanied by artifices. Even when it does not deceive the debtor and does not adopt a savage aspect in the saddest moments of life, it is always a crime, because it is founded on the desire to obtain illicit profit from the exceptional position of the debtor, who consents through inexperience or necessity to assume a debt without a loan and to subscribe the act of his own ruin. In such a case, usury, which for various reasons is a special crime, is more closely related to extortion, but the conception of neither extortion nor fraud include all of the usurious attributes. Usury, it may be said, always takes advantage of extortion and not always of fraud and has its own peculiarities, and is abhorrent in its financial and legal aspects. Such a crime does not rationally demand the element of custom which the French law requires since we can find in the case of a single usurious act the unjust profit of a debt without a loan brought about by the inexperience or stringent needs of the debtor. Its continuance is only an aggravation.

§ 399. *Usury is a Crime against Private Property.* The special features of the crime of usury are generally connected with the crimes against economic life and especially with those which refer to exchange and credit, since usury involves debts without corresponding loans, or debts enormously disproportionate to their loans, and since credit includes property and usury is destructive of private wealth, so we can state that usury is referable not mediately but immediately to crimes against private property. The nature of usury is such that it is always criminal, be it between traders or not. From the ethico-juristic aspect, it is a matter of pure indifference whether the act is commercial or not. Here we must observe that if the penal laws did not apply to commercial matters, usury would abandon its customary civil forms and assume commercial attitudes. On this account, the German law which applies to traders and to commercial matters is preferable to the Austrian law which does not regard traders. It is true that in business it is very difficult to determine accurately the point where legal profits end and illegal profits begin. But this difficulty is met as well in private life although to a less degree. The net account is always a difficult thing to obtain in business and generally in all human affairs, because they are complicated in their nature. If the trader gains great development and freedom of procedure, the criterion with which usury in trade should be judged would be rougher than the criterion in private life, but the definition which we have given of usury would remain substantially the same.

§ 400. *Usury will Never be Eradicated by a Statute.* A law against usury which has so many diverse causes will certainly never destroy that. Usury depends upon the financial condition of society, especially upon the scarcity of capital and deficient development of credit. It depends upon custom in which bad faith takes no little part, and on human nature itself, in which overreaching and egoistical tendencies are not foreign, and which is marked by folly, improvidence, and transient enthusiasm. Education and statutes can restrain, modify, and correct these tendencies, which are now more and now are less marked, but it will never succeed in uprooting them. And this is true because usury goes on its pace when it is forbidden and penalized, and when it is free. Is it on that account necessary to make no effort? Should the legislator wait with arms folded for the spontaneous development of those social harmonies which we have heard so much about? He will have to wait many and many a year to see this plague diminished or on the way to be cured, because capital is not yet sufficiently productive and credit so far has not become so general and well-organized as to foreshadow the approach of the time when usury will have lost its strength. Punishments, it is true, have appeared with economic and civil progress and in a great number of cases have lessened and limited usury. Fear has ordinarily in private relations been the backbone of legislation, and the branch of the law which prescribed penalties for usury was most important in the years gone by. In our own time, civil law bears a larger proportion in relation to the ancient penal law than before, but the fear of conviction has by no means ceased to exercise a salutary restraint upon the conduct of men. It is true that usury threatened by the statutes will seek better means of concealment and in many cases will probably succeed in escaping prosecution. But the attack under the civil and penal aspect must be equal to the force expended in the breaking of the law, hence the system of civil law remedies and of criminal penalties which we have mentioned in this chapter. This system should be developed in a way which will not harm true credit and good faith, getting its inspiration from the rules of a wise economic legislative policy. In a word, penal laws against usury, if they do not always and effectively punish the guilty because of imperfections to which all penal laws are subject, produce two not unimportant advantages; on one side, they keep some from the crime who are disposed to commit it, and on the other, they preserve the high reputation of the administration of justice, not forcing it to protect contracts of a potently immoral character, and which are contrary to universal opinion.

CHAPTER XVI

PARTNERSHIP, EXCHANGE, TRANSPORTA-
TION, AND SUNDRY WAGERING
CONTRACTS

THE CONTRACT OF PARTNERSHIP AND ITS FORMS. — PART-
NERSHIP AND INCORPOREAL PERSONS. — THE REGIME OF
AUTHORIZATION AND OF SUPERVISION. — ANCIENT AND
MODERN EXCHANGE. — THE NATURE OF THE CONTRACT OF
TRANSPORTATION. — INSURANCE AND ITS NEW THEORIES. —
GAMBLING CONTRACTS.

§ 401. *Three Kinds of Partnerships.* A partnership
is generally defined as a contract under which two or
more persons control something in common in order
to get gain therefrom. Civil partnerships accomplish
their object in civil life; commercial partnerships
make speculations by the exercise of commercial acts.
These last are not full partnerships but particular, since
their objects are always clearly marked. These are
distinguished into three kinds according to the amount
of liability to third parties. The first is a general
partnership in which the partnership obligations are
guaranteed by the full and unlimited liability of every
partner. The second is the limited partnership in which
the partnership obligations are guaranteed by the full
and unlimited liability of the general partners and
by the sums deposited by the special partners. The
third is the special partnership or joint stock company; in it the partner is only liable to the amount
invested.

§ 402. *Subdivisions of Partnerships.* A general partnership offers the greatest guaranty to third parties, incites the great activity on the part of the partners, and is useful in those industries which need the presence of directing partners in different places at the same time. This form of partnership, requiring unlimited confidence among the partners, does not include many people. Large and hazardous undertakings can only be accomplished through limited or special partnerships, which are better able to concentrate a large capital, impossible where there is unlimited personal liability. There are other kinds of partnerships, differing among themselves, which fall under the main division into the three classes. The Italian Commercial Code, for example, allows partnerships for mutual insurance. It looks upon them as collective entities distinct from the individuals who compose them, but enforces the requirements of a special partnership as to the responsibilities of the managers, the publication of partnership acts, failure, change of charter, and accounts. So, in the case of the coöperative partnerships, as to publication of their partnership acts and the obligation and liability of the directors, the code applies the same rules as to special partnerships. The partnership of the German Code corresponds to the Italian dormant partnership and does not enter into the three categories. A partnership with a dormant partner is not an entity separate from its members like the other partnerships, but is a trade union of one or more persons with a participation in the profits and losses in one or more operations, or even in an entire business.

§ 403. *Partnerships are not Legal Entities, but are More than the Sum of the Component Wills.* Partnerships in general, derived from the interpenetration of the wills in respect to an object and presupposing a common will, are ethical organisms in the broad sense of the word. But this common will, although easily distinguishable from the particular wills from which it arises, is not such as to constitute the definite and self-existing unity of a corporation, because its purpose is not fixed and therefore is not independent of the desires of the individuals. A partnership looks to the immediate advantage of its members; the corporation works for its own ends. A partnership is dissolved by death or at the will of its members; a corporation in these cases does not dissolve. Partners are owners and upon the dissolution of the partnership they divide the goods among them. Members of a corporation are not owners of its property and do not divide it when the corporation ceases to exist. A partnership, therefore, in the true sense of the word, is not, like a corporation, a juridical or incorporeal person. Nevertheless, there is in a partnership something more than the collection of its members or the sum of particular wills, because it is founded on a common will. That kind of a will is a natural element which is found in the maxim of the oldest Italian jurisconsults. "Aliud est corpus unius societatis et aliud est quilibet ipsius societatis." The maxim was well illustrated by examples of Roman law which recognized in some forms of partnership an entity distinct from the members. The common will is the rational principle of juristic individuality, which the law establishes as a means or vehicle for relations between strangers and the partners, who are in fact the subjects of the rights and obligations. A suit for partner's share in fact is the suit for the quota of the partner in the property of the society which is held in joint ownership. If the theory of Ihering[1] did not recognize incorporeal persons it could well be applied to partnership. We

[1] Cf. § 214 ante.

must not forget that the conditions for an incorporeal person understood in full and broad sense are two — the capacity to will, and the authorization of the State. There is not complete personality without recognition, as we have shown before.[1]   Therefore, Puffendorf and Troplong were wrong when they said that a partnership of itself constituted a juridical or moral being without need of authorization, which was demanded, they said, only in the cases of public moral entities.   Recognition must necessarily be given by the State or not at all. Positive law can admit the individuality of either civil or trading partnerships, or those of trading alone, or both of trading and civil, if the latter assume the form of a trading society.   It all depends upon the motives and general utility which the legislature may determine in different ways, but in the philosophy of law every kind of partnership, whether civil or commercial, has the virtue of bring raised to the state of juridical individuality.   Positive law ordinarily does not consider the civil partnerships as collective entities because they are not founded necessarily, as trading partnerships are, on relations with third parties, and because they have not purposes as definite, certain, and manifest as the latter.   Civil partnership can develop in many ways, unknown or insufficiently clear, to reach presumptive recognition.   On the contrary, the trading partnerships do not meet these obstacles and are therefore regarded by the laws as collective entities.   The same laws allow civil societies to assume trading forms without losing their essential characteristics, since their nature does not depend upon their form.   In this case, they acquire juridical individuality because they are founded upon relations with third parties which must be governed by the creation of a means or vehicle, as Ihering says.

[1] *Cf.* § 220 *ante.*

§ 404. *Association is Old, but Associations are New.*
Troplong writes that there is no need for new legislative rules on the subject of partnerships because association is a fact existing in all ages.   And truly Roman history shows us a type of partnership for the collecting of taxes besides the celebrated example of a private association; while the Middle Ages gives us that of the great Florentine families, and the Lombards scattered in all regions of the earth but always creditors of their king.   The history of the XVIIth and XVIIIth centuries is full of maritime companies for trade and colonization. But although Troplong gives an exact description of the spirit of association which is as old as history, he has not understood the profound difference between the old and the new trading societies.   The first, which were composed of a few members, were all founded on monopoly, which in its turn demanded slave labor, while the second lived and developed power in the régimes of freedom.   Who is ignorant that the Roman equestrian order had the privilege of leasing out the taxes? After the discovery of America, have not the distant undertakings of particular companies been a kind of governmental emanation?   And was not the East India Company given the tremendous privilege of exclusive trade in its territory?   The same society, it must not be forgotten, was made owner of an immense expanse of land.

§ 405. *Coöperative Societies.*   The French Revolution in its love for freedom of labor looked askance at every kind of association among operatives, fearing that under the semblance of a recognized society a revolutionistic order would arise.   From this suspicion came that isolation of the operative later so deeply deplored and eliminated in part through the splendid application of the great principle of mutual aid, the real base of coöperation, whose success demands the presence of the highest gifts of intellectual and moral human nature. Coöperation is principally concerned with consumption, credit, and production. The coöperative societies of consumption and credit, furnishing means of accumulation and instruments of labor, are the best adapted to realize production. It can be said, to adopt a phrase of Vico, that coöperation in its application to consumption and credit makes its own material. In coöperation are interwoven ethics, economics, and politics, because the individual in a system of reciprocal aid ceases to be egoistic, makes larger profits, and becomes a factor in society. In fact, in the coöperative associations of consumption are united the sentiments of mutuality and individual responsibility together with the love of family. They obtain just prices, good quality, and exact weight. The love of family always develops and becomes stable through building societies. When an operative obtains a modest home in which his wife can be with the children, a large incentive to that bad habit of tavern life is destroyed, the number of crimes diminishes, and the beneficial sentiment of house-holding appears, and the real base of the workmen's credit is established. The people's coöperative banks begin a state of personal and democratic credit, because they do not require the deposit of capital and conciliate the two diverse objects of mutualism and individual-ism, which constitute a problem which has not, as yet, been well considered. The coöperation of production does not add fuel to the antagonism between capital and labor, but presupposes a capitalistic laborer. Neither does it owe its origin to a dependent right to labor; it asks nothing of the State. Such societies cannot be considered as fantastic communities; they do not absorb the individual, nor are they opposed to competition, because there are large and small industries which have a great need of help in order to make both ends meet through the exorbitant prevalence of the bigger industries.

§ 406. *Need to Regulate Coöperative Societies.* With these statements as a premise, it becomes evident that modern commercial legislation has (despite the contrary opinion of Troplong) to recognize and regulate these new forms of association, which are the effect of the natural development of freedom, which never resuscitates old economic forms of civil society. It is, however, necessary to notice that if the coöperative societies from one point of view are commercial societies, because they have speculation for an object and live by trade, from another point of view they are something greater, since they tend to harmonize the desires and personal interests with the principles of social stability and fraternity through the development of the laboring classes. In this sense such coöperative societies are involved in social legislation.

§ 407. *Governmental Authorization of Partnerships.* The principle of economic freedom, which has generated new forms of association, is destined to produce still more general and notable changes in the relations between such entities and the State. Even now the day of governmental authorization nears its end in the codes of civilized people. It is entirely contrary to contractual freedom and cannot fail to seem strange that for the completion of a private contract (which a partnership is) there is need of governmental authorization, while it is demanded in no other kind of contract. It is an anomaly that the administrative power can interfere in affairs of individual interests, protected and limited by law. Now this interference is contrary to principles of civil equality, and does not exist except when the law makes general rules and not special rules for different cases.   Law to-day should not take care of him who ruins himself and loses his fortune, when he is in a position to understand what he is doing and is effectively free, because the individual cannot remain eternally a minor escaping thus from a sense of responsibility upon which moral progress largely depends.   Law should not look upon the State as an Argus or a Briareus, since the public power is not competent to judge correctly about the economic conditions of an industrial project, jeopardizing, perhaps, the confidence of the citizens in the State, because of frequent cases of bankruptcy more or less shameful in operations which had received the governmental *placet*. History shows that authorization has not efficiently hindered the triumph of deceit, neither has it prevented the bold effrontery of swindlers and adventurers to the harm of many who believed themselves sufficiently protected by the prior governmental examination of an undertaking conducted under the form of a limited or special partnership.   On the other hand, it is possible that projects capable of great utility might not meet the approval of the governmental advisers ordinarily unversed in industrial matters, and therefore blinded by scruples and by their education.   In such a case the refusal of the authorization is an incalculable loss to civil society.

§ 408. *Governmental Supervision of Partnerships.* The fate of the system of vigilance is one with that of authorization because both are based on the forethought of a paternal government.   Governmental supervision has disappeared in the progressive nations.   The general opinion on this subject is that the government should abstain from all direct interference leaving to the persons interested the care and responsibility of taking

account of the doings of a partnership of which they are
members or with which they are connected. It is clear
that they can always bring it before a competent court
for any violation of law. Governmental supervision
has the same vices as authorization; it is incompetent
to hinder the maladministration of the partnership.
Thus on one hand, it is pernicious to private interests,
because it creates a false belief that they are subject to
investigation, and on the other hand, it harms the good
name of the government to whose negligence are imputed
all the maladministrations. A watchfulness exercised
only over the important companies would result in an
illegal and odious inequality of treatment.

§ 409. *Publicity in Partnership Business and Personal Liability.* We believe that the dangers resulting
upon partnerships in business can be avoided by following the principle of freedom with its necessary and
practical consequences. From this it follows that the law
should, above all things else, establish the greatest publicity in respect to the number and nature of the acts
and greater and more active efficacy in regard to the
method of carrying them out. It should provide, too,
for fuller and more rigorous liability for obligations
assumed on the part of the managers, promoters, officers,
and all those who are active in the partnership. The
law finally should render the watchfulness of those interested easy without disturbing the organization of the
associations by foreign factors such as instruments of
government protection. The ideas enunciated here have
already begun to have their influence on modern law,
as can be seen from such laws as are in existence.

410. *Freedom to Associate is Necessary.* The conception of freedom of business, gathered by us in an
inductive manner from economic history, positive law,
and all recent experience on the subject, becomes also de-

ductive and necessary, connected as it is with the law of the respect due to private property, and therefore to the principle of individual personality. Because it follows from the recognition that the individual personality is the very freedom of individual man, and that property is the investiture of the person and his free will applied to objects, that the individual can dispose of his possessions as he will and that he can render them subject to infinite agreements as long as he does not offend against custom, the social well-being, and public order. Such limitation as we have seen he enacted in regard to forest and mining property[1] can easily be understood when we recollect that in the ethical organism so different from the natural, the whole should respect the responsibility of the parts as the parts should act in consideration of the conscious and free life of the whole.

§ 411. *Bills of Exchange.* Many writers, like some legislators, among whom the French take an important place, consider a bill of exchange as a proof or symbol of a contract for the transportation of money, by which the contractor assumes the obligation of paying a sum of money to another or upon his order at a certain time or place for value given. There are three conditions to a bill of exchange, understood in this manner: the transportation from one place to another, a contract between the drawer and drawee, and the indication of value received. A bill of exchange differs from a promissory note, because the latter is an act by which the maker obligates himself to pay the creditor or his order at a definite time, declaring that he has received value. The former is always commercial, while the note is such only if signed by a trader or issued in commerce, and because it has a drawee and is drawn on a distant place. In a note, he who pays is the maker, and he pays in the

[1] *Cf.* Chap. VII, Bk. II, *ante.*

same place in which the note is made. Now this theory is substantially modified by science and law; and the radical modification is sanctioned by the philosophy of law. A man can easily employ a bank and draw a letter of exchange thereon to his own credit. In such a case there is no transportation, but there is a simple title of credit or an instrument of exchange given. A true bill of exchange is an obligation surrounded by rigorous formalities to distinguish it from other obligations and to render commerce more efficacious and certain. It must be a written obligation, by which one is bound to pay a sum of money to whomsoever presents the paper at maturity. This understood, it does not presuppose transportation from one place to another, and furthermore, the drawer can draw upon himself and pay it without the intervention of a drawee. A bill of exchange does not really demand a contract between a drawer and drawee, neither has it any need of containing the statement of value received, because, as Thöl says, writing on this subject, the contract of a bill of exchange arises when the bill is drawn. The indispensable conditions are delivery and presentation. A bill of exchange is the promise to pay a sum of money to the payee; it is performed by the drawee or indorser, if he accepts. There is no counterpromise on the part of him who takes the bill of exchange, because he, having the title, has the rights and is not bound by any duties. (It is true that he should present it to the drawee for acceptance and that, in case he does not accept or pay, he should have it protested, an act by which the failure to accept or pay is stated, but these are the only conditions for the exercise of the right of the holder and they are not real obligations, as Marghieri has shown in "La Cambiale.") From what has been said of the nature of a bill of exchange it is clear that it is not a

mixture of buying and selling or of bailment and loan
for use, as Trendelenburg thinks.

§ 412. *Transportation.* Transportation has the greatest possible importance because a large part of the
objects of wealth and value is brought into circulation by its aid. We can state without fear of error
that almost all the commercial life of society centres
about this business which at the present day is largely
conducted through railroads. A railroad is the use of
the steam-engine for transportation. It demands large
capital and the formation of collective entities for its
construction and exercise. Upon it the transportation
of the greater part of the merchandise, the objects of exchange, depends, and it brings the other means of transportation into coördination and harmony with it. Thus
it is the principal factor of travel. The State has been
obliged to fix the general plan of railroad construction
by statute and to regulate its functions, because this
means of transportation, like the others that are connected with it and depend on it, is an object of public
service. It is here a question both of the circulation of
wealth and the granting of a monopoly, since the laws of
competition cannot take part. For experience shows
that where there is one railroad, another will not be
built alongside, because the cost as well as the governmental grant forbids such a struggle for trade. One is
usually sufficient to unite the whole countryside. The
determination of the railroad plan and the relation
between the State and the company is a matter of
administrative law. The regulation of the relative
duties of shipper, carrier, and consignee is a question
of commercial law, which is not, however, a conventional
and voluntary law on this subject, preserving as it does
in the typical means of transportation the character of
public service. A contract of transportation does not

regard an isolated act, however complicated, but the whole business. The isolated act is simply an act of civil life and not commercial. Transportation implies a legal relation between him who sends the goods and him to whom they should be brought, and the third who should take them from the first and second. A contract of transportation, says De Tullio in a book of that name, is complex, presupposing rights and duties between the shipper, consignee, and common carrier from the moment of its formation. The identity of the consignee is of little importance, but at the moment of the formation of the contract there must be some consignee, although he need not be certain. In such cases the consignment is made to the bearer in the bill of lading, because the shipper must say that he has contracted an obligation with somebody, though he is ignorant what individual it is. The initial carrier in regard to the shipper acts as agent of the other common carriers and in regard to the other common carriers he acts as agent of the shipper. The contract is a unit despite the number of intermediate carriers; the bond which holds the shipper, consignee, and common carrier is one. The carrier accepts the obligation of providing the transportation, and he is responsible for its execution as if it were his own act, even if he must employ other carriers.

§ 413. *Insurance and Socialism.* Insurance is a wagering contract by which the insurer obligates himself to guarantee the insured from a certain risk for a stipulated sum, called a premium, which is determined by the nature of the risk. Insurance eliminates misfortunes by the division of the risk and can be considered, as Hermann considered it, as the commerce of indemnity for loss. He says that the prevention and repression compete with insurance. Prevention demands great care and is very expensive; repression costs less though it often has no effect; insurance costs still less, but the accident happens. Wagner and the other champions of the socialism of the State, moved by an erroneous conception, which we have criticized before[1] (that is, that with the progress of time the functions of the State increase to the detriment of the activities of private citizens), tend to make public law re-absorb a great part of private law. We have observed that society thus would travel over a road that it has already been over and return to the epoch of imperative law, in which the statutes provided for everything and the State took part in all the business of economic and civil existence. Conforming to this principle, the same writers affirm that insurance is not a business of free and private trade, but a public institution, that is, it is the fulfillment of a duty on the part of the State which must be substituted for the companies. Public administration, they say, carries on the business of communication, water supply, sanitation, and city illumination; if it represses the causes of injury, it can well complete the system by assuming the business of insurance. The insurance companies are very complex and often resemble petty States and are governed by men whose only interest lies in their salary. The State should take over the business of insurance, not with an object of gain, but as a means of general well-being, for it would have no need to make deceitful promises or pay large commissions to solicitors. Private insurance contains always a great injustice in the relation of the premium to the risk. It is not equitable that the farmer should pay a greater premium for fire insurance for his home than the millionaire in the city pays for his magnificent home. In general, the degree of risk is not the effect of a free act

[1] *Cf.* § 191 *ante.*

of will as in the case cited and a thousand others.   Private insurance is not possible for those who need it most; justice demands that the premium should have a relation to the wealth of the insured, and the State becoming insurer, could provide it for the poor and needy.

§ 414.   *Criticism of the Socialistic View of Insurance.* A criticism of these articles has been made with great acumen by Salandra, in his book "Un Caso di Socialismo di Stato."   Above all, we must note that a modern State is not generally disposed to assume economic functions. We have already seen that it has sold its land and no longer competes in business with its citizens, but gets its income chiefly from the customs.[1]   To realize its conception of its duties to protect the law and the progress of culture and well-being, it takes part in economic pursuits, if the private citizens have not sufficient initiative, if it must destroy the pernicious effects of a monopoly, or if it is a question of promoting an industry.   Such cases of governmental intervention alleged by the socialists of the Wagnerian school are related to public security and help, and not with economic ends.   City lighting, hygiene, and police are examples of this.   The prevention or repression of causes of injury are duties of a State, since it must preserve individuals from dangers that threaten all.   The benefit of insurance is obtained when an accident has happened and the burden has fallen on the life or estate of some individual.   An injury must be avoided or repaired by him who caused it.   Furthermore, it is indubitably clear that individual management is more economic than management by a society and the latter more economic than administration by the State because they are smaller and controlled by persons who are trained managers and have an interest in the gains

[1] *Cf.* § 192 *ante.*

and are watched by the stockholders, who have certainly a more direct and keen interest than the members of a civil government or political assembly chosen by election. Insurance as an industrial enterprise which renders cheap services, adapting itself to the habits, needs, and prejudices of its members, is always better entrusted to private citizens. Experience is the strongest proof of the truth of this judgment which shows that the attempts by the State to carry on insurance have generally been failures.

§ 415. *Insurance Rates are Determined by Calculation.* We must reflect that the essence of insurance is the proportion of the premium to the risk. Insurance rates are ascertained through mathematical principles by calculation and cannot logically be subordinated to ethical purposes. No one would wish to pay a higher rate than was due so that another's rate might be lower. Take away the principle of proportion and insurance will vanish. Admitting that everyone is obliged to insure and that some pay higher and some less premiums than they should, it is clear that the first would pay a tax so that the State could give an almost gratuitous service to the second. Such beneficence may be a special duty of the State, whose legitimacy and convenience it is not necessary to examine now, but certainly it is not true insurance. Insurance is not a method of equalizing fortunes and solving social difficulties. It does not tend towards an equal division of wealth, as Wagner believes. If it is true, says Zammarano in "L'Intrapresa delle Assicurazioni," that the farmer cannot build his house of brick or stone, but must build it of wood; if it is true that he who does not enjoy good health cannot be insured or must pay a higher premium; and if he who has a field exposed to the destructive force of hailstorms must pay more than he who has a field less

exposed to this plague, insurance has no duty to repair
the social inequalities or to give wealth, strength, or
health to them that lack it.

§ 416.   *Insurance is more Economic than Ethical.*
The insurance business is not really a protective institution, because it looks to profits; charitable institutions, as savings banks, mutual aid societies, and
such, have no financial aim.   Even the mutual insurance
companies (a kind of coöperative society) have really
a financial aim, the insured wishing to pay a less premium
for the risk with the increase in the number of policies.
He does a protective act who insures his life, house,
or harvest and not the company which gains thereby.
Insurance companies are of great social importance
dividing the total loss among a great number of stockholders.   On one hand, they limit the individual loss, and
on the other hand they prevent great losses by the banks
and corporations, due to wide-reaching accidents, and
thus avoid a diminution of income.   The great obstacle
to their development is the rate which remains high,
because competition is difficult.   Zammarano observes
that the old life-insurance companies increase the commissions of the soliciting agents to take business from
their new rivals, and that the new associations are forced
to raise theirs more, creating thus an excess of expense
and not keeping, therefore, a reserve equal to the risks
assumed.   The companies for their insurance against
injury unite and refuse any reinsurance to the younger
societies which do not adopt their rate.   Mutual societies have no less need of agents, who demand the same
rate as the business companies pay;   and they cannot
deny it because they must extend the sphere of their
business.   It is futile to dream of a more efficacious and
economic control of insurance through the State with
the object of establishing competition among the private

concerns, because in all the civilized countries of Europe these attempts have been made and have not succeeded, except in Germany, where there is a peculiar combination of circumstances. A deficiency of the reserve fund, in consequence of heavy expense, does not in short policies ruin the concern, if it acquires every year a certain number of new policies. In such cases the new insurance pays for the old and the business goes on until the ascending movement stops, or many losses occur. The salient point of the question is always the obtaining of a reserve fund, the exact value of which should be prescribed by law. It must not be forgotten that the matter of insurance is too complicated and delicate to be easily understood. Often the directors of the companies do not understand it well. The insured knows nothing about it and is without the company, and therefore can exercise no supervision. The observations of Zammarano are true and his deduction valid. The law is called upon to harmonize the principle of freedom of trade with the necessity of a serious protection of the rights of the insured. If it were shown that this protection could not be obtained except by the intervention of the State, there would be a case where a reasonable exception existed for preventive authorization and control by the government in the case of trading corporations. And this exception is not the only one, since no one doubts the legality and propriety of the State board of bank examiners for banks that issue notes.

§ 417. *The Law should Guard against Trickery.* The law should promote moral conditions for the better development of social life and should give a free field for productive labor. It should not protect wagering contracts which are based on thoughtlessness and idleness, creating, on one side, sudden and enormous fortunes, and on the other, instantaneous desolating ruin and misery. While the law, however, cannot watch all the games of chance, it can watch the tricks which lie within the exercise of corporations. This guardianship can be exercised against speculation, that is, to those contracts which do not entail the acquirement of stock or the payment of money at the moment of formation, but the payment in the future of the difference in value not dependent on blind luck. In the same way that particular knowledge is required for the race course, the pursuit of arms and other exercises, in the present case a knowledge of a special kind is necessary in order to foresee the flux and reflux of the values quoted on the exchange. Such knowledge regards the commercial movement of values and their tendencies. It is not blind luck which decides, but certain facts which can only be foreseen after attentive study and long experience.

CHAPTER XVII

THE PRIMITIVE FAMILY.— THE FAMILY AS THE PROTOTYPE OF THE STATE

MATING AND THE INSTINCT OF REPRODUCTION IN ANIMALS. — THE THEORIES OF LUCRETIUS AND VICO. — PRIMITIVE UNIONS. — MATRIARCHY. — EXOGAMY AND RAPE. — THE BEGINNINGS OF THE DEVELOPMENT OF THE PATRIARCHAL FAMILY. — THE PROGRESSIVE INDIVIDUALIZATION OF RELATIONSHIP. — THE PROCESS OF SPECIFICATION, AND THE OBJECT OF THE FAMILY.

§ 418. *The Primitive Family. The Family as the Prototype of the State.* Individual man expands through property, which represents acquired means, and develops through reciprocal acts, the result of a common will working for determinate useful objects. He begins his development with family relations, which are the closest and first form of society. The family is an ethical organism in which many consciousnesses interpenetrate, many wills agree, forming a common consciousness with a common spirit and will. It is the intimate union of nature, based on feeling, and for a definite need. In the evolution of ethico-juridical forms, it shows progress as it affects individual property and obligations, because man is no longer merely individual, but connotes an ethical organism. It is through the family that the individual becomes the abstract man, who is seen more fully in civilization, in a State, and in a system of States. If the family is a real union, civilization and the State are human communities based on the distinction of interests and the principles of

reason. The system of States presupposes the human
factor in every nation.

§ 419. *Elementary Family among Animals.* The
state of matrimony and the family have their distinct
prototypes in some forms of intercourse and co-existence among species of animals. The lowest and most
general satisfaction of the instinct of reproduction is promiscuity. The sexual life of most animals follows
organic impulses, blindly, without showing preferences
or attachments which amount to anything like choice
or fidelity. Polygamy exists among the animals which
live in groups, where there is a predominance of females
over males. Polyandry is very rare, because the female
is not as strong as the male and cannot curb and check
the extravagances of a male seraglio. Monogamy is not
rare among the species which are scattered, living in
couples either because of difficulty in finding food or
because of their unsociable nature. Some species give
marvelous examples of monogamy, where widowhood
ordinarily results in the death of the survivor. There
are examples among animals, too, where the instinct of
reproduction has lost its original egoistic character.
Among the ants reproduction, following a system for
the division of labor, is assigned. The search for any
kind of domestic life, however, has been fruitless in the
lower species, which pay but little attention to their offspring, and leave preservation to chance. With reptiles,
the female gives some care to her eggs, while the male
gives her food. It is in the female that the love of young
first awakens; in the male it comes later and with less
intensity. With both parents, this love lasts only until
the time of weaning; hence the short duration of domestic
relations even among the monogamic animals. Filial
affection is a pure exception; the larger apes have a kind
of family, in which the children and the parents live to-

gether for a certain length of time. The head is a male adult who keeps his authority only until he is abandoned or murdered by his own children. The basis of domestic obedience is force, making a command binding as long as the father is in a position to punish those who disobey. As a general rule, the female, among the mammiferous animals, is the centre about which the family is grouped. If the male remains a member, it is due more to her attractions than to love of progeny.

§ 420. *Former Views of the Human Family.* Coming now to regard the phases of human matrimony and family relations, we see to-day in all science which deal with man and civil institutions that what existed in the past is still observable in the living species. As in like studies, not a few types, believed primitive for many years, have been shown to be posterior forms more or less imperfect, so some social facts, though original and initial, appear, in the light of later analysis, derivative and historic in the true sense. One of these facts is the patriarchal family, which until recently has been represented as an elementary natural group, existing from the beginning of humanity, and consisting of a father with one or more wives, and their offspring. The relationship was determined through the father, who was the absolute owner of the wives, children, and property. So the patriarchal families, growing larger, brought about the "γένος," "gens," or "clan." From the multiplication of such unions the tribe was born; whence civil communities were derived.

§ 421. *The Modern View of the Origin of Human Families.* Recent studies of the oldest records and profound researches into legends and the customs of modern savages have led to the belief that the patriarchal family was not the beginning of society. It has been demonstrated by these studies and researches that at the beginning there was a horde, ignorant of individual relationships, because its members were not considered as children of certains persons, but rather as children of all the fathers and mothers in the community. Only later did the horde break up into smaller groups which began to lead separate lives. From that moment can be traced the genesis of matrimony, or the union, more or less stable, of a great or less number of individuals, and consequently the genesis of the family. Primitive families were based on maternal relationship, because of the customary uncertainty of the father's identity, and had a feminine genealogy, differing from the patriarchal family, which developed in a way which presupposes the certainty of the father.

§ 422. *The Maternal Family Preceded the Paternal.* As this was the course of development it is clear that in the remote times of the common ownership of women, the right of the horde must be considered as the "jus naturæ," and that afterwards the "jus naturæ" was the right of the mother, through whom the son of a dead man's sister succeeded to his goods, and sometimes to his political dignity or sacerdotal office, together with the obligation of revenge. It is easy to understand that the father's right could be changed to a natural right only by the slow and incessant development of ages.

§ 423. *History of Researches into the Origin of the Family.* It has been said that these studies were begun in the XVIIth century by Lafitau, in his work "Les Coutumes des Sauvages Americaines," and that in the XIXth century they were followed, extended, and systematized by D'Eckenstein, and Bachofen in his "Antiquarische Briefe," by McLennan in "Origin of Consanguinity and Primitive Conditions of Matrimony," by Morgan in "System of Consanguinity and Affinity," by Lubbock in "Origin of Civilization and the Primitive

Condition of Man," by Girard-Teulon in "Les Origines du Mariage et de la Famille," by Spencer in his "Principles of Sociology," and by Letourneau in "Sociologie d'après l'Ethnologie." We may add that Lafitau, D'Eckenstein, and Letourneau furnish only data and special facts, while the others coördinate general philosophical and historical discoveries. Vico, however, has been forgotten, who, before all the writers mentioned, published his theory, almost identical with the modern doctrine, as we will see in the following paragraph. Lucretius also has been overlooked, who in the Fifth Book of his immortal poem, "De Natura Rerum," in speaking of the primitive ages, says: —

> "*Et Venus in silvis jungebat corpora amantium:*
> *Conciliabat enim vel mutua quamque cupido,*
> *Vel violenta viri vis atque impensa libido,*
> *Vel prælium, glandes, atque arbuta, vel pira lecta.*

And in picturing the character of a later date and more advanced period, the Latin poet writes: —

> "*Inde casas postquam, ac pelleis, ignemque pararunt,*
> *Et mulier coniuncta viro concessit in unum:*
> *Castaque privatæ Veneris connubia læta*
> *Cognita sunt, prolemque ex se videre creatam:*
> *Tum genus humanum primun mollescere cœpit.*"

§ 424. *Vico's Theory of the History of Family.* Providence, teaches Vico, at the first beginning of nations decreed that the strongest men of gigantic stature should wander on the heights of the mountains like beasts, which too are strong. Frightened by the first thunderbolts after the Flood, they fled into caves and surrendered themselves to a superior force, which they called Jove; and though proud and cruel, they

humiliated themselves in their terror before a divinity.
In such a state of human affairs, we can imagine no
other plan which Divine Providence could have adopted
to cure them of their bestial vices in the great forests of
the earth in order to introduce the ways of human civilization.   Thereupon there were formed republics called
monastic, with one ruler who was guided by the Most
High, who they believed made and hurled those thunderbolts in which they saw the true light of God, the
Ruler of mankind.   To Him all things were subject.
They imagined the rulers to be divine.   As subjects they
feared and revered them as His representatives.   Therefore, torn in the struggle between frightful superstition
and bestial lust (in such men most violent) and feeling
that the aspect of heaven was terrible to them and
forbade them the use of love, these men held the promptings of the lusts of the flesh in check.   And beginning
to use human liberty, which restrains the emotions of
desire and gives them the direction which (not coming
from the body from which desire comes) must come
from the mind, and therefore be proper to man, their
nature was changed, and seizing the women, whose
nature was unwilling and resisting, they dragged them
within their caves and kept them in life-long slavery.
These unions, the first which were modest and religious,
were the beginning of matrimony, by which, of known
women there were born known children by known
fathers; thus the family began.   The fathers ruled with
Cyclopean control, governing their children and wives
as their unbending and cruel nature prompted them.
Taught in such a school, at the founding of the cities
men were found to fear the imperial edicts.   Providence
created certain economic governments of monarchical
form under the family rulers who excelled in sex, age,
and worth, in a state which could be called a state of

nature, but which was the patriarchal age.   They had
formed the first natural states of a religious, chaste, and
binding order; and limited to their own land, no longer
able to wander over the country as they had done before in their savage ways, they had to kill the beasts
for food' for their families.   And since they could no
longer wander to find pasturage, they had to conquer
the earth and sow seeds.   And all this was caused by
the savagery of human nature.   After a long period,
hunted down by their own evil deeds, which were bringing about an infamous communion of possessions and
women, men who were impious, with no fear of God,
shameless and weak, unbridled in incest and bestial
love, wandering and alone on the great plains and in
the valleys, with their lives in danger as the result of
their infamous communion, sought refuge with the
fathers, who received them into their protection, together with their followers, who increased the family
kingdoms.

§ 425. *Vico's Theory of the History of the Family
Reviewed.*   We can briefly repeat that part of the conclusions of the "Scienza Nuova," of which some fragments have been cited before (*seriatim*) for a different
reason.   Vico says in the most open manner that before the modest and religious human marriages, that is,
before matrimony and the family, of certain fathers
with certain mothers and certain children, there was
a shameful communion of things and women in which
impious, shameless, and wicked men lived their
lives.   This communion ended, says Vico, when they
forcibly carried off to their grottoes the unwilling and
resisting women.   The women were not modest or
pure, but did not wish to be reduced to the service of
man.   The men were solitary sovereigns or princes,
the heads of economic governments of monarchical form.

Now a kingdom is a derivative of strong control, as a popular republic is a derivative of freedom, and the oligarchy is a result of protection. Control, freedom, and protection are the three elements of the idea of law corresponding to knowledge, will, and power. In Vico's judgment matrimony is bound up with the right of property, and does not result from monarchical government. It was accompanied by the need of killing beasts, of conquering the earth, and of sowing seed in order to nourish the families by which and for which the fields were cultivated. Vico, however, is wrong in transforming the wild state so suddenly into the age when men were modest, pious, and wise; thus the heroic age which follows the divine seems to be a step in the wrong direction, through which man passed from the age of shameful communion to the times of modest and religious marriage with certain fathers, that is, to the time of the patriarchal family. Naturally, Vico, as in his day there were not the many aids from different modern studies, did not discover and could not discover all those factors found or surmised to-day by Bachofen, McLennan, Morgan, Tyler, Lubbock, and Giraud-Teulon. But the great author of the "Scienza Nuova" left the question open, so to speak, and recognized implicitly the correctness of deductions from the customs of modern savages. He taught that when men can form no idea of distant and unknown things, they can imagine them by the aid of things known and present. But we must not forget a wise warning of Darwin that quite frequently the licentiousness of savages is the result of decadence.

§ 426. *Modern Example of the Community of Women.* Bachofen, McLennan, Morgan, Lubbock, and Giraud-Teulon agree with Lucretius and Vico in recognizing a primitive period of the communion of women, and invoke the authorities of ancient and modern writers. In China, women were common until the end of the reign of Fouhi, and in Greece until the days of Cecrops; the Massageti, Nasimonisans, and Auseans did not know of matrimony according to Herodotus and Strabo. Strabo and Solon say that the Garamantians were in the same condition, and Zenophon adds to this class the Mosynocians, who scandalized the soldiers of Cyrus by their lack of any sense of shame. The authors cited adduce many facts to prove that the most absolute communism exists in some parts of New Zealand, South America, of the Andaman and Nicobar Islands. The system is found, too, among some negro people who have no family names and distinguish the individuals only by some peculiarity, as "Long" or "Lame."

§ 427. *History Proves Original Communion of Women.* Among the facts alleged as methods of determining relationship, the homes and some of the strange nuptial rights, which belong exclusively to the system of preëxistent community of women, demand special attention. The careful researches of Morgan show that relationship was not originally between individuals, but a relation between the individual and the tribe. The child at first recognized as his fathers all the adults of the tribe, and as mothers all the women of the tribe who could have borne him. The inhabitants of the Sandwich Islands, for example, until the last century, had only five classes of relations. The first included the individual, his brothers, sisters and cousins; the second included the father, mother, and their brothers, sisters, and cousins, who were, however, all called fathers and mothers; the third consisted of the grandfather, the grandmother, and their brothers, sisters, and cousins, and formed the class of grandparents; the fourth consisted of the children and their cousins, all recognized as children; the fifth class included the grandchildren and their cousins, and was the class of grandchildren. According to this classification or relationship, all the members of a tribe were brothers and sisters to each other; the uncle looked upon his nephew as his son, and the nephew was regarded as the son of his aunt. In a country where a man calls his nephew or niece his child, it is reasonable to suppose that marriages are allowed between brothers and sisters. Travelers say that the missionaries encounter the greatest difficulty in those islands in teaching the women chastity. Adultery, incest, and fornication are sanctioned by custom and religion. In conclusion we may add that incest was a general rule in antiquity, as can be seen from the fact that the gods and heroes married their sisters. The Egyptians and Persians imitated this custom. Diodorus says that the Egyptian king was in duty bound to marry his sister; Plato testifies that the Pythian oracle held such a union legal and proper according to the laws of nature. The other fact worthy of study is the houses situated in the Indian territories of the central and southern United States. From one hundred to one hundred and fifty feet long, they are capable of giving shelter to forty or fifty families, that is, to three or four hundred persons. The huge cabin of the Indians of Columbia could hold a hundred people, and there are villages in that country which consist of one or two houses of this size. Mexico, the regions of Yucatan and of Guatamala, were, before the arrival of Europeans, full of such villages, which furnish good testimony of the promiscuity of life. The early Spaniards who discovered these countries believed these constructions were palaces.

§ 428. *Traces of Primitive Promiscuity in Many Marriage Rites.* When the exclusive possession of one woman by one man appears in history, we must consider whether this institution of positive law violates and is contrary to the primitive law of the community called the "jus naturæ." It was recognized as an infraction of natural and religious law because the fecundity of women like that of the earth or the Great Mother should not suffer limitations, whence arose the need of a tribute to be paid to the offended deity and of an expiation to be rendered to the gods; tribute and expiation consisting in enforcing a period of provisional promiscuity on the woman to be married. The old customs show this, which are found in strange and scandalous cults, celebrated in homage of the god, protector of fecundity. The Lydians, Sardinians, and Babylonians made a sacrifice of their chastity before the wedding (as Herodotus and Strabo report), and in crises all the women of war were forced to offer their shame as an expiation to placate the divinity outraged by their violation of the marriage law of nature. The magistrate of Locros demanded in a day of public danger the sacrifice of the chastity of the women in the Temple of Venus. Strabo himself says that the daughters of good family, who devoted themselves for a certain time to the cult of Anaitis, were most sought after as wives; that such expiation was necessary in Armenia and in some parts of the Island of Cyprus. Herodotus speaks of the same custom among the Thracians. And Diodorus Siculus states that in the Balearic Islands, at Majorca and Minorca and in other places, the bride for the first night belongs to all the guests. In the Mahabharata, we read that women, like cattle, were held in common, and that Cwetaketom was the first to introduce private possession. In India there is a religious sect called "Vira-Sriva," that hold men equal by the "lingam." The priestesses of Siva and Krishna obey the same religious commands, and their depravity is famous. In that country a woman without a husband and a widow can sacrifice to the idol in a temple of Tulava, but from the moment of sacrifice is forced to give herself to all. Strabo says on this subject that a Parthian who has had two or three children by one woman can leave her and marry another. To-day the Eskimos and Indians of North and South America, the tribes of Polynesia and Australia, the negroes of East and West Africa, like the Caffirs, give their guest temporarily some of their wives. Some Brazilian tribes do the same for their prisoners of war whom they can kill and eat. Among the ancient Peruvians, in Ethiopia and even now among many aboriginal tribes of India, in Burma, Cashmir, southern Madagascar and New Zealand, the bride belongs for the first night to all the relatives and friends. In some parts of India, in ancient Abyssinia, among some classes in Brazil and Peru, this "jus primæ noctis" is exercised by the chieftain and priests. In the primitive nations of Greece, which were in closer relations with Asia, — Corinth for example, — there were a special body of priestesses with the object of forcing their fellow-women to the sacrifice of their shame. Courtesans are treated with great regard in some societies because they continue an old custom, sanctioned by religion. The constant discussion of poetry, philosophy, and politics developed the ideas and taste of Athenian courtesans. Their houses became the places of profitable leisure. Who does not know that Socrates argued with them and that Pericles was often in the house of Aspasia? In India, Abyssinia, and Java, they enjoy a good name and are treated with respect. All these facts disprove Spencer's claim that the primitive community of women contained no legal idea.

§ 429. *Love a Later Development.* The primitive unions must have been without sentiment or love.

They consisted in animal intercourse, being founded on the slavery of women. They must have been temporary and completed without rites, if we argue from the union of modern savages. Lubbock gets together the different reports from all travelers on this point and teaches things of no small interest for our theme. Hottentots and Caffirs are so cold and indifferent as to induce those who have studied their customs to affirm that there is no love in their union. There are Indian tribes in both Americas who have no word for "fear," and there are several languages which have no verb "to love." Missionaries, in translating the Bible into these languages, are forced to invent a vocabulary to express this idea. Among the Osages and Cherokees, there cannot be found a single poetical or musical expression that reveals love. At Yariba in central Africa, the natives marry with the greatest indifference, as if they were engaged in buying or selling grain. The tribes inhabiting the hills in Chittegong (India) look upon matrimony as simply a bodily union and a utility or means of getting their food cooked. The young men in Australia pay the women for the quality of services they can render. They are treated with the greatest brutality, being beaten and struck with spears upon every occasion. Travelers have seen women with their backs entirely covered with scars. In some parts of Paraguay and Abyssinia, the marriage bonds are so light that the husband and wife can separate upon mutual consent. They have no sense of shame according to the stories of all the travelers. The Hassaniyeh Arabs have a form of matrimony which lasts three days; on the fourth, the woman is entirely free. In Ceylon they have trial marriages for five days; at the end of this time the marriage can be annulled or confirmed. Among certain tribes of southern India, girls of fifteen or twenty years are married

to boys of five or six. The girl lives with her father-in-law
or with a maternal uncle or cousin. If there are children
of that union, the boy is the legal father, who in his turn
has issue by a woman married to some other child, his
own children being half grown. In almost all marriages
between savages there is a dearth of rites or ceremonies.
The Badagas of Hindustan, the Kirumbas, a tribe living
in the hills of Nilgherry, the Keriahs of central India,
the Indians of California, the Kutchin Indians, the Redskins of the United States, the Asawaks of South America,
the tribes of Australia and Brazil, the people of Abyssinia, of West Africa, the Ashantis and Hottentots, have
no witnesses, magistrates, or priests for a wedding, but
reserve them for the ceremonies accompanying circum-
cision and tattooing. Montesquieu is wrong, therefore,
when he says that in all ages marriage has been a religious ceremony.

§ 430. *Development from Promiscuity and Monogamy.*
It is probable that, as time went on, the system of
communion was restricted by means of maternal relationship; thus the family was created, that at first was
formed by the mother, the father being generally unknown. The family began to be formed through
the mother. The name of the mother alone descended
and the husband represented only a secondary consideration. Now, matriarchy, although unilateral, is
always superior from an ethical and civil point of view
to generic relationship, which is a relation between the
individual and the community and excludes the family
as a particular and distinct society. Bachofen regards
the passage from communion to matriarchy as a revolt
by the women who were ashamed of their state and
succeeded in gaining supremacy. He calls the second
state material, and the third, or the period of paternal
rights, in which the father is recognized as the author

of life, and the mother as the nurse, the spiritual period.
It seems that Bachofen is right in calling the second
period material, because in it the family appears on its
natural foundation. But we believe him wrong in stating
that the cause of the change from the first to the second
state was a revolt by the women, because we cannot believe that in those barbarous times, the sense of shame and
unity of action should have been so developed among
women as to allow a determined reaction to conquer the
men who were the stronger. The legend of the Amazons,
so general and extensive, has probably been formed
through a fantastic attraction of the existence of women
familiar with politics. Bonghi, in his "Lezioni di Storia
Antica," says that popular fancy has thus drawn the
change from the feminine rule to masculine, from the
two different states of the family. It was believed the
rule of the women preceded that of the men, and
that the women, when heads of the family, were heads of
the State as well.

§ 431. *The Sandwich Island Example.* The transition from the system of community to that of matriarchy is clearly illustrated by the natives of the
Sandwich Islands. Communion in these islands is
becoming restricted, and the union of brothers and
sisters are few. On one hand, the brothers begin by
owning women in common; on the other, the sister lives
in more easily broken conjugal relations with a certain
number of men. In the last century, there has been a
great change, because the family of feminine relationship
has been instituted. The system of relationship through
women still exists in Australia, in the Ladrone Islands,
in Fiji and Tonga, and in other parts of the Pacific Archi-
pelago; in the Caroline Islands, among the people who
live between Burma and Siam, in some of the tribes of
Ceylon, in the Maldives, upon the coasts of Malabar,

among some of the primitive peoples of India, among the greater number of the Indians of North America, among the Arawaks of South America, in Senegal, in Loango, in Congo, among the Herreros and Caffirs, on the coasts of Guinea, and among the Touareng.

§ 432. *Example of Ancient Matriarchy.* The ancient Iberians, the primitive people of Asia Minor, the Lycians, according to Herodotus, the inhabitants of Locros, according to Polybius, and the Etruscans, who have left mortuary inscriptions with the name of the mother and not the name of the father of the deceased, lived under the same system. There are bilingual Etruscan inscriptions which give the name of the deceased and of his or her mother, as in the following examples: "L. Caius Caulia natus; Thania Sudernia nata." In other inscriptions, there is found the name of the mother alone and not that of the deceased, for example, "Perrica natus." There are still others to which there is added a Latin translation which does not contain the name of the father. This addition is a result of Roman custom or of the personal knowledge of the lapidary, as Corssen says, in his book, "Ueber die Sprache der Etrusker." In the museum at Naples the only bilingual Etruscan inscription is of the last kind: "Vl, Alfni Nuvi Cainal." This Corssen translates, "Velus Albinus Novius Caina (mother) natus." Cainal is a feminine proper name found in twelve other inscriptions. The Latin translation of the inscription is as follows: "C. Alfius A. F. Cainnia natus." Writing this verse in full we have, "Caius Alfius Auli filius Cainnia natus." Herodotus observes that in Egypt the women took part in public life, carrying on business and managing industries, while the men stayed at home and did the weaving. Diodorus adds that among the many benefits of Isis, the Egyptian queen had more power

and was more respected than the king, and that a
private citizen was part of his wife's property according
to the terms of the nuptial contract. Many mortuary
inscriptions in Egypt contain the name of the mother
and not that of the father of the deceased, and if they
give the name of the latter, they always give the name
of the mother too. In fact, Isis is represented as the
immortal beginning of things, the great life-giving
divinity, while Osiris was the principle of fecundity,
but was only temporary and mortal. With the importance of Isis came the power of the sister-wives of
the Pharaohs and the legal duty, reported by Herodotus,
of the sons and daughters to support their aged parents.
Similar relations between the sexes is found in the
countries of Angola, among the Timannians, the
Kurankos, the Sulimas, among the Bazes of southern
Egypt, among the Bogos and the Beni-Amer. And
the great power of the queen or sister-wife is found
to-day in the greater number of the African kingdoms in
which by the side of the chief there is a woman given
the dignity of "makonda," a dignity and power generally
belonging to the chief's sister who is at the same time
his chief-wife. In ancient Athens, according to Varro,
in a passage preserved by St. Augustine, the children
received the name of the mother. In the Orestes of
Æschylus there is preserved a mark of relationship
through the mother, because the Erinnyes, representing
the old law, demand the condemnation of Orestes, the
murderer of his mother, by saying that Clytemnestra
was no relation of her son, though the blood of the
man who had been murdered and Apollo, the champion
of the new law, implore mercy for Orestes, claiming that the mother was not the creator of her son,
but the nurse of the seed placed in her breast. The
Erinnyes interrupt the discourse and say that the

young god wishes to destroy the old law, and therefore the old gods.

§ 433. *Inheritance where the Genealogy is Maternal.*
As we have observed before, in those countries where
there is a feminine genealogy, the son of a man's sister
and not his own is his heir.   Such was the law of inheritance among the Ethiopians, according to the statement of
Herodotus and Strabo.   The Mahabharata tells of
King Vasuki, who wanted an heir and defender.
This prince did not think of taking unto himself a wife,
but sought a husband for his sister, who was a man
marked by the gods, to lay with the bride but one night,
and in due time the hero Astika was born, who was the
king's heir.   The legend of the Mahabharata shows that
the same law of inheritance existed in India in the
same form that it to-day holds among the natives.
It is still existent in Nubia, in the Soudan, in Negrizia,
on the coasts of New Guinea, along the lakes and streams
of East Africa, and along the Zambese, among the Bassutos, the Tourarengs, the Herreros, in Madagascar,
among the Bogos, Battas of Lunatra, and on certain
islands of the Pacific, with the Tlinkithes, the Kenayes
of Russian America, in Mexico, in Peru, among the
Indian tribes of North America, and in Malabar.   In
Africa, the son inherits from his father only his weapons.
In Madagascar, among the Touarengs, the Herreros,
and among the Redskins, a son of a sister inherits
the political dignity and sometimes the sacerdotal
duties of his uncle under this system of relationship.
The duty of revenge follows the feminine genealogy
where the latter exists, and falls to the lot, not of the
son of the murdered man, but to his maternal nephews.

§ 434. *Endogamy and Exogamy.* If humanity has
developed from the state of communion to a period
of relationship by means of women, it is logical to pre-

sume that the first tribes or groups of relatives were
constituted under the system of descent from woman
to woman. McLennan thinks that the organic principle of the tribe (in the oldest antiquity) has been
exogamy, that is, the prohibition of marriage between
individuals of the same totem. Exogamy must owe
its existence to marriage by capture, and the capture
was at first actual and real, later symbolic.   He has
found exogamy in China, Siberia, Tartary, India,
Circassia, in both the Americas, Australia, the Islands
of the Pacific, among the Celts, and in Scotland.
The law had little regard for women among primitive
people who used to kill whatever girls were born, looking upon them as a cause of weakness likely to become
later an incentive for attacks by their neighbors.   It
seems to us that this doctrine sheds much light on certain facts which have been but little understood until
our own day. Exogamy produces rapid changes of
nationality without immigration or war because the
mother is of a hostile tribe.   It furnishes us the reason
of the custom that the Redskins, for example, have
of calling a woman's son the son of her brother and the
nephew the son of the sister.   The Chinese still call
boys the children of their uncle, and the nephews, descendants of their aunt.   It is clear that where exogamy
prevails promiscuity is restricted, and thus a great
progress is made because there can be no marriage between brother and sisters; but the promiscuity does not
cease, as is often argued from this.   It forces us to wonder
at what period these marriages of brothers and sisters
disappeared. As a natural consequence of the necessity
which brought about exogamy, the idea of incest was
born, which made its appearance in strange forms.
In Ceylon, the father is forbidden to look at his own
daughter after she has reached the age of puberty,

and the same prohibition is placed upon the mother in respect to her son. In Asia, among the Mongols, in Africa, among the Bassutos, the daughter-in-law must hide when she sees her father-in-law. Among the Arawaks, a man is not allowed to look at his mother-in-law. Among the Caffirs and Redskins, the latter cannot pronounce the name of her son-in-law. In the Fiji Island, the brothers, sisters, cousins, parents, and children-in-law cannot speak nor eat together. There are analogous customs in Australia, India, Borneo, and West Africa. Lubbock believes that marriage by capture could coexist and did coexist with the system of communion. But marriage by capture has probably been the beginning of individual marriages. The woman stolen from another tribe became by right of war the exclusive property of the captor. From this Lubbock argues that exogamy is the result of capture, while McLennan looks upon it rather as the cause. The former disagrees with the latter upon the alleged motive of exogamy because infanticide was not limited to the girls, but extended as well to the boys, as it does in Australia. Besides, there are some tribes who have marriages by capture and at the same time are endogamous; the Bedouins, for example, recognize the right of marriage by capture, and can at the same time marry a cousin upon the payment of a certain fine. Giraud-Teulon does not think that the murder of the girls was a cause of exogamy, because the custom of infanticide must have been common and reciprocal to the various tribes, and therefore would have rendered exogamy and capture impossible. Spencer adds that the murder of the girls must have been equalized by the great mortality of the young men in the almost constant state of war. He adds that polyandry, the consequence of McLennan's theory, does not always accompany exog-

amy. Spencer tries to base exogamy upon a theory of
booty, because the woman is one of the main objects
to be taken from the enemy, and such is the purpose of
the warriors. Since the warriors were the most important men in the community, the practice of marrying
foreign women became general, and acquired a religious
sanction. Endogamy is found among the peaceful
tribes, while exogamy is found in the warlike and victorious ones; but how could it happen, we must ask
Spencer, that the warlike tribes of New Zealand are
endogamous? But in whatever way we look at it, it is
certain that there was, in the age of which we speak, a
necessity of obtaining by capture the women of another
tribe. In fact, without this necessity, the men would not
have at great risk of life sought their wives from the
enemy. The capture at first is brutal and ferocious, as in
Australia, New Zealand, some of the islands of the Pacific and South America. The men of Australia, when
they discover a woman without protection, stun her with
a blow of a "dowak," drag her by the hair to the neighboring brush, and wait until the poor creature comes to
herself. So it is in the country around Sidney, at Bally,
and in other places. Later on, the capture acquires a
symbolic form; as a symbol it exists in India, in the
interior of Asia, among the Malasians, in Africa, and
among the ancient Greeks and Romans.

§ 435. *Maternal Genealogy is Physical, the Paternal,
Spiritual.* The relationship by means of women, being
derived from a physical certainty, should appear as
an institution of natural law. On the contrary, the
relationship by means of men should be regarded as a
creation of civil law, because it presupposes a free
recognition of the bonds of relationship, a voluntary
and reflective act which is connected with an abstract
presumption. A child can only be the child of one

woman, but it may be the child of any of several men. If the relationship by means of men requires reflective acts and abstract presumptions, it is evident that it must be posterior. The sentiment of paternity in its origin has not, nor can it have, a character truly ethical. Paternity at first was a relation of slavery and later became a method for the acquisition of wealth among modern savages, as it is with those that live on the coast of Guinea. The father himself is often seen selling his own children as slaves and the children, when grown, ambush the father and sell him in his turn with the greatest pleasure. In some countries in South Africa, the children are considered animals to be given as food to the wild beasts, and the natives protect themselves from lions by making traps, with babies as bait.

§ 436. *Wide Extent of Polyandry.*   It seems that the collection of a group around a man was not always personal; polyandry among brothers is a proof of this. And polyandry is not a result of poverty because it existed in rich tribes or among rich individuals of the tribes.   If not universal, it was most extensive, to judge from the traces of it.   For example, the five brothers Pandava, heroes of the Mahabharata, all married the beautiful Draupadi.   The Bretons lived in polyandry, according to Caesar.   To-day, polyandry is found in Asia; Thibet, Buchavia, in the Himalayas, in Cashmir; and on the coasts of Malabar, in Ceylon, New Zealand.   Among the inhabitants of Thibet, the children and goods belong to the head of the family, and descend by right of primogeniture.   Among the Todas, the first born is given to the primogenitus; the second child is assigned to the second eldest of the brothers.   A man among a polyandrous race who has no brother associates with some stranger, or if he does not so desire, remains single.

§ 437. *Paternity a Derivation of the Right of Property.*
Paternity is shown in history when there is established
an individual control in the form of matrimony. That paternity is a derivation of the right of ownership is proved
by divers facts. One of these proofs is found in the ancient Aryan language. A father, in Sanscrit, is called a
"patar," owner, or "ganitor," creator. In the Vedas the
two terms are joined, forming "pitaganita." Such a
conjunction and later such a confusion of the conceptions
in the language are sure indications of the influence of
property rights in the development of the masculine
family. And here we must notice that a man can become
for a certain time a woman's master in two ways, by
right of conquest, or by bargain and sale. In a warlike
tribe, the captor of a woman of another tribe makes her
his own, like any other booty, by virtue of the capture.
And in this connection, we must note what Lubbock
says of the possibility of the coexistence of individual
marriages and community of wives. In other tribes, the
masculine family was brought about through bargain
and sale, because woman was considered part of the family's property, and always remained part of the inheritable estate. The family sold a right of use but did not
sell the women. The husband, therefore, had to stay in
the cabin and village of his wife's family. In Sumatra,
the husband and his descendants became the absolute
property of his wife's family, if the marriage was celebrated in a form called "ambel-anak," now fallen into
disuse. Not very dissimilar customs existed among the
Kochs of India, in Ceylon, and ancient China. Clearly,
the difficulties in the way of getting a wife in the primitive
ages, when poverty was all supreme, were many. Often
the price of a wife was temporary slavery in the house
of the father-in-law, such as Jacob spent in the house of
Laban, and as it still is in Asia, Africa, and the two Amer-

icas. In some tribes of American Indians, the husband is forced to move into his father-in-law's house, but can have his own, if he pays a tribute from the hunt until a daughter is born. This child, who becomes the property of his maternal uncle, completes the price due from her mother. Among the Makololos, the southern Kimbundas, and some races of the Gold Coast, at Timon and among the Limbus of India, the price of the mother does not include the children, who must be bought separately, if the father wishes to keep them. Along all the coast of Guinea, and among several African tribes, the law forbids the acquisition of a son by his father. His life and liberty depend absolutely upon the caprice of his maternal uncle. It can be easily seen that the masculine family by right exists from the moment when the purchase of the mother includes the children. According to the ways and law of the Kimbundas, the Fellatahs, and of the kingdom of Fanti, the only way in which a man can possess his own wife or daughter is by union with a slave. In such a case, he has true power over his wife and descendants, and his personalty is not inherited by children of a legitimate wife, but by the children of the slave, or if she has none, by adopted children. The union of the owner and his slave is a symptom of deep alteration in the marriage states in several African peoples. There is a marked tendency to such unions, as man wants to rule and not to be ruled. For women of such races are absolute masters of their husbands and their children who received their name. They control all their husband's acts. The unfortunate husbands have no means of opposing the conduct of their wives, who follow their own way, and exercise an absolute supremacy.

§ 438. *Symbolic Recognition of Paternity.* In the primitive world abstract ideas cannot prevail because the intellect, at the beginning, departs but little from the senses, and is bound to the particular. And so when the notion of paternity had appeared, the general presumption of the maxim, "Pater est is quem nuptiæ demonstrant," was not immediately applied. But there was had recourse to a symbol peculiar to an uncivilized and mute age; the father had to imitate the pains of childbirth, thus making himself another mother. Strabo states that this was the practice of the Iberians; Apollonius reports this custom among the savages living around the Black Sea; Diodorus and Plutarch attribute it to the islanders of Corsica and Cyprus; Marco Polo found it in eastern Asia; and to-day, we find it still in South America and on the west coast of Africa. In lower Guinea and in some other places there is a ceremony of the mixture of the blood by which an apparent consanguinity is established and the paternity is recognized. This ceremony consists in making a few drops of the blood from the veins of one pass into the veins of the other, by two slight incisions, and by drinking a drop or so. This mixture of the blood is called "fatti draha" in Madagascar.

§ 439.   *Different Types of the Patriarchal Family.* The patriarchal type developed among the Semites in the Hebrew family, among the Aryans, the associated Indian family, in the Hellenic γένος, in the Roman agnative family, in the Celtic, "sept," in the Teutonic and Slavic, domestic community. Maine, in his "Lectures on the Early History of Institutions," explains with clearness and precision the formation of the Irish "sept"; and in his "Dissertations on Early Law and Custom," he outlines the early domestic communities of eastern Europe, availing himself of Bogisc's important discoveries. The Irish family is divided into four classes, "geilfine," "deirbhfine," "irafine" and "indfine," of which the youngest, "geilfine," has five members; the others have twelve,

four each. When there is a birth in the "geilfine," its oldest
member is advanced into the "deirbhfine," and so in each
class. The oldest member of the "indfine," however, goes
out of the organization, for declassification is allowed.
The word "geilfine" has the same meaning as the Latin
"manus," "familia"; "deirbhfine" means true family;
"irafine," subsequent family; and "indfine" means the
ultimate family. It seems that the principle of its conception was that of the "patria potestas," because the
"geilfine" consists of the father and four children or
adopted children under his immediate authority, while
the other groups contain emancipated descendants, whose
dignity decreased with the distance from the true and
typical group. The Roman and this kind of family have
a common base in paternal authority, but there are many
notable differences; for example, the institution of emancipation is systematic in the Irish family, while in the
Roman it is entirely arbitrary. There is a similar English custom in which the youngest son, and not the
eldest, is the heir and stays with his father, never being
emancipated. All the other sons leave home emancipated, but the last remains and is dependent on his father
all his life. The domestic community of the southern
Slav is a union of natural families descended from a
common ancestor. These essentially patriarchal families
are governed by the oldest member; the relationship is
through the "grand sang," that is, is agnative, and not
through the "petit sang," or cognative. And the prevalence of agnation is the surest testimony of a masculine
form of descent. From one aspect, these communities
are democratic, because each member has the right to
be fed, clothed, and lodged by the corporation; he also
has a voice in the assembly or "skuptchina," held under
the presidency and direction of the older members.
From another aspect, it seems despotic, because the sum

of everything is found in the hands of the head of the house or "domacin," who may be the eldest son of the deceased chief, or his brother, or even a woman of exceptional ability. The election is governed in part by relationship, in part by the necessities of life. These elections are found in the associated Indian family and in the "sept." The capital in agriculture or enterprise of the community is inalienable like the "res mancipi" of the Romans, which formed the basis of the agrarian community of Latium. The "peculium," consisting at first in some heads of cattle in a common pasture, works as the dissolving force of the corporation using its influence the same as among the Indians and the Romans. The daughters had a right to marry and to have a dowry. They enjoyed a certain liberty of choice and took as women to the house which they entered what they could take of the herd or personal property, which sometimes went to the feminine heirs by a particular rule of inheritance. Most extensive was the list of impediments to marriage, which sprang from relationship and were shown in many ways. There is the adoption of individuals of the families and a curious series of conventional and spiritual affinities. In the primitive world, the prejudice was paramount that men not bound together by blood relationship were either enemies or slaves.

§ 440. *Development of the Family.* From all that has been said two conceptions can be gotten; the most immediate is that of the derivation of the patriarchal group (that Maine still believes primitive) as the system of paternal administration of the property in the interest of the family. Spencer says, and with a great deal of justice, that the existence of such a system cannot be reconciled with the fact of the "jus vitæ ac necis" of the father in remote ages. It is not conceivable that a savage, with his selfishness and

without any idea of justice or sentiment of responsibility, should administer the goods and chattels in the
interest of his family.   And if in the patriarchal group
there are found many domestic animals, we must believe
that the group is not primitive, because the domestication must have taken time.   The other conceptions
includes the law of the development of property, the
family rights over property and towards other men in
primitive times, which we have studied in other places.
At the beginning, there existed a communion of both
women and chattels.   Relationship was a connection
between an individual and his group, which had all the
property rights.   Then the communion began to be
restricted, and there appeared first the feminine family
and then the masculine, and property no longer belonged
to the community but was assigned to the home.   There
was a true "dominium a domu."   As time went on, the
individual was emancipated from the patriarchal power
and family and obtained that extended liberty which
he has, for example, in the American family.   In that
country, the boys of fifteen or sixteen years of age choose
their careers with the greatest independence and proceed to effect their choice in the same manner; the girls
go out alone, travel alone, and freely choose their husbands.   The individual destroys trusts, family estates,
and many other limitations established in the interest
of the preservation of the family; and proclaims the
absoluteness of his property.   The weakening of the
family bonds go hand in hand with absolute property.

§ 441.   *Evolution Tends to Individualism.*   Evolution
is progressive individualization, a growing intimacy of
parts.   Now relationship is essentially a product of
evolution because it began by being generic and little
by little became specific and reached distinction in
different degrees unknown to the primitive world; it

became more conscious and intimate, passing from a
state of homogeneity and incoherence to one of heterogeneity and coherence.   The great connotation of primitive relationship was entirely superficial.   With the
appearance of the family, the relationship was manifested in a smaller sphere but became richer in ramifica-
tion and degree.   It became a real union.   With the
flight of time, it acquired greater variety and intimacy.
It made qualitative progress, for promiscuous life is from
an ethical standpoint inferior to the matriarchal family,
and the latter in its turn to the patriarchal family, which
is founded in the last analysis on the double certainty
of the father and mother. Divers systems of relationships succeeded one another in a struggle to reach the
most suitable.   And the prevalence in history, now of
one, now of another, has always been the election of the
relative best.   Promiscuity and even the matriarchal
family are not very favorable for the preservation and
development of society, since they lack strong domestic
unity, power to control, and respect for ancestry.   The
children are entrusted entirely to the care of the mother
who is weak and not in a condition to be effectively able
to protect them.   When the father reaches old age he is
without the help of children or wife.   Polyandry has
the advantage of stopping an excessive increase of population, but it cannot be of long duration because it always
lessens fecundity and lacks cohesive force, while lack of
subordination between the fathers renders the good education of the children impossible, and harms society.
Polygamy (the result in some countries of the honor
derived from the possession of many wives and in others
from the advantage of having many slaves) is better than
polyandry.   In polygamy, the bonds between the father
and his children are strong, and there is formed a line
of masculine ancestors, which favors the development

THE PRIMITIVE FAMILY

mission of power in the same family. Polygamy diminishes infant mortality through maternal and paternal
care, and rapidly fills the places of men killed in war.
Its great evil lies in the continual discords between the
women and children. Monogamy is a necessity in these
regions, where the life demands a dispersion of the tribe
over a vast area. Monogamy depends upon the phases
of the conception of property, the numerical equality
of the two sexes, and the experience of the benefits
which it brings. In truth, it determines fully the relations between the parents and children and relatives in
every line. It produces peace and cohesion. It perfects the support, improves the education, and is more
fecund in most cases than polygamy, except where the
men are much fewer than the women. Spencer shows
the connection of polygamy with the military communities, and of monogamy with industrial communities. In
the first, war is the rule, captures frequent, the number of
women excessive through death in the tribal wars, and
great the reputation of bravery derived from the possession of many women captured from the enemy, and the
despotic character of the warrior is prevalent; in the
second, the principle of freedom and voluntary coöperation predominates. As militarism declines, and industrialism expands, the number of the two sexes approaches
equality, and monogamy generally becomes the rule. The
despotic power of the father ceases, and the life of the
children becomes sacred and develops towards freedom.

§ 442. *The Origin of Relationship in Love.* Relationship, whatever its form, has its origin in love, which
is also subject to the laws of evolution. Love has
its stages, progress, and history. It began by including many individuals without being deep. In that
phase it was vague and external, but it gained strength

and learned the use of its wings.   As it gained strength,
and was restricted, it became more concrete and real
by specialization.   It tended to individualization and
then became individual and could not brook company.
Love has grown richer.   It includes new points of view
of the loved object.   As man develops, it becomes always
more various.   Monogamy is the full individuality of
love.   It is the last selection of human love.   The love,
shown in polygamy and polyandry, in which a man does
not give himself entirely to a woman and a woman does
not abandon herself entirely to a man, has not attained
full self-realization.   Free love and that which is not
foreign to a fidelity which is content with several loved
objects are primitive facts.   Has the family yet reached
its final limit of specification?   Some think this possible,
alleging as proof the antagonism of the family to society,
which can be observed among animals and the human
race.   Experience, they say, shows that where the
social instinct is most developed and alive, the family
is always a unity less strong and less lasting, and that
where the sentiment of the family includes all the activity of its components, society suffers thereby and becomes
weakened.   They add that it is not right to state the derivation of society on the family, because sexual love is
of itself selfish and exclusive, and because there are associations of animals which are in no sense families, not
making for procreation.   Political society is not a development of the family because one is bound by reason
and the other not, because one is based on reward according to merit and the other on the principle of assistance
of the weak, who are not able to provide for their needs.
It seems to us that the growing individualization and
intimacy in the system of relationship cannot bring
about the destruction of the family.   These factors
only mean that relationship, little by little, will be

concentrated within natural limits, and that the parts of the ethical organism will have more freedom. The restriction of relationship, the greater intensity of domestic bonds, and the emancipation of the individual from the despotic prevalence of the head of the family, are not signs of the disappearance of the family nucleus. The nucleus will remain, though more limited and intimate. It will acquire a higher character, since it will be founded on monogamic marriage. It will fully recognize the freedom of its elements, but it will always remain safe and sound. If such freedom becomes excessive, it will have to be tempered and harmonized by the principle of authority, so that the nucleus may be saved. An ethical organism, which is becoming more typical and which conforms to the laws of reason, is not destined to disappear, but tends to persevere in its existence, to take on such higher coördinations as nature and reason dictate. In mankind, society and family are in no wise antagonistic, because primitive society was created through relationship broadly construed, that is, not only on natural and blood relationship but on civil and fictitious relationship. The members of the first civil and political communities were bound together by ties of blood either real or fanciful. It is only recently that the fact of the common habitation or life became the base of the city or State. The religious and warlike fraternities of remote times all assumed a family character. A primitive society can always be regarded as an amplified family. Now the social sentiment among men is born from the family centre, but it cannot on the other hand deny that the latter, with the progress of time, can become distinct and have its own development dependent upon particular causes.

§ 443. *Society and Family are Distinct.* Society and family have diverse functions but are not mutually ex-

clusive; they are rather complementary. Society is a
community of civil interest and becomes a political
union; the family is a community based on domestic
affection and piety. One is larger and higher than the
other and includes it from various points of view, either
by reinforcing the individual activities with reciprocal
exchange of services or by organizing the ethical whole
in its single elements. The family without civil society
or the State is an incomplete and rudimentary nucleus;
the State cannot be imagined without the family, because it originated in the latter. The idea of the human
community develops in various ways, depending upon
whether affections approximate interests or whether interests are dignified into reason. Affection, interest,
and reason form the three bases of the human union
and determine its form. With the single principle, by
which the family is governed, society would be badly
organized and would dissolve, because help would be
extended to those cases in which it would be unjust and
dangerous, strengthening, increasing, and aggravating
through love the evil derived from individual weaknesses. With the single principle on which society is
governed, that is, on reward according to merit, there
would be wanting the assiduous care for that portion
of the human race which, without its fault, is incapable
of providing for its needs. Society would not fulfill its
duty and would not attain its object. The family will
live as long as the individual and as long as the sentiments and conceptions which are referable to care or
ownership. Family and society are terms which work
together and presuppose one another. And in the human species they advance side by side because the perfection of the family exercises an influence on the moral
development of civil society and the State. And good
civil and political government cannot fail to bring great

advantages to the life of the family.   In other words, the greater ethical elevation that the family attains, the more will civilization and politics be raised; and as civilization and the State approach their true end, the family will profit thereby.   But this does not prevent the two objects being distinct and sometimes opposite.   In fact, sometimes society absorbs the family and sometimes the family absorbs society.

CHAPTER XVIII

THE CONJUGAL RELATION

LOVE AS THE FOUNDATION OF MATRIMONY. — THE IDEA OF
MATRIMONY. — CONDITIONS. — CIVIL MATRIMONY. — THE PRE-
CEDENCE OF THE CIVIL CEREMONY. — RELATION BETWEEN
THE PARTIES. — MARITAL AUTHORITY. — BEBEL'S BOOK, AND
THE IDEA OF SPENCER. — THE SYSTEM BY WHICH PROPERTY
IS REGULATED IN MATRIMONY.

§ 444. *Family is Divided into the Paternal and Conjugal Relations.* The family is composed of two relations
intimately bound together, one of which germinates in
the other. These relations are the conjugal and the
parental. The conjugal relation is the object of matrimonial law, the other of domestic law. According to
Aristotle, every society and ethical organization arises
and is preserved by a bond, by common affection, and
by the friendship of the two parties. Love, the foundation of matrimony, is a friendship suggested by
nature and accompanied by cupidity. It is taught us
by considering someone as a cause of one's own happiness, by feeling the desire of living and reliving in others.
This same conception is shadowed in the fable of the
division into the two parts of primitive and hermaphro-
dite man, a kind of robust and strong composite of both
sexes, and of the fancied meeting of two opposites,
wearied by the fear of the gods, who of their own will
come together and make one, as you can read in the
"Symposium." Through generation, love can be said to
be the attempt of the mortal to be immortal, as Socrates

says in the same Dialogue. Love, the cause of matrimony, is not the winged child of the myth, otherwise the conjugal union would be fleeting; neither is it the impulse to the production of the beautiful in a beautiful mind and body, as Plato believed, because this would deprive it of the natural tendency to generation, and furthermore, in this case, it could exist between individuals of the same sex. Love is rather the inclination of the senses, an affection, a desire untrammelled by reason. This fleeting appetite is raised to an enduring sentiment, to a constant will becoming a duty, and existing in fidelity and mutual sacrifice. Here, as elsewhere, it is the mind which makes the elements of the senses necessary and keeps them true. Plato did not thoroughly understand the nature of love on another score, for he allows polygamy, while true and living love is a feeling which will not brook it. Aristotle, on the other hand, had a true conception of love, calling matrimony the union exclusive, lasting, and divine, which results from the interpenetration of the two opposite characters of man and woman. Such a conception was common to the minds of the Roman jurisconsults, who defined matrimony as "conjunctio maris et fœminæ, consortium omnis vitæ, divini et humani juris communicatio," and as "conjunctio viri et mulieris individuam vitæ consuetutinen continens." Hegel is right when he says that Kant presents matrimony in its shamelessness, in his definition of it as a bond of the persons of different sex for the interchange and constant possession of mere sexual pleasures.

§ 445. *Marriage is a Union.* Rosmini has written strongly on the subject. Inner man, he says, is one and identical; thus there arises in him a continual tendency to reduce plurality to unity. Hence, as plurality reduced to unity in an object pleases the mind

which contemplates it, in whose eyes it is beautiful,
so plurality reduced to unity in sentiment is pleasant
to the sentiments and is called eudemonistic well-being
Beauty in plurality becomes unity in the ideal world.
Rosmini's idea of beauty, which has its source in Leibnitz's doctrine, may not satisfy everybody, because it is
formal. Yet even in consciousness and knowledge there
is the same reduction of the various to identity that is
observable in beauty. The specific difference between
truth and beauty lies in the æsthetic sense, in the imagination which clothes conceptions in more suitable sensible forms. The unification, our philosopher goes on,
which makes a man and his possessions one, produces
the fact of property; the unification of individuals produces the fact of society, and the conjugal relation above
all others. Matrimony, it must be remembered, is the
union not of things, but of human beings; it is the full
and perfect natural union of two individuals of different
sex. From this it follows that the two sentiments of the
husband and wife should on every score be so responsive
as to find the complement of each in the other. The spiritual element should respond to the spiritual, the physical to the physical, so that the man and the woman are
bound together by a three-strand rope of soul, mind,
and body. In the sentence, "erunt tuo in carne una,"
the first phrase, "erunt tuo," expresses this individuality
and the impossibility of the fusion of two personalities;
the other, "in carne una," expresses the unity of life.
And now it must be remembered that the union of the
sexes is a vital, not a mere phyiscal union, though in the
physical act the two fundamental sentiments of the individuals seem to become one.

§ 446. *The Union must be Spiritual, Mental, and Physical.* There is a true union of man and woman only
when the spiritual and mental bond precedes the physi-

cal, which is only the complement or completion of the former. When one human being joins himself to another, he should join fully with all that makes the man. For every union, to be fixed and stable, should begin at the apex of human nature and thereafter descend to the other elements, if those who unite do not want to subject reason to desire. From this can be seen the reason for the illegality of concubinage; the law cannot recognize it, because it lacks an ethical basis. An immoral marriage law is based on the right of might; it is based on the strength of man and is the legal dishonor of woman. From what has been said, it is clear that matrimony has a primary object—full personal union,—and a secondary object—generation. The personal union is the primary object because there can be no matrimony without it; and generation is only secondary, because the matrimony exists despite the sterility of the union. Generation was the chief object in the days of the Old Testament, when sterile unions were dissolved; in the time of the New Testament the personal union has become the main and primary purpose.

§ 447. *Conditions and Impediments to Marriage.* From these attributes of matrimony its conditions and impediments are deducible. The first condition clearly is an age necessary for the "conjunctio maris et fœminæ" and for the "consortium omnis vitæ." There must be physical capacity and moral maturity for a marriage; the law should do all in its power to hinder marriages of precocious appetites or of folly. The second condition is bound up with the first; it is the necessity of parental consent until the children have reached an age in which a full discernment of the facts and relations of life can be presumed. But to avoid an arbitrary prohibition on the part of the parents, an appeal to the courts is allowed. A law requiring the consent of the State for the marriage of persons of certain classes, for example, of members of the wage-earning or proletarian classes, is a violation of the most sacred individual rights, that is, the right to find one's own fulfillment in others with absolute freedom of choice. Legislation requiring such consent in order to reduce the excess of population, following the old pagan theory of political thought, markedly increases the number of illegitimate births. The objection of the infringement of personal liberty cannot be applied to the requirement of a certificate for the marriage of those engaged in military pursuits for discipline and the general good of the service.

§ 448. *Marriage between Relatives.* The third condition is the degree of consanguinity. The judgment of mankind is opposed, says Rosmini, to marriage between lineals, because in the progress which nature has assigned to sexual love, the child is the result of the activity which has ceased to exist, having developed and been satisfied. This progress shows that it would be unnatural for sexual love to begin when nature has decreed it to end, that is, in the descendant. As to collaterals, if human instinct was considered in its perfection, it is evident that it would force men to marry where there was no consanguinity, or else where the common stock was so distant as to have been lost to memory. The reason of this is that where the common ancestor is known and remembered, he seems to be reproduced in the children or with this paternal image in the mind, it seems as if the marriage was contracted with him in marrying a brother, in whom, in every man's mind, is the father made young once more. If the nature of matrimony is considered, which unites the individuals, it can be seen that the cognates of one cousin are the agnates of the other; hence, the same rule for them.

§ 449. *Adoption and Marriage.* In adoption, the adoptor has the feelings of a parent, and assumes his duties; the adopted should consider himself as a son. What has already been said concerning the impediments of lineal relatives should be applied to this knot of legal relationship. In general, the intrinsic motives for the prohibition of intermarriage, besides those already given (that marriage is ideally the union of diverse, not similar elements), can be roughly reduced to two: to the protection of family morals, and to the dangers arising from the marriage of relatives, whose descendants are often weak, sickly, with a disposition towards insanity, and frequently deaf and dumb. These unions result in the inheritance of such diseases, as long and constant experience shows. The prohibition is not absolute, allowing for exception where the relationship is slight, or where there are potent reasons of domestic necessity. So among collaterals, while the marriage of brothers and sisters is always forbidden, yet sometimes it is permitted between relatives of the same degree, — between uncle and niece, or nephew and aunt. It is necessary, in such cases, to take account of all positive and relative factors in the family.

§ 450. *The Impediment of Attempted Murder.* The fourth condition refers to an attempt upon the life of the consort of the person, whom the criminal desires to marry. Such an attempt is an impediment, since matrimony cannot be the reward for a crime. The fifth is the disregard to solemn formalities, prescribed under penalty of nullity, which serve to give certainty and publicity to matrimony.

§ 451. *Annulment of Marriage.* It is easy to understand that impediments are caused by the failure to observe the above conditions. These impediments annul the marriage, making it void or voidable. The

impediments which produce absolute nullity, that
is, those which can be invoked by anyone who
has an interest, are, for example, that the contracting parties are not of age, or that one of them has
entered into a prior marriage. The impediments which
produce relative nullity, that is, those which can be
invoked by certain persons, are lack of consent or impotency. A person without the power of sexual intercourse cannot enter matrimony, because a specific
object of marriage is lacking. This impotency must be
manifest, that is, such as can be known and recognized
by a doctor; it must be incurable and not transitory,
anterior to the wedding, and then existing. Some impediments are temporary, and have nothing to do with
the essential requisites of marriage. They prevent the
marriage being fully legitimate, but allow it to be
sustained. Of this kind is the prohibition against a
widow's marriage within ten months of the death of
her husband. The theory of these impediments is the
same as that of the conditions required for a marriage,
and have to do with the philosophy of the law as well
as with positive law.

§ 452. *Betrothals.* The custom of a betrothal has,
Trendelenberg says, a good basis; because the engage-
ment serves not only as a preparation for the marriage,
but also tends to implant in the couple (who begin
forthwith a more intimate life) true will in place of
wavering faith, and also because in this way it is
possible to test their desire to marry, which should be
neither a romantic sentiment nor an unfeeling calculation. And yet the betrothal, though well sanctioned
by use and by the weight of tradition, cannot, in case of
breach, have any other legal result than indemnification
for the injury caused. If it had greater legal force and
could compel the marriage, it would defeat its own pur-

pose, which is to put a certain time between the date of the promise and the marriage in order to test the character and vocation of the couple for a more intimate life.

§ 453. *Marriage is Ethical, Religious, and Juridical.* Marriage is an ethical, religious, and legal institution. Marriage laws have been the subject of a long and bitter struggle between the Church and State. The former considered the sacrament as the essence of a conjugal union, and therefore claimed the right to regulate it with its canons and in its courts. The Council of Trent made the triune proclamation of marriage before the Church; it imposed upon the couple the duty of declaring their intentions before a parish priest, and of receiving his benediction. Following St. Thomas, it was admitted that the rite of the sacrament was to be given upon the desire of the couple, while the solemnity comes from the sacerdotal benediction. Civil governments began to take up the right to enact marriage laws at the time of the Reformation. Civil marriage first appeared in England under the laws of Cromwell, who gave justices of the peace authority to celebrate marriages, and jurisdiction over them, — a law defended by Milton, but doomed to fall with the other republican institutions. In the Catholic countries canon law controlled, but was enforced by the State. Some royal orders in France and in the Kingdom of Naples began the vindication of the State's jurisdiction. In France civil marriage was permitted to the Protestants by the laws of Louis XVI. The Revolution, by means of the Constitution of 1791, and the Legislative Assembly of 1792, treated marriage as any other contract, and prescribed a civil form, obligatory upon all citizens. To the Code belongs the credit of having restored to marriage its high ethical character, taken away by

the laws of 1791 and 1792. The Code allowed impediments upon the basis of its ethical character, reaffirmed
the jurisdiction of the civil courts and the right of
the State to pass marriage laws; it prohibited the celebration of the religious ceremony before the civil. The
French Code was introduced into Italy, but, upon the
Restoration, the ancient state of the law was brought
back in nearly all its forms. The Italian Code prescribes for the civil marriage, but allows it to be
celebrated before or after the religious ceremony.

§ 454. *State Control of Marriage.* The State is not
an atheistic but a lay power. It has no authority in
religious matters, and therefore cannot look upon marriage except as a civil contract, *sui generis*, recognizing,
however, that the complete union is a divine bond.
The incompetence of the State is not due to ignorance of religion or the Church, nor indifference to those
high human interests so vital and powerful. In the State
there is contained and developed the same human nature
on which religion is based; but the State considers human
nature only from the juristic point of view. It should
prevent the clergy inspiring the multitude to rebellion or
fanaticism, but at the same time, it should not encourage
the development of atheism. The State, therefore, cannot discredit the religious ceremony, but can add the
legal duty of a civil ceremony as an essential necessity.
To look upon marriage as a civil contract does not mean
to lower it to the condition of a bargain and sale partnership or ordinary contract, in which there is great usefulness, or an exchange of value, but it connotes the recognition of the perfect union of two persons of different sex.
Marriage, looked upon as a civil contract, has a distinct
and particular nature in its meaning and its end, and is
essentially different from all other contracts. The State,
in the case of marriages, not only exercises its functions

of guaranty, but intervenes as an ethical power, an organ of natural law, and realizes the conception of matrimony, determines its conditions, taking account of the various historical needs of the people. Consequently it cannot as Trendelenburg would wish, give over without abdication to the Church the contract of marriages, nor can the institution of civil marriage be considered as a return of the days of the struggle with the Church, as the same philosopher adds. Civil marriage is not a backward step of any kind, but is the marriage of natural law, in which the State is an effectual factor in social relations, without passing the confine of its authority. For the same reason we must not be misled by Rosmini, who teaches that the laws should follow the religious forms allowed by the State, as in the case of freedom of conscience. If the State did this, it would not have its own forms of marriage, but would be forced to regulate it in many different and various ways. For the same reason, permissive civil marriage cannot be recognized where an election is given between the religious and civil ceremonies; and if the former is chosen, the Church celebration must be registered in the books provided by the State for the purpose. Upon the same theory is based the legality of punishing the contracting parties and the priest who performs the religious ceremony before the civil. In such an act are found the common elements of fraud and injury. Clearly, the religious marriage, examined by itself, is not a fraudulent act, but it becomes such when it entails the breaking the laws of the State, the denial of the conjugal relation and of the rights of children, both undermining the moral sense of the community and inflicting the greatest harm upon the two families. Religious marriage is the effectuation of true matrimony in one of its branches, and is not a kind of concubinage in which the sexual passions are appeased, but in which no

sacred or profane bonds are entered, and no duty towards
the public taken. Gabbi, in "I Due Matrimonii," has
said that those who are married by the Church desire
a form of moral union without conjugal or domestic burdens, letting the future look out for itself; many therefore
disregard the civil marriage, and a moral degeneration of
society results. The institution of marriage is here broken
by both families, and is broken also by the priest who
blesses such a union contrary to the law of the State.
The parties being the chief actors deserve the greater
punishment. There is here no reason for appealing to
the theory of the separation of Church and State, because
the latter's rights or prerogatives are injured by such
an act. The clericals can be interested in opposing civil
marriages, but not in opposing the prohibition of cele-
brating it before the religious ceremony. Neither can
the principle of civil liberty be invoked, for it has not
been infringed, since the religious marriage has in no wise
been made into concubinage. The prohibition in question eliminates an easy method of masculine egotism and
power, and conforms to the prudence of those who want
both ceremonies, because one of the parties might die
after the religious, and before the civil marriage. In
this case, the other would be left in an equivocal, undefined and injurious position. But marriages *in extremis*
seem a reasonable exception to the rule, for they tran-
quilize the conscience of a dying man and for this reason
should entail no punishment either for the parties or
the priest. The parties, if the one who was dying recovers,
must be penalized unless they have a civil ceremony performed within a certain time. The priest, of course, being free from blame, should not be punished even if the
parties refuse to have the second marriage. The State,
besides enacting this prohibition, should take part in
stopping the abolition of the rights of widowhood,

which are brought about either by action of law or by will. The *conditio viduitatis* presupposes that the deceased wished his survivor to keep inviolate the conjugal faith. With the entrance into a religious marriage by the survivor, such faith is destroyed. The law cannot act in the case of an illegal ceremony, for the deceased has trusted to the honor of the survivor, and we must adopt a phrase of the law of contracts, that the law cannot enter the sphere of personal judgments and valuations.

§ 455. *The Equality of the Sexes.* There are many different relations between husband and wife, a great number of which lie within the sphere of custom, and are not subject to legal enforcement. The law recognizes only those which it can enforce, such obligations, that is, as those of cohabitation, faithfulness, and support. Certainly a family must have a head to avoid inaction and anarchy, and the head should be appointed by law, in accordance with the dictates of nature. It is of little profit in discussing if the parents or children should be the head, entrusted, as it is, with the power of controlling the domestic fate. But should the law give the decision to the husband and father? Is it reasonable that the husband must join the wife in many of her important acts, such as the alienation of realty, in making a loan, or gift? Plato believed in the identical nature of man and woman and a congenital diversity of functions, but this idea had not been fully recognized by all the presuppositions of political thought. Aristotle, in his turn, declared with great precision the natural difference of the sexes, and looked upon it as one with the unity of divine determination. He pointed out that in the conjugal coöperative society the man is stronger and better suited for the acquisition and defense of property than his wife, while she is calm, cautious, domestic, prudent, imploring help and aid against injustice, particularly that arising from external relations.   If Plato accentuated the identity of the sexes and did not see the difference between them, Aristotle erred on the other side.   Xenophon and Plutarch, however, kept the balance between these facts, which they developed in a practical manner in lectures and arguments.   Xenophon said that God destined man and woman to freedom in the social community, adding, however, that woman tends to domesticity, and man to the affairs of the world.   Plutarch, while recognizing that in the initiative, in poetry, and morals, women have equalled men in merit, did not wish to praise women for any similarity to men, or men for any similarity to women.   Among the Romans, the identity of the natures of the sexes and their equality of rights were the base of the Roman theories and institutions in historical times.   Cicero was opposed to the Voconian Law that excluded women from the greater part of the inheritance.   Seneca believed that the duty of fidelity was as binding upon a man as a woman, on the grounds of the equality of the sexes.   Yet the Romans were opposed to a woman's mixing in politics, and wanted her to be the housewife.   Christianity proclaimed the principle of the unity in nature of man and woman, in teaching that God made woman out of Adam, and gave them the same name, though at the same time it admitted the control of the man, as is shown by the above fact and by the sentence: "Vir caput est uxoris, mulier autem gloria viri est."   St. Augustine, like Cicero, called the Voconian Law unjust, and considered adultery as grave a fault in the husband as in the wife.   St. Jerome writes: "Apud nos quod non licit fœminis, æque non licit viris, et eadum servitus pari conditione censatur."

§ 456. *Comparison of the Sexes.* It has been said with truth, that as to their body, man is superior in

that he has more power, and woman in that she is more
delicately made.   The heavier bones and muscles, the
great lung capacity, and the big brain will always make
man the conqueror in the struggles of life.   Woman
is marked by a greater excitability of the nervous system.   Mentally, we must agree with Beneke that in
man thought has a greater and more intimate power,
auto-consciousness is more developed, reflection more
sustained, firmness, coherence, and seriousness are better
marked, and the mental functions more complex and
difficult.   In woman, on the contrary, sentiment predominates over thought, involving memory and imagination; in her, too, ideas of the outside world, and of life
among her fellows predominate; she is less self-analyti-
cal, and has less abstract virtue.   Her intuitions about
things of moment are finer, but because of sudden reactions lead to unhappiness and distress.   In her you
find greater adaptability, delicacy, timidity, docility, and
sacrifice.   In woman, too, are found greater sudden
bursts of passion; and love is longer and more calculat-
ing.   Man's mind easily masters general ideas, while
woman's does so with the greatest difficulty, always by
way of her heart; man enjoys creative faculties and
reaches the heights of genius.   Woman feels more than
she analyzes truth, and individualizes everything.   In
history we find that she pays more attention to single
characters than to general causes.   In deeds of benevolence she tends more to charity, which alleviates particular cases of suffering, than to philanthropy, which takes
forethought against the suffering of mankind.   In business a man risks more than a woman and gains more,
while a woman saves more and is a better manager.

§ 457.   *Inequality of the Sexes*.   Stuart Mill, the
modern writer most renowned in sustaining the above
theory of the emancipation of woman, disagreeing with

Comte and Spencer, conceives the harmony of the
sexes as a result of the abstract identity of nature
and mere organic opposition. He thinks that the
original and important difference of organism can
be transformed, as experience shows in psychological
determination; that the difference between man and
woman can be reduced to organic contrast. If there
was but a single tone, true harmony would be lacking,
because the effectiveness increases with the greater
variety of elements. Stuart Mill believes that the cause
of the psychic differences between the sexes is education.
But education in this case would not be natural development aided by art; it would be rather a foreign importation contrary to nature, a contradictory mark in the
feminine mind presupposing a clean slate at the start,
a mark that has been made throughout centuries. The
power of education should not be exaggerated when it
extends beyond the confines of nature. Huxley says
on this subject that the ancient Salic law of nature will
never be abrogated nor will there be changes of dynasty.
And although he is the closest follower of Darwin, he
adds that he would not dare to state seriously that a
different system of education would ever be successful
in removing the physical obstacles by which woman is
always made weaker than man in the struggles of life.
Spencer further affirms that in the progress of civilization the masculine and feminine characters modify in
adaptation to higher social demands, and in the woman
particularly certain mental and moral qualities, taught
by necessity for protection against the greater strength of
man in barbarous times, disappear; but the habits and
original activities of the two sexes do not disappear.
Furthermore, Mill is wrong in likening the form of the
family community to that of a trading company, in which
the control is entrusted to the more expert and is not

determined by law; because the family is a society formed of unequal persons and has an ethical existence higher than that of mere association for exchange, including the relations between husband and wife and between children and parents — relations which have to do with the most intimate fact of human existence.

§ 458. *The Husband Must Have the Authority.* From this analysis it can be seen that the institution of marital authority is not repugnant to the principles of reason if organized in a way to forbid the presupposition of feminine incapacity, rendering thus marital caprice more difficult. The modern foundation of this institution is the idea of the unity of the family; the freedom of the woman is limited not because she is woman but because she is wife. Though between the two sexes there should be an equality of civil rights, in the family rules of harmony and preservation should not be lacking. Unity is obtained by giving the husband the predominating vote, because he possesses the strength and therefore must be the head or treasurer, and because he has the broader, deeper, and more concentrated mind. The general control of the family, therefore, belongs to the man; to the woman, gifted with a mind more capable of grasping particulars, belongs the care of the house, which, accepted as a duty and not as a burden, is a vast field where kindness, taste, the virtue of saving, and domestic piety form a beautiful whole. A husband should protect his wife, and the protection would be useless if it could not prevent her wasting the estate. The authority of the judge, whose protecting intervention is necessary, especially when it is a question of a business in which the husband has a particular interest, controls the unreasonable disagreement of the husband. It has been observed that if this intervention is removed on the pretext of emancipating the wife,

she is made a slave to the caprices of a stingy or specu-
lating husband.   The wife generally wants peace in the
house even at the cost of the sacrifice of her money, and
therefore consents to its waste.   In ancient times the
marital authority was practically the result of the
domestic power, of the conviction of the inferiority of
the woman, and of the right of self-defense in Germanic
law. In India and Rome the woman was not allowed the
"patria potestas," and was subject to a life-long guardianship.   In Attic law the power that a husband, father,
and grandfather exercised over a woman had a character of defense very similar to that of the "mundium"
among the Germans.   The "manus" and the "patria
potestas" of the Romans were, on the other hand, part of
the "dominium," of which they seem to have been forms.
With time the "manus" weakened, especially in the Anto-
nine epoch, and the tendency to the legal equality of the
two sexes began to prevail.   Canon law could not
forget that woman was made of the rib of a man and did
not favor the Roman tendency. On the other hand, there
was the "mundium" of barbaric law exercised at first by
the relatives of the wife and then by her husband.   A
transition period sprang up in which an unmarried woman
was subject to the Roman law and was considered as
the free owner of her own possessions, while to the wife
the canon and barbaric law was applied.   Marital
authority originated thus, but in the fullness of time it
did not fail to change its significance and to adopt the
humanity of the Romans.   Criscuolo, in his monograph
"La Condizione della Donna nel Diritto Italiano,"
states with great clearness the different phases of marital
power.

    § 459. *Socialistic Equality of the Sexes.*   Bebel has
written a book entitled "Die Frau und der Socialmus,"
with the evident purpose of finding a great aid to

socialistic principles in women's interests and feelings. Bebel, by a rapid examination of the condition of women in various times and among various peoples, in which he avails himself of the researches of Bachofen, Morgan, McLennan, and of the work of Engels, "Die Ursprung der Familie, des Privat-eigenthemus und des Staats," tries to show that the oppression of woman, like all social oppression, is a derivative of economic dependence and individual ownership. Such dependence did not exist in the primitive times of the right of the order and of feminine relationship, but arose in the epoch of the patriarchal family and the right of the father-owner. The enslaving of woman, made stronger and developed in ancient society, continued in the Middle Ages favored by Christianity, with its preference for celibacy and monasticism, and has been mitigated only under the progressive civilization of Western countries. In contemporaneous society woman finds no satisfaction allowed her sexual instinct outside of indissoluble and monogamic marriage, a distinct form of individual ownership. Marriage, in the wealthy classes, is a business and investment, a method for the production of capital; in the disinherited classes, it is a union to which poverty accompanied by roughness and brutality is not foreign. Even worse is the condition of the great number of women condemned to remain unmarried because of the accumulation of property in the hands of a few, militarism, and the quantitive disproportion of the sexes. Only when woman is equal to man in every respect and in her variety of opportunities will her cause be brought to the front and put in a condition favorable to development. The differences will disappear, placing woman in the same position and conditions as man, freeing her from the subjection in which she has been kept for centuries. The statutes are only the social state of a country, mirrored in a certain number of legal decisions. The marital authority is an institution founded on the "manus" and "mundium;" the prohibition of the franchise is a survival of an old prejudice. Justice demands the perfect similarity of the two sexes as to rights, because there is no natural difference. There will come a time, says Bebel, when capitalism will be routed and in its place collective property and equality will reign. Then woman will be socially and economically independent of man. Educated, like man, she will be able to direct her efforts to what pleases her, she will choose in matrimony the man of her heart or will be chosen, and will be able with perfect freedom to accept or refuse. Marriage will be perfectly free and will be completed without the intervention of a magistrate, and will last only until the love which caused it has disappeared. In this way humanity will return to its starting place, reaching that happiness to which it always aspires and which it does not and cannot find in society as constructed at present. Marriage is evil, since its constructive principle is private property.

§ 460. *Criticism of the Socialistic Equality of the Sexes.* Bebel falls into the same error as the other contemporaneous socialists, supposing that the whole social evolution owes its origin to a single cause, the economic factor, an error which we have criticized above.[1] Like the other socialists, he does not understand the theory of evolution because he does not realize the process of increasing specification or individualization, and confuses it with the artificial control of capital. Wherever he sees the form of a human individuality, there he recognizes a production of capital and private ownership. Of course, private property is the result of the principle of individual personality, but not every mani-

[1] *Cf.* § 310 *ante.*

festation of this principle is property. The individual—
let us repeat it with Aristotle—is shown not only by
possession but also by affection. It is beyond dispute
that the patriarchal family owes its origin to the right
of the father as owner. But it cannot be denied that
this right later became an ethical power of a character
entirely different from the domestic authority; a power
belonging to the father and mother founded upon the
duty of nourishment, education, and instruction of
their young. Monogamy has a base entirely different
from the right of private property because it is the
deepest demand of the love and intimacy of an absolute
union of man and woman. The patriarchal family
itself, though so closely connected with ownership, is a
product of the evolution of relationship which was first
generic, then depended upon the physical certainty of
the mother, and finally was based on the spiritual certainty of the father. These phases of relationship
comprehend economic causes accentuating in full the
periods of the development of ownership, but at the
same time they represent phases of human love.
The condition of woman before the patriarchal age
could not have been better than her later state, because
woman in the days of bestial lust and infamous communion must have depended in whole or in good part
upon the components of the tribe. In matriarchal
families promiscuity was limited but not destroyed, and
woman could not have been protected from the violence
of the strong, although she was the centre of the family,
and apparently free. The revolution of women and
their consequent social supremacy, idealized by Bachofen, cannot be considered as an event in history. A
matriarchy understood as a government organized by
women was not possible in primitive times, in which their
sense of shame and consciousness of self were not fully

developed, and when strength was all dominant. Nor is it true that Christianity was the greatest enemy of the freedom of women, because it makes the conception of her sublime. The ideal of the woman of antiquity lay in childbearing, and in being a servant to the man, in the education of the children until a certain age, in acting as cook or handmaid, and in remaining in her home. Christ, as Bonghi writes in "La Donna e l'Avvenire," discovered the spirit of woman and understood the love which redeemed and saved her. The women loved him, followed him, and touched his garments to be made whole in body and soul. Christ forgave the sins of the woman who bathed his feet with her tears, because she had loved much. He refused to punish the sinner, and cursed him who coveted woman as an instrument of pleasure; he desired marriage to be the complete union of soul and body. He denied man the right of repudiation. He loved his mother tenderly. He wrought his first miracle at a wedding banquet. He liked little children to be about Him. He exalted woman, because his father's wife and his mother was a virgin. In this supernatural conception of the virgin wife and mother lies the combination of the idealization of the Christian woman. But, thus idealized, woman could no longer be content with the Roman praise. "She wove the wool, and kept her home." Her soul was enflamed; she turned Christian before man; she felt that Christ had done more for her than for him, since he had raised her from the lowest degradation — had done more than her happiest dreams had pictured, or than Greek or Latin mind or fancy has imagined.

§ 461. *Facts of the Socialists are Untrue.* The description that Bebel gives of the actual state of women has many false tints and is far from true; it not being true that the greater part of the marriages among the wealthier class are due entirely to financial calculations and that almost all the unions in the lower classes are marked by poverty, roughness, and brutality. It is undoubtedly true that selfishness and short-sightedness are the rules of the human conduct but we must not forget that the sentiments of sympathy and reason are also active, and that they develop with the progress of time. The relation between the sexes is not actually what it should be. It is still far from perfect, but it cannot be said that it is profoundly perverted or that it constitutes a continual manifest and general negation of morals. And would women return to their normal state if society admitted that the sexual instinct could be legitimately satisfied out of wedlock? Bebel lamented that society furnished woman no means for the satisfaction of the sexual instinct except in marriage, as if it could furnish any other with the consent of the ethical essence of man. Contemporaneous society admits woman to certain lucrative employments, which can be especially enjoyed by those who do not marry. In some countries the employment of the woman in public and private offices is greater, in others, there is an effort to regulate it, with a regard to the particular characteristics of woman, in order not to destroy her real end, and to control competition with man. To-day woman has acquired civil equality, and it will not be long before she will in all cases be capable of being guardian, trustee, of being one of the family council, and arbitratrix. The legal equality of woman even in respect to the obligations of conjugal fidelity, is fiercely sought and will soon gain recognition. The legal incapacities of the married woman, of which we have written in this chapter, do not exist in all countries, and are strongly combated. The *patria potestas* is given to the mother, who retains it after the dissolution of the marriage. It cannot be said that woman, in a civilized country, is very far from the day of her enfranchisement, because the common opinion in all such States is not absolutely opposed to it, apart from all theoretical questions of the political rights. They enjoy public rights;for example, that of petition, association, etc. Can, by chance, this condition of women be called servitude? Such condition may not be perfect, we may need to draw all the logical consequences of the admitted principles of civil equality, we may even need to recognize others besides, but certainly we can no longer speak of the enslavement of women. Bebel wishes absolute equality because he starts out with the erroneous hypothesis of the complete identity of the nature of the two sexes, and sees only differences due to education and environment, disagreeing thus even with the Darwinists. In his mind the future of woman lies in a recourse to the remote past and free love, involving only temporary and private responsibility. Love, accepting the conceptions of the German socialists, would have to retravel its road, destroying all its history, in which it has always grown more individualistic and ideal. Even in human times love has striven to be free, but its freedom has been interpenetrated with reason, which transfigures the affections and makes them permanent and not capricious. The necessity of consent in such times is not the denial of the nature of things. Woman, concludes Bonghi, will not be in the future the handmaid or careful housekeeper of the husband, but will be his real helpmate and friend. Woman, more cultured and more versed in the affairs of life, will not lose the eternal feminine. She will be intellectually vivacious, affectionate, ruled by sentiment, quick of perception, keen in discernment, pitying, helping, pious, and kind, as she is now, and at the same time she will be active in the factory, office, courts, and assemblies, and will expand the treasure of her mind as she does not do now.

§ 462. *Woman Should, however, be given Equal Opportunity.* Spencer, in his last book, "Justice," asks if the sphere of action of the individual gifted with the higher faculties should not be larger than that of him who is inferior. If a man of large stature and body occupies a greater space than one who is little and thin, it is just that the activities of the great and the small, of the strong and the weak, of the superior and inferior should have boundaries too restricted for one and too extended for the other. But he hastens to add that the metaphor must not be taken literally, because the freedom of single individuals is not the fact presented in that simple cubical form. The man gifted with higher faculties, inasmuch as he has rights to physical safety, the development of his energies and their derivative products, makes no attempt upon the physical health, the free development and ownership of his fellow-being, who is his inferior. The refusal to the inferior man of a sphere of action equal to that given the superior is equivalent to the addition of a disadvantageous, artificial rule to his natural infirmity, which sympathy and pity will sooner or later lead us to destroy. Neither is it possible to proportion a man's freedom to his capacity, since neither can be measured. Putting aside every other motive, practical considerations force us to treat men equally as to freedom, whatever be the degree of development of which they are potentially capable. Now this conception with changed terms is applied by the same author to the relations between the rights of men and women. There are women who have a forced intelligence greater than that of not a few men. If the quantum of freedom should be controlled by the capacity (admitting that the operation be possible) there should in such cases be no attention paid to the difference of sex. Starting out with the fact that the average of physical and mental

force in woman is inferior to that in man, we do not overcome the obstacle because we have no means of establishing the proportion between the two averages, and are
then forced by sentiment to compensate the inferiority
with greater artificial advantages. Equity demands that
if we do not do anything to advance woman artificially,
we should at least abstain from placing difficulties in the
path of the development of her natural energies. If men
and women are considered as independent members of
the same society, in which each should take care for his
needs as best he can it is not equitable to subject woman
to restrictions concerning occupation, profession, or ca-
reer. Woman must enjoy the same freedom as man and
enjoy the fruits of her knowledge and ability. Of the
equal rights which woman has before marriage, equity
demands she should preserve thereafter all those which
are not contradictory of that state;—such as the rights to
physical well-being, property in acquired chattels, freedom
of belief and speech. Such rights should not be subject
to any limitations except as they are opposed to explicit
clauses in the contract. The limitations vary with time
and place, and upon the failure of fixed data we must be
content with approximation. As cases differ and conditions vary it is very difficult to be precise about the reciprocal rights of control of the two consorts. It is necessary to take so many circumstances into account which
it is not possible to foresee, even in the case of a disagreement between two wills. But this much is certain: the
balance of authority should always incline to the side of
man who is ordinarily gifted with better judgment. But
in such questions reasoning has a limited force, because
all depends upon the character of the parties. From
what Spencer says we draw two conclusions: the first is
that he, like ourselves, believes in the principle of the
civil equality of women; the second is favorable to the

idea of Stuart Mill, that the regulation of the rights of husband and wife should depend more upon the variety of the contract than upon law. But Spencer seems to admit what Mill does not; that in case of a dispute between the husband and wife we should in the abstract give preference to the man. In respect to political rights we may say preliminarily that Spencer declares himself opposed to giving them to woman, since she does not bear some burdens imposed on man, such as military service.

§ 463. *System of Property in Matrimony.* There are four systems which control property in marriage; two of them can be called absolute, and two relative or medial. The system of communion is that in which the goods of the husband and wife, both prior and posterior to marriage, are put in a fund whose property is common but whose administration is given to the husband. Such a system is preferred by the philosophers, for example, by Trendelenburg and Rosmini, because it makes for the ideal of a full union. Then the system of the separation of goods (preferred by the jurists who are friends of precaution and of the personal freedom of woman) means that the goods of the husband and wife, without difference as to priority or posteriority to coverture, are kept entirely distinct. The two relative systems are the system of dowry (dos) and of common ownership of utilities; the first is nearer the system of separation, and the second nearer to that of communion. The dowry consists of a quantity of goods which the woman contributes upon her .marriage to bear some of the burdens of matrimony. The husband has the administration and enjoyment but the property is in the wife. In the communion of utilities, the property remains separate, the enjoyment is common, and the husband has the right of administration. Law furnishes a remedy of separation against the possible

consequences of a poor administration in the two
relative systems.

§ 464. *History of Property in Matrimony.* Among
the Romans marriage entered into with the "conventio
in manu" caused the transfer of all the goods from the
wife to her husband, but without the "conventio in
manu," a wife preserved the free disposition of her property. The "conventio" was first the rule and later the
exception. Side by side with the system "sine con-
ventione" developed, little by little, with many precautions. There was a prohibition against mortgaging a
dotal estate, there was absolute inalienability of the
dotal property, and through this came the general
mortgage of the husband's goods. Such a system of
protection flourished for a long time in Europe, but
in the countries of the Frankish common law the communion of goods, an institution of the Germanic people,
was allowed and generally followed. The French Code
allows the communion of the common law, and the dower
rule much changed. In Italy, on the other hand, the
Roman rule of dowry prevails. This dotal property, intended to support the burdens of the marriage, must be
inalienable. But it has been observed that the logic of
absolute inalienability demands that the legislature
impose the dower system as a necessity, so that all the
goods of the wife be made her dowry. The alienation of
the dowry can, however, be permitted by judicial authority, whenever there is necessity or an evident
advantage in it. It is necessary that law protect the
interests of the children, and at the same time place
confidence in the affection of the parents. An absolute
and inflexible protection of the children's interest is
blind and sometimes produces an opposite effect.

§ 465. *History of Dowry.* The system by which a
husband could not alienate the goods of his wife was

recognized in India under the name of "stridhan." Her own property included (according to Mitakshara, one of the oldest treatises on Indian law) what was given to her by her father, mother, brother, or husband before marriage and (added this same treatise extending the conception of "stridhan" and quoting Manu) what she acquired by heredity, partition, purchase, occupancy, or discovery. Maine thinks that "stridhan" was a derivative of the custom of paying the price of the bride on the eve of the wedding, part to the father as an indemnity for the transmission of authority, and part to the bride herself. A certain number of Aryan customs, it seems probable, gave the woman the goods which she acquired and rights which she enjoyed as part of the purchase price, once thought the only type of her personal property. The relation between the Indian "stridhan" and the Roman "dos" is evident, though the "stridhan" was rudimentary. We know that the Brahmins combated the privileges accorded by the ancient law to women. In the old law there is no trace of the custom of burning the widow alive upon the funeral pyre of her husband. They were influenced by the belief that the condition of the deceased would be ameliorated in the world to come by the expiatory rites, and they considered heredity as the foundation of such rites, which were a kind of compensation or great sacrifice on the part of the heir, with the purpose of helping the spirit of the dead. They taught that woman, through her physical weakness and retired life, was not fit to fulfill the sacred rites, and therefore they tried to restrict the sphere of her personal property in conformity with their progressive tendencies of subjecting private ownership in general to religious servitude. The most liberal legal school of India, that of Bengal, accords to the widow without children a life estate in her husband's property. In this country suttee, that is, the immolation of a childless widow, was general. The Brahmins encouraged the victim to the sacrifice on the pyre to avoid her being clothed with property rights. From every point of view, the "stridhan" and the "dos" are Aryan customs common to all the peoples of that race. They have different destinies in history through the influences of causes sometimes infavorable to their development, or suited to give them a rigorous and long existence.

CHAPTER XIX

INDISSOLUBLE MARRIAGE AND DIVORCE

THE IDEAL OF INDISSOLUBILITY. — THE CONCRETE DEMANDS OF LIFE. — THE QUESTION OF DIVORCE IN RELATION TO INDIVIDUAL RIGHTS AND SOCIAL AND HISTORICAL FACTS. — DIVORCE AND THE CHURCH. — CAUSES OF DIVORCE. — PRECAUTIONS.

§ 466. *Marriage should be Indissoluble.* There is no doubt that the ideal marriage is indissoluble. Matrimony is the absolute union of a man and woman. It is the perfect interpenetration of the various sensual and spiritual qualities of the two sexes. It is the "viri et mulieris conjunctio, individuam vitæ consuetudinem continens." Such a union would not be perfect and absolute in the eyes of rational law if it lacked the irrevocability which is shown in an ardent affection's promise of eternal love, in the solemnity of the celebration of matrimony, which accompanies no other contract, in the pure emotion of the parents at the cradle, in the need of educating the growing children, who are always binding their parents to them by new and stronger ties. The irrevocability is shown, too, by the mutual duties and rights which make the adult children repay the care spent upon them in their infancy and early youth. And it is necessitated by the inequality of the sexes, by which a woman once married is never the woman of her youth, as it is said in the Bible.

§ 467. *Morality, Religion, and Politics Demand Indissoluble Matrimony.* Morality recognizes, in indissoluble matrimony, love controlled by reason, which gives the bond of passion its character of necessity and permanence. At the touch of reason passion loses its blind and violent element of sensuality, and by idealization, becomes a duty. It is not true that indissolubility destroys freedom, by decreeing a perpetual love. What it destroys is the wavering and sensual desire; for love, transfigured by reason, is not the negation, but the base of moral freedom, which only exists when impulses are governed by practical mind, that is, a mind which follows the laws of the good. Human freedom, to quote Vico, comes from the mind, and consists in restraining and directing the prompting of lust which comes from the body. Religion consecrates the ideas of indissolubility, making marriage a sacrament, and proclaiming, "Quod Deus conjunxit, non homo separet." The Church believes that the marriage rite is a sacrament, because the conjugal union, as a participation by man in God's attribute of creation, is objectively a religious act, regardless of the intent. And for politics, too indissoluble marriage is the ideal, because the stability of the State and its departments rests upon the stability and peace of its families: both are the result of a complete, and therefore indissoluble union.

§ 468. *Civil Marriages can be Indissoluble.* The conception of civil marriage is not opposed to the principle of indissolubility, as the members of the clerical school and the champions of the theories that made the French laws of 1792 claimed. For marriage is a special contract, since it comprehends the absolute union of persons of different sexes. In fact, there is legislation which looks upon marriage as a civil contract but holds it indissoluble, as there is legislation making it religious, but allowing divorce. From the legal and civil point of view the orthodox doctrine can be followed that consent is necessary for the creation of the contract, but not for its preservation. It can easily be held that consent is a necessary prerequisite of marriage, which, however, must conform to natural laws and be absolute and irrevocable. In this respect the subjective element should be subordinate to the objective. So in contract law, it is not always true that the contractual acts depend upon consent. The jurists say, "Quæ ab initio sunt voluntatis, post factum sunt necessitatis," if society or third parties have an interest in the contract. Civil marriage is not based on the principle of arbitrary and individualistic ethics. It is a result of the conception of a lay State, and of liberty of conscience. In other words, logic does not prevent the civil marriage, and refutes the theory of Grotius, Puffendorf, and Thomasius. For Grotius, in his definition of marriage, laid emphasis on the physical side, practically allowing for no difference between it and concubinage. The difference, he says, is one of positive law: "Concubinatium quemdam verum ac ratum esse conjugium etsi effectibus quibusdam juris civilis propriis privetur aut etiam effectus quosdam naturales impedimento legis civilis, amittat." Puffendorf believed that matrimony, being consensual in origin, was subject to all the laws of contract. Thomasius believed that indissolubility, conjugal fidelity, and marital authority are all parts of the conjugal contract, and not consequences of natural law. This ideal of indissolubility should not be disregarded on the ground that law does not recognize contracts which result in the abnegation of civil personality, for marriage is not a mutual renunciation, but, on the other hand, it is the acquisition of a new status. Even if a husband and wife make their two natures one, as Rosmini says, yet it is impossible for them to become one and to preserve distinct and inalienable individuality.

In fact law protects their distinct personalities. The law does not recognize irrevocable contracts, implying a full or partial alienation of personality, but recognizes those which, without producing such an alienation, create a higher order of ethical relations.

§ 469. *Arguments For and Against Divorce.* The idea of indissolubility is generally accepted, both by those who combat divorce, and by those who are not partizan. Kant, Fichte, Hegel, Stahl, Trendelenburg, Rosmini, Gioberti, and Ahrens agree with Hume and Bentham among the English in condemning it. Comte, the founder of positivism, and Proudhon believe in it. While Hegel, Trendelenburg, and Ahrens agree that the idea of matrimony tends to indissolubility, they permit divorce on the old principle that the absolute is the highest but the relative is easier of attainment. The absolute union is founded on love, and when love dies the union is broken and matrimony is left without its true base. Reason, to which conjugal love is subject, in many cases cannot without inconsistencies keep up throughout life the appearance of affectionate relations which are dead, when respect, which man should keep in proportion to the intrinsic worth of its objects, is lost. The law is not in proper relation to the facts, when, for example, in case of flagrant breach of fidelity, it converts the heroism of a Christian into a contractual duty. The law, in such and similar cases, in preserving marriage bonds, in the attempt to reawaken love where reason cannot keep alive respect, is content with a nominal union deprived of all ethical substance. It leaves the natural order of things, because love presupposes respect and there cannot be an effect without a cause; love without respect is not true love, but lust. The legal preservation of a union which no longer exists is at best a mask. Even Rosmini, a formidable enemy of divorce, wishing to explain its existence among the Hebrews, writes that absolute union, the ideal marriage, demands for its realization a man or woman perfect by nature.   If they are not so gifted, to use Rosmini's words, if their individual natures are so vitiated as not to be worthy to receive the completeness of union, which human perfection demands, we must make some indulgence.   This indulgence, one philosopher adds, gives men a little leeway, which is wrong in itself, but whose vice is based upon and attributable to the same vice in nature.   The indulgence, the allowance so different from approval, is divorce, which is not *per se* good.   It is only proper to ask if the hardness of heart that necessitated divorce among the Hebrews has really disappeared from the earth, and if human nature has so changed to-day as to make perfection attainable.   It is true that education has made great strides, that customs were brutal of old, that now we are more delicately strung, but human nature retains its old vices, if we can judge from the actual relation of the sexes.   They say that love is unending, because one being cannot cease loving another who completes his life, but they forget that in becoming unworthy of love or respect the completion ceases.   Proudhon's statement that the subordination of love to justice, the foundation of marriage, can even deny love is a paradox, because the act of subordination logically presupposes the existence of the end subordinated, which cannot exist, according to Proudhon.   It is neither true nor human justice which is obtained by the ruin of life, of the utilities and interests, as there is no concrete moral good to be had by the elimination of the inclinations, affections, and passions.   Let justice rule, but do not let this world perish.   In marriage let marriage be ruled by justice, but do not destroy love, the informing principle of the absolute union.   It is

said that the actuality is always inferior to the idea;
but it need not be opposed to it. From the idea of
indissolubility to the remedy of divorce there is no
descent. The two terms are mutually exclusive. To
prove this, put a full union on one side and divorce on
the other. The truth is that, when divorce makes its
appearance, the real union has ceased. It is not the
violent destruction of marriage, but the legal end of a
union, which no longer exists in fact. Defining divorce
as a remedy and not as a good *per se*, after having proclaimed indissolubility as the ideal, it is impossible to
say that divorce attains the ideal. Only a true eternal
union corresponds to the ideal: divorce marks the
end of a union. It begins where the ideal of indissolubility ends, and therefore is not in fact a contradiction
of it. If divorce is opposed to the nature of matrimony,
it must be regarded as the greatest of evils. If, however, it is looked upon as one of the serious disorders
which are derived from the defects of matrimony, it
can be considered as a lesser ill. The ends of the relation are the defect of the legal bond and divorce. It is
not claimed that divorce is not a remedy *per se*, though
it is not positive, being only the annulment of the marriage. A remedy is that which fills what the evil has
emptied, that repairs what the latter destroys; and yet
there is no contradiction between the conception of a
cessation and a remedy, since there are many cases where
the ceasing of an act, habit, or condition is a remedy.
Some remedies aim only at destruction of the evil, while
others have only a reparatory virtue, but most are both
destructive and reparatory.

§ 470. *Divorce a Necessity because of Human Frailty.*
Philosophy of law should not look upon divorce in relation to individuals or from their view-point, as ancient
natural law did, but should study it in its social aspects,

weighing the advantages and evils which can come to
society from personal separations and dissolution of
marriage.   It must not be forgotten that social interests
and conventionalities should not destroy individual rights,
as the latter should not be raised above social rights.
In this case, as in others like it, the two terms tend
rationally to the harmony which comes from looking
upon the State as an ethical organism.   A State would
be a single physical or natural organism, in which the
part lives the life of the whole, if it absorbed in its
eminent right the rights of the individuals, who have
their own personality, and realize the idea of man in one
of his branches.   If divorce were not possible, but in its
place there was only legal separation, which keeps the
bonds in force and dispenses only with cohabitation,
the evil would be great.   Separation necessitates solitude, embitters one's nature, and beclouds one's mind.
It is a cause of concubinage, and of the increase in the
number of illegitimate births.   Sometimes, too, the
nominal bond which remains increases the dishonor of
the innocent party, since it imposes upon him, if rich, a
duty of paying with a brave mien for the continual and
irremedial infidelity of the other.   The prosecution for
adultery allowed by law is of no useful service,
since no one cares to become ridiculous by a lawsuit,
to enforce a possible imprisonment of a few months
or a year.   Cases are not lacking, too, when murder
has been the result; and not rare are the acquittals
upon the plea of the unwritten law.   In other cases,
suicide brings an end to suffering which the victim
cannot bear.   When the system of separation prevails, the children find their parents living in illicit
unions, a fact which endangers the respect which
they should bear towards the authors of their days.
It is not true that this system makes reunions of those

once separated possible, because the cause of the division
cuts deep before they deliberately place themselves
before judicial authorities in order to obtain the sentence
of separation. The proceedings themselves increase the
division, and, in the majority of cases, destroy all reasonable hope of reconciliation. And it has been observed
that the few reunions which have taken place in the
higher classes of society are *pro forma*, temporary, and
dependent almost every time upon extrinsic reasons.
On the other hand, we are forced to agree, with those
who combat divorce, that not all who want to be freed
from conjugal bonds would be willing to marry again,
but from this it cannot be supposed that the greater
number of innocent husbands and wives would not
avail themselves of the opportunity of remarriage given
by divorce. There are not many men whose reflection
is deep and critical; old impressions are strong and
tenacious. The decision has its roots in a complexity
of peculiar and variable conditions, in the degree of
excitability, in the power of reaction against impressions,
in examples of well assorted unions. If it is true that
some people, who had reached a certain age, victims of
conjugal disillusions, would restrain their instincts, this
cannot be said of most. This is no exaggeration of the
animal tendencies of human beings. Impulses of primitive vivacity, although they may decrease, still continue; and not all succeed in stifling them. And until
that end is reached, the two great evils of the system of
absolute personal separation, concubinage, and the illegitimate births, will go on. "Malo electio est in culpa";
a wrong gives no rights, say the enemies of divorce; and
clearly no few disillusions are born of an improvident
choice made with a light heart. But in the choice one is
never bound to demand what is truly perfect, and to
abstain from all that is not so in the fullest sense of the

word.   All aspire to the absolute, but no one attains it.
Sometimes imperfections are potential, in embryo at
the first, and develop later.   In other cases they can
be learnt only through intimate experience.   And even
if known at the moment of choice, there is always a
hope of destroying or eradicating them by the new life,
by the controlling force of affection which has the
nobility to disallow the existence of refractory or un-
amenable nature.   Would you make a fable of the soul's
generous nature, where love and worth act together to
make men good, and refuse it recognition?

§ 471.   *Divorce has Real Evils.*   We must not, however, deny the real evils of divorce.   Above all,
society would be forced often to submit to the scandal
of the marriage of the divorced and culpable party
with the person who was the cause of his fault.   For
the statutes forbidding this are useless because of
the legal uncertainty of the adultery.   In the second
place, it cannot be in accord with the sentiments of
civilized nations, particularly those of southern Europe,
that a woman who has been the wife of a man still living,
should be the wife of another, or that a man should be
the husband of two women, both of whom are living,
or further, that the children should have at the same
time a stepfather, a stepmother, and their own parents.
It is true, however, that customs alter with years, and
perhaps this repugnance may become markedly modified.
In the third place, it is not an unfounded fear that
divorce will be obtained for causes prepared, with malice
prepense, by those who wish without cause to break the
marital yoke.   Acts of severe injustice, cruelty, and
desertion will be committed with the secret intention
of forcing a divorce.   Cases will not be impossible
where husbands will make opportunities for their wives'
unfaithfulness in order to gain a divorce and remar-

riage. All these evils will develop, threatening to undermine the family and society, if divorce comes to be looked upon as a new form of freedom, which can be availed of as any other. A people which has such a conception of divorce is in a state of moral decadence, no longer understanding the worth of marriage or of ethical relationships. With them divorce will aid the work of corruption, and hasten their ruin. The Romans were corrupt when they began to avail themselves of the rights of repudiation and divorce as means for the attainment of their individual wishes, falling into the excesses of which history tells us. Justinian even made marriage dissolvable by mutual consent, without the introduction of the judiciary, or preliminary allowance of alimony. In France, too, in the past century, morality was at a low ebb, and the law considered divorce as a result of the great principle of freedom. ˏThe Assembly allowed divorce upon the desire of either husband or wife for incompatibility of temper. The Convention gave more rein, abolishing the prohibitions of remarriage within a year after the declaration of divorce by mutual consent, and allowed divorce for six months desertion. Matrimony was, therefore, a status to be proved, as it is among the savage tribes; the Convention itself was forced to repeal its decrees which had produced infinite scandals. But if divorce is not a new form of freedom, but rather as an enforcement of conjugal duties, social morality, far from being lessened, may be strengthened by it. The fear of divorce in uncorrupted ages, with people of deep rooted customs will insure the fulfillment of conjugal duties, and make divorce a remedy of little frequency. It has been shown that divorce can coexist with good morals and not affect them: take the example of ancient Rome for hundreds of years. In England it was allowed for many years, and was rare. The morality of a nation depends on many causes, among which must be placed divorce and separation. But in combination with many different causes it is impossible to determine what influence each factor bears to the resultant state of morality.

§ 472. *The History of the Catholic Church and Divorce.* Such are the standards by which divorce must be weighed in history. Allowed in America, England, Germany, Switzerland, Norway, Denmark, Belgium, Holland, France, and in Austria for the Protestants, and at the present forbidden only in Italy, Spain, and Portugal, divorce has different results upon the various moral conditions of the nations dependent upon what point of view is taken. The Church from the beginning endeavored to inculcate the principle of indissolubility as better conforming to Christian beliefs, but met with complete success only in the XIth century. It was in that century that the conception of marriage as a sacrament, formed stage by stage, developed in its fullest vigor and became a universal theory and belief of the Church. The victory of the Church was connected with the formation of this belief and its decided prevalence at that time. The influence of Christianity is manifest in the laws of Constantine, which restrict the power of repudiation, extended again by the emperors who succeeded him. This influence is seen, too, in the limitation of divorce introduced in the Germanic laws. The Church carried out its original plan better with the Germans than the Romans, for many reasons. The first was the want of the sacramental idea among the Romans; the second, that the right of repudiation with the German belonged to the husband only, and was unpopular on the score of being a privilege, while with the Roman it could be availed of either by husband or wife. The Christian influence must have had, and in fact did have, greater influence where there was inequality. We can see that the Church in its long struggle against divorce was constrained to make not a few serious compromises, but this does not mean that it ever abandoned its ideal. The Church did what every being must do in order not to vanish from the earth; it adapted itself to the experience of time and customs. We must not forget that life is a constant struggle for the supremacy of the subjective over the objective, a never ending compromise with external contingencies. And it is only just to recollect that the exceptions to indissolubility allowed by the Church are not due to the Germanic element, but to its own principle and Christian belief, in which the law of the spirit was opposed to that of the flesh, the celestial city to the terrestrial, faith to knowledge, voluntary poverty to labor. It should not be a cause of wonder that celibacy was encouraged, and that marriage came to be looked upon as a remedy of an evil, the instinct of fornication. The ideal is always the resistance and victory of the spirit over the lusts of the flesh; marriage, willingly or unwillingly entered into, is not perfection, since it presupposes a carnal union. The ideal of marriage which the Church followed is a sufficient reason for the exceptions that it made in the French Capitularies, the result of an agreement between clergy and laity in council, legislation of a time when kings suffered for their inability to convert canons into statutes. The Capitularies recognized the right of the woman to marry again, because she could not smother her instincts. It decreed that if an individual committed adultery with his mother-in-law, he could never marry, and she could never lie with her innocent spouse, and the latter could marry again. The husband can marry again if the wife commits adultery with her brothers- or father-in-law, because she must abstain from all carnal intercourse. The marriage of a priest and his niece is invalid; both can marry, but since "reprehensible est ut relictam sacerdotis alius homo habeat," this marriage can be voided, and the second husband, "si se continere non potest, aliam accipiat." So when the principle of indissolubility became a dogma, through moral precepts becoming law, the Church again adapted itself to the needs of life. In fact, the dogma of the Council of Trent was so drawn up as not to wound the people living in divorce in the bosom of the Greek Church and the Venetian Republic. With the establishment of this dogma, the Church felt the need of increasing the causes of nullity, thus continuing to allow some divorces. But it cannot be said, on this account, that canon law recognized divorce, because the causes of nullification are prior to the marriage, or are so imagined, while those of divorce are posterior.

§ 473. *Causes for Divorce; Adultery.* The kind and number of causes for divorce must be determined by principles of justice harmonized with social conditions. The number of causes should not be increased except upon a clearly shown necessity, in order to hinder, or at least not to hasten the destruction of custom, nor should it be so small as to exclude just and impelling causes; for divorce should be a sufficient remedy. The causes ordinarily recognized by wise legislation and reason are adultery, cruelty, indignities, convictions for infamous crimes, or life imprisonment, and desertion. Adultery is always destructive of marriage, according to the German word "ehebruch." Many think that the adultery of man or woman is the same of itself, but that the consequences are different, because an adulteress destroys the paternal relation, which is not the case with an adulterer. Hence, statutes should require peculiar circumstances to make his adultery grounds for a divorce, as, for example, that he keeps his mistress in the home, or openly elsewhere, or at least that the act is accompanied by circumstances which made it an indignity to his wife. This theory holds that adultery in either spouse has the same moral character, but with different consequences. If this difference in result be accepted, it follows logically that the adulteress, who does more harm, should be more severely punished, but it does not follow that the husband, except in the above cases, has a right to fail in respect and honor due his wife, to interrupt or perhaps destroy by secret adultery the continuity of the conjugal relation, and to disturb the rational relation by making some other woman the mother of his children. Justice in the interest of woman's morals and dignity demands that there be equality in the crime, and that the easy privilege of man be done away with.

§ 474. *Cause for Divorce, Excesses, Cruelty, and Indignities.* And to excesses, cruelty, and indignities, Savoye-Rollin spoke truly before the Tribunal: "Think that the hand that should protect dealt the blow, that the mouth which uttered the insults should have used the tones of love; think that all the conditions of this contract which bind the victim to the executioner are violated by him, and that all are kept by the victim." The conviction for infamous crime destroys the respect and moral value of the criminal. Life imprisonment does the same, but further renders the object of marriage impossible. Desertion is also a just cause for divorce, but the statute should be carefully made for the determination of its characters, otherwise it will serve as a cloak for fraud and trickery, as under the French laws of 1792. We need not admit as causes, insanity, diseases, or change of religion, because this is contrary to the feeling of kindness and piety, which would destroy the most intimate union of pleasures and griefs through an involuntary misfortune in homage to the most abject selfishness.   As difference in belief does not hinder the contraction of marriage, it should not, upon subsequent development, be a ground for its dissolution.   As absolute union in practice is obtained only more or less imperfectly, it does not seem necessary to introduce these causes.

§ 475.   *Divorce by Mutual Agreement.* Should divorce be allowed upon mutual consent? Montesquieu says that the law establishes causes for divorce where incompatibility is greatest.   The statement is true, because the effective mutual incompatibility is the clearest denial of the absolute union of matrimony.   In this case, mutual consent is not the cause of the dissolution of the marriage, but is only the sign.   It cannot be alleged that allowing such a cause of divorce is reducing marriage to contract. It would serve to hide the woes and shame of the home, it would avoid the ridicule, and prevent the necessity of a legal accusation, which sometimes results in imprisonment.   But to ward off a series of abuses fatal to matrimony, the law should surround it with the greatest precautions.   It should declare, in imitation of the French Code, that this cause could not be availed of before or after a certain age, and that the consent of parents or grandparents should be obtained, that half the estate should be given to the children, that no other marriage should be contracted for three or four years, and that a long time should precede the granting of the divorce.   It is clear that non-reciprocal incompatibility cannot be a cause of divorce, because marriage is not a contract, but something more than a contract, and therefore cannot be dissolved without mutual consent.   Marriage cannot lie in the caprice of a single person, as happened in France in the XVIIIth Century.

§ 476. *Some Precautions in Divorce.* From others precautions of the French Code are not to be disregarded, which tend to restrain possible abuses of divorce. The culpable party, since he is in fault, should lose all benefits; the innocent party should lose nothing. In the interest of morality and family peace, the culpable consort should not be able to marry his accomplice. Any second marriage, in fact, should be allowed only after a long interval. Because of the seriousness of marriage, the divorced couple should not be allowed to remarry, as happened in France. The position of the children in divorce should be the same as a case of annulment by canon law, or separation by civil law. The innocent party should keep the children, who lose no advantages given them by law or by the nuptial agreement, except those consequent on a second marriage. Remarriage can certainly not be forbidden because of the children. The father and mother retain their authority, and contribute to their education according to their financial ability. It is evident that law, owing respect to the principles of liberty, cannot deny equal recognition to the separation of the Catholics and the divorce of the Protestants or atheists. The law acts upon all in their quality of citizens, and gives them a choice of method.

CHAPTER XX

THE PARENTAL RELATIONSHIP

THE TENDENCY TO RE-LIVE IN OTHERS. — THE BASIS AND
PHASES OF THE "PATRIA POTESTAS." — GUARDIANSHIP, ITS
KINDS, AND TRUSTEESHIP. — ADOPTION. — CHILDREN BORN OUT OF
MATRIMONY. — THE RIGHT TO PURSUE THE FATHER. — LEGITI-
MATION.

§ 477. *Parental Relationship a Derivative of the Conjugal.* From the conjugal relation upon the birth of children springs the parental relation. At first this kind of
union is more abstract than concrete, since the children
are not able to join their will and act to the will and
act of their parents, and a partnership is not generally
effective without the union of wills and acts. It becomes
concrete from the moment when the children acquire
knowledge of their relations and ends. From that
moment the coöperation of will is a fact.

§ 478. *Parental Relationship is Fundamental.* Human
nature feels the need of self-amplification. Man by
marriage lives in another; by generation he relives in
others. By the profound and wonderful act of generation, writes Rosmini, the father extracts and multiplies his own feeling, to which he admits a new
person who is of the same quality as the father, and
forever joined to him in sentiment, intelligence, and
affection. The act of generation is accomplished by
the coöperation of the three fundamental divisions of
man, since with true sentiment at the point of highest
excitement he spurs himself to the attainment of his

act, that is, the creation of a son; therefore between father and child there is a close and intimate communication, through the common end, which is the result of common feeling. And, although the corporeal union ceases when the child sees the light of day, there always remains the union of objects, because the son in Holy Writ is called increment of the parents, their offspring, and Dante speaks of the child as the flower and fruit of the parents. From this it appears, Rosmini goes on, that the father has at first a causal relation with his child, since he created the new life; to this is added a second necessary chain, a communication of sentiment between the father and his child, which can never be broken. Upon this double tie depends the parental relation. In the causal relation the parents are always superior to their children and can exercise a power which is not licit over any other persons. In that of unity of sentiment they are urged to a special and strange love for their children, and this love, as every other true sentiment of mankind, is a duty. From the connection of blood between parents and children are born the "jura sanguinis," common to the father and mother, indestructible until the child leaves the domestic circle. Such rights are essentially individual, seigneurial, and appertain to ownership. From the social relation, originating in the blood relationship, but not indissoluble as the former, are derived the "jura familiæ" and the rights of the domestic society, belonging in particular to the head of the house. Nature infuses in the mind of parents two sentiments, the sentiment of having children for their own good, and that of having children for the good of the children and their descendants. Children, without loss of personal dignity, are medial in the joy and good which their parents can obtain through them, and on the other hand, are ultimate in respect to the care to which they are entitled. The rights of the parents growing out of the children's medial condition, their duties emanate from the ultimate condition which the children enjoy in their own personality. To take a child's earnings is a right of lordship and contract, founded on the sentiment of having children for one's own advantage; the right of providing for a child's welfare is founded on the sentiment of having children for their good and the good of their descendants. If these two sentiments exist in perfection, it is found that the first is easily satisfied and is willing to sacrifice itself to the second. It seems that the *patria potestas* is a seigneurial right, subordinate, however, to the right of control of the domestic society which makes for the utility and good of the children.

§ 479. *Rosmini's Theory not that of the Natural Cause.* Rosmini's theory must not be confused with the old belief in the deduction of the parental rights and the *patria potestas* from natural and causal forces acquired in the completion of marriage or procreation. This natural force was raised to the level of spiritual principles and ethical purposes in order to become the human basis of the *patria potestas*. Rosmini has been careful to reinforce the causal reasons with the necessary bond of a communion of sentiment between the parents and children, by which the parents are constrained to a strong love for their children, a love which is a duty as well, he says. Now the duty of loving one's children resolves into that of procuring their good, of protecting them, of supporting and educating them, transfusing, in Plato's words, the benefits of maturity and old age into adolescence and youth, adding wisdom to strength. Thanks to this duty, the institution becomes rational, and the primary law, or that of the "antecedents" of nature of the Stoic School, interpenetrates with the "consequents," or secondary law, and receives formality and strength from the latter. In this duty chiefly, and also in the sentiment of procreation of children, must be found the true and ultimate foundation of *patria potestas*. That Rosmini's conception is always the *patria potestas* is shown by his expressed subordination of the seigneurial right, contained therein, to the right of control of the domestic society. The seigneurial right is an immediate consequence of causality, as the right of control owes its origin to the parents' love, which is a duty. The expressions which he sometimes uses could give rise to ambiguity, but an attentive reading of the pages devoted to the parental relationship will destroy all doubt. Control, lordship, and mediality have a different meaning, when used of persons and things. The child is subject to his father's control and lordship, and is medial, as far as a person can be, keeping always his personal dignity, Rosmini says. The father is the cause of his children, as far as man can be such a cause, so a son can be called the effect of his father. Antiquity, he says, developed in the child such an extension of the existence of his parents, that it went to the excess of considering the son as the property of the father. It seems in this connection that modern legislation is inclined to look upon the father as merely medial to the welfare of the son.

§ 480. *Patria Potestas Governed by Essential Reason.* In primitive law the *patria potestas* was born from the passive obedience of the children, because the father had strength and practical sense. In India religion counselled the faithful to study twice the sacred books, to retire from active life, in old age becoming ascetics and hermits. This never meant that the sons, at any time or against their father's will, could demand a division of the estate. Paternal authority, judging from the rules of Manu and Nerada, has always been

absolute among the Indians. In Sparta the lack of
patria potestas resulted in the destruction of the family.
In Athens it existed, though it has no special name, allowing a certain guardianship and protection, based on the
presumption of the intelligence of the father, according
to Socrates. This principle, absolutely enforced, did
not insure filial piety or obedience, because the son was
encouraged to measure his father's intellect with his
own, and in such a struggle he may find his own superiority, and feel no longer bound to obedience. In Aristotle's time the insufficiency of this foundation for the
patria potestas began to be felt. It began to decay, preparing the way for the dissolution of the State. In
Rome the *patria potestas* was extensive, absorbing the
personalities of the children. It approximated ownership, "plena potestas in re," and was limited only by the
magistracy of the son, or by a war, which separated the
son from his father. The *patria potestas* was so controlled by the Romans as to oppose its rights to those
of the State. Through this almost unlimited power
there was a kingdom, existing within a free republic,
making it strong and vigorous. Neither was domestic
piety lacking in the family, but was developed, even
where paternal authority was severe, and tempered the
latter's vigor. In the Middle Ages the *patria potestas*
assumed, as a result of barbaric law, that character of a
power of defense and guardianship, appertaining to the
"mundium," which it had in Athens. With the prevalence of individualism, the institution became a means for
individual advantages. It is not a cause of surprise,
therefore, that the father came to be looked upon as
the means for the welfare of his sons, and not as ultimate in himself. In homage to personal freedom there
was an effort to lessen the *patria potestas*, for it was
thought that a free constitution could not coexist with

a family founded on its vigorous authority, forgetting the example of Rome, and the others offered by Greece, where the decay of the State began with the weakening of family ties and paternal power.   In our age the *patria potestas* has lost all its ancient ferocity and severity, and has become stronger when rationally exercised.   True strength lies in the intellect, Spinoza says; the senses and passions are weaknesses.   Paternal rights are not placed above the duties of taking thought, instructing, and educating the young, but are made subordinate, and founded on the duty.   The ethical relations are now recognized again in their integrity and intimate organic connection.   But the father ceases to be considered as medial only, and is ultimate. We can repeat in this regard what has been said before of man and the State in this reciprocal medial and ultimate relation.[1]

§ 481. *The Mother Enjoys the Patria Potestas.*   From what has been said, it is a logical inference that the *patria potestas* belongs without distinction to both parents, because both are bound to support, instruct, and educate their children. It certainly cannot be denied the mother, who takes so great and so important a part in the up-bringing. It must, however, be exercised during coverture by the father in order to give unity to the family through the gifts and powers belonging to man, which have been discussed under the head of marital authority.   After coverture the *patria potestas* should not cease nor be changed to guardianship as under the French Code, but should be exercised by the survivor as in the Italian Code. This Italian innovation conforms perfectly to natural law, since there is no reason why this authority, common during coverture, should upon the death of either consort be converted into

[1] *Cf.* § 173 *ante.*

a guardianship. The law in that hypothesis would distrust the judgment of the parents, in which, as far as the domestic relations are concerned, it has always put the greatest confidence. As to the rights of the *patria potestas*, we must point out that if the power of imprisoning a recalcitrant son is no longer accorded to the father, he cannot be denied the power of driving him from the house, or of putting him in a house of correction. If the *patria potestas* be strictly enforced, it is clear that no action for partition of the estate can be allowed the children. As to the estate, the father has the right of administrating the estate of the children, because of their incapacity, and he can enjoy the income. This interest is given to the father to his own use, and is seigneurial in its origin, being subordinate to the administrative power of the domestic society. It is, therefore, subject to certain conditions, and is exercised only over certain possessions. The *patria potestas* is not uncontrolled; the laws have methods of tempering and ending it, if the parents are unworthy through some grave fault.

§482. *Guardianship.* During the *patria potestas* there is no place for guardianship as an institution by itself, since the latter is included in the former. But the *patria potestas* can come to an end while there are still persons in the family who, because of age, have need of education, support, and protection. In this case there must be a guardianship which appears as a substitute for the lost paternal power. It is a social duty, since everyone must aid those who cannot take care of themselves or their property. Guardianship is developed within the domestic sphere, and enters into private law in that aspect, though it has at the same time both a public and social element, because of the duty involved. It is connected, therefore, with the function of the State and with the principles of public law.

This public character of guardianship does not presuppose any relationship between guardian and ward,
nor can it be called a substitute for paternal authority
even in case of mental weakness. The rights of the
patria potestas, however, are always included, though
in a restricted manner, in guardianship, whether of a
minor or adult. The Roman law of guardianship was
concerned with the administration of the estate; modern
law tends to the development of the educational
functions, the especial property of the *patria potestas*,
so important in our days, in which a good education
is a fruitful asset. From this premise it can be inferred
that guardianship, in its ethical character, should not be
confused with the "negotiorum gestio," because on
one hand guardianship is a domestic institution and
includes to a certain extent the rights of the *patria
potestas*, and on the other, it is a "munus publicum."
In fact the agent can be appointed at choice, while the
guardian is appointed by the father, the law, a magistrate, or a family council. Testamentary guardianship is the first and predominating form, for the father
is better fitted than anyone else to designate his successor
in the education of his son. Upon a failure to appoint
by will, the law can with due regard to circumstance
appoint a guardian following the degrees of consanguinity
in which it always places confidence. If there are no
relatives, the guardianship is donative, that is, it lies in
the gift of the court or family or guardianship council.
To-day a guardianship can be decreed because of mental
weakness

§ 483. *History of Guardianship*. In Greece guardianship was testamentary and donative, because there
was not enough confidence in the heir presumptive
of the ward to trust him as guardian. In Rome it
began by being testamentary, became agnative, and

finally donative. Among the Germans it was part of the "mundium," and belonged only to the nearest relative. With the Lombards the guardian had to have judicial authorization for any important act. The judge had to call together the family in many cases, for example, in the alienation of realty. Such assemblies were the beginning of the family councils presided over by a magistrate.

§ 484. *The Creation of a Guardianship.* The law of guardianship should not presume the fulness of paternal love in the guardian, nor true filial devotion in the ward. It should adopt the greatest precautions to insure the guardian's care and attention to the need of the ward, placing great confidence in consanguinity. If the deliberation is the act of many, and the execution the act of one, if the State should watch the exercise of the guardian's authority, it is a good plan to entrust the deliberation to a family council presided over by a magistrate, and the execution to the guardian. This surveillance on the part of the State can be exercised by a magistrate alone, or by the family council presided over by a magistrate. The Italian Code follows the second plan. A guardian differs from a trustee, who acts for emancipated minors or spendthrifts. The trustee has control of the estate alone, while the guardian is invested with all the rights of the father to a limited extent. We must note that the *cestui que trust* cannot do anything without the intervention of the trustee. Also, according to the Italian Code, he needs for certain acts the authorization by the family council, and for others the sanction of the court.

§ 485. *Adoption.* We have said that man not only wants to live in others, but wants to relive in others.[1] The first want is satisfied in marriage, the second in

[1] *Cf.* § 441 *ante.*

generation. A couple may remain childless, and some men do not marry because of sickness or from reasons of prudence. The childless couple are unhappy because they do not relive in others; those who abstain from marriage because of disease or prudence are doubly so, since they neither live nor relive in others. The State has no right to condemn these individuals to solitude and unhappiness, or to deny them civil recognition of spiritual generation, which is not less real than the corporeal, and is a result of philogamy. And so some assume willingly the care of supporting and educating children who have been abandoned or left to their care, acquiring in time sentiments not unlike those of true paternity, and awaiting in return the filial devotion of these children, when they have grown. Man feels that in the family relation, and in the affections which are based on it, is the only true happiness that is given him to enjoy, and when they fail him, he seeks their closest substitute, tired of the loneliness in which he sees himself condemned to live. Before legal adoption, there was *de facto* adoption founded on the desires of human nature. "Adoptio imitatur naturam," taught the ancients, "atque in eorum solatio inventa est, qui liberos non susceperunt, aut susceptos amiserunt." From another point of view, adoption helps the preservation of a family threatened with dissolution. It has its motive in philogamy, and at the same time perpetuates the ethical and organic unity which is the molecule and centre of the highest and larger ethical organism, the State. In history, the more the family has appeared as an organized and powerful nucleus with religious, civil, and political characteristics, the more has the need for adoption been felt, which strengthens this nucleus and prevents its dying out.

§ 486. *History of Adoption.* Adoption is in accord with the constitution and principles of the oldest republics. We may note that adoption is based upon the relationship of the parties to it, and when the relationship was not natural it must have been civil. Adoption at that time could not have been entered into with the object of comfort, but with the social and political object of the preservation of the family. In fact the Roman conception of "solatio liberorum amisorum" is found in the early law in the exceptional cases of adoption by a woman. In modern times, since the family is still a unit, the need of adoption, though less strongly felt, still exists. The unity is not as strong or as complex as is the Roman family, but it exists nevertheless, and cannot fail so to do, since the family is an ethical body. The difference between the two unities lies in the former being in the interest of the father, the latter in the interest of the family itself. This understood, it is clear that adoption, which is the legal act by which there is established a relation of paternity and filiation between two strangers, cannot be considered as of exclusive private import, conclusive merely of the personal satisfaction of the parties. Adoption produces a change of status, because the adopted child becomes the child of the adoptors and acquires rights of inheritance under the intestate laws, besides the right to support and to the name of the adoptors. A personal status is not within the scope of contract, but of law, hence the reason for the solemnity of adoption and the intervention of a court. An adoption is always the image of nature, and therefore cannot break the ties of blood relationship between the child and his family. Its motive lies in a personal sentiment, though consecrated by law, and from this it follows that its effect should be limited to adoptor and adopted and should not extend to their respective families. The above breach and extension have no part in the true and genuine conception of adoption. Adoption is advantageous in hindering tardy marriages, ordinarily of short duration, and seldom happy.

§ 487. *Opposition to Adoption not Founded on Reason.* Adoption has met not a little opposition, especially in France, where it had no traditions. The French jurisconsults, followed in Italy by Pisanelli, state that nature alone can create the relation of paternity and filiation, and that law cannot destroy the sacred affection derived from ties of blood. But they do not reflect that adoption is not introduced to destroy natural ties, or to give the artificial relation greater effects than the natural. They do not remember that it is only the image and cannot have the appeal of the true family, whose interest it cannot prejudice, since it cannot exist if there are legitimate children. It only prejudices collaterals and relatives, who would inherit upon failure of closer heirs, but it is not just to sacrifice the individual's freedom and happiness to these ties, which do not belong to the family in the strict sense. The enemies of adoption go further, saying that it is a useless institution since there is such testamentary freedom allowed, that the beneficence can be shown by a legacy without need of introducing any artificial relations. These have not thought that ordinary benevolence is not the motive of adoption but benevolence which is part of philogamy and assumes the forms of paternal and filial devotion. Furthermore, adoption should not be considered only in its relation to the individuals, whose comfort it is, but in relation to the family which it tends to preserve. Nor have they showed that adoption is a feudal institution, for it flourished under primitive law, in India, Greece, and Rome. It is not essentially feudal, because the grant of titles and arms did not depend upon the will of the individual. Adoption, it is at last argued, is employed to avoid the legal prohibition of the recognition of hidden filiation. But does not the court supervise an adoption, seeing that it does not cloak a crime? The Italian lawyer, Vigliani, argued that point in the Senate; "Either the paternity of the adoptor will be known or suspected, and the court will refuse the petition for adoption, or will be unknown and hidden, and the adoption will take place, and it does not seem just to complain that an unfortunate child, deprived of help and family, should find both in adoption without scandal to society, ignorant of the hidden ties of nature which bind him to the adoptor."

§ 488. *The Status of Illegitimate Children.* Law, being an ethical principle, should not encourge illicit unions. It should, however, protect children born out of matrimony from the acts of the parents, in whom often love is lacking, or is smothered by the interest of their legitimate families or by conventionality. It should visit all the consequences of the fault upon its authors, and not extend it to others. Law cannot make the condition of children born out of matrimony equal to that of legitimates, because it must guard the morality and order of family life. Children born out of matrimony can be either natural, adulterous, or incestuous. The last two are sprung *ex nefario coitu*, from criminal unions. But should the crime and tort of their parents subject them to the payment of damages and penalties, and mark them from innocent children? The disgrace and loss of certain rights under the civil law belong, Rosmini states, to that age of the world in which the individual principle was involved in general nature, and operative only therein, the stock was punished for the acts of the individual. Now that age has passed. Through the New Testament, human nature has been awakened and fully developed.   Public opinion has changed.   Now law should punish severely the fault of the parents, — with penalties, however, which affect them alone, protects the innocent victims, and declares them clear of all infamy and free from all consequent harm.   Justice demands that adulterous and incestuous children should be considered in the same manner as natural children (as the Austrian Code decrees) and should not have only *pietatis gratia* necessaries.   Adulterous and incestuous children also have rights to upbringing, instruction, and support by their parents, whose legal responsibility, like the *patria potestas*, should be extended over them.   The law can allow the recognition of these classes of children without fear of more scandalous suits than are possible to-day in actions for the disinheritance of children, and for the annulment of the bonds of matrimony for incest.   Through their recognition adultery and incest will be discovered, and justice will therefore be rendered capable of punishing its violators, the victim will have a money indemnity, and individual responsibility will be increased, making criminal unions much fewer.   Neither can a limited right of inheritance be denied such offspring for the same reason that they must be given rights (which are in Italy actully given to natural children), that is, because of their innocence, and because "factum cuique suum nocere debet."   But though the rights of adulterous and incestuous children should be the same as those of natural children, the rights of illegitimates cannot be made equal to those of legitimates, because the scope of personal integrity lies wholly within matrimony, since all reproduction and educational functions belong to the true family, as ordered by the State, in accordance with the dictates of natural law and the conditions of civilization.   We must harmonize the sacred rights to life, and the obligations of parentage, with the demands of the whole, or society. In history, when marriage was regulated rather by custom than by statutes, and everything was controlled by the head of the family, there was but little difference made between legitimates and illegitimates. Examples of this are the heroic times among the Greeks, and the patriarchal times with the Hebrews. The Greek law, subsequent to the heroic ages, treated illegitimates with severity. This severity continued until Pericles, who had no legitimate offspring, made his natural son legitimate. In Rome concubinage was recognized, owing to the disparity of conditions. Children thus born had the right of pretorian inheritance from the mother and her family, but from the father could obtain only necessaries. In the day of the Empire they were considered as natural children of the father, who was given the *patria potestas*, and who could legitimize them, without having the power of making any will in their favor, a power given over a portion of the estate by Valentinus. Justinian admitted them to the inheritance if the father died intestate, or upon failure of wife and children, if he had left them nothing. In all cases the natural children had a right to necessaries. According to Justinian, however, children *ex nefario coitu* had not even this right, while in the time of Gaius they were recognized as cognates, and enumerated among the "vulgo quæsiti," admitted to pretorian inheritance. The children *ex damnato coitu* had no right of action against their father, but the relation could be proved to stop or declare an incestuous marriage, or to annul a legacy in their favor. Finally, concubinage was forbidden by canon law. There immediately arose, on one hand, morganatic marriages, contracted by persons of unequal conditions, giving a right of inheritance to a portion of the estate, set apart at the time of the marriage, and on the

other hand, the marriage of conscience, secretly celebrated, and not producing special or definite legal effects.
Concubinage continued too, despite the prohibition, but
the illegitimates (though they sometimes ascended
thrones) were considered incapable of inheritance or of
ecclesiastical preferment, and were the subjects of the
right of necessaries only. Their estates upon their
death belonged to the lord or the State. Only after a
long period were they given the power to will. The
French Revolution championed the rights of all to partake equally in the inheritance except adulterous children. The Code gave the natural children a right of
inheritance of a smaller portion than the legitimate,
but gave the offspring of adultery and incest the right
to necessaries alone, dividing them into natural children recognizable and natural children non-recognizable.

§ 489. *Inquiry into Paternity.* If the laws assigned
a certain position in the family to illegitimates, they
should not be deprived of the means of finding their
father and claiming that position. Some codes, like the
French and Italian, recognize the right to prove maternity, but forbid the inquiry into the paternity,
though the French Code allows the latter in cases of
rape, and the Italian in cases of rape by force, if the
act coincides with the time of conception. It is evident
that the codes are unjust, because they protect the
monstrous privilege of the seducer, who escapes all
responsibility for his acts, leaving the unsophisticated
and well meaning girl to face great trouble, and wreaking
the effect of his brutal selfishness upon an innocent
creature. The inquiry into the paternity would not be
an innovation. It has the evidence of history in its
favor because, allowed by the Roman, it was retained by
the German and canon laws, and flourished until the end
of the XVIIth Century, here surrounded by precaution

and guards, here without them, to the ease and frequency of scandalous abuse.   In France this abuse was possible, and the honor of respectable men and the peace of the family was often in the power of a cunning harlot, helped by bribed witnesses and blackguards.   When the right of action was done away with in France, because of the continual injustice which it permitted, the civil law was divided into two classes, one of which followed the old law, and one the French.   In the nations which followed the French law, and especially in France itself, through the study of comparative legislation, there arose a doubt of the intrinsic justice of the prohibition, and subsequently a reaction against it.   The prohibition of the inquiry into paternity was regarded as an obvious and unreasoning form of the supremacy of the male, who is stronger than the female.   It was noted that there was no need to regard the forced recognition of the fruits of seduction or a passing intimacy as an offense against morality, if the law recognizes a spontaneous recognition, and admits the children of a mistress to intestate inheritance.   The ending of the brutal privilege and the awakening of feeling of responsibility might exercise an effective restraint.   This is the opinion of several philosophers of the law, for example, Ahrens and Trendelenburg.   Rosmini criticizes the plan, because in illicit unions the mother can always be found, while often the father cannot.   The father is often not found, he says; but why exclude him from punishment the times that he is?   We can find many imperfections in the statutes due to the poor development of the power of abstraction.   At first, legislation was content with reasoning on principle, which was sometimes right but not always.   In those cases in which the principle failed, natural law suffered from their decrees, as in the case for which there was no statute, or where a statute was

violated. On this score, therefore, the perfection of the
law lies in acting upon the general principle, which governs the majority of cases, and upon other principles and
special rules, which one by one embrace the refractory
cases, and cover the whole field of rational law. The
marriage ceremony, to quote Rosmini, cannot be considered as the only proof of paternity; there are others.
All are sometimes inefficient. A wedding establishes
rather a legal presumption than a logical proof. It is
not, therefore, a source of wonder that the presumption
should yield to the truth of the fact of the illegitimacy of
the son, otherwise proved. And if it is right to give
the adulterous and incestuous children the same rights
as the natural, it follows that the first can be recognized
and legitimized, and that they too can inquire into the
identity of their father, if such search be reasonably
conducted.

§ 490. *Proof of Paternity.* There are two methods
by which the paternity of a child born out of wedlock can be determined, — by the belief of the father,
and by circumstantial evidence. The father's belief
can be enforced by proof of his written statement,
proved by witnesses, or by other evidence about his
relations with the mother, and should not be restricted
to a formal recognition. In countries where the priority of civil marriage is not required, the religious
ceremony supplies such proof, and is always considered
by the State as a formal recognition. It is clearly an
implied recognition if the son is called, and treated, and
generally reputed to be the son. The proof of paternity
from circumstantial evidence now allowed in case of
rape, should be extended to other cases in which there
are sufficient motives to admit it. The "custodia
ventris," for example, consisting in cohabitation "more
uxorio," in the watching of the man over the woman

in the period of conception, joined with the honorable behavior of the woman herself, the simple seduction of a young girl, and the seduction of an honest woman of any age through false promises of marriage, should be considered the principal prerequisites for inquiry into the paternity. Justice demands it, and the proof is possible and not always difficult. It must be remembered that only the girl who has been seduced, not the woman of many affairs, can be allowed to testify. The abuse of proof was possible when the sworn statement of the pregnant woman, the victim of seduction, was enough by itself. The possibility was lessened when the other requirement of lack of customary intimate relations was added, and was not much to be feared when a writing by the father was necessary, as the Convention decreed.

§ 491. *Legitimation.* The law should also provide that what is not originally moral may become so. And therefore it should allow, as a reparation of an injustice, legitimation by subsequent marriage, or by decree in cases in which the subsequent marriage is not possible. It follows, of course, that the legitimated son has the same rights as the legitimates. This principle, and that of responsibility, is connected with the existence of receptacles[1] for abandoned children, which is the end of the civil estate of thousands and thousands of men, and which increases the number of abandoned children, and is the infamous cause of the abandonment of legitimates, especially in large cities. These receptacles are a worn-out form of blind and irrational charity, and are closed in most civilized countries, giving way to various maternity hospitals which take children at their birth. Such institutions have the merit of

[1] These receptacles are placed in public places in the cathedrals of Southern Europe. In them a child can be placed, who is supported by the money placed in the receptacle by charitable persons. They are described by Victor Hugo in "Notre Dame de Paris."

preventing the abandonment of legitimate children, and often provide for the future life of the disgraced infant. Some laws permit the parents to remain unknown; others declare that the mothers must give their name. Without doubt the latter, based upon the principle of responsibility, conforms better to rational law. The first do not enforce vigorous justice, because they fear infanticide. In fact, the fear is not unfounded, since it is a question of saving one's honor and of avoiding disastrous consequences. But on this subject, as on every other, much depends on the morals and customs of the people. The fear is baseless, however, as far as the closing of the receptacles is concerned, since it has been seen that there is more infanticide where the receptacles are in use than where they are not. This does not mean that the presence or absence of the receptacles is an effective cause of the increase or decrease of this kind of crime. Experience shows that infanticide generally is committed before the mother feels the emotions of maternity, and also where there is no one whom she trusts, to whom she can temporarily give the fruit of her dishonor. If the emotions are felt, if the confidant is there, the baby is saved, and it little matters whether it is the receptacle or the charity, provided the mother need not give her name at the birth. The receptacle should be placed by the bedside to avoid infanticide.

CHAPTER XXI

DEFINITION, HISTORY, AND BASIS OF INHERITANCE

THE CONCEPTION OF HEREDITY. — INTESTACY AND TESTACY IN HISTORY. — INHERITANCE AND ANCESTOR WORSHIP. — DOCTRINES AS TO THE BASIS OF INHERITANCE. — DOMESTIC CO-OWNERSHIP AND THE RIGHT OF PROPERTY, AS BASES FOR INHERITANCE.

§ 492. *Law of Inheritance Affects all Relations of Life.* Death extinguishes man and many of his relations, but his goods, rights, and obligations continue to exist and form that "nomen" or "universitas juris" which is called his estate. "Hereditas," says the early Roman law, "nihil aliud est quam successio in universum jus quod defunctus habuit." The "heres" is placed in the position of the "herus" and represents his personality, becoming the new subject of the rights which are the "universum jus defuncti." He is the successor with full title and is held bound to pay the debts of the decedent and bear the burdens of inheritance, differing from the successor under a particular or testamentary title, who does not represent the personality of the deceased and inherits only what is left to him and must bear only the burdens inherent therein or those imposed by the testator. Now inheritance, on one hand, is connected with the family, because it appears when that is decomposed into its elements or another family; on the other hand, it is connected with property, since it effects a transfer of the estate. The law of inheritance, therefore, logically presupposes the parental and conjugal relations and domestic and matrimonial law. It can be considered as the last phase of family law and even of private law, since the private relations have their end in individual and domestic life. The foundations of this kind of law lie in the family community and the free will of the owner. If all the law of heredity were based on the family, the individual could be entirely absorbed by the collective entity and would lose his personality; no form of inheritance save the statutory and unalterable would be recognized. If, however, it were based entirely upon the will of the disposing individual, the family would be denied, and the individual would have an untrammelled right to decide upon his own duties. In this case there would be no laws of intestacy, and testamentary inheritance would cover everything. The law of inheritance should, therefore, harmonize the rights of the family with the just claims of the individual, without forgetting that the right of succession, being directly referable to the family touches the "seminarium republicæ," and therefore is of great interest to the State.

§ 493. *Inheritance Among the Older Nations.* In primitive times the right of the community prevailed, and not that of the part or individual. In such times intestate succession, which represented the absorbing right of the family, was the only and prevalent right, and not testacy, which is the act of an individual. Traces of true testacy are not found in the Book of Genesis although the patriarchs had a certain right of conferring their goods in case of death. In Athens there was an institution of appointing an heir, in the form of an adoption, provided there were no children. This shows that at first only children could inherit. In the earlier days there was no power of will among the Spartans, but it was introduced by the laws of Epithadeus.

Neither did it exist among the Germans, nor does it to-day among the tribes and people who are in the condition of the ancient Germans. In Rome inheritance was first regulated exclusively by statute, which considered the "sui," then the "agnati," and later the "gentiles." The earlier and solemn form of the "testamentum calatis comitiis" was a law, and needed the consent or sanction of the people. The first manner of making a will, perhaps because it was the first, could not be availed of independently of the "lex," and could not be free from customary forms. Testacy is not a primitive fact, but neither is it an institution of mere civil or positive law, as we will see. Not all that is of latter development, however, is artificial; it is true that the nature of things is nothing but their birth, but this understood in its fullness includes genetic development or evolution. Human nature consists more in the *fieri* than in the *esse*, whence it follows that the natural is not that alone which develops first. And furthermore, it can be noted that what is natural, rational, and universal at the beginning seems to be introduced by art and appears as a simple particular fact. It is only later that it comes to be recognized in its true character, when the mind is fully developed, as the great Neapolitan philosopher said. A will, properly so called, was a Roman invention. In Rome the freedom of the testator was untrammelled, as can be seen from the laws of the Twelve Tables, in which it is written, "Pater familias uti legassit super pecunia tutelave rei suæ, ita jus esto." It must not be supposed, however, that the power of willing in Rome was a method of disposing in favor of strangers. It was simply a means by which that complexity of rights included in the *patria potestas* passed from one individual to another. The inheritance was always "universitas juris," and included the "sacra" and domestic ceremonies. This was

true not only in Rome but also in Athens, when the power
to will began there, and in Bengal. Neither can it be said
that the will in Rome was a method of creating inequal
ities, because it served equitable purposes and was a cor-
rective of the law which excluded from the inheritance
the natural children and those who had been emancipated. Great, therefore, was the horror of the Romans of
dying intestate. The real inequality arose with feudal
law which recognized primogeniture. A feud once having become hereditary, the overlord had an interest in
keeping a single son responsible for military service.
Wherever, says Maine, the patriarchal power became
political there arose the right of primogeniture which is
of two kinds. In India and western Europe, primogeniture is the passing from father to son, while with the
Celts upon the death of the first son the second takes his
place, excluding the sons of the first because of the
desire to have a mature man as the head of the house.

§ 494. *Forms of Roman Wills.* The first form of
Roman will was that "calatis commitiis." It is a
question whether the people intervened in the Commi-
tia to convert the will of the testator into a statute, or
acted merely as witnesses. But it seems probable that
at the time when the transformation from intestacy to
testacy was taking place the people had to make the disposition of the testator a law and that later they merely
acted as witnesses. The second form was "per æs et libram" to which recourse was had when one could not make
a will in the solemn manner. It existed at the same time
as the will "calatis commitiis." The "emptor familiæ"
was not an heir-at-law but was "loco heredis" and took
the estate without the debts, for which reason some
people have likened him to the adopted son under the
laws of arrogation. The will "per æs et libram" consisted, when coexisting with the "calatis commitiis," as

a method of necessity. It was divided into two parts, the "mancipatio" and the "rogatio." The "mancipatio" transferred the property, and the "rogatio" gave the title of trustee to the "emptor familiæ" of particular legacies. Gaius says: "Acessit deinde tertium genus testamenti, quod per æs et libram agitur, qui enim neque calatis commitiis neque in procinctu testamentum fecerat si subita morte urgebatur amico familiam suam id est patrimonium suum mancipio dabat eumque rogabat, quid cuique post mortem suam dari vellet." Then the testament "per æs et libram" ceased being supplementary and became the ordinary form. The "mancipatio" was considered a formality, not productive of the transference of ownership in favor of the "emptor familiæ," who was no longer "in loco heredis." When the "mancipatio" took on this form the testator could revoke it. Gaius says: "Sed illa quidem duo genere testamentorum in desuetudinem abierunt; hoc vero solum quod per æs et libram fit in usu retentum est sane nunc aliter ordinatur atque olim solebat; namque olim familiæ emptor, id est qui a testatore familiam accipiebat mancipio heredis locum obtinebat; et ob ei mandabat testator, quid cuique post mortem suam dari vellet; nunc vero alius heres testamento institutur, a quo etiam legata relinquuntur, alius dicis gratia propter veteris juris imitationem familiæ emptor adhibetur." The "nuncupatio," the other part of the will, consists in the declaration before witnesses that the writing contained the last dispositions. Ulpian states: "In testamento, quod per æs et libram fit, duæ res aguntur, familiæ mancipatio et nuncupatio testamenti. Nuncupatur testamentum in hunc modum, tabulas testamenti testator tenens ita dicit: Hæc uti his tabulis cerisve scripta sunt ita do, ita lego, ita testor, itaque vos, quirites, tesitmonium præbitote; quæ nuncupatio et testatio vocatur." It seems that the second phase of mancipatory will was determined by reasons of utility, as, for example, the need of creating several heirs at the same time, or of creating them conditionally. The third form of will was the pretorian. The pretorian will was written because it was fundamentally only the will "per æs et libram" without the formality of the "mancipatio" and "nuncupatio." Cicero, Gaius, and Ulpian speak of the pretorian will, "septem signis testium signatum," or of "tabulas quæ septem testium signis signatæ sunt." Some fragments emphasize the "bonorum possessio secundum nuncupationem," and from this it can be seen that the will proper could sometimes be nuncupative.

§ 495. *History of Wills in the Middle Ages.* We have said that there was no form of will among the Germans. The right of relationship and the active and passive solidity of the connotation of the family were absolute. Tacitus writes of them: "Heredes, successoresque sui cuique liberi, et nullum testamentum. Si liberi non sunt, proximus gradus in successione, frates, patrui avunculi." The inheritance contracts or bilateral and irrevocable disposition which bound one or both of the parties in the acquisition or loss of rights of inheritance were admitted by the German laws and prepared the way for testacy. Such agreements were prohibited by Roman law because they affected the revocability of the will and because the spectacle of a contractual heir who looks with avid eye upon the estate of him who is still alive, and who wastes loving care upon his future successor certain of the estate, is not moral. It is clear that the introduction of hereditary agreements makes the will possible, being in contradiction to that absolute predominance of family rights which existed at the beginning. The irrevocability of such dispositions remaining always intact, at first property and possession were transmitted, afterwards property alone and not possession, and finally the transmission of both was postponed until the death of the owner. The growing influence of the Roman idea over the clergy and a recognition of bequests for the good of the soul and of donations *pia causa*, which approached nearer and nearer to a will, hastened its reappearance in the Middle Ages. The Church was interested in holding as valid dispositions in its favor which did not wholly conform to civil law because unaccompanied by all the formality and prescribed conditions. It concerned itself only with the certainty of the will of the testator; in this canon law approximated natural law. Now from these notes on the history of inheritance it can be seen that the right was not born like the Minerva from the head of Jove, because at the first it was public, oral, and irrevocable, later it became secret, written, and revocable. Perfection is always found in development and not in the initial form.

§ 496. *Testacy and Ancestor Worship,* The historical development of succession is connected also with the evolution of property and of the family, which we have mentioned before.[1] Here we may notice the connection between inheritance and ancestor-worship in primitive times. This old cult does not refer to remote and fabled ancestors, but to the great-grandfather, grandfather, and father, and in general to persons known to the worshipers who, transformed into divinities, continue to protect the family and to exercise their authority, rewarding good actions and punishing bad. This cult was practised by the greater number of nations, among whom were the Indians, Greeks, Romans, Chinese, and ancient Japanese. Sacrifices to ancestors were not unknown to the Hebrews as a foreign custom or pro-

[1] *Cf.* §§ 242, 440, *ante.*

hibited idolatry. The "sacra privata" of the Romans had great importance and influence over the laws and edicts. Little by little the restrictions placed on inheritance by such a cult to the advantage of the pontifical authorities disappeared and the domestic gods became mere larvæ. Lubbock and Spencer and, before them, Vico, looked upon ancestor-worship as an imaginative attribute of primitive men such as we have just said. Lubbock says that the savage is unable to understand death and is apt to confuse it with sleep. In sleep the spirit lives, although the body seems dead. It is natural, therefore, that savages should introduce food into the tomb, because death is analogous to sleep. The spirits of the dead live in another world and have, therefore, great power; whence the custom of praying to the dead. Spencer classifies society by the criterion of a belief in a spiritual world. All people admit the return to life of another self after death. Among them, a large number suppose that this self exists a long time after death. In this number are those nations which practise the propitiation of spirits. Among these nations there are some unprogressive and stationary in which the cult of ancestors perpetuates itself like a belief in the immortality of the soul, and among the last there are not lacking some that confer a preëminence upon a series of illustrious ancestors. For example, they exalt the leaders of a conquering race into a group of obscure ancestors. A savage, says Spencer, believes in another self because he looks in springs and listens to echoes, noticing the reflection and the sound. It was a common belief among the Indians that the living relations rendered the fate of the soul of the dead more comfortable by oblations. The Brahmins, the ministers of the oblations and ceremonies, had an interest in the division of ownership on account of the multiplication of acts of piety and gifts. Wherever ancestor-worship was established, paternity was recognized, judging from the fact that the ancestor worshiped and the worshiper both belong to the masculine sex. The ancestor worshiped had all the appearance of the Roman *paterfamilias*, or the subject of the *patria potestas*, writes Maine, the author of the greatest researches in primitive law on this subject. In India the eldest legitimate son could offer sacrifices for the soul of the deceased with the greatest efficiency. But if he was lacking, there succeeded to the rights and inheritance (that was a kind of state of spiritual servitude) the son of the daughter designated by the father. Among the Athenians there was the same custom, because a father who feared to die without sons had the right to bequeath his cloak to his daughter and her future husband; the son of this marriage grown to a certain age became a member of the family of his maternal grandfather, taking his name and his estate. If the father died intestate, the daughter was bound to marry a relation. So too, in the Middle Ages, it seems that where a daughter could not inherit, her son sometimes had the right of succession. There being no right in India to designate a daughter through whom the line of inheritance should go, it fell to the adopted children and then to the illegitimate children of women living in the family and subject to the authority of the decedent. These sons could fulfill all the rights, as even a slave could in Rome. If all these persons were lacking, there was the means of "niyoga" for the celebration of rites, which was practised even by the Hebrews and which shows, according to McLellan, the reality of the succession of polyandry to promiscuity. The sacrifices by this institution had to be celebrated by the son whom the widow had by a cognate relative, or, if there was none such, by an agnate, a member of the same family as her husband, or of the same caste. Moses ordered that if anyone died without a son, his brother could marry his widow and thus give children to the decedent, of whom the first bore his name. In India the inheritance of collaterals presents no little obscurity and at the beginning was not clearly determined. Upon the failure of relations in the descending line, the spiritual relations, the master, the co-disciple or king were called to the inheritance. It was believed that a collateral could not celebrate the sacrifices with sufficient efficiency. Later the hierarchic repugnance to fictitious affiliations necessitated their admittance. At the beginning, when the patriarchal family was formed, the mother was not worshiped, nor the maternal grandfather in his turn, since they were not equal in importance to the paternal ancestors.

§ 497. *Foundation of the Testamentary Right.* Various have been the theories of foundation of inheritance and especially of testamentary inheritance. The theories of Plato and of Aristotle on this subject were inspired directly by the political conditions of the place and time in which they were formed. Plato taught that the right to make a will is the result of the excessive condescension of the legislature, since the testator did not have full consciousness at his last moments; that for such a right there should be substituted the perpetual transmission of the estate in the same family; and that upon the failure of sons, the father should have the power to dispose of only one-tenth of his estate, the remainder going to his adopted son. Aristotle saw no other means for the preservation of the estate in the family than the abolition of the testamentary power, for which he would have substituted perpetual transmission in the male line. Roman philosophers, on the other hand, preferred the will, largely Roman in its birth and development. Cicero, Seneca, and Quintilian, assigning to this right the natural base of the sentiment of friendship and benevolence, were careful to bring to light the close connection between testamentary power and foresight for the future. The jurisconsults did not seek philosophical principles, but they did not know how to conceive of the power to will as the result of indulgent laws. Testamentary power in the eyes of Ulpian had but one relation to law, and that was to find in it no obstacle. "Lege obvenire hereditatem non improprie quis dixeret et eam quæ ex testamento defertur; quia lege XII. Tabularum testamentariæ hereditates confirmantur." And if Papinianus says, "Testamenta factio non priviti sed publici juris est," he did not mean to deny the natural base of the act of the last will, but was emphasizing external and incidental forms. The commentators discuss whether a will be "jure naturæ et gentium," or simply "juris civili." Theophilus accepts the belief that it is "jure naturæ et gentium," and enlarges the catalogue of Hermongenianus in the law "ex hoc jura," of the Digest. The Glossists and Alciati combat the natural origin of the will, basing their arguments on various citations from the early law. Bartolus and Baldo cite other places in opposition, and follow the contrary belief. Donnellus and Cujas develop the belief of Theophilus, and state that the right to will is based on the real connection between the individual and posterity. Among the writers on natural law who represent the two opposite doctrines, Grotius and Puffendorf are the most distinguished. Grotius believed that the power to will lies in natural law and likened it to a contract, defining it as an alienation, conditional upon death, revocable until the last moment of the life of the alienor, with reservation of possession and enjoyment in his favor. Wolff, Burlamaqui, Lampredi, Kant, and among the modern authorities, Troplong, accept the idea of Grotius.

Kant finds in the acquisition of an inheritance not a common and regular acquisition but an ideal one. He observes that the right conferred by a will upon the heir is the right of accepting after the death of the testator his promise made in his last moments to give his goods under certain conditions. The acquisition of the inheritance is based on a fictitious or ideal contract between the alienor and his heir which presumes acceptance in the manner indicated, because everyone wishes to enrich himself. The heir acquires a right of inheritance, not an inheritance, of which he has the property but not the possession, since he has only an *actio* for it. On the other hand, Puffendorf argues that a will is a creation of civil law and opposes its assimilation to contract, because a contract presupposes a meeting of two minds, which does not happen in the case of a will. Puffendorf is followed by Hennecius and St. Thomas, who cannot be persuaded that one man can transfer his estate to another when his will is no longer efficacious and he is no longer the owner. The French law of 1791, which abolished almost entirely the right to will, is the logical consequence of the conception that testacy has its foundation not in the nature of things but rather in convention and social utility. The speeches of Mirabeau, Robespierre, and Tronchet were inspired by the principles of Puffendorf, as Gabba says in his book on inheritance. First Bodin, afterwards Mably and Rousseau, accepted the Aristotelean theory that the State should dispose of the deceased's possessions, trying to keep them as far as possible in the family. Among the jurists prior to the codification, Bynkershoek says that when a man dies his goods are vacant, and by natural law anyone can take them. Cardinal De Luca and D'Aguesseau hold that the will belongs to positive law. Vinnio and Voet approve of the theory of Grotius. Gravina thinks that the origin of the right to will is natural. Finally, Leibnitz, in order to find a principle on which to base his theory of testacy, had recourse to the immortality of the soul. In the discussion which preceded the formation of the Code Napoleon, Bigot-Preameneu claimed that the will of the owner was the rule and intervention of the law,—an exception, because intestacy rested entirely upon the presumption of the will of the testator. Treilhard thought that the will had a natural origin. Portalis, finding the inseparability of the right to will and ownership, admitted that both rights were of the same nature. Such a conception has become common to philosophers and jurists of our century who think that intestate succession is the effect of family ownership. The philosophers and jurists of our age sometimes oppose the principle of individual ownership to that of family control, and *vice versa*, wishing to base the right of succession exclusively on one or the other of them. So some base the right of succession on the express will of the owner and succession *ab intestato* upon the presumption of his will, excluding the idea of domestic co-ownership. Others, on the contrary, like Hegel, Gans, and Stahl, make intestacy a primitive and normal succession and testamentary succession secondary and imitative, thus depriving the latter of a strong foundation. The real harmony lies in the antithesis of the two principles, as we will see; but first it is necessary to remark that the socialists, hostile to private property, combat (as is logical) the right of inheritance. Lassalle is distinguished in our day for the criticism of such a right, founded according to him on two antiquated notions, the absurd continuation of the will of a dead man, and the aristocratic co-ownership of goods in the Roman family. We may remark too, that the modern collectivists limit their denial of the right of inheritance to land and instruments of labor and recognize them for personalty, in which they recognize private property.

§ 498. *Intestacy is Founded on Family Co-ownership.* Before determining the foundation of inheritance, it is necessary to make two observations. The first is that the right of inheritance refers to social man and not to man in a hypothetical state of nature or isolation, and secondly to point out that a will is not essentially connected with the last instance of life but can be made at any time. These two considerations save the mind from prejudices which have had no little influence on the erroneous solution of the question. Now coming to intestacy, it cannot be doubted that its principle lies in consanguinity or in that ethical organism of the family which shows itself by a community of goods. When the family becomes certain and establishes itself in certain places, its definiteness prompts its members to the cultivation of land and later makes the beginning of ownership, which appears as a collection of means suitable to the preservation and development of that collective body. Ownership in a family should undergo modification according to the nature and purpose of the family itself, which is an interpenetration of persons, a communion of sentiments, affections, ideas, and wills. There cannot fail to be co-ownership. In every age and country the members of the conjugal and domestic societies have made assignments of family goods upon the death of one of them and have thought themselves injured if a stranger took possession of any. The sons, participators in the community, did not acquire upon the death of the father a new right but merely obtained greater freedom in the administration of the goods. In the early Roman law we have found this conception, which is not aristocratic but directly the opposite. "In suis heredibus evidentius apparet continuationem domini eo rem perducere, ut nulla videatur hereditas fuisse,

quasi olim hi domini essent qui etiam vivo patre quodam-
modo domini existimantur: unde etiam filiusfamilias
appelantur, sicut paterfamilias, sola nota hac adjecta per
quam distinguitur genitor ab eo qui genitus est; itaque post
mortem patris non hereditatem percipere videntur: sed
magis liberam bonorum administrationem consequuntur:
hac ex causa licet non sint heredes instituti, domini sunt."
The domestic co-ownership of the Romans, however, is
so rigorously conceived as to render the goods of the
family inalienable, acquiring the quality of "sui et
necessari." The inalienability of family goods not only
descends from the ancient Roman law but is the principle of all primitive laws, which always regard the entity
and not the individual as the subject. True domestic
co-ownership should not be understood in this manner,
which is a breach of individual rights, neither should
it be looked upon as a "communio pro indiviso" in
which the co-owner has an equal right to individual
ownership on the "pars pro indiviso," that is, where the
family is an unequal society with superiors and inferiors.
The inequality does not render co-ownership impossible,
but only makes the different members enjoy an unequal
property right. Domestic co-ownership is *sui generis*
and presupposes that important distinction between relative and absolute property originally conceived by Rosmini. It is founded on the full and absolute right of the
father, head, governor and representative of the family
and on the relative rights of its members, who have a right
conditioned upon the death of the father. Whoever,
teaches Rosmini, has a full property right in something
over which another person has a relative property right
can use and consume the thing to a definite and reasonable extent. If there is co-ownership, which is an association between him who has a full right and him who has a
relative right, the first must use it for the purposes of the

co-ownership and society. To the absolute owner, that is, to the head, belongs the decision of what are necessary or useful expenses of the family according to the norm of a wise control. The nature of relative property being what it is, and this right of property not being limited except in relation to a full owner, it follows that he has a right above all other persons to its use and control; and that upon the death of the full owner these goods become his absolutely. From this, Rosmini goes on, comes the right of the relative owners not to limit in the hands of the full owner the use and consumption of goods gotten or acquired by him, but to demand that they be so placed that at the death of the full owner they can be distinguished so that he can succeed to all his property. With this premise it is easy to overcome the beliefs and doctrines of those who wish to base intestacy on the necessity of educating children, consent, benevolence, the presumption of the will of the deceased, or occupancy. If heredity exists only in the necessity of educating the children, it loses its own nature and becomes a simple pension established for educational purposes, a pension which has no reason for continued existence when it has attained its end. The mere sentiment of benevolence is not of itself a claim or right. The conception of a presumption of will denies the right of the family and is the result of the principle of individual caprice, express, tacit, or presumed, and supposes a prior testamentary inheritance. The theory of occupancy considers man as unattached and vagrant, without any thought of the future. Man, according to this way of looking at it, is a force which cannot be effective after death. Such theory, besides, lays open the way to general warfare, because everyone would enter the struggle to occupy the inheritance and, what is worse, the victory in this bitter struggle would not always belong to the relations.

§ 499. *Testacy is Founded on Ownership.* If the immediate foundation of intestacy rests on consanguinity and domestic co-ownership, that of testamentary succession is based on the right of property; he who is owner of something can dispose of it freely, saving always that he fulfills his duties. The right to will is inseparable from ownership, from which it gets its reason and intention. It has its deepest roots in the heart of man, who is a social and collective subject, and responds to the natural impulse by which everyone more or less tends to prolong his memory in future generations. In general, the right of inheritance connects the activity of the person whose inheritance it is with that of those dear to him who survive him. It represents the connecting bonds of humanity in history. Without inheritance history could not proceed, because the present is the continuation of the past and the germ of the future. Heredity is the indispensable condition for the multiplication of capital, the increase of production and wealth, because it is clear that man would not have the impulse to work and to subject himself to privations and pain if he were not sure of being able to leave his estate to his family and to dispose of his goods. Neither do the facts that according to natural law testamentary dispositions were not recognized, or that the act takes place when the will of the testator is no longer efficient through death, or that after death one feels neither pain or injury, contradict this theory. Those who believed that these facts show the theory untenable hold that the statutes give an "actio violati sepulcri" and "actio injuriarum" for a slandered memory, through a sentiment of humanity for the insult to the honor of the existing family. But in the first place, the will of the testator is efficient at the moment when he makes his disposition, since it is the will of a living

owner; and the volitive act of an individual in legal
form acquires a substance and a duration independent
of the life of the subject from whom it emanates.   A
will is an act that stands by itself, differing from a contract or gift.   It is not a contract because the testator can
always revoke it, and a transference of goods revocable
at any time cannot be called an agreement.   Nor can it
be a conditional contract because the conditions would be
potential and would lie entirely in the "si voluero;" in other
words, the testator would transfer his goods to the heir on
condition that he wished to keep his promise.   It is clear
that the actions for desecration of a grave and for defa-
mation are given for the purpose which we have noted
above; but besides such objects there is another, the protection of the physical and moral inviolability of a man
that has continued a past and begun a future generation.
The tomb is the resting place of the human remains and
the home of the soul, — of a will and a personality in decomposition.   A man's memory, reputation, and honor
constitute the projection of his existence, forming his
moral life, which continues beyond the tomb.   The recognition of such a life does not include necessarily the idea
of the immortality of the soul as a legal principle.   The
moral life finds its existence in the estimation and honor
of the person; both continue in the memory and consciousness of his survivors without need of recognizing
the immortality of the soul, on which Leibnitz and Rosmini found the testamentary right.   The republic of the
souls, for these two philosophers, is not a chimera.
Admitting the immortality of the soul, it is incredible,
they say, that a soul after the loss of its body should
not still have some relation with other persons, which
binds it and gives it what is its natural due, the desire
for its last will to have weight with its fellow-beings.   The
dead have rights not of themselves, but through those

who hold them dear, and by those who take their inheritance. "Heredes una cum defuncto persona reputantur," the early Romans teach us. Now a spirit exercises its rights most beneficially when in virtue of its desires the surviving heirs enjoy the property left behind, which enjoyment is a virtual exercise of its rights because it is the effecting of its last will. If this will is not observed, the exercise of its rights is denied, and it is robbed of its property. There are some who have not placed the true value on this beautiful and noble theory of Leibnitz and Rosmini, because we must recognize that legal relations and institutions should be derived from principles of reason and not from religious beliefs. For many, the immortality of the soul is not philosophically demonstrable nor can it be considered as a postulate of practical reason although accepted as an object of faith.

CHAPTER XXII

INTESTACY AND THE WILL

THE DEGREE AND QUALITY OF RELATIONSHIP. — THE CAPAC-
ITY OF SUCCESSION. — THE CLASSES OF HEIRS. — REPRESENTA-
TION. — CAPACITY TO MAKE A WILL OR TO RECEIVE THROUGH
A WILL. — KINDS OF WILLS. — INTESTACY. — THE RIGHT OF REP-
RESENTATION AND TESTAMENTARY SUCCESSION. — MISTAKES
IN THE UNDERLYING AND IMMEDIATE CAUSE. — CONDITIONS. —
THE RIGHT TO THE INCREASE. — SUBSTITUTION AND TRUSTS. —
PRINCIPLES COMMON TO ALL KINDS OF SUCCESSION.

§ 500. *Intestate Succession Follows the Degrees of Relationship.* Intestacy is founded on the ties of blood and
should be regulated by the quality of relationship. Relationship is the bond existing between persons of the same
stock. Its degree is measured by the number of generations, each generation forming a degree. In quality of
relationship, first come descendants, then ancestors, and
lastly collaterals; relations of a nearer degree exclude any
of a greater degree. These are principles of natural law
which Justinian recognized in regulating ascending inheritance, decreeing that the nearer ancestors, paternal and
maternal, should be preferred to the remote without regard to the origin of the inheritance, and that only with
the ancestors of equal degree should the inheritance be
divided, a moiety going to the paternal and a moiety to
the maternal ancestors, regardless of their relative numbers. Modern legislatures have followed the Novella
and have thus sanctioned the precepts of natural reason.

§ 501. *Incapacities of Intestate Succession.* Everybody, as a general rule, has a right of inheritance. In

our day, foreigner, monk, or prisoner for life can inherit
as they are no longer considered to have ceased to be persons. A foreigner has civil rights which belong to him in
his quality of man; a monk, if a citizen, has civil and
political rights; a prisoner for life can be deprived
only of those rights which cannot be reconciled with his
condition. He no longer has political rights, nor the *patria potestas*, nor can he be appointed a guardian; he will
be subject to a legal prohibition by which he cannot administer his own estate, but there is no reason for denying him the right of inheritance. And yet there are some
persons incapable of inheritance, though these are the
exception. The incapable properly so called are incapable in respect to any inheritance and can never acquire
property by succession. Some incapable through crime,
are excluded, only inheriting from him against whom
they have committed the culpable act.[1] Those also are
incapable of inheritance who at the time of the vesting
of it are not yet conceived, as they have no existence.
Those who are conceived can take the inheritance when
they are born, by what we have said before.[2] Those are
incapable through crime who have murdered or tried to
murder the person from whom they would inherit, and
also those who have calumniously accused the deceased
of an infamous crime; and those who have hindered
him from making a will or have caused him to make one,
or have suppressed, altered, or changed any disposition
of it. Incapacity properly so called exists and acts of
itself; incapacity through crime presupposes a legal
conviction.

§ 502. *Four Kinds of Intestate Succession; Relations.*
There are four classes of heirs *ab intestato*, legitimate
relations, natural relations, surviving husband or wife,

[1] They lose the inheritance if they had acquired it.
[2] *Cf.* § 180 *ante.*

and the State. The first class is divided into three orders, descendants, ancestors, and collaterals. Love of descendants is the most intense and therefore there is no doubt as to their inheritance. "Nullum dubium est quia omnia quæ nostra sunt liberis nostris ex voto paremus," says the early Roman law. Children, therefore, whether male or female, of any marriage should be preferred above all other heirs. The descendants of children come next, according to proximity of degree to the deceased; the quality of consanguinity should prevail over the degree. The legitimated and the adopted children who are in every way like the legitimate should be numbered among the latter. After the children come the ancestors, because "amor primum descendit deinde ascendit." The parents take equal shares in an inheritance from a son, since the son's affection for his father and mother should be equal. If he dies leaving no father or mother, the inheritance should belong to the nearest ancestor without distinction of lineage. The third order is formed by the collaterals, all bound together by strict bonds and constituting a family living under the same roof, brought up and educated with equal care. If with the parents are brothers and sisters of the whole blood, they inherit equally. Half brothers and sisters cannot be excluded from participation because they are bound by sufficiently strong affection to the descendant, but they should take in smaller proportions than the brothers and sisters of the whole blood, who are more closely bound together. If brothers and sisters are the nearest survivors of the decedent they should be preferred to all others. When there are no brothers and sisters, the descendants should take by representation and succeed to the positions of their uncles and aunts, or if they are lacking, the nearest relation. There is a point, however, where the inheritance of collaterals stops because the consciousness of family unity and relationship fails. At this point the State becomes the heir, as is reasonable, because relationship beyond a certain degree is not felt.

§ 503. *Natural Relatives in Intestacy.* The second class is formed of natural relatives. Children born out of matrimony recognized voluntarily or through judicial declaration can share in the inheritance of their parents. And it is right that they should not be deprived of it, because they are more intimately and deeply bound to the authors of their days than collaterals. On the other hand, the law cannot make the position of natural children equal to that of the legitimate children if it wishes to protect morality and to preserve the true rational family. It is true that natural children come into the world without any fault of their own; but this is no reason to treat them equally with legitimate children though it should give them some right to participate in the inheritance.

§ 504. *Husband and Wife under the Intestate Laws.* The surviving husband or wife represents the third kind or class of heir even by natural law, because in matrimony there is that deep and full interpenetration of two persons, often spoken of before, which cannot fail to be sufficient title to make the surviving consort share in the inheritance of the decedent. The survivor must not be exposed to danger of poverty through the perversity of heirs; his existence should not depend upon the pleasure of the children and he should have a share not less than theirs. The Roman "quarta uxoria" does not conform to this conception since it is given only to the poor and undowered wife who must undergo the humiliation of proving her own need in order to obtain the hereditary alms. If the right of succession belongs to the surviving consort, provision must be made that the estate of one family should not enter another through a second marriage.

The statute should distinguish in the protection given to the surviving consort when these are their children and when there are only distant and remote relations.

§ 505. *The State is the Ultimate Heir*. The fourth class of heir is the State. The estate of a decedent who has not any relatives must be regarded as vacant, and therefore belong to the State. It is right that the goods should devolve to the State, for no one beyond the degrees of consanguinity that have ethical weight should inherit by the intestate laws. The county with which the individual is connected by closer ties would not be an irrational beneficiary which could use it for works of beneficence, possibly in his name.

§ 506. *Transmission; Succession per Stirpes and per Capita*. If, in intestacy, those first entitled are lacking or are incapable of inheriting, their descendants take their place and rights, not of themselves but by representation. They inherit of their own right when they have a right of immediate inheritance by the statutes. By transmission (*transmitio*) the heir of him takes in whose favor the inheritance first lay, and who died without having tacitly or expressly accepted it or without having renounced it. Succession by representation is immediate, and that by transmission is mediate, because in the first the inheritance has not devolved to him who has died or been declared incapable, and in the second the "delatio heretatis" has happened in favor of him who takes by transmission. They inherit *per capita* who are of the same degree and participate in the inheritance in equal parts; the others who are substituted in the place of another inherit *per stirpes*. The representatives take what would have belonged to the man whom they represent and divide it among themselves or according to their branches, all *per stripes*. Representation has a natural reason because the affection is constant and the love of ancestors intense towards their descendants both of the second and greater degrees, and because the children as members of the family and clothed with family rights, among which is that of inheriting the estate of their parents, are put in their place. It is not equitable to make the misfortune for a son in the death of his father greater by depriving him of his inheritance from his grandfather or uncle. Neither is it right to inflict the effects of incapacity upon innocent individuals because "peccata suos teneant auctores." Representation, therefore, conforms to the principles of the family and of equity and cannot be reduced to a mere invention of civil law, since it is a derivative of ties of blood. Its reasons are found in the direct line of descent indefinitely and in the collateral lines up to a certain point. Representation among the descendants of brothers and sisters of the decedent can be admitted because the children of a brother or sister are considered part of the family to which he or she belongs. The nephew considers his uncle almost like a father and the uncle feels a semi-paternal love for his nephew. Further the reason for representation does not go. It is not at all possible among ancestors, since love descends and does not ascend; a stream never flows to its source; the ancestor is always the head of the family of descendants. It is a matter of general belief that the inheritance from distant descendants cannot take place immediately; but the son of a man who has renounced the inheritance from his father inherits from his grandfather by his own right, being the nearest cognate.

§ 507. *Testamentary Succession.* Coming now to testamentary succession, we must remember that everybody is capable of making a will or of taking through a will except certain persons determined by law. The same principle is applied here as in the case of intestate succession, because inheritance is a natural right.   They clearly are incapable of making a will who through immaturity have not fullness of judgment, and those not of sane mind.   The testator who has become blind with anger against his legal heirs can be considered not of sane mind and they will have, therefore, an action "ab irato"; neither can a will be made under in‐ fluence of violence, trickery or duress.   Fraud has two forms, — undue influence and deceit.   Undue influence consists in gifts, demonstrations of affection generally sim‐ ulated, services, complacency, and prayers, with the object of winning liberality.   Deceit that differs from illicit per‐ suasion is accompanied by a series of acts intended to surprise the mind of the testator, inspiring in him a dis‐ position different from what he really has, as if a reply were suggested to an equivocal question contrary to the understanding of the testator.   Then those who are not conceived and those that are guilty of crime are incapable of inheriting.   But the law of testamentary inheritance can admit the children of a person living at the time of the testator's death to the inheritance although they are not conceived.   In doing this it does not make a precept con‐ trary to the dictates of reason, because it allows the testa‐ tor to benefit the children of a dissipated person and does not tie up the inheritance for a long time.   There are those who are incapable of inheriting from certain per‐ sons, as the executor before the approval of his account, the notary, the witness to his will, and he who has writ‐ ten a secret will in which there is no approval of the leg‐ acy in the handwriting of the testator.   For other persons there is a partial relative incapacity.   They cannot receive more than a definite fraction from certain descendants.   For example, it is not permissible to leave children born out of matrimony, even if recog‐ nized, more than the proportion established by law.

A widower who marries again cannot leave to his second wife a greater proportion then he leaves to the children of the first.

§ 508. *Forms of Ordinary Wills.* There are ordinary and special wills: the ordinary are of two kinds, one the holograph, written throughout, dated and subscribed by the hand of the testator, and the other by notarial act. A holographic will separates the testator from every foreign influence and gives him full freedom of providing for his inheritance without the dangers of an anticipated publicity. It presents, however, some inconveniences because it is uncontrolled by any kind of legal form and remains essentially a private act. It is evident that the legislature should not hinder the free expression of the will of a disponer by many and grave formalities, but it must insist upon some to establish the certainty and the freedom of testamentary dispositions. In our day the art of forgery is well developed, and handwritings are difficult to prove. And the opportunities of forging a will are many when there is no necessity of depositing it with a public official. Let us, therefore, preserve the holographic will, but impose an obligation of filing or recording. It is necessary in general to lessen the formalities in cases of plague, or voyages, wars, and residence abroad. To these requirements the laws regulating special wills are made to conform.

§ 509. *Coexisting Testacy and Intestacy; The Reserve.*[1] In Roman legislation the principle, "Nemo pro parte testatus pro parte intestatus decedere potest," was strong. The reasons for this principle were two, — the desire to avoid division of the "sacra privata" and the supposed impossibility of the division of the "universum jus defuncti." The first reason has fallen into the realm

[1] The reserve is the portion which by Continental law the testator is not allowed to will, but which is governed by the intestate laws. J. L.

of history; the second is founded on a conception foreign
to the "universum jus" because it is not dismembered
but remains one in the multiplicity of individual representatives, successors of a common identity who continue the personality of the decedent in this world.
Intestacy and testacy can therefore coexist. And their
coexistence is essentially necessary since it can be shown
that intestacy alone would absorb the whole right of
the individual and testacy alone would deny the right
of the family. The wisdom of centuries has found harmony in the coexistence of the two kinds of inheritance,
in the division of the estate of the "de cujus" into a
devisable part and a reserve. This system conforms
to reason because it sacrifices the right neither of the
family nor the individual, but pays them equal regard.
There is no doubt that the foundation of the reserve
lies in the "jura sanguinis," in the right of the family.
It is enjoyed by the heirs, but at the same time its
preservation is of general interest since it looks to the
hereditary transmission of goods, a powerful means for
the preservation of the family and therefore of civil
society. It is not a derivative of the obligation to supply
necessaries because it cannot be reduced to a simple
pension, neither is it an offshoot of the civil and legal conversion of natural duties of parents, because if so conceived it would be able to take the same position as the
right of a creditor and be at the absolute disposal of the
legislator. The reserve brings into existence the principle of domestic co-ownership. It is the quota of the
inheritance due by law and inviolable. The reserve
as a quota of the inheritance cannot be demanded or
renounced during the life of the "de cujus." It can be of
any kind, personal or real, or consist of choses in action,
existing at the date of the vesting of the inheritance.
It entails an obligation for the payment of debts. Since

the reserve is ordered by law, it protects the family rights and it follows that the heir who takes under the will can claim besides his legacy a right to the reserve itself, of which he cannot be deprived even by the testator. Disinheritance (allowed by Roman law before and after Justinian and by many modern civil laws) allows the testator to follow any unreasonable caprice and is not necessary when the "hereditas" can be lost through unworthiness. Causes of unworthiness can be sufficiently increased to allow the complete abolishment of disinheritance. And it is necessary, therefore, to consider as unworthy those who are guilty of insults, maltreatment, or injury towards the "de cujus." The reserve, founded on the substantial right of the family and established by law, is inviolable, whence it belongs in property and possession to the heir and is not subject to conditions, terms, or burdens.

§ 510.   *The Criticism of the Reserve*.[1]   The institution of the reserve, not recognized by the common law, has been the subject of much criticism and discussion among jurists and economists.   It has been said, for example, that a father has no obligation to leave his children a part of his property, but is only bound to give them a good education; that the idea of domestic co-ownership is aristocratic and feudal; and that the centre of modern society is the individual.   This objection should have no weight because it confuses the substance with the method.   Co-ownership is the intrinsic ideal of the intimate communion of the family; it has acquired different forms because the family itself has passed through many phases.   Should we perhaps destroy property and family because they had at one time a feudal character?   It is not true that the centre of modern society is the individual.   The affirmation of that means

[1] *Cf.* § 509, n. 1, *ante*.

falling into individualism, where every man is considered as an abstract entity, as an atom, and not in relation to his diverse qualities and positions in the family, bodies corporate, and the State.   It is said that the children may have special resources; that is no reason for depriving them of their rights.   It can be said further that the children may be unworthy, without reflection that either their unworthiness is great and then the law will exclude them from the inheritance, or else it is small and then it is not right to deny them their reserve because a father will always be able to reward or punish them with the part at his disposition.   For this part can serve to equalize the conditions of the children when some are not able to help themselves by their own intelligence and activity.   The accusation of producing inertia among the heirs has been brought against the reserve but following this to its logical conclusion we could decide that in order to increase individual activity we should dispossess them by taxation because in this way we would make them more active. Not enough regard is given to the fact that this reserve fund may be the first capital to work with and that it is much more difficult to get together the first few pennies than to acquire the second quarter of a million.   Finally, the reserve is accused of dividing the estate.   But it has been observed that the condition of property is good because it produces an equality and independence conferring on many, means suitable to sustain life, and makes labor possible by the application of capital to industry. It is, therefore, a guarantee of order; it increases love of country, since it attaches the owner to the soil.   Division of property is an evil only when it breaks it up into petty values.   This evil can be guarded against in many ways.   In conclusion, the reserve has the merit of preserving the family from thoughtless liberality and of dividing the property and capital.   It impedes, if but slightly, the increase of population in the aristocratic classes which are generally incapable of giving work to society in any considerable quantity or quality, as the economist, Rossi, a champion of the reserve, has said, whose authority can well be opposed to that of Stuart Mill, the champion of unlimited testamentary power.

§ 511. *Extent of the Reserve.*[1] The reserve belongs to the legitimated and adopted children and their descendants, as they enjoy all the rights of the family. Adoption makes the adopted son the equal of the legitimate but a personal relation always differentiates them. Grandchildren and descendants come in by the right of representation. If the testator does not leave children or descendants the reserve belongs to the ancestors who are debtors of their descendants to the amount of the reserve. There is here a reciprocal obligation of true natural law. To the wife and natural son a reserve is given by the principles of justice. It is not always considered as a quota of the inheritance since an effort is made to favor children, ancestors, and in general the legitimate family. In fact, the law sometimes prescribes that the portion belonging to the wife can be satisfied by the heirs through a life estate or an assignment of interest, and that due a natural son can be paid off in money. The law establishes a determinate portion for a widow and natural son if taken from the portion which can be willed, in order not to prejudice the stronger title to the intestate part, which is the right of the descendants and ancestors. The reserve for collaterals is not possible when the system of private and acquired goods is destroyed which tends to the destruction of the family estate. The development of industry and commerce and the knowledge of

[1] *Cf.* § 509, n. 1, *ante.*

the effective limits of the family understood in a particular sense have destroyed the last vestige of the mediæval system, unknown to the Romans. A collateral reserve is not based on the philosophy of law because the brothers and sisters are centres of other families, neither is it based on social interest which does not need a limitation of the testamentary power through the enjoyment of a modern reserve by the brothers and sisters. If the testator wishes to benefit either of these he can very easily do it. We can note that these persons *per se* had no right of inheritance in Roman law. To fix the measure of the reserve rationally, it is necessary to take into consideration both the degree and kind of relationship and the economic situation of the family. To harmonize the economic situation and principles of justice, it is necessary that the reserve be neither too little nor too great. If it is too little, it will not be a reserve but rather a pension for necessaries and would lead to the same evils as unlimited testamentary power. If it is too large, it will absorb the right of individual property. The right of the family must be balanced with the right of individual. The system of absolute proportionality between the reserve and the number of heirs, which was adopted at the time of the French Revolution, absorbs the testamentary power; the other of the limited proportionality accepted by Justinian and the French Code is unjust and often ineffective. It does not always attain its object, because the ratio should be stopped at a certain point unless one wishes to destroy testamentary power; and by stopping it one decrees an equal portion for five children as for eight or ten. Besides it is not just because it limits capriciously the right of the individual owner and disposer. It can be noted that such a system renders the inheritance of the estate uncertain in case of the survivorship of the children. The system of the invariable quota, whatever the number of heirs, followed by the Custom of Paris, by the Code Napoleon and the Italian Code, seems preferable because it considers equally the two contradictory rights and takes account of economic factors in a general way. In the most cases, the number of the descendants to inherit is greater than the number of ancestors (and descendants are more frequently heirs); the quota, therefore, reserved for descendants should be greater than for ancestors. It is true that the result of this system is that the intestate inheritance is very small if there are many children. But it is impossible to hope to conform to the indefinite variety of economic needs in all the combinations of life. The law should consider what ordinarily happens, "id quod plerumque accidit." When a reserve is allowed it is evident that the acts of liberality *inter vivos* or by the will should be reduced if they exceed the disposable part. Above all the legacies should be reduced proportionally among "hæredes" and then the legatees; if that is not enough the "donationes" should be disregarded, proceeding from the last to the first. The legacies should be reduced first because they are acts and not contracts as the "donationes"; the last gift goes first because this is often enough to supply the reserve. The testator has always the power of foreseeing the possibility of a reduction and of giving a preference to a legacy or gift.

§ 512.   *No Representation in Testamentary Succession.* The question arises if the right of representation is applicable to testamentary succession. After serious reflection on this subject it does not seem to be regularly applicable because in testamentary succession the reasons on which the right of representation is based are lacking; there is a mediate transference of estate. Often the legatee is no relation to the testator and therefore ties of blood, domestic equity, principles of family life should not be relied on. The affection of the testator is directed to the person to whom the realty or personalty is given if he is a stranger and does not extend to his descendants. In other words, the descendants of a legatee obtain the realty or personalty by transmission and not by representation presupposing a "delatio hereditatis" or transfer of the right in favor of the legatee, and do not immediately come into the inheritance by act of law as happens in the case of representation. A representative is placed in the position and given the rights of the man he represents by the virtue of the law without the necessity of the devolution of the inheritance in his favor. This is in force in inheritance *ab intestato*. A testamentary inheritance, on the contrary, depends directly on the will of the testator and does not come into the power of the legatee unless by possession. It cannot as a rule pass to the descendants of the heir without "delatio;" therefore their inheritance is mediate and transmissive. The effects of transmission are different from those of representation, because the descendants of an "hæres" take the inheritance as representatives and do not exclude the co-heir or substituted heir and would not hinder the right of accrual. But descendants taking by transmission would exclude the co-heir and the substituted heir, and would prevent the right. But sometimes a legatee is bound to the testator as a descendant, brother, or sister. In such a case the same reasons for representation as in intestacy are found, because the descendants of the legatee are in respect to the testator in that line or degree of relationship in which there would have been representation if it were a question of inheritance *ab intestato*. If the legatee is predeceased or unworthy, his descendants will receive the inheritance by a right analogous to that of representation in intestacy, which is considered as a kind of tacit or legal surrogation not extended to the descendants of legatees in general, as is easily understood, because it is based on the ties of blood. It was different under Theodosian transmission introduced into Roman law by a law of Theodosius the Second and Valentinian: "Filios seu filias, nepotes aut neptes, pronepotes vel proneptes a patre vel matre, avo vel avia, proavo vel proavia scriptos heredes, licet non sint invicem substituti, seu cum extraneis, seu soli sint instituti, et ante apertas tabulas defunctis (sive se noverint scriptos heredes, sive ignoraverint), in liberos suos cuiuscumque sint.sexus vel gradus, derelictam sibi hereditariam portionem posse transmittere, memoratasque personas (si tamen hereditatem non recusant) nulla huiusmodi præscriptione sibi obstante, eam tamquam debitam vindicare. Quod scilicet etiam super legatis, seu fideicommissis a patre vel matre, avo vel avia, proavo vel proavia derelictis locum habet." Justinian confirmed the Theodosian transmission but it was very different from representation because it supposed that the legatee should die before the reading of the will and not before the death of the testator. It was, therefore, a true case of transmission and not of representation. The Italian Code holds with the above enunciated principle that the descendants of a predeceased or incapable legatee will be given the inheritance or legacy in cases in which representation in their favor would have been lost, if it were a case of intestacy, unless the testator has otherwise disposed of it; provided that it is a question of a legacy of rent or a right of a personal nature.

§ 513. *Requisites of Wills.* There are many more things to note about the disposable part of an estate. In the first place, a legatee may be designated in any manner whatsoever, the only requisite being that he should not be so uncertain as not to be determinable. Every disposition of the testator must be certain and original, that is, not dependent on the will of a third party. In the second place, an error in respect to the underlying cause of the will cannot have the same effect as one that refers to the immediate cause. The first renders the will invalid because the testator would not have made that disposition if he had known of a fact, for example, the existence of an only son whom he believed dead. The second has not an annulling effect because the impulsive cause is accessory and not determining; the will to dispose is followed with the impulse taken away. A legacy given to one of the children of a father in consideration of a numerous offspring holds good even if at the moment of the testator's death the number of children has been much reduced. In the third place, it is necessary to notice that the testator can impose burdens upon the legatee, or if he has left it *sub modo* he can impose conditions. Conditions can be of as many kinds as those in contract. The Romans taught that immoral, impossible, and illegal conditions in a will "vitiantur et non vitiant" because they were looked upon as the effects of mental weakness which should not make innocent third parties suffer who had not consented to them. But the Roman doctrine, received by some codes, should not be followed, because mental disturbance destroys the will. If the testator knows what he is doing he cannot be ignorant of the fact that the fulfillment of the above kind of condition is contrary to nature and law, and therefore it is logical to infer that he has not true desire to leave his substance to the legatee. The validity or invalidity of the legacy depends less upon the regard which the heirs merit than upon the state of mind of the testator at the moment in which he makes his will. Conditions which prevent a marriage are considered contrary to the principle of freedom but the "conditio viduitatis" is not, it being inequitable that the wife should violate the faithfulness which her deceased husband wished kept by contracting a second marriage, and still profit by his generosity. It is true that the survivor can live an immoral life without losing the legacy. But this cannot be helped because the deceased has trusted to morality the faithfulness of the survivor. The recognition of the above condition is bound up with the desire to favor the interest of the children. In the fourth place, we must mention the right of accrual and substitution. The right of contribution is the right by which the portion of a legatee who cannot take his legacy devolves upon the co-heirs named jointly in a single clause of the same will without distribution. It must be presumed that the legatees named this way are considered by the testator as a single person, and therefore if one fails his part should go to the profit of the others. If the legatees are given unequal parts the presumption ceases and the part which fails falls into the intestate estate. Whoever has full right of disposal of part of the goods not reserved can name an heir or legatee in the second degree, that is, to take upon the failure of the legatee of the first degree. This is substitution which can be direct or indirect. Direct substitution is that by virtue of which the substitute inherits directly from the decedent. Simple substitution is of this kind because it is for relatives made by the testator in the second or greater grades in case the heir of the preceding grade does not take the inheritance. Simple substitution is called reciprocal when testamentary co-heirs are substituted one in place of the other. Another example of direct substitution would be the "pupillare" of the Roman law, which takes place when a father appoints an heir in place of a son who may die a minor. Of the two direct substitutions, the simple conforms to reason because the right of disposition of the testator is not exercised in a manner to bind the property. On the other hand, the testator has the right to an actual heir chosen by him and can provide for the case in which the first named does not wish or cannot take. The Roman pupillary substitution is no longer admissible because it is the consequence of the *patria potestas* which no longer exists, by which the will of the father took the place of the will of a minor son in making final disposition of his property. Indirect and uncertain substitution is the "fidei commissus," dependent upon the obligation of reserving or restoring some part of the inheritance or all of it to a third person. This kind of substitution is no longer recognized because it is the effect of the unreasonable caprice of an old man with one foot in the grave and ties up the commerciability of the legacy. We must not confuse this kind of substitution with a trust estate which exists where someone is made heir with the secret agreement of being only an administrator or bailee of the inheritance until it can be restored to the legatee. Fideicommissary substitution is patently accompanied by the burden of preserving and restoring and prevents the alienation of the goods, but the legatee can enjoy them, while a trustee can keep nothing, and must return the inheritance with the interest. To-day, testamentary trusts are recognized, but the Italian Civil Code forbids the proof of a trust in order to avoid many difficulties except where the trust was employed to aid a person incapable of inheritance. In that case alone, one is allowed to prove that the legatee is a trustee. The making of a legatee by a certain day or until a certain day is not permissible, since it is trust. For if a legatee is only appointed after a given day, the heir at law will inherit from the testator with the duty to preserve and restore, and if the legatee is appointed from a certain day the heir-at-law will have to restore the inheritance to the estate or to the subsequent legatee.   Finally we must mention a few dispositions under particular bequests and trusts. A trust is a disposition under a particular clause by which the testator imposes an obligation in favor of a third person.   It is logical that the testator to make a trust should have the faculty of disposing or willing.   The trustee on his side must have the capacity of receiving by will because the legacy is a part of the inheritance. Any legatee can be burdened by a trustee's duties, even an "hæres," as well as legatees and adopted or substituted "hæredes."   You must note that on the reserve no burdens, conditions, or obligations can be thrown because it is the part consecrated to the family by statute. Everything can be willed which is in the trade of the legatee or can be useful to him.   Things not in the trade of the testator or for the legatee but in the trade of the beneficiary can be willed.   Existing things, future, realty, personalty, particular objects, titles to rights and corporeal and incorporeal objects are the subject of trusts.

§ 514.   *The Vesting of a Legacy.*   The common principles of every kind of inheritance refer to vesting, devolution, acceptance, refusal, the division of the inheritance, and to collation.[1]   The inheritance vests at the death of the testator or the person from whom the inheritance comes.   Inheritance from a living man is not possible because whoever is alive has and exercises as pleases him the right of property.   The vesting of the inheritance makes the moment certain in which it begins to exist and can devolve; and at that instant, therefore, one should find conditions which make the heirs capable of inheriting.   The devolution, as conceived by the German law and by the French and Italian Codes, is the passage of the inheritance into the power of the heirs, accompanied by the power of acceptance or refusal.   They

[1] *Cf.* § 516 *post.*

have full right from the moment of the vesting of the inheritance, both in respect to property and possession. This is the signification of the old German and French motto, "the dead give to the living." We must observe that the maxim would be true if the inheritance was irrefusable, if there still existed, as there did in Rome, "heredes necessari" who inherited even "invito animo," slaves, for example, or "heredes sui," who at first were involuntary heirs as were the sons and descendants of the deceased, so made by the *patria potestas* at the moment of death. But these two kinds of heirs no longer exist, because modern law only recognizes voluntary heirs out of respect for principles of individual liberty. If an act of will is necessary for the renunciation of the inheritance, it would be logical and just to demand for its acquisition the act of "aditio" established by the Romans for "heredes voluntarii" or "extranei." The modern conception of devolution is contradicted, because the acquisition *ipso jure* is not in accord with the contemporaneous existence of the faculty of accepting or refusing; neither can it be reconciled with the existence of unclaimed legacies. Acquisition is the result of the exercise of such a faculty and cannot logically come first. The three Roman principles, the "acquisitio ipso jure" for the "heredes sui," the "aditio" for strangers, and the judicial act for the "bonorum possessor" form the base of the three existing legislative systems existing in Europe to-day. The first principle is followed by the French, Prussian, and Italian law, the second by Saxon law, the third by the Austrian Code.

§ 515. *Acceptance of a Legacy.* The acceptance of an inheritance can be simple or with an inventory. The first is express, when one assumes the title and quality of heir by an act, or tacit if the heir does some act that necessarily shows an intention of accepting and which he would have no right to do except as heir; it is presumed, if by force of law and in consequence of his acts he is retained as heir without the contrary being admissible or provable; this happens where one conceals the inheritance.   The effect of acceptance pure and simple exists in the commingling of the estate of the heir and that of the decedent and therefore the heir is personally liable to the creditors of the decedent "ultra vires hereditatis." Acceptance with the benefit of the inventory, always express, prevents the commingling of the two estates. Therefore, the heir is obligated to the creditors of the deceased only to the extent of his inheritance. The renunciation must always be express and never presumed. Both acceptance and renunciation can be made during the life of the "de cujus" or when the inheritance vests.   An inheritance in common between heirs can produce much inconvenience and many disadvantages but they can proceed amicably or legally to a partition which is a declarative or specific setting aside of their quota of a common inheritance.   The quota of each co-heir is certain in quality but uncertain in quidity.   With the division this uncertainty ceases and each heir is held the single and immediate owner of his part.

§ 516. *Collation.* A collation is the restitution which a descendant co-heir makes to the hereditary estate in favor of brothers, sisters, and their descendants, of all he has received from the deceased common ancestor during his life as a direct or indirect gift. It is founded on the presumed desire of the deceased ancestor not to alter the equality among his descendants. It is reasonable to suppose that the deceased ancestor would have made his gifts under a title of set-off and with the intent of obliging the donee to return all gifts to the hereditary fund. "Pater," say the Glossists, "non debet sua inæqualitate ex pluribus filliis unum facere legitimum et alium bastardum." From this we see that collation takes place only in favor of descendent co-heirs and in an inheritance from a common ancestor. Collation can be actual or fictitious. It is actual when the very goods to be returned are given back to the hereditary fund; fictitious when the value of the goods is deducted from the portion of the donee.

§ 517. *Three Factors in Inheritance.* In inheritance in general it is necessary to distinguish three elements, the individual, the family, and society. Ownership presumes these three factors and law should attribute to each of them in inheritance what belongs to it. Law must recognize the right of the owner, and the family and social ties; two ties which give rise to two rights. It must conform not only to the principles of reason but to the conditions of time, place, and civilization.

INDEX

[The numbers refer to the pages.]

782 INDEX

Incorporeal persons—(*continued*).
the "Quid Simile" theory
(§ 213), 364.
rights without a subject
(§ 215), 366.
will (§ 218), 370.
wealth cannot be subjective
(§ 216), 368.
Individualism and the feudal system (§ 257), 421.
Individualism — modern (§ 260),
427.
"Individualismo ed il Socialism
nel Diritto Contrattuale,
L'," by Giantureo, 591.
Individuality and Christianity
(§ 256), 420.
Induction, Duty of (§ 32), 115.
four methods (§ 23), 105.
in the critic of law (§ 27), 105.
statistical and mathematical
(§ 30), 112.
"Infortuni del Lavoro, Gl'," by
Fusinato, 594.
Ingram, 276.
Inheritance, factors (§ 517), 773.
affects all relations of life
(§ 492), 732.
among the ancients (§ 493),
733.
Instinct (§ 77), 179.
"Institutes" 245, 298, 345, 346.
Insurance, more economic than
ethical (§ 416), 630.
fraud (§ 417), 631.
rates are calculable (§ 415),
629.
Insurance and socialism (§ 413),
626.
socialistic view, criticism of
(§ 414), 628.
Interest is legitimate (§ 386), 597.
abrogation of legal maximum
(§ 390), 601.
is economic (§ 391), 602.
is legal (§ 388), 599.
recognition of (§ 387), 599.
Intestacy, founded on family co-
ownership (§ 498), 745.
husband and wife (§ 504), 754.
incapacities (§ 501), 751.

Intestacy—(*continued*).
kinds of succession (§ 502),
752.
natural relative (§ 503), 754.
the state the ultimate heir
(§ 505), 755.
and testacy co-existing, the
reserve (§ 509), 758.
succession (§ 500), 751.
the reserve, extent of (§ 511),
762.
the reserve, criticism of (§ 510)
760.
transmission (*transmuttio*),
Succession *per stirpes* and
per capita (§ 506), 755.
"Intrapresa delle Assicurazioni,
L'," by Zammarano, 629.
Ionic philosophers, 1.

Jacobi, 79.
Jamblichus, 408.
Jesuits, 13.
Jurisprudence, distinct from cus-
tom (§ 161), 305.
industrial (§ 305), 491.
industrial, divisions of (§ 306),
491.
Juristic man. See Man.
"Jus Naturæ Methodo Scienfico
Tractatum," by Wolff, 267.
"Justice," by Spencer, 224, 226,
258, 662.
Justinian, 207, 208, 475, 726, 757,
766.

Kant, 46, 95, 97, 137, 163, 168,
180, 191, 210, 228, 229, *et
seq.*, 238, 241, 246, 251, 267,
269, 298, 357, 367, 384, 386,
387, 388, 391, 549, 584, 586,
668, 697, 742.
"Kant e l'Empirismo," by Spaventa, 139.
"Kapital, Das," by Marx, 440, 497.
Kerbaker, 121.
Knowledge is *a priori* (§ 74), 174.
criticism of positivist theory
of (§ 72), 171.
is subjective (§ 73), 172.
Krause, 78, 98, 241, 289.

784INDEX

784 INDEX

[The numbers refer to the pages.]

INDEX

juristic, two prerequisites
(§ 172), 321.
the origin of economic relations (§ 276), 453.
"Man versus the State, The," by
Spencer, 299.
Manu and Nerada, 208, 715.
Marezoll, 306.
Marghieri, 624.
Marius Paganus. See Paganus.
Marriage (§ 445), 668.
a spiritual, mental, and physical union (§ 446), 669.
annulment (§ 451), 672.
between relatives (§ 448), 674.
civil and indissoluble (§ 468),
697.
conditions and impediments
(§ 447), 670.
ethical, religious, and juridical
(§ 453), 674.
husband must have authority
(§ 458), 682.
impediment of attempted murder (§ 450), 672.
indissolubility (§ 446), 696.
indissolubility, demanded by
morality, religion, and politics (§ 467), 696.
property (§ 463), 692.
property, history of (§ 464),
693.
state control of (§ 454), 675.
Marriage and adoption (§ 449), 672.
Marsh, 464, 468.
Marsilius, 8.
Martial, 132.
Martiis, Cognetti de, 276, 516.
Marx, Karl (§ 311), 98, 283, 440,
458, 493, 494, 495, 497, 507,
508, 509, 510.
Masci, 145, 148, 164, 181, 187.
Materialism, Bacon's (§ 49), 135.
the result of illegitimate deduction (§ 50), 136.
psychological and physical
(§ 51), 137.
Maternal and paternal genealogy
(§ 435), 653.

Matriarchy (§ 432), 648.
inheritance (§ 433), 650.
Melanchthon, 14, 297.
Menger, 590.
Mengotti, 463, 465.
Merlo, 123.
Messedaglia, 279, 466, 468.
Metaphysics and necessity (§ 5),
90.
"Metaphysische Aufangründe der
Rechslehre," by Kant, 95.
Mill, 106, 107, 115, 138, 160, 214,
216, 222, 240, 254, 262, 386,
680, 681.
Milone, 543.
Mind, attributes of (§ 76), 175.
Mines not land (§ 278), 460.
economics favor freedom
(§ 295), 478.
history of law of (§ 289), 471.
no title by accession (§ 291),
474.
objection to emancipation
(§290), 471.
special conditions special laws
(§ 287), 470.
title by "fictiones" (§ 292), 474.
Minghetti, 284, 285, 286.
Mirabeau, 743.
Mistake (§ 366), 576.
Modern philosophy, 19.
character of, as foreshadowed
by Vico (§ 7), 92.
Modestinus, 195.
Mohl, 286, 292.
Molineo, 559, 560.
Molitor, 547.
Mommsen, 406, 409.
Monad, Spirit as (§ 63), 157.
Monogamy, development from promiscuity (§ 430), 646.
development from promiscuity. Sandwich Islands ex-
amples (§ 431), 647.
Montesquieu, 17, 26, 27, 62, 309,
386.
"Moral Statistik," by Oettingen,
190.
"Moralische Statistik und die Men-
schliche Willensfreiheit, Die,"
by Drobisch, 189.

INDEX

INDEX 789

"Proprietà, La," by Lampertico, 439.

"Proprietà Collettiva nell' Apennino Marchigiano, La," by Valenti, 412.

"Proprieté et ses Formes Primitives, De la," by Laveleye, 389, 405, 406.

Protagoras, 348, 349.

Protestantism, 13.

Proudhon, 699, 700.

Puchta, 301, 363, 406, 542, 547, 710.

Puffendorf, 33, 95, 357, 617, 698, 742, 743.

Pythagoras, 130, 131, 285, 408.

Pythagoreans, 1, 3, 114.

Quesnay, 344.

Quetelet, 189, 258.

"Quintessenz der Socialismus, Die," by Schaffle, 496.

Quintilian, 741.

Rae, 445, 493.

Randa, 364, 547, 548.

Rational Law. See Law.

Reactionary period, 62.

Realism, 8.

"Realtà delle Persone Giuridiche, Sulla," by Fisichella, 375.

Reason, a result of evolution (§ 110), 228.

development of (§ 202), 350.

"Recht des Besitzes in Mittelalten und in der Gegenwart," by Bruns, 542.

"Recht des Besitzes," by Savigny, 540.

"Recht und Verhältnisse von Standpunkte in Volkwartschaftlich Gutenlehre," by Böhm-Bawerk, 284.

Reclus, 465.

Release, 564.

"Reliquie della Proprietà Collettiva in Italia," by Venezia, 412.

Renaissance, 12, 19.

Renan, 119.

Renazzi, 61.

Representation (§ 67), 165.

"Republica delle Api, La," by Bonifazio, 345.

Rescission, 564.

Retroactivity. See Law.

Ribot, 164, 182, 183.

Ricardo, 447, 448, 486, 497, 498 507, 508.

Riehl, 171.

Rights, individual, the sujects of (§ 214), 365.

absolute and relative duties (§ 173), 322.

correlation of duties and (§ 193), 341.

development of (§ 178), 326.

increase with man's development (§ 175), 324.

inherent and acquired (§ 174), 323.

inherent equality of and property (§ 236), 395.

invention and discovery is economic (§ 326), 519.

member of corporation (§ 224) 377.

not abstract, but components of life (§ 206), 356.

of competition (§ 323), 514.

of exemption (§ 323), 514.

of invention and discovery (§ 325), 515.

of invention is a property right (§ 327), 520.

of invention is economic (§ 326), 519.

of property, fundamental basis (§ 227), 383.

personal and property (§ 329), 523.

subsidiary inherent (§179), 327.

subsidiary inherent in struggle for development (§ 205), 355.

to aid (§ 190), 339.

to associate (§ 189), 337.

to freedom (§ 187), 335.

to freedom and self-defense (§ 183), 329.

to honor and good name (§ 185), 333.

to life (§ 180), 327.

to life, suicide (§ 181), 328.

[The numbers refer to the pages.]

792   INDEX

"System der Finanzwissenschaft,"
by Roscher, 499.
"System der Heutigen Römischen
Rechts," by Savigny, 301.
"System der Oestreichischen Almeinen Rechts," by Unger,
363.
"System der Pandekten," by Thibaut, 541.
"System des Römischen Civilrechts," Gans, 547.

Tabula rasa, 26, 149, 179.
Tacitus, 419.
"Temperamenti della Proprietà
Prediale, I," by Lomonaco,
394.
"Teoria della Retroactività delle
Leggi," by Gabba, 314.
"Teorie Sociali dei Sofisti Greci,
Sulla," by Chiappelli, 130.
"Terra e la Sistema Sociale, Le,"
by Loria, 450.
Testacy, foundation of (§ 497),
741.
  and ancestor worship (§ 496),
738.
  and intestacy, coexisting. The
reserve (§ 509), 758.
  founded on ownership (§ 499),
748.
  no representation (§ 512), 764.
  succession (§ 507), 756.
Theophilus, 742.
Theophrastus, 109.
"Théorie du Code Penal," by
Chauveau and Helie, 334.
Theory that the useful, just, and
honest are three aspects of
the good (§ 126), 252.
Theosophy, 17.
Thibaut, 63, 541.
Thiers, 384.
Thilo, 370.
Thomas Aquinas. See Aquinas.
Thomasius, 34, 246, 698.
Thornton, 339.
Thought (§ 68), 166.
Thrasimachus, 348, 349.
Tocco, 184.

"Tractatus Theologico-Politicus,"
by Spinoza, 211.
Tracy, 37.
"Traité de Legislation," by Comte
309.
Transmission (transmittio) (§ 506),
755.
Transportation (§ 412), 615.
"Treatise on Civil Government,"
by Locke, 386.
Trendelenburg, 76, 96, 239, 240,
263, 268, 270, 271, 310, 314,
320, 325, 361, 370, 384, 547,
585, 586, 673, 692, 699, 728.
Tronchet, 743.
Troplong, 617, 742.
Tullio, 213, 387, 626.
Turgot, 83, 344, 486, 513.
Tyler, 258.
Tyndall, 155.

Ulpian, 112, 244, 300, 736, 737, 742.
Ulrici, 240.
Unger, 363.
Unions, basis (§ 301), 486.
  history of (§ 302), 487.
  legal (§ 303), 486.
  potentiality of harm (§ 304),
489.
Unus homo, nullus homo, 77.
"Ursprung der Familie, des Privat-
eigenthums und des Staats,
Die," by Engels, 684.
Usury (§ 389), 600.
  a debt without consideration
(§ 398), 610.
  a crime against private property (§ 399), 611.
  and high interest (§ 393), 605.
  ineradicable by law (§ 400),612.
  is a crime (§ 396), 607.
  its abolition (§ 395), 605.
  methods of (§ 392), 603.
  simple and seductive (§ 393),
604.
  Stein distinction (§ 397), 608.
Utilitarianism, the material of law
(§ 104), 218.
  Maine's criticism of (§ 105),
219.
"Utilitarianism," by Mill, 214.